Lecture Notes in Computer Science 13291

Esma Aïmeur · Maryline Laurent · Reda Yaich ·
Benoît Dupont · Joaquin Garcia-Alfaro (Eds.)

Foundations and Practice of Security

14th International Symposium, FPS 2021
Paris, France, December 7–10, 2021
Revised Selected Papers

 Springer

Editors
Esma Aïmeur ⓘ
University of Montreal
Montreal, QC, Canada

Reda Yaich ⓘ
IRT SystemX
Palaiseau, France

Joaquin Garcia-Alfaro ⓘ
Télécom SudParis
Palaiseau, France

Maryline Laurent ⓘ
Télécom SudParis
Palaiseau, France

Benoît Dupont
University of Montreal
Montreal, QC, Canada

ISSN 0302-9743   ISSN 1611-3349 (electronic)
Lecture Notes in Computer Science
ISBN 978-3-031-08146-0   ISBN 978-3-031-08147-7 (eBook)
https://doi.org/10.1007/978-3-031-08147-7

Preface

The 14th International Symposium on Foundations and Practice of Security (FPS 2021) was hosted by IRT SystemX, Paris, France, from December 7 to December 10, 2021. FPS 2021 received 62 submissions from authors based in countries all over the world. Each paper was reviewed by at least two Program Committee members, and up to four in the case of divergent evaluations.

The Program Committee selected 18 regular papers and ten short papers for presentation. The conference was held in a fully hybrid mode, with the efficient and full involvement of the IRT SystemX host. The agenda was rich and dense. The program included five in-person sessions, four virtual sessions, and a two-day workshop on Secure Digital Manufacturing.

We had three excellent invited keynotes given by Huan Liu (Arizona State University), Solange Ghernaouti (Université de Lausanne), and Mark Hunyadi (Université catholique de Louvain).

An additional cross-disciplinary international panel, addressing cybersecurity and privacy threats and challenges in artificial intelligence, completed the agenda with the participation of Karim Benyekhlef (Professor, Université de Montréal), Julien Chiaroni (Director of Grand Défi on "Trustworthy AI for Industry" at SGPI), Jean-Gabriel Ganascia (Professor, Sorbonne University), Vanessa Henri (Lawyer, Emerging Tech and Data Governance, Fasken), Claire Levallois-Barth (Associate Professor, Télécom Paris), and Félicien Vallet (AI Lead, CNIL).

Several people contributed to the success of FPS 2021. First, we would like to thank all the authors who submitted their research results. The selection was a challenging task, and we sincerely thank all the Program Committee members, as well as the external reviewers, who volunteered to read and discuss the papers.

We are very grateful to the General Chairs, Reda Yaich (Head of Cybersecurity and Networks, IRT SystemX) and Benoît Dupont (Professor, Université de Montréal), and the IRT SystemX team for their great efforts in organizing the logistics, both in person and online, during the symposium and for managing the conference website.

Finally, we also want to express our gratitude to the Publication Chair, Joaquin Garcia-Alfaro (Professor, Télécom SudParis), for the huge endeavor to plan and edit the proceedings.

Protecting the communication and data infrastructure of an increasingly interconnected world has become vital to the normal functioning of all aspects of our world. Security has emerged as an important scientific discipline whose many multifaceted complexities deserve the attention and synergy of the mathematical, computer science, and engineering communities.

The aim of FPS is to exchange theoretical and practical ideas that address privacy and security issues in interconnected systems. Special attention has been given this year to artificial intelligence and cybersecurity.

We hope the papers in this proceedings volume will be valuable for your professional activities in this area.

December 2021   Esma Aïmeur
                                                        Maryline Laurent

Organization

General Chairs

Benoît Dupont   Université de Montréal, Canada
Reda Yaich   IRT SystemX, France

Program Committee Chairs

Esma Aïmeur   Université de Montréal, Canada
Maryline Laurent   Télécom SudParis, France

Publications Chair

Joaquin Garcia-Alfaro   Télécom SudParis, France

Program Committee

Mohamed Abid   University of Sfax, Tunisia
Manar Alalfi   Ryerson University, Canada
Dima Alhadidi   University of Windsor, Canada
Man Ho Au   Hong Kong Polytechnic University, Hong Kong
Ken Baker   University of Calgary, Canada
Sébastien Bardin   CEA, France
David Barrera   Carleton University, Canada
Adrien Bécue   Airbus Defense and Space, France
Anis Bkakria   IRT SystemX, France
Yosra Ben Saied   National School of Computer Science,
                                   United Arab Emirates
Abdelmalek Benzekri   Université Toulouse III - Paul Sabatier, France
Gregory Blanc   Télécom SudParis, France
Guillaume Bonfante   Université de Lorraine and Loria, France
Samia Bouzefrane   CNAM, France
Driss Bouzidi   Mohammed V University in Rabat, Morocco
Francesco Buccafurri   University of Reggio Calabria, Italy
Jordi Castellà-Roca   Universitat Rovira i Virgili, Spain
Ana Rosa Cavalli   Télécom SudParis, France
Yacine Challal   Higher School of Computer Science, Algeria
Isabelle Christment   TELECOM Nancy, France

Mohmed Mejri	Laval University, Canada
Ali Miri	Ryerson University, Canada
Benoit Morgan	IRIT, France
Paliath Narendran	University at Albany–SUNY, USA
Guillermo Navarro-Arribas	Autonomous University of Barcelona, Spain
Gabriela Nicolescu	Polytechnique Montréal, Canada
Jun Pang	University of Luxembourg, Luxembourg
Marie-Laure Potet	Vérimag, France
Isabel Praça	Instituto Superior de Engenharia do Porto, Portugal
Silvio Ranise	FBK-Irst, Italy
Jean-Marc Robert	Ecole de technologie superieure, Canada
Michael Rusinowitch	Inria Nancy, France
Giovanni Russello	University of Auckland, Australia
Kazuo Sakiyama	University of Electro-Communications, Japan
Zakaria Sahnoun	University of Blida, Algeria
Jarno Salonen	VTT Technical Research Centre, Finland
Florence Sedes	Paul Sabatier University, France
Siraj Shaikh	Conventry University, UK
Kalpana Singh	IRT SystemX, France
Natalia Stakhanova	University of Saskatchewan, Canada
Douglas Stebila	University of Waterloo, Canada
Chamseddine Talhi	École de technologie superieure, Canada
Qiang Tang	Luxembourg Institute of Science and Technology, Luxembourg
Nadia Tawbi	Université Laval, Canada
Renaud Sirdey	CEA, France
Natalija Vlajic	York University, Canada
Ahmad Samer Wazan	Université Toulouse III - Paul Sabatier, France
Edgar Weippl	SBA Research, Austria
Stephen B. Wicker	Cornell University, USA
Nicola Zannone	Eindhoven University of Technology, The Netherlands
Nur Zincir-Heywood	Dalhousie University, Canada

Steering Committee

Frédéric Cuppens	Polytechnique Montréal, Canada
Nora Cuppens-Boulahia	Polytechnique Montréal, Canada
Mourad Debbabi	Concordia University, Canada
Joaquin Garcia-Alfaro	Télécom SudParis, France
Evangelos Kranakis	Carleton University, Canada
Pascal Lafourcade	Université d'Auvergne, France

Jean-Yves Marion   Mines de Nancy, France
Ali Miri   Ryerson University, Canada
Rei Safavi-Naini   Calgary University, Canada
Nadia Tawbi   Université Laval, Canada

Additional Reviewers

Carles Anglés-Tafalla   Kalikinkar Mandal
Stefano Berlato   Gaël Marcadet
Gaurav Choudhary   Qian Mei
Kimberly Cornell   Mohamed Amine Merzouk
Romain Dagnas   Philip Nelson
Cristòfol Dauden-Esmel   Luong Nguyen
Rup Deka   Huu Nghia Nguyen
Armando Miguel Garcia   Charles Olivier-Anclin
Rami Haffar   Mustafizur Rahman Shahid
Houda Jmila   Sourav Saha
Ashneet Khandpur Singh   Mathieu Turuani
Wissam Mallouli

Contents

IoT Security

Attacks and Code Security

Cryptography and Privacy

Secure and Robust Cyber Security Threat Information Sharing

Anis Bkakria[⊠], Reda Yaich, and Walid Arabi

SystemX Technological Research Institute, 91120 Palaiseau, France
{Anis.Bkakria,reda.yaich,walid.arabi}@irt-systemx.fr

Abstract. In recent years, several laws have been decreed, at both national and European levels, to mandate private and public organizations to share their Cyber Security related information. However, existing threat sharing platforms implement "classical" access control mechanisms or at most centralized attribute-based encryption (ABE) to prevent data leakage and preserve data confidentiality. These schemes are well-known to be suffering from a single point of failure on security aspects. That is, if the central authority is compromised, the confidentiality of the shared sensitive information is no longer ensured. To address this challenge, we propose a new ABE scheme combining both the advantages of centralized and decentralized ABE while overcoming their weaknesses. It overcomes the centralized ABE's single point of failure on security by requiring the collaboration of several entities for decryption key issuing. In addition, in contrast to existing decentralized ABE schemes, our construction does not require the data providers to fully trust all attributes authorities, only a single authority should be trusted. Finally, we formally prove the security of our ABE construction in the generic group model.

Keywords: Information sharing · Fine-grained access control · Attribute based encryption · Cyber security

1 Introduction

Several studies and experts have recognised Cyber Security Threat Information Sharing among European operators of critical infrastructures (and essential services) as a mandatory step for continuous improvement of the national security posture [7]. It enhances the pro-activeness of security practitioners through the exchange of actionable information related to network and information security, such as threats, incidents, vulnerabilities, mitigating measures and best practices. Therefore, the European Council resolution 68/01 of 2007 *"encourage, where appropriate in cooperation with The European Network and Information Security Agency (ENISA), effective exchanges of information and cooperation between the relevant organisations and agencies at national level; to commit to fighting spam, spyware and malware"* [21].

More recently, the European legislation such as NIS Directive or the Cyber Security Act advocated and incentivised the creation of sectoral Information

© Springer Nature Switzerland AG 2022
E. Aïmeur et al. (Eds.): FPS 2021, LNCS 13291, pp. 3–18, 2022.
https://doi.org/10.1007/978-3-031-08147-7_1

Sharing and Analysis Centers (ISACs) both at national and Europe Levels. ISACs are non-profit structures that aim to provide a federated structure to gather, analyses and share threat information among sectorial communities of private and public stakeholders. However, setting up and running ISACs is facing several technical, financial and legal barriers [1,14]. Alongside cost-saving and poor management, the lack of trust and potential reputational risks are the most critical barriers to effective information sharing [1].

In the next subsection, we use an illustrative case-study to further motivate the need for a fine-grained and secure threat information sharing mechanism as a mean to mitigate the risk of sensitive information leakage and to incentive critical operators and legal authorities to share valuable information.

1.1 Illustrative Case-Study

France was the first European country to have gone through the regulatory process to implement an adequate and mandatory Cyber Security for "Critical Infrastructures Information Protection" (CIIP). As such, a dedicated CIIP regulatory framework was established in 2013 under the name of "CIIP law". As the national authority for Cyber Security and cyber defence, the ANSSI is in charge of coordinating the Cyber Security aspect of the framework and accompanying the critical operators (called "operators of vital importance") in implementing the new measures. In this law, a critical operator is defined as "operator[s] whose unavailability could strongly threaten the economical or military potential, the security or the resilience of the Nation". As part of the CIIP law, critical operators must notify the national authority ANSSI of any cyber incident targeting their critical information systems. The type of incidents to be notified have also been specified by sectorial orders (Fig. 1).

Fig. 1. Illustrative use-case (adapted from [2])

As illustrated in the figure above, the cyber incident handling process is coordinated by the French Authority ANSSI. The process starts when a cyber incident occurs in a critical operator (1). If the incident concerns an Information System of Vital Importance (SIIV), the critical operator sends an incident form to the national authority ANSSI (2). The critical operator will receive ANSSI support that can take the form of remote recommendations or onsite technical assistance to handle the incident (3). The completed incident declaration form is a "confidential" document as it may contain sensitive information that disclosure can lead to criminal prosecution. Thus only secure communication means or post can be used to send the document in order to preserve its integrity and confidentiality. CIIP law imposes ANSSI to preserve incidents information at State level (4–5). However, ANSSI is allowed to use technical information to analyse and anticipate cyber-crisis. These analyse, after being anonymised, can be shared further with other critical operators at the national or European level to strengthen their capacity to detect sophisticated attacks.

Nowadays, the above incident management and threat information sharing process is for the most important part manual. The critical operator need to download a form, complete it and send it by post or secure communication channel. The advent of cyber threat management platforms such as OpenCTI[1] will bring progressively higher degree of automation and accelerate detection and response of new security threats. Figure 2, illustrates how such platforms can be used to automate the process described in the case-study.

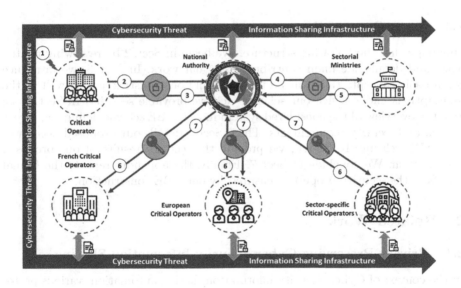

Fig. 2. Automation of cyber threat information sharing

However, using such platforms to share confidentials data as presented above requires a *Secure and Robust Cyber Security Threat Information Sharing* mechanism. The next section presents the main contributions of the article to address security and robustness (e.g. Single Point of Failure) challenges raised by the use of such platforms.

---

[1] https://www.opencti.io/en/.

1.2   Our Contributions

In this paper, three main contributions are proposed. First, we propose a secure and robust cyber threat intelligent (CTI) sharing solution. That is, we use a novel ABE based construction to ensure fine grained access control on shared data items. Compared to existing CTI sharing solutions, ours provides higher robustness level as it does not involve any single point failure on security. Second, we propose a novel ABE construction combining both the advantages of centralized and decentralized ABE while overcoming their weaknesses. Our ABE construction overcomes the centralized ABE's single point failure on security by requiring the collaboration of several entities for decryption key issuing. Moreover, our construction does not require the data providers to fully trust all attributes authorities, only a single authority should be trusted by data providers. Finally, we formally prove the security and the robustness of our solution in the generic group model.

1.3   Paper Organization

Our paper has the following structure. We begin in Sect. 2 by reviewing related work and details the main contributions of our work. In Sect. 3, we introduce some basic concepts that will be used to build our construction as well as the assumptions under which our schemes achieve provable security. In Sect. 4, we give the overview of the considered system model, ABE scheme definition, threat model, and security requirements. Then, Sect. 5 details our proposed decentralized ABE scheme. In Sect. 6, we provide the security results of our proposed construction. We conclude in Sect. 7. Finally, the appendix reports the formal proofs of the security properties ensured by our ABE construction.

2   Related Work

2.1   Privacy-Preserving Cyber Security Information Sharing

In the context of Cyber Security information sharing automation, various protocols and standards have been proposed, such as TAXII, STIX, CybOX, VERIS, MAEC, SCAP and IODEF [9,19]. Security information sharing in competitive environments with the game theory approach has been studied in [10]. The study of privacy issues in Cyber Security information sharing in [22,23]. Several information sharing programs, such as CISSP, NCCIC, ISAC, have also been developed in [9].

The recent studies [24,26] review the current state of the art on cyber threat intelligence (CTI) sharing, identifying associated benefits and barriers. These works highlight that issues of security, trustworthiness, provenance, and privacy remain open research challenges in cyber threat intelligence sharing in that they have not been comprehensively addressed.

Therefore, in this paper, we focus at the most recent and elaborate work on CTI sharing, in order to make it more secure, especially against attackers who target the sharing mechanism itself. One of the most recent Framework using Ciphertext-Policy Attribute Based Encryption (CP-ABE) scheme is [16]. It allows to address several issues related to CTI sharing not resolved by previous works, namely: the confidentiality of personal information, fine-grained access control, reliability, auditability. The authors propose to combine the TATIS security framework, which provides fine-grained protection for the threat intelligence platform API, with the capabilities of the distributed registry to enable trusted and reliable sharing of threat intelligence, with the ability to verify the provenance of the threat intelligence.

Nevertheless, After reviewing the current state of the art in cyber threat intelligence (CTI) sharing, we came to the conclusion that all ABE based CTI sharing approaches use a single authority. In a single-authority-system, all trust rests on the single authority, so if the authority is compromised, the entire system and there is an overhead on the Central Authority (CA) for key management.

Hence, to deal with a single point of failure (SPOF), we propose in our work to use the decentralized systems approach which distribute the responsibility among several entities. Moreover, to address the SPOF flaw, our ABE approach, allows to keep the data contrability, namely, among the chosen attribute authorities that ensure the responbility of sharing, one of them will be identified as a trusted attribute authority (TAA) by the data provider and at each new access to its data it will have the control to generate a key decryption or not. More technical details to address these failures will be given in the following section.

2.2   ABE Access Control

Attribute-based encryption (ABE) was introduced in 2005 by Sahai and Waters [17]. It is a one-to-many public key encryption scheme, i.e. we encrypt with a single key and we have the possibility to generate several keys to decrypt. ABE provides highly granular access control, scalable key management and flexible data distribution [11]. It allows data to be encrypted and shared on the basis of descriptive attributes, without any prior knowledge of the identity of recipients. Only entities with attributes that satisfy a data access policy can decrypt a text. ABE has been widely studied in the literature resulting in many ABE constructions [11]. These constructions can be classified into single-authority [4] and multi-authority [6] ABE. In single-authority setting, the attributes as well as the access key (decryption key) issuing are managed by a single authority, while in the multi-authority setting, the attributes are generated by multiple authorities, yet each authority is responsible of issuing access keys for the data that has been encrypted using its public key. As pointed out in [12], both single and multi-authority ABE constructions suffer from a single-point of failure on security. That is, once an authority is compromised, an adversary can easily obtain the authority's master key that can be used to generate private keys of any subset of the attributes managed by the compromised authority to access (decrypt) the encrypted data. To deal with the previous security weakness, Li et al. [12] proposed a new ABE multi-authority ABE construction called TMACS, where the set of authorities collaboratively manage the whole set of attributes and no one of the authorities has full control of any specific attribute. Thanks to the usage of the (t, n) threshold secret sharing proposed in [15], TMACS is proved to be secured when less that t authorities are compromised by an adversary.

The robustness of the TMACS construction comes at the expense of data access controllability. That is, regardless the access policy that will be enforced by the data owner on the encrypted data, any set of t authorities can issue a decryption key for the encrypted data. Hence, the data owner needs to fully trust all the involved authorities in the system, which is seldom satisfied in real world secure data sharing use cases, including our secure CTI sharing use case.

Compared to existing ABE constructions, the ABE scheme we are proposing in this paper achieves a high level of robustness while providing a better data access controllability to data provider. That is, instead of requiring all attribute authorities to be trusted by all data providers, each data provider needs only to trust a single attribute authority.

3   Preliminary

In this section, we give background information on bilinear maps and the security assumption we are considering. Then, we give a brief description of the trusted third party free secret sharing method proposed by Pedersen in [15].

3.1   Bilinear Maps

Let $\mathbb{G}$ and $\mathbb{G}_T$ be two multiplicative cyclic group of prime order p. Let g be a generator of $\mathbb{G}$ and $e : \mathbb{G} \times \mathbb{G} \to \mathbb{G}_T$ be a bilinear map having the following properties:

- Symmetric bilinearity: for all $g_1, g_2 \in \mathbb{G}$ and $a, b \in \mathbb{Z}_p$, we have $e(g_1^a, g_2^b) = e(g_1^b, g_2^a) = e(g_1, g_2)^{a \cdot b}$.
- Non-degeneracy: e(g,g) $\neq 1$.
- The group operations in $\mathbb{G}$ and $e(\cdot, \cdot)$ are efficiently computable.

In the sequel, the we refer to the tuple $(\mathbb{G}, \mathbb{G}_T, p, e(\cdot, \cdot))$ as a bilinear environment.

Definition 1 (Independence [5]). *Let $P, Q \in \mathbb{F}_p[X_1, \cdots, X_n]$ be two s-tuples of n-variate polynomials over $\mathbb{F}_p$. Write $P = (p_1, \cdots, p_s)$ and $Q = (q_1, \cdots, q_s)$. We say that polynomial $f \in \mathbb{F}_p[X_1, \cdots, X_n]$ is dependant on the sets (P, Q) if there exists $s^2 + s$ constant $\{\vartheta_{i,j}^{(a)}\}_{i,j=1}^s$, $\{\vartheta_k^{(b)}\}_{k=1}^s$ such that*

$$f = \sum_{i,j} \vartheta_{i,j}^{(a)} \cdot p_i \cdot p_j + \sum_k \vartheta_k^{(b)} \cdot q_k$$

We say that f is independent of (P, Q) if f is not dependent on (P, Q).

Definition 2 (GDHE assumption [5]). *Let* $(\mathbb{G}, \mathbb{G}_T, p, e(\cdot, \cdot))$ *be a bilinear environment and* s, n *be positive integers. Let* $P, Q \in \mathbb{F}_p[X_1, \cdots, X_n]$ *be two s-tuples of n-variate polynomials over* $\mathbb{F}_p$ *and let* $f \in \mathbb{F}_p[X_1, \cdots, X_n]$. *Let* g *be a generator of* $\mathbb{G}$ *and* $g_t = e(g, g) \in \mathbb{G}_T$. *The GDHE assumption states that, given the vector*

$$H(x_1, \cdots, c_n) = (g^{P(x_1, \cdots, x_n)}, g^{Q(x_1, \cdots, x_n)}) \in \mathbb{G}^s \times \mathbb{G}_T^s$$

it hard to decide whether $U = g_t^{f(x_1, \cdots, x_c)}$ *or* U *is random if* f *is independent of* (P, Q).

3.2 Trusted Third Party Free Threshold Secret Sharing

In a secret sharing scheme, a secret is distributed among several participants organized in an access structure listing all groups that can access the secret. The objective is to provide information specific to each participant so that only a specific group of participants can reconstruct the secret. Several practical secret sharing schemes have been proposed [3, 8, 15, 18]. In this work, we use the trusted third party free threshold secret sharing construction proposed in [15], which we briefly describe as following.

Consider a system involving a set $\mathcal{P} = \{P_1, P_2, \cdots, P_n\}$ of n participants and a threshold t ($t \leq n$). Let us suppose that to each participant $P_i \in \mathcal{P}$ is associated a unique scalar $z_i \in \mathbb{Z}$ ($\forall P_i, \forall P_j \in \mathcal{P} : P_i \neq P_j \Leftrightarrow z_i \neq z_j$) representing the public identifier of the participant in the system. First, each participant P_i selects a random scalar $s_i \in \mathbb{Z}_p$ that will represent his/her sub-secret and generates a random polynomial $f_i(x)$ of degree $t - 1$ such that $f_i(0) = s_i$. The sum of sub-secrets $S = \sum_{i=1}^{n} s_i$ will represented the master secret that will be shared by the participant. Nevertheless, S is not known to any participant. Second, each participant P_i computes the sub-shares $s_{i,j} = f_i(z_j), 1 \leq j \leq n, j \neq i$ and securely sends $s_{i,j}$ to P_j. Once a participant P_i receives sub-shares from all other $n - 1$ participants, he/she/it computes $s_{i,i} = f_i(z_i)$ and computes it own master share as $S_i' = \sum_{j=1}^{n} s_{j,i}$. Once each participant P_i has computed his master share S_i', the master secret key S can be constructed using the Lagrange interpolating formula by any t out of n participants. Let us denote by $S_k', 1 \leq k \leq t$ the set of master shares to be used, the master secret can be constructed as following.

$$\sum_{k=1}^{t} \left(S_k' \cdot \prod_{j=1, j \neq k}^{t} \frac{z_j}{z_j - z_i} \right) = \sum_{i=1}^{n} S_i = S$$

4   System and Security Models

In this section, we introduce the system model, system definition, threats model and security requirements of our construction.

4.1 System Model

The architecture we consider in our approach involves five entities: A certificate authority, multiple attribute authorities, data providers, and data consumsers (users), and a cloud server.

- The certificate authority (CA) is a blockchain-based PKI management system e.g., [20,25] that is charged of setting up the system parameters such as the bilinear environment to be used, the set of attributes and their respective public keys. CA is responsible of registering attribute authorities as well as data consumers. Finally its responsible of choosing the robustness level that should be satisfied, i.e., the number of attribute authorities that should collaborate to issue a decryption key. We emphasis that the CA is not involved in any decryption key issuing operation.
- Attribute authorities are mainly responsible of issuing decryption keys to data consumers. In addition, they collaborate together with the CA to set up the master public key of the system.
- Cloud storage server is an entity that provides data storage capabilities.
- The data provider is the entity aiming to share its data. It encrypts the data to be shared using a chosen access structure formulated over a set of attributes that defines who can access the shared data.
- The data consumer (data user) is the entity that will access and use the shared data. He/She/It is labeled by a set of attributes. Data consumers can download any encrypted (shared) data from the cloud service. However, only those who are labeled with proper attributes can successfully decrypt the encrypted data.

4.2 Definition of Our Construction

Our construction is defined using seven algorithms that we denote *CASetup, AASetup, CAKeyGen, AAKeyGen, DecKeyGen, Encrypt, Decrypt*. The algorithms *CASetup* and *CAKeyGen* are performed by CA, *AASetup* and *AAKeyGen* are performed by the attribute authorities, *Encrypt* is performed by data providers, finally *DecKeyGen* and *Decrypt* are performed by data consumers.

- **CASetup(λ)** is a probabilistic algorithm that takes as input the security parameter λ and outputs the public parameters of the system pp.
- **AASetup(pp)** is a probabilistic algorithm that takes as input the system parameters pp and returns a secret key share sk and a master public key share pk.
- **CAKeyGen(pp)** is a probabilistic algorithm that takes as input the system parameters pp and outputs a global public master key PMK_{CA}.
- **AAKeyGen(PMK_{CA})** is a probabilistic algorithm performed by an attribute authority A_i that takes as input the public master key PMK_{CA} and outputs a (local) public master key PK_i.

- **Encrypt**$(M, \mathbb{M}, A_i)$ is a probabilistic algorithm that takes a message M, and access structure $\mathbb{M}$, and the attribute authority A_i chosen (trusted) by the data provider for validating the access to the data and outputs an encrypted data item bundle χ.
- **DecKeyGen**$(PMK_{CA}, \mathbb{A})$ is a probabilistic algorithm that takes as input the global public master key PMK_{CA} and the set of registered attribute authorities $\mathbb{A}$ and output a secret decryption key $\mathcal{K}$.
- **Decrypt**$(\chi, \mathcal{K})$ is a deterministic algorithm that takes as input an encrypted data item bundle χ and a decryption key $\mathcal{K}$ and outputs the plaintext M if and only if (1) the access structure used to encrypt the the data item is satisfied by the attributes involved in $\mathcal{K}$, and (2) $\mathcal{K}$ is approved and signed by the authority attribute trusted by the data item provider.

4.3 Threat Model

In our construction, the CA is assumed to be a trusted entity, that is, he is supposed to issue correct certificates to the different entities of the system. As the CA capabilities are supposed to be provided by a blockchain-based PKI management system e.g., [20,25], then we fairly assume that the CA is a single point of failure-free entity. The attribute authorities are honest but curious entities. That is, they are supposed to honestly perform the different operations the proposed construction, however some of them may be corrupted by an adversary that aims to learn as much information as possible about the shared data. Moreover, we assume that the cloud server is also honest but curious as it will correctly follow the proposed protocol, yet may collude with malicious data consumers or compromised attribute authorities to get unauthorized access privileges. Finally we assume the data consumers to be malicious entities that can collude with each other, with the cloud server, and/or with compromised attribute authorities.

4.4 Security Requirements

Multiple malicious users may collude to access a data item that none of them can decrypt alone. We require our construction to be secure against such collusion attack. This requirement can be formalized as following.

Definition 3 (Collusion Resistance). *Let λ be the security parameter, $\mathcal{A}$ be the adversary, and $\mathcal{C}$ be the challenger. We consider the following game that we denote $Exp_{\mathcal{A}}^{Col}$.*

1. *Setup: $\mathcal{C}$ executes CASetup, AASetup, CAKeyGen, and AAKeyGen algorithms. It then transmits the public parameters pp, the global public master key PMK_{CA}, and the public master keys PK_{A_i} ($i \in [1, n]$) to $\mathcal{A}$.*
2. *Query – Phase 1: $\mathcal{A}$ can make a set of n adaptive secret decryption key queries. For each query Q_i, it submits the set of attributes Δ_i that should be involved in the decryption key and the attribute authority A_i that validate and sign the secret decryption key. For each query Q_i, $\mathcal{C}$ executes the algorithm DecKeyGen to generate a valid secret decryption key $\mathcal{K}_{A_i}$.*

3. *Challenge: $\mathcal{A}$ chooses two equal-length messages M_0, M_1, the public master key $PK_{A_{i*}}$ of $A_{i*} \in \mathbb{A}$ to be use for message encryption, and a challenge access structure $\mathbb{M}^*$ such that $\forall i \in [1,n], \Delta_i$ does not satisfy $\mathbb{M}^*$. Then it sends them to $\mathcal{C}$. The latter chooses a random $\beta \in \{0,1\}$, encrypts M_β under $\mathbb{M}^*$ to get the challenge ciphertext C^*, and sends C^* to $\mathcal{A}$.*

4. *Query – Phase 2: $\mathcal{A}$ can make adaptive secret key queries as in phase 1. The only restriction here is that the set of attributes Δ_i involved in each query does not satisfies $\mathbb{M}^*$, otherwise, $\mathcal{A}$ will trivially win the game by running the Decrypt algorithm.*

5. *Guess: $\mathcal{A}$ outputs its guess β' of β.*

We define $\mathcal{A}$'s advantage by $Adv^{Exp_{\mathbb{A}}^{Col}}(\lambda) = |Pr[\beta = \beta'] - 1/2|$. Our construction is said to be collusion resistant if $Adv^{Exp_{\mathbb{A}}^{Col}}(\lambda)$ is negligible.

In addition, we require our construction to be robust. That is, any data item encrypted by a data consumer u remains fully protected as far as no more than $t - 1$ attribute authorities including the one trusted by the data provider are compromised. This requirement is formalized using the following definition.

Definition 4 ((t,n)-Robustness). *Let λ be the security parameter, $\mathcal{A}$ be the adversary, and $\mathcal{C}$ be the challenger. We consider the following game that we denote $Exp_{\mathcal{A}}^{Rob}$. We omit the first four steps of the game since they are the same as defined in $Exp_{\mathbb{A}}^{Col}$.*

5. *Compromise: In this step, $\mathcal{A}$ can perform only one of the following actions:*
   (a) *Adaptively chooses $t - 1 < n$ attribute authorities including A_{i*} and compromises them to get their master secret key shares $sk_i, i \in [1, t-1]$.*
   (b) *$\mathcal{A}$ compromise all attribute authorities except A_{i*}.*
6. *Guess: $\mathcal{A}$ outputs its guess β' of β.*

We define $\mathcal{A}$'s advantage by $Adv^{Exp_{\mathbb{A}}^{Rob}}(\lambda) = |Pr[\beta = \beta'] - 1/2|$. Our construction is said to be (t,n)-Robust if $Adv^{Exp_{\mathbb{A}}^{Rob}}(\lambda)$ is negligible.

5   Our Proposed Scheme

In this section we give a detailed description of our construction. It is composed of the following four phases: System initialization, user registration and key generation, data encryption, and data decryption.

System Initialization. In this phase, the system parameters are set up using the following steps.

1. **CA setup:** This sub-process is performed by CA. The CA first chooses a bilinear environment $(\mathbb{G}, \mathbb{G}_T, p, e(\cdot, \cdot))$ and choose g as a generator of $\mathbb{G}$. Then, CA defines a cryptographic hash functions $H : \mathbb{G}_T \to \{0,1\}^m$ for some m. Finally, the CA chooses an unforgeable under adaptive chosen message attacks signature system Ξ and generates a signature key CMK and a verification key VMK. This process outputs the set parameters $pp = (\mathbb{G}, \mathbb{G}_T, p, e(\cdot, \cdot), H, \Xi, VMK)$.

2. **AA registration:** Each attribute authority sends a registration request to CA. If it is a legal authority, the CA generate a random unique identifier $id_{A_i} \in \mathbb{Z}_p$ and generates a signed certificate Υ_{A_i}.

3. **Robustness level selection:** According the number n of the registered authorities, CA chooses the robustness level t ($t < n$) that should be satisfied and publishes its public master key $PMK_{CA} = (pp, n, t)$.

4. **AA setup:** Let us denote $\mathbb{A} = \{A_1, A_2, \cdots, A_n\}$ the set of registered attribute authorities. In this step, the n attribute authorities will collaborate to build a shared secret using the trusted third party free threshold secret sharing described in Sect. 3.2. Each $A_i \in \mathbb{A}$ selects a secret random $\alpha_i \in \mathbb{Z}_p$ and generates a random $t-1$ degree polynomial $f_i(x)$ such that $f_i(0) = \alpha_i$. Then it calculates the sub-shares $s_{i,j} = f_i(id_{A_j}), \forall i \in [1,n]$ and securely sends the sub-share $s_{i,j}$ to the entity A_j. Once, receiving $n-1$ sub-shares form all other attribute authorities, A_i computes its master secret key share $sk_i = \sum_{i=1}^{n} s_{j,i}$ and its master public key share $pk_i = e(g,g)^{sk_i}$. We emphasis here that the master shared key $\alpha = \sum_{i=1}^{n} \alpha_i$ is decided in the system, but it should not be known to any entity in the system.

5. **Global public key computation:** this step performed by the CA which randomly selects t out of the n master public key shares. Let us denote by $\mathcal{I}$ the set of indices of the t chosen master public key shares. The global public key of the system is then computed as follows:

$$\prod_{i \in \mathcal{I}} pk_i^{\prod_{j \in \mathcal{I}, j \neq i} \frac{id_{A_j}}{id_{A_j} - id_{A_i}}} = \prod_{i \in \mathcal{I}} e(g,g)^{sk_i \cdot \prod_{j \in \mathcal{I}, j \neq i} \frac{id_{A_j}}{id_{A_j} - id_{A_i}}}$$
$$= e(g,g)^{\alpha}$$

Then, the CA chooses a random master key $a \in \mathbb{Z}_p$ and computes g^a. Moreover, it chooses, for each attribute δ in the universe of attributes to be used Δ, a random public key $o_\delta \in \mathbb{Z}_p$ and computes $\Theta_\delta = g^{o_\delta}$. Then, the CA updates its public master key $PMK_{CA} = (pp, n, t, g^a, e(g,g)^{\alpha}, \{\Theta_\delta\}_{\delta \in \Delta})$.

6. **AA public key computation:** each $A_i \in \mathbb{A}$ chooses a random $\beta_i \in \mathbb{Z}_p$ and computes its master public key $PK_i = e(g,g)^{\alpha \cdot \beta_i}$. The master secret key of A_i is $SK_i = \{sk_i, \beta_i\}$.

We note here the global master secret $MSK = (a, \alpha)$ does not need to be obtained by any entity of the system. In addition, a does not need to be preserved by CA. It's also worth mentioning that all the information transferred between the different entities are encrypted and signed by their sender.

Data Encryption. The data encryption operation Encrypt is performed by the data provider independently. Similarly to most recent ABE schemes, the data to be shared M will be firstly encrypted using a secure symmetric key algorithm such as AES. Then, the chosen symmetric key will be encrypted we described in the following steps.

1. The data provider starts by choosing the attribute authority $A_i \in \mathbb{A}$ he/she trusts for validating the access to the data to be encrypted and shared. Afterwards, he/she defines the access policy that should be enforced as a monotone boolean formula. Then he/she executes the Encrypt algorithm who picks a random $s \in \mathbb{Z}_p$ and uses the master public key PK_i of the chosen attribute authority A_i to generate the symmetric key as:

$$\kappa = H(PK_i^s) = H\left(e(g,g)^{\alpha \cdot \beta_i \cdot s}\right)$$

   Then the Encrypt algorithm encrypts M using κ to get $E_\kappa(M)$.

2. In the second step, the Encrypt algorithm uses the method presented in [13] to transforms the access policy into an LSSS access structure $(\mathbb{M}, \rho)$. $\mathbb{M}$ is an $l \times k$ LSSS matrix and $\rho(x)$ maps each row of $\mathbb{M}$ to an attribute $\rho(x)$. Then, to hide the random element s used to generate the symmetric key, the Encrypt algorithm chooses a random vector $\boldsymbol{v} = \{s, v_2, \cdots, v_k\} \in \mathbb{Z}_p^k$. For each row vector $\mathbb{M}_i$ of $\mathbb{M}$, $\lambda_i = \mathbb{M}_i \cdot \boldsymbol{v}^\top$ is calculated and a random scalar $r_i \in \mathbb{Z}_p$ is chosen. The Encrypt algorithm computes the ciphertext $\mathcal{C}$ as follows:

$$\mathcal{C} = \left(C = g^s, \forall i \in [1, l] : C_i = (g^a)^{\lambda_i} \cdot \Theta_{\rho(i)}^{-r_i}, D_i = g^{r_i}\right)$$

   The Encrypt algorithm output the encrypted data $E_\kappa(M)$ and the ciphertext $\mathcal{C}$. Finally the data owner sends the encrypted data item bundle $\chi = (A_i, E_\kappa(M), \mathcal{C})$ to the cloud server for storage.

User Registration and Key Generation. When a user u_i joins the system, he/she sends a registration query to the CA to get a unique id_{u_i} and a signed certificate Υ_{u_i}. Then, to get a decryption key, the user has to perform the following two steps.

1. The user u chooses t out of the n attribute authorities according to his/her own preferences and individually queries each of the chosen attribute authorities a decryption key share. The user can generate his secret decryption key if and only if he/she gets t decryption key share from t different attribute authorities. To get a decryption key share from the attribute authority A_i, the user sends a signed query containing its identity id_u and its certificate Υ_u. A_i verifies the signature of the CA on Υ_u then authenticates the request by verifying the signature of the *user* on the request. If the user is legitimate, A_i assigns a set of attributes $\Delta_u^{(i)}$ to the user according to the access that A_i wants to grant to the u. Then A_i chooses a random $z_i \in \mathbb{Z}_p$ and generate a decryption key share as following:

$$\mathcal{K}_i = \{K_i = g^{sk_i} \cdot g^{a \cdot z_i}, \quad L_i = g^{b_i}, \quad \forall \delta \in \Delta_u^{(i)} : K_\delta = \Theta_\delta^{z_i}\}$$

   We note here that each attribute authority may assign different set of attributes to the user. In this case, the user will be able only to compute a decryption key that involves the set of attributes $\Delta_u = \cap_{i=1}^t \Delta_u^{(i)}$ that has been assigned by all t attribute authorities.

Once u gets t decryption key shares from t different attribute authorities, he/she computes its decryption key as following.

$$K = \prod_{i=1}^{t} K_i^{\prod_{j=1,i\neq j}^{t} \frac{id_{A_j}}{id_{A_j}-id_{A_i}}}$$

$$= \prod_{i=1}^{t} \left(g^{sk_i \cdot \prod_{j=1,i\neq j}^{t} \frac{id_{A_j}}{id_{A_j}-id_{A_i}}} \cdot g^{a \cdot z_i \cdot \prod_{j=1,i\neq j}^{t} \frac{id_{A_j}}{id_{A_j}-id_{A_i}}} \right)$$

$$= g^{\alpha} \cdot g^{a \cdot \sum_{i=1}^{t} \left(z_i \cdot \prod_{j=1,i\neq j}^{t} \frac{id_{A_j}}{id_{A_j}-id_{A_i}} \right)}$$

$$L = g^{\sum_{i=1}^{t} \left(z_i \cdot \prod_{j=1,i\neq j}^{t} \frac{id_{A_j}}{id_{A_j}-id_{A_i}} \right)}$$

$$\forall \delta \in \Delta_u : \quad K_{\sigma} = \Theta_{\delta}^{\sum_{i=1}^{t} \left(z_i \cdot \prod_{j=1,i\neq j}^{t} \frac{id_{A_j}}{id_{A_j}-id_{A_i}} \right)}$$

Now, by using $d = \sum_{i=1}^{t} \left(z_i \cdot \prod_{j=1,i\neq j}^{t} \frac{id_{A_j}}{id_{A_j}-id_{A_i}} \right)$, we can simplify the different elements of the user decryption key as follows.

$$\mathcal{K} = \{K = g^{\alpha} \cdot g^{a \cdot d}, L = g^d, \forall \delta \in \Delta_u : K_{\delta} = \Theta_{\delta}^d\}$$

2. As it is, the decryption key obtained in the previous step does not allow the user to decrypt any encrypted data. To be able to decrypt data items that has been encrypted using A_i public key, the user decryption key has to be approved and signed by A_i. For this, the user chooses a random scalar $q \in \mathbb{Z}_p$ and randomizes its decryption key as follows:

$$\overline{\mathcal{K}} = \{\overline{K} = K^q, \overline{L} = L^q, \forall \delta \in \Delta_u : \overline{K}_{\delta} = K_{\delta}^q\}$$

Then the user sends a signed query containing its randomized decryption key $\overline{\mathcal{K}}$ and its certificate Υ_u to A_i. Once A_i receives the query, it authenticates the request using the user certificate, then, based on the attributes that are included on the key Δ_u, A_i decides whether or not the received key should be validated. If not, the user query is aborted. Otherwise, A_i uses its master secret key SK_i to compute the validated decryption key $\overline{\mathcal{K}}_{A_i}$. Then, it sends the latter to the user.

$$\overline{\mathcal{K}}_{A_i} = \{\overline{K}' = \overline{K}^{\beta_i}, \overline{L}' = \overline{L}^{\beta_i}, \forall \delta \in \Delta_u : \overline{K}'_{\delta} = \overline{K}_{\delta}^{\beta_i}\}$$

Once u receives the signed decryption key $\overline{\mathcal{K}}_{A_i}$, it removes the randomization to compute the final signed (by A_i) decryption key we denote $\mathcal{K}_{A_i}$.

$$\mathcal{K}_{A_i} = \{K' = \overline{K}'^{q^{-1}}, L' = \overline{L}'^{q^{-1}}, \forall \delta \in \Delta_u : K'_{\delta} = \overline{K}'^{q^{-1}}_{\delta}\}$$

$$= \{K' = (g^{\alpha} \cdot g^{a \cdot d})^{\beta_i}, L' = g^{d \cdot \beta_i}, \forall \delta \in \Delta_u : K'_{\delta} = \Theta_{\delta}^{d \cdot \beta_i}\}$$

We emphasis here that in the key generation process, no interaction is required between the involved attribute authorities.

Decryption. The decryption process is performed by a data consumer (user) u who runs the Decrypt algorithm. The user starts by downloading from the cloud server the data item $(A_i, E_\kappa(M), \mathcal{C})$ that is supposed to be decrypted. To be able to decrypt the data item, the decryption key issued to the data consumer needs to fulfill two requirements: (1) It needs to be approved and signed by A_i, and (2) the attribute sets Δ_u involved in the decryption key satisfies the access structure $(\mathbb{M}, \rho)$ used to encrypt the data item. Let $\mathbb{M}_u$ be a sub-matrix of $\mathbb{M}$, where each row of $\mathbb{M}_u$ corresponds to an attribute in Δ_u, and $\mathbb{I} = \{i : \rho(i) \in \mathbb{A}\}$ be a subset of $\{1, 2, \cdots, l\}$. Let us denote by $\mathbb{M}_i$ the ith row of the matrix $\mathbb{M}$. The Decrypt algorithm computes a set of constants $\{w_i\}_{i \in \mathbb{I}}$ such that $\sum_{i \in \mathbb{I}} w_i \cdot \mathbb{M}_i = (1, 0, \cdots, 0)$. Then, it uses the $\{w_i\}_{i \in \mathbb{I}}$ to decrypt the data item as following.

$$
\begin{aligned}
\overline{\mathcal{C}} &= \frac{e(C, K')}{\prod_{i \in \mathbb{I}} \left(e(C_i, L') \cdot e(D_i, K'_{\rho(i)}) \right)^{w_i}} \\
&= \frac{e(g,g)^{\alpha \cdot \beta_i \cdot s} \cdot e(g,g)^{a \cdot d \cdot \beta_i \cdot s}}{\prod_{i \in \mathbb{I}} \left(e(g,g)^{a \cdot d \cdot \lambda_i \cdot \beta_i} \cdot e(\Theta_{\rho(i)}, g)^{-r_i \cdot d \cdot \beta_i} \cdot e(g, \Theta_{\rho(i)})^{r_i \cdot d \cdot \beta_i} \right)^{w_i}} \\
&= \frac{e(g,g)^{\alpha \cdot \beta_i \cdot s} \cdot e(g,g)^{a \cdot d \cdot \beta_i \cdot s}}{\prod_{i \in \mathbb{I}} \left(e(g,g)^{a \cdot d \cdot \lambda_i \cdot \beta_i} \right)^{w_i}}
\end{aligned}
$$

By considering that

$$
\begin{aligned}
\sum_{i \in \mathbb{I}} w_i \cdot \lambda_i &= (w_1, w_2, \cdots, w_{|\mathbb{I}|}) \cdot \boldsymbol{\lambda}_{\mathbb{I}}^\top \\
&= (w_1, w_2, \cdots, w_{|\mathbb{I}|}) \cdot \mathbb{M}_u \cdot \boldsymbol{v}^\top \\
&= (1, 0, \cdots, 0) \cdot (s, v_2, \cdots, v_n) = s
\end{aligned}
$$

we get $\overline{\mathcal{C}} = e(g,g)^{\alpha \cdot \beta_i \cdot s}$. Then, the Decrypt algorithm computes the symmetric key $\kappa = H(\overline{\mathcal{C}})$. Using κ, it decrypts the encrypted data $E_\kappa(M)$ to get M.

6   Security Analysis

We now demonstrate the security and robustness of the proposed construction by proving that it fulfills the security requirements defined in Sect. 4.4.

Theorem 1. *Our construction is collusion resistant under the GDHE assumption.*

Theorem 2. *Our construction is (t,n)-robust under the GDHE assumption.*

7   Conclusion

In this paper, we propose a formally proved secure and robust Cyber Security information sharing solution relying on a novel attribute-based encryption scheme that combines both the advantages of centralized and decentralized ABE while overcoming their weaknesses. In contrast to centralized ABE schemes, our construction is a single point of failure-free on security since it requires the collaboration of several entities for decryption key issuing. In addition, in contrast to existing decentralized ABE schemes, our construction does not require the data providers to fully trust all attributes authorities, only a single authority should be trusted.

Acknowledgments. This research is funded by the European Union's Horizon 2020 research and innovation programme under the Secure Collaborative Intelligent Industrial Automation (SeCoIIA) project, grant agreement No 871967. Additionally, part of this work was done as part of IRT SystemX project PFS (Security of Smart Ports).

References

1. Incentives and Barriers to Information Sharing - ENISA. https://www.enisa.europa.eu/publications/incentives-and-barriers-to-information-sharing
2. The French CIIP Framework—Agence nationale de la sécurité des systèmes d'information. https://www.ssi.gouv.fr/en/cybersecurity-in-france/ciip-in-france/
3. Bertilsson, M., Ingemarsson, I.: A construction of practical secret sharing schemes using linear block codes. In: Seberry, J., Zheng, Y. (eds.) AUSCRYPT 1992. LNCS, vol. 718, pp. 67–79. Springer, Heidelberg (1993). https://doi.org/10.1007/3-540-57220-1_53
4. Bethencourt, J., Sahai, A., Waters, B.: Ciphertext-policy attribute-based encryption. In: 2007 IEEE Symposium on Security and Privacy (SP 2007), pp. 321–334. IEEE (2007)
5. Boneh, D., Boyen, X., Goh, E.-Jn.: hierarchical identity based encryption with constant size ciphertext. In: Cramer, R. (ed.) EUROCRYPT 2005. LNCS, vol. 3494, pp. 440–456. Springer, Heidelberg (2005). https://doi.org/10.1007/11426639_26
6. Chase, M.: Multi-authority attribute based encryption. In: Vadhan, S.P. (ed.) TCC 2007. LNCS, vol. 4392, pp. 515–534. Springer, Heidelberg (2007). https://doi.org/10.1007/978-3-540-70936-7_28
7. ENISA: ENISA NCSS Good Practice Guide. No. November (2016). www.enisa.europa.eu
8. Ito, M., Saito, A., Nishizeki, T.: Secret sharing scheme realizing general access structure. Electron. Commun. Japan (Part III: Fund. Electron. Sci.) **72**(9), 56–64 (1989)
9. Kampanakis, P.: Security automation and threat information-sharing options. IEEE Secur. Privacy **12**(5), 42–51 (2014). https://doi.org/10.1109/MSP.2014.99
10. Khouzani, M., Pham, V., Cid, C.: Strategic discovery and sharing of vulnerabilities in competitive environments. In: Poovendran, R., Saad, W. (eds.) GameSec 2014. LNCS, vol. 8840, pp. 59–78. Springer, Cham (2014). https://doi.org/10.1007/978-3-319-12601-2_4
11. Kumar, P., Alphonse, P., et al.: Attribute based encryption in cloud computing: a survey, gap analysis, and future directions. J. Network Comput. Appl. **108**, 37–52 (2018)

12. Li, W., Xue, K., Xue, Y., Hong, J.: TMACS: a robust and verifiable threshold multi-authority access control system in public cloud storage. IEEE Trans. Parallel Distrib. Syst. **27**(5), 1484–1496 (2015)
13. Liu, Z., Cao, Z.: On efficiently transferring the linear secret-sharing scheme matrix in ciphertext-policy attribute-based encryption. IACR Cryptol. ePrint Arch. **2010**, 374 (2010)
14. Nweke, L.O., Wolthusen, S.: Legal issues related to cyber threat information sharing among private entities for critical infrastructure protection. In: International Conference on Cyber Conflict, CYCON 2020-May, pp. 63–78 (2020). https://doi.org/10.23919/CyCon49761.2020.9131721
15. Pedersen, T.P.: A threshold cryptosystem without a trusted party. In: Davies, D.W. (ed.) EUROCRYPT 1991. LNCS, vol. 547, pp. 522–526. Springer, Heidelberg (1991). https://doi.org/10.1007/3-540-46416-6_47
16. Preuveneers, D., Joosen, W., Bernal Bernabe, J., Skarmeta, A.: Distributed security framework for reliable threat intelligence sharing. Secur. Commun. Networks **2020**, 1–15 (2020). https://doi.org/10.1155/2020/8833765
17. Sahai, A., Waters, B.: Fuzzy identity-based encryption. In: Cramer, R. (ed.) EUROCRYPT 2005. LNCS, vol. 3494, pp. 457–473. Springer, Heidelberg (2005). https://doi.org/10.1007/11426639_27
18. Shamir, A.: How to share a secret. Commun. ACM **22**(11), 612–613 (1979)
19. Steinberger, J., Sperotto, A., Golling, M., Baier, H.: How to exchange security events? overview and evaluation of formats and protocols. In: 2015 IFIP/IEEE International Symposium on Integrated Network Management (IM), pp. 261–269. IEEE (2015)
20. Talamo, M., Arcieri, F., Dimitri, A., Schunck, C.H.: A blockchain based PKI validation system based on rare events management. Future Internet **12**(2), 40 (2020)
21. UNION, T.C.O.T.E.: Strategy for a Secure Information Society in Europe (2007/C 68/01). https://eur-lex.europa.eu/legal-content/EN/TXT/HTML/?uri=CELEX:32007G0324(01)
22. Vakilinia, I., Tosh, D.K., Sengupta, S.: 3-way game model for privacy-preserving cybersecurity information exchange framework. In: MILCOM 2017–2017 IEEE Military Communications Conference (MILCOM), pp. 829–834 (2017). https://doi.org/10.1109/MILCOM.2017.8170842
23. Vakilinia, I., Tosh, D.K., Sengupta, S.: Attribute based sharing in cybersecurity information exchange framework. In: 2017 International Symposium on Performance Evaluation of Computer and Telecommunication Systems (SPECTS), pp. 1–6 (2017). https://doi.org/10.23919/SPECTS.2017.8046770
24. Wagner, T.D., Mahbub, K., Palomar, E., Abdallah, A.E.: Cyber threat intelligence sharing: survey and research directions. Comput. Secur. **87**, 101589 (2019). https://doi.org/10.1016/j.cose.2019.101589, https://www.sciencedirect.com/science/article/pii/S016740481830467X
25. Yakubov, A., Shbair, W., Wallbom, A., Sanda, D., et al.: A blockchain-based PKI management framework. In: The First IEEE/IFIP International Workshop on Managing and Managed by Blockchain (Man2Block) Colocated with IEEE/IFIP NOMS 2018, 23–27 April 2018. Tapei, Tawain (2018)
26. Zibak, A., Simpson, A.: Cyber threat information sharing: perceived benefits and barriers. In: Proceedings of the 14th International Conference on Availability, Reliability and Security, pp. 1–9 (2019)

Revisiting Stream-Cipher-Based Homomorphic Transciphering in the TFHE Era

Adda-Akram Bendoukha, Aymen Boudguiga$^{(\boxtimes)}$, and Renaud Sirdey

Université Paris-Saclay, CEA-List, Palaiseau, France
{adda-Akram.bendoukha,aymen.boudguiga,renaud.sirdey}@cea.fr

Abstract. Transciphering allows to workaround the large expansion of the size of FHE encrypted data, thanks to the use of symmetric cryptography. Transciphering is a recryption technique that delegates the effective homomorphic encryption to the cloud. As a result, a client only has to encrypt (once) a symmetric key SYM.sk under a homomorphic encryption system, while his payload data are encrypted under SYM.sk using the chosen symmetric encryption algorithm.

In this work, we study the performances of some symmetric encryption algorithms in light of the TFHE cryptosystem and its properties. This allows us to unleash the use of additional existing symmetric algorithms which were not viable candidates for efficient encrypted domain execution with levelled-FHEs. In particular, we provide experimental evidences that Grain128-AEAD, a well established and well respected stream-cipher which is a finalist of the NIST competition for light-weight cryptography, is amenable to practical performances when run in the encrypted domain. As such, our work extends practical transciphering capabilities to include authenticated encryption for the first time.

Keywords: FHE · Stream-ciphers · Transciphering

1 Introduction

Fully Homomorphic Encryption (FHE) provides end-to-end confidentiality of personal and sensitive data by allowing general computations in the encrypted domain. Indeed, FHE is well suited for services requiring clients data offloading to computation servers in the Cloud. Yet, such offloading necessarily implies sending data over a network at some point, and the intrinsic expansion factor of FHE ciphertexts becomes an issue for their transmission and a potential show stopper for FHE usage with some use-cases. Indeed, large FHE ciphertexts are a

The research leading to these results has been funded in part from the European Union's Preparatory Action on Defence Research (PADR-FDDT-OPEN-03-2019). This paper reflects only the authors' views and the Commission is not liable for any use that may be made of the information contained therein.

E. Aïmeur et al. (Eds.): FPS 2021, LNCS 13291, pp. 19–33, 2022.
https://doi.org/10.1007/978-3-031-08147-7_2

bottleneck, especially in infrastructures with small bandwidth such as IoT infrastructures using for example LoRa or Sigfox for communication with a gateway to the cloud.

Transciphering works around this expansion issue by combining both symmetric cryptography and FHE. This results in a mean for compressing FHE ciphertexts prior to their transmission, with the ability to recover the homomorphic encryption of the message later without any security breaches and with additional computational cost only on the server.

While transciphering has been studied in depth in the state-of-the-art between 2015 and 2018 [3, 4, 8, 9, 19, 21–23], most existing works have done so in the context of levelled FHE cryptosystems which suffer from limitations due to the increased computational cost of FHE calculations at larger multiplicative depth. As such, there is a need to revisit these works as well as the portfolio of symmetric algorithms amenable to practical performances when run in the encrypted domain in light of the TFHE cryptosystem which enabled practical bootstrapping and which, as such, does not induce multiplicative-depth related limitations. To the best of our knowledge, this has not yet been done in the state of the art.

Contribution − In this work we investigate stream-cipher-based transciphering by means of TFHE. We consider the following steam-ciphers: Trivium [15], Kreyvium [8], Grain-128a [1] and Grain128-AEAD [18]. We show that TFHE leads to practical performances when transciphering with the aforementioned stream-ciphers. In particular, as it removes the burden of multiplicative-depth constraints imposed by levelled FHE schemes, we show that TFHE allows to perform transciphering with a much smaller amount of homomorphic calculations (requiring to perform only one rather than many warm-ups in the encrypted domain). Also, this paper is, to the best our of knowledge, the first to demonstrate practical performances when running Grain-128a and Grain-AEAD in the FHE domain and to bring anthenticated encryption into the picture of transciphering (thanks to Grain-AEAD). In addition, we discuss several optimized implementations for these stream-ciphers with words which are 8 or 32-bits long. Finally, we detail the timing performances obtained when running each of these algorithms over TFHE by means of Cingulata [12], a well-established homomorphic applications compiler.

Paper Organization − The remainder of this paper is organized as follows. In Sect. 2, we briefly recall the principle of transciphering. In Sect. 3, we briefly present TFHE as our target FHE scheme for transciphering. In Sect. 5 and 6, we review the stream-ciphers that we intend to use for transciphering with TFHE. And in the last Sect. 7, we discuss implementation details and performance results.

2   Tranciphering

In a typical homomorphic encryption usage scenario, a first party (e.g., a client) aims at delegating the evaluation of a certain function f over a confidential message m to a distant Cloud server. In a direct approach, The client would encrypt m using a Fully Homomorphic Encryption scheme (FHE). The size expansion

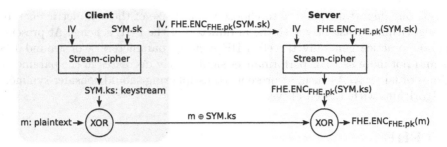

Fig. 1. Transciphering with a stream-cipher

factor is defined as $\frac{|\mathsf{FHE.Enc}(m)|}{|m|}$. In most FHE cryptosystems this factor is very large. In can reach some mega-bytes with respect to the chosen cryptosystem, its parameters and the chosen security level. This by opposition to protocols involving symmetric algorithms which usually lead to negligible or small overheads. This fact yielded the idea to bind FHE and symmetric cryptography to workaround this size expansion issue.

Indeed, with transciphering, we aim at lessening the quantity of homomorphically encrypted data to be sent to the Cloud by encrypting it symmetrically instead, and preserving the ability to recover the entire homomorphic encryption of the initial data. To do so, a client encrypts his message m using a symmetric cryptosystem with key SYM.sk, and the key SYM.sk is encrypted using a homomorphic cryptosystem with key FHE.pk. At the reception of $(\mathsf{SYM.Enc_{SYM.sk}}(m), \mathsf{FHE.Enc_{FHE.pk}}(\mathsf{SYM.sk}))$, the Cloud server homomorphically runs the symmetric cryptosystem decryption function i.e., runs SYM.Enc using $\mathsf{FHE.Enc_{FHE.pk}}(\mathsf{SYM.sk})$. In the case of stream-cipher, an FHE encrypted keystream is the output of the previous evaluation. On the Cloud side, we would have both $m \oplus keystream$ and FHE.Enc(keystream). FHE.Enc(m) is then easily computed by performing a homomorphic xor between $m \oplus keystream$ and FHE.Enc(keystream) (as depicted in Fig. 1). The size of m can be arbitrarily large, while the size of SYM.sk is fixed and is usually small enough to be homomorphically encrypted and transmitted once and for all. This is how compression is obtained (at the computational cost, of course, of homomorphically running the symmetric scheme decryption function on the server).

In terms of security, as most practically-used symmetric encryption algorithms do not have formally established indistinguishability properties, it should be emphasized that using transciphering jeopardizes the IND-CPA property of the FHE scheme (FHE schemes can be at most IND-CCA1 and most the schemes used in practice are only IND-CPA). This should however not be considered an issue in practice provided that symmetric encryption more often than not teams with provably-secure public-key encryption for efficiency reasons in practical scenarios, and FHE is no exception. Nevertheless, if we assume a perfect PRF on the symmetric side, the resulting construction would be IND-CPA [10].

Yet, one important point is to choose the key size of the symmetric encryption algorithm consistently with the parameters of the FHE scheme. At present, common practice generally targets FHE security parameters λ of around 128 bits and not more as FHE performances significantly decreases in the parameter regimes of larger λ. As such, at present, transciphering should consider symmetric algorithms with 128 bits keys.

3   TFHE

In this section, we present a high-level description of TFHE to justify its suitability for transciphering.

3.1   Learning with Errors

The Learning With Errors (LWE) assumption states that given an arbitrary number of samples $(a, b = \langle a, s \rangle + e) \in \mathbb{Z}_q^{n+1}$ where a and s are both in $\mathbb{Z}_q^n$ and $e \in \mathbb{Z}_q$ is a small error sampled from a Gaussian distribution over $\mathbb{Z}_q$, finding s is a computationally hard problem. The hardness of LWE has been proved by Regev in [24].

LWE is adapted to the real torus $\mathbb{T} = \mathbb{R}/\mathbb{Z}$ (i.e. $(a, b) \in \mathbb{T}^n \times \mathbb{T}$). We call TLWE and TRLWE the LWE instances over the torus and the polynomial ring $\mathbb{T}_N[X] = \mathbb{T}[X]/(X^N + 1)$, respectively. For a matter of efficiency binary keys are used in both TLWE and TRLWE

3.2   TLWE/TRLWE Encryption

Given a TLWE sample $(a, b = \langle a, s \rangle + e)$ and a message $m \in \mathbb{Z}_p$. Integer messages are mapped to elements of $\mathbb{T}$. The encryption of an integer m is given by $(a, b) + (0, m')$ where $m' = \frac{q}{p} \cdot \bar{m}$ and $\bar{m}$ the mapping of m over $\mathbb{T}$.

The decryption computes a dot product and then rounds the result to the nearest integer: $\frac{p}{q} \cdot (b, a)^T \cdot (1, -s) = \frac{p}{q} \cdot \lfloor \frac{q}{p} \cdot \bar{m} + e \rceil = \bar{m}$.

The same idea applies to the TRLWE settings. The aforementioned encryption scheme is an additive homomorphic scheme. In TFHE, the multiplication is ensured using GSW samples and a gadget decomposition algorithm [13,17].

3.3   Bootstrapping

In order to decrypt a message correctly, the noise e has to remain under a certain bound $e < \frac{q}{2 \cdot p}$. Obviously, the noise grows while evaluating operations on a ciphertext. The original idea of Gentry [16] was to boostrap a ciphertext to bring its noise to a fixed level. Bootstrapping consists in decrypting a ciphertext homomorphically. In practice, TFHE proposes the most efficient bootstrapping that takes 13 milliseconds per boolean gate computation. TFHE bootstrapping is explained in details in [13].

3.4   Impact on Transciphering

Thanks to its bootstrapping, TFHE offers greater freedom in the choice of the symmetric cryptosystem used for transciphering. Indeed with TFHE, we can perform more operations and even relax the constraints imposed by the multiplicative depth[1], since we have an efficient way to reduce the noise. This gives us access to a whole new set of symmetric cryptosystems eligible for transciphering.

In parallel, when stream-ciphers are used for tranciphering with a levelled homomorphic encryption scheme such as BFV, we have to bound their multiplicative depth. That is, we fix the size of the output keystream in advance with respect to the size of the data chunk to be encrypted. Bounding the stream-cipher size is suited for parallel implementation and batching. Otherwise, higher parameters have to be chosen for the cryptosystem in order to handle the required multiplicative depth. This solution has an impact on the general performance, not only of transciphering, but also on the computation on the message m initially planned.

4   Choice of the Symmetric Scheme

When it comes to transciphering, as stated in [8], stream-ciphers are more attractive than block-ciphers for two main reasons. First, when encrypting using a stream-cipher, keystream generation is independent of the data to be encrypted/decrypted. Consequently, almost all of the homomorphic calculations required for transciphering (i.e., the homomorphic keystream calculations) can be performed offline, outside of the critical latency path. Then, when the data to be tranciphered are available, there only remains to homomorphically XOR them with the precomputed homomorphically encrypted keystream. So, stream-cipher-based transciphering offers this advantage over block-cipher-based transciphering.

Second, modern stream-ciphers generally follow the pattern of a relatively expensive warm-up phase which enables the subsequent generation of an (almost) arbitrary long sequence of keystream. The keystream bits are generated in a very lightweight way. This is more interesting than block-cipher-based designs, since the warm-up has to be paid only once (or infrequently) and can be done offline. Note that one block-cipher run is more or less equivalent to one stream-cipher warm-up, in terms of computational cost.

Still, as shown in [8], when using levelled FHE scheme the warm-up had to be frequently redone (stream-ciphers were then preferred because they have an intrinsically lower multiplicative depth than block-ciphers) leading to a kind of CTR mode of operation for an IV-based stream-cipher such as Trivium. However, in this work, we remove the multiplicative-depth constraint by using TFHE, and avoid these regular warm-ups. As such, we enable a more natural use of a stream-ciphers with one (rather expensive) homomorphic warm-up for many (cheap)

---

[1] The multiplicative depth of a circuit is the maximum number of successive multiplications in the circuit.

homomorphic keystream bits generation (which can still be performed offline). As a consequence, the use of TFHE allows to drastically reduce the amount of homomorphic operations required for transciphering[2].

5 Trivium/Kreyvium

5.1 Trivium

When we search for a suitable stream-cipher to build an efficient transciphering scheme, we tend to give a particular interest to hardware-oriented and lightweight cryptosystems. Since they focus on providing a high throughput while using a small internal state and small arithmetic circuits, and of course an appropriate level of security. These specifications are quite similar to the ones we have for building transciphering schemes.

Trivium is part of the eSTREAM portofolio for hardware oriented encryption and fits the aforementioned requirements. Indeed, it is able to produce up to 2^{64} keystream bits from an 80-bits KEY and IV, by updating an internal state (S_i) composed of 3 registers of sizes 93, 84, and 111 by the mean of additions and multiplications and reinserting the output of each round back into the internal state (which is 288-bits long).

$$t_1 = s_{66} + s_{93} + s_{91} \cdot s_{92} + s_{171}$$
$$t_2 = s_{162} + s_{171} + s_{175} \cdot s_{176} + s_{264}$$
$$t_3 = s_{243} + s_{288} + s_{286} \cdot s_{287} + s_{69}$$
$$(s_1, \ldots, s_{93}) \longleftarrow (t_3, s_1, \ldots, s_{92})$$
$$(s_{94}, \ldots, s_{177}) \longleftarrow (t_1, s_{94}, \ldots, s_{176})$$
$$(s_{178}, \ldots, s_{288}) \longleftarrow (t_2, s_{178}, \ldots, s_{287})$$

Trivium's structure can be viewed as a composition of three main functions. First, an initialization step (Init(KEY, IV)) sets the internal state value using bits from KEY, IV and zeros. Second, a Warmup step increases the internal state's entropy by iterating 1152 times, linear and non-linear operations, to mix bits from the different registers. Finally, a keystream generation step (KeyGen(t)), similar to Warmup, outputs the tth keystream bit by computing $z_t = $ KeyGen(t) ∘ Warmup ∘ Init(KEY, IV). For more details about Trivium specification and security analysis, interested readers can refer to [15].

5.2 Kreyvium

Canteaut et al. [8] proposed Kreyvium to increase Trivium security from 80-bits to 128-bits. That is why, the design of Kreyvium is almost identical to Trivium. However, Kreyvium has an 128-bits key and IV each. The internal state of Kreyvium is composed of an extra pair of 128-bits registers initialized with the key and the IV. Thus, Kreyvium has 544-bits internal state. The key and IV bits are constantly re-injected by a XOR operation into the computation of the state update.

---

[2] As a general guidelines, the first rule of optimization for FHE is to find (legitimate) ways of doing less FHE calculations.

6 Grain128a/Grain128-AEAD

6.1 Grain128a

Grain128a [1] is a hardware-oriented stream-cipher from the eSTREAM portofolio and thus, a lightweight cryptosystem with well-respected security. It supports a 128-bits key and a 128-bits IV. Its internal state is composed of an LFSR and an NFSR[3], initialized respectively with the key and the IV. It comes with the possibility to perform an authenticated encryption by the mean of a MAC of size 32-bits.

6.2 Grain128-AEAD

Grain128-AEAD is a well-established stream-cipher which is widely inspired from Grain128a. It is a finalist of the NIST competition on lightweight cryptography and has slight modifications compared with its predecessor. Its Authenticated Encryption with Associated Data mode (AEAD) is compulsory and refers to the possibility of encrypting a subset of the plaintext bits using a mask d as: $c_i = m_i \oplus (ks_i \cdot d_i)$, as well as computing a larger MAC (64-bits long) on it. Grain128-AEAD internal state is 256-bits long and is formed by a 128-bits NFSR and a 128-bits LFSR. It relies also on two 64-bits accumulator and shift registers for MAC computation.

After 384 rounds of warm-up, Grain128-AEAD produces two streams of bits: the encryption keystream ks and the MAC keystream ms. They are extracted from the main keystream using bit parity i.e., $ks_i = y_{384+2i}$ and $ms_i = y_{384+2i+1}$ (where y_{383} denotes the last output bit from the warmup phase of the cipher).

6.3 MAC Computation

After Grain128a-AEAD warm-up for 384 rounds, the accumulator and the shift registers are initialized with the first 128-bits of keystream. Then, a message authentication code (MAC) can be computed for the plaintext bitstream m of size $M = |m|$. The MAC computation consists in updating the accumulator and the shift registers as follows:

$$a_k^{i+1} = a_k^i + m_i \cdot r_k^i, \quad 0 \leq i \leq M, \quad 0 \leq k \leq 63$$
$$r_k^{i+1} = r_{k+1}^i, \quad r_{63}^{i+1} = ms_i, \quad 0 \leq k \leq 62$$

where a_i^t and r_i^t denote the accumulator and shift register bits, respectively and ms the aforementioned MAC keystream. The MAC corresponds to the obtained accumulator at the end of this iteration.

Note that this MAC computation can be generalised to any stream-cipher, such as Trivium or Kreyvium, to extend it to support an authenticated encryption mode.

---

[3] Linear/Non-linear feeadback shift register.

6.4   MAC Usage in the Context of Transciphering

Now that we have a method to perform an authenticated encryption, the question of how to exploit the MAC after it has been homomorphically computed arises, i.e., how to fully achieve authenticated encryption within transciphering. So, when an authenticated encrypted message is received by the cloud it gets a message XORed by a portion of keystream and the associated MAC. Note that both of these are in the clear domain with respect to the FHE encryption layer. The cloud then homomorphically computes both an (homomorphic) encryption of the portion of keystream as well as (homomorphic) encryptions of the bits which *will* be used for (homomorphically) recomputing the MAC (from the message bits) as in Sect. 6.3. When appropriate, all these homomorphic ciphertexts can be precomputed offline. The cloud can then use the homomorphic keystream to retrieve (homomorphic) encryptions of the message bits which can then be used to homomorphically compute the associated MAC. The received MAC (a cleartext with respect to the FHE layer) can then be compared to the (homomorphically) computed one (a ciphertext with respect to the FHE layer) to lead to an (homomorphically) encrypted bit[4] equal to either 1 (if the MAC match) or 0 (otherwise). At this point, the cloud is by construction not able to know whether or not the two MAC match. Now assume that post transciphering the cloud need to (homomorphically) compute $f(m)$ or rather $[f(m)]$ (from $[m]$ which is the homomorphic encryption of the message obtained after transciphering). Then, if μ denotes the received MAC and $[\mu']$ the (homomorphically) computed one, we may want the cloud compute an encrypted result $[r]$ such that

$$[r] = \left[\left\{ \begin{array}{ll} f(m) \text{ if } \mu = \mu' \\ \text{NIL} \quad \text{otherwise} \end{array} \right. \right], \tag{1}$$

where NIL is out of f range. As such, post (FHE) decryption, the client can make the difference between valid outputs and invalid ones (due to integrity errors on the transmission channel). Note that, in order to comply with FHE requirements, Eq. (1), eventually has to be implemented by means of conditional assignments[5] which can be performed by means of algebraic operations[5]. That way, of course, the cloud cannot distinguish between the case where it computed (an encryption of) NIL or (that of) a valid result.

7   Experimental Results

7.1   The Cingulata Homomorphic Compiler

Cingulata, formerly known as Armadillo [12], is a toolchain and run-time environment (RTE) for implementing applications running over homomorphic

---

[4] Of course, comparison cannot be done per se in the encrypted domain, so if the μ_i's denotes the bits of the received MAC and the $[\mu'_i]$'s denote the FHE encryptions of the bits of the (homomorphically) computed one, the cloud has to compute $\prod_i (1 \oplus \mu_i \oplus [\mu'_i]) = [b]$.

[5] I.e., putting a into x when c is true, b otherwise, can be written has $x := ca \oplus (1 \oplus c)b$.

encryption. Cingulata provides high-level abstractions and tools to facilitate the implementation and the execution of privacy-preserving applications.

Cingulata relies on instrumented C++ types to denote private variables, e.g., CiInt for integers and CiBit for Booleans. Integer variables are dynamically sized and are internally represented as arrays of CiBit objects. The Cingulata environment monitors/tracks each bit independently. Integer operations are performed using Boolean circuits, which are automatically generated by the toolchain. For example a full-adder circuit is employed to perform an integer addition. The Boolean circuit generation is configurable and two generators are available: focused on minimal circuit size or on small multiplicative-depth. More generally, it is possible to implement additional circuit generators or to combine them.

A CiBit object can be in either plain or encrypted state. Plain-plain and plain-encrypted bit operations are optimized out, in this way constant folding and propagation is automatically performed at the bit-level. Bit operations between encrypted values are performed by a "bit execution" object implementing the IBitExec interface. This object can either be a HE library wrapper, simply a bit-tracker object or even a plaint bit execution used for algorithm debugging purposes. When a HE library wrapper is used the Cingulata environment directly executes the application using the underlying HE library.

Another option is to use the bit-tracker in order to build a circuit representation of the application. The later allows to use circuit optimization modules in order to further optimize the Boolean circuit representation. The hardware synthesis toolchain ABC[6] is used to minimize circuit size. It is an open-source environment providing implementations of state-of-the-art circuit optimization algorithms. These algorithms are mainly designed for minimizing circuit area or latency but, currently, none of them is designed for multiplicative depth minimization. In order to fill this gap, several heuristics for minimizing the multiplicative depth are available in Cingulata, refer to [5,11] for more details.

The optimized Boolean circuit is then executed using Cingulata's parallel run-time environment. The RTE is generic, meaning that it uses a HE library wrapper, i.e. a "bit execution" object as defined earlier, in order to execute the gates of the circuit. The scheduler of the run-time allows to fully take advantage of many-core processors. Besides, a set of utility applications are provided for parameter generation (given a target security level), key generation, encryption and decryption. These applications are also generic, in the same vein as the parallel RTE.

7.2 Implementation Details

First, we did a simple implementation of Trivium, Kreyvium, Grain128a and Grain128-AEAD by following their original specifications using a binary representation [1,9,15,18]. We developed these algorithms with Cingulata as it provides all the necessary tools for implementing applications with a binary

---

[6] http://people.eecs.berkeley.edu/alanmi/abc/.

plaintext space, efficiently. Indeed, Cingulata specifies all the boolean operators needed for updating the bits of the internal state of each stream-cipher.

Second, we followed [6] and implemented each stream-cipher using longer words (8 or 32-bits long). Indeed, our selected stream-ciphers admit fairly efficient compact 8 and 32-bits software implementations which are suitable for more constrained platforms. Let us consider the example of Trivium, since it takes 64 (bit-level) cycles for the re-injection of t_3 to have an effect on t_1 [15], up to 64 cycles can be performed in parallel leaving the possibility for byte-oriented, 32-bit-word-oriented and 64-bits-word-oriented implementations requiring only 36 bytes of memory for the internal state (slightly more for 64-bits implementations as 288 is not a multiple of 64). The same analysis applies to Kreyvium, Grain128a and Grain128-AEAD.

Finally, we did a separate implementation for the MAC computation algorithm described in Sect. 6.3. Indeed, this MAC computation is adaptable to any stream-cipher once we are able to separate its keystream bits using their parity.

Dividing the keystream into two seperate keystreams was straightforward in Cingulata for the original implementation which outputs 1-bit of keystream at a time (i.e., at every keystream generation round). Indeed, we have just to take odd bits as the MAC computation keystream (ms in Sect. 6.3).

However, this task of keystream division using bits parity will become more challenging when we consider the compact 8-bits or 32-bits implementations without using Cingulata (which in fine works on a per-bits basis and, as such, gives an access to individual encrypted bits). When a true n-bits implementation is done, if our considered stream-cipher outputs 8-bits at a time, we will need to separate these 8-bits into 4-bits for encryption and 4 others for MAC computation. To do so, the most appropriate approach is to use a static look up table, with 256 entries, which outputs two 4-bits values using the initial (encrypted) 8-bits value as the selector.

7.3   Performance Results

As presented in Table 1, we see that the warm-up phase in each of the studied stream-ciphers remains time-consuming when performed homomorphically over TFHE (between 4 to 6 min). Trivium, Kreyvium and Grain128a remain somewhat inside the same range. This is due to the fact that Trivium and Kreyvium have a lightweight internal state update[7] but perform a large number of iterations (1152). On the other hand, Grain128a has a heavier update function[8] but only performs 256 iterations for warming-up. Lastly, for Grain128-AEAD the warm-up time significantly increases, because it does 128 additional iterations (384 in total) to initialize the accumulator and the shift register for MAC computation.

---

[7] A small number of additions and multiplications (only three) per round.

[8] LFSR/NFSR update, non linear function application and register shifting (register shifting being almost free).

However, following the operating mode defined in Sect. 4, when using TFHE, the warm-up phase can be performed (almost) once and for all and offline. As such, warm-up durations of a few minutes are easliy amortized and have no impact on latency. Hence, one can make sure, within a given protocol, that when some payload data is transmitted, the internal state of the stream-cipher, on the server side, has already been (homomorphically) warmed-up and is ready to produce the keystream bits required to transcipher that data. In fact, as a further optimization, the server may even start producing and internally storing homomorphically encrypted keystream bits as soon as the warm-up is done and prior to the reception of the symmetrically encrypted message. This results in an almost latency-free decompression process since only the remaining (homomorphic) XORs need to be done upon message arrival. Of course, the server still has to pay the computational cost of homomorphically computing the (FHE encrypted) keystream bits but that cost does not necessarily translate into additional latency.

Things are a little more complicated when authenticated encryption is implemented since, as discussed in Sect. 6.4, the MAC (homomorphic) computation has to be finalized when the message is received. Still, that finalization can be performed in parallel to the homomorphic evaluation of $f(\mathsf{FHE.Enc}(m))$ (the payload of the system). Upon completion of both, the two results can then combined following (1) for generating the final result.

With respect to our multi-bit implementations, recall that the Cingulata compiler automatically (and transparently to the programmer) turns them into (optimized) single-bit ones. As such, if Cingulata does its job properly we should expect that the comfort obtained by programming over words rather than bits does not translate into a degradation of the performances. Nicely, this is what we observed as the difference in execution times between single-bit and multi-bit implementations are not significant. Even if this test is slightly far-fetched for the considered algorithms (since they have natural single-bit expressions). This illustrates that Cingulata provides a higher level programming interface without significant losses in terms of performances (approximately $+2\%$ of computation time). See the two rightmost columns in Tables 1 and 3. Note additionally that the multi-bits implementation are more easily amenable to (automatic) parallelization.

We ran *single core* performance tests on an Intel(R) Xeon(R) CPU E3-1240 v5 @ 3.50 GHz and 8 GB RAM. However, contrary to the CTR mode of operation suggested in [9] (Sect. 4) we are now considering a more sequential more of operation. In the case where high parallelization is required to achieve low latency objectives we may thus need to interleave several keystreams (generated from several independant internal states). In that case, those keystreams can be computed in parallel (of course to the detriment of memory usage since several internal states would then have to be simultaneously stored).

We compare our results to the ones presented in [9]. In that paper, they used the BGV and BFV cryptosystems provided in HELib and Cingulata (respectively) with Trivium and Kreyvium, as well as LowMC which we do not consider in this paper (see Sect. 8). The parameters of the underlying FHE scheme (levelled) were firstly selected to fit the exact multiplicative depth of the symmetric cryptosystem, which is not representative of a real-world scenario, since, obviously, the goal is to perform further computations on the decompressed ciphertexts. They then selected parameters for an additional multiplicative depth of 6 (i.e. for a total depth of 6 plus the multiplicative depth of either Trivium or Kreyvium). The single-slot and single-core throughputs (the number of keystream bits generated per minute) they obtained were between 3.15 and 3.66 bits/min[9]. Meanwhile, we obtain a throughput of around 120 bits/min, without any constraints on post-decompression computations, nor on the keystream size to be produced, and thus the size of the message to be decompressed. We use the default parameters of TFHE which provide a security level of 128-bits, and we ran the tests on a low end PC. In addition, [9] intensively used *batching* which is an optimization, not available in TFHE, consisting in packing several cleartexts in a single ciphertexts with FHE operations applying in a SIMD fashion. While in our work no major optimization were added than those automatically done by Cingulata. Also we would like to emphasize that Grain-128a and Grain128-AEAD would not be runable with a levelled FHE, at least not without a large increased in FHE parameters (in order to cope with the increase in multiplicative depth) which would dramatically impact performances. With that respect, this paper works changes the status for the homomorphic execution of Grain128a and Grain-AEAD from "practically undoable" to "only 3 times slower than Trivium/Kreyvium" (over TFHE).

Table 1. Warm-up time in minutes

	1-bit	8-bits	32-bits
Trivium	4.23	4.64	4.84
Kreyvium	4.98	5.52	5.83
Grain128a	4.12	4.15	4.21
Grain128-AEAD	6.55	6.68	6.71

8   Other Algorithms

In this work, we chose to investigate only stream-ciphers based on conservative designs and which are either standardized or in the process of being so. However, since the first proposal of transciphering as a technique for FHE ciphertext compression [7], many symmetric (block and stream) ciphers have been designed

---

[9] To be fair, these throughputs could be increased to around 2000 bits/min with 600 slots of batching, however with FHE security parameters which are now outdated (due to recent advances in LWE-based systems cryptanalysis); so as an order of magnitude we should expect all the throughputs given in [9] to be divided by around 5. Still, as already stated, batching-based improvements in throughput are not applicable when using TFHE.

Table 2. 64-bits stream generation time in minutes

	1-bit	8-bits	32-bits
Trivium	0.29	0.30	0.32
Kreyvium	0.33	0.36	0.39
Grain128a	1.09	1.05	1.06
Grain128-AEAD	1.13	1.12	1.14

Table 3. Homomorphic MAC computation time in minute of a 32-bits message

1-bit	8-bits	32-bits
0.65	0.66	0.68

in order explicitly fit FHE operations cost model, and as such, achieve improved FHE performances. These "FHE friendly" algorithms consider the requirement of leading to circuits with very few multiplications and a low multiplicative depth. FLIP [23], LowMC [2], FiLIP [20], and FASTA [14] are examples of new algorithms designed following this philosophy. Even though their efficiency in the FHE context is effective by construction, some of these forward-looking designs still have not yet stand the test of time in terms of security, at least compared to the algorithms which we considered in this paper (Table 2).

9 Conclusion

In this work we demonstrate the improvement brought by the TFHE cryptosystems and its practical bootstrapping capabilities to the issue of transciphering. In particular, on top on demonstrating much better homomorphic execution performances on stream ciphers already suitable for transciphering, this paper also demonstrates that additional algorithms and functionalities are within reach of practical homomorphic execution performances. This is the case, for the well-respected Grain algorithms family including their authenticated-encryption flavor which can further be adapted to pretty much any other stream cipher to enable them with message integrity checking.

Yet, even if we implemented and tested multi-bit versions of the algorithms, the Cingulata compiler has automatically turned them back to bit-wise implementation (without a significant performance loss which shows that the compiler does its job properly). As a result, this paper is only the first part of the story since we have thus (implicitly) limited ourselves to bit-wise implementations over TFHE in gate-bootstrapping mode (i.e. with $\mathbb{Z}_2$ as message space and a bootstrapping applied after each XOR and AND gates involved). The second part of the story which will be the scope of a subsequent paper will be to use the programmable bootstrapping feature of TFHE to design higher-level homomorphic operators allowing to run transciphering directly over larger message spaces (e.g., $\mathbb{Z}_{2^4}$ or $\mathbb{Z}_{2^8}$) with further efficiency gains.

References

1. Ågren, M., Hell, M., Johansson, T., Meier, W.: Grain-128a: a new version of Grain-128 with optional authentication. IJWMC **5**, 48–59 (2011)
2. Albrecht, M., Rechberger, C., Schneider, T., Tiessen, T., Zohner, M.: Ciphers for MPC and FHE. Cryptology ePrint Archive Report 2016/687 (2016). https://eprint.iacr.org/2016/687
3. Albrecht, M.R., et al.: Feistel structures for MPC, and more. In: Sako, K., Schneider, S., Ryan, P.Y.A. (eds.) ESORICS 2019. LNCS, vol. 11736, pp. 151–171. Springer, Cham (2019). https://doi.org/10.1007/978-3-030-29962-0_8
4. Albrecht, M.R., Rechberger, C., Schneider, T., Tiessen, T., Zohner, M.: Ciphers for MPC and FHE. In: Oswald, E., Fischlin, M. (eds.) EUROCRYPT 2015. LNCS, vol. 9056, pp. 430–454. Springer, Heidelberg (2015). https://doi.org/10.1007/978-3-662-46800-5_17
5. Aubry, P., Carpov, S., Sirdey, R.: Faster homomorphic encryption is not enough: improved heuristic for multiplicative depth minimization of Boolean circuits. In: Jarecki, S. (ed.) CT-RSA 2020. LNCS, vol. 12006, pp. 345–363. Springer, Cham (2020). https://doi.org/10.1007/978-3-030-40186-3_15
6. Boudguiga, A., Letailleur, J., Sirdey, R., Klaudel, W.: Enhancing CAN security by means of lightweight stream-ciphers and protocols. In: Romanovsky, A., Troubitsyna, E., Gashi, I., Schoitsch, E., Bitsch, F. (eds.) SAFECOMP 2019. LNCS, vol. 11699, pp. 235–250. Springer, Cham (2019). https://doi.org/10.1007/978-3-030-26250-1_19
7. Brakerski, Z., Gentry, C., Vaikuntanathan, V.: (Leveled) fully homomorphic encryption without bootstrapping. In: Proceedings of the 3rd Innovations in Theoretical Computer Science Conference, ITCS 2012, pp. 309–325. Association for Computing Machinery, New York (2012). https://doi.org/10.1145/2090236.2090262
8. Canteaut, A., et al.: Stream ciphers: a practical solution for efficient homomorphic-ciphertext compression. In: FSE, pp. 313–333 (2016)
9. Canteaut, A., et al.: Stream ciphers: a practical solution for efficient homomorphic-ciphertext compression. J. Cryptol. **31**(3), 885–916 (2018). https://doi.org/10.1007/s00145-017-9273-9
10. Canteaut, A., et al.: Stream ciphers: a practical solution for efficient homomorphic-ciphertext compression. J. Cryptol. **31**(3), 885–916 (2018). https://doi.org/10.1007/s00145-017-9273-9. https://hal.inria.fr/hal-01650012
11. Carpov, S., Aubry, P., Sirdey, R.: A multi-start heuristic for multiplicative depth minimization of Boolean circuits. In: Brankovic, L., Ryan, J., Smyth, W.F. (eds.) IWOCA 2017. LNCS, vol. 10765, pp. 275–286. Springer, Cham (2018). https://doi.org/10.1007/978-3-319-78825-8_23
12. Carpov, S., Dubrulle, P., Sirdey, R.: Armadillo: a compilation chain for privacy preserving applications. In: Bao, F., Miller, S., Chow, S.S.M., Yao, D. (eds.) Proceedings of the 3rd International Workshop on Security in Cloud Computing, SCC@ASIACCS 2015, Singapore, Republic of Singapore, 14 April 2015, pp. 13–19. ACM (2015). https://doi.org/10.1145/2732516.2732520
13. Chillotti, I., Gama, N., Georgieva, M., Izabachène, M.: TFHE: fast fully homomorphic encryption over the torus. Cryptology ePrint Archive Report 2018/421 (2018). https://eprint.iacr.org/2018/421
14. Cid, C., Indrøy, J.P., Raddum, H.: FASTA - a stream cipher for fast FHE evaluation. Cryptology ePrint Archive Report 2021/1205 (2021). https://ia.cr/2021/1205

15. De Cannière, C., Preneel, B.: TRIVIUM. In: Robshaw, M., Billet, O. (eds.) New Stream Cipher Designs. LNCS, vol. 4986, pp. 244–266. Springer, Heidelberg (2008). https://doi.org/10.1007/978-3-540-68351-3_18
16. Gentry, C.: Fully homomorphic encryption using ideal lattices. In: Proceedings of the Forty-First Annual ACM Symposium on Theory of Computing, STOC 2009, pp. 169–178. ACM, New York (2009). https://doi.org/10.1145/1536414.1536440
17. Gentry, C., Sahai, A., Waters, B.: Homomorphic encryption from learning with errors: conceptually-simpler, asymptotically-faster, attribute-based. In: Canetti, R., Garay, J.A. (eds.) CRYPTO 2013. LNCS, vol. 8042, pp. 75–92. Springer, Heidelberg (2013). https://doi.org/10.1007/978-3-642-40041-4_5
18. Hell, M., Johansson, T., Maximov, A., Meier, W., Yoshida, H.: Grain-128AEADv2: strengthening the initialization against key reconstruction. Cryptology ePrint Archive Report 2021/751 (2021). https://ia.cr/2021/751
19. Hoffmann, C., Méaux, P., Ricosset, T.: Transciphering, using FiLIP and TFHE for an efficient delegation of computation. In: Bhargavan, K., Oswald, E., Prabhakaran, M. (eds.) INDOCRYPT 2020. LNCS, vol. 12578, pp. 39–61. Springer, Cham (2020). https://doi.org/10.1007/978-3-030-65277-7_3
20. Hoffmann, C., Méaux, P., Ricosset, T.: Transciphering, using FiLIP and TFHE for an efficient delegation of computation. Cryptology ePrint Archive Report 2020/1373 (2020). https://eprint.iacr.org/2020/1373
21. Lepoint, T., Naehrig, M.: A comparison of the homomorphic encryption schemes FV and YASHE. In: Pointcheval, D., Vergnaud, D. (eds.) AFRICACRYPT 2014. LNCS, vol. 8469, pp. 318–335. Springer, Cham (2014). https://doi.org/10.1007/978-3-319-06734-6_20
22. Méaux, P., Carlet, C., Journault, A., Standaert, F.-X.: Improved filter permutators for efficient FHE: better instances and implementations. In: Hao, F., Ruj, S., Sen Gupta, S. (eds.) INDOCRYPT 2019. LNCS, vol. 11898, pp. 68–91. Springer, Cham (2019). https://doi.org/10.1007/978-3-030-35423-7_4
23. Méaux, P., Journault, A., Standaert, F.-X., Carlet, C.: Towards stream ciphers for efficient FHE with low-noise ciphertexts. In: Fischlin, M., Coron, J.-S. (eds.) EUROCRYPT 2016. LNCS, vol. 9665, pp. 311–343. Springer, Heidelberg (2016). https://doi.org/10.1007/978-3-662-49890-3_13
24. Regev, O.: On lattices, learning with errors, random linear codes, and cryptography. J. ACM 56(6) (2009). https://doi.org/10.1145/1568318.1568324

Generic Construction for Identity-Based Proxy Blind Signature

Xavier Bultel[1] , Pascal Lafourcade[2] , Charles Olivier-Anclin[2]([⊠]) ,
and Léo Robert[2]

[1] LIFO, INSA Centre Val de Loire, Université d'Orléans, Orléans, France
[2] Université Clermont-Auvergne, CNRS, Mines de Saint-Étienne, LIMOS,
Clermont-Ferrand, France
charles.olivier-anclin@uca.fr

Abstract. Generic constructions of blind signature schemes have been
studied since its appearance. Several constructions were made leading to
generic blind signatures and achieving other properties such as identity-
based blind signature and partially blind signature. We propose a generic
construction for identity-based Proxy Blind Signature (IDPBS). This
combination of properties has several applications in the real world, in
particularly in e-voting or e-cash systems and it has never been achieved
before with a generic construction. Our construction only requires two
classical signatures schemes: a blind EUF-CMA blind signature and a
SUF-CMA unique signature. The security of our generic identity-based
proxy blind signature is proven under these assumptions.

1 Introduction

Designed in 1982 by D. Chaum [7], blind signatures are well known primitives,
enabling anonymous system for banking and electronic voting. The end of the
twentieth century and the beginning of the twenty-first was a golden age for
blind signatures. Multiple improvements were made, *e.g.,* a scheme based on
discrete logarithm proposed by J. L. Camenisch [6]. Several new properties were
developed such as *proxy blind signature* [27], *partially blind signature* [2], or *fair
blind signature* [25].

At the same time, identity-based cryptography has been introduced by
A. Shamir in 1985 [23]. It took until 2002 to produce the first identity-based
blind signature [34].

Recently, with the development of cryptocurrency and practical e-voting systems, blind signature returns to the centre of the attention. For instance self-
sovereign identity is a new approach to digital identity. It gives an independent control of the identity information that are given by people when certified

This study was partially supported by the French ANR, grants 18-CE39-0019 (MobiS5),
the French government research program "Investissements d'Avenir" through the
IDEX-ISITE initiative 16-IDEX-0001 (CAP 20-25), the IMobS3 Laboratory of Excel-
lence (ANR-10-LABX-16-01), the French ANR project DECRYPT (ANR-18-CE39-
0007) and SEVERITAS (ANR-20-CE39-0009).

E. Aïmeur et al. (Eds.): FPS 2021, LNCS 13291, pp. 34–52, 2022.
https://doi.org/10.1007/978-3-031-08147-7_3

information needs to be provided. In particularly, it addresses the difficulty of establishing trust in an interaction. Another application can be found in digital cash. In July 2021 was launch by the European Central Bank a project for digital euro to issue a new means of payment through electronic money. In order to be competitive with existing cryptocurrencies this digital euro should allow anonymity of payments. Identity-based blind signature could be the solution to facilitate the adoption of citizens. Moreover, the proxy property is needed to fit properly with the real world structure. In the case of the banks, they might want to distribute to several agencies located in different countries the ability to sign. In the case of e-voting, multiple polls are needed to organize an election. The delegation in several local pools is needed in order to distribute the election in each states or cities. In such a setup, identity-based proxy blind signature (IDPBS) is the solution for a secure voting protocol. There exist 14 IDPBS in the literature, 10 schemes use pairing [12,13,16,22,28–31,33,35] and the four others are paring free [15,19,20,26].

Concerning generic constructions, D. Galindo *et al.* [10] shown that only a EUF-CMA (Existential UnForgeability under Chosen Message Attack) signature scheme and a EUF-CMA blind signature scheme are necessary to achieve an *Identity-based Blind Signature* (IDBS). Hence our aim is to design a generic construction for an IDBS but with an additional property: ability to delegates right to sign messages (*i.e.,* proxy).

Contributions: We first define the security notions of IDPBS that are not completely formalised in the literature. In order to prove our construction we need to have clear security experiments for all required properties.

We then propose the first generic construction for *Identity-based Proxy Blind Signature*. Our construction uses two building blocks:

- a SUF-CMA (Strong Existential Unforgeability under Chosen Message Attack) *unique signature scheme* $S = (KeyGen_S, Sign_S, Verif_S)$
- a EUF-CMA *blind signature scheme* $BS = (KeyGen_{BS}, Protocol_{BS}, Verif_{BS})$.

We combine these two primitives in order to design a blind signature. In the literature there exist several SUF-CMA unique signature schemes, also known as Verifiable Unpredictable Functions (VUFs). For instance RSA-FDH [3] or [18] are unique signature schemes. There are also other unique signature schemes based on Diffie-Hellman assumption in bilinear groups [1,8,14,17].

We formally prove the security of our construction that only relies on the security properties of the two primitives used. Our construction can be instantiated with any unique signature such as BLS [5] and any blind signature *e.g.,* a blind ECDSA [21,32].

Related Work: Since blind signature exists, numerous generic constructions are investigated. When they can be achieved, they allow to directly adapt new advances on more basic primitives. Few generic constructions have been presented for blind signatures. In [9], Fischlin *et al.* proved that blind signatures can be constructed by assembling a signature scheme with a zero-knowledge proof and an encryption scheme. The same year, another construction of identity-based (partially) blind signature was proposed by D. Galindo *et al.* [10]. This construction consists in two building blocks, a SUF-CMA signature scheme and a EUF-CMA blind signature scheme. They were all proved secure under some basic assumptions such as reliability of the underlying scheme in their respective settings.

Outline: In Sect. 2, we introduce the cryptographic material and notations for all building blocks of our construction. We also formally define the models of all the security properties of IDPBS. In Sect. 3, we present our main result *i.e.*, the generic construction for IDPBS. In Sect. 4 we propose the security of our construction. Analysis of the efficiency is considered in Sect. 5. The conclusion is given in Sect. 6.

Notations: In this paper we will be using the following notations. Take $\mathcal{D}$ and $\mathcal{E}$ two algorithms, $\langle \mathcal{D}, \mathcal{E} \rangle$ will correspond to an interactive protocol in between both algorithms. We will also denotes by $[\mathcal{D}]$ the set of all possible outputs of the specified algorithm. We will refer to the set of all values returned by an algorithm $\mathcal{D}$ using $Out(\mathcal{D})$.

2   Formal Security Definitions and Properties for IDPBS

The definition of *identity-based proxy blind signature* varies in the literature. We give a definition based on [35] since it is the most generic one if we do not specify the ability to the original signer to actually sign messages (this ability is held to the proxy only). This feature could be added to the definition but there is no relevance for it. Note that our choice of definition is arbitrary yet we believe to be best suited.

Definition 1 (Identity-Based Proxy Blind Signature - IDPBS). *An* IDPBS *with security parameter $\mathfrak{K}$ is a 5-tuple of polynomial-time algorithms and protocols (*Setup, Extract, $\langle \mathcal{S}, \mathcal{P} \rangle$, $\langle \mathcal{P}, \mathcal{U} \rangle$, PBVerif*) involving a public key generator* PKG, *an original signer $\mathcal{S}$, a proxy signer $\mathcal{P}$ and a user $\mathcal{U}$. Algorithms work as follows:*

- Setup($1^{\mathfrak{K}}$): *this protocol is run by* PKG. *It calls $\mathfrak{K}$ to generate the global parameters* params *of the system and a master key-pair (mpk, msk).*
- Extract(params, msk, ID): *this protocol is run by the* PKG. *It takes as input an identity ID and a master key msk and return the corresponding secret key $sk[ID]$ via a secure channel.*
- $\langle \mathcal{S}, \mathcal{P} \rangle$ *is the* proxy-designation protocol *between $\mathcal{S}$ and $\mathcal{P}$. The inputs are the two identities $ID_{\mathcal{S}}$ and $ID_{\mathcal{P}}$ of the signers, their respective secret keys (query to* PKG *via* Extract*) and a delegation warrant m_w. As a result of the interaction, the expected local output of $\mathcal{P}$ is a secret key $sk_{\mathcal{P}}$ and a public agreement $w_{\mathcal{S} \to \mathcal{P}}$ that can be verified by any user. Formally $(sk_{\mathcal{P}}, w_{\mathcal{S} \to \mathcal{P}}) \leftarrow \langle \mathcal{S}(ID_{\mathcal{S}}, ID_{\mathcal{P}}, sk[ID_{\mathcal{S}}], m_w), \mathcal{P}(ID_{\mathcal{S}}, ID_{\mathcal{P}}, sk[ID_{\mathcal{P}}]) \rangle$.*

- *Signature issuing is an interactive protocol between the proxy signer $\mathcal{P}(sk_\mathcal{P})$ with its secret key and the user $\mathcal{U}(mpk, ID_\mathcal{S}, ID_\mathcal{P}, m)$ knowing a message $m \in \{0,1\}^*$ and both identities $ID_\mathcal{P}$ and $ID_\mathcal{S}$. It generates the signature for the user $\sigma \leftarrow \langle \mathcal{P}(sk_\mathcal{P}), \mathcal{U}(mpk, ID_\mathcal{S}, ID_\mathcal{P}, m) \rangle$.*
- Verif$(mpk, ID_\mathcal{S}, ID_\mathcal{P}, w_{\mathcal{S} \rightarrow \mathcal{P}}, m, \sigma)$ *it outputs 1 if the signature σ is valid with respect to m, $ID_\mathcal{S}$, $ID_\mathcal{P}$, $w_{\mathcal{S} \rightarrow \mathcal{P}}$ and mpk, otherwise 0.*

The security of proxy signature has been defined in [4]. For this type of schemes, the adversary is allowed to corrupt an arbitrary number of users and learn their secret keys. Moreover, the adversary can register public keys on behalf of new users, possibly obtained otherwise than running the key-generation algorithm, and possibly depending on the public keys of already registered users. The adversary is also allowed to interact with honest users playing the role of a original signer or of a proxy signer.

Oracles. The adversary has access to oracles during this process. Elements returned by the adversary should not have been received from an oracle's query.

- **Query of Extraction:** $\mathcal{O}_{\mathsf{Extract}}(msk, \cdot) \rightarrow (sk[ID_i], \mathsf{cert}_{ID_i})$
  $\mathcal{A}$ request extraction for an identity ID_i, he sends ID_i to the PKG and receive the consistent answer $sk[ID_i]$ with the certificate cert_{ID_i}.
- **Query of Keys Delegation:** $\mathcal{O}_{ID \rightarrow \mathcal{A}}(ID, sk[ID], m_w, ID_i)$
  The adversary produces an identity ID_i, a warrant m_w and request to the user with identity ID a delegation. The following protocol is executed $\langle \mathcal{A}(ID_i, ID, m_w), \mathcal{C}(ID, sk[ID]) \rangle \rightarrow (sk_{ID_i}, w_{ID \rightarrow ID_i})$
- **Query of Issuing Delegation:** $\mathcal{O}_{\mathcal{A} \rightarrow ID}(ID_i, sk[ID_i], m_w, ID)$
  For an already existing identity ID, $\mathcal{A}$ asks to delegate to an user with identity ID_i chosen by himself. The protocol $\langle \mathcal{A}(ID, sk[ID], ID_i, m_w), \mathcal{C}(ID_i, ID) \rangle \rightarrow (sk_{ID_i}, w_{ID \rightarrow ID_i})$ is executed. The transcript of the interactions is given to $\mathcal{A}$ but he does not learn the secret key.
- **Query of Secret Key:** $\mathcal{O}_{\mathsf{Exposure}}(ID_i) \rightarrow sk[ID_i]$
  For any already existing ID_i different to the identity of the user under attack, $\mathcal{A}$ can request a secret key to $\mathcal{S}$.
- **Query of Proxy Secret Key:** $\mathcal{O}_{\mathsf{PExposure}}(ID_i) \rightarrow sk_{ID_i}$
  For any already existing ID_i different to identity of the user under attack, $\mathcal{A}$ can request a proxy secret key.
- **Query of Transcript of Delegation:** $\mathcal{O}_{ID_i \rightarrow ID_j}$
  $\mathcal{A}$ chooses two identities ID_i and ID_j with ID_i already extracted. Then $\langle \mathcal{C}(ID_i), \mathcal{P}(ID_j) \rangle$ is executed and the adversary gets the transcript of the interactions. The identities ID_i and ID_j are not necessarily different.
- **Query of signature:** $\mathcal{O}_{\mathsf{S}}(ID_i, m) \rightarrow \sigma_m$
  $\mathcal{A}$ can ask for a blind signature from ID_i (an already claimed identity). $\mathcal{A}$ chooses the message and a signature σ is produced and returned to him.
- **Query of proxy signature:** $\mathcal{O}_{\mathsf{PS}}(ID_i, m) \rightarrow \sigma_m$
  $\mathcal{A}$ chooses a message m and two identities ID_i, ID_j with ID_i already extracted and ID_j provided with a delegation from ID_i. The proxy signature protocol is run with $\mathcal{A}$ playing the role of the user and the user associated to ID_j the proxy signer.

Security Properties. We formally defined all security properties that a IDPBS scheme should satisfy as follows:

- *Blindness* has to be consider from two points of view since attackers could be either S^* or P^*. Both are still required to win the experiment $\mathsf{Exp}^{bl}_{\mathsf{IDPBS},*}(\mathfrak{K})$ of the game defined in Fig. 1. A proxy blind signature achieves *blindness* if for any polynomial time adversary $\mathcal{A}$, $\mathsf{Adv}^{bl}_{\mathsf{IDPBS},\mathcal{A}}(\mathfrak{K}) = |\mathsf{Exp}^{bl}_{\mathsf{IDPBS},\mathcal{A}}(\mathfrak{K}) - 1/2|$ is negligible.
- *Unforgeability* is quite similar to the context of identity-based proxy signature schemes defined in [4]. The experiment is given in Fig. 2.
- *Verifiability* means that the verifier $\mathcal{V}$ can always be convinced of the original signer's agreement on the signed message. We formalise this property thanks to the experiment of Fig. 3.
- *Prevention of misuse* requires that the proxy signer cannot use the proxy key for other purposes than generating proxy signatures within the terms of a delegation made by S to P. In case of misuse, the responsibility of the proxy signer should be determined explicitly. This is formalized in Fig. 4.
- *Strong Identifiability* requires anyone to be able to determine the identity of the corresponding proxy signer from the signature as described by the experiment of Fig. 5. This is to allow linkability of a signature to a proxy signer in case of a fraud. In the context of identity-based proxy signature, it is straight forward achieved.

$\mathsf{Exp}^{bl}_{\mathsf{IDPBS},S^*}(\mathfrak{K}):$
1. $(mpk, msk) \leftarrow \mathsf{Setup}(1^{\mathfrak{K}})$
2. $(ID_S, ID_P, m_0, m_1) \leftarrow \mathcal{A}(mpk)$
3. $b \overset{\$}{\leftarrow} \{0, 1\}$
4. $\sigma_b, w_{S \rightarrow P,b} \leftarrow \langle \mathcal{A}, \mathcal{C}(ID_S, ID_P, m_b) \rangle$
5. $\sigma_{1-b}, w_{S \rightarrow P,1-b} \leftarrow \langle \mathcal{A}, \mathcal{C}(ID_S, ID_P, m_{1-b}) \rangle$
6. $b^* \leftarrow \mathcal{A}((m_0, \sigma_0, w_{S \rightarrow P,0}), (m_1, \sigma_1, w_{S \rightarrow P,1}))$
7. Return $b^* = b$

Fig. 1. Security experiment for blindness of IDPBS [36].

$\mathsf{Exp}^{uf}_{\mathsf{IDPBS},\mathcal{U}^*}(\mathfrak{K}):$
1. $(mpk, msk) \leftarrow \mathsf{Setup}(1^{\mathfrak{K}})$
2. $(ID_S, ID_P, m_w) \leftarrow \mathcal{A}(mpk)$
3. $sk[ID_S] \leftarrow \mathsf{Extract}(msk, ID_S)$
4. $(sk_P, w_{S \rightarrow P}) \leftarrow \langle \mathcal{C}(ID_S, ID_P, sk[ID_S], m_w), \mathcal{C}(ID_S, ID_P, sk[ID_P]) \rangle$
5. $\{(ID_{P_i}, m_i, \sigma_i)\}_{1 \leq i \leq l'} \leftarrow \mathcal{A}(mpk, ID_S, ID_P, m_w, w_{S \rightarrow P})$
6. If $\exists i \neq j, m_i = m_j$ or $\exists i, \mathsf{Verify}(ID, m_i, \sigma_i) = 0$: Return 0
7. Else Return 1

Fig. 2. Security experiment for unforgeability of IDPBS [4]. In this game, l is the number of succeeding call to the signing oracle $\mathcal{O}_{\mathsf{PS}}$.

– *Strong Undeniability.* Once a proxy signer creates a valid proxy signature with the delegation of an original signer, it cannot repudiate the produced signature. Here the validity of the signature holds as a proof against deniability of the proxy user as we can see in the experiment of Fig. 6.

An adversary breaks an identity-based proxy blind signature if for any of these experiments he has non negligible probabilities of winning the corresponding game.

$\mathsf{Exp}^{veri}_{\mathsf{IDPBS},\mathcal{P}*}(\mathfrak{K})$:
1. $(mpk, msk) \leftarrow \mathsf{Setup}(1^{\mathfrak{K}})$
2. $(ID_\mathcal{S}, ID_\mathcal{P}, m_w) \leftarrow \mathcal{A}(mpk)$
3. $sk[ID_\mathcal{S}] \leftarrow \mathsf{Extract}(msk, ID_\mathcal{S})$
4. $sk_\mathcal{P}, w_{\mathcal{S} \rightarrow \mathcal{P}} \in Out(\mathcal{A}) \leftarrow \langle \mathcal{C}(ID_\mathcal{S}, ID_\mathcal{P}, sk[ID_\mathcal{S}], m_w), \mathcal{A}(ID_\mathcal{S}, ID_\mathcal{P}, sk[ID_\mathcal{P}]) \rangle$
5. $(m, \sigma, m'_w, w'_{\mathcal{S} \rightarrow \mathcal{P}}) \leftarrow \mathcal{A}$
6. If $\mathsf{Verif}(mpk, ID_\mathcal{S}, ID_\mathcal{P}, m, \sigma, m'_w, w'_{\mathcal{S} \rightarrow \mathcal{P}}) = 1$,
   $w'_{\mathcal{S} \rightarrow \mathcal{P}} \notin Out(\mathcal{O}_{\mathsf{DelGen}}(ID_\mathcal{S}, ID_\mathcal{P}, sk[ID_\mathcal{S}], m'_w))$ and $m'_w \neq m_w$: **Return** 1
7. **Else Return** 0

Fig. 3. Security experiment for verifiability of IDPBS.

$\mathsf{Exp}^{PoM}_{\mathsf{IDPBS},\mathcal{P}*}(\mathfrak{K})$:
1. $(mpk, msk) \leftarrow \mathsf{Setup}(1^{\mathfrak{K}})$
2. $(ID_\mathcal{S}, ID_\mathcal{P}, m_w) \leftarrow \mathcal{A}(mpk)$
3. $sk[ID_\mathcal{S}] \leftarrow \mathsf{Extract}(msk, ID_\mathcal{S})$
4. $sk_\mathcal{P}, w_{\mathcal{S} \rightarrow \mathcal{P}} \in Out(\mathcal{A}) \leftarrow \langle \mathcal{C}(ID_\mathcal{S}, ID_\mathcal{P}, sk[ID_\mathcal{S}], m_w), \mathcal{A}(ID_\mathcal{S}, ID_\mathcal{P}, sk[ID_\mathcal{P}]) \rangle$
5. $(ID, m, \sigma, m'_w, w'_{\mathcal{S} \rightarrow \mathcal{P}}) \leftarrow \mathcal{A}$
8. If $\mathsf{Verif}(mpk, ID_\mathcal{S}, ID, m, \sigma, m'_w, w'_{\mathcal{S} \rightarrow \mathcal{P}}) = 1$ with $ID \neq ID_\mathcal{P}$, $m'_w \neq m_w$ and
   $w'_{\mathcal{S} \rightarrow \mathcal{P}} \notin Out(\mathcal{O}_{\mathsf{DelGen}}(ID_\mathcal{S}, ID_\mathcal{P}, sk[ID_\mathcal{S}], m'_w))$: **Return** 1
7. **Else Return** 0

Fig. 4. Security experiment for prevention of misuse of IDPBS.

$\mathsf{Exp}^{st-id}_{\mathsf{IDPBS},\mathcal{P}*}(\mathfrak{K})$:
1. $(mpk, msk) \leftarrow \mathsf{Setup}(1^{\mathfrak{K}})$
2. $(ID_\mathcal{S}, ID_\mathcal{P}, m, m_w) \leftarrow \mathcal{A}(mpk)$
3. $sk[ID_\mathcal{S}] \leftarrow \mathsf{Extract}(msk, ID_\mathcal{S})$
4. $sk_\mathcal{P}, w_{\mathcal{S} \rightarrow \mathcal{P}} \in Out(\mathcal{A}) \leftarrow \langle \mathcal{C}(ID_\mathcal{S}, ID_\mathcal{P}, sk[ID_\mathcal{S}], m_w), \mathcal{A}(ID_\mathcal{S}, ID_\mathcal{P}, sk[ID_\mathcal{P}]) \rangle$
5. $\sigma \leftarrow \mathsf{Protocol}\langle \mathcal{A}(mpk, sk_\mathcal{P}, w_{\mathcal{S} \rightarrow \mathcal{P}}), \mathcal{C}(ID_\mathcal{S}, ID_\mathcal{P}, m) \rangle$
6. $ID \leftarrow \mathcal{A}(\sigma)$
7. If $\mathsf{Verif}(mpk, ID_\mathcal{S}, ID, m, \sigma, m_w, w_{\mathcal{S} \rightarrow \mathcal{P}}) = 1$ with $ID \neq ID_\mathcal{P}$: **Return** 1
8. **Else Return** 0

Fig. 5. Security experiment for strong identification of IDPBS.

$\mathsf{Exp}^{st-und}_{\mathsf{IDPBS},\mathcal{P}^*}(\mathfrak{K})$:
1. $(mpk, msk) \leftarrow \mathsf{Setup}(1^{\mathfrak{K}})$
2. $(ID_\mathcal{S}, ID_\mathcal{P}, m_w) \leftarrow \mathcal{A}(mpk)$
3. $sk[ID_\mathcal{S}] \leftarrow \mathsf{Extract}(msk, ID_\mathcal{S})$
4. $sk_\mathcal{P}, w_{\mathcal{S} \to \mathcal{P}} \in Out(\mathcal{A}) \leftarrow \langle \mathcal{C}(ID_\mathcal{S}, ID_\mathcal{P}, sk[ID_\mathcal{S}], m_w), \mathcal{A}(ID_\mathcal{S}, ID_\mathcal{P}, sk[ID_\mathcal{P}]) \rangle$
5. $(Id, (m, \sigma), m'_w, w'_{\mathcal{S} \to \mathcal{P}}) \leftarrow \mathcal{A}$
6. If $\mathsf{Verif}(mpk, ID_\mathcal{S}, ID_\mathcal{P}, m, \sigma, m_w, w_{\mathcal{S} \to \mathcal{P}}) = 1$,
$\mathsf{Verif}(mpk, ID_\mathcal{S}, ID, m, \sigma, m'_w, w'_{\mathcal{S} \to \mathcal{P}}) = 1$ with $ID \neq ID_\mathcal{P}$: Return 1
7. Else Return 0

Fig. 6. Security experiment for strong undeniability of IDPBS.

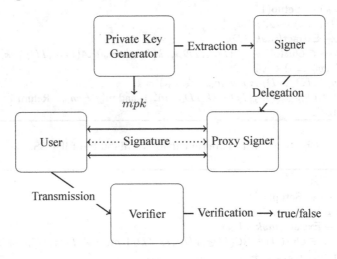

Fig. 7. General framework for our generic construction of IDPBS.

3   Our **IDPBS** Construction

A general idea of the interactions of our construction is given in Fig. 7. $\mathcal{S}$ and $\mathcal{P}$ both start with their respective identities $ID_\mathcal{S}$ and $ID_\mathcal{P}$. We suppose them known by the user. A message m is generated by $\mathcal{U}$ prior to the signature protocol.

We now give the description of each step of the issuing of a new signature. The algorithms are presented in Fig. 8.

Key Generation. KeyGen is executed first and retruns the keys for the PKG.

Extraction. The private key generator (PKG) produces a signing key for $\mathcal{S}$ and the associated certificate cert$_\mathcal{S}$ following algorithm Extract. The PKG sends the User Secret Key associated to the identify $ID_\mathcal{S}$, $USK[ID_\mathcal{S}] = (\mathsf{cert}_\mathcal{S}, vk^\mathsf{S}_\mathcal{S}, sk^\mathsf{S}_\mathcal{S})$ to $\mathcal{S}$ via a secure channel and $\mathcal{S}$ verifies the signature cert$_\mathcal{S}$.

At the end of this phase, $\mathcal{S}$ is provided with public/private keys $(vk^\mathsf{S}_\mathcal{S}, sk^\mathsf{S}_\mathcal{S})$ and a certificate cert$_\mathcal{S}$ linking the public key to its identity. Later, the user is able to verify this certificate with the master public key mpk. $\mathcal{U}$ can thus be convinced that this key was produced by a private key generator.

Delegation. Proceeding to the delegation from the signer $\mathcal{S}$ to the proxy signer $\mathcal{P}$ is generally described as an interactive protocol. Here, we chose to proceed as follows. Let m_w be a contract produced after a negotiation prior to that step. The signer produces a link in between the contract m_w, a blind signature public key $vk_{\mathcal{P}}^{\mathsf{BS}}$ and both identities $ID_{\mathcal{S}}$ and $ID_{\mathcal{P}}$. For the creation of the proxy signer, $\mathcal{S}$ only has to be in procession of its identity $ID_{\mathcal{P}}$. The procedure is described in algorithm DelGen.

After running the algorithm $\mathcal{S}$ sends $(w_{\mathcal{S}\to\mathcal{P}}, \mathsf{cert}_{\mathcal{S}}, vk_{\mathcal{S}}^{\mathsf{S}})$ to $\mathcal{P}$. It is also necessary to send information through a secure channel $USK[ID_{\mathcal{P}}] = (vk_{\mathcal{P}}^{\mathsf{BS}}, sk_{\mathcal{P}}^{\mathsf{BS}})$.

When receiving this information, the proxy $\mathcal{P}$ runs the mandatory verification of certificates $\mathsf{cert}_{\mathcal{S}}$ and $w_{\mathcal{S}\to\mathcal{P}}$. If both pass, $\mathcal{P}$ accepts the keys and the certificates.

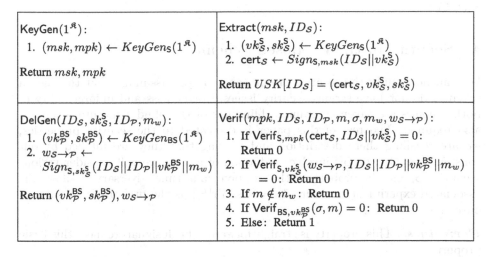

Fig. 8. Algorithm of the generic construction of IDPBS.

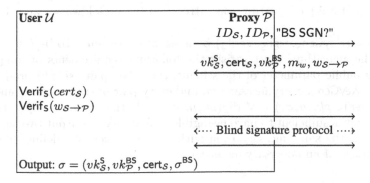

Fig. 9. Signature issuing of IDPBS.

Signature Issuing. At this point $\mathcal{P}$ is in possession of: $mpk, ID_\mathcal{S}, ID_\mathcal{P}, vk_\mathcal{S}^\mathsf{S}$, $\mathrm{cert}_\mathcal{S}, (vk_\mathcal{P}^\mathsf{BS}, sk_\mathcal{P}^\mathsf{BS}), m_w, w_{\mathcal{S}\to\mathcal{P}}$. He now interacts with $\mathcal{U}$ in possession of a message m in order to issue a blind signature on m. The final signature is composed of $\sigma = (vk_\mathcal{S}^\mathsf{S}, vk_\mathcal{P}^\mathsf{BS}, \mathrm{cert}_\mathcal{S}, \sigma^\mathsf{BS})$, where σ^BS is the signature obtained from the blind signature scheme. Figure 9 describes these interactions. Note that the two first steps can be combined with the upcoming ones if the user speaks first in the blind signature protocol. Thus, it is possible to achieve the round optimal property with this construction *i.e.,* reaching the minimum of two communications in the issuing of an IDPBS signature.

Verification. $\mathcal{U}$ transmits the inputs of the algorithm to the verifier. The validity of the signature is assessed by running Verif.

As we can see in algorithm Verif of Fig. 8 the verification process implies to attest the validity of all certificates and adding to that checking the final signature. It needs 2 executions of $Verif_\mathsf{S}()$ and 1 execution of $Verif_\mathsf{BS}()$, thus leading to a relatively long process of verification compare to other blind signatures (see Sect. 5).

4   Security of the Proposed Scheme

We can now study the security of our construction, assuming that the chosen schemes do not have serious security issues. Correctness and unforgeability of both schemes are taken as granted, blindness of the blind signature scheme is also required. The rest of this paper is dedicated to the security properties, we are recalling there description and proving that they are fulfilled by our construction. Our proofs involves reduction of games, we will consider various scenarios S_i and the probability that a polynomial time adversary $\mathcal{A}$ allows the associated experiment to return 1. We use $\Pr[S_i]$ as the probability of such an outcome.

Correctness. This property is straightforward if both signature meet this basic property.

Blindness. The blindness of the scheme require a unique signature scheme. The notion of unique signature was introduced by S. Goldwasser and R. Ostrovsky [11].

Let $\mathsf{S} = (\mathsf{KeyGen_S}, \mathsf{Sign_S}, \mathsf{Verif_S})$ be a signature scheme. To be a unique signature, the algorithms must satisfy the following requirements of uniqueness: For every public parameter of the scheme, every key pair (sk, pk) produced by algorithm $\mathsf{KeyGen_S}$, every message m, and every pair of signatures σ_1 and σ_2, if we have $\mathsf{Verif_S}(pk, m, \sigma_1) = \mathsf{Verif_S}(pk, m, \sigma_2) = 1$, then it must imply $\sigma_1 = \sigma_2$. In our case it is sufficient to have negligible probability to output two signatures verifying for the same message even with the secret key. We define $\mathsf{Adv}_{\mathsf{S}, \mathcal{A}_\mathsf{S}}^{uni}$ as the advantage of an adversary against it.

Lemma 1 (Blindness). *Given* S *a unique signature scheme and* BS *a blind signature scheme with blindness, our construction gives rise to a blind identity-based proxy blind signature scheme. In particular, we show that:* $\mathsf{Adv}_{\mathsf{IDPBS},\mathcal{A}}^{bl} \leq \mathsf{Adv}_{\mathsf{BS},\mathcal{A}_{\mathsf{BS}}}^{bl} + 3 \cdot \mathsf{Adv}_{\mathsf{S},\mathcal{A}_{\mathsf{S}}}^{uni}.$

Proof. Fix $\mathcal{A}$, a polynomial time adversary. Let us define Game 0 to be the security game against for blindness of our scheme. The game can be described as follows.

Game 0_1:

1. $(mpk, msk) \leftarrow \mathsf{KeyGen}_\mathsf{S}(1^{\hat{R}})$
2. $(ID_\mathcal{S}, ID_\mathcal{P}, m_0, m_1, m_w) \leftarrow \mathcal{A}(mpk)$
3. $b \xleftarrow{\$} \{0, 1\}$
4. $\sigma_b, w_{\mathcal{S}\rightarrow\mathcal{P},b} \leftarrow \mathsf{Protocol}\langle \mathcal{A}, \mathcal{C}(ID_\mathcal{S}, ID_\mathcal{P}, m_b)\rangle$
5. $\sigma_{1-b}, w_{\mathcal{S}\rightarrow\mathcal{P},1-b} \leftarrow \mathsf{Protocol}\langle \mathcal{A}, \mathcal{C}(ID_\mathcal{S}, ID_\mathcal{P}, m_{1-b})\rangle$
6. $b^* \leftarrow \mathcal{A}((m_0, \sigma_0), (m_1, \sigma_1))$

If we define S_0 to be the event that $b = b^*$ in Game 0_1, then the adversary's advantage is $\mathsf{Adv}_{\mathsf{IDPBS},\mathsf{B}}^{bl} = |\mathsf{Pr}[S_0] - 1/2|$. First we need to investigate more in depth the interactive protocol of the proxy blind signing. For that we consider lines 4 and 5 and put forward their description in Game 0_2. For each $i \in \{0, 1\}$,

Game 0_2:

1. $vk_\mathcal{S}^\mathsf{S}, \mathsf{cert}_{\mathcal{S},i}, vk_\mathcal{S}^\mathsf{BS}, w_{\mathcal{S}\rightarrow\mathcal{P},i} \leftarrow \mathcal{A}$
2. If $(\mathsf{Verif}_\mathsf{S}(\mathsf{cert}_{\mathcal{S},i}) \neq 1)$ or $(\mathsf{Verif}_\mathsf{S}(w_{\mathcal{S}\rightarrow\mathcal{P},i}) \neq 1)$, Abort
3. $\sigma_i^\mathsf{BS} \leftarrow \mathsf{Protocol}_\mathsf{BS}\langle \mathcal{A}, \mathcal{C}(vk_\mathcal{S}^\mathsf{BS}, m_i)\rangle$
4. $\sigma_i \leftarrow (vk_\mathcal{S}^\mathsf{S}, vk_\mathcal{S}^\mathsf{BS}, \mathsf{cert}_{\mathcal{S},i}, \sigma_i^\mathsf{BS})$

We now make one small change to the underlying Game 0_2. The warrant $w_{\mathcal{S}\rightarrow\mathcal{P}}$ will be fixed for both execution of the protocol and produced by $\mathcal{A}$ in the second step. Line 2 of Game 0_1 becomes $(ID_\mathcal{S}, ID_\mathcal{P}, m_0, m_1, m_w, w_{\mathcal{S}\rightarrow\mathcal{P}}) \leftarrow \mathcal{A}(mpk)$ in Game 1_1. Let S_1 be the event that $b = b^*$ in Game 1. Here the difference between S_0 and S_1 correspond to the event $F = $ "non unique determination of the signature $w_{\mathcal{S}\rightarrow\mathcal{P}}$ of a warrant m_w". Thus $|\mathsf{Pr}[S_0] - \mathsf{Pr}[S_1]| \leq 2 \cdot \mathsf{Adv}_\mathsf{S}^{uni}(k)$ by the difference lemma [24]; this probability is considered negligible by hypothesis.

Game 2_1:

1. $(mpk, msk) \leftarrow \mathsf{KeyGen}_\mathsf{S}(1^{\hat{R}})$
2. $(ID_\mathcal{S}, ID_\mathcal{P}, m_0, m_1, m_w, w_{\mathcal{S}\rightarrow\mathcal{P}}, \mathsf{cert}_\mathcal{S}) \leftarrow \mathcal{A}(mpk)$
3. $b \xleftarrow{\$} \{0, 1\}$
4. $\sigma_b, w_{\mathcal{S}\rightarrow\mathcal{P},b} \leftarrow \mathsf{Protocol}\langle \mathcal{A}, \mathcal{C}(ID_\mathcal{S}, ID_\mathcal{P}, m_b)\rangle$
5. $\sigma_{1-b}, w_{\mathcal{S}\rightarrow\mathcal{P},1-b} \leftarrow \mathsf{Protocol}\langle \mathcal{A}, \mathcal{C}(ID_\mathcal{S}, ID_\mathcal{P}, m_{1-b})\rangle$
6. $b^* \leftarrow \mathcal{A}((m_0, \sigma_0), (m_1, \sigma_1))$

Game 2_2:

1. $vk_{\mathcal{S}}^{\mathsf{S}}, vk_{\mathcal{S}}^{\mathsf{BS}}, w_{\mathcal{S} \to \mathcal{P}} \leftarrow \mathcal{A}$
2. If $(\mathsf{Verif_S(cert_S)} \neq 1)$ or $(\mathsf{Verif_S}(w_{\mathcal{S} \to \mathcal{P}}) \neq 1)$, Abort
3. $\sigma_i^{\mathsf{BS}} \leftarrow \mathsf{Protocol_{BS}}\langle \mathcal{A}, \mathcal{C}(vk_{\mathcal{S}}^{\mathsf{BS}}, m_i)\rangle$
4. $\sigma_i \leftarrow (vk_{\mathcal{S}}^{\mathsf{S}}, vk_{\mathcal{S}}^{\mathsf{BS}}, \mathsf{cert}_{\mathcal{S}}, \sigma_i^{\mathsf{BS}})$

Just like we did for certificate $w_{\mathcal{S} \to \mathcal{P}}$, we restrict our adversary to output an unique $\mathsf{cert}_{\mathcal{S}}$ at the beginning of the game. Only signature containing this certificate are accepted, otherwise the procedure fails. After changing Game 1 into Game 2 as described, we can define an event S_2 representing the event $b = b^*$ after Game 2. $\mathsf{cert}_{\mathcal{S}}$ is supposed to be fixed at the beginning of the session. Applying the difference lemma a second time, we obtain a difference of happening between the two game with an upper bound $|\mathsf{Pr}[S_0] - \mathsf{Pr}[S_1]| \leq \mathsf{Adv}_{\mathsf{S}}^{uni}(k)$. This step has the same consequences as for the previous one and $\mathcal{A}$ gained the same advantage.

Our thirds step consist of neutralising the ability $\mathcal{A}$ has to distinguish in between σ_0^{BS} and σ_1^{BS}. Let us restate the games and draw a random value from the possibles outputs of the blind signature protocol without executing it. Hence, the adversary obtains no information from the element σ_i^{BS} he receives at the last step. We have assumed blindness of the blind signature scheme, thus the gained advantage is negligible.

Game 3_2:

1. $vk_{\mathcal{S}}^{\mathsf{S}}, vk_{\mathcal{S}}^{\mathsf{BS}}, w_{\mathcal{S} \to \mathcal{P}} \leftarrow \mathcal{A}$
2. If $(\mathsf{Verif_S(cert_S)} \neq 1)$ or $(\mathsf{Verif_S}(w_{\mathcal{S} \to \mathcal{P}}) \neq 1)$, Abort
3. $\sigma_i^{\mathsf{BS}} \xleftarrow{\$} [\mathsf{Protocol_{BS}}\langle \cdot, \cdot \rangle]$
4. $\sigma_i \leftarrow (vk_{\mathcal{S}}^{\mathsf{S}}, vk_{\mathcal{S}}^{\mathsf{BS}}, \mathsf{cert}_{\mathcal{S}}, \sigma_i^{\mathsf{BS}})$

An extra bridging steps would be to reformulate line 4 of Game 3,2 to ignore this random value that has no impact on the choice of $\mathcal{A}$ and set $\sigma_i \leftarrow (vk_{\mathcal{S}}^{\mathsf{S}}, vk_{\mathcal{S}}^{\mathsf{BS}}, \mathsf{cert}_{\mathcal{S}})$ in line 4 of Game 4_2. This formulation leads to a complete incapability of the adversary to decide anything as all of its input are produced directly by himself. Therefore, by the triangular inequality, $\mathsf{Adv}_{\mathsf{IDPBS}, \mathcal{A}}^{bl} = |\mathsf{Pr}[S_0] - \mathsf{Pr}[S_3]| \leq \mathsf{Adv}_{\mathsf{BS}, \mathcal{A}_{\mathsf{BS}}}^{bl} + 3 \cdot \mathsf{Adv}_{\mathsf{S}, \mathcal{A}_{\mathsf{S}}}^{uni}$.

Unforgeability. The unforgeability of our construction relies on this theorem.

Lemma 2 (Unforgeability). *Given a signature scheme* S *and a blind signature scheme* BS *both with unforgeability, our construction has unforgeability. In particular, we show that:* $\mathsf{Adv}_{\mathsf{IDPBS}, \mathcal{A}}^{uf} \leq q \cdot (\mathsf{Adv}_{\mathsf{BS}, \mathcal{A}_{\mathsf{BS}}}^{uf} + \mathsf{Adv}_{\mathsf{S}, \mathcal{A}_{\mathsf{S}}}^{uf})$.

Proof. Fix an adversary $\mathcal{A}$ against the unforgeability of our scheme given access to the previously described oracles. $\mathcal{A}$ is allowed to make any number of queries to each of them, but the final outputs of the game should be no element obtained from an oracle. We may write the security game as follows.

Game 0:

1. $(mpk, msk) \leftarrow \mathsf{Setup}(1^{\mathcal{R}})$
2. $(ID_{\mathcal{S}}, ID_{\mathcal{P}}, m_w) \leftarrow \mathcal{A}(mpk)$
3. $sk[ID_{\mathcal{S}}] \leftarrow \mathsf{Extract}(msk, ID_{\mathcal{S}})$
4. $(sk_{\mathcal{P}}, w_{\mathcal{S} \rightarrow \mathcal{P}}) \leftarrow \mathsf{DelGen}(ID_{\mathcal{S}}, ID_{\mathcal{P}}, sk[ID_{\mathcal{S}}], m_w)$
5. $\{(ID_{\mathcal{P}_i}, m_i, \sigma_i)\}_{1 \leq i \leq l'} \leftarrow \mathcal{A}$
6. If $\exists i \neq j, m_i = m_j$ or $\exists i, \mathsf{Verify}(ID_{\mathcal{P}_i}, m_i, \sigma_i) = 0$: Return 0
7. Else Return 1

We can define the event S_0 corresponding to Game 0 outputting 1. If such an outputs happens this would be considered as a valid forgery, thus $\mathsf{Adv}^{uf}_{\mathsf{IDPBS}, \mathcal{A}} = \Pr(S_0)$. Let l be the number of proxy blind signature queries that are successfully completed. With probability $\mathsf{Adv}^{uf}_{\mathsf{IDPBS}, \mathcal{A}}(\mathcal{R})$, the adversary $\mathcal{A}$ succeeds and outputs a valid forgery $i.e.$, a list of l' tuples $\{(ID_{\mathcal{P}_i}, m_i, \sigma_i)\}_{1 \leq i \leq l'}$ with $l < l'$. Since $l < l'$, there exists at least some identity ID_i in the output list such that the number $l(ID_i)$ of completed blind signature queries during the attack involving ID_i is strictly less than the number $l'(ID_i)$ of tuples involving identity ID_i in the output list. This has to hold by the pigeonhole principal. If we outputted a forgery for the right identity $ID = ID_{\mathcal{P}_*}$, then we have completed $l(ID)$ executions of the blind signature protocol during our attack $\mathsf{F}_{\mathcal{BS}}$ against the blind signature scheme BS, with public key $vk^{\mathsf{BS}}_{\mathcal{P}_*}$ and we can easily obtain $l'(ID)$ valid signatures under the same public key from the list output by $\mathcal{A}$ satisfying $l(ID) < l'(ID)$ for that identity. Hence, we can modify our game to restrict our adversary to output a forgery on a specified identity. He has probability $1/q$ to get a forgery for the right identity. Game 1 is modified accordingly. This gives the relation $1/q \cdot \Pr[S_0] = \Pr[S_1]$ between the probability of the two events S_0 and S_1.

Game 1:

1. $(mpk, msk) \leftarrow \mathsf{Setup}(1^{\mathcal{R}})$
2. $(ID_{\mathcal{S}}, ID_{\mathcal{P}}, m_w) \leftarrow \mathcal{A}(mpk)$
3. $sk[ID_{\mathcal{S}}] \leftarrow \mathsf{Extract}(msk, ID_{\mathcal{S}})$
4. $(sk_{\mathcal{P}}, w_{\mathcal{S} \rightarrow \mathcal{P}}) \leftarrow \mathsf{DelGen}(ID_{\mathcal{S}}, ID_{\mathcal{P}}, sk[ID_{\mathcal{S}}], m_w)$
5. $\{(m_i, \sigma_i)\}_{1 \leq i \leq l'} \leftarrow \mathcal{A}$
6. If $\exists i \neq j, m_i = m_j$ or $\exists i, \mathsf{Verify}(ID_{\mathcal{P}}, m_i, \sigma_i) = 0$: Return 0
7. Else Return 1

$\mathcal{A}$ has the capability to forge new signatures $\mathsf{cert}_{\mathcal{S}}$ embedded proxy blind signature, leading to new signature. In Game 2, we will ask $\mathcal{A}$ to output $\mathsf{cert}_{\mathcal{S}}$ at the beginning. As a consequence, modification of the key $vk^{\mathsf{S}*}_{\mathcal{S}}$ will lead to failure. Define event S_2 as "$\mathcal{A}$ wins the Game 2", the probability of realisation of these event only differ by $\mathsf{Adv}^{uf}_{\mathsf{S}}(k)$ from $\Pr[S_1]$, which is supposed negligible.

Game 2:

1. $(mpk, msk) \leftarrow \mathsf{Setup}(1^\mathfrak{K})$
2. $(ID_\mathcal{S}, ID_\mathcal{P}, m_w) \leftarrow \mathcal{A}(mpk)$
3. $sk[ID_\mathcal{S}] \leftarrow \mathsf{Extract}(msk, ID_\mathcal{S})$
4. $(sk_\mathcal{P}, w_{\mathcal{S} \to \mathcal{P}}) \leftarrow \mathsf{DelGen}(ID_\mathcal{S}, ID_\mathcal{P}, sk[ID_\mathcal{S}], m_w)$
5. $\mathsf{cert}_\mathcal{S} \leftarrow \mathsf{Sign}_{\mathsf{S}, msk}(ID_\mathcal{S} \| vk_\mathcal{S}^\mathsf{S})$
6. $\{(m_i, \sigma_i = (vk_\mathcal{S}^\mathsf{S}, vk_\mathcal{S}^\mathsf{BS}, \mathsf{cert}_\mathcal{S}, \sigma_i^\mathsf{BS}))\}_{1 \le i \le l'} \leftarrow \mathcal{A}$
7. If $\exists i \ne j, m_i = m_j$ or $\exists i$, $\mathsf{Verify}(ID_\mathcal{P}, m_i, \sigma_i) = 0$: Return 0
8. Else Return 1

A second restriction can now be put forward: inability to forge blind signatures on scheme BS. In Game 3, $\sigma_{m_i}^\mathsf{BS}$ is the blind signature given by a legit execution of the blind signature scheme for the key pair $(vk_\mathcal{S}^\mathsf{BS}, sk_\mathcal{S}^\mathsf{BS})$. This time we have have $|\Pr[S_2] - \Pr[S_3]| \le \mathsf{Adv}_\mathsf{BS}^{uf}(k)$.

Game 3:

1. $(mpk, msk) \leftarrow \mathsf{Setup}(1^\mathfrak{K})$
2. $(ID_\mathcal{S}, ID_\mathcal{P}, m_w) \leftarrow \mathcal{A}(mpk)$
3. $sk[ID_\mathcal{S}] \leftarrow \mathsf{Extract}(msk, ID_\mathcal{S})$
4. $(sk_\mathcal{P}, w_{\mathcal{S} \to \mathcal{P}}) \leftarrow \mathsf{DelGen}(ID_\mathcal{S}, ID_\mathcal{P}, sk[ID_\mathcal{S}], m_w)$
5. $\mathsf{cert}_\mathcal{S} \leftarrow \mathsf{Sign}_{\mathsf{S}, msk}(ID_\mathcal{S} \| vk_\mathcal{S}^\mathsf{S})$
6. $\{(m_i, \sigma_i = (vk_\mathcal{S}^\mathsf{S}, vk_\mathcal{S}^\mathsf{BS}, \mathsf{cert}_\mathcal{S}, \sigma_{m_i}^\mathsf{BS}))\}_{1 \le i \le l'} \leftarrow \mathcal{A}$
7. If $\exists i \ne j, m_i = m_j$ or $\exists i$, $\mathsf{Verify}(ID_\mathcal{P}, m_i, \sigma_i) = 0$: Return 0
8. Else Return 1

All part of each signature have to be legit, thus the adversary is totally unable to conduct any action that could lead to a new signature. We conclude that $l = l'$. In that Game 3, any signature outputted by $\mathcal{A}$ was produced directly by the proxy signer. We observe a total advantage of an adversary against the generic IDPBS scheme of $\mathsf{Adv}_{\mathsf{IDPBS}, \mathcal{A}}^{uf} \le q \cdot (\mathsf{Adv}_{\mathsf{BS}, \mathcal{A}_\mathsf{BS}}^{uf} + \mathsf{Adv}_{\mathsf{S}, \mathcal{A}_\mathsf{S}}^{uf})$.

Verifiability. From a proxy signature, a verifier can be convinced of the original signer's agreement on the signed message.

Lemma 3 (Verifiability). *The adversary's advantage against the verifiability of the generic IDPBS scheme is* $\mathsf{Adv}_{\mathsf{IDPBS}, \mathcal{A}}^{veri}(\mathfrak{K}) \le \mathsf{Adv}_{\mathsf{S}, \mathcal{A}_\mathsf{S}}^{uf}$.

Proof. It is possible for an adversary $\mathcal{A}$ against verifiability to issue any blind signature by executing the protocol with himself. Thus any $\mathcal{A}$ is able to produced proxy signature under warrant m_w due to the settings of that game. Modifying Game 0 into Game 1, changes correspond to the inability of the adversary to forge a new certificate $w_{\mathcal{S} \to \mathcal{P}}$.

Game 1:

1. $(mpk, msk) \leftarrow \mathsf{Setup}(1^\mathfrak{K})$
2. $(ID_\mathcal{S}, ID_\mathcal{P}, m_w) \leftarrow \mathcal{A}(mpk)$

3. $sk[ID_S] \leftarrow$ Extract(msk, ID_S)
4. $(sk_P, w_{S \rightarrow P}) \leftarrow$ DelGen$(ID_S, ID_P, sk[ID_S], m_w)$
5. $(m, \sigma, m'_w, w'_{S \rightarrow P}) \leftarrow \mathcal{A}(sk_P, w_{S \rightarrow P})$,
   with $w'_{S \rightarrow P} \in Out(\mathcal{O}_{\mathsf{DelGen}}(ID_S, ID_P, sk[ID_S], m'_w))$
6. If Verif$(mpk, ID_S, ID_P, m, \sigma, m'_w, w'_{S \rightarrow P}) = 1$, $m'_w \neq m_w$
   and $w'_{S \rightarrow P} \notin Out(\mathcal{O}_{\mathsf{DelGen}}(ID_S, ID_P, sk[ID_S], m'_w))$: Return 1
7. Else Return 0

Let S_0 and S_1 by the respective event "Game i returns 1". By the difference lemma, we can conclude that $|\mathsf{Pr}[S_0] - \mathsf{Pr}[S_1]| \leq \mathsf{Adv}_S^{uf}(k)$. Differences in the games would directly lead to another adversary exploiting it to forge new signatures.

Note that, in Game 1 lines 5 and 6 contradict themselves, hence it is impossible for the adversary to win Game 1. We conclude that $\mathsf{Adv}_{\mathsf{IDPBS}, \mathcal{A}}^{veri}(\mathfrak{K}) \leq \mathsf{Adv}_{S, \mathcal{A}_S}^{uf}$.

Prevention of Misuse. Relatively similar to *verifiability*, *prevention of misuse* require that a proxy signing key cannot be used for purposes other than generating valid proxy signatures. In such a case of fraud it should be possible to identify the proxy signer.

Lemma 4 (Prevention of misuse). *The advantage of an adversary against prevention of misuse is* $\mathsf{Adv}_{\mathsf{IDPBS}, \mathcal{A}}^{PoM}(\mathfrak{K}) \leq \mathsf{Adv}_S^{uf}(k)$.

Proof. Start with Game 0 being the experiment $\mathsf{Exp}_{\mathsf{IDPBS}, \mathcal{P}^*}^{st-id}$.

Adversary $\mathcal{A}$ receives a warrant m_w with certificate $w_{S \rightarrow P}$. If he wants to use his keys for an unauthorised message, $\mathcal{A}$ has to produce a fake warrant and its associated certificate, otherwise the signature would not verify. But latter he could be identify as the cheater and be reprimand. In order not to be identify, $\mathcal{A}$ has to produced this certificate of delegation for another identity. We introduce change in our previous experiment and obtain Game 1.

Game 1:

1. $(mpk, msk) \leftarrow$ Setup$(1^{\mathfrak{K}})$
2. $(ID_S, ID_P, m_w) \leftarrow \mathcal{A}(mpk)$
3. $sk[ID_S] \leftarrow$ Extract(msk, ID_S)
4. $(sk_P, w_{S \rightarrow P}) \leftarrow$ DelGen$(ID_S, ID_P, sk[ID_S], m_w)$
5. $(ID, m, \sigma, m'_w, w'_{S \rightarrow P}) \leftarrow \mathcal{A}(sk_P, w_{S \rightarrow P})$,
   with $w'_{S \rightarrow P} \notin Out(\mathcal{O}_{\mathsf{DelGen}}(ID_S, ID_P, sk[ID_S], m'_w))$
6. If Verif$(mpk, ID_S, ID, m, \sigma, m'_w, w'_{S \rightarrow P}) = 1$ with $ID \neq ID_P$, $m'_w \neq m_w$ and
   $w'_{S \rightarrow P} \notin Out(\mathcal{O}_{\mathsf{DelGen}}(ID_S, ID_P, sk[ID_S], m'_w))$: Return 1
7. Else Return 0

In Game 0, $\mathcal{A}$ was able to output a forgery of a signature, this not the case in Game 1. We consider the adversary's advantage $\mathsf{Adv}_S^{uf}(k)$ as negligible. We obtain $|\mathsf{Pr}[S_0] - \mathsf{Pr}[S_1]| \leq \mathsf{Adv}_S^{uf}(k)$. In Game 1, condition of lines 5 and 6 of Game 1 cannot be fulfilled both at the time, we conclude to $\mathsf{Pr}[S_1] = 0$, from this fact we can conclude to the upper bound $\mathsf{Adv}_{\mathsf{IDPBS}, \mathcal{A}}^{PoM}(\mathfrak{K}) = \mathsf{Pr}[S_0] \leq \mathsf{Adv}_S^{uf}(k)$.

Strong Identifiability. Anyone can determine the identity of the corresponding proxy signer from a proxy signature. Let now be $\mathcal{A}$ an adversary against strong identifiability of the IDPBS. Set Game 0 as the experiment $\text{Exp}^{st-id}_{\text{IDPBS},\mathcal{P}*}(\mathfrak{K})$ for this scheme.

Lemma 5 (Strong Identifiability). *The advantage of an adversary $\mathcal{A}$ against strong identifiability is* $\text{Adv}^{st-id}_{\text{IDPBS},\mathcal{A}}(\mathfrak{K}) \leq \text{Adv}^{uf}_{\text{S}}(k)$.

Proof. In order to win the experiment $\text{Exp}^{st-id}_{\text{IDPBS},\mathcal{P}*}(\mathfrak{K})$ an adversary $\mathcal{A}$ has to outputs a second identity ID such that $ID_{\mathcal{P}}$ and ID verifies:

$$w_{\mathcal{S}\to\mathcal{P}} = Sign_{\text{S},sk^{\text{S}}_{\mathcal{S}}}(ID_{\mathcal{S}}||ID_{\mathcal{P}}||vk^{\text{BS}}_{\mathcal{P}}||m_w)$$
$$= Sign_{\text{S},sk^{\text{S}}_{\mathcal{S}}}(ID_{\mathcal{S}}||ID||vk^{\text{BS}}_{\mathcal{P}}||m_w) = w'_{\mathcal{S}\to\mathcal{P}}.$$

If this equality holds, even if $w_{\mathcal{S}\to\mathcal{P}}$ was given to $\mathcal{A}$ during the game, it is clear that $\text{Adv}^{st-id}_{\text{IDPBS},\mathcal{A}}(\mathfrak{K}) = \Pr[(m,m') \leftarrow \mathcal{A}|Sign_{\text{S},sk^{\text{S}}_{\mathcal{S}}}(m) = Sign_{\text{S},sk^{\text{S}}_{\mathcal{S}}}(m')] \leq \text{Adv}^{uf}_{\text{S}}(k)$.

Strong Undeniability. A proxy signer cannot repudiate a proxy signature it created. Given the information that $\mathcal{U}$ has at the end of a blind signing session, he has enough knowledge to expose $\mathcal{P}$. This would lead to ability to revoke the signature $w_{\mathcal{S}\to\mathcal{P}}$ of $\mathcal{S}$.

Lemma 6 (Strong Undeniability). *Strong undeniability of our scheme holds. The adversary's advantage against this property is* $\text{Adv}^{st-und}_{\text{IDPBS},\mathcal{A}}(\mathfrak{K}) \leq \text{Adv}^{uf}_{\text{S}}(k) + \text{Adv}^{uni}_{\text{S}}(k)$.

Proof. Let Game 0 be the experiment associated to strong undeniability. Once published a signature cannot be repudiated as all information were revealed to the public, in particularly, in an identity-based setup $ID_{\mathcal{S}}$ and $ID_{\mathcal{P}}$ were transited. Using the Verif algorithm we will output 1 if the signature is valid. Thus $\mathcal{A}$ as to trick around this and propose an alternative possibility. $\mathcal{A}$ can output a second ID that could work for the same setup and thus causing doubts. We have modify our experiment in Game 1.

Game 1:

1. $(mpk, msk) \leftarrow \text{Setup}(1^{\mathfrak{K}})$
2. $(ID_{\mathcal{S}}, ID_{\mathcal{P}}, m_w) \leftarrow \mathcal{A}(mpk)$
3. $sk[ID_{\mathcal{S}}] \leftarrow \text{Extract}(msk, ID_{\mathcal{S}})$
4. $(sk_{\mathcal{P}}, w_{\mathcal{S}\to\mathcal{P}}) \leftarrow \text{DelGen}(ID_{\mathcal{S}}, ID_{\mathcal{P}}, sk[ID_{\mathcal{S}}], m_w)$
5. $(Id, (m, \sigma), m'_w, w'_{\mathcal{S}\to\mathcal{P}}) \leftarrow \mathcal{A}(sk_{\mathcal{P}}, w_{\mathcal{S}\to\mathcal{P}})$,
   with $w'_{\mathcal{S}\to\mathcal{P}} \in Out(\mathcal{O}_{\text{DelGen}}(ID_{\mathcal{S}}, ID, sk[ID_{\mathcal{S}}], m'_w))$:
6. If $\text{Verif}(mpk, ID_{\mathcal{S}}, ID_{\mathcal{P}}, m, \sigma, m_w, w_{\mathcal{S}\to\mathcal{P}}) = 1$,
   $\text{Verif}(mpk, ID_{\mathcal{S}}, ID, m, \sigma, m'_w, w'_{\mathcal{S}\to\mathcal{P}}) = 1$ with $ID \neq ID_{\mathcal{P}}$: Return 1
7. Else Return 0

The difference in between our games 0 and 1 is the ability of the adversary to forge new delegations. It would lead to a forgery against the scheme S if $\mathcal{A}$ was able to outputs such a certificate. Hence $|\Pr[S_0] - \Pr[S_1]| \leq \mathsf{Adv}_S^{uf}(k)$. We can now consider the probability such that $\mathsf{Verif}(mpk, ID_\mathcal{S}, ID_\mathcal{P}, m, \sigma, m_w, w_{\mathcal{S} \to \mathcal{P}})$ $= \mathsf{Verif}(mpk, ID_\mathcal{S}, ID, m, \sigma, m_w', w_{\mathcal{S} \to \mathcal{P}}') = 1$ for $ID \neq ID_\mathcal{P}$. From the steps of the Verif algorithm, it is equivalent to $\mathsf{Verif}_{S, vk_\mathcal{S}^S}(w_{\mathcal{S} \to \mathcal{P}}, ID_\mathcal{S} || ID_\mathcal{P} || vk_\mathcal{P}^{BS} || m_w) = \mathsf{Verif}_{S, vk_\mathcal{S}^S}(w_{\mathcal{S} \to \mathcal{P}}', ID_\mathcal{S} || ID || vk^{BS'} || m_w') = 1$. But S is an unique signature scheme and thus this advantage is negligible. We directly conclude that $\mathsf{Adv}_{\mathsf{IDPBS}, \mathcal{A}}^{st-und}(\mathcal{R}) \leq \mathsf{Adv}_S^{uf}(k) + \mathsf{Adv}_S^{uni}(k)$.

5   Analysis of the Construction

Warrant Modification. The type of delegation used for our scheme implies to generates a new key pair to issued or change the contract m_w for a proxy user. Otherwise anyone getting a signature for the first contract could easily get a forgery for the new contract. This specificity requires a new communication with the signer when the warrant is changed and the issue of new keys for the proxy. This is similar to most IDPBS schemes.

Efficiency. Let S $=$ (KeyGen$_S$, Sign$_S$, Verif$_S$) and BS $=$ (Commit$_{BS}$, Blind$_{BS}$, Sign$_{BS}$, Unblind$_{BS}$, Verif$_{BS}$) respectively be a unique signature scheme and a blind signature scheme with the desired properties to assemble them and get a generic IDPBS as it is described above. For any IDPBS signature issuing in between a proxy signer $\mathcal{P}$ and a user $\mathcal{U}$ algorithm that need to be executed are reported in Table 1. The efficiency of this generic construction is not competitive with the best IDPBS schemes of the literature (see Sect. 1 for an exhaustive list), this is mostly due to the multiple sub-signature verifications that have to be processed during the verification of the signature.

Table 1. Underlying algorithm to issue or verify generic IDPBS signatures. ($\mathcal{U}$: User, $\mathcal{P}$: Proxy, $\mathcal{V}$: Verifier, T: Total)

	Verif$_S$	Commit$_{BS}$	Blind$_{BS}$	Sign$_{BS}$	Unblind$_{BS}$	Verif$_{BS}$
$\mathcal{U}$	2		1		1	1
$\mathcal{P}$		1	1		1	
$\mathcal{V}$	2					1
T	4	1	1	1	1	2

Communication Efficiency. Both communications specified in protocol Fig. 9 (*i.e.*, between the user and the proxy signer) can be merged into the first interaction of the blind signature scheme to obtain a round optimal blind signature. The number of communications can thus be reduced to the minimum as long as round optimal signature scheme is used in the generic construction.

6 Conclusion

We propose a new generic construction for identity-based proxy blind signature, based on two basic primitives, namely a unique signature scheme and blind signature scheme. The purpose of such generic construction is to reunite fundamental, "low level" primitives with blind signature construction with additional properties. Another contribution is a formalisation of the security for identity-based proxy blind signature based on the 6 usual statements of security property that are proposed in numerous articles. We formally prove that our construction is secure. For this, we only require blindness and unforgeability of the blind signature and unforgeability and hardness to determined two different signatures for the same message. The latest property is clearly achieved by some existing schemes such as the well known BLS signature. Adding up this result with the previous literature, it is now possible to construct a secure identity-based proxy blind signature from only a few building blocks such as a signature scheme, a zero-knowledge proof, a commitment and an encryption scheme.

References

1. Abdalla, M., Catalano, D., Fiore, D.: Verifiable random functions: relations to identity-based key encapsulation and new constructions. J. Cryptol. **27**(3), 544–593 (2013). https://doi.org/10.1007/s00145-013-9153-x
2. Abe, M., Fujisaki, E.: How to date blind signatures. In: Kim, K., Matsumoto, T. (eds.) ASIACRYPT 1996. LNCS, vol. 1163, pp. 244–251. Springer, Heidelberg (1996). https://doi.org/10.1007/BFb0034851
3. Bellare, M., Rogaway, P.: The exact security of digital signatures-how to sign with RSA and Rabin. In: Maurer, U. (ed.) EUROCRYPT 1996. LNCS, vol. 1070, pp. 399–416. Springer, Heidelberg (1996). https://doi.org/10.1007/3-540-68339-9_34
4. Boldyreva, A., Palacio, A., Warinschi, B.: Secure proxy signature schemes for delegation of signing rights. J. Cryptol. **25**(1), 57–115 (2010). https://doi.org/10.1007/s00145-010-9082-x
5. Boneh, D., Lynn, B., Shacham, H.: Short signatures from the Weil pairing. In: Boyd, C. (ed.) ASIACRYPT 2001. LNCS, vol. 2248, pp. 514–532. Springer, Heidelberg (2001). https://doi.org/10.1007/3-540-45682-1_30
6. Camenisch, J.L., Piveteau, J.-M., Stadler, M.A.: Blind signatures based on the discrete logarithm problem. In: De Santis, A. (ed.) EUROCRYPT 1994. LNCS, vol. 950, pp. 428–432. Springer, Heidelberg (1995). https://doi.org/10.1007/BFb0053458
7. Chaum, D.: Blind signatures for untraceable payments. In: Chaum, D., Rivest, R.L., Sherman, A.T. (eds.) Advances in Cryptology, pp. 199–203. Springer, Boston, MA (1983). https://doi.org/10.1007/978-1-4757-0602-4_18
8. Dodis, Y.: Efficient construction of (distributed) verifiable random functions. In: Desmedt, Y.G. (ed.) PKC 2003. LNCS, vol. 2567, pp. 1–17. Springer, Heidelberg (2003). https://doi.org/10.1007/3-540-36288-6_1
9. Fischlin, M.: Round-optimal composable blind signatures in the common reference string model. In: Dwork, C. (ed.) CRYPTO 2006. LNCS, vol. 4117, pp. 60–77. Springer, Heidelberg (2006). https://doi.org/10.1007/11818175_4

10. Galindo, D., Herranz, J., Kiltz, E.: On the generic construction of identity-based signatures with additional properties. In: Lai, X., Chen, K. (eds.) ASIACRYPT 2006. LNCS, vol. 4284, pp. 178–193. Springer, Heidelberg (2006). https://doi.org/10.1007/11935230_12

11. Goldwasser, S., Ostrovsky, R.: *Invariant* signatures and non-interactive zero-knowledge proofs are equivalent. In: Brickell, E.F. (ed.) CRYPTO 1992. LNCS, vol. 740, pp. 228–245. Springer, Heidelberg (1993). https://doi.org/10.1007/3-540-48071-4_16

12. He, J., Qi, C., Sun, F.: A new identity-based proxy blind signature scheme. In: 2012 IEEE International Conference on Information Science and Technology (2012)

13. Heng, P., Ke, K., Gu, C.: Efficienct ID-based proxy blind signature schemes from pairings. In: 2008 International Conference on Computational Intelligence and Security (2008)

14. Jager, T.: Verifiable random functions from weaker assumptions. In: Dodis, Y., Nielsen, J.B. (eds.) TCC 2015. LNCS, vol. 9015, pp. 121–143. Springer, Heidelberg (2015). https://doi.org/10.1007/978-3-662-46497-7_5

15. James, S., Thumbur, G., Reddy, P.: An efficient pairing-free identity based proxy blind signature scheme with message recovery. ISC Int. J. Inf. Secur. **13**(1), 59–72 (2021)

16. Lang, W., Tan, Y., Yang, Z., Liu, G., Peng, B.: A new efficient ID-based proxy blind signature scheme. In: ISCC 2004 (2004)

17. Lysyanskaya, A.: Unique signatures and verifiable random functions from the DH-DDH separation. In: Yung, M. (ed.) CRYPTO 2002. LNCS, vol. 2442, pp. 597–612. Springer, Heidelberg (2002). https://doi.org/10.1007/3-540-45708-9_38

18. Micali, S., Rabin, M., Vadhan, S.: Verifiable random functions. In: 40th Annual Symposium on Foundations of Computer Science (Cat. No. 99CB37039), pp. 120–130. IEEE (1999)

19. Padhye, S., Tiwari, N.: An efficient ID-based proxy blind signature with pairing-free realization. In: ICIET 2016 (2016)

20. Prabhadevi, S., Natarajan, A.: Utilization of ID-based proxy blind signature based on ECDLP in secure vehicular communications. IJEIT **3**(5), 55–60 (2013)

21. Qin, X., Cai, C., Yuen, T.H.: One-more unforgeability of blind ECDSA. In: Bertino, E., Shulman, H., Waidner, M. (eds.) ESORICS 2021. LNCS, vol. 12973, pp. 313–331. Springer, Cham (2021). https://doi.org/10.1007/978-3-030-88428-4_16

22. Sarde, P., Banerjee, A.: A secure ID-based blind and proxy blind signature scheme from bilinear pairings. J. Appl. Secur. Res. **12**(2), 276–286 (2017)

23. Shamir, A.: Identity-based cryptosystems and signature schemes. In: Blakley, G.R., Chaum, D. (eds.) CRYPTO 1984. LNCS, vol. 196, pp. 47–53. Springer, Heidelberg (1985). https://doi.org/10.1007/3-540-39568-7_5

24. Shoup, V.: Sequences of games: a tool for taming complexity in security proofs. IACR Cryptology ePrint Archive 2004/332 (2004)

25. Stadler, M., Piveteau, J.-M., Camenisch, J.: Fair blind signatures. In: Guillou, L.C., Quisquater, J.-J. (eds.) EUROCRYPT 1995. LNCS, vol. 921, pp. 209–219. Springer, Heidelberg (1995). https://doi.org/10.1007/3-540-49264-X_17

26. Tan, Z.: Efficient pairing-free provably secure identity-based proxy blind signature scheme. Secur. Commun. Netw. **6**(5), 593–601 (2013)

27. Tan, Z., Liu, Z., Tang, C.: Digital proxy blind signature schemes based on DLP and ECDLP. MM Res. Prepr. **21**(7), 212–217 (2002)

28. Wang, B., Liu, W., Wang, C.: ID-based proxy blind signature scheme with proxy revocation. In: 2nd International Workshop on Computer Science and Engineering, WCSE (2009)

29. Wang, C.H., Fan, J.-Y.: The design of ID-based fair proxy blind signature scheme with weak linkability. In: ISIC (2012)
30. Wei-min, L., Zong-kai, Y., Wen-qing, C., Yun-meng, T.: A new ID-based proxy blind signature scheme. Wuhan Univ. J. Nat. Sci. **10**(3), 555–558 (2005). https://doi.org/10.1007/BF02831144
31. Yang, M., Wang, Y.: A new efficient ID-based proxy blind signature scheme. J. Electron. **25**(2), 226–231 (2008). https://doi.org/10.1007/s11767-006-0146-x
32. Yi, X., Lam, K.-Y., Gollmann, D.: A new blind ECDSA scheme for bitcoin transaction anonymity. Cryptology ePrint Archive Report 2018/660 (2018)
33. Yu, Y., Zheng, S., Yang, Y.: ID-based blind signature and proxy blind signature without trusted PKG. In: Sarbazi-Azad, H., Parhami, B., Miremadi, S.-G., Hessabi, S. (eds.) CSICC 2008. CCIS, vol. 6, pp. 821–824. Springer, Heidelberg (2008). https://doi.org/10.1007/978-3-540-89985-3_111
34. Zhang, F., Kim, K.: ID-based blind signature and ring signature from pairings. In: Zheng, Y. (ed.) ASIACRYPT 2002. LNCS, vol. 2501, pp. 533–547. Springer, Heidelberg (2002). https://doi.org/10.1007/3-540-36178-2_33
35. Zhang, F., Kim, K.: Efficient ID-based blind signature and proxy signature from bilinear pairings. In: Safavi-Naini, R., Seberry, J. (eds.) ACISP 2003. LNCS, vol. 2727, pp. 312–323. Springer, Heidelberg (2003). https://doi.org/10.1007/3-540-45067-X_27
36. Zhu, H., Tan, Y.-A., Zhu, L., Zhang, Q., Li, Y.: An efficient identity-based proxy blind signature for semioffline services. Wirel. Commun. Mob. Comput. **2018**, 1–9 (2018). https://doi.org/10.1155/2018/5401890

Optimizing Anonymity and Performance in a Mix Network

Mathieu Jee[1], Ania M. Piotrowska[2], Harry Halpin[2(✉)], and Ninoslav Marina[1]

[1] Haute Ecole Arc, Neuchâtel, Switzerland
`mathieu.jee@protonmail.ch`, `ninoslav.marina@he-arc.ch`
[2] Nym Technologies, Neuchâtel, Switzerland
`{ania,harry}@nymtech.net`

Abstract. Mix networks were developed to hide the correspondence between senders and recipients of the communication. In order to be usable and defend user privacy, anonymous communication networks like mixnets need to be parameterized in an optimal manner. This work uses a mixnet simulator to determine reasonable packet size and parameters for the real-world Nym mixnet, a stratified continuous-time mixnet that uses the Sphinx packet format. We analyzed network parameters, such as the sending rate, cover traffic overhead, and mixing delay, to determine the impact of various configurations on the anonymity and performance.

Keywords: Mix networks · Anonymity · Privacy · Scalability · Simulation

1 Introduction

The Internet was designed in a trusted academic environment and so privacy was not considered essential in the design of network protocols like TCP/IP and UDP. However, privacy can be added to existing internet protocols by using an anonymous communication network as an overlay network on top of the existing internet, with the most widely deployed being Tor [6]. Yet Tor's threat model explicitly excludes a powerful *global passive adversary* that can monitor all the inputs and outputs of the network – such as claimed to be possible by intelligence agencies like the NSA – and Tor's current threat model is increasingly vulnerable to various traffic analysis attacks [8]. This has recently led to a revival of research into alternative anonymous communication networks such as mix networks (mixnets) [1] and dining cryptographer networks (DC-nets) [4].

One such alternative anonymous communication system, that pre-dates Tor, is a *mixnet*, which uses relay servers called mixes (or mix nodes) to counter a global passive adversary that could monitor all the input and output of every node to link senders to receivers of packets [1]. Multiple mix nodes are typically put in a cascade as a single mix node could be compromised easily. In a mixnet, messages between a sender and a receiver are layer-encrypted and transited through a cascade of multiple mix nodes before reaching their recipient, similar

© Springer Nature Switzerland AG 2022
E. Aïmeur et al. (Eds.): FPS 2021, LNCS 13291, pp. 53–62, 2022.
https://doi.org/10.1007/978-3-031-08147-7_4

to onion-routing in Tor [6]. Unlike Tor, mixnets eliminate information leakage as each mix node forwards the packets in a different order than it was received, and a passive eavesdropper cannot predict the reordering process inside each mix node [1]. However, even newer cascade-based mix network designs such as cMix [2] suffer from limits on their anonymity and performance, as the bandwidth of the entire mixnet is limited to the bandwidth of the smallest capacity mix node in the cascade [11].

Loopix [10] can both resist global passive adversaries and also be competitive in terms of performance with existing solutions like Tor [4]. Loopix does this by using the continuous time-mixing technique, in which a mix delays each packet independently before forwarding it to the next hop. The amount of time a packet needs to wait in each mix is chosen by the sender, who picks it at random from an exponential distribution $Exp(\mu)$. The average delay μ can be set as a parameter. However, the original Loopix design [10] does not provide sample parameters. Hence a purely theoretical analysis has been done in comparison to Tor, because there has been no empirically deployed "real world" mixnet and no clear methodology for determining the parameters [4]. The Nym project[1] is deploying an advanced mixnet design using a Loopix-style stratified topology that can add more interconnected nodes dynamically to match the incoming traffic. The design of the Nym mixnet is more fully described in the whitepaper [5]. Yet the Nym mixnet requires parameters such as packet size and the amount of cover traffic to be set as system parameters before the network can be used.

Next, we outline the problem of parameterizing real-world mixnets, in Sect. 2. In Sect. 3, we outline our experimental setup that uses a simulator [11] to determine realistic parameter settings for the Nym mixnet. The results of our simulation work are presented and discussed in Sect. 4, while the conclusions and the future steps for real-world mix networking are shown in Sect. 5.

2   Problem

The main problem facing a real-world mixnet is the ideal packet size and parameters so that user's traffic has the best possible anonymity and an acceptable level of performance. The problem is not completely amendable to a purely theoretical analysis as given by formal frameworks [4], as the exact anonymity and latency provided by a mix network depends on interactions between the exact number of the mix nodes used, their topology, and the precise pattern of traffic. Therefore, the best route to determine these parameters is via either empirical data or simulated data, where simulations can take into account the complex structure and interdependencies of the various parameters needed by the mixnet, and then calculate the latency and anonymity provisioned by the mixnet. In prior work, an open-source discrete network simulator has been used to compare different mixnet designs [11]. This work extends the prior work by determining the parameters needed for a real-world mix network for performance

---

[1] https://nymtech.net.

with reasonable latency, as well as determining if these trade-offs are affected by changes in the size of the underlying Sphinx packet [3].

The goal of this paper is to measure the performance and the level of anonymity of the Nym network for different parameters. This includes the size of the Sphinx payload and the cover traffic rates. The motivation is to tweak these parameters in order to increase the performance, as measured in *goodput*. Note that throughput defines the overall amount of data going through the network per time unit, while the goodput measures only the useful information (e.g., without the overhead). In the second part of our analysis, we modify the client sending rate and the average packet delay at each hop, called mixing delay. Finally, we explore using different packet sizes and different sending rates depending on the kind of traffic transmitted.

3   Methodology

3.1   Experimental Setup

All simulations were run on a model of the Nym network that reflects the current state of the Nym testnet. At the time we deployed our study, there was a total of 1500 mix nodes with 100 clients. This number of 100 active clients does not reflect the targeted number of clients when deploying mainnet, since as the Nym mixnet matures, the number of clients will be larger than the number of mix nodes.

Each user's client routes traffic on behalf of their user via the Nym mixnet. Each of the three layers in the mixnet is composed of 500 mix nodes. The traffic in the Nym network is divided into the *user traffic*, which is sent by the user through the network and *cover traffic*, which is traffic sent through the network to increase the anonymity of the packets [10]. These packets are indistinguishable from normal packets carrying user data.

In continuous-time mixes like Loopix and Nym (as opposed to cascade mixnets like cMix [2]), a parameterized Poisson process is used by a sender to determine the *delay* at each mix. Therefore, the average time of packet delivery through the mixnet can be estimated, although the exact delivery time of each packet is not possible to discover. While the delay increases the latency, it increases the amount of mixing and thus the anonymity of the mixnet.

The output of each client is composed of two separate streams of data where the first stream of data is in charge of sending the packets from the user. If the client does not have any packets to send, this Poisson process sends an indistinguishable 'dummy' packet in lieu of a user-defined packet in order to always have a constant sending rate of packets, regardless of the fact that some of these packets are genuine or dummy packets. A second Poisson process, completely independent from the first one, is used to send cover traffic. The first Poisson process is controlled by parameter λ_1, while the second is controlled by λ_2.

We do not consider the case where the adversary controls one or more mix nodes (forcing them to drop packets), as there exist already techniques to detect and reject these malicious mix nodes from the topology network [7]. In this work, we consider passive global adversaries and honest mix nodes.

3.2 Measuring Anonymity with Entropy

In their well-known work, Pfitzmann and Hansen define anonymity as the state of being not identifiable within a set of subjects, also called *anonymity set* [9]. Thus, a common measure of anonymity is the anonymity set, which reflects the size of the set of other packets with which our message can be confused by the attacker. However, this is a very imprecise way of accounting for mixnet traffic as it does not take into account multiple observations through multiple mix nodes by an adversary who thus gains knowledge over time. An adversary observing mix nodes in the network for a while may assign different probabilities for each outgoing packet being linked to the observed incoming packet. Therefore, we use the Shannon entropy to measure anonymity, as proposed by Danezis et al. [12]. Shannon entropy measures uncertainty. So if the entropy is smaller, the anonymity is weaker, while if the entropy is larger, more uncertainty brings better anonymity. A system with no anonymity has an entropy of zero.

According to this measurement of anonymity, the maximum anonymity is reached when an adversary is seeing every packet as potentially equally being a specific packet from the targeted user. Probabilistically, it means that the adversary sees each packet with uniform probability with respect to the source of that packet. This means that the adversary observes each packet with probability $\frac{1}{L}$, where L is the number of all packets traversing the network.

3.3 The Mix Simulator

We analyse how different packet sizes and network parameters impact anonymity, measured by empirically quantifying entropy via multiple simulations using a virtual mix network via a mix simulator [11]. This software is able to simulate traffic transiting between clients and mix nodes by modeling interactions between network components as a sequence of events in time, where each event marks a change of state. The software can simulate various network configurations and parametrization, including the number of mix nodes and clients, network topology, sending rates, average mixing delays or packet size. Given a configuration, the software runs the simulated network and evaluates the entropy of each packet transiting the network. Since it is a discrete-event simulator, the events are processed sequentially and one unit of time (tick) of the simulation is interpreted as one second in a real deployed mixnet.

For the purpose of our experiments, the mix simulator creates a virtual stratified mix network with three layers of 500 mix nodes and initializes 100 clients (100). Each client will send its traffic into the mix network using two distinct Poisson processes (as described in Sect. 3.1). Once the simulator is in a steady-state, the simulator selects randomly one of the client's as a *target client*. This targeted client will start sending a specific number of real messages to random other clients. The entropy of each packet in the face of a global passive adversary is then calculated.

Entropy Measurements. We denote the target client as C. Each packet sent into the mix network has an assigned probability P_i, where i can go from 1 to N. All packets sent by non-target clients have initially probability 0. Once the network is in a steady state the target client C sends a packet with initial probability 1. At each hop between layers, the probability mass assigned to packet i is updated as follows

$$P_i = \frac{P_i}{l} + P_{M_k}.$$

Here l denotes the total number of packets (both real and dummy) that are already inside the mix node's pool (i.e., the packets being mixed) and P_{M_k} is the probability of the current mix node. Once the probability of packet i is updated, probability P_{M_k} of the mix node is also updated as:

$$P_{M_k} = P_i.$$

All packets have their probability mass updated at each mix node while traversing the network. The overall entropy is updated each time a packet exits the mix network as:

$$H(p_C) = -\sum_{j=1}^{L} P_j \cdot \log_2(P_j)$$

where L is the number of all the packets traversing the mix network.

In order to ensure that our entropy measurement is precise and not biased, we have to repeat the measurement multiple times and take the average result. To speed up our simulations, we run multiple entropy measurements in parallel so that each packet and each mix node are assigned a vector of probabilities. The probability of packet i is denoted by P_i, while the probability stored by mix node M_k is denoted by P_{M_k}. We repeat our entropy measurement N times, where N denotes the total number of packets sent by the target client C. Therefore, $P_i[j]$, for $j = 0, 1, 2, \ldots, N - 1$, is the probability that a given packet i is the $j-$th packet sent by the target client C. Furthermore, at each hop, the probability mass assigned to packet i is now updated as:

$$P_i[j] = \frac{P_i[j]}{l} + P_{M_k}[j].$$

4   Results

4.1   Impact of Sending Rates and Mixing Delay on Anonymity and Performance

The *mixing delay* greatly influences the anonymity and the performance of the network. To recall, mix nodes hold each packet for μ milliseconds on average

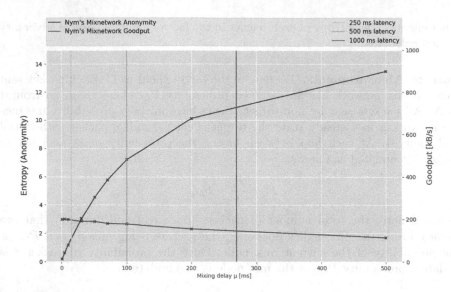

Fig. 1. Anonymity and Goodput plotted against the mixing delay with latency levels.

before forwarding it to the next hop. The amount of time a packet is kept by a mix node is specified by the sender, who selects it at random from the exponential distribution with parameter μ.

This mechanism is in charge of mixing packets: the larger parameter μ is, the more packets are present at the same time inside the mix node, leading to higher entropy. On the contrary, with a small value of μ, fewer packets will be mixed together resulting in a lower entropy. However, augmenting the mixing delay has a side effect on the latency: if packets are held longer inside each mix node, the average latency will also increase. The use-cases of the Nym mixnet generally do not require low latency usage. Since Nym is designed to be used for cryptocurrency transactions and instant messaging, so a medium to high latency is acceptable.

The simulator was run with a 2048 byte packet size, with the user traffic being 150 packets/second and the cover traffic being 50 packets/second. As can be seen in Fig. 1, we see that the mixing delay has a huge impact on the quality of anonymity with only a small drop of the goodput. Interestingly, when increasing the mixing delay the impact of performance is not reflected on the goodput value but rather on the latency of the network. The three vertical lines represent *different levels of latency* that map to low, medium and high latency tolerance. Each vertical line shows from which value of mixing delay the various latency thresholds are reached.

4.2   Simulations with Different Packet Sizes

Each message sent via the Nym mixnet is layer-encrypted using the Sphinx cryptographic packet format [3]. First of all, it is important to clarify what we mean by *modifying Sphinx packet sizes* and *goodput*. When we increase (or decrease) Sphinx packet sizes, we actually only modify the size of the payload of the packet. The Sphinx header is not taken into consideration because it does not contain the actual data of communications, but only routing information and cryptographic parameters for message authentication [3] (Fig. 2).

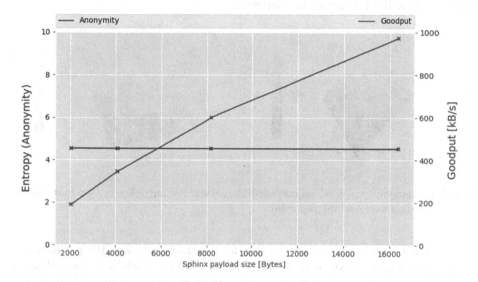

Fig. 2. Anonymity and Goodput plotted against different sizes of Sphinx payloads

To understand the effects of different payloads sizes on the network, we simulate the network's state with different Sphinx packet sizes (in bytes) with a sending rate of 50 packets a second for both user and cover traffic and a constant mixing delay of .05 s. As can be seen in Table 1, this simulation verifies the hypothesis that varying the packet sizes has an impact on the performance of the network without having any effect on the quality of anonymity. When increasing payload sizes, we reduce the number of real packets needed to transmit a single user-defined message. As could be deduced, regardless of the size of the payload and the amount of packets generated by clients, the traffic flowing inside the mix network remains the same as the first Poisson process keeps the sending rate at a constant value even if there are fewer real packets. Hence the entropy is not impacted by the different payload sizes as could be predicted, but the goodput is proportionally increasing in relation to packet size while the anonymity remains at the same level.

4.3   Finding the Best Combination of Sending Rates and Mixing Delay

Now that we have analyzed the mixing delay with a constant sending rate, we illustrate the impact the sending rate and mixing delay has together on the anonymity (Fig. 3a) and the goodput (Fig. 3b). Anonymity and goodput do not grow in the same direction. As expected, the entropy increases when both mixing delay and sending rate are increasing. On the other hand, the slope of the goodput plotted surface on the *mixing delay axis* is rather flat, meaning that the mixing delay has not much impact on the goodput, as explained earlier (Fig. 1), but rather on the latency of the network.

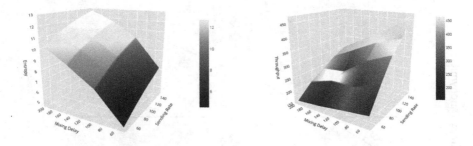

Fig. 3. a: Anonymity plotted against sending rate and mixing delay. b: Goodput plotted against sending rate and mixing delay.

To find an optimal parameterization for the anonymity and the performance of the network, we have to take into account multiple variables. First of all, a second Poisson process dedicated to cover traffic is needed to keep a higher level of anonymity without sacrificing too much of the goodput. As per Fig. 3a, 3b, a larger sending rate enhances both the anonymity and the goodput. As the maximum a CPU can handle is 200 per Sphinx packets a second at this moment, the sum of both stream sending rates should not be higher than 200 packets per second. Therefore, we select $\lambda_1 = 150$ as the maximum sending rate for the first Poisson process.

The choice of the best mixing delay value is a bit more difficult since we have to be aware that mixing delays impact the latency of the network. To keep a high level of anonymity and still be able to fulfill Nym's use-cases requirements, the latency of the network does not need to be the lowest possible. Hence, we can stick with a maximum of 500 to 1000 ms of end to end latency, meaning that the best value of mixing delay parameter μ for Nym's network varies from 100 to 270 ms. In Table 1 we present detailed anonymity and performance results for various mixing delays from 100 to 270 ms, with 2048 byte and 4096 byte Sphinx payloads and selected sending rates.

For everyday usage like instant messaging, we propose the combination of 100 ms of mixing delay alongside 200 Sphinx packets generated per second for each client is suitable, with 150 ms for user traffic and 50 ms for cover traffic.

Table 1. Resulting network parameters from simulator.

Packet [bytes]	Delay [ms]	Sending rate [ms]	Entropy	Goodput [kB/s]	Latency [ms]
2048	100	150 + 50	10.13	400.83	500
2048	150	150 + 50	11.70	349.84	651
2048	200	150 + 50	12.76	300.47	798
2048	250	150 + 50	13.48	243.35	951
2048	270	150 + 50	13.72	229.05	1011
4096	100	150 + 50	10.08	565.95	499
4096	150	150 + 50	11.66	429.85	650
4096	200	150 + 50	12.71	403.60	796
4096	250	150 + 50	13.44	360.68	948
4096	270	150 + 50	13.69	325.17	1008

These parameters are optimal in terms of anonymity with acceptable throughput and 500 ms of latency.

As expected, increasing the payload size only impacts the goodput and does not affect the anonymity or the latency. Thus, having an even larger packet size would further enhance the goodput. In our opinion, increasing the size of Sphinx payloads to 4096 bytes is the optimal size to increase the goodput and have the same level of anonymity while keeping the required bandwidth below 1 megabyte per second. When comparing the two different packet sizes, we note the increase of goodput by approximately 40%, which is a significant improvement in terms of performance for Nym.

5 Conclusion

We studied the effects of parameters like mixing delays and packet sizes on the network and proposed an optimal size of Sphinx packet and parameters for the Nym mixnet. By combining the previously optimized network parameters and the new 4096-byte Sphinx payload, we enhance the goodput up to 40%, while keeping the same level of latency. The anonymity of the network does increase with the increase of the mix delay, but an acceptable entropy can be gained even with small 100 ms delays. This parameter optimization offers a concrete improvement to the existing Nym testnet mixnet, allowing the mixnet to to enable the support of real world applications while increasing the privacy of all.

References

1. Chaum, D.: Untraceable electronic mail, return addresses, and digital pseudonyms. Commun. ACM **24**, 84–88 (1981)
2. Chaum, D., et al.: cMix: mixing with minimal real-time asymmetric cryptographic operations. In: Gollmann, D., Miyaji, A., Kikuchi, H. (eds.) ACNS 2017. LNCS, vol. 10355, pp. 557–578. Springer, Cham (2017). https://doi.org/10.1007/978-3-319-61204-1_28

3. Danezis, G., Goldberg, I.: Sphinx: a compact and provably secure mix format. In: Proceedings of 30th IEEE Symposium on Security and Privacy, pp. 269–282 (2009)
4. Das, D., Meiser, S., Mohammadi, E., Kate, A.: Anonymity trilemma: strong anonymity, low bandwidth overhead, low latency-choose two. In IEEE Symposium on Security and Privacy (SP), pp 108–126 (2018)
5. Diaz, C., Halpin, H., Kiayias, A.: The next generation of privacy infrastructure, The Nym Network (2021)
6. Dingledine, R., Mathewson, N., Syverson, P.F.: Tor: the second-generation onion router. In: Proceedings of the 13th Conference on USENIX Security Symposium, pp. 13–21 (2004)
7. Leibowitz, H., Piotrowska, A.M., Danezis, G., Herzberg, A.: No right to remain silent: isolating malicious mixes. In: Heninger, N., Traynor, P., (eds.) 28th USENIX Security Symposium, pp. 1841–1858 (2019)
8. Panchenko, A., et al.: Website fingerprinting at internet scale. In: 23rd Annual Network and Distributed System Security Symposium (2016)
9. Pfitzmann, A., Hansen, M.: Anonymity, unlinkability, unobservability, pseudonymity, and identity management - A consolidated proposal for terminology (2005)
10. Piotrowska, A., Hayes, J., Elahi, T.: The loopix anonymity system. In: Proceedings of the 26th USENIX Conference on Security Symposium, pp. 1199–1216 (2017)
11. Piotrowska, A.M.: Studying the anonymity trilemma with a discrete-event mix network simulator. In: WPES 2021: Proceedings of the 20th Workshop on Workshop on Privacy in the Electronic Society, pp. 39–44 (2021)
12. Serjantov, A., Danezis, G.: Towards an information theoretic metric for anonymity. In: Dingledine, R., Syverson, P. (eds.) PET 2002. LNCS, vol. 2482, pp. 41–53. Springer, Heidelberg (2003). https://doi.org/10.1007/3-540-36467-6_4

Homomorphic Evaluation of Lightweight Cipher Boolean Circuits

Kalikinkar Mandal[1]($\boxtimes$) and Guang Gong[2]

[1] Faculty of Computer Science, University of New Brunswick,
Fredericton E3B 5A3, Canada
kmandal@unb.ca
[2] Department of Electrical and Computer Engineering, University of Waterloo,
Waterloo, ON N2L 3G1, Canada
ggong@uwaterloo.ca

Abstract. Motivated by a number of applications of lightweight ciphers in privacy-enhancing cryptography (PEC) techniques such as secure multiparty computation (SMPC), fully homomorphic encryption (FHE) and zero-knowledge proof (ZKP) for verifiable computing, we investigate the Boolean circuit complexity of the core primitives of NIST lightweight cryptography (LWC) round 2 candidates. In PEC, the functionalities (e.g., ciphers) are often required to express as Boolean or arithmetic circuits before applying PEC techniques, and the size of a circuit is one of the efficiency factors. As a use case, we consider homomorphic evaluation of the core AEAD circuits in the cloud-outsourcing setting using the TFHE scheme, and present the performance results.

Keywords: Lightweight cryptography · Homomorphic evaluation · TFHE · Privacy-preserving computation

1 Introduction

Pervasive and ubiquitous computing has been integrating the physical world into the digital world where billions of physical devices such as smart devices, sensors and actuators are deployed at different applications for operational, monitoring and data collection. The collected data are processed at backend servers/cloud for operation, automation, and optimizing costs. Despite the use of lightweight cryptographic algorithms such as authenticated encryption (AE) for protecting communication in resource-constrained applications, it may be used for secure storage of data from constrained applications. Such stored data will not solely be used for storage or backup (securing while at rest) purposes, but also be used for performing analytics computations for extracting useful information for operational, automation, and optimizing cost purposes. To enable computation on encrypted data by a lightweight cipher, a friendly (computationally-efficient) interface of the lightweight cipher with privacy-enhancing cryptography (PEC)

© Springer Nature Switzerland AG 2022
E. Aïmeur et al. (Eds.): FPS 2021, LNCS 13291, pp. 63–74, 2022.
https://doi.org/10.1007/978-3-031-08147-7_5

techniques such as secure multiparty computation (SMPC) and fully homomorphic encryption (FHE) is required.

The idea of friendliness of a symmetric-key algorithm with SMPC protocols or FHE schemes or bridging the gap between a symmetric-key algorithm and a public-key algorithm using key/data encapsulation mechanisms is not new [3,12,15,17,23,32]. In the literature of SMPC, FHE and zero-knowledge proof. (ZKP), AES has not only been widely used as a benchmarking cipher, but also used to develop privacy-preserving applications using secure computation techniques [16,21,25,26,28,30,34]. Block ciphers namely Triple-DES and SIMON are also used as benchmarking ciphers for SMPC and FHE applications [26,29]. Symmetric-key primitives are also used in cryptocurrency and blockchain applications along with zero-knowledge proof techniques. For example, Zcash [36], the latest version (2019) adopted CHACHA20_POLY1305 [24] for authenticated encryption, and the BLAKE2 hash function (the top 2 finalist in the NIST SHA3 competition for hash). Hawk [27] uses lightweight block cipher Speck [9] for encryption in the CBC mode, and SHA-256 for pseudorandom functions (PRFs) and commitments, and achieves only 80-bit security.

The NIST lightweight cryptography (LWC) standardization competition has aimed at standardizing lightweight authenticated encryption with associated data (AEAD) schemes and hash functions [8]. Although lightweight authenticated ciphers have aimed at providing security in constrained environments, their real-world deployment would not only be limited to resource-constrained environments, rather be used at heterogeneous computing environments, depending upon their efficiencies. Therefore, the friendliness of lightweight ciphers with PEC techniques should be evaluated.

In this work, we consider the secure evaluation of lightweight ciphers for FHE as a use case. Due to the heterogeneity of the AE modes in the NIST LWC round 2 candidates, we consider the core underlying primitives of the AEAD schemes, which are the nonlinear components that are the bottleneck in privacy-enhancing computations. First, we generate the optimized Boolean circuits of the core primitives of the NIST LWC AEAD schemes, and present the circuit complexity statistics in terms of the number of gates. The importance of studying the circuit complexity is that, in PEC, the functionalities (e.g., ciphers) are often required to express as Boolean or arithmetic circuits before applying PEC techniques, and the running time (efficiency) of the privacy-preserving scheme relies on the size of the circuit. We homomorphically evaluate the performance of the AEAD core primitives in the computation-outsourcing setting where we develop an implementation in C++ on top of the TFHE scheme [13,14] which is one of the schemes in the homomorphic encryption standard [2]. Finally, we present the experimental results on the performance of the core AEAD primitives.

2   Related Work

Lightweight Cryptography and NIST LWC Standardization Competition. The advent of lightweight cryptography is due to providing security in resource-constrained environments such as RFID, IoT and sensors where traditional ciphers may be heavy [10]. Lightweight cryptography exists for more than a decade. There have been numerous symmetric-key ciphers such as block and stream ciphers, and authenticated encryption developed in the past years targeting to hardware efficiency. Some notable examples are PRESENT, CLEFIA, and LEA in the ISO/IEC standards [37], Grain and Trivium from the eStream project [18], and ASCON and ACORN from the CAESAR competition [11]. In response to the call for proposal of the NIST LWC standardization competition, there were 56 proposals for authenticated encryption (many with both AE and hash) accepted as round 1 candidates, 32 candidates were moved to round 2, and currently 10 candidates are chosen as finalists [8].

Symmetric-Key Ciphers for Privacy-Enhancing Cryptography. There is a growing interest in the development of symmetric-key ciphers dedicated to privacy-enhancing applications such as secure multiparty computation, fully homomorphic encryption and zero-knowledge proofs. Some examples of stream ciphers designed for FHE are FILP [32], Kreyvium [12], and Rasta [17], and the block cipher examples for MPC, FHE and ZKP applications include LowMC [5], MiMC [3], GMiMC [4], and MARVELlous [6]. Examples of hash functions for MPC and ZKP applications include GMiMC [4], MARVELlous [6,7], and Poseidon [22]. [35] presents the constructions of parallel nonce-based authenticated encryption based on the MiMC and Legendre symbol PRFs for MPC applications. To the best of our knowledge, the suitability of these primitives, especially block ciphers and stream ciphers have not been investigated for resource-constrained applications where the hardware efficiency is a major consideration.

3   Preliminaries

3.1   Authenticated Encryption

An authenticated encryption with associated data (AEAD) scheme is a tuple of algorithms AEAD = (AKeyGen, AEnc, ADec). The key generation AKeyGen outputs a key, i.e., $K \leftarrow$ AKeyGen(1^λ) for security parameter λ, AEnc accepts a key K, a nonce N, an associated data AD and a message M and produces a ciphertext and a tag, i.e., $(C, T) \leftarrow$ AEnc(K, N, AD, M). Similarly, ADec accepts a key, a nonce, an AD, a ciphertext and a tag and produces a message if the tag verification is successful, i.e., $\{M, \perp\} \leftarrow$ ADec(K, N, AD, C, T). The encryption algorithm AEnc has four phases: an initialization phase, an AD processing phase, an encryption phase and a tag generation phase, and similarly for the decryption algorithm, the encryption phase is replaced by a decryption phase.

3.2 Fully Homomorphic Encryption and Outsourcing Protocol

Fully Homomorphic Encryption. A fully homomorphic encryption (FHE) scheme consists of a tuple of four probabilistic polynomial-time algorithms FHE $=$ (HKeyGen, HEnc, HDec, HEval) [20]. The key generation algorithm HKeyGen generates secret, public, and evaluation keys, i.e., (pk, sk, evk) $\leftarrow$ HKeyGen(1^λ) for a security parameter λ, HEnc encrypts a plaintext message (m) using the public key, i.e., $c \leftarrow$ HEnc(pk, m), HDec decrypts a ciphertext (c) using the private key, i.e., $m \leftarrow$ HEnc(sk, c), and HEval evaluates a function f (typically represented using a circuit) on a set of ciphertexts $(\{c_i\}_{i=0}^{\ell-1})$ using the evaluation key (evk), and produces a single ciphertext HEnc($f(m_0, \cdots, m_{\ell-1})) \leftarrow$ HEval(evk, f, $\{c_i\}_{i=0}^{\ell-1})$ which is the encrypted output of f on plaintext messages $(\{m_i\}_{i=0}^{\ell-1})$.

Hybrid-Encryption Based Outsourcing Protocol. Figure 1 shows a computation and data outsourcing protocol combining a symmetric-key encryption scheme and a fully homomorphic encryption scheme. It follows the paradigm of key and data encapsulation mechanisms (KEM/DEM) for hybrid encryption where the data is encrypted using a symmetric encryption and the key of the symmetric-key encryption is encrypted using a public key scheme (e.g., FHE), i.e., $KEM\|DEM =$ HEnc(pk, K)$\|$AEnc(K, $Data$) [15]. Note that the client generates the keys for both FHE and AE schemes. The ciphertext conversion step from an AEAD to a FHE ciphertext, denoted by CTC, needs the *homomorphic evaluation* of the AEAD decryption algorithm.

Client		Cloud/Server
(pk, sk) $\leftarrow$ HKeyGen(1^λ)		
K $\leftarrow$ AKeyGen(1^λ)		
C^h(K) $\leftarrow$ HEnc(pk, K)	$\xrightarrow{\text{pk}, C^h(\text{K})}$	pk, C^h(K)
$C^a(M_i) \leftarrow$ AEnc(K, M_i)	$\xrightarrow{C^a(M_i)}$	$C^a(M_i)$
		$C^h(M_i) =$ CTC(evk, ADec, C^h(K), $C^a(M_i)$)
f	$\xrightarrow{f}$	$C^h(f(M_0, \cdots, M_{\ell-1})) =$ HEval(f, evk, $C^h(M_i)$)
	$\xleftarrow{C^h(f(M_0,\cdots,M_{\ell-1}))}$	
$f(M_0, \cdots, M_{\ell-1}) =$		
HDec(sk, $C^h(f(M_0, \cdots, M_{\ell-1}))$)		

Fig. 1. An FHE-based client-server computation and data outsourcing protocol using symmetric-key encryption [32].

A concrete instance of the client-server computation and data outsourcing protocol in Fig. 1 is the smart energy management system. Consider a scenario where a smarthome thermostat sends temperature readings of a house in every an hour basis to a cloud, who processes the temperature readings and instruct the thermostat to automate the heating in the house. Note that cleartext temperature readings leaks information about individuals' presence or absence in the house. The cloud can do the profiling of houses from temperature readings, which invades privacy. This can be prevented by a conjunction of lightweight AEAD algorithms with FHE algorithms. Assume the thermostat has implemented a lightweight AEAD scheme. For each day, it uses a nonce that can be a time stamp of the day and encrypt each hour's temperature reading using a block of AEAD encryption where a temperature reading can be represented using a 32, 64 or 128 bit number. Thus, for each day 24 readings are sent to the cloud, and by the end of the day, it converts to AEAD ciphertexts to FHE ciphertexts, and then performs statistical/analytical computations on encrypted readings.

4 Circuit Complexity of NIST LWC Round 2 Candidates

In this section, we generate and report the Boolean circuits of the core primitives of the NIST LWC round 2 candidates. The reason for this is that, in many privacy-enhancing applications, the functionalities are required to represent as a Boolean circuit before applying the privacy-enhancing techniques.

4.1 Generating Boolean Circuits of Core Primitives

Boolean Circuits Generation. We call a component of an AEAD scheme a *core primitive* if it is the nonlinear component of the AEAD scheme. For instance, for a permutation-based AEAD scheme, the core primitive is the permutation as it provides the nonlinearity and the mode part involves linear operations. We generate the circuits for the underlying permutations, block ciphers or state update functions of the AEAD or hash schemes. We use the CBMC-GC compiler [19] to generate the circuits where circuits are represented using XOR, AND and NOT gates in the Bristol fashion [1]. Table 1 summarizes the list of circuits with the numbers of XOR, AND and NOT gates. The multiplicative depth and the total depth of the LWC circuits are also reported. The description of the circuits can be found in [31]. We do not claim that the circuit sizes are minimal.

Table 1. Summary of the circuit complexity of some NIST LWC core primitives in round 2.

Cipher	State size	Total gates	Individual gates			AND depth	Total depth	% AND
			AND	XOR	NOT			
AES [38]	128	33616	6800	25124	1692	–	–	20.23
ACE	320	46182	12288	27648	6246	128	475	26.61
ASCON	320	25466	3712	15932	5822	12	93	14.58
ASCON(r6)	320	12408	1792	7868	2748	6	47	14.58
ASCON(r8)	320	16760	2432	10556	3772	8	62	14.58
CHAM-64	64	12244	4960	6464	820	204	386	40.51
CHAM-128	128	26324	11200	13184	1940	528	818	42.55
GASCON	320	13889	2240	9408	3405	7	52	16.13
GASCON (r11)	320	23757	3520	14784	5453	11	82	14.82
GIMLI	320	35427	8640	17760	9027	24	75	24.39
GIFT-128	128	20657	5120	10240	5297	160	449	24.79
TweGIFT-64	64	7427	1803	3686	1938	112	304	24.28
TweGIFT-64-INV	64	7700	1803	3686	2211	84	241	23.42
KECCAK-200	200	19985	3600	10800	5585	18	174	18.01
KECCAK-400	400	44394	8000	24000	12394	20	192	18.02
KNOT-256	256	49770	13312	23296	13162	104	260	26.75
KNOT-384	384	109140	29184	51041	28980	152	380	26.74
KNOT-512	512	191665	51200	89600	50865	200	500	26.71
PHOTON	256	43706	3072	35136	5498	36	209	7.02
SATURNIN	256	45643	7680	22465	15627	120	331	16.83
SKINNY-ENC-128-384	128	45178	7168	24176	13834	169	762	15.86
SKINNY-DEC-128-384	128	46903	7168	24256	15479	169	774	15.28
sLiSCP-LIGHT-192	192	20366	5184	12096	3086	108	437	25.45
sLiSCP-LIGHT-256	256	34588	9216	20736	4636	144	542	26.65
sLiSCP-LIGHT-256 (r9)	256	17324	4608	10368	2348	72	271	26.65
SPARKLE-256	256	59588	25440	31360	2788	200	554	42.69
SPARKLE-384	384	98422	41976	51920	4526	220	613	42.65
SPARKLE-512	512	143524	61056	75648	6820	240	703	42.54
SPECK-64	64	22900	9688	11450	1762	364	713	42.31
SPONGENT-160	160	67261	24000	28800	14461	160	430	35.68
SPONGENT-176	176	82658	29700	35640	17318	180	483	35.93
SPOOK: SHADOW-512	512	35420	6144	29184	92	19	94	17.35
CLYDE-128-ENC	128	13655	1536	12096	23	24	132	11.25
CLYDE-128-DEC	128	13655	1536	12096	23	37	161	11.25
SUBTERRANEAN	257	1319	265	772	290	2	7	20.09
TINYJAMBU-INIT[†]	128	11696	2118	8422	1156	50	276	18.11
TINYJAMBU (P_{1024})[†]	128	5638	1024	4096	518	24	134	18.16
WAGE	259	105739	37745	62121	5873	333	2220	35.70
XOODOO	384	25275	4608	13824	6843	12	93	18.23

[†] TinyJambu offers 112-bit security

Optimizing S-box Implementations. The CBMC-GC compiler accepts a high-level C code and produces a straightline program representation of the circuit. We use the reference C code from the NIST LWC competition [8], but we modify the code to apply the bitslice implementation to produce optimized circuits if the bitslice implementation is not used. We wrote the bitslice representations of the Sboxes in the circuit generation process for the following ciphers. For PHOTON, we used the bitslice representation of the Present Sbox proposed in [33]. For SPONGENT, SKINNY, and TweGift, we use the bitslice representations of the respective Sboxes, and for WAGE, we use the bitslice implementation of the SB Sbox.

Multiplicative Depth. The multiplicative depth of a Boolean circuit is the maximum number of sequential multiplications (AND operations) in the circuit. For instance, for ACE, the Feistel round function in the Simeck-box is a quadratic function of an AND depth 1 and the total of rounds is 128, the multiplicative depth is 128, which can be verified in Table 1. In general, if d is the multiplicative depth of a Boolean circuit of a round function composed of a substitution-permutation network (SPN) or Feistel network based cipher, the multiplicative depth of a r-round cipher is rd where r is the number of rounds. The multiplicative depth of the Boolean circuits of the core primitives is an important consideration for the FHE applications where for some FHE scheme, the key setup parameters are chosen based on the depth of the circuit. Moreover, the noise growth due to the multiplication operation is larger than the noise growth due to that of the addition operation.

5   Homomorphic Evaluation of Core AEAD Circuits

As shown in Sect. 3.2, converting an AEAD ciphertext to an FHE ciphertext requires the homomorphic evaluation of the core AEAD circuits. In this section, we first show how to convert an AEAD ciphertext to an FHE ciphertext, and perform the homomorphic evaluation of the core AEAD circuits of the NIST LWC AE schemes using TFHE and present experimental results.

5.1   Conversion of AEAD Ciphertexts to FHE Ciphertexts

We use a sponge-based AEAD scheme as an example to explain the process of converting an AEAD ciphertext to an FHE ciphertext and focus only on the encryption and decryption process. Figure 2 presents a high-level description of the homomorphic evaluation of the sponge mode (without subtle details). Let S be the state of the permutation π after initialization and associated data processing phases. Assume the encryption of a message is performed, like a stream cipher encryption, as $C_i = M_i \oplus K_i$ where K_i is served as a keystream block that is obtained from the rate part of the state of the permutation after processing previous $(i-1)$ message blocks, i.e., $K_i \leftarrow \lfloor \pi^i(S) \rfloor_r$ where $\lfloor \cdot \rfloor_r$ denotes the contents from the rate part. For simplicity, assume that there is no AD and a cloud receives ciphertexts $C = (C_0, \cdots, C_{\ell-1})$ and the encrypted key of the AEAD scheme, i.e., $\mathsf{HEnc}(K\|N)$ where $C = \mathsf{AEnc}(K, N, M)$. The cloud performs the following steps to obtain $\mathsf{HEnc}(M)$ from the AEAD ciphertexts C as follows:

Step 1: Compute an FHE ciphertext of the AE ciphertext: It first computes the FHE ciphertexts of all C_i's using the public key of the FHE scheme as $\mathsf{HEnc}(C) = (\mathsf{HEnc}(C_0), \mathsf{HEnc}(C_1), \cdots, \mathsf{HEnc}(C_{\ell-1}))$.

Step 2: Homomorphically evaluate the permutation circuit $\mathcal{C}_\pi$: Using the encrypted key $\mathsf{HEnc}(K\|N)$ of the AEnc scheme, it homomorphically evaluates the permutation circuit $\mathcal{C}_\pi$ sequentially for each ciphertext block and obtain $\mathsf{HEnc}(K_i) \leftarrow \lfloor \mathsf{HEnc}(\pi^i(S)) \rfloor_r$ where $\mathsf{HEnc}(S) \leftarrow \mathsf{HEnc}(K\|N)$, and then computes the FHE ciphertext of M_i from $\mathsf{HEnc}(K_i)$ and $\mathsf{HEnc}(C_i)$ as $\mathsf{HEnc}(M_i) = \mathsf{HEnc}(K_i \oplus C_i) \leftarrow \mathsf{HEval}(\mathsf{XOR}, \mathsf{HEnc}(K_i), \mathsf{HEnc}(C_i))$. where HEval performs homomorphic XOR operations on $\mathsf{HEnc}(K_i)$ and $\mathsf{HEnc}(C_i)$.

In the above steps, the most expensive operation is the homomorphic evaluation of the permutation. As we have considered the binary circuit, the choice of the FHE scheme determines whether the ciphertext $\mathsf{HEnc}(C_i)$ is a single ciphertext (packed using SIMD) or r ciphertexts where each ciphertext is an FHE encryption of one-bit of AEAD ciphertexts.

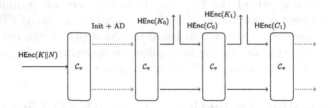

Fig. 2. Homomorphic evaluation of the sponge mode in the decryption phase. Two blocks of decryption are shown where $\mathcal{C}_\pi$ is the circuit for the permutation π.

Note that for the permutation-based AEAD schemes such as ACE and ASCON, the same underlying permutation is required to evaluate for both encryption and decryption operations. As there are several FHE schemes such as BGV, BFV, and TFHE in [2], in this preliminary work, we focus on the homomorphic evaluation of the core primitives of the AEAD schemes using TFHE that provides the flexibility on any arbitrary depth circuit.

5.2   Experimental Evaluation

Experimental Setup. We have developed a generic implementation for the homomorphic evaluation of the core-AEAD circuits in C++ on top of the TFHE scheme [13,14], which is a candidate in the homomorphic encryption standard [2]. TFHE supports homomorphic evaluations of 10 binary gates including XOR, AND, and NOT, and does not need to know the depth of the circuit during the parameter generation phase. For the details about TFHE, the reader is referred to [13,14]. As the circuit is represented using only XOR, AND and NOT gates, our implementation uses homomorphic computations of these three gates. In our implementation, we feed the core circuit of an AEAD scheme and an encrypted state, and obtain the encrypted output through its homomorphic evaluation. For instance, for a permutation, we provide the TFHE encrypted key and nonce, and homomorphically evaluate the permutation circuit and obtain the encrypted output. We use the default parameters of TFHE providing the 110-bit security. We conduct the experiments on a desktop with a 3.00 GHz Intel Core i7-9700 CPU and 32 GB RAM running on Ubuntu 18.04. Note that the homomorphic evaluation is done using a single thread (no parallelism is exploited).

Performance. We now present the Wall-clock running time for homomorphically evaluating the core-AEAD circuits in Table 1. We micro-benchmark the timings of homomorphic computation of XOR, AND and NOT gates in TFHE. For instance, in TFHE, the homomorphic XOR computation time for 128 ciphertexts is about 4.96 s. The micro-benchmarking results show that the homomorphic operations for XOR and AND takes almost the same amount of time. Table 2 reports the computation time (in second) of the homomorphic evaluation of core AEAD circuits given in Table 1. The homomorphic evaluation time of the ACE permutation circuit is about 16 min and the AES circuit takes about 21 min in a single CPU. As a summary, our experimental results that Subterranean AEAD core takes the smallest amount of time (41 s) and WAGE takes the largest time (64 min). Note that in the AEAD modes, the different AEAD cores process data of different lengths for each call of the core.

Table 2. Homomorphic evaluation times of core AE circuits using TFHE with security 110 bits. Timings are given in second (s), and the fractional part is omitted.

	ACE	AES	Ascon	Gimli	GIFT-128
Total Time	1562 s	1257 s	775 s	1047 s	605 s
	TweGIFT-64	TweGIFT-64-inv	Keccak-200	Keccak-400	Knot-256
Total Time	217 s	216 s	566 s	1256 s	1437 s
	Knot-384	Knot-512	Photon	Saturnin	Skinny-enc
Total Time	3144 s	5533 s	2336 s	1178 s	1242 s
	Skinny-dec	sLiSCP-light-192	sLiSCP-light-256	Sparkle-256	Sparkle-384
Toral time	1243 s	675 s	1180 s	2255 s	3663 s
	Sparkle-512	Spongent-160	Spongent-176	Shadow-512	Clyde-128-Enc
Total Time	5346 s	2117 s	2616 s	1400 s	542 s
	Clyde-128-Dec	Subterranean	TinyJambu-init	TinyJambu (P_{1024})	WAGE
Total Time	542 s	41 s	417 s	203 s	3892 s
	Xoodoo	Ascon (r6)	Ascon (r8)	sLiSCP-light-256 (r9)	
Total Time	730 s	381 s	507 s	588 s	

Estimating Time for Individual AEAD Modes. Table 2 presents the homomorphic evaluation time only for the core primitives. The modes of operation for different ciphers are different and process different number of message blocks in each call of a core primitive. The homomorphic evaluation time of a particular AEAD mode using TFHE can be estimated based on the number of invocations of the core primitive and the homomorphic operation cost of the mode. As we have focused on the performances of only the core primitives, we do not provide any comparison with existing schemes in [12,17,32].

6   Conclusions and Future Work

In this work, we considered the homomorphic evaluation of lightweight authenticated ciphers from the NIST LWC competition for privacy-enhancing cryptographic applications. To our knowledge, this work is the first that reports the Boolean circuits of the core primitives of NIST lightweight cryptography round 2 candidates. We implemented the homomorphic evaluation scheme of the lightweight AEAD schemes using the TFHE library, and presented the performance results for the NIST LWC round 2 ciphers.

As a future work, we are currently working on specialized implementations of homomorphic evaluation techniques for lightweight ciphers and also applying for blockchain applications.

Acknowledgement. The work of Kalikinkar Mandal was supported by the NBIF TRF202-010 award. The research of Guang Gong was supported by NSERC SPG and Discovery Grants. The authors would like to thank the reviewers for their insightful comments to improve the quality of the paper.

References

1. Bristol fashion MPC circuits. https://homes.esat.kuleuven.be/~nsmart/MPC/old-circuits.html
2. Albrecht, M., et al.: Homomorphic encryption security standard. Technical report, HomomorphicEncryption.org, Toronto, Canada (2018)
3. Albrecht, M., Grassi, L., Rechberger, C., Roy, A., Tiessen, T.: MiMC: efficient encryption and cryptographic hashing with minimal multiplicative complexity. In: Cheon, J.H., Takagi, T. (eds.) ASIACRYPT 2016. LNCS, vol. 10031, pp. 191–219. Springer, Heidelberg (2016). https://doi.org/10.1007/978-3-662-53887-6_7
4. Albrecht, M.R., et al.: Feistel structures for MPC, and more. In: Sako, K., Schneider, S., Ryan, P.Y.A. (eds.) ESORICS 2019. LNCS, vol. 11736, pp. 151–171. Springer, Cham (2019). https://doi.org/10.1007/978-3-030-29962-0_8
5. Albrecht, M.R., Rechberger, C., Schneider, T., Tiessen, T., Zohner, M.: Ciphers for MPC and FHE. In: Oswald, E., Fischlin, M. (eds.) EUROCRYPT 2015. LNCS, vol. 9056, pp. 430–454. Springer, Heidelberg (2015). https://doi.org/10.1007/978-3-662-46800-5_17
6. Aly, A., Ashur, T., Ben-Sasson, E., Dhooghe, S., Szepieniec, A.: Design of symmetric-key primitives for advanced cryptographic protocols. Cryptology ePrint Archive, Report 2019/426 (2019). https://eprint.iacr.org/2019/426
7. Ashur, T., Dhooghe, S.: Marvellous: a stark-friendly family of cryptographic primitives. Cryptology ePrint Archive, Report 2018/1098 (2018). https://eprint.iacr.org/2018/1098
8. Bassham, L., Calik, C., Chang, D., Kang, J., McKay, K., Turan, M.S.: Lightweight cryptography (2019). https://csrc.nist.gov/projects/lightweight-cryptography

9. Beaulieu, R., Shors, D., Smith, J., Treatman-Clark, S., Weeks, B., Wingers, L.: The simon and speck lightweight block ciphers. In: Proceedings of the 52nd Annual Design Automation Conference. DAC 2015, Association for Computing Machinery, New York, NY, USA (2015). https://doi.org/10.1145/2744769.2747946
10. Bogdanov, A., et al.: PRESENT: an ultra-lightweight block cipher. In: Paillier, P., Verbauwhede, I. (eds.) CHES 2007. LNCS, vol. 4727, pp. 450–466. Springer, Heidelberg (2007). https://doi.org/10.1007/978-3-540-74735-2_31
11. CAESAR: Competition for Authenticated Encryption: Security, Applicability, and Robustness. https://competitions.cr.yp.to/caesar.html
12. Canteaut, A., et al.: Stream ciphers: a practical solution for efficient homomorphic-ciphertext compression. J. Cryptol. **31**(3), 885–916 (2018)
13. Chillotti, I., Gama, N., Georgieva, M., Izabachène, M.: Faster fully homomorphic encryption: bootstrapping in less than 0.1 seconds. In: Cheon, J.H., Takagi, T. (eds.) ASIACRYPT 2016. LNCS, vol. 10031, pp. 3–33. Springer, Heidelberg (2016). https://doi.org/10.1007/978-3-662-53887-6_1
14. Chillotti, I., Gama, N., Georgieva, M., Izabachène, M.: TFHE: fast fully homomorphic encryption library (2016). https://tfhe.github.io/tfhe/
15. Cramer, R., Shoup, V.: Design and analysis of practical public-key encryption schemes secure against adaptive chosen ciphertext attack. SIAM J. Comput. **33**(1), 167–226 (2003)
16. Damgård, I., Keller, M.: Secure multiparty AES. In: Sion, R. (ed.) FC 2010. LNCS, vol. 6052, pp. 367–374. Springer, Heidelberg (2010). https://doi.org/10.1007/978-3-642-14577-3_31
17. Dobraunig, C., et al.: Rasta: a cipher with low ANDdepth and Few ANDs per bit. In: Shacham, H., Boldyreva, A. (eds.) CRYPTO 2018. LNCS, vol. 10991, pp. 662–692. Springer, Cham (2018). https://doi.org/10.1007/978-3-319-96884-1_22
18. eSTREAM: the ecrypt stream cipher project. http://www.ecrypt.eu.org/stream/
19. Franz, M., Holzer, A., Katzenbeisser, S., Schallhart, C., Veith, H.: CBMC-GC: an ANSI C compiler for secure two-party computations. In: Cohen, A. (ed.) Compiler Construction, pp. 244–249. Springer, Heidelberg (2014). https://doi.org/10.1007/978-3-642-54807-9_15
20. Gentry, C.: Fully homomorphic encryption using ideal lattices. In: Proceedings of the forty-first annual ACM symposium on Theory of computing, pp. 169–178 (2009)
21. Gentry, C., Halevi, S., Smart, N.P.: Homomorphic evaluation of the AES circuit. In: Safavi-Naini, R., Canetti, R. (eds.) CRYPTO 2012. LNCS, vol. 7417, pp. 850–867. Springer, Heidelberg (2012). https://doi.org/10.1007/978-3-642-32009-5_49
22. Grassi, L., Khovratovich, D., Rechberger, C., Roy, A., Schofnegger, M.: Poseidon: a new hash function for zero-knowledge proof systems. In: 30th USENIX Security Symposium (USENIX Security 21), pp. 519–535. USENIX Association (2021). https://www.usenix.org/conference/usenixsecurity21/presentation/grassi
23. Grassi, L., Rechberger, C., Rotaru, D., Scholl, P., Smart, N.P.: MPC-friendly symmetric key primitives. In: Proceedings of the 2016 ACM SIGSAC Conference on Computer and Communications Security, pp. 430–443. CCS 16, Association for Computing Machinery, New York, NY, USA (2016). https://doi.org/10.1145/2976749.2978332
24. Housley, R.: Using chacha20-poly1305 authenticated encryption in the cryptographic message syntax (CMS). Technical report, RFC 8103 (2017)

25. Kamara, S., Mohassel, P., Riva, B.: Salus: a system for server-aided secure function evaluation. In: Proceedings of the 2012 ACM Conference on Computer and Communications Security, pp. 797–808. CCS 2012, Association for Computing Machinery, New York, NY, USA (2012). https://doi.org/10.1145/2382196.2382280

26. Keller, M., Orsini, E., Rotaru, D., Scholl, P., Soria-Vazquez, E., Vivek, S.: Faster secure multi-party computation of AES and DES using lookup tables. In: Gollmann, D., Miyaji, A., Kikuchi, H. (eds.) ACNS 2017. LNCS, vol. 10355, pp. 229–249. Springer, Cham (2017). https://doi.org/10.1007/978-3-319-61204-1_12

27. Kosba, A., Miller, A., Shi, E., Wen, Z., Papamanthou, C.: Hawk: the blockchain model of cryptography and privacy-preserving smart contracts. In: 2016 IEEE Symposium on Security and Privacy (SP), pp. 839–858 (2016)

28. Laur, S., Talviste, R., Willemson, J.: From oblivious AES to efficient and secure database join in the multiparty setting. In: Jacobson, M., Locasto, M., Mohassel, P., Safavi-Naini, R. (eds.) ACNS 2013. LNCS, vol. 7954, pp. 84–101. Springer, Heidelberg (2013). https://doi.org/10.1007/978-3-642-38980-1_6

29. Lepoint, T., Naehrig, M.: A comparison of the homomorphic encryption schemes FV and YASHE. In: Pointcheval, D., Vergnaud, D. (eds.) AFRICACRYPT 2014. LNCS, vol. 8469, pp. 318–335. Springer, Cham (2014). https://doi.org/10.1007/978-3-319-06734-6_20

30. Lindell, Y., Riva, B.: Blazing fast 2pc in the offline/online setting with security for malicious adversaries. In: Proceedings of the 22nd ACM SIGSAC Conference on Computer and Communications Security, p. 579?590. CCS 2015, Association for Computing Machinery, New York, NY, USA (2015). https://doi.org/10.1145/2810103.2813666

31. Mandal, K.: Boolean circuits for ae cores of NIST lightweight ciphers (2020). https://www.cs.unb.ca/~kmandal/nistlwc/lwc_circuit.html

32. Méaux, P., Journault, A., Standaert, F.-X., Carlet, C.: Towards stream ciphers for efficient FHE with low-noise ciphertexts. In: Fischlin, M., Coron, J.-S. (eds.) EUROCRYPT 2016. LNCS, vol. 9665, pp. 311–343. Springer, Heidelberg (2016). https://doi.org/10.1007/978-3-662-49890-3_13

33. Nicolas T. Courtois, D.H., Mourouzis, T.: Solving circuit optimisation problems in cryptography and cryptanalysis. Cryptology ePrint Archive, Report 2011/475 (2011). https://ia.cr/2011/475

34. Pinkas, B., Schneider, T., Smart, N.P., Williams, S.C.: Secure two-party computation is practical. In: Matsui, M. (ed.) ASIACRYPT 2009. LNCS, vol. 5912, pp. 250–267. Springer, Heidelberg (2009). https://doi.org/10.1007/978-3-642-10366-7_15

35. Rotaru, D., Smart, N.P., Stam, M.: Modes of operation suitable for computing on encrypted data. IACR Trans. Symm. Cryptol. **2017**(3), 294–324 (2017). https://doi.org/10.13154/tosc.v2017.i3.294-324, https://tosc.iacr.org/index.php/ToSC/article/view/775

36. Sasson, E.B., et al.: Zerocash: decentralized anonymous payments from bitcoin. In: 2014 IEEE Symposium on Security and Privacy, pp. 459–474 (2014)

37. Standards, I.: Information security - lightweight cryptography - part 2: Block ciphers (2019). https://www.iso.org/standard/78477.html

38. Tillich, S., Smart, N.: AES circuit. https://homes.esat.kuleuven.be/~nsmart/MPC/AES-non-expanded.txt

Breaking Black Box Crypto-Devices Using Laser Fault Injection

Bodo Selmke[1]([✉]), Emanuele Strieder[1], Johann Heyszl[1], Sven Freud[2], and Tobias Damm[2]

[1] Fraunhofer Institute for Applied and Integrated Security (AISEC), Garching, Germany
{bodo.selmke,emanuele.strieder,johann.heyszl}@aisec.fraunhofer.de
[2] Federal Office for Information Security (BSI), Bonn, Germany
{sven.freud,tobias.damm}@bsi.bund.de

Abstract. Laser fault injection attacks on hardware implementations are challenging, due to the inherently large parameter space of the fault injection and the unknown underlying implementation of the attacked device. In this work we report details from an exemplary laser fault attack on the AES-based authentication chip Microchip ATAES 132A, which lead to full secret key extraction. In addition we were able to reveal some details of the underlying implementation. This chip claims to feature various countermeasures and tamper detection mechanisms and is therefore a representative candidate for devices to be found in many different applications. On this basis we describe a systematic approach for Laser fault attacks on devices in a black-box scenario. This includes the determination of all relevant attack parameters such as fault locations, timings, and energy settings.

Keywords: Fault injection · Fault attack · Laser fault injection · Security · Physical device security

1 Introduction

Fault attacks are a variant of implementation attacks, which can be used to extract secret keys or to bypass security mechanisms of a device by manipulating internal data values or altering the program flow in an exploitable manner. Various methods for fault injection are established, ranging from low-cost glitching attacks, to expensive but highly precise Laser fault injection (LFI) attacks. Beside many theoretical publications or proof-of-concepts, there are also some published practical examples of such attacks. Cui et al. [5] demonstrated that electromagnetic fault injection can be used to compromise the secure boot of a multi-core ARM processor. O'Flynn [16] managed to dump the memory of a SoloKey authentication token using EMFI. Without physical device access, Tang et al. demonstrated that a root-user is able to mount fault attacks on secure execution environments [22]. Murdock et al. [15], as well as Qui et al. [18], showed a similar attack principle based on manipulation of on-chip power regulators.

© Springer Nature Switzerland AG 2022
E. Aïmeur et al. (Eds.): FPS 2021, LNCS 13291, pp. 75–90, 2022.
https://doi.org/10.1007/978-3-031-08147-7_6

With regard to LFI-attacks in particular, Woudenberg et al. [24] managed to skip a PIN-check on an unknown smartcard, without naming the actual device. Vasalle et al. [25] compromised the secure boot process of a smartphone and thus received the highest privilege level on the device using LFI. Recently Hériveaux [12] described an LFI-attack against Microchip's ATECC 508A crypto-device, which extracts data from the secure memory of the chip by manipulating the PIN check. Those examples show which threat fault injection attacks impose, even though the attack methods are partly low-cost. Therefore, certified security controllers include countermeasures against such attacks. Fault attacks on these devices are frequently seen as a threat where attackers largely rely on luck, because little is usually known about implementation details and the vast parameter space. Indeed, attackers often handle such large parameter spaces by employing randomized brute-force strategies to succeed. Also, the precise internal effects which lead to successful attacks often remain unclear. However, in this contribution we want to point out that the path to successful fault injection is in fact a structured approach. We show this for LFI-attacks by means of a representative chip that implements various security features but still remains vulnerable. We break the cryptographic implementation and recover the internal key from an AES implementation. Though an LFI-setup is used, we would like to emphasize that a similar outcome is most likely achievable with lower-cost setups.

2   Laser Setup and Device Under Test

We demonstrate a systematic LFI campaign on Microchip's ATAES132, a HW security module for embedded systems. This device is based on an AES-128 core with little information about its implementation details. It can be used as authentication device with secure key storage capabilities for up to 16 keys. These key slots can only be *written* through the external interface, while it is not possible to read any of the internally stored keys. The chip additionally offers the use of a single volatile key. The AES core can be utilized in two different block cipher encryption modes, the simple *Electronic Codebook (ECB)* mode for single block encryption, and the *Counter with CBC-MAC (CCM)* mode for authenticated encryption of multi-block data.

The manufacturer describes it to be a *high security device* [1], which incorporates various physical security mechanisms. It is described to "prevent or significantly complicate most algorithmic, timing, and side-channel attacks". Laser-based fault injection is not explicitly mentioned but light sensors are, which are commonly used to prevent laser-based attacks. The following protection measures are explicitly listed in the user guide [2,14]: tamper detectors against voltage, temperature and frequency manipulations, light sensors, active metal shield covering the circuitry, internal memory encryption, and further not specified protection measures. In summary, the protection level against hardware attacks seems high, even though the specification of security measures is imprecise.

2.1 Device Preparation

The ATAES132 is available in SOIC and UDFN packages. We chose the SOIC type for our experiments due to easier preparation and soldering. For the LFI experiments, we used a backside prepared sample. Even though LFI is in principle applicable from both sides of a chip, the better and common method is injecting faults from the substrate side. On the frontside the numerous metal layers of modern CMOS chips block the light and thus impede Laser attacks.

Backside preparation of the SOIC package was achieved by mechanical grinding. Figure 3 (bottom left) shows the open chip from the backside. For optical analysis of the chip structure we also prepared a frontside decapsulated sample using wet-etching (cf. Fig. 2). We investigated a sample of the chip with an electron microscope, and estimate the technology node to be approximately 250 μm.

The DUT was soldered to a generic SOIC-16 breakout board, in which a hole was drilled at the center of the SOIC footprint to enable backside access. We use an SPI connection to an STM32 Nucleo board to control the DUT. The Nucleo board acts as an UART to SPI converter relaying the commands from the control PC to the DUT. Its second task is to control the power supply of the DUT and perform a power cycle when the device e.g. goes into a short-circuit or latch-up fault state which is characterized by high current consumption. This is detected through monitoring the supply voltage using an analog input.

2.2 Laser System and Triggering

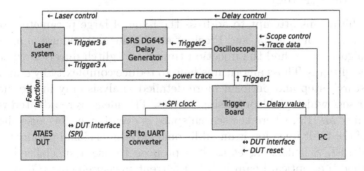

Fig. 1. Fault injection setup and DUT

A stable trigger signal is important for fault injection attacks. Unlike for side-channel attacks where captured traces can be aligned later, this is not possible for fault attacks. We used the SPI clock for synchronization with the DUT by feeding this signal into an FPGA-based trigger generation board. This board is configured to count a specific number of SPI clock cycles[1] after which the trigger

---

[1] The exact SPI clock edge on which was triggered on is not specified on request of the manufacturer.

signal is generated. This trigger signal has a constant offset to the communication input for the DUT and is input to a digital sampling oscilloscope (DSO). The DSO is configured as a second stage, triggering on a distinctive pattern in the power signal of the DUT, which is measured using a differential probe over a shunt resistor. This stage ensures, that a time variation between communication inputs and internal operation of the DUT is mitigated. Without this second stage, we observed a jitter of about 2 clock cycles relative to the power trace.

The trigger signal from the DSO is fed into a programmable delay generator (Standford Research Systems DG645), which delays the signal by a configurable value before triggering the laser. Figure 1 shows a schematic overview of the used experiment setup.

The Laser system used for our experiments is based on two identical diode-pumped solid state lasers (Nd:YAG) with a wavelength of 1064 nm. The pulse length of the lasers is 800 ps and the maximum possible pulse frequency is 1 kHz. The beams of both laser sources are fed into separate laser scanners which enable independent positioning of both laser beams. Subsequently these beams are coupled and projected by the same objective onto the DUT. Hence, this setup allows for an independent spatial and temporal configuration of the laser beams.

3   Preceding Search Space Reduction

In the following section, we describe how the search space can be reduced before the Laser scan process.

3.1   General Strategy

Several publications attempt to address the issue of large parameter spaces for fault attacks. Carpi et al. [3] and Picek et al. [17] suggest the use of a genetic or memetic algorithm to find the injection timing and glitch duration when applying voltage glitches. Those algorithms help to reduce complexity by starting with a coarse search step and perform more detailed analysis only in the vicinity of parameter sets which yield promising results. The ideas were adapted to EMFI by Maldini et al. [13], where the search space is even bigger, because the spatial location of the fault injection is an additional two-dimensional parameter. In the context of LFI, Schellenberg et al. [20] propose to use a specialized measurement method, i.e. optical beam induced current measurements (OBIC), to find locations of registers on a chip for fault injection. Their method is based on pattern recognition and requires applicable reference patterns, as well as specialized measurement equipment.

Our approach is to reduce the search space by excluding a priori areas on the die, which most likely do not include the functionality to be attacked. Further the time span considered for the attack is narrowed down with a side channel analysis. For the Laser scan process of the DUT, we prepared a database of known output values for specific and expected faults to simplify the evaluation process. Once we observed faults in the device output, we run a tuning algorithm to optimize the laser focal plane and the required energy level.

3.2   Identifying the AES Core Area

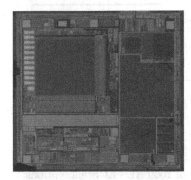   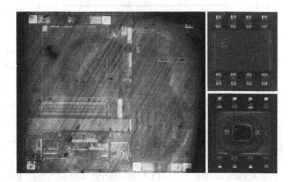

Fig. 2. Frontside photography of the die (flipped to match the backside view in Fig. 3) (Color figure online)

Fig. 3. Chip package (right) before and after mechanical decapsulation. Left: corresponding IR image from die backside.

Figure 2 shows a topside image of the chip after wet-chemical decapsulation (mirrored to match the backside view in Fig. 3), which allows to identify several parts: A large block of memory on the upper left side (A) is the EEPROM of the DUT, because of the clearly visible sense amplifiers its borders. On the bottom left there is a block of analog circuits identifiable by an in-homogeneous and loose placement (B). This part most likely includes an RC-oscillator for generation of the internal clock signal. There are two separated areas with densely placed standard cells (D, E), which we identified as the core logic area of the chip. In direct proximity, there are four smaller memory blocks on the bottom right (F), and two more memory blocks at the top (C). We suppose, that these are in fact SRAM blocks or register banks. It can be assumed that the AES hardware engine is implemented in standard cell logic, therefore it can be part of either of the two standard cell areas. Given that an AES engine could likely be re-used as hard-macro in multiple chips by the manufacturer after it has been synthesized and evaluated, it seems likely that the engine is contained in the smaller standard cell area (E).

3.3   Identifying the AES Execution Time

To narrow down the time-span that must be considered for fault injection, the AES execution is searched using side-channel traces captured with the setup described in Sect. 2.2. The DUT is configured to run the AES core in ECB mode. A mean of 1000 power traces is depicted in Fig. 4a. The figure depicts the entire time span between the command and response of the device. For this first test,

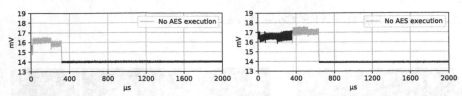

(a) Mean of 1000 AES ECB operations us- (b) Mean of 1000 AES ECB operations using an invalid key.   ing a valid key.

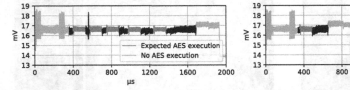

(c) Mean of 1000 AES CCM encryptions.   (d) Mean of 1000 AES ECB encryptions.

Fig. 4. Side-channel power consumption recordings of AES operations to narrow down to actual AES execution. (Color figure online)

an invalid key is used which means that no AES operation is actually performed. In a second test, a valid key from the volatile memory is used (cf. Fig. 4b). For both cases the long periods with a stable low signal can be disregarded. From the remaining trace, the orange marked part can be excluded as well because it is present in the first test where no AES execution is performed.

As a next step we captured 1000 traces with the DUT running the CCM mode (cf. Fig. 4c). This test uses a valid key from non-volatile memory. This leads to a new pattern at the beginning which likely corresponds to the loading of this key from EEPROM. This pattern is marked in orange and can be excluded, because it is not present in the mean trace using the volatile key slot shown in Fig. 4b. For the encryption of 16 plain text bytes in CCM mode, five AES operations are necessary in the case for the ATAES132A because of the associated data. Indeed, an according repeating pattern can be identified which is marked in green in Fig. 4c. The same pattern is evident in the mean power trace of a single ECB mode execution using a key from non-volatile memory as shown in Fig. 4d. In summary, the AES operation can be narrowed down to a significantly smaller time span.

Testing for Side-Channel Leakage. We also performed a side-channel leakage test on the input and output data of the AES operation to further narrow down the time-span. Figure 5 depicts the results of a correlation-based leakage test [9] targeting plain- and ciphertext bytes of the AES ECB mode execution for the previously identified time-span using 10.000 traces. The respective mean trace is shown at the top of the figure. The result shows statistically significant leakage for both plain- and ciphertexts with correlation coefficients as up to 0.4 which is clearly significant when compared to the noise floor. Hence, the AES operation must be in between the spikes of the green and the orange correlation coefficient

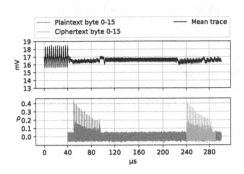

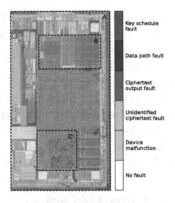

Fig. 5. Results of a correlation-based side-channel leakage test targeting plain- and ciphertext. (Color figure online)

Fig. 6. Outcome of fault injections. (Color figure online)

trace. This finally enables to narrow down the operating time of a single AES block encryption to only 146 μs which corresponds to approximately 151 clock cycles.

To determine if a side-channel attack on the power signal is possible, we performed further leakage tests on approx. 500.000 traces targeting intermediate values. We tested for correlation on S-Box input values and on the Hamming-Distance between the S-Box inputs of round one and two. Both tests did not show any detectable leakage, most likely due to included countermeasures.

4   Laser Fault Injection Scans

The subsequent steps are based on the insights about location and time-span described in the previous section. The goal in the next steps is to generate faulty device behavior, hence, faulty outputs. The success of a fault injection can be assessed based on the fault injection outcome. The output ciphertext of the device is used for the classification of the effect of a fault injection. Each ciphertext output is compared to two databases containing results for all possible faults under a certain fault model and known values for key and data input. The databases cover all possible two byte faults (any combination of affected bits) in any of the AES rounds for both data path and key schedule. The restriction to two bytes allows a reasonable memory vs. probability of classification trade-off. We distinguish six types of test outcomes:

Data path fault – These faults are caused by a fault injection into the data path logic. This category is most promising for actual fault attacks such as DFA.

Key schedule fault – A fault injection into the key schedule logic or the key storage. Such cases are interesting but harder to exploit.

Ciphertext output fault – The ciphertext itself was faulted. These faults are caused by faulting either the last round key in the key schedule or the data path state in the last round. Such faults are less interesting for actual attacks (as are the following types).

Device malfunction – This class contains all other types of irregular device behavior after fault injection (e.g. no answer).

Unidentified ciphertext fault – The ciphertext was incorrect, but could neither be found in the database for data path faults, nor in the database for key schedule faults

No fault – Regular device behavior i.e. no effective fault injection.

4.1 Large Area Scans

Through the power analysis, the AES execution timing was already narrowed down as much as possible in the time domain. As a next step a first laser scan is performed over a large area. As described in Sect. 3.2 the relevant parts of the AES engine are likely to be found on the right chip side in the standard cell areas. Therefore we start by scanning this part of the chip in a relatively coarse grid of 5 μm. No die-thinning was performed for this stage. The triggering time for the fault injection is set to the middle of the time-span identified in the power trace in Sect. 3.3. In this phase, only the first trigger stage was used. With the lack of synchronization to the internal clock of the DUT, timing variations are expected, which is not necessarily a disadvantage at this point. Since the required timing is unknown, a small temporal randomization of the fault injection can even be advantageous. Optimal parameter settings for the laser (energy, silicon thickness) are also unknown at this point, so we focus the beam slightly below the surface of the die and set the pulse energy to 30 nJ based on empirical knowledge from previous analyses. By setting the focus near the backside surface (instead of attempting to focus on the active regions below) the laser intensity in the active layers of the chip stays relatively low. Since the required energy level to induce faults is unknown at this point, and due to the "damage susceptibility" of the device, it is recommended to utilize a relatively low setting for the pulse energy.

Figure 6 depicts an overlay of three different scan results with the respective die image and shows in area A this initial scan. No data path or key schedule faults were observed in this scan, the results within area C did not occur in this scan. Solely the faults in area B were observed and this area and scanned with higher spatial resolution in the following (cf. Sect. 4.2). Mostly device malfunctions or output of corrupted ciphertext was observed. Locations which lead to faulty outputs are colored according to the classification scheme described above. However, the scan reveals an area where the output ciphertext is only slightly faulted with faults in at most two bytes, suggesting that the ciphertext itself is altered. This proves that the laser intensity is sufficient to affect the device.

Furthermore Fig. 6/A shows that the locations where device malfunction were observed are areas which contain analog circuitry. Generally these parts of the chip are not interesting in respect to fault injection attacks because they likely affect the entire chip at once. The locations where the ciphertext is altered originates from a memory block. Depending on the underlying system design, the memory blocks may contain keys and even intermediate values of the AES computation. With this state of results, a more detailed analysis of this section of the chip is a reasonable next step.

4.2   LFI Scan of Memory Blocks

The area covering the memory blocks (cf. Fig. 6/B) was scanned with an increased spatial resolution. The delay for the trigger signal was varied from $40\,\mu s$ to $240\,\mu s$ (cf. Fig. 5). The measurement shows injected *data path* faults in the range from $40\,\mu s$ to $65\,\mu s$ delay. The comparison with the database indicates that these are faults injected into the plaintext. Faults injected with a trigger delay in the range from $190\,\mu s$ to $240\,\mu s$ lead to manipulations of the ciphertext. Consequently, the AES computation must be in between this time interval. Injections with a respective delay did however not lead to any exploitable faults in this area, hence the intermediate data values are stored elsewhere. Nevertheless, it can be derived that the timing for the AES computation is even shorter than found in Sect. 3.3, since the encryption is already completed at $190\,\mu s$, $50\,\mu s$ earlier.

4.3   Laser Parameter Calibration

In order to obtain precise fault injection results with a low number of simultaneously affected bits, it is necessary to minimize the effective spot size of beam on the DUT. Since the laser beam has to pass through the silicon substrate to reach the active layer of the die, the focal point has to be set below the surface of the backside. Furthermore, the pulse energy must be minimized to reduce the area reaching a critical intensity. Both parameters vary, depending on the substrate thickness and the doping level. An IR camera can be use to directly adjust the focus of the objective system on the DUT, but was not installed in our system. Hence a different method must be used for calibration. We used the observable fault effect at a known location to tune the laser parameters. This can be achieved by reducing the pulse energy until no effect is observable and subsequently lowering the focal point. Repeating these two steps until no further reduction is feasible results in the optimal settings.

4.4   Successful DFA

The fault injections into the memory region C (cf. Fig. 2) helped to calibrate the trigger timing and LFI parameters. Using these settings, a repeated scan of the standard cell area E (cf. Fig. 2) was performed. Figure 6/C depicts the results. Two important clusters can be identified: Faults marked in blue represent faulted round-key bytes, while red ones represent data path faults during the AES. This marks a major milestone during the investigation, since faults in the datapath during an AES computation will allow successful DFA attacks.

Once the area scans revealed locations where faults in the data path are observed, the remaining attack required only marginal effort. Analysis of the generated faults reveals mostly single bit faults in individual rounds. This hints a high precision of the calibrated setup. The fault model of the DFA described by Tunstall et al. [23] requires one single byte fault in round 7 of the AES to determine the secret key. We adjusted the trigger delay until a number of received faulty ciphertexts could be attributed to round 7, which we successfully verified as exploitable. Hence, we are able to perform a DFA attack and extract the full key used by the device. However, only part of the injected faults were in round 7, therefore multiple faulty ciphertexts have to be tested. This could impair DFA attacks which require multiple ciphertext pairs.

Attacking the CCM-Mode. The DFA attack in the previous section is performed against the plain ECB-mode encryption. However, the use of the CCM-mode is the recommended usage. This raises the question, if the device is vulnerable in CCM-mode *encryption*. Note that attacking the *decryption* would fail because faulty data would not pass the authenticity check. The CCM mode is a combination of the CBC-MAC mode for authentication and the counter mode for data encryption/decryption. [10] using the same key for both parts. Both, the generation of the MAC and the encryption rely on the use of a nonce. Since a DFA requires a pair of faulty and correct ciphertext outputs, an attack is only feasible if it is possible to repeat an encryption with the same input data. This requires to keep the nonce and the MAC counter constant. The MAC counter of the device is automatically reset whenever a new nonce is generated. Individual keys can be configured to use an external nonce, hence, in this case a DFA is feasible. If the device is configured to use a random internally generated nonce, a DFA is not possible, because on each encryption a fresh nonce is used.

In this case the attacker can use *Statistical Fault Analysis* (SFA) [11]. SFA does not require the repetition of the identical encryption operations. Dobraunig et al. demonstrated that SFA is applicable to attack nonce-based encryption schemes [7]. The underlying concept is to generate faults in one of the latter rounds of the AES and to calculate the resulting intermediate byte value based on a key hypothesis. The attack exploits the fact, that the distribution of the faulted byte values is most likely biased (cf. Sect. 4.5), hence the correct hypothesis is easily distinguishable from the uniform distribution of the other cases. With regard to this DUT, the variation means that different rounds are affected in repeated injection tests. Due to the statistical approach of SFA, this is not necessarily a problem, since it will only increase the number of necessary fault injections.

Attacking the decryption is detected by the MAC verification and an error is output. Interestingly, *Statistical Ineffective Fault Analysis* [6,8], which are a variant of SFA, exploit so-called *ineffective* faults, i.e. fault injections that did not result in a fault. Hence, this method can be applied to attack the decryption, since only the information which inputs lead to an error is evaluated. In comparison to SFA, SIFA requires more fault injections to succeed because fault injections are partly dismissed, thus, not useful to the attacker. Given our results of injected faults with significant biases, we deem that these statistical attacks are feasible on this device.

4.5 Repeatability and Fault Model

In our experiments we were able to target specific bytes of the AES state. Figure 7a shows the results of a scan of the area including all 16 state bytes using a trigger delay of 150 μm. As can be seen, the fault sensitive locations of the individual bytes do not follow a regular pattern, but are more randomly clustered, typical for automatically placed logic cells. The individual byte locations can be further disaggregated into bit locations, exemplarily shown in Fig. 7b for the first two bytes. About 95% of all fault injections of this scan resulted in single bit faults in the AES state. In previous publications the observed fault model for SRAM cells [19] or D-type Flip-Flops [4,21] is strictly biased in the sense that depending on the exact location, LFI results in single specific type of fault (set or reset). Additional tests revealed that specific locations were predominantly sensitive for Bit-Flips in a particular direction. In the near vicinity of these locations, we observed less biased faults at a reduced success rate for the fault injection.

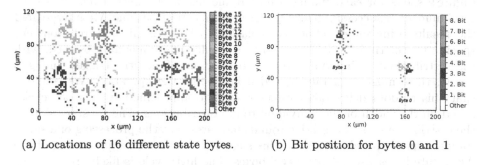

(a) Locations of 16 different state bytes.   (b) Bit position for bytes 0 and 1

Fig. 7. Detailed analysis of the fault sensitive locations

4.6 Revealing Details About the AES Implementation

Unlike the high spatial precision of the setup, we were not able to inject faults with precise and consistent timing. Through special tests described in this paragraph, we were able to reveal certain implementation and countermeasure details of the AES.

No Masking. The measurement result in Sect. 4.5 showed a significant location dependent bias in the fault model. This indicates that no masking mechanism is implemented. If the intermediate values would be masked, the test for the fault model should show an unbiased distribution. A fault injection would still lead to set or reset faults on the *masked* values, but this bias will be destroyed with the removal of the mask.

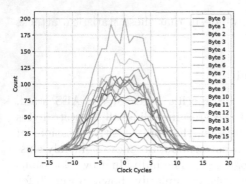

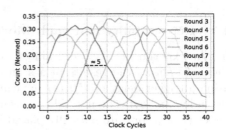

Fig. 8. Byte-wise fault occurence for the 6th round.

Fig. 9. Number of observed faults in different rounds for every injection time. Number is relative to total number of successful faults per injection time.

Round Processing. For a temporal analysis of the round processing we tested different LFI timings for all 16 bytes of the state. At specific locations for each byte, we tested the same timing range with 400 fault injections for each timing. Figure 9 shows for each timing, which round has been affected relative to the total number of successful fault injections at this injection time. We interpolated the results using cubic spline interpolation to help visual interpretation. For specific trigger timings, faults in up to six different rounds are observed, with the distributions of individual rounds overlapping. Since the trigger timing is stable, there must be a randomized delay before the operation. We estimate that this random delay takes values from 0 to approximately 25 clock cycles based on the width of the individual round distributions. The constant shift of the distributions for consecutive rounds indicates that the processing of a single round requires five clock cycles. This suggests a *column-wise* processing of the AES state bytes using 4 parallel S-boxes. The fifth cycle is likely used for the round key computation which also requires 4 S-box calls (cf. Fig. 6, key schedule and data path can be faulted using similar trigger delays). There is no further randomized delay between the rounds, since this would result in a widening in the distribution for later rounds.

Intra-round Processing Sequence of Bytes. During round computation, the columns of the AES state can be processed independently of each other. This sequence can be randomized at the beginning of the block encryption, or even at the beginning of each round. Figure 8 uses the same data as Fig. 9, but evaluates byte-faults which affected round 6. Since there is no apparent difference in the distribution of bytes over time, this seems to indicates that there is no general tendency for several bytes to be processed earlier than others. Hence this would mean that there is no fixed sequence of columns and fixed starting point, but a randomized ordering for the individual round computations. However, with these

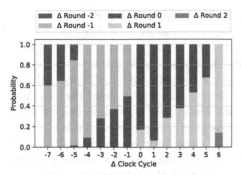

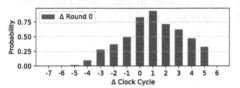

(a) Affected round count normalized by successful fault injections per time

(b) Distribution of double faults within same round.

Fig. 10. Double LFI on different bytes within single execution with different time offsets

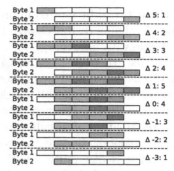

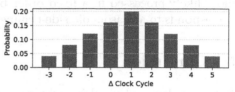

(a) Illustration of which triggering differences lead to faults in the same round.

(b) Resulting histogram of occurrence of deltas.

Fig. 11. Illustration of double LFI into sequentially processed AES-columns.

results it is still ambiguous how the column processing is implemented. Therefore we performed a test using two lasers, in order to inject faults into two different bytes of the same encryption and hence avoid the influence of triggering jitter: Based on the results from Fig. 7a the first laser was configured to target byte 1 and the second laser to target byte 2. A constant trigger timing was used for the first Laser and a variable timing for the second Laser. Figure 10 depicts the results of this test, evaluating the temporal distance in terms of rounds for both faults. For both figures, the x-axis states the time difference between the both laser shots in terms of clock cycles, the y-axis displays the relative frequency of the observed distance in affected AES rounds. Figure 10a shows that one round is hit over a time interval of roughly 5 clock cycles. Figure 10b evaluates only the cases where both faults affected the same round. This distribution is roughly triangle-shaped and can only be the result of a fixed sequence in the column processing of the AES computation.

As a model of a fixed processing sequence of columns, Fig. 11a shows all possibilities for two faults in consecutive columns to occur in the same round. A state byte can be faulted in a given round from time where the computed value is stored in the register until this register value is overwritten. Hence, this fault be injected during more than one clock cycle and even during the subsequent round. The boxes for both bytes represent the 5 cycle long processing window during which the byte can be faulted in order to affect the given round. Each line refers to a specific timing distance, with the corresponding individual cases illustrated by the boxes with matching colors. E.g. if the second laser shot is 4 clock cycles after the first, there are two possible combinations to affect the same round. Figure 11b depicts a histogram showing the number of double fault possibilities for each of the nine possible clock cycle deltas. As can be seen, the possible range for the timing distance between both shots is at most nine clock cycles and the distribution of possible combinations per timing interval has a triangle shape. A randomization of the column-processing between individual rounds would lead to a distribution with wider variance and without a single peak. Therefore, we conclude from our measurements that the columns are processed in a fixed order. Combining this with the previous insight, the columns are most likely processed in a fixed order but with a random starting point which corresponds to a reasonable side-channel countermeasure.

5   Conclusion

In this work we outline the necessary steps for a Laser fault attack in a black box scenario. We demonstrate this, with an actual attack on an AES-based security device. Though this chip includes several security features, it was found that it is vulnerable to optical fault attacks. Hence, with the device configured in ECB-mode, we were able to determine the internal keys using DFA. However, since there is no detection of the fault injection, we conclude that statistical attacks on the CCM mode will work as well. Our results suggest that many non-certified devices will likely be susceptible to similar attacks. In addition, we demonstrate how several details of the underlying implementation can be revealed using fault injection.

References

1. Atmel Corporation: CryptoAuthentication Family of Crypto Elements with Hardware-Based Key Storage (2015). Rev.: Atmel-8756F-ATSHA204A-ATEAS132-ATECC508A_E_US_112015
2. Atmel Corporation. 32K AES Serial EEPROM Specification, SUMMARY DATA SHEET, 2016. Atmel-8914BS-CryptoAuth-ATAES132A-Datasheet-Summary_02 2016
3. Carpi, R.B., Picek, S., Batina, L., Menarini, F., Jakobovic, D., Golub, M.: Glitch it if you can: parameter search strategies for successful fault injection. In: Francillon, A., Rohatgi, P. (eds.) CARDIS 2013. LNCS, vol. 8419, pp. 236–252. Springer, Cham (2014). https://doi.org/10.1007/978-3-319-08302-5_16
4. Courbon, F., Loubet-Moundi, P., Fournier, J.J.A., Tria, A.: Adjusting laser injections for fully controlled faults. In: Prouff, E. (ed.) COSADE 2014. LNCS, vol. 8622, pp. 229–242. Springer, Cham (2014). https://doi.org/10.1007/978-3-319-10175-0_16

5. Cui, A., Housley, R.: BADFET: defeating modern secure boot using second-order pulsed electromagnetic fault injection. In: Enck, W., Mulliner, C. (eds.) 11th USENIX Workshop on Offensive Technologies, WOOT 2017, Vancouver, BC, Canada, 14–15 August 2017. USENIX Association (2017)
6. Dobraunig, C., Eichlseder, M., Gross, H., Mangard, S., Mendel, F., Primas, R.: Statistical ineffective fault attacks on masked AES with fault countermeasures. In: Peyrin, T., Galbraith, S. (eds.) ASIACRYPT 2018. LNCS, vol. 11273, pp. 315–342. Springer, Cham (2018). https://doi.org/10.1007/978-3-030-03329-3_11
7. Dobraunig, C., Eichlseder, M., Korak, T., Lomné, V., Mendel, F.: Statistical fault attacks on nonce-based authenticated encryption schemes. In: Cheon, J.H., Takagi, T. (eds.) ASIACRYPT 2016. LNCS, vol. 10031, pp. 369–395. Springer, Heidelberg (2016). https://doi.org/10.1007/978-3-662-53887-6_14
8. Dobraunig, C., Eichlseder, M., Korak, T., Mangard, S., Mendel, F., Primas, R.: SIFA: exploiting ineffective fault inductions on symmetric cryptography. IACR Trans. Cryptogr. Hardw. Embed. Syst. 2018(3), 547–572 (2018)
9. Durvaux, F., Standaert, F.-X.: From improved leakage detection to the detection of points of interests in leakage traces. In: Fischlin, M., Coron, J.-S. (eds.) EURO-CRYPT 2016. LNCS, vol. 9665, pp. 240–262. Springer, Heidelberg (2016). https://doi.org/10.1007/978-3-662-49890-3_10
10. Dworkin, M.: Recommendation for block cipher modes of operation: the CCM mode for authentication and confidentiality. Technical report, National Institute of Standards and Technology (2004)
11. Fuhr, T., Jaulmes, É., Lomné, V., Thillard, A.: Fault attacks on AES with faulty ciphertexts only. In: Fischer, W., Schmidt, J.-M. (eds.) 2013 Workshop on Fault Diagnosis and Tolerance in Cryptography, Los Alamitos, CA, USA, 20 August 2013, pp. 108–118. IEEE Computer Society (2013)
12. Hériveaux, O.: Black-box laser fault injection on a secure memory. In: Conférence francophone sur le thème de la sécurité de l'information, SSTIC (2020)
13. Maldini, A., Samwel, N., Picek, S., Batina, L.: Genetic algorithm-based electro-magnetic fault injection. In: 2018 Workshop on Fault Diagnosis and Tolerance in Cryptography, FDTC 2018, Amsterdam, The Netherlands, 13 September 2018, pp. 35–42. IEEE Computer Society (2018)
14. Microchip Technology Inc.: ATAES132A 32K AES Serial EEPROM Complete Data Sheet (2018). Document Number: DS40002023A
15. Murdock, K., Oswald, D., Garcia, F.D., Van Bulck, J., Piessens, F., Gruss, D.: Plundervolt: how a little bit of undervolting can create a lot of trouble. IEEE Secur. Priv. 18(5), 28–37 (2020)
16. O'Flynn, C.: Min()imum failure: EMFI attacks against USB stacks. In: Gantman, A., Maurice, C. (eds.) 13th USENIX Workshop on Offensive Technologies, WOOT 2019, Santa Clara, CA, USA, 12–13 August 2019. USENIX Association (2019)
17. Picek, S., Batina, L., Jakobovic, D., Carpi, R.B.: Evolving genetic algorithms for fault injection attacks. In: 37th International Convention on Information and Communication Technology, Electronics and Microelectronics, MIPRO 2014, Opatija, Croatia, 26–30 May 2014, pp. 1106–1111. IEEE (2014)
18. Qiu, P., Wang, D., Lyu, Y., Qu, G.: VoltJockey: breaching TrustZone by software-controlled voltage manipulation over multi-core frequencies. In: Cavallaro, L., Kinder, J., Wang, X., Katz, J. (eds.) Proceedings of the 2019 ACM SIGSAC Conference on Computer and Communications Security, CCS 2019, London, UK, 11–15 November 2019, pp. 195–209. ACM (2019)

19. Roscian, C., Sarafianos, A., Dutertre, J.-M., Tria, A.: Fault model analysis of laser-induced faults in SRAM memory cells. In: Fischer, W., Schmidt, J.-M. (eds.) 2013 Workshop on Fault Diagnosis and Tolerance in Cryptography, Los Alamitos, CA, USA, 20 August 2013, pp. 89–98. IEEE Computer Society (2013)

20. Schellenberg, F., et al: On the complexity reduction of laser fault injection campaigns using OBIC measurements. In: Homma, N., Lomné, V. (eds.) 2015 Workshop on Fault Diagnosis and Tolerance in Cryptography, FDTC 2015, Saint Malo, France, 13 September 2015, pp. 14–27. IEEE Computer Society (2015)

21. Selmke, B., Heyszl, J., Sigl, G.: Attack on a DFA protected AES by simultaneous laser fault injections. In: 2016 Workshop on Fault Diagnosis and Tolerance in Cryptography, FDTC 2016, Santa Barbara, CA, USA, 16 August 2016, pp. 36–46. IEEE Computer Society (2016)

22. Tang, A., Sethumadhavan, S., Stolfo, S.J.: CLKSCREW: exposing the perils of security-oblivious energy management. In: Kirda, E., Ristenpart, T. (eds.) 26th USENIX Security Symposium, USENIX Security 2017, Vancouver, BC, Canada, 16–18 August 2017, pp. 1057–1074. USENIX Association (2017)

23. Tunstall, M., Mukhopadhyay, D., Ali, S.: Differential fault analysis of the advanced encryption standard using a single fault. In: Ardagna, C.A., Zhou, J. (eds.) WISTP 2011. LNCS, vol. 6633, pp. 224–233. Springer, Heidelberg (2011). https://doi.org/10.1007/978-3-642-21040-2_15

24. van Woudenberg, J.G.J., Witteman, M.F., Menarini, F.: Practical optical fault injection on secure microcontrollers. In: Breveglieri, L., Guilley, S., Koren, I., Naccache, D., Takahashi, J. (eds.) 2011 Workshop on Fault Diagnosis and Tolerance in Cryptography, FDTC 2011, Tokyo, Japan, 29 September 2011, pp. 91–99. IEEE Computer Society (2011)

25. Vasselle, A., Thiebeauld, H., Maouhoub, Q., Morisset, A., Ermeneux, S.: Laser-induced fault injection on smartphone bypassing the secure boot. In: 2017 Workshop on Fault Diagnosis and Tolerance in Cryptography, FDTC 2017, Taipei, Taiwan, 25 September 2017, pp. 41–48. IEEE Computer Society (2017)

Authentication and Content Protection

Employing Feature Selection to Improve the Performance of Intrusion Detection Systems

Ricardo Avila[1][✉], Raphaël Khoury[1][✉], Christophe Pere[2][✉], and Kobra Khanmohammadi[3][✉]

[1] University of Quebec at Chicoutimi, Saguenay, Canada
{ricardo.avila,raphael.khoury}@uqac.ca
[2] La Capitale Financial Group Inc., Quebec City, Canada
christophe.pere@lacapitale.com
[3] Geotab Inc., Oakville, Canada
kobrakhanmohammadi@geotab.com

Abstract. Intrusion detection systems use datasets with various features to detect attacks and protect computers and network systems from these attacks. However, some of these features are irrelevant and may reduce the intrusion detection system's speed and accuracy. In this study, we use feature selection methods to eliminate non-relevant features. We compare the performance of fourteen feature-selection methods, on three ML techniques using the UNSW-NB15, Kyoto 2006+ and DoHBrw-2020 datasets. The most relevant features of each dataset are identified, which show that feature selection methods can increase the accuracy of anomaly detection and classification.

Keywords: Feature selection · Machine learning · Intrusion detection systems

1 Introduction

The Anomaly-based Detection (AD) methods identify anomalous events in the network system. Anomalies are patterns in the data that do not conform to a well-defined notion of normal behavior. These anomalies can be identified by monitoring or evaluating regular activities, connections, hosts, or users of the network over a period of time [16]. On the other hand, Signature-based Detection (SD) methods rely upon a database containing traffic patterns associated with known attacks, which makes it a very effective strategy [22]. However, this database must be constantly updated since any new attacks, not present in the database, will otherwise go undetected. Finally, the Stateful Protocol Analysis (SPA) method is the process of comparing predetermined profiles of generally accepted definitions of benign protocol activity for each protocol state with observed events to locate deviations [27]. Unlike AD, which uses specific host or network profiles, the SPA

© Springer Nature Switzerland AG 2022
E. Aïmeur et al. (Eds.): FPS 2021, LNCS 13291, pp. 93–112, 2022.
https://doi.org/10.1007/978-3-031-08147-7_7

relies on the vendor's universal profiles that specify how specific protocols should or should not be used. This method thus allows the Intrusion Detection Systems (IDS) to understand and track the network's state.

In AD, the use of Machine Learning (ML) techniques proved to be an efficient approach to develop classifiers capable of distinguishing attacks from normal examples [7]. However, many research articles that apply ML for intrusion detection focus only on evaluation metrics (e.g. accuracy, precision, recall, and F-measure), ignoring other important aspects of classifier implementation and evaluation, such as feature extraction and selection [14,15].

Several researchers recommend using public datasets to develop intrusion detection systems using data mining and ML techniques [3,7,11,14]. Researchers widely use public datasets because they exhibit different types of attack and are labeled.

Feature Selection (FS) is the process of removing non-informative or redundant predictors from the model [18], which improves the accuracy of the classifiers and increasing both classification time and the model's explainability. As far as we know, no prior research compares several FS methods in the context of intruding detection and identifies the most relevant features in each of the datasets mentioned above. To address this lacuna, in this paper, we identified the most relevant features of UNSW-NB15, Kyoto 2006+ and DoHBrw-2020 datasets by applying fourteen different FS techniques and three ML algorithms in the context of intrusion detection. In this process, each dataset, FS method, and classifier is examined to identify the optimal algorithm for intrusion detection.

The remainder of this paper is organized as follows. In Sect. 2, we provide a general description of the datasets used in our study. Section 3 provides an overview the FS techniques used in this line of research. Then, in Sect. 4, the proposed methodology is explained. Section 5 provides a summary of the experiments and a discussion of the main results obtained. Related works and concluding remarks are given in Sect. 6 and 7 respectively.

2   Datasets

A large amount of network traffic is required to train and test an IDS that relies upon ML techniques. Unfortunately, for security and privacy reasons, such network traffic can be difficult to obtain. Nonetheless, several datasets are publicly available to security researchers. An analysis of the main public datasets available is presented in the study by Avila et al. [5]. In this section, we discuss the three datasets used in this study. The description of each feature of the datasets is available in their respective download repositories. To aid in the analysis, features are grouped into four categories:

- Metadata (M) - features that contain information about the network connection. This type of data can be observed/captured by most network monitoring systems, and is present in the vast majority of public datasets.
- Correlations across several connections (C) - features that present datum concerning multiple connections, such as the number of connections on the

server or the count or percentage of connections that are live for a certain period of time.

– Behavior (B) - features that present the underlying behavior such as the protocol used or type of service requested.
– Errors and error codes (E) - features that display the count or percentage of connections where a failure occurred.

2.1 UNSW-NB15

This dataset was created by the Cyber Range Lab, at the Australian Center for Cyber Security (ACCS) and consists of real and synthetic access activities classified as normal or attack behaviors. The dataset is available for download on the website of the University of New South Wales (UNSW)[1].

Table 1 presents the categories of all features of the UNSW-NB15 dataset. It has 49 features including the class label indicating whether each sample consists of normal activity or attack, and contains approximately 2.5 million records. This dataset's distribution is 44.9% normal and 55.1% intrusion. The dataset is not anonymous, contains records from a small network, and has a feature (*attack_cat*) that classifies nine types of attacks.

Table 1. Categories of features in the UNSW-NB15 dataset.

Category	Feature name
M	srcip, sport, dstip, dsport, proto, state, dur, sbytes, dbytes, sttl, dttl, swin, dwin, stcpb, dtcpb, trans_depth, res_bdy_len, sjit, djit, stime, Ltime, sintpkt, dintpkt, tcprtt, synack, ackdat, attack_cat
B	service, is_ftp_login
E	sloss, dloss
C	sload, dload, spkts, dpkts, smeansz, dmeansz, is_sm_ips_ports, ct_state_ttl ct_flw_http_mthd, ct_ftp_cmd, ct_srv_src, ct_srv_dst, ct_dst_ltm, ct_src_ltm ct_src_dport_ltm, ct_dst_sport_ltm, ct_dst_src_ltm

2.2 Kyoto 2006+

The Kyoto 2006+ dataset contains data which was collected through the implantation of various types of honeypots, and other systems in five networks inside and outside Kyoto University. The dataset is available for download on the author's website at the Information Technology Center (ITC) at Nagoya University[2].

---

[1] https://cloudstor.aarnet.edu.au/plus/index.php/s/2DhnLGDdEECo4ys.
[2] https://www.takakura.com/Kyoto_data/.

Table 2 presents the categories of all features of the Kyoto 2006+ dataset. The dataset contains 24 features, including the class label indicating whether each sample consists of normal activity or attack. The complete dataset contains data captured between November 2006 and December 2015. In this study, only data from the year 2015 was used, totaling approximately 12.4 million records. This dataset's distribution is 90.18% benign and 9.82% intrusion. However, the dataset is not anonymized and displays several types of attacks (e.g., DoS, scan, brute-force, backdoor, others).

Table 2. Categories of features in the Kyoto 2006+ dataset.

Category	Feature name
M	duration, source_bytes, destination_bytes, flag, IDS_detection, start_time, protocol, malware_detection, ashula_detection, source_ip_address, source_port_number, destination_ip_address, destination_port_number
B	service
E	serror_rate, srv_serror_rate, dst_host_serror_rate, dst_host_srv_serror_rate
C	count, same_srv_rate, dst_host_count, dst_host_srv_count, dst_host_same_src_port_rate

2.3   DoHBrw-2020

This dataset was created by the Canadian Institute for Cybersecurity (CIC) and contains benign and malicious DNS over HTTPS (DoH) traffic as a two-layered approach to detect and characterize DoH traffic. The dataset is available for download on the website of the University of New Brunswick (UNB)[3].

Table 3 presents the categories of all features of the DoHBrw-2020 dataset. The dataset contains 35 features, including the class label indicating whether each sample is characterized as benign DoH and malicious DoH. Our study used the data files *l2-malicious.csv* and *l2-benign.csv*, containing 249.836 and 19.807 records, respectively. This dataset's distribution is 92.7% intrusion and 7.3% benign. We selected this dataset because it is one of the newest publicly available, is not anonymized, and uses the RFC8484 protocol, which enhances privacy and combats eavesdropping and man-in-the-middle attacks by encrypting DNS queries and sending them in a covert channel.

---

[3] https://www.unb.ca/cic/datasets/dohbrw-2020.html.

Table 3. Categories of features in the DoHBrw-2020 dataset.

Category	Feature name
M	SourceIP, DestinationIP, SourcePort, DestinationPort, TimeStamp, Duration
B	no feature in this category
E	no feature in this category
C	FlowBytesSent, FlowSentRate, FlowBytesReceived, FlowReceivedRate, PacketLengthVariance, PacketLengthStandardDeviation, PacketLengthMean, PacketLengthMedian, PacketLengthMode, PacketLengthSkewFromMedian, PacketLengthSkewFromMode, PacketLengthCoefficientofVariation, PacketTimeVariance, PacketTimeStandardDeviation, PacketTimeMean, PacketTimeMedian, PacketTimeMode, PacketTimeSkewFromMedian, PacketTimeSkewFromMode, PacketTimeCoefficientofVariation, ResponseTimeTimeVariance, ResponseTimeTimeStandardDeviation, ResponseTimeTimeMean, ResponseTimeTimeMedian, ResponseTimeTimeMode, ResponseTimeTimeSkewFromMedian, ResponseTimeTimeSkewFromMode, ResponseTimeTimeCoefficientofVariation

3 Background

Feature selection (FS) is the task of eliminating irrelevant and redundant features in order to improve the performance of ML processes, resulting is a smaller model with fewer features for both classification and training. In general, FS is used for two reasons. First, a high number of features will result in the *curse of high dimensionality*, specially, when there is a paucity of training data [18]. The curse of dimensionality makes data sparser which worsens the accuracy of ML algorithms. Second, FS reduces the amount of time and memory needed to create a ML model.

Typically, datasets used for intrusion detection contain a large number of features, making them candidates for FS. Several FS methods exist, each having its own advantages and disadvantages. In the literature, FS methods are broadly classified in 4 categories, namely Filter, Wrapper, Embedded, and Hybrid [1]. A description of each category is given below.

Filter Methods - Many researchers apply FS using some filter method (FM) because such methods are independent of any specific learning algorithms and are considered a low computational cost method [1]. FM depends on the characteristics of the data for the selection process. Filters examine each feature individually and determine how predictive it is to the classification task at hand. As a result, filter methods are typically more computationally efficient than other FS methods (e.g. wrapper methods). In this study, we apply the following FM:

- Constant features (COF) - Features that present only one value for all the entries in the dataset (same value for that attribute).
- Quasi-constant features (QCF) - Features for which a single value is observed for nearly all entries. A threshold value must be determined, which varies between 95% and 99% of all entries with the same value in the dataset.
- Duplicated features (DUF) - Two or more features for which every entry is the same, and which can naturally be considered a single feature.
- Correlation features (CRF) - Two or more features for which the entries are highly correlated, making it possible to predict one feature from the other with a high degree of precision. Such highly correlated features only provide redundant information.
- Statistical and ranking (STR) - Finally, statistical metrics are used to rank each feature based on its interaction or relationship with the target. Any feature whose evaluation falls above a specified threshold is then retained for classification. In this way, each feature is classified independently of the other features based on its interaction or relationship with the target.

Wrapper Methods - Wrapper methods (WM) depend on the performance of a specific learning algorithm to estimate the importance of the selected features. WM examine all or almost all possibilities of feature combinations to discover the most favorable feature set [26]. For that reason, they are known as greedy algorithms. In this study, we apply the following WM:

- Step forward (STF) - This techniques reduces an initial d-dimensional feature space to a k-dimensional feature subspace (where $k < d$). This method begins by evaluating all features individually and selects the one that generates the best performing algorithm. The second step evaluates all possible combinations of the that feature and a second feature, and again selects the pair that produces the best performance. This process continues until a subset of k features is obtained.
- Step backward (STB) - This technique starts by fitting a model using all features. It then creates new subsets by removing one feature at a time, and re-applying the ML model. Each subset is evaluated until the removal of an additional feature doesn't decrease performance past a specific arbitrary threshold.
- Exhaustive (EXH) - When using this method, the optimal subset of all combinations of features is chosen by optimizing a specified performance metric for a certain ML algorithm. For example, if the classifier is a decision tree and the dataset has four features, the algorithm will measure all fifteen feature subsets combinations. Then select the one that shows the best performance (i.e., precision) of the decision tree classifier. This method is costly from a computational perspective, but it can identify the optimal subset of features.

Embedded Methods - Embedded methods (EM) are a combination of FM and WM methods that incorporate FS as part of the model learning process [1]. EM approaches inherit the best properties of wrapper and filter methods: (i) they take into consideration the interaction between each feature and the learning algorithm; and (ii) they are much more efficient than WM as they do not need to evaluate resource sets iteratively, because they fit the ML model only once. In our study, we applied the following EM methods:

- Lasso regularization (LAR) - This method works by adding a penalty to the model to reduce overfitting. In the regularization of the linear model, the penalty is applied to the coefficients that multiply each of the predictors. Lasso (also called L1-penalty with absolute beta/norm) has reduced the coefficients to zero. In this way, some features can be removed from the model using Lasso regularization.
- Regression coefficients (RGC) - Linear regression is a simple approach for predicting a quantitative response Y based on predictor variables $X_1, X_2, ...X_n$. It assumes that there is a linear relationship between $X(s)$ and Y. The magnitude of the coefficients directly influences the scale of the features. Therefore, to compare coefficients between features, they all must be on the same scale. Consequently, regression includes a necessary normalization phase.
- Tree importance (TIM) - When using FS with tree importance, for each feature, the decision tree asks a question of the form: "Is the value of observation A as high as possible for feature X?". If the answer is positive, the observation is allocated to one side of the tree node; if it is negative, the observation is carried to the other side of the node. The answer that leads to the greatest possible reduction of impurities means that it gives the best possible separation from the class.

Hybrid Methods - Hybrid methods (HM) can be considered a composition of several FS algorithms (WM, FM, and EM). The main objective is to correct the instability problems and limitations of some existing FS algorithms, like not having to examine all possible feature combinations, as the case of WM. In this study, we applied the following HM:

- Feature shuffling (FES) - This method consists of randomly shuffling the values of a specific variable and determining how this permutation affects the performance metric of the ML algorithm. This is done by exchanging the values of each resource, one at a time, and measuring how much the permutation decreases the precision, the ROC-AUC, or another metric of evaluation of the ML model.
- Recursive feature elimination (RFE) - This method creates a subset of features by starting with all features in the training dataset and successively removing features until removing a feature causes the performance metric (e.g. ROC-AUC) to decrease.
- Recursive feature addition (RFA) - Conversely, this method constructs a feature set by iteratively adding features one by one, starting from an empty set, until the addition of another feature causes the performance metric (e.g., ROC-AUC) to decrease.

4 Methodology

All the experiments were conducted using a Python environment with Scikit-learn, an open-source ML library. The code were implemented on a desktop computer with a Intel Xeon eight-core CPU (3.9 GHz) and 128 GB memory. The methodology of this study is shown in Fig. 1 and described as follows.

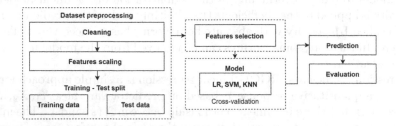

Fig. 1. Steps used in the proposed methodology

4.1 Dataset Preprocessing

A data pre-processing step must be performed before we can proceed with the classification itself. This step is usually the most time-consuming process of the ML methodology. There is no single technique that can be applied to obtain a satisfactory representation in all domains, requiring many experiments with empirical data to arrive at an appropriate representation.

- Cleaning - The first step of prepossessing consists of the removal of duplicate records, null values, or empty values present in the dataset. In this step, we also transform the non-numeric instances into a numeric representation. Usually, the estimator (classifier) defined in the Scikit-learn works well with numerical inputs. Furthermore, many ML algorithms cannot be employed directly with categorical data. This method can also be applied to encode integer variables, creating a new binary variable for each unique integer value.
- Features scaling is used to avoid features with large values that may weigh heavily on the final results. Normalization is one of the most common techniques of feature scaling that harmonizes the scales of attribute values.
- Training - Test Split - The training-test split is used to evaluating the performance of the ML algorithms. The dataset was divided into two subsets. The first subset with 80% fits the model and is referred to as the training dataset. The second subset with 20% tests the model. The predictions are made and compared to the expected values using the second subset.

4.2 Feature Selection

This step aims to reduce the number of features available to the model. The inclusion of this step is the crux of the current paper. The features that are removed do not add value to the model, and their removal improves most experiments that use it. All the FS methods used in our study are presented in the Subsect. 3.

4.3   Model Creation

Various techniques can be employed to address the intrusion detection problem. Liao et al. [16] identify three classes of intrusion detection methodologies: Signature-based Detection (SD), Anomaly-based Detection (AD), and Stateful Protocol Analysis (SPA).

In this experiment, we focus on AD. This category of intrusion detection methods is used to identify unusual behavior on a computer or network. They work from the assumption that attacks are different from normal activity and that the differences are sufficiently salient to permit automated detection.

AD has the capacity to identify zero-day attacks without previous knowledge of them [4]. Additionally, it can be used to produce information about new attacks, and define new signatures for Signature-based detectors. However, it usually produces many false alarms due to users' and systems' unpredictable behavior, requiring constant data collection to classify normal behavior patterns.

In our experiment, we compare the effectiveness of three classifiers, namely Logistic Regression (LR) [25], Support-Vector Machines (SVM) [23], and K-Nearest Neighbors (KNN) [2]. The evaluation metrics used in the test data are accuracy (AC), F-measure (F1), precision (PR), and recall (RE), which have their usual meaning. The classifiers' performance was evaluated based on 10-fold cross-validation, dividing the datasets into ten consecutive folds, and taking each of them for testing in turn, and the rest were used as training data.

Regardless of the AD method used, three related problems remain: (i) the rate of false alarms, (ii) the difficulty in selecting the appropriate features, and (iii) the high cost to process the growing volume of data. So if we can combine the advantages of selecting the appropriate features in conjunction with ML methods, this approach can detect anomalous attacks according to their characteristics in the problem domain.

5   Experiments and Results

5.1   Experiments

The experiments were carried out in two main steps. In the first step, we performed anomaly detection using all features of the UNSW-NB15 (49 features), Kyoto 2006+ (24 features), and DoHBrw-2020 (35 features) datasets. In this study, we are only interested in detecting intrusions, rather then categorizing them, and consequently approach this problem as a Binary Classification problem. The network system characteristics can denote either *Normal* (no intrusion detected) or *Intrusion* (intrusion detected). To this end, we replaced the values in the *attack* column of each dataset which categorizes anomalies with a boolean value that simply indicates the presence or absence of an anomaly.

After specifying the target column, in second step, we applied fourteen feature-selection methods to identify the most relevant fields from the input feature set. We applied the methods of FS individually to the datasets. The description of each of the FS methods used was presented in Sect. 3, and the source code developed was made available in a public repository on GitHub[4].

Tables 4, 5, and 6 report the results of the binary classification scheme using each of the different reduced feature set. In each table, results present the accuracy obtained upon evaluation. It is important to highlight that all these metrics were computed using the weighted average. When selecting the weighted average, the objective is to calculate each class label's performance.

5.2   Results and Discussion

The experiments aim to answer four Experimental Questions (EQ). Each EQ is answered in the following subsections.

5.2.1   (EQ1) Are There Features that Are Consistently Removed Across Multiple FS Methods?

Table 8 presents features removed from the UNSW-NB15 dataset according to fourteen FS methods. The features most likely to be removed were: 12 times for *ackdat* (M), *is_ftp_login* (B), and *ct_ftp_cmd* (C), and 11 times for *dloss* (E), *spkts* (C), *tcprtt* (M), *is_sm_ips_ports* (C), *ct_srv_src* (C), and *ct_dst_ltm* (C). In the Kyoto 2006+ dataset, according to Table 9, the most removed features were: 10 times for *malware_detection* (M) and *serror_rate* (E), and 8 times for *dst_host_same_src_port_rate* (C), *dst_host_srv_serror_rate* (E), *ashula_detection* (M), and *start_time* (M). Finally, in the case of the DoHBrw-2020 dataset,

Table 4. Accuracy of fourteen feature-selection methods on three ML algorithms using the UNSW-NB15 dataset.

Methods	No. of used features	Logistic regression					Support vector machine					K-nearest neighbors				
		PR	RE	F1	AC	ET	PR	RE	F1	AC	ET	PR	RE	F1	AC	ET
-	48	75.75	75.45	75.60	84.48	1.93 s	78.21	60.24	68.05	81.98	80 m01 s	86.45	77.88	81.94	89.06	5.99 s
COF	45	75.75	75.45	75.60	84.48	1.36 s	77.96	60.77	68.30	82.02	78 m04 s	86.45	77.88	81.94	89.06	4.56 s
QCF	42	75.75	75.45	75.60	84.48	1.69 s	78.14	60.63	68.28	82.05	76 m05 s	86.45	77.88	81.94	89.06	4.60 s
DUF	47	75.75	75.45	75.60	84.48	1.86 s	78.21	60.24	68.05	81.98	79 m25 s	86.45	77.88	81.94	89.06	5.90 s
CRF	31	73.30	71.94	72.62	82.71	1.62 s	78.10	60.63	68.27	82.03	47 m42 s	86.29	77.95	81.91	89.03	3.51 s
STR	15	93.81	90.09	80.39	90.37	2.05 s	73.73	99.95	84.86	86.97	22 m38 s	93.05	95.98	94.49	92.38	2.03 s
STF	15	74.78	84.93	79.53	77.51	1.57 s	70.34	90.83	79.28	71.76	29 m52 s	92.76	95.83	94.27	96.78	2.32 s
STB	15	93.20	89.12	79.82	90.37	2.11 s	73.73	99.95	84.86	86.10	24 m17 s	92.81	95.80	94.28	96.98	2.71 s
EXH	13	94.43	91.23	80.11	90.38	2.64 s	73.73	99.95	84.86	86.32	23 m27 s	92.98	95.61	94.28	97.07	2.62 s
LAR	16	93.62	89.91	79.61	90.39	1.96 s	73.72	99.95	84.86	84.43	25 m30 s	92.76	95.93	94.32	96.81	2.25 s
RGC	15	91.00	83.79	83.24	90.44	1.85 s	73.73	99.95	84.86	85.77	23 m14 s	92.93	96.20	94.54	96.89	1.98 s
TIM	14	91.00	83.79	83.23	90.41	1.88 s	73.73	99.95	84.86	85.21	23 m23 s	92.93	96.23	94.56	96.88	2.05 s
FES	13	89.60	94.34	91.91	93.23	3.81 s	78.99	99.20	87.95	88.81	20 m29 s	92.21	95.48	93.81	96.30	2.73 s
RFE	5	90.47	90.39	90.43	89.44	1.84 s	89.99	87.48	88.72	90.70	20 m54 s	94.91	96.23	95.57	97.94	1.63 s
RFA	10	90.68	85.57	88.05	88.70	3.72 s	82.96	96.65	89.28	89.84	22 m12 s	91.75	89.51	90.62	94.09	2.34 s

---

[4] https://github.com/theavila/EmployingFS.

Table 5. Accuracy of fourteen feature-selection methods on three ML algorithms using the Kyoto 2006+ dataset.

Methods	No. of used features	Logistic regression					Support vector machine					K-nearest neighbors				
		PR	RE	F1	AC	ET	PR	RE	F1	AC	ET	PR	RE	F1	AC	ET
-	23	95.80	62.71	75.80	78.43	8.93s	98.37	96.36	97.35	95.58	30m40s	98.82	98.70	98.76	97.35	18.3s
COF	23	95.80	62.71	75.80	78.43	8.91s	98.37	96.36	97.35	95.58	30m41s	98.82	98.70	98.76	97.35	18.4s
QCF	22	95.79	62.73	75.81	78.64	11.5s	98.23	94.33	96.25	95.63	19m17s	98.82	98.70	98.76	96.97	17.4s
DUF	21	95.79	62.74	75.82	79.29	7.5s	97.87	93.87	95.83	95.33	19m16s	98.82	98.70	98.76	97.35	17.3s
CRF	21	97.51	66.12	78.81	75.65	5.79s	97.93	94.63	96.25	95.48	18m49s	98.82	98.70	98.76	97.35	17.1s
STR	15	96.13	60.89	74.55	80.35	9.52s	98.71	94.84	96.74	95.90	18m40s	99.07	99.40	99.23	98.49	12.8s
STF	15	96.13	81.70	64.48	71.93	3.25s	98.40	89.73	93.86	94.62	21m19s	99.20	99.13	99.16	98.18	10.7s
STB	15	90.12	70.84	43.19	63.58	3.16s	98.64	84.23	90.87	23.58	25m14s	99.54	99.84	99.69	99.45	10.2s
EXH	10	91.97	69.51	53.10	61.12	2.05s	97.37	87.55	92.20	92.93	21m25s	99.19	99.30	99.25	98.16	9.96s
LAR	8	96.90	68.56	80.30	82.03	2.47s	92.91	78.61	85.17	46.19	11m52s	94.31	98.39	96.31	89.49	9.63s
RGC	14	96.96	67.05	79.28	81.83	6.42s	92.33	79.95	40.32	49.11	13m27s	94.78	98.64	96.67	93.28	9.12s
TIM	6	97.22	63.45	76.79	68.63	1.9s	98.66	84.28	90.91	84.76	10m30s	99.55	99.83	99.69	99.46	7.01s
FES	17	96.99	64.78	77.68	78.95	10.4s	98.57	93.84	96.15	95.54	21m47s	99.07	99.40	99.23	98.49	13.8s
RFE	6	**99.53**	**98.58**	**48.32**	**67.63**	**2.59s**	**98.68**	**88.86**	**93.51**	**88.86**	**16m11s**	**99.52**	**99.80**	**99.66**	**99.46**	**8.03s**
RFA	9	99.53	98.58	48.32	71.22	3.09s	98.56	88.61	93.32	88.54	18m25s	99.52	99.80	99.66	99.43	10.1s

Table 6. Accuracy of fourteen feature-selection methods on three ML algorithms using the DoHBrw-2020 dataset.

Methods	No. of used features	Logistic regression					Support vector machine					K-nearest neighbors				
		PR	RE	F1	AC	ET	PR	RE	F1	AC	ET	PR	RE	F1	AC	ET
-	34	99.87	99.37	99.62	99.99	15.4s	96.72	99.31	98.00	99.48	10m28s	99.18	91.55	95.21	99.62	6.63s
COF	31	99.87	99.37	99.62	99.99	14.5s	96.72	99.31	98.00	99.48	9m35s	99.18	91.55	95.21	99.62	6.12s
QCF	31	99.87	99.37	99.62	99.99	14.9s	96.72	99.31	98.00	99.48	9m37s	99.18	91.55	95.21	99.62	6.18s
DUF	33	99.87	99.50	99.68	99.99	15.1s	96.72	99.31	98.00	99.48	10m20s	99.18	91.55	95.21	99.62	6.61s
CRF	22	94.62	99.75	97.11	99.99	12.7s	91.11	77.55	83.79	99.71	8m32s	99.10	96.85	97.96	99.69	3.94s
STR	15	93.78	98.87	96.26	99.98	13.4s	89.71	76.92	82.82	99.59	7m15s	99.34	94.83	97.03	99.67	2.43s
STF	13	95.30	99.75	97.47	99.99	13.1s	86.68	62.42	72.58	99.61	6m42s	99.08	95.59	97.30	99.79	2.41s
STB	14	94.73	99.75	97.17	99.99	13.2s	86.69	62.42	72.58	99.61	6m47s	99.08	95.59	97.30	99.79	3.54s
EXH	15	99.62	99.62	99.62	99.99	9.77s	85.25	56.12	67.68	99.58	7m00s	99.07	94.20	96.57	99.69	3.68s
LAR	7	99.94	99.17	99.55	99.96	2.34s	91.34	87.77	89.52	99.80	5m34s	99.23	97.10	98.15	99.79	1.11s
RGC	15	99.87	99.50	99.68	99.99	13.7s	86.86	57.60	69.20	99.48	7m01s	99.18	91.55	95.21	99.62	3.81s
TIM	8	91.55	99.75	95.47	99.97	2.86s	91.54	76.42	83.3	99.87	5m17s	99.25	97.19	98.21	99.79	1.14s
FES	16	99.87	99.50	99.68	99.99	14.1s	85.71	52.96	65.47	99.55	6m49s	99.45	91.93	95.54	99.61	3.64s
RFE	4	**95.87**	**99.50**	**97.65**	**99.98**	**1.29s**	**91.54**	**76.42**	**83.30**	**99.85**	**4m38s**	**99.72**	**89.28**	**94.21**	**99.99**	**1.08s**
RFA	5	97.06	99.87	98.45	99.99	1.74s	91.40	76.42	83.24	99.81	4m52s	99.78	97.23	98.59	99.51	1.17s

according to Table 10, the most removed features were: 12 times for *PacketTime-CoefficientofVariation* (C) and 11 times for *PacketLengthCoefficientofVariation* (C), *ResponseTimeTimeVariance* (C), and *RespTimeTimeMean* (C).

The datasets used in this study had few features removed by FM. Even so, these methods must be applied together with others FS methods, improving the performance of ML algorithms and decreasing the execution time.

5.2.2 (EQ2) Are the Same Features Removed by Every FS Method Across Different Datasets?

The results of Tables 8, 9, and 10 show that the STR method removed the feature that indicates the source port number used in the session (*sport* in UNSW-NB15, *source_port_number* in Kyoto 2006+, and *SourcePort* in DoHBrw-2020). The feature that indicates the source IP address used in the session (*dstip* in UNSW-

NB15, *destination_ip_address* in Kyoto 2006+, and *DestinationIP* in DoHBrw-2020) was removed by the LAR method. Finally, the RFE method removed the feature that has the length (number of seconds) of the connection (*dur* in UNSW-NB15, *duration* in Kyoto 2006+, and *Duration* in DoHBrw-2020).

The removal of the same features in the three datasets proves the consistency of the FS methods, showing that the same techniques can be applied to other datasets.

5.2.3   (EQ3) Which ML Algorithms Achieve the Best Results When Used FS in the Context of Anomaly Detection? Which Are the Most Relevant Features?

Analyzing the results of UNSW-NB15 dataset presented in Table 4, the optimal accuracy obtained was 97.94%, when using 5 features selected using the RFE method with the KNN algorithm. According to Fig. 2b, the most representative features are *sbytes* (M), *sttl* (M), *smeansz* (C), *ct_srv_dst* (C), and *service* (B).

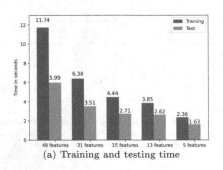

(a) Training and testing time

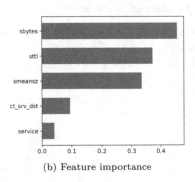

(b) Feature importance

Fig. 2. Training and test runtimes and representative features of UNSW-NB15 dataset.

In the case of the Kyoto 2006+ dataset, as shown in Table 5, the optimal accuracy was 99.46%, when using 6 features, RFE method and KNN algorithm. Figure 3b presents the most representative features, which are *source_ip_address* (M), *destination_ip_address* (M), *destination_bytes* (M), *source_bytes* (M), *destination_port_number* (M), and *service* (B).

Finally in the case of the DoHBrw-2020 dataset, as shown in Table 6, the optimal accuracy was 99.99%, when using 4 features, RFE method and KNN algorithm. Figure 4b presents the most representative features, which are *TimeStamp* (M), *SourcePort* (M), *DestinationPort* (M), and *PacketTimeMode* (C). As the TimeStamp feature was ranked the most relevant, we can say that the traffic capture could have been influenced by the periods of the controlled attacks.

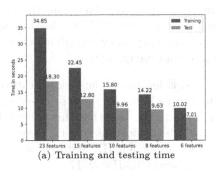 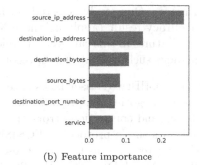

(a) Training and testing time   (b) Feature importance

Fig. 3. Training and test runtimes and representative features of Kyoto 2006+ dataset.

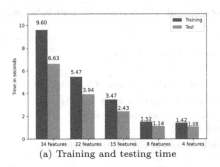 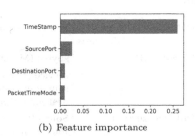

(a) Training and testing time   (b) Feature importance

Fig. 4. Training and test runtimes and representative features of DoHBrw-2020 dataset.

The most relevant features are presented in Table 7, with their category, name, and respective dataset being displayed. According to the obtained results, the categories have different characteristics of importance for anomaly detection:

- Metadata - Among the 15 features selected as the most relevant in our study, 10 are part of this category. These features are significant for anomaly detection, highlighting the feature *sbytes* (number of data bytes transferred from source to destination in single connection) selected in two datasets.
- Correlations - Two of the selected features in this study were from the UNSW-NB15 dataset (*smeansz*, *ct_srv_dst*), with the *PacketTimeMode* feature being the only one selected in the DoHBrw-2020 dataset.
- Behavior - The feature *service* was selected in two datasets. Also, other studies recognized this feature as one of the most relevant features after using FS methods. Even presenting only two features of this category in this study (*service*, *is_ftp_login*), this type of feature helps in better accuracy results in different types of attacks like DoS, exploits, and fuzzers [12].

– Errors - Our study selected no feature in this category based on the best accuracy result (applying the KNN algorithm and the RFE method). Even so, features in this category are relevant because they allow identifying various attacks such as brute force, reconnaissance, and analysis [8].

The DoHBrw dataset lacks category B and E features. The lack of features in these categories can prejudice identifying attacks based on the type of service, protocol, and connection errors or failures. Despite the fact that this dataset is based on a single protocol (RFC8484), it would be important to have resources in these categories, as they are present in other important IDS datasets such as KDD'99, NSL-KDD, ISCX-IDS-2012, CTU-13, and CIC-IDS-2017.

Table 7. Selected features based on best accuracy of 14 FS methods and KNN algorithm.

Dataset	No. of features	Selected features based on best accuracy
UNSW-NB15	5	sbytes (M), sttl (M), service (B), smeansz (C), ct_srv_dst (C)
Kyoto 2006+	6	service (B), source_bytes (M), destination_bytes (M), source_ip_address (M), destination_ip_address (M), destination_port_number (M)
DoHBrw-2020	4	SourcePort (M), DestinationPort (M), TimeStamp (M), PacketTimeMode (C)

5.2.4   (EQ4) What Is the Reduction Time Obtained with FS?

The number of features is an essential metric of the quality of an ML solution since it affects the training and test time of the model. Figures 2a, 3a, and 4a illustrate the training and test time, and results show that the number of features affects the time needed to evaluate the model. The number of features in the UNSW-NB15 dataset (Fig. 2a) reduced from 48 to 5 features and the execution time from 5.99 s to 1.63 s, during model test. On average, the execution time was decreased by 72.78% of the total model processing time in the training and test. Similarly, the number of features in the Kyoto 2006+ dataset (Fig. 3a) was reduced from 23 to 6 features and the execution time from 18.30 s to 7.01 s. On average, the execution time was decreased by 61.94% of the total model processing time in training and test. Finally, in the DoHBrw-2020 dataset (Fig. 4a), the number of features was reduced from 34 to 4 features and the execution time from 6.63 s to 1.08 s. On average, the execution time decreased by 83.71% of the total processing time of the model in training and test.

6 Related Work

Janarthanan and Zargari [13] investigated FS for learning models over the KDD'99 and UNSW-NB15 datasets. They used two subset of features for their experiment. The first subset consists of the most frequently used features in the previous studies while the second subset is set of features selected using FS methods over UNSW-NB15 datasets. They showed that the subset obtained by applying FS approaches provides better results, and showed that the results in UNSW-NB15 outperformed those obtained from KDD'99. They hypothesized that this result might be due to an imbalance in the number of attack types in the training and testing datasets of KDD'99.

Hajisalem and Babaie [9] used Correlation-based FS to remove irrelevant feature in their proposed hybrid classification method. They simulated their approach on NSL-KDD and UNSW-NB15 datasets and reached 99% detection rate and 0.01% false positive rate.

Pham et al. [17] used FS, in combination with ensemble methods, to improve the accuracy of classifiers. They used two subset of selected features. First, 25 features were selected using "leave-one-out" techniques and Naive Bayes classifier. The second subset consisted of 35 features and was selected using Gain the Ratio technique. The models were then evaluated using the NSL-KDD datasets.

Binbusayyis and Vaiyapuri [6] applied four different feature evaluation measures including correlation, consistency, information, and distance, to select the more crucial features for intrusion detection. They applied the subset combination strategy to merge the output of the four measures and achieve a potential feature set. They then tested these features on four evaluation datasets, namely KDD'99, NSL-KDD, UNSW-NB15, and CIC-IDS-2017.

Prasad et al. [19] proposed a FS approach that combines compromising Rough set theory and the Bayes theorem. The proposed FS method proceeds by identifying the core features and ranking them based on the probability that a feature belongs to a class. They tested their approaches on multiple datasets, including KDD'99, Kyoto2006+, ISCX2012, LBNB, DEFCON, CAIDA, ADFA-LD, and CICIDS2017.

FS has also received significant attention in other areas and several surveys of existing approaches have been published. Li et al. [15] surveyed FS approaches alongside with a brief historical background of the field, followed by a selection of challenges like FS for high-dimensional small sample size data, large-scale data, and secure FS, and finally presented recent advances on this area.

Sheikhpour et al. [21] surveyed semi-supervised FS methods which use both labeled and unlabeled data to evaluate feature relevance. Harish and Revanasiddappa [10] presented an empirical study of the most widely used FS methods in text categorization. Venkatesh and Anuradha [24] also surveyed FS approaches and conclude that most of the FS methods are effective only on static data. They do not perform well with noisy big data such as IoT and web-application data.

Sharma and Kaur [20] analyzed the nature-inspired meta-heuristics used in FS. Meta-heuristics are problem-independent optimization techniques that provide an optimal solution by exploring and exploiting the entire search space iteratively. They categorized nature-inspired meta-heuristic techniques and identified research gaps and analyzed the performance of divergent meta-heuristic techniques in the solving FS problem.

7   Conclusion and Future Works

At the term of the of experiment performed in this study, we showed that FS improves of evaluation metrics was obtained for all classification algorithms when using FS methods, with KNN outperforming other algorithms. FS was also found to yeild substantial improvements in execution time.

Most resource selection methods are computationally costly, since they usually involve a large number of evaluations. FM is generally more efficient than WM, but our experiments shows that this is not always true. In general, the EM and HM had better accuracy performance and reduced the execution time of the ML algorithms during the training and testing stages. Therefore, to reduce the computational cost, two points must be considered: (i) an efficient search technique; and (ii) a rapid assessment measure. The creation of a FS methods that meets these requirements remains an open problem.

The experiments results show that the selection of features has merits in reducing the models' complexity and increasing the accuracy of the intrusion detection, as measured using different classification metrics. In future work, we intend to create a new dataset and an adaptive IDS method for real-world network traffic data. We also aim to study the interplay between FS and the unbalanced dataset problem, which is endemic in this field.

Appendix A - Complementary Tables

Table 8. Selected and removed features from the UNSW-NB15 dataset according to each of the fourteen feature-selection methods.

Feature name	Feature selection methods													
	COF	QCF	DUF	CRF	STR	STF	STB	EXH	LAR	RGC	TIM	FES	RFE	RFA
srcip	✓	✓	✓	✓	x	x	x	x	x	x	x	x	x	x
sport	✓	✓	✓	✓	x	x	x	x	x	x	x	x	x	x
dstip	✓	✓	✓	✓	x	x	x	x	x	x	x	x	x	x
dsport	✓	✓	✓	✓	x	x	x	x	x	x	x	x	x	x
proto	✓	✓	✓	✓	x	x	✓	x	x	✓	x	x	x	x
state	✓	✓	✓	✓	x	✓	✓	✓	✓	✓	✓	✓	x	x
dur	✓	✓	✓	✓	✓	✓	✓	✓	✓	✓	✓	✓	x	x
sbytes	✓	✓	✓	x	✓	✓	✓	✓	✓	✓	✓	✓	✓	✓
dbytes	✓	✓	✓	x	✓	✓	x	x	x	x	x	x	x	✓
sttl	✓	✓	✓	✓	✓	✓	✓	✓	✓	✓	✓	✓	✓	x
dttl	✓	✓	✓	x	✓	✓	✓	✓	✓	✓	✓	✓	x	x
sloss	✓	✓	✓	x	x	x	x	x	x	x	x	x	x	✓
dloss	✓	✓	✓	x	x	x	x	x	x	x	x	x	x	x
service	✓	✓	✓	✓	✓	✓	✓	✓	✓	✓	✓	✓	✓	x
sload	✓	✓	✓	✓	✓	✓	✓	✓	✓	✓	✓	x	x	x
dload	✓	✓	✓	✓	✓	x	✓	✓	✓	✓	✓	✓	x	x
spkts	✓	✓	✓	x	x	x	x	x	x	x	x	x	x	x
dpkts	✓	✓	✓	x	✓	x	✓	✓	✓	✓	✓	✓	x	x
swin	✓	✓	✓	x	x	x	x	x	✓	x	x	✓	x	x
dwin	✓	✓	✓	✓	x	x	x	x	x	x	x	x	x	x
stcpb	✓	✓	✓	✓	x	x	x	x	x	x	x	x	x	x
dtcpb	✓	✓	✓	✓	x	x	x	x	x	x	x	x	x	x
smeansz	✓	✓	✓	✓	✓	✓	✓	✓	x	x	x	✓	✓	✓
dmeansz	✓	✓	✓	✓	✓	✓	✓	✓	x	✓	✓	x	x	✓
trans_depth	✓	✓	✓	✓	x	x	x	x	x	x	x	x	x	x
res_bdy_len	✓	✓	✓	✓	x	x	x	x	x	x	x	x	x	x
sjit	✓	✓	✓	✓	x	x	✓	x	✓	x	✓	x	x	x
djit	✓	✓	✓	✓	x	x	x	x	x	x	x	x	x	x
stime	✓	✓	✓	✓	x	x	x	x	x	x	x	x	x	x
Ltime	✓	✓	✓	✓	x	x	x	x	x	x	x	x	x	x
sintpkt	✓	✓	✓	x	✓	✓	✓	✓	✓	✓	✓	✓	x	x
dintpkt	✓	✓	✓	✓	✓	✓	✓	x	x	x	x	x	x	x
tcprtt	x	x	✓	x	x	x	x	x	✓	x	x	x	x	✓
synack	x	x	✓	✓	x	x	x	x	✓	✓	x	x	x	✓
ackdat	x	x	✓	✓	x	x	x	x	x	x	x	x	x	x
is_sm_ips_ports	✓	x	✓	✓	x	x	x	x	x	x	x	x	x	x
ct_state_ttl	✓	✓	✓	✓	✓	✓	x	x	x	x	✓	x	x	x
ct_flw_http_mthd	✓	✓	✓	✓	x	x	x	x	x	x	x	x	x	x
is_ftp_login	✓	x	✓	x	x	x	x	x	x	x	x	x	x	x
ct_ftp_cmd	✓	x	x	✓	x	x	x	x	x	x	x	x	x	x
ct_srv_src	✓	✓	✓	x	x	x	x	x	x	x	x	x	x	x
ct_srv_dst	✓	✓	✓	✓	✓	✓	x	x	✓	✓	✓	✓	✓	✓
ct_dst_ltm	✓	✓	✓	x	x	x	x	x	x	x	x	x	x	x
ct_src_ltm	✓	✓	✓	✓	x	x	x	x	x	x	x	x	x	x
ct_src_dport_ltm	✓	✓	✓	x	x	x	x	x	✓	x	x	x	x	x
ct_dst_sport_ltm	✓	✓	✓	x	x	✓	x	x	✓	x	x	✓	x	x
ct_dst_src_ltm	✓	✓	✓	x	x	x	x	x	x	x	x	x	x	✓
attack_cat	✓	✓	✓	x	x	x	x	x	x	x	x	x	x	x

✓ = Selected, x = Removed

Table 9. Selected and removed features from the Kyoto 2006+ dataset according to each of the fourteen feature-selection methods.

Feature name	Feature selection methods													
	COF	QCF	DUF	CRF	STR	STF	STB	EXH	LAR	RGC	TIM	FES	RFE	RFA
duration	✓	✓	✓	✓	✓	✓	✓	x	x	✓	x	✓	x	✓
service	✓	✓	✓	✓	✓	x	✓	✓	✓	✓	✓	✓	✓	✓
source_bytes	✓	✓	✓	✓	✓	✓	✓	✓	x	✓	x	✓	✓	✓
destination_bytes	✓	✓	✓	✓	✓	x	✓	✓	x	✓	✓	✓	✓	✓
count	✓	✓	✓	✓	✓	✓	✓	x	x	✓	✓	✓	x	✓
same_srv_rate	✓	✓	✓	✓	x	✓	✓	x	x	✓	x	✓	x	x
serror_rate	✓	✓	✓	✓	x	✓	x	x	x	✓	x	x	x	x
srv_serror_rate	✓	✓	✓	✓	x	x	✓	x	✓	✓	✓	✓	x	x
dst_host_count	✓	✓	✓	x	✓	✓	✓	✓	✓	✓	✓	✓	x	x
dst_host_srv_count	✓	✓	✓	✓	✓	x	x	x	✓	✓	x	✓	x	x
dst_host_same_src_port_rate	✓	x	✓	✓	x	x	✓	x	x	✓	x	✓	x	x
dst_host_serror_rate	✓	✓	✓	x	✓	✓	x	x	x	✓	x	✓	x	x
dst_host_srv_serror_rate	✓	✓	✓	✓	✓	x	✓	x	x	x	x	x	x	x
flag	✓	✓	✓	✓	✓	x	x	x	✓	x	x	✓	x	x
IDS_detection	✓	✓	✓	✓	x	✓	✓	✓	x	x	x	✓	x	x
malware_detection	✓	✓	x	✓	x	✓	x	x	x	x	x	x	x	x
ashula_detection	✓	✓	x	✓	x	✓	✓	✓	x	x	x	x	x	x
source_ip_address	✓	✓	✓	✓	✓	✓	✓	✓	x	x	✓	✓	✓	✓
source_port_number	✓	✓	✓	✓	✓	x	x	x	✓	✓	x	✓	x	x
destination_ip_address	✓	✓	✓	✓	✓	✓	✓	✓	x	x	✓	✓	✓	✓
destination_port_number	✓	✓	✓	✓	✓	✓	x	x	✓	✓	x	✓	✓	✓
start_time	✓	✓	✓	✓	x	✓	x	✓	x	x	x	x	x	x
protocol	✓	✓	✓	✓	✓	✓	✓	✓	✓	x	x	x	x	✓

✓ = Selected, x = Removed

Table 10. Selected and removed features from the DoHBrw-2020 dataset according to each of the fourteen feature-selection methods.

Feature name	Feature selection methods													
	COF	QCF	DUF	CRF	STR	STF	STB	EXH	LAR	RGC	TIM	FES	RFE	RFA
SourceIP	✓	✓	✓	✓	✓	✓	✓	✓	✓	✓	✓	✓	x	✓
DestinationIP	✓	✓	✓	✓	✓	✓	✓	✓	x	✓	✓	✓	x	x
SourcePort	✓	✓	✓	x	x	✓	✓	✓	x	✓	✓	✓	✓	✓
DestinationPort	✓	✓	✓	✓	x	x	x	✓	x	x	x	✓	✓	✓
TimeStamp	✓	✓	✓	✓	✓	✓	✓	✓	✓	✓	✓	✓	✓	✓
Duration	✓	✓	✓	x	✓	✓	✓	✓	✓	✓	✓	x	x	x
FlowBytesSent	✓	✓	✓	x	✓	✓	✓	✓	x	x	x	x	x	x
FlowSentRate	✓	✓	✓	x	x	✓	✓	✓	x	x	x	✓	x	x
FlowBytesReceived	✓	✓	✓	✓	✓	x	x	x	✓	✓	x	✓	x	x
FlowReceivedRate	✓	✓	✓	✓	x	x	x	x	x	x	x	✓	x	x
PacketLengthVariance	✓	✓	✓	x	✓	✓	✓	✓	x	x	x	✓	x	x
PacketLengthStandardDeviation	✓	✓	✓	x	✓	x	x	x	x	x	x	✓	x	x
PacketLengthMean	✓	✓	✓	✓	✓	✓	x	x	x	✓	✓	x	x	x
PacketLengthMedian	✓	✓	✓	✓	✓	✓	✓	✓	x	x	x	✓	x	x
PacketLengthMode	✓	✓	✓	✓	✓	✓	✓	x	✓	✓	✓	✓	x	x
PacketLengthSkewFromMedian	✓	✓	✓	x	x	✓	✓	✓	x	x	x	✓	x	x
PacketLengthSkewFromMode	✓	✓	✓	✓	✓	x	x	✓	x	x	x	✓	x	x
PacketLengthCoefficientofVariation	x	x	✓	✓	✓	x	x	x	x	x	x	x	x	x
PacketTimeVariance	✓	✓	✓	x	✓	x	x	x	x	x	x	✓	x	x

(continued)

Table 10. (*continued*)

Feature name	Feature selection methods													
	COF	QCF	DUF	CRF	STR	STF	STB	EXH	LAR	RGC	TIM	FES	RFE	RFA
PacketTimeStandardDeviation	✓	✓	✓	x	✓	x	x	x	x	x	x	x	x	x
PacketTimeMean	✓	✓	✓	x	x	x	x	x	✓	✓	x	x	x	x
PacketTimeMedian	✓	✓	✓	✓	x	x	x	x	x	x	x	x	x	x
PacketTimeMode	✓	✓	x	✓	x	✓	✓	✓	x	x	x	✓	✓	✓
PacketTimeSkewFromMedian	✓	✓	✓	✓	x	✓	✓	✓	x	x	x	x	x	x
PacketTimeSkewFromMode	x	x	✓	✓	x	x	✓	✓	x	x	x	x	x	x
PacketTimeCoefficientofVariation	x	x	✓	✓	x	x	x	x	x	x	x	x	x	x
ResponseTimeTimeVariance	✓	✓	✓	x	x	x	x	x	x	x	x	x	x	x
RespTimeTimeStandardDeviation	✓	✓	✓	✓	x	x	x	x	x	✓	✓	x	x	x
RespTimeTimeMean	✓	✓	✓	x	x	x	x	x	x	x	x	x	x	x
RespTimeTimeMedian	✓	✓	✓	✓	x	x	x	x	x	x	x	x	x	x
RespTimeTimeMode	✓	✓	✓	✓	x	x	x	x	x	x	x	x	x	x
RespTimeTimeSkewFromMedian	✓	✓	✓	✓	x	x	x	x	✓	✓	x	x	x	x
RespTimeTimeSkewFromMode	✓	✓	✓	✓	x	x	x	x	x	x	x	x	x	x
RespTimeTimeCoefficientofVariation	✓	✓	✓	✓	x	x	x	x	x	x	x	x	x	x

✓ = Selected, x = Removed

References

1. Salem, A., Tang, J., Liu, H.: Feature selection for clustering: a review. In: Data Clustering: Algorithms and Applications, pp. 29–60. CRC Press (2013)
2. Aha, D., Kibler, D., Albert, M.: Instance-based learning algorithms. Mach. Learn. **6**(1), 37–66 (1991)
3. Ahmed, M., Mahmood, A., Hu, J.: A survey of network anomaly detection techniques. J. Netw. Comput. Appl. **60**, 19–31 (2016)
4. Alazab, A., Hobbs, M., Abawajy, J., Alazab, M.: Using feature selection for intrusion detection system. In: ISCIT, pp. 296–301. IEEE (2012)
5. Avila, R., Khoury, R., Khoury, R., Petrillo, F.: Use of security logs for data leak detection: a systematic literature review. Secur. Commun. Netw. **2021**(1), 29 (2021)
6. Binbusayyis, A., Vaiyapuri, T.: Identifying and benchmarking key features for cyber intrusion detection: an ensemble approach. IEEE Access **7**, 106495–106513 (2019)
7. Buczak, A.L., Guven, E.: A survey of data mining and machine learning methods for cyber security intrusion detection. IEEE Commun. Surv. Tutor. **18**, 1153–1176 (2016)
8. Jie, G.: An effective intrusion detection model based on pls-logistic regression with feature augmentation. Cyber Secur. **1**(1), 133–140 (2020)
9. Hajisalem, V., Babaie, S.: A hybrid intrusion detection system based on ABC-AFS algorithm for misuse and anomaly detection. Comput. Netw. **136**, 37–50 (2018)
10. Harish, B.S., Revanasiddappa, M.B.: A comprehensive survey on various feature selection methods to categorize text documents. Int. J. Comput. Appl. **164**, 1–7 (2017)
11. Idhammad, M., Afdel, K., Belouch, M.: Semi-supervised machine learning approach for DDoS detection. Appl. Intell. **48**(10), 3193–3208 (2018)
12. Iglesias, F., Zseby, T.: Analysis of network traffic features for anomaly detection. Mach. Learn. **101**(1–3), 59–84 (2015)
13. Janarthanan, T., Zargari, S.: Feature selection in UNSW-NB15 and KDDCUP'99 datasets. In: ISIE, pp. 1881–1886. IEEE (2017)

14. Koushal, K., Jaspreet, S.: Network intrusion detection with feature selection techniques using machine-learning algorithms. Int. J. Comput. Appl. **150**(12), 1–13 (2016)
15. Li, J., et al.: Feature selection: a data perspective. ACM Comput. Surv. **50**(6), 45 (2017)
16. Liao, H.-J., Lin, C.-H.R., Lin, Y.-C., Tung, K.-Y.: Intrusion detection system: a comprehensive review. J. Netw. Comput. Appl. **36**(1), 8 (2013)
17. Pham, N.T., Foo, E., Suriadi, S., Jeffrey, H., Lahza, H.: Improving performance of intrusion detection system using ensemble methods and feature selection. In: ACSW, pp. 2:1–2:6. ACM (2018)
18. Poggio, T., Mhaskar, H., Rosasco, L., Miranda, B., Liao, Q.: Why and when can deep-but not shallow-networks avoid the curse of dimensionality: a review. Int. J. Autom. Comput. **14**(5), 16 (2017)
19. Prasad, M., Tripathi, S., Dahal, K.P.: An efficient feature selection based Bayesian and rough set approach for intrusion detection. Appl. Soft Comput. **87**, 12 (2020)
20. Sharma, M., Kaur, P.: A comprehensive analysis of nature-inspired meta-heuristic techniques for feature selection problem. Arch. Comput. Methods Eng. **1**(25), 1103–1127 (2021)
21. Sheikhpour, R., Sarram, M.A., Gharaghani, S., Chahooki, M.Z.: A survey on semi-supervised feature selection methods. Pattern Recognit. **64**, 141–158 (2017)
22. Sy, B.K.: Signature-based approach for intrusion detection. In: Perner, P., Imiya, A. (eds.) MLDM 2005. LNCS (LNAI), vol. 3587, pp. 526–536. Springer, Heidelberg (2005). https://doi.org/10.1007/11510888_52
23. Tian, S., Yu, J., Yin, C.: Anomaly detection using support vector machines. In: Yin, F.-L., Wang, J., Guo, C. (eds.) ISNN 2004. LNCS, vol. 3173, pp. 592–597. Springer, Heidelberg (2004). https://doi.org/10.1007/978-3-540-28647-9_97
24. Venkatesh, B., Anuradha, J.: A review of feature selection and its methods. Cybern. Inf. Technol. **19**, 26 (2017)
25. Wang, Y.: A multinomial logistic regression modeling approach for anomaly intrusion detection. Comput. Secur. **24**(8), 662–674 (2005)
26. Xue, B., Zhang, M., Browne, W.N., Yao, X.: A survey on evolutionary computation approaches to feature selection. IEEE Trans. Evol. Comput. **20**(4), 606–626 (2016)
27. Yang, Y., McLaughlin, K., Sezer, S., Yuan, Y.B., Huang, W.: Stateful intrusion detection for IEC 60870-5-104 SCADA security. In: 2014 IEEE PES General Meeting, vol. 1, p. 5 (2014)

Implementation of Lightweight Ciphers and Their Integration into Entity Authentication with IEEE 802.11 Physical Layer Transmission

Yunjie Yi[1], Kalikinkar Mandal[2(✉)], and Guang Gong[1]

[1] Department of Electrical and Computer Engineering, University of Waterloo,
Waterloo, ON N2L 3G1, Canada
{y22yi,ggong}@uwaterloo.ca
[2] Faculty of Computer Science, University of New Brunswick, Fredericton, Canada
kmandal@unb.ca

Abstract. This paper investigates the performance of three lightweight authenticated ciphers namely ACE, SPIX and WAGE in the WiFi and CoAP handshaking authentication protocols. We implement the WiFi and CoAP handshake protocols and the IEEE802.11a physical layer communication protocol in software defined radio (SDR) and embed these two handshaking protocols into the IEEE802.11a OFDM communication protocol to measure the performance of three ciphers. We present the construction of KDF and MIC used in the handshaking authentication protocols and provide optimized implementations of ACE, SPIX and WAGE including KDF and MIC on three different (low-power) microcontrollers. The performance results of these three ciphers when adopted in WiFi and CoAP protocols are presented. Our experimental results show that the cryptographic functionalities are the bottleneck in the handshaking and data protection protocols.

Keywords: Internet of Things (IoT) · Security and privacy ·
Lightweight cryptography · Microcontroller implementation ·
Authentication protocol · IEEE 802.11a OFDM transmission ·
Software defined radio

1 Introduction

The rapid growth of the Internet of Things (IoT) penetrates our daily life deeply and poses extraordinary effects on us. The IoT connects a wide range of devices, spanning from tiny smart devices to computers and servers. Most of those IoT devices such as sensors, actuators and radio frequency identification (RFID) tags are wirelessly connected through Internet, bluetooth, vehicular ad-hoc

---

Yunjie Yi is now with Huawei Canada, Waterloo and the work was done when he was with University of Waterloo.

© Springer Nature Switzerland AG 2022
E. Aïmeur et al. (Eds.): FPS 2021, LNCS 13291, pp. 113–129, 2022.
https://doi.org/10.1007/978-3-031-08147-7_8

networks (VANETs) and equipped with microcontrollers and radio frequency (RF) transceivers. They communicate with each others to collect various types of data from applications such as industrial and building control, e-health (e.g., medical devices embedded in our body or skin), smart home (e.g., lights, TV, thermostats, cameras, washing machines, dryers, and refrigerators), smart grid, self-driving cars, and other embedded systems.

As an IoT system consists of heterogeneous devices, the devices are connected through different types of wireless communication protocols. The major organizations such as IEEE and Internet Research Task Force (IRTF) for standardizing communication and security protocols have moved to support IoT systems. The newly amended IEEE 802.11ax for WiFi systems targets to support established frequency bands with low power and low complexity operations, meaning it may support the access point (AP) to interact with the client device (and vice versa) at data rates as low as 375 Kbps [15,17]. On the other hand, new lightweight protocol standards such as MQTT [24] and CoAP [29] and MAC protocols [18,27] for tiny IoT devices are developed while considering the factors such as limited resources, communication patterns, and interoperability. Recently several protocols and key generation techniques have been developed [19,20,26]. In [20], a lightweight secure transport protocol is proposed which provides implicit mutual authentication. In [19], a lightweight authentication with key agreement protocol is developed for smart wearable devices. A key generation technique for symmetric-key ciphers is proposed based on the channel feature for smart home applications [26]. The upcoming cellular 5G system aims to enable IoT for connecting a growing number of cars, meters, machinery sensors, etc. [1,4].

Recently, the National Institute of Standards and Technology (NIST) has initiated the lightweight cryptography (LWC) competition to standardize cryptographic algorithm(s) for providing security in resource-constrained environments in the applications of healthcare, Internet of Things, cyber physical systems, and distributed control systems [9]. As a response to the call for proposals, there are 56 submissions received as round 1 candidates in February 2019, and out of 56 candidates, 32 candidates are selected as round 2 candidates in August 2019 [9], and 10 finalists are announced in March 2021 [10]. Investigating the performance of such lightweight cryptographic algorithms as cipher suits in different IoT protocols such as WiFi and CoAP running on different IoT devices are important to understand the suitability of such ciphers in the mutual authentication protocols.

Microcontrollers are a key computing element in IoT. The devices and sensors are equipped with microcontrollers with limited memory, power and processing speed. Microcontrollers essentially perform all computations including the security algorithms. As commercial WiFi-enabled devices do not allow developers to implement new algorithms using their APIs, we are unable to leverage existing communication protocols due to the closed platform. One way of implementing an OFDM communication system is using software defined radio [8,12]. In this work, we implement the IEEE 802.11a orthogonal frequency-division multiplexing (OFDM) communication protocol using the GNU radio and USRPs and cryptographic algorithms in microcontrollers to measure the performance of new lightweight cryptographic algorithms. The goal of this paper is to investigate the performance of three NIST LWC round 2 candidates namely ACE, SPIX and WAGE in the WiFi and CoAP handshaking mutual authentication and key agreement protocols. Our contributions in this paper are summarized as follows.

(a) **Implementation of three lightweight ciphers and their induced KDF and MIC.** We present optimized implementations of three LWC schemes, namely ACE [2], SPIX [5] and WAGE [3] on three different (low-power) microcontrollers (8/16/32-bits). We propose a construction of a key derivation function (KDF) and a message integrity check (MIC) generation function along with their implementations on microcontrollers. Our implementations are written in the assembly language and exploit microcontroller resources to achieve a better speed up.

(b) **Implementing WiFi and the CoAP handshaking authentication in SDR.** We implement the WiFi transportation layer security protocol and the CoAP UDP security protocol using three LWC ciphers, and the IEEE802.11a physical layer communication protocol in SDR in real-time, and embed these two security protocols into the IEEE802.11a communication protocol.

(c) **Experimental evaluation and comparison.** We benchmark the performances of three core permutations, their KDF and MIC, and present the results for handshaking and data protection protocols on three microcontrollers ATmega128, MSP430 and Cortex-M3. Our experimental results show that ACE, SPIX and WAGE take about 2,966 ms, 2,831 ms, and 2,808 ms, respectively to complete the IEEE802.11X authentication protocol using Cortex-M3. In the data protection protocol, ACE, SPIX and WAGE achieve a throughput of 109 Kbits/s, 63 Kbits/s, and 53 Kbits/s, respectively on Cortex-M3 to encrypt and authenticate a plaintext of 1024 bits and an associated data of 128-bits. Our experimental results show that the cryptographic operations are the dominating factors for authentication and data protection protocols.

2 Preliminaries

In this section, we provide brief backgrounds on three lightweight authenticated encryption schemes, IEEE 802.11X handshake and data protection protocols, and CoAP protocol. For the details on IEEE 802.11a OFDM standard and software defined radio, we refer the reader to the full version of this paper [28].

2.1 Three Lightweight Authenticated Encryption Schemes

We consider three lightweight authenticated encryption with associated data (AEAD) schemes, namely ACE, SPIX and WAGE, which are round 2 candidates in the NIST lightweight cryptography competition [9].

- ACE is a lightweight AEAD and hash scheme which operates in the unified sponge duplex mode [2] to offer both functionalities. At the core of ACE is a lightweight permutation of width 320 bits built upon bitwise XORs and ANDs, left cyclic shifts and 64-bit word shuffles. ACE provides a 128-bit security for both AE and hash functionalities.

– SPIX is a lightweight AEAD scheme which operates in the unified sponge duplex mode [5] built upon the sLiSCP-light permutation of width 256 bits [6]. It offers a security level of 128 bits.
– WAGE is a lightweight AEAD scheme which also operates in the unified sponge duplex mode [3]. The construction of the WAGE permutation is based on a Galois-style nonlinear feedback shift register (NLFSR) over the finite field $\mathbb{F}_{2^7}$. It accepts a key and a nonce of size 128 bits and offers a 128-bit security.

For the details about the ciphers and their modes, the reader is referred to [2,3,5]. Table 1 lists the parameters for AEAD for these three schemes. The length of each parameter is given in bits and d denotes the amount of processed data (including both associated data (AD), for authentication only, and message (M) for both encryption and authentication) before a re-keying is done. n denotes the internal state size of the permutation, k denotes the key size, r denotes the rate in the sponge mode, and t denotes the size of the authentication tag. For each execution of an AEAD algorithm, it processes $r\ell_{AD}$ bits of AD data and $r\ell_M$ bits of plaintext (the padding is applied if AD/M is not a multiple of r).

Table 1. Parameters for ACE, SPIX and WAGE

Algorithm	State	Rate	Key	Tag	Data
	n	r	k	t	$\log_2(d)$
ACE	320	64	128	128	124
SPIX	256	64	128	128	60
WAGE	259	64	128	128	60

2.2   IEEE 802.11i: IEEE 802.11X 4-Way Handshake and Data Protection

In IEEE 802.11X, it is specified that the wireless network consists of supplicants (clients) which wish to be connected to the network, and an access point (or authenticator/server) in the IEEE 802.11X and extensible authentication protocol (EAP) [14,25]. The supplicant and the access point share a pairwise master key (PMK) ahead of time. The IEEE 802.11 security solution is specified in the IEEE802.11i amendment. To join a network, the device or supplicant executes the 4-way handshake protocol with the authenticator to establish a fresh session key, followed by installing the key. Once the key is installed, it is used to encrypt and authenticate traffic data frames using the data protection algorithm. These two phases are summarized as follows:

(a) **4-way handshake protocol**: This process conducts a mutual entity authentication and generates the session keys. The 4-way handshake protocol first generates a pairwise transient key (PTK) from the pre-shared pairwise master key PMK, and then conducts a challenge-response protocol for mutual authentication.

(b) **Data protection:** After a successful execution of the 4-way handshake protocol, the data protection is performed using either CCMP (AES in counter mode for encryption and CBC MAC for integrity check and message authentication) or GCMP (AES in counter mode for encryption and polynomial hash for generating a MAC).

The WiFi data field contains identifiers, key information, replay counter, nonce, initial vector, message integrity code (MIC), and transported data. For the details of the protocol and a diagram, the reader is referred to the full version of the paper [28].

PKT and MIC Generation in 4-Way Handshake. The pairwise transit key (PTK) is generated as follows

$$PTK = \text{KDF}(PMK, ANonce||SNonce||\text{AP MAC adr}||\text{STA MAC adr})$$
$$= KCK||KEK||TK$$

where KDF is a key derivation function, the nonces namely $ANonce$ and $SNonce$ are 128 bits. The first 128-bit in PTK is the key confirmation key (KCK) that is used to generate a MIC over the message, the second 128-bit is the key encryption key (KEK) that is used for encrypting the group key, and the last segment is the temporal key (TK) used for protecting traffic data where the length depends on a cipher suite selected.

$$MIC_A = \text{MIC}(KCK, ANonce, RC); MIC_S = \text{MIC}(KCK, SNonce, RC)$$
$$MIC_{all} = \text{MIC}(KCK, D, RC + 1)$$

where RC is a replay counter of 128 bits (see [13]), and D carries the cipher suite of 128 bits.

2.3 CoAP: DTLS Handshake and Data Protection Protocols

The Constrained Application Protocol (CoAP) enables an efficient transmission of information for resource-limited devices [29]. The security in CoAP is provided using Datagram TLS (DTLS) over the user datagram protocol (UDP). See the full version of the paper [28] for the message flow of the protocol when a server authenticates an IoT client device in an IoT network. There are four security modes available in CoAP, namely NoSec, PresharedKey, RawPublicKey and Certificates [22,29]. NoSec means the security is not provided in the CoAP message transmission. PresharedKey mode is used for symmetric-key algorithms for authentication and message protection. RawPublicKey mode is used for the public-key algorithms without certificate, and the devices are programmed with a list of pre-installed keys. Certificates mode provides authentication based on the X.509 public-key certificate.

Note that both Certificates and RawPublicKey use elliptic curve (EC) based public key cryptography, and PresharedKey uses TLS-PSK based on symmetric-key algorithms with the cipher suit TLS-PSK-WITH-AES128-CCM-8 for authentication. Certificates mode uses the cipher suit TLS-ECDHE-ECDSA-WITH-AES-128-CCM-8 with X.509 certificate. RawPublicKey mode uses the cipher suit TLS-ECDHE-ECDSA-WITH-AES-128-CCM-8.

In our work, we consider only the PresharedKey mode for authentication. Note that *ClientHello* contains the client's version number ($ver._C$), client random nonce ($Nonce_C$), session ID (ID_C), cipher suit ($Ciphersuit_C$) and compression method ($Compress_C$) [16]. Similarly, for the server, *ServerHello* contains the server's nonce ($Nonce_S$), session ID (ID_S), cipher suit ($Ciphersuit_S$), and compression method ($Compress_S$). Like IEEE 802.11X, the client and server share a pairwise master key (PMK). To joint the network, the device executes the 6-way handshaking with the server to establish a fresh session key, followed by installing the key (TK) after the 6-th round of the handshake. After that, the device uses the installed key to encrypt and authenticate traffic data frames using the protection algorithms. We summarize these two phases below:

(a) **CoAP 6-way handshake protocol:** This conducts the mutual entity authentication and generation of session keys.
(b) **Data protection:** After a successfully handshaking, the data protection algorithm, which is AES128 in counter mode with CBC-MAC and 8-octet Integrity Check Value (ICV), is applied to secure the traffic.

Similar to IEEE 802.11X, the 6-way handshake generates a pairwise transient key (PTK) from PMK, and conducts a challenge-response protocol for mutual authentication. The PTK and MIC generation are similar to that of IEEE 802.11X, except the following

$$PTK = \texttt{KDF}(PMK, ClientHello||ServerHello) = KCK||KEK||TK$$

where KDF is a key derivation function. We omit the MIC generations for CoAP as it is similar to the one in Sect. 2.2.

3   Construction and Implementation of KDF and MIC in CoAP and IEEE 802.11i

3.1   ACE, SPIX, and WAGE as Cipher Suites in CoAP and IEEE 802.11i Protocols

In IEEE 802.11X 4-way and CoAP 6-way handshake protocols, the key derivation function (KDF) and message integrity check (MIC) are two fundamental cryptographic functionalities for authentication. The data protection protocol requires an AEAD algorithm for encryption and tag generation to protect the traffic. Our idea is to use a single cryptographic primitive (e.g., AEAD) to serve all cryptographic functionalities required in the handshake and data protection protocols. We now show how to construct KDF and MIC algorithms from the ACE, SPIX, and WAGE AEAD schemes. Let $\mathcal{F}$ be the underlying permutation instantiating an AEAD scheme where $\mathcal{F} \in \{\text{ACE}, \text{SPIX}, \text{WAGE}\}$. As all three ciphers operate in the sponge duplex mode [7,11] with different permutations of different widths and the rate for absorbing messages are the same, we provide a generic construction that works for $\mathcal{F} \in \{\text{ACE}, \text{SPIX}, \text{WAGE}\}$.

Constructing KDF. We now show how to configure a sponge-based AEAD as a key derivation function in both handshake protocols. As an AEAD scheme has three phases, we use only the initialization and encryption phases to construct a KDF, but with a subtle difference that for each key type KCK, KEK or TK, we use different domain separation values.

Construction 1 (Key Derivation Function) *Let $S = (S_r, S_c)$ be the state of the permutation $\mathcal{F} \in \{\text{ACE}, \text{SPIX}, \text{WAGE}\}$ where S_r with $|S_r| = r$ and S_c with $|S_c| = c$ denote the rate part and capacity part of the state, respectively, and $n = r+c$ denotes the state size. Let M^C and M^S be the inputs of length 256 bits from the client (or supplicant) and server (or access point) in KDF to derive session keys using PMK. Let $M^C = M_0^C \| M_1^C \| M_2^C \| M_3^C$ and $M^S = M_0^S \| M_1^S \| M_2^S \| M_3^S$ where $|M_i^C| = |M_i^S| = r = 64$. Then the key derivation function to derive $PTK = KCK \| KEK \| TK$ is defined below.*

Loading master key:	**Outputting $KEK = KEK_0 \| KEK_1$:**
1: $S \leftarrow load(M_0^S \| M_0^C, PMK)$	11: $KEK_0 \leftarrow S_r \oplus M_2^S$;
2: $S \leftarrow \mathcal{F}(S)$	12: $S \leftarrow (KEK_0, S_c \oplus (0^{c-2}\|10))$
Absorbing key:	13: $S \leftarrow \mathcal{F}(S)$
3: $S \leftarrow (S_r \oplus PMK_0, S_c); S \leftarrow \mathcal{F}(S)$	14: $KEK_1 \leftarrow S_r \oplus M_3^S$;
4: $S \leftarrow (S_r \oplus PMK_1, S_c); S \leftarrow \mathcal{F}(S)$	15: $S \leftarrow (KEK_1, S_c \oplus (0^{c-2}\|10))$
Outputting $KCK = KCK_0 \| KCK_1$:	16: $S \leftarrow \mathcal{F}(S)$
5: $KCK_0 \leftarrow S_r \oplus M_1^S$;	**Outputting $TK = TK_0 \| TK_1$:**
6: $S \leftarrow (KCK_0, S_c \oplus (0^{c-2}\|01))$;	17: $TK_0 \leftarrow S_r \oplus M_2^C$;
7: $S \leftarrow \mathcal{F}(S)$	18: $S \leftarrow (TK_0, S_c \oplus (0^{c-2}\|11))$;
8: $KCK_1 \leftarrow S_r \oplus M_1^C$;	19: $S \leftarrow \mathcal{F}(S)$;
9: $S \leftarrow (KCK_1, S_c \oplus (0^{c-2}\|01))$	20: $TK_1 \leftarrow S_r \oplus M_3^C$
10: $S \leftarrow \mathcal{F}(S)$	

Note that the size of the capacity part depends on $\mathcal{F}$. In practice, the MAC address of a device is a 48-bit number. However, we convert it into a 128-bit number by applying the padding 1 followed by 79 zeros (i.e., 10^{79}). The reason for making the length of MAC addresses is due to the output length of PTK.

Constructing MIC. Our idea for adopting a sponge-based AEAD scheme to construct a MIC is by computing a tag on a non-empty associated data and an empty plaintext (with no padding). Note that in the IEEE 802.11X 4-way and CoAP 6-way handshake protocols, the session key KCK is used to generate three MICs on $ANonce(ServerHello)$, $SNonce(ClientHello)$ and D fields. Below we provide a construction of a MIC based on an AEAD scheme.

Construction 2 (Message Integrity Code). *Let $CTR = CTR_0 \| CTR_1$ be a counter and $M = M_0 \| \cdots \| M_{\ell-1}$ be a message of ℓ blocks after padding. Following the notations in Construction 1, the message integrity code on M and CTR is constructed as follows.*

Loading and absorbing KCK:
1: $S \leftarrow load(CTR, KCK); S \leftarrow \mathcal{F}(S)$
2: $S \leftarrow (S_r \oplus KCK_0, S_c); S \leftarrow \mathcal{F}(S)$
3: $S \leftarrow (S_r \oplus KCK_1, S_c); S \leftarrow \mathcal{F}(S)$
Absorbing M: For $i = 0 \cdots \ell - 1$
4: $S \leftarrow (S_r \oplus M_i, S_c \oplus (0^{c-2} \| 01)); S \leftarrow \mathcal{F}(S)$

Absorbing KCK again:
5: $S \leftarrow (S_r \oplus KCK_0, S_c)); S \leftarrow \mathcal{F}(S)$
6: $S \leftarrow (S_r \oplus KCK_1, S_c); S \leftarrow \mathcal{F}(S)$
Outputting MIC:
7: $MIC \leftarrow tagextract(S)$

For example, in IEEE 802.11X, while generating MIC_A, $M = ANonce$ and $CTR = RC$, while generating MIC_S, $M = SNonce$ and $CTR = RC$, and while generating MIC_{all}, $M = D$ and $CTR = RC + 1$ for the above construction.

Security and Efficiency. Intuitively, the security of Constructions 1 and 2 relies on the security of the AEAD algorithm. Following the parameters and security of ACE, SPIX and WAGE, the security of both KDF and MIC is 128 bits [2,3,5]. The efficiency of both KDF and MIC is measured by the number of permutation calls required to complete the functionality. As the rate r is 64, the KDF in Construction 1 needs *eight* calls to the permutation as it outputs three session keys and each of length 128 bits. On the other hand, the MIC in Construction 2 needs *($\ell+5$)* calls to the permutation as the initialization and finalization needs five calls and absorbing the message needs ℓ calls.

3.2 Optimized Microcontroller Implementations of ACE, SPIX and WAGE

This subsection presents the details about the microcontroller platforms and the implementations of three ciphers.

Microcontroller Platform. We implement ACE, SPIX, and WAGE and corresponding KDF and MIC algorithms described in Sect. 3.1 in assembly on three different microcontrollers, namely 8-bit Atmega128, 16-bit MSP430F2013/2370 and 32-bit Cortex-M3LM3S9D96. The IAR embedded workbenches for MSP430 and Cortex-M3 and the Atmel Studio 7.0 for Atmega128 have been used to import the codes into microcontrollers and to calculate the number of clock cycles and the execution time for the AEAD, KDF and MIC algorithms. See the full paper [28] for the resources such as the flash memory size, the RAM size and the number of general-purpose registers available on three microcontrollers. The throughput, denoted by η, is calculated as $\eta = \frac{m \times f}{C}$ where m is the length of the message, f is the CPU frequency and C is the total number of clock cycles. The CPU frequency for all three microcontrollers used in our experiment is 16 MHz. We report the memory usage, the number of clock cycles from the IAR embedded workbenches and the Atmel Studio in the debug mode.

SPIX and ACE. In our implementation, we target to achieve the highest throughput. For the 8-bit Atmega128 implementation, the state of the SPIX permutation is stored in registers so that we can avoid data exchange between the memory and registers while executing the round function of the permutation. On the other hand, for the 16-bit and 32-bit microcontroller implementations, the states of SPIX and ACE are stored into the memory due to not having available registers to entirely store the state. While executing the permutation, the partial state is stored into registers and then after partial state update, it is again stored back to the memory. The most expensive operation is shifting state words, so that the method above saves clock cycles by managing the position of the state instead of shifting the contents of the state. Note that the ACE permutation requires more registers than that of the SPIX permutation due to the larger state size.

WAGE. For the 16-bit implementation of WAGE, we use the microcontroller MSP430F2370, instead of MSP430F2013, due to a larger memory space to save the round constants. The design of the WAGE permutation is based on a shift register which requires shifting the entire state for each execution of the round function, which consumes 36 shift operations in each iteration. Instead of loading the state of 259 bits into registers, the state is contiguously stored in the RAM. To execute the permutation, we extract the corresponding 7-bit words from the RAM into registers and apply the permutation operations such as lookup table and bitwise XOR operations. After computing the feedback, the updated value is stored next to the memory location of the current state. In this way, for each iteration we allocate a new memory byte, which results in $148 \ (= 37 + 111)$ bytes for 111 rounds of the WAGE permutation.

The absolute locations of those extracted content in the RAM are not fixed but the relative locations to the first byte of the 259 bits are fixed. Therefore, we only need the initial memory location of the first byte of the 259 bits, which is the same for each round, denoted as init, the integer numbers of the relative locations, denoted as set λ, and an integer variable init to record the current round number. Then, the current locations of the extracted contents will be the set $\{\text{init} + \text{init} + t \,|\, t \in \lambda\}$. After finishing 111 rounds, we set init $= 0$ and copy the final state to the initial state location in the RAM. Then, we proceed to the next evaluation of the WAGE permutation.

4 Implementation of OFDM System, IEEE 802.11X and CoAP in SDR

We implement the OFDM system in the GNU software defined radio (SDR). In our implementation, the OFDM system consists of an OFDM sender, an OFDM receiver, and the GNU radio companion. Figure 1 provides our experimental setup for the OFDM system. We now describe the implementation details of the OFDM sender and the OFDM receiver.

4.1 Experimental Setup for OFDM Sender and Receiver

IEEE 802.11a OFDM Sender. Figure 2 shows an overview of the OFDM sender. The file-source block in the GNU radio is used to output bytes from a binary file to its next block, and it is set to repeatedly sending the message bit stream automatically during each test. Each 96 bytes from the file-source block will be tagged in the stream-to-tagged-stream block. After that, the following blocks will manipulate each 96 message bytes at a time. For example, the packet-header-generator block generates 48 header bytes for each tagged message which is the tagged 96-byte.

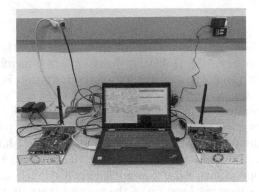

Fig. 1. Experimental setup of software defined radio

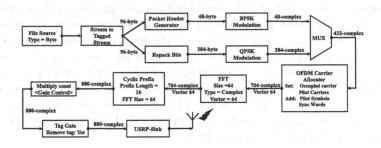

Fig. 2. A block diagram of the OFDM sender

The repack-bits block in Fig. 2 operates 1-byte at a time. We denote a 1-byte input as $\mathbf{a} = (a_0, a_1, a_2, a_3, a_4, a_5, a_6, a_7)$. The repack-bits block converts $\mathbf{a}$ to $\mathbf{d} = (d_0, d_1, d_2, d_3)$ by converting each 2-bit (a_{2i}, a_{2i+1}) to a decimal number d_i. After that, each decimal number is converted to a byte $\mathbf{b}$ which is $\mathbf{b} = (b_0, b_1, b_2, b_3)$. The output of the repack-bits block is $\mathbf{b} = (b_3, b_2, b_1, b_0)$ which is in the endianness of LSB. Comparing the input $\mathbf{a}$ with the output $\mathbf{b}$, it indicates that each input byte corresponds to four output bytes, which explains that each 96-byte input has 384 bytes for the repack-bits block in Fig. 2.

The BPSK-modulation block also converts each byte to an 8-byte complex number. More specifically, it maps the tuple of bytes $(00, 01)_{hex}$ to complex numbers $((-1, 0), (1, 0))_{decimal}$. Similarly, the QPSK-modulation block converts each byte input into a complex number. It maps the input bytes $(00, 01, 02, 03)_{hex}$ to output complex numbers $((-1/\sqrt{2}, -1/\sqrt{2}), (1/\sqrt{2}, -1/\sqrt{2}), (-1/\sqrt{2}, 1/\sqrt{2}), (1/\sqrt{2}, 1/\sqrt{2}))_{decimal}$, respectively.

The MUX block is used to combine each 48-complex header and 384-complex payload at a time. Therefore, the output of the MUX block is 432 complex numbers in total, and is sent to the OFDM-carrier-allocator block, which is described as follows.

The OFDM-carrier-allocator block maps the stream of 432 complex numbers into 11 complex vectors, which are shown in Fig. 3. The complex vectors are labeled as M_i for $i = 1, 2, \ldots, 11$, and each vector contains 64 complex numbers as 64 subcarriers, where M_1 and M_2 are two synchronization words. Additionally, each header prime and each message prime in Fig. 3 come from the header and message data after inserted 4 pilot carriers and 0 DC subcarrier. Namely, the pilot complex numbers $[1, 1, 1, -1]$ are inserted into the subcarriers $[-21, -7, 7, 21]$ respectively for each of 64 subcarriers. Furthermore, the subcarriers from -32 to -27 and from 27 to 31 and subcarrier 0 are set to be complex value zeros.

The size of the IFFT block is set to 64 so that it can manipulate 64 complex subcarriers at a time. More specifically, it converts 64 complex numbers that are discrete samples in the frequency domain to 64 complex numbers that are discrete samples in the time domain.

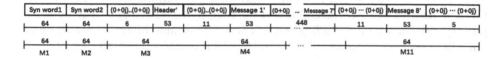

Fig. 3. Complex number stream after the OFDM carrier manipulator block

The cyclic prefix block inserts a cyclic prefix (CP) consisting of 16 complex numbers at the beginning of every stream of 64 complex numbers. The prefix is the copy of the last 16 complex numbers out of the 64 complex numbers. The multiply-const block is used to multiply each input complex number by a constant number in order to adjust the gain of signals. The constant number is set from 0.01 to 0.03 for the implementation by using USRPs. In other words, if the constant number is lower than 0.01, then the signal-to-noise ratio (SNR) will be too small. In contrast, if the constant number is higher than 0.03, the USRP will be saturated for a high SNR. The SDR will receive a high bit-error-rate (BER) for both situations. Note that this constant number is the reference number for the USRP devices which may not be linearly proportion to the sending signal's power, and its range is not accurate for each USRP device. Finally, the tag-gate block is used to remove the tag which is an internal variable passed by blocks.

The USRP-sink block in the GNU radio companion provides an interface to setup the parameters of the USRP device, which has parameters, namely IP address, center frequency and sample rate. In our experiment, the USRP-sink block is used to set the parameters for the USRP sender whose IP address is set to be $addr = 192.168.10.2$ and the center frequency is set to 892 MHz.

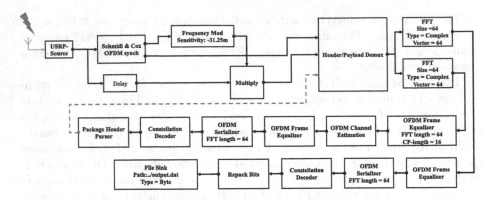

Fig. 4. A block diagram of the OFDM receiver

IEEE 802.11a OFDM Receiver. The OFDM receiver is shown in Fig. 4. The OFDM demodulation procedures include a header detector, FFT, frame equalizer, OFDM serializer, underlying demodulation and repack are put in one block which used Schmidl OFDM Synchronization block given by [23] in order to increase the efficiency of frequency and timing synchronization. The file-sink block is used to save the demodulated message bytes and to get BER by comparing with the original sending data. The USRP-source block for the receiver and the sender is the same, except the IP, which is $addr = 192.168.60.2$.

4.2 Experiment Setup for the IEEE 802.11X and CoAP Handshaking Mutual Authentication

We implement the 4-way and 6-way handshake protocols using Atmel Studio, IAR, and two USRP N210 devices to generate, send and receive messages. We record the time for transmitting each 96 bytes message in the tag debug block and calculate the time of generating tags from IAR. The OFDM system is a tagged system, the sending message has to be the multiple of 96 bytes or the last 96 bytes won't be sent. The 4-way or 6-way handshake protocols transmit $4 \times 96 = 384$ or $6 \times 96 = 576$ bytes.

We implement the KDF and MIC algorithms described in Sect. 3 for ACE, SPIX and WAGE and record the key derivation and MIC computation times in the IAR and Atmel Studio. The 4-way and 6-way transmission timings are captured in the SDR. Finally, the total time for the 4-way or 6-way handshake protocol is the sum of the 4-way or 6-way transmission time, the session key generation time and the MIC computation time.

To assess the efficiency of the data protection phase, we consider associated data (AD) and plaintext messages of two different lengths: (1) we choose no AD and a 1024-bit plaintext message; and (2) we choose an AD is of 128 bits and a plaintext message of 1024 bits. We record the execution times for ACE, SPIX and WAGE in the AEAD mode in the USRP interface.

5   Experiment Results and Comparisons

Performance of the IEEE802.11X and CoAP Protocols. Table 2 presents the execution time of the IEEE802.11X and CoAP handshake protocols where the execution times for the communication module and cryptographic functionalities are separately shown for a clear understanding. In our experiments, the frame size of the USRP is 1472 bytes, and the average frame rate of USRP is about 16.82 Kbps. In Table 2, the 4-way-Tx-time and 6-way-Tx-time is the 4-way and 6-way transmission time for the handshake protocols, which is the time required by the USRP. It takes about 700 and 1050 milliseconds (ms) to transmit the messages in the 4-way and 6-way communications, respectively. The "Gen-time" is the execution time for one KDF or MIC according to Constructions 1 and 2. The "WiFi-Auth" ("CoAP-Auth") in Table 2 is the total time to complete a mutual authentication, which includes the 4-way (or 6-way) transmission time and the execution times of 2 KDFs and 6 MICs (or 2 KDFs, 2 hash, 6 MICs) computations. For instance, with ACE, SPIX, and WAGE, the execution time to complete the handshake protocol is about 2,831, 2,966, and 2,808 ms, respectively.

Table 2. Performance of KDF and MIC on microcontrollers at a clock frequency of 16 MHz and time for the IEEE 802.11X and CoAP handshake mutual authentication and key establishment protocols

Cryptographic primitives	Platform	Function	Memory usage [Bytes] SRAM	Flash	Setup [Cycles]	Throughput [Kbps]	Gen-time [ms]	4-way-Tx-time [ms]	WiFi-Auth [ms]	6-way-Tx-time [ms]	CoAP-Auth[†] [ms]
SPIX	8-bits	KDF	175	1,586	705,314	23.23	44.08	700	3,176.64	1,060	6,857
	ATmega128	MIC	175	1,590	833,251	2.46	52.08				
	16-bits	KDF	50	1,562	286,679	57.15	17.92	690	2,912.84	1,050	6,502
	MSP430F2013	MIC	50	1,580	338,106	6.06	21.13				
	32-bits	KDF	408	1,230	59,140	277.04	3.70	700	2,831.58	1,050	6,342
	LM3S9D96	MIC	408	1,294	69,770	29.35	4.36				
ACE	16-bits	KDF	330	1,720	550,752	29.75	34.42	710	3,089.68	1040	6,567
	MSP430F2013	MIC	330	1,740	551,016	3.72	34.44				
	32-bits	KDF	599	1,826	102,762	159.44	6.42	730	2,966.56	1,070	6,481
	LM3S9D96	MIC	599	1,790	102,746	19.93	6.42				
WAGE	8-bits	KDF	808	4,448	139,478	117.47	8.72	710	2,903.22	1060	6,443
	ATmega128	MIC	808	4,476	139,309	14.70	8.71				
	16-bits	KDF	46	4,518	166,993	98.11	10.44	720	2,955.78	1,050	6,399
	MSP430F2013	MIC	46	4,538	166,865	12.27	10.43				
	32-bits	KDF	3,084	6,278	107,071	153.02	6.69	690	2,808.54	1,060	6,424
	LM3S9D96	MIC	3,084	6,326	106,977	19.14	6.69				

† For CoAP-Auth, SPIX and WAGE provide 112-bit security due to the security of SPIX and WAGE hash.

Performance of the Data Protection Protocol. The execution time in the data protection protocol includes the execution time of encrypting a plaintext message and producing a tag using an AEAD algorithm and the transmission time of sending the ciphertext and the tag. The transmission time is recorded in the SDR for transmitting 1024-bit ciphertext and 128 bit tag from one USRP to another USRP, which takes about 1,060 ms. Tables 3, 4, and 5 present the transmission time and the AEAD execution times of SPIX, ACE, and WAGE, respectively. As in all three AEAD algorithms, the permutation is at the core, we present its performance, the memory usage, setup, and throughput results.

Note that "Gen-time" in Tables 2, 3, 4 and 5 is the time to one execution of the respective AEAD algorithm. For example, the total time to complete the data protection protocol with a plaintext message of 1024 bits and an AD of 128 bits is about 1,304 ms using SPIX on ATmega128. Note that in our experiment the emulation of SDR does not affect the results of the handshake protocols.

Table 3. Performance of SPIX AE mode on microcontrollers at a clock frequency of 16 MHz IEEE 802.11i data protection protocol

Cryptographic	Platform	Memory usage [Bytes]		Setup [Cycles]	Throughput [Kbps]	Gen-time [ms]	Tx-time [ms]
		SRAM	Flash				
SPIX Perm-18	8-bits ATmega128	161	1,262	128,377	31.91	8.02	N/A
	16-bits MSP430F2013	24	1,409	52,294	78.33	3.27	
	32-bits LM3S9D96	352	946	10,900	375.78	0.68	
SPIX-AE ($l_{AD} = 0$, $l_M = 16$)	8-bits ATmega128	175	1,550	1,667,042	9.83	104.19	1,060
	16-bits MSP430F2013	50	1,845	677,818	24.17	42.36	1,080
	32-bits LM3S9D96	408	1,210	139,569	117.39	8.72	1,050
SPIX-AE ($l_{AD} = 2$, $l_M = 16$)	8-bits ATmega128	175	1,644	1,795,322	9.13	112.21	1,080
	16-bits MSP430F2013	50	1,891	730,340	22.43	45.65	1,050
	32-bits LM3S9D96	424	1,326	150,313	109.00	9.39	1,070

Table 4. Performance of ACE AE and Hash modes on microcontrollers at a clock frequency of 16 MHz IEEE 802.11i data protection protocol

Cryptographic	Platform	Memory usage [Bytes]		Setup [Cycles]	Throughput [Kbps]	Gen-time [ms]	Tx-time [ms]
		SRAM	Flash				
ACE Perm	16-bits MSP430F2013	304	1,456	69,440	73.73	4.34	N/A
	32-bits LM3S9D96	523	1,598	13,003	393.76	0.81	
ACE-AE ($l_{AD} = 0$, $l_M = 16$)	16-bits MSP430F2013	330	1,740	1,445,059	11.34	90.32	1,060
	32-bits LM3S9D96	559	1,790	26,9341	60.83	16.83	1,070
ACE-AE ($l_{AD} = 2$, $l_M = 16$)	16-bits MSP430F2013	330	1,786	1,582,892	10.35	98.93	1,080
	32-bits LM3S9D96	559	1,858	294,988	55.54	18.44	1,080
ACE-Hash ($l_M = 2$, $j = 4$)	16-bits MSP430F2013	330	1,682	413,056	4.96	25.82	N/A
	32-bits LM3S9D96	559	1,822	77,114	26.56	4.82	
ACE-Hash ($l_M = 16$, $j = 4$)	16-bits MSP430F2013	330	1,684	1,375,672	11.91	85.98	
	32-bits LM3S9D96	559	1,822	256,524	63.87	16.03	

Comparing with AES and Other NIST Lightweight Ciphers. We compare the throughput of the SPIX, ACE and WAGE permutations with the AES-128 permutation. The results of AES on 8-bit AVR microcontrollers (written in C) from [21] show that the throughput of AES-128 is $\frac{10180 \times 8 \times 2}{1000} = 162.880$ Kbps when the CPU frequency is set to 16 MHz. When we compare the results of AES-128 with WAGE, our implementation results of WAGE give a higher throughput, which is 217.98 Kbps, on the same 8-bit microcontroller platforms. Moreover, SPIX and ACE permutations give higher throughput on 32-bit microcontrollers which are 393.76 Kbps and 286.78 Kbps, respectively.

When written in assembly, the throughput of the AES-128 permutation is $\frac{43671 \times 8 \times 2}{1000} = 698.74$ Kbps, which is higher than that of our implementations. However, the internal state size of SPIX, ACE and WAGE are 256, 320 and 259 bits, respectively, which are more than twice as much as that of AES-128.

Software microcontroller benchmarking of NIST round 2 candidates can be found in [10], and the performance results are obtained from the reference C code (not optimized). Thus, we do not compare our results with those for fairness.

Scaling up the Speed for WiFi System. In our experiment, the USRP transmission rate is about 16.82 Kbps. However, the real WiFi systems have a transmission rate in the range of 50 Mbps and 320 Mbps at distance of 100 m from devices to an access point, which is much higher than that of the USRP.

We compute the equivalent 4-way transmission time for the WiFi system by scaling the 4-way transmission time of the USRP. For the 4-way transmission time with SPIX that takes about 700 ms, the equivalent transmission time for the WiFi system at a transmission rate of 50 Mbps is $\frac{0.7 \times 16.82}{50000} = 0.235$ ms. Similarly it can be computed for the 6-way transmission time. Therefore, from Table 2, we can observe that the execution time for the cryptographic operations is the dominating factor in the 4-way or 6-way handshake protocols.

Table 5. Performance of WAGE AE mode on microcontrollers at a clock frequency of 16 MHz in IEEE 802.11i data protection protocol

Cryptographic	Platform	Memory usage [Bytes]		Setup [Cycles]	Throughput [Kbps]	Gen-time [ms]	Tx-time [ms]
		SRAM	Flash				
WAGE Perm	8-bits ATmega128	802	4132	19011	217.98	1,190	N/A
	16-bits MSP430F2370	4	5031	23524	176.16	1.47	
	32-bits LM3S9D96	3076	5902	14450	286.78	0.9	
WAGE-AE ($l_{AD} = 0$, $l_M = 16$)	8-bits ATmega128	808	4416	362888	45.15	22.68	1,080
	16-bits MSP430F2370	46	5289	433105	37.83	27.07	1,090
	32-bits LM3S9D96	3084	6230	278848	58.76	17.43	1,060
WAGE-AE ($l_{AD} = 2$, $l_M = 16$)	8-bits ATmega128	808	4502	397260	41.24	24.83	1,050
	16-bits MSP430F2370	46	5339	474067	34.56	29.63	1,060
	32-bits LM3S9D96	3084	6354	305284	53.67	19.08	1,060

6   Conclusion and Future Work

In this paper, we presented optimized microcontroller implementations of three LWC schemes ACE, SPIX and WAGE and implemented the IEEE 802.11X 4-way and CoAP 6-way handshake protocols and the IEEE 802.11a physical layer OFDM transmission protocol in software defined radio and embed the handshake protocols into the IEEE 802.11a protocol to simulate the 4-way and 6-way handshake modulation and communication. We proposed and implemented the constructions of KDF and MIC algorithms using the above three LWC schemes, including KDF and MIC on three different types of microcontrollers. We reported the experimental results for two IoT authentication protocols namely IEEE 802.11X and CoAP and data protection protocols. Our results show that for authenticated encryption all three ciphers achieved the highest throughput on Cortex-M3.

As a future work, we extend our experiment setup for the SDR and the LWC schemes to provide performance evaluations of upcoming 5G security mechanisms and other new IoT protocols.

Acknowledgement. The research of Yunjie Yi and Guang Gong, and partial work of Kalikinkar Mandal were supported by NSERC SPG and Discovery Grants. The authors would like to thank the reviewers for their insightful comments to improve the quality of the paper.

References

1. 5G PPP: 5G PPP phase1 security landscape. In: 5G PPP Security WG, European Commission, June 2017
2. Aagaard, M., AlTawy, R., Gong, G., Mandal, K., Rohit, R.: ACE: an authenticated encryption and hash algorithm. NIST LWC Round 2. https://csrc.nist.gov/CSRC/media/Projects/lightweight-cryptography/documents/round-2/spec-doc-rnd2/ace-spec-round2.pdf
3. Aagaard, M., AlTawy, R., Gong, G., Mandal, K., Rohit, R., Zidaric, N.: WAGE: an authenticated cipher, NIST LWC round 2 (2019). https://csrc.nist.gov/CSRC/media/Projects/lightweight-cryptography/documents/round-2/spec-doc-rnd2/wage-spec-round2.pdf
4. Alliance, L.: (2021). https://lora-alliance.org/
5. AlTawy, R., Gong, G., He, M., Mandal, K., Rohit, R.: SPIX: an authenticated cipher, NIST LWC round 2. https://csrc.nist.gov/CSRC/media/Projects/lightweight-cryptography/documents/round-2/spec-doc-rnd2/spix-spec-round2.pdf
6. Altawy, R., Rohit, R., He, M., Mandal, K., Yang, G., Gong, G.: sLiSCP-light: towards hardware optimized sponge-specific cryptographic permutations. ACM Trans. Embed. Comput. Syst. **17**(4), 81:1–81:26 (2018). https://doi.org/10.1145/3233245. http://doi.acm.org/10.1145/3233245
7. AlTawy, R., Rohit, R., He, M., Mandal, K., Yang, G., Gong, G.: sLiSCP: Simeck-based permutations for lightweight sponge cryptographic primitives. In: Adams, C., Camenisch, J. (eds.) SAC 2017. LNCS, vol. 10719, pp. 129–150. Springer, Cham (2018). https://doi.org/10.1007/978-3-319-72565-9_7
8. Arslan, H., Mitola, J., III.: Cognitive radio, software-defined radio, and adaptive wireless systems. Wirel. Commun. Mob. Comput. **7**(9), 1033–1035 (2007)
9. Bassham, L., Calik, C., Chang, D., Kang, J., McKay, K., Turan, M.: Lightweight cryptography (2019). https://csrc.nist.gov/projects/lightweight-cryptography/round-2-candidates
10. Bassham, L., Calik, C., Chang, D., Kang, J., McKay, K., Turan, M.: Lightweight cryptography - finalists (2021). https://csrc.nist.gov/Projects/lightweight-cryptography/finalists
11. Bertoni, G., Daemen, J., Peeters, M., Van Assche, G.: Duplexing the sponge: single-pass authenticated encryption and other applications. In: Miri, A., Vaudenay, S. (eds.) SAC 2011. LNCS, vol. 7118, pp. 320–337. Springer, Heidelberg (2012). https://doi.org/10.1007/978-3-642-28496-0_19
12. Bloessl, B., Segata, M., Sommer, C., Dressler, F.: Performance assessment of IEEE 802.11P with an open source SDR-based prototype. IEEE Trans. Mob. Comput. **17**(5), 1162–1175 (2018). https://doi.org/10.1109/TMC.2017.2751474
13. Chen, L., Gong, G.: Communication System Security. Chapman and Hall/CRC, London (2012)
14. Congdon, P., Aboba, B., Smith, A., Zorn, G., Roese, J.: IEEE 802.1 x remote authentication dial in user service (radius) usage guidelines. RFC 3580, pp. 1–30 (2003)

15. Group, I.W., et al.: 802.11ax - IEEE draft standard for information technology - telecommunications and information exchange between systems local and metropolitan area networks. IEEE STD (2019)
16. Hamdane, B., Serhrouchni, A., Montfaucon, A., Guemara, S.: Using the HMAC-based one-time password algorithm for TLS authentication. In: 2011 Conference on Network and Information Systems Security, pp. 1–8, May 2011. https://doi.org/10.1109/SAR-SSI.2011.5931396
17. Khorov, E., Kiryanov, A., Lyakhov, A., Bianchi, G.: A tutorial on IEEE 802.11ax high efficiency WLANs. IEEE Commun. Surv. Tutor. **21**(1), 197–216 (2019)
18. Kim, D., Jung, J., Koo, Y., Yi, Y.: Bird-MAC: energy-efficient mac for quasi-periodic IoT applications by avoiding early wake-up. IEEE Trans. Mob. Comput. **19**(4), 788–802 (2020)
19. Li, J., Zhang, N., Ni, J., Chen, J., Du, R.: Secure and lightweight authentication with key agreement for smart wearable systems. IEEE Internet Things J. **7**(8), 7334–7344 (2020)
20. Li, P., Su, J., Wang, X.: iTLS: lightweight transport-layer security protocol for IoT with minimal latency and perfect forward secrecy. IEEE Internet Things J. **7**(8), 6828–6841 (2020)
21. Meiser, G., Eisenbarth, T., Lemke-Rust, K., Paar, C.: Efficient implementation of eSTREAM ciphers on 8-bit AVR microcontrollers. In: 2008 International Symposium on Industrial Embedded Systems, pp. 58–66, June 2008. https://doi.org/10.1109/SIES.2008.4577681
22. Rahman, R.A., Shah, B.: Security analysis of IoT protocols: a focus in CoAP. In: 2016 3rd MEC International Conference on Big Data and Smart City (ICBDSC), pp. 1–7, March 2016. https://doi.org/10.1109/ICBDSC.2016.7460363
23. Schmidl, T.M., Cox, D.C.: Robust frequency and timing synchronization for OFDM. IEEE Trans. Commun. **45**(12), 1613–1621 (1997). https://doi.org/10.1109/26.650240
24. ISO/IEC 20922:2016 [ISO/IEC 20922:2016] information technology - message queuing telemetry transport (MQTT) v3.1.1. https://www.iso.org/standard/69466.html
25. Vollbrecht, J., Aboba, B., Blunk, L., Levkowetz, H., Carlson, J.: Extensible authentication protocol (EAP) (2004)
26. Wang, L., An, H., Zhu, H., Liu, W.: Mobikey: mobility-based secret key generation in smart home. IEEE Internet Things J. **7**(8), 7590–7600 (2020)
27. Ye, Q., Zhuang, W.: Distributed and adaptive medium access control for internet-of-things-enabled mobile networks. IEEE Internet Things J. **4**(2), 446–460 (2017)
28. Yi, Y., Gong, G., Mandal, K.: Implementation of three LWC schemes in the WiFi 4-way handshake with software defined radio (2021). https://arxiv.org/pdf/1909.11707.pdf
29. Shelby, Z., Hartke, K., Bormann, C.: The constrained application protocol (COAP). RFC 7252 (2014). https://tools.ietf.org/pdf/rfc7252.pdf

HistoTrust: Ethereum-Based Attestation of a Data History Built with OP-TEE and TPM

Dylan Paulin, Christine Hennebert[✉], Thibault Franco-Rondisson,
Romain Jayles, Thomas Loubier, and Raphaël Collado

Univ. Grenoble Alpes, CEA, Leti, 38000 Grenoble, France
christine.hennebert@cea.fr

Abstract. Device- or user-centric system architectures allow everyone to manage their personal or confidential data. But how to provide the trust required between the stakeholders of a given ecosystem to work together, each preserving their interest and their business? HistoTrust introduces a solution to this problem. A system architecture separating the data belonging to each stakeholder and the cryptographic proofs (attestations) on their history is implemented. An Ethereum ledger is deployed to maintain the history of the attestations, thus guaranteeing their tamper-resistance, their timestamp and their order. The ledger allows these attestations to be shared between the stakeholders in order to create trust without revealing secret or critical data. In each IoT device, the root-of-trust secrets used to attest the data produced are protected at storage in a TPM ST33 and during execution within an ARM Cortex-A7 TrustZone. The designed solution aims to be resilient, robust to software attacks and to present a high level of protection against side-channel attacks and fault injections. Furthermore, the real-time constraints of an embedded industrial application are respected. The integration of the security measures does not impact the performance in use.

Keywords: Attestation · Secure hardware · TPM · OP-TEE · Trust · Data history · Ledger · Embedded industrial application · IoT · Real-time performance

1 Introduction

Logs trace the activity of a device in the form of a data history of various kinds, such as its internal states, connection, communication activity or the data it produces. Their audit engages the accountability of the owner of the device as a legal entity. Within an ecosystem of stakeholders, each one is thus accountable to provide a trusted history of the data produced by its devices to an auditor in the event of a litigation. This confidential data is of great value for the business of the stakeholders.

Attestation schemes based on the use of a TPM offer standard solutions allowing the authentication of a platform by a remote device [1,2], or even

© Springer Nature Switzerland AG 2022
E. Aïmeur et al. (Eds.): FPS 2021, LNCS 13291, pp. 130–145, 2022.
https://doi.org/10.1007/978-3-031-08147-7_9

making the user anonymous [3]. But these schemes do not consider the real time data emitted by the industrial applications embedded on the trusted IoT devices [4,9]. The authors of [5] highlight this issue through the delicate question of the certification of sensor data, even by a trusted platform. The tension between privacy, which requires the protection of confidential data, and trust which requires guarantees between the stakeholders working in a given ecosystem is tangible.

The blockchain provides a technology that maintains by design a history of proofs or transactions [6]. Histotrust introduces a device-centric [10] solution based on Ethereum technology that conciliates the need for data security and privacy with the trust required between stakeholders. HistoTrust provides an architecture that ensures end-to-end security and privacy by design while satisfying the real-time data transmission needs of the embedded industrial application. The design of an enhanced wallet is outlined. It serves as root-of-trust for the data emitted by the IoT device.

The following section positions the work done in HistoTrust in relation to existing solutions. The use case, the threat model and requirements are then described in Sect. 3. Section 4 outlines HistoTrust solution, its secure system architecture and the embedded implementation based on off-the-shelf secure hardware components for IoT devices. Section 5 is dedicated to the presentation of the results and discussions before the conclusion.

2   Related Works

2.1   Secure Data History with Trusted Hardware

The paper [7] shows the added value of blockchain technology to meet the specificities of a smart manufacturing use case. Compared to a centralized solution based on digital certificates and PKI, the Ethereum-based solution shows a more refined management of security and privacy at the expense of performance. In this paper, HistoTrust solution demonstrates that performance can also be maintained and met the needs of the use case when using a blockchain.

The authors of EmLog [4] present their framework as *"the first attempt at preserving off-the-shelf ARM development board hosting OP-TEE"*. EmLog implements a secure logging system from end-to-end between embedded constraint devices and a remote database. HistoTrust introduces an architecture design and an on-board implementation design using off-the-shelf secure hardware components, as OP-TEE and TPM 2.0 [11], that goes beyond EmLog solution and achieves the EmLog perspectives. Preserving forward security thanks to the one-way hash chain scheme introduced by Shneier and Kelsey [8], EmLog and SGX-Log [9] are not designed for multi-stakeholders contexts and may suffer of data losses in case of power failure.

In the Logs system EngraveChain detailed in the paper [12], the data history is ciphered, then registered in an Hyperledger Fabric ledger. This implementation lacks agility because the blockchain is not designed to store large volumes of data, nor confidential data even encrypted. Moreover, the ciphering of recorded data in a ledger implies a complex key management.

The blockchain technology provides by design the tamper-resistance of the recorded transactions history forming the ledger. HistoTrust provides an attestation scheme securing the history of data issued from distributed devices. An Ethereum ledger maintains the history of cryptographic attestations of data produced by distributed devices owning by multiple stakeholders. The blockchain technology enables to share these cryptographic proofs between the involved stakeholders providing trust. In addition, the raw data is kept by their owner who ensures their persistence and confidentiality.

Based on an Ethereum blockchain, BlockPro [13] presents a decentralised architecture of IoT devices. The authenticity of the devices issuing data is achieved through a challenge to the IoT device submitted to its PUF (Physical Unclonable Function). Several improvements can be made to this scheme, in particular it is not mentioned how the account address issuing the transactions is built and how it is linked to the PUF. Paper [14] shows that dissociating IoT devices and validator nodes is a powerful architecture that is exploited by HistoTrust.

2.2   Attestation Scheme

The principle of remote attestation is described in depth in [2]. The Trusted Platform Module (TPM) is the targeted device enabling the endorsement of attestation keys that may be owned by the manufacturer, the vendor or the owner. The attestation scheme follows recommendations and standards provided by the Trusted Computing Group (TCG) [1]. Attestation aims at proving to a remote verifier the property of a target by supplying a proof over a network. It consists in three stages: 1) key provisioning, 2) attestation process, 3) verification process.

TPM 2.0 includes an endorsement hierarchy enabling to derive from a secret seed, an attestation key named ak identifying the device. For HistoTrust purpose, ak is endorsed by the stakeholder owner of the device. In remote attestation schemes, this key is used to sign the TPM's PCR registry in order to prove to a remote verifier the state of the device. This scheme is employed in [15] where an infrastructure provider authenticates a smartphone before issuing confidential data to a service provider. HistoTrust provides an elegant solution to this problem in a decentralized context without infrastructure provider. Others studies as [16] or [17] exploit this attestation scheme to verify software and device integrity. [16] highlights that the real-time requirements of industrial IoT application must be tackled in complement. HistoTrust brings solutions to this request.

In a decentralized root-of-trust architecture, each device is responsible for protecting its secret. With HistoTrust, each device integrates a TPM provisioned with secret keys endorsed by its owner, ensuring root-of-trust. The ST33 TPM provides an EAL-5+ security level. An OP-TEE environment is used in addition through an ARM cortex-A7 to execute operations that are not supported by TPM 2.0 standard. Papers [10] and [18] provide an in-depth analysis of the security level offered by these two components against logical and physical attacks. HistoTrust goes beyond the TrustZone-based wallet detailed in [19] and introduces an Ethereum compliant enhanced wallet relying on a TPM.

3 System Requirements

3.1 Use Case

In a factory, many actuators participate in the assembly of a product (a car for example) on a production line (see Fig. 1). These actuators are driven by physical devices that generate digital commands. These devices embed industrial applications that may include embedded artificial intelligence (AI). So, when an incident occurs, creating a financial loss (by stopping the production line for example), it is necessary to find the cause and eventually to charge the costs to the accountable stakeholder. However, the presence of AI makes it difficult to reproduce commands. In some cases, only the analysis of the logs allows to understand what happened and to find the origin. In this context, sharing the attestations of the digital data generated by independent devices that operate on the same production line provides transparency and trust to the stakeholders involved. Moreover for stakeholders who are not physically present in the factory and have left their devices. In case of litigation, each stakeholder should be able to provide its raw data that verifying the shared recorded attestations to an independent auditor, an insurance expert for example, proving that its raw data is authentic, not tampered, complete and ordered.

3.2 Threat Model

The profile of the attacker is that of a powerful stakeholder who, in a multi-stakeholders context, places the blame on another stakeholder of the eco-system for lack of proofs. So, HistoTrust should be able to bring solution to these threats:

- a stakeholder who deletes or falsifies his data implicating him
- a stakeholder who falsifies another's data to put blame on him
- infiltration of a malware that generates fake data
- a user who makes a mistake turns off the device to erase the proofs

3.3 Requirements

The requirements are formalized below. For a given stakeholder, the aim is to prove that its devices are genuine and the data they issued are complete and of integrity.

- R1: *maintaining performance*: the security and privacy features shall not impact the industrial application performances.
- R2: *forward integrity*: the data attestation history must be immutable and transparent to the stakeholders. The raw data must be persistent and of integrity.

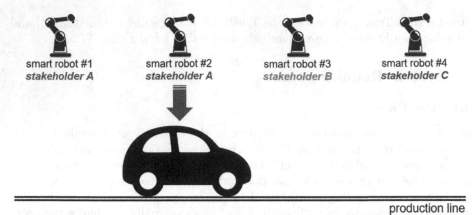

Fig. 1. Illustration of the use-case

- R3: *public authentication*: any stakeholder should be able to authenticate the devices issuing data at a given time through the attestations history.
- R4: *power failure*: no raw data or attestations should be lost in the event of a power failure.
- R5: *privacy-preserving data*: The raw data shall not be exposed to the other devices.
- R6: *verifiability*: An accredited auditor must be able to verify the data attestations.
- R7: *multiple stakeholders*: the scheme shall support multiple-stakeholders owning multiple devices issuing data concurrently.

4   Design

This section details the architecture and implementation choices to meet the requirements of the use case.

4.1   Architecture Design

All the devices are distributed on a local network in the factory, with an access point to communicate with the outside world. A consortium (permissioned and private) blockchain is deployed. Each stakeholder involved has a validator node, represented by a computer in the Fig. 2. Thus, the governance of the system is ensured with equity by all the stakeholders involved.

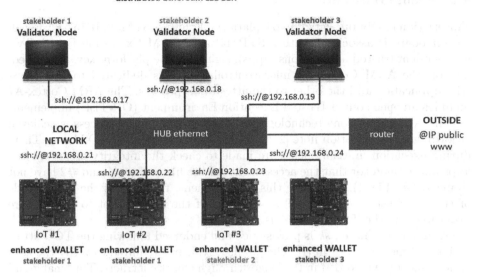

Fig. 2. Network architecture

The IoT devices acting in the production line, are provided with an enhanced wallet, enabling to send transactions to the validator nodes. Each device is the root-of-trust of the data it produced, forming a distributed root-of-trust network. IoT provisioning is done independently by each stakeholder, prior to the deployment of the hardware in the factory. The management of access rights and authorizations is done through smart contracts.

We make the choice to use the Ethereum Go open-source solution to implement a permissioned blockchain based on a Proof-of-Authority (PoA) "Clique" [20]. Table 1 presents the features of the main blockchains used in the cross-industry domain. This choice is motivated by the availability of a large amount of code and open-source projects coming from the ethereum community, in particular the web3 library. Aiming to be implemented on constrained embedded devices, the code must be optimized at low level.

Table 1. Main blockchain features

Blockchain	Type	Smart contract	Open source	Crypto wallet	Consensus algorithm
Ethereum geth	Permissioned	Yes	Yes	secp256k1	PoA Clique
Ethereum mainnet	Permissionless	Yes	Yes	secp256k1	PoW etash
Hyperledger fabric	Permissioned	Yes	Yes	pkcs#11	PBFT
Hyperledger sawtooth	Permissioned	Yes	Yes	secp256k1	PBFT or PoET
Iota	Permissionless	No	No	Winternitz	Fragment of PoW

4.2   Secure Hardware

This section briefly presents the IoT platform design. A STM32MP157-EV1 evaluation board is associated with a STPM4RasPI TPM Expansion Board. Two independent trusted applications (apps), signed by the platform key, are embedded on the ARM Cortex-A7 microcontroller. One is dedicated to the industrial application and the other to the attestation process. The ARM Cortex-A7 includes an open source Trusted Execution Environment (OP-TEE) implementing the ARM TrustZone technology. At start, a secure boot process is achieved according the application note [21] relying on Brainpool 256 ECDSA key. Then, during execution, measurements are made to check the integrity of the trusted apps and to monitor that the access rights to the file buffer #1 and #2 have not changed (see Fig. 4). To enable this measurement, the hash of the binary code of the two trusted apps as well as the hash of the access right to the files are provisioned in the TPM PCR registry.

A private key noted sk is provisioned and endorsed following the TCG attestation scheme described in [1]. The public certificates required to verify the keys endorsement are recorded in the ledger through smart contracts. This enables all stakeholders to verify that devices issuing data are genuine in the system. The digital signature with the elliptic curve secp256k1 required for Ethereum transaction is not supported by the TPM 2.0 standard. So, we have implemented this cryptographic function in the TrustZone in order to avoid exposing the private key sk to software attacks. This key is ciphered in the TPM key vault and is accessed from the TrustZone via the SPI bus. The evaluation board EV1 presents the benefit to enable the security of the SPI bus at low level.

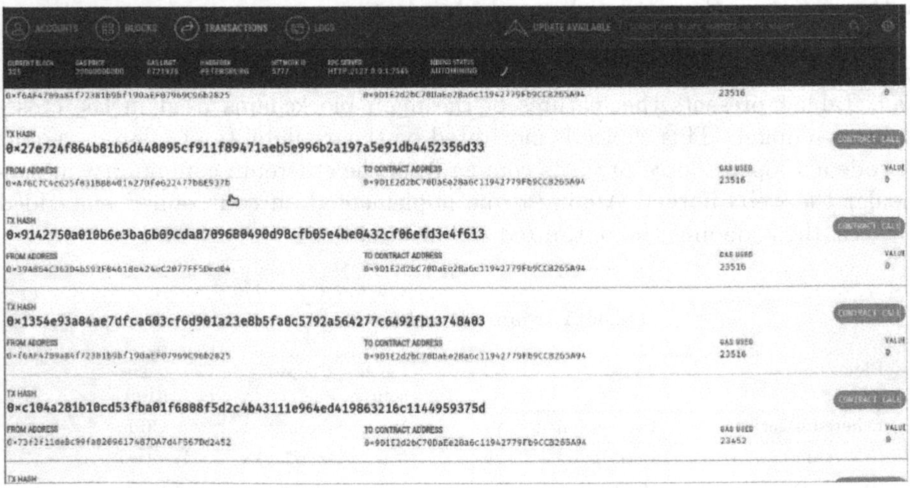

Fig. 3. History of data attestations recorded in the ledger

The attestation process uses *sk* to attest the data produced by the industrial application. During the production phase, the cryptographic attestations are registered in Ethereum ledger through a smart contract. The attestation history is transparent and available to all stakeholders. The Fig. 3 shows a portion of the ledger with the history of attestations on the data. Each record is a transaction signed by *sk*, emitted from the account of the issuing device, and sent to the smart contract. It includes the hash of the attested data set.

4.3   Implementation

The embedded system depicted Fig. 4 aims to integrate the security needed to meet the requirements without impacting the industrial application performances. All the data needed to be attested are timestamped and written in the file buffer #1 in real-time. The size of this buffer is not limiting, as it is stored on the SD card which has several GB available. Only the industrial application is allowed to write in this file. The attestation process is implemented as an independent trusted application allowed to read the file buffer #1. The reading of the freshly written data set is triggered by the receipt from the blockchain confirming that the transaction attesting the previous data set is recorded in the ledger.

The attestation process consists in computing the hash of the latter data set produced, that is included in the 'data' field of an ethereum transaction. This transaction is signed with the private key *sk* which is also used to build the account address issuer. To achieve this signature, the private key *sk* is accessed in the TPM vault through the SPI bus. The signed transaction is sent to the blockchain for validation and a receipt is returned if the registration in the ledger is confirmed. This receipt is written in a second file buffer #2. Only the attestation trusted app is allowed to write in this file.

The files #1 and #2 are stored in persistent memory. If a power failure occurs, the data is saved and the attestation process resumes where it left off when the power returns. The content of these files may also be ex-filtrated by their owner stakeholder via VPN through the access point. The read and write access rights to the two files are supervised by the TPM measurement process and an alert is raised if they are modified.

5   Evaluation

The evaluation aims at qualifying the performance of the embedded scheme in order to ensure the security and privacy requirements while keeping the rate and the efficiency of the industrial application.

Four IoT devices are deployed for the experiments. Each is composed of a STM32MP157-EV1 board and a STPM4RasPI TPM Expansion Board including a secure element STSAFE-TPM ST33. Each embeds one of the following configurations concerning the access to the private key *sk*, in order to evaluate the overhead of security on the overall system:

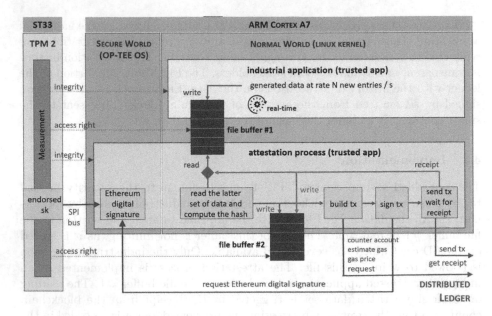

Fig. 4. Embedded design in the IoT devices

- Iot #1: *sk* is in clear in the OP-TEE non-volatile memory
- Iot #2: *sk* is ciphered in the OP-TEE non-volatile memory
- Iot #3: *sk* is in clear in the STSAFE-TPM ST33 vault
- Iot #4: *sk* is ciphered in the STSAFE-TPM ST33 vault

Each device produces digital data, builds attestations and emits transactions to the Ethereum ledger composed of three validator nodes. In a first stage, we use the Ethereum Ganache simulator to emulate the validator nodes in order to focus on the embedded design and the implementation of the IoT devices. In a second stage, one validator node is deployed per stakeholder involved in the consortium of the distributed system. Each one hosts and accesses the content of the ledger.

5.1   Performance

In this section, the aim is to evaluate the performance of the embedded implementation in the IoT devices according the architecture depicted in the Fig. 2, in presence of three stakeholders and four IoT devices producing data. One goal is to qualify the impact of security and privacy on the user experience and the execution of the industrial task. Another goal is to evaluate the security and privacy level with respect to the requirements defined in Sect. 3.

The methodology followed consists in a first stage of implementing functional benchmarks of the applications including cryptographic operations on a personal computer (PC) in C language and performing intensive tests. In a second stage, the code is well structured and transferred to the embedded devices. The functions embedded in the OP-TEE environment that accesses to the TPM, are isolated from those implemented in the Linux userland. Thus, the performances obtained on the PC are presented as functional benchmarks in Fig. 5, noting that no hardware security is present.

In the following, several experiments are launched with different data rates issued by the industrial application, from 33 entries per second to 10000 entries per second. For each experiment, 20000 entries are considered. An entry is a set of data composed of 50 bytes including such fields:

$$[index][timestamp][rawdata]$$

The *index* field enables to order the data entries. It is followed by the timestamp and the raw data produced by the application. The application used produces data of fixed size. For the purpose of performance testing, the rate of data produced is variable.

The left-hand graph in Fig. 5 shows the number of transactions (abbreviated "tx number") sent to Ganache for each data rate. The green curve corresponds to the real-time of production of 20000 entries for each data rate, while the orange curve shows the processing time of the processor Core i5-7200U that fluctuates between 1 and 4 ms. The numbers of transactions sent to Ganache follows the needs of the real-time constraints. When the data rate increases, more entries are included in the attested data set in a given transaction and globally the number of transactions is reduced. The total processing time follows the amount of transactions built.

The right-hand graph illustrates the amount of entries attested per transaction with regards to the processing time required for one cycle, i.e. the process to build and issue a transaction to Ganache. The timing of the Ethereum ECDSA signature is quite stable whatever the data rate, while the timing of the process to build one transaction increases with the data rate. An in-depth analysis shows that the rise comes from the hash operation that takes more time when the amount of data increases.

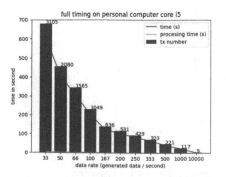 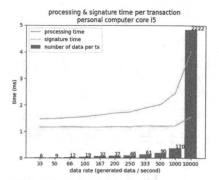

Fig. 5. Benchmark on personal computer with Core i5

The Fig. 6 illustrates the results obtained once deployed onto the four boards running simultaneously. 20000 entries are generated by each board, leading to a different number of transactions according to the transaction processing time, illustrated board by board on Figs. 7 and 8. The real-time curve shows that the constraint is the same for the boards and for the benchmark PC. The total processing time is close regardless of the board configuration, showing that the use of a TPM to protect the private key with a higher security level, has not a big impact on the whole system performances.

The right-hand graph illustrates the ratio of transactions emitted by each board at a given data rate. When the private key is accessed in the TPM, this increases the timing process to sign the transaction and mechanically, more data entries are included in an attestation and the number of transactions sent to Ganache decreases.

The timings presented in the Figs. 7 and 8 show that the processing time to build a transaction is quite stable whatever is the data rate for each configuration of access to the private key. The impact of storing sk in the TPM rather than disposing of the key directly in the OP-TEE memory is 70 ms for

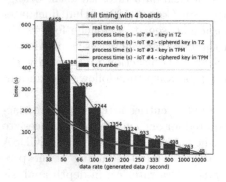 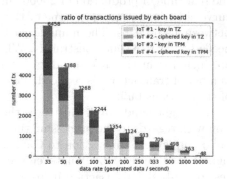

Fig. 6. Full time processing with 4 boards

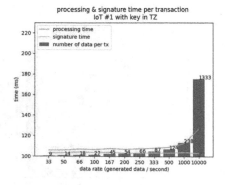 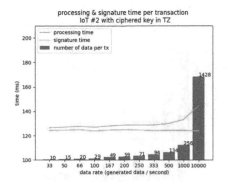

Fig. 7. One cycle processing with private key sk in TrustZone

one transaction processing time. Ciphering *sk* takes 25 ms additional to execute the AES deciphering before signing.

As reference and comparison, the paper [22] highlights the implementation performances of a IOTA light node on different ARM Cortex-M4, Cortex-M7, Cortex-M3 and Cortex-A53. These microcontrollers do not include secure hardware, but their firmware may be protected from tampering. IOTA uses Winternitz One-Time Signature Scheme [23] known to be robust to side-channel attacks. The processing time of this signature scheme takes 80 ms on ARM Cortex-M7, 135 ms on Cortex-M4, 683 ms on Cortex-M3, 328 ms on Cortex-A53. Our implementation of the Ethereum ECDSA signature on the Cortex-A7 TrustZone takes 102 ms when *sk* is present in the OP-TEE memory, 173 ms when *sk* is accessed in the TPM vault, and 20 ms additional if the deciphering of *sk* is done in TrustZone. These results seems very good with regard to the state of the art. These performance analysis show that:

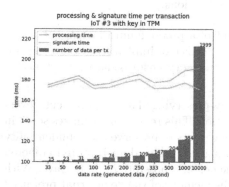 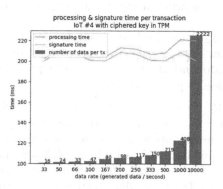

Fig. 8. One cycle processing with private key *sk* in TPM vault

1. the architecture and the embedded implementation design enable to follow real-time application constraints even for high data rates.
2. the storage of the private key *sk* in the TPM does not impact the global performances.
3. the implementation of Ethereum ECDSA signature on the elliptic curve secp256k1 in the TrustZone of the ARM cortex-A7 is quite efficient compared to the state of the art of similar studies.

As conclusion of this section, the implementation of security and privacy by design in embedded devices including TrustZone and TPM does not impact the performances of the industrial application, even when high data rates are considered. So the requirement R1 is fulfilled.

5.2 Security and Privacy

In this section, we examine whether the security and privacy requirements are satisfied.

R2: Forward Integrity. Solutions such as EmLog [4] or SGX-log [9] ensure forward integrity by forming a history of secure data blocks, based on Schneier technique [8], enhanced by the diversification of encryption keys forming a hash-key-chain, involving complex key management. Based on blockchain technology, which ensures by design the forward integrity of the information recorded in the ledger, HistoTrust introduces a new solution to the problem of log security. The history of cryptographic attestations of the data is maintained in the ledger, each attestation being a pointer to the raw data maintained outside the blockchain by its owner. Thus, any tampering or removal of raw data is detectable.

R3: Public Authentication. The recorded attestation authenticates the device issuer. It may also authenticate the stakeholder owner if its identity is public to the consortium. The consultation of the attestations history allows any stakeholder having access to the ledger to know:

- the devices that have issued data in a given time interval,
- the order in which the devices performed actions.

R4: Power Failure. Resilience in the event of a power failure means not losing raw data or cryptographic attestations. The choice of implementation using two independent files monitored in permanent memory ensures data persistence in case of power failure.

R5: Privacy-Preserving Data. The privacy-preserving data requirement covers raw data at storage and during transportation. This requirement makes sense in a multi-stakeholders context where everyone wants to preserve the confidentiality of his data. With EmLog, SGX-log and EngraveChain, data is stored ciphered on a remote back-end common to all stakeholders, possibly in an enclave. With HistoTrust, raw data is stored locally in the memory of the device that produced it, and can be ex-filtrated via a VPN link by its owner. So, the privacy between devices is ensured. However, someone with physical access to the device can read the newly generated data before it is ex-filtrated. Thus, physical protection of the device in the factory is required to make access to the board peripherals difficult and detectable.

R6: Verifiability. The correctness of the data history is achieved knowing both the raw data and the recorded attestations. In the context of HistoTrust, how a stakeholder proves to others that his data history is correct without providing them with his raw data? Two solutions are considered: An accredited stakeholder, an insurance expert or a judicial officer for example, could have access to the raw data of each stakeholder, as well as to the ledger, in order to carry out the verifications. Another solution is to share between stakeholders a trusted application that verifies the data history in an OP-TEE environment. Once a secure channel has been established between the OP-TEE and the server hosting a stakeholder's raw data, access to the ledger being authorized to all, the verification is carried out in the OP-TEE and the output report shared with all.

R7: Multiple Stakeholders. EmLog and SGX-log offer solutions where the number of stakeholders is limited by the technology. HistoTrust brings a solution where the number of stakeholders is not limited by using blockchain technology as a complement to existing technologies. The stakeholders ensure the governance together, each having a validator node.

The Table 2 resumes this discussion.

Table 2. The satisfaction of needs by the main schemes

Scheme	R1	R2	R3	R4	R5	R6	R7
EmLog [4]	✓	✓	>	>	>	✓	>
SGX-log [9]	✓	✓	x	✓	>	✓	>
EngraveChain [12]	x	✓	✓	x	>	✓	✓
HistoTrust	✓	✓	✓	✓	>	✓	✓

requirement: ✓ met, > to improve, x not met

6   Conclusion

HistoTrust brings several contributions beyond the existing ones:

1. a scheme for attesting data histories produced at real-time by industrial applications embedded on independent IoT devices,
2. the deployment of a decentralized root-of-trust network based on the use of a TPM and an OP-TEE environment specific to each IoT device,
3. an architecture ensuring by design end-to-end security and privacy and providing trust within an ecosystem of independent stakeholders.

Among the perspectives considered, we will tackle the privacy-preserving data requirement in order to protect the data confidentiality in the device that produces it. For this, the structure of the embedded code will be revised: some parts of the code will be ported to the TPM in the form of a Java applet and thus becomes resistant to physical attacks. Others will be implemented in the OP-TEE to reinforce the confidentiality of the solution. It is also envisaged to test HistoTrust on mobile IoT devices.

Acknowledgement. This work is a collaborative research action that is partially supported by (CEA-Leti) the European project ECSEL InSecTT (www.insectt.eu, InSecTT: ECSEL Joint Undertaking (JU) under grant agreement No 876038. The JU receives support from the European Union's Horizon 2020 research and innovation program and Austria, Sweden, Spain, Italy, France, Portugal, Ireland, Finland, Slovenia, Poland, Netherlands, Turkey. The document reflects only the author's view and the Commission is not responsible for any use that may be made of the information it contains.) and by the French National Research Agency (ANR) in the framework of the Investissements d'avenir program (ANR-10-AIRT-05, irtnanoelec).

References

1. Trusted Computing Group: TCG Trusted Attestation Protocol (TAP) Use Cases for TPM Families 1.2 and 2.0 and DICE, Version 1.0, Revision 0.35, November 2019. https://trustedcomputinggroup.org/wp-content/uploads/TCG_TNC_TAP_Use_Cases_v1r0p35_published.pdf
2. Coker, G., et al.: Principles of remote attestation. Int. J. Inf. Secur. **10**, 63–81 (2011). https://doi.org/10.1007/s10207-011-0124-7
3. Yang, K., Chen, L., Zhang, Z., Newton, C.J.P., Yang, B., Xi, L.: Direct Anonymous Attestation with Optimal TPM Signing Efficiency, eprint 1128 (2018). https://eprint.iacr.org/2018/1128.pdf
4. Shepherd, C., Akram, R.N., Markantonakis, K.: EmLog: tamper-resistant system logging for constrained devices with TEEs. In: Hancke, G.P., Damiani, E. (eds.) WISTP 2017. LNCS, vol. 10741, pp. 75–92. Springer, Cham (2018). https://doi.org/10.1007/978-3-319-93524-9_5
5. Saroiu, S., Wolman, A.: I am a sensor, and I approve this message. In: Proceedings of the Eleventh Workshop on Mobile Computing Systems and Applications, HotMobile 2010. ACM Publisher (2010). https://citeseerx.ist.psu.edu/viewdoc/download?doi=10.1.1.155.242&rep=rep1&type=pdf. https://doi.org/10.1145/1734583.1734593
6. Hardjono, T., Smith, N.: An attestation architecture for Blockchain networks, arXiv:2005.04293 [cs.CR] (2020). http://export.arxiv.org/abs/2005.04293
7. Hennebert, C., Barrois, F.: Is the blockchain a relevant technology for the industry 4.0? In: Proceedings of the 2nd IEEE Conference on Blockchain Research & Applications for Innovative Networks and Services, BRAINS 2020, pp. 212–216. IEEE Publisher (2020). https://ieeexplore.ieee.org/document/9223290. https://doi.org/10.1109/BRAINS49436.2020.9223290
8. Schneier, B., Kelsey, J.: Cryptographic support for secure logs on untrusted machines. In: Proceedings of the 7th Conference on USENIX Security Symposium, vol. 7, SSYM 1998. USENIX Association (1998)
9. Karande, V., Bauman, E., Lin, Z., Khan, L.: SGX-log: securing system logs with SGX. In: Proceedings of the 2017 ACM on Asia Conference on Computer and Communications Security, ASIA CCS 2017, pp. 19–30. ACM Publisher (2017). https://doi.org/10.1145/3052973.3053034
10. Chakraborty, D., Hanzlik, L., Bugiel, S.: simTPM: user-centric TPM for mobile devices. In: Proceedings of the 28th Conference USENIX Security Symposium, SSYM 2019, pp. 533–550. USENIX Association (2019). https://www.usenix.org/conference/usenixsecurity19/presentation/chakraborty. ISBN 978-1-939133-06-9
11. Shepherd, C., et al.: Secure and trusted execution: past, present, and future - a critical review in the context of the internet of things and cyber-physical systems. In: Proceedings of the IEEE Trustcom/BigDataSE/ISPA, pp. 168–177. IEEE Publisher (2016). https://eprint.iacr.org/2016/454.pdf. https://doi.org/10.1109/TrustCom.2016.0060
12. Shekhtman, L., Waisbard, E.: EngraveChain: tamper-proof distributed log system. In: Proceedings of the 2nd Workshop on Blockchain-enabled Networked Sensor, BlockSys 2019. ACM Publisher (2019). https://dl.acm.org/doi/pdf/10.1145/3362744.3363346. https://doi.org/10.1145/3362744.3363346

13. Javaid, U., Aman, M.N., Sikdar, B.: BlockPro: blockchain based data provenance and integrity for secure IoT environments. In: The 1st Workshop on Blockchain-enabled Networked Sensor Systems, BlockSys 2018. ACM Publisher (2018). https://dl.acm.org/doi/pdf/10.1145/3282278.3282281. https://doi.org/10.1145/3282278.3282281

14. Elsts, A., Mitskas, E., Oikonomou, G.: Distributed ledger technology and the internet of things: a feasibility study. In: The 1st Workshop on Blockchain-enabled Networked Sensor Systems, BlockSys 2018. ACM Publisher (2018). https://dl.acm.org/doi/pdf/10.1145/3282278.3282280. https://doi.org/10.1145/3282278.3282280

15. Hengartner, U.: Location privacy based on trusted computing and secure logging. In: Proceedings of the 4th International Conference on Security and Privacy in Communication Networks, SecureComm 2008. ACM Publisher (2008). https://core.ac.uk/download/pdf/21748895.pdf. https://doi.org/10.1.1.216.7307

16. Koutroumpouchos, N., et al.: Secure edge computing with lightweight control-flow property-based attestation. In: Proceedings of the IEEE Conference on Network Softwarization, NetSoft 2019, pp. 84–92. IEEE Publisher (2019). https://ieeexplore.ieee.org/stamp/stamp.jsp?tp=&arnumber=8806658. https://doi.org/10.1109/NETSOFT.2019.8806658

17. Casado-Vara, R., de la Prieta, F., Prieto, J., Corchado, J.M.: Blockchain framework for IoT data quality via edge computing. In: Proceedings of the 1st Workshop on Blockchain-Enabled Networked Sensor Systems, BlockSys 2018, pp. 19–24. ACM Publisher (2018). https://dl.acm.org/doi/pdf/10.1145/3282278.3282282. https://doi.org/10.1145/3282278.3282282

18. Sabt, M., Achemlal, M., Bouabdallah, A.: Trusted execution environment: what it is, and what it is not. In: Proceedings of the 14th IEEE International Conference on Trust, Security and Privacy in Computing and Communications, TrusteCom 2015. IEEE Publisher (2015). https://hal.archives-ouvertes.fr/hal-01246364/document. https://doi.org/10.1109/Trustcom.2015.357

19. Gentilal, M., Martins, P., Sousa, L.: TrustZone-backed bitcoin wallet. In: Proceedings of the 4th Workshop on Cryptography and Security in Computing Systems, CS2 2017, pp. 25–28. ACM Publisher (2017). https://dl.acm.org/doi/pdf/10.1145/3031836.3031841. https://doi.org/10.1145/3031836.3031841

20. Szilágyi, P.: EIP-225: Clique proof-of-authority consensus protocol. Ethereum Improvement Proposal. https://eips.ethereum.org/EIPS/eip-225

21. STMicroelectronics: STM32MP15ROM code secure boot. https://wiki.st.com/stm32mpu/wiki/STM32MP15_ROM_code_secure_boot

22. Stucchi, D., Susella, R., Fragneto, P., Rossi, B.: Secure and effective implementation of an IOTA light node using STM32. In: The Proceedings of the 2nd Workshop on Blockchain-enabled Networked Sensor, BlockSys 2019. ACM Publiher (2019). https://dl.acm.org/doi/pdf/10.1145/3362744.3363344. https://doi.org/10.1145/3362744.3363344

23. Buchmann, J., Dahmen, E., Ereth, S., Hülsing, A., Rückert, M.: On the security of the winternitz one-time signature scheme. In: Nitaj, A., Pointcheval, D. (eds.) AFRICACRYPT 2011. LNCS, vol. 6737, pp. 363–378. Springer, Heidelberg (2011). https://doi.org/10.1007/978-3-642-21969-6_23

Automatic Annotation of Confidential Data in Java Code

Iulia Bastys[1]([envelope]), Pauline Bolignano[2], Franco Raimondi[2,3], and Daniel Schoepe[2]

[1] Chalmers University of Technology, Gothenburg, Sweden
bastys@chalmers.se
[2] Amazon Prime Video, London, UK
{frai,pln,schoeped}@amazon.com
[3] Middlesex University, London, UK
f.raimondi@mdx.ac.uk

Abstract. The problem of *confidential information leak* can be addressed by using automatic tools that take a set of *annotated* inputs (the *source*) and track their flow to public *sinks*. Unfortunately, manually annotating the code with labels specifying the secret sources is one of the main obstacles in the adoption of such trackers.

In this work, we present an approach for the automatic generation of labels for confidential data in Java programs. Our solution is based on a graph-based representation of Java methods: starting from a minimal set of known API calls, it propagates the labels both intra- and inter-procedurally until a fix-point is reached.

In our evaluation, we encode our synthesis and propagation algorithm in Datalog and assess the accuracy of our technique on seven previously annotated internal code bases, where we can reconstruct 75% of the pre-existing manual annotations. In addition to this single data point, we also perform an assessment using samples from the SecuriBench-micro benchmark, and we provide additional sample programs that demonstrate the capabilities and the limitations of our approach.

1 Introduction

A number of information flow trackers for automatically detecting leaks of confidential data have been developed for roughly every programming language: Joana [14] or the Checker framework [1] for Java, JSFlow [15] for JavaScript, TaintDroid [13] for Android apps are just a few examples of such tools. Whether they operate dynamically, statically, or in a mixed fashion, the trackers usually require the *manual* intervention of the developer for *explicitly* marking the variables that contain confidential information (the secret sources) and the methods that output on public channels (the public sinks). Then, based on these annotations, the trackers automatically detect any (explicit or implicit) information flow from the secret sources to the public sinks.

Confidential data leak issues are difficult to catch by standard engineering testing strategies. Therefore, at first glance, information flow trackers seem to be

© Springer Nature Switzerland AG 2022
E. Aïmeur et al. (Eds.): FPS 2021, LNCS 13291, pp. 146–161, 2022.
https://doi.org/10.1007/978-3-031-08147-7_10

the ideal solution to the problem of detecting such leaks. However, in practice, a different picture is displayed. Developers are burdened with an error-prone, manual task of figuring out what is sensitive, adding annotations to their code to highlight it, and keeping them up-to-date in a consistent way. As previously highlighted [11], this manual process of annotating (or labelling) the code is one of the main obstacles in the adoption of programming analysis tools at large scale. Furthermore, annotations generate risks of their own, as they may introduce compilation issues due to lack of support for them in the future. In a number of cases, these factors tip the balance between benefit and risk in favour of avoiding the use of automated tools that require manual annotation.

In this paper, we describe a method for *automatically* detecting and annotating confidential data in Java code. Once annotated, the code can be passed on to an information flow tracker for detecting data leaks. By employing an automatic labelling mechanism, we reduce the burden for developers and remove the risk associated with code changes.

More in detail, our approach is based on a graph-based representation of Java programs and consists of rules that characterise confidentiality. We refer to these rules as the confidentiality policy. For example, the policy includes the assumption that if a variable is encrypted, then it is highly likely that is confidential and it should be labeled as such. Our analysis is parametric in the confidentiality policy, so the policy can be extended or modified for different application domains.

Naturally, without any input from the developer, not *all* confidential data will be annotated. For example, variables that are not encrypted, or that do not match our algorithm's "selection" criteria will not be detected. Developers can still extend the policy with other cases, or even resort to manual annotations.

The paper is structured as follows: we introduce background material on graph-based representations for Java programs and the underlying Datalog-based solver in Sect. 2. Our method is described in Sect. 3, while details about its implementation and evaluation are reported in Sect. 4. A discussion on its limitations and possible extensions is presented in Sect. 5, while related work is discussed in Sect. 6. Finally, we conclude in Sect. 7.

2   Background: Graph-Based Representations for Java

Several graph-based representations of Java objects have been used in the past and their variations have appeared under different names such as Groums (Graph-based Object Usage Models) [21], BigGroums [19], and AUGs (API Usage Graphs) [7]. These representations are typically directed acyclic graphs capturing control and data flows, and interactions within and between objects, such as object instantiations, method calls, and data field accesses. While previous work has focussed mainly on detecting mis-uses of APIs [7,19], our aim is slightly different: we employ the graph-based representation to construct a set of potentially sensitive variables based on their usage in the code. We also extend previous representations by introducing *inter-procedural edges* (Sect. 3.4). For simplicity, we further refer to our graphs as *Groums*.

In the following, we give a brief overview of Groums, and for more details we refer the reader to the original work [7,19,21].

Definition 1 (Groum). *A Groum is a directed acyclic multi-graph with a single entry node and a single exit node. Nodes can be of three types: action, control, and data. Edges can be of two types: control- and data-flow.*

Nodes. There are three types of nodes in a Groum: action, control, and data. Data nodes (depicted as ellipses) denote the program literals and variables, control nodes (depicted as diamonds) denote the instructions altering the control flow of the program (such as conditional and loop statements, but also exception raising), and action nodes (depicted as boxes) denote all other instructions, such as method invocation (MI), assignments, etc. As a convention, each Groum has a single start and exit node, which have no corresponding instruction in the program they model, and are represented as data nodes.

Edges. A Groum has two types of edges: data flow and control flow. Data flow edges (depicted as directed dotted edges) are either outward edges connecting to an action or control node if the literal or variable they represent is used in that action or control statement, or inward edges if the data they represent is a result of an action, such as method return. Control flow edges (depicted as directed solid edges) connect action and control nodes and denote the order of instruction execution in the program.

Data flow edges are refined further, as follows: condition (`cond`) between a data node and a control node denoting the result of expression guarding the conditional or loop statement or the exception raised, definition (`def`) between an MI action node and a data node, parameter (`param`) between a data node and an MI action node, and receiver (`recv`) between a data node depicting an instance of a class object and a method of that class.

Control flow edges are also refined further, as follows: dependence (`dep`) between two action nodes or between an action node and a control node (not necessarily in that order) denoting the order of instruction execution in a program, exception throwing (`throw`) between an MI action node and a control node representing a `try` statement or `catch` clause, true/false (`T/F`) between a control node denoting the guard of a conditional or loop statement and the action/control node denoting the instruction to be executed after the guard evaluation.

An example of Groum, together with the corresponding Java code it models, is depicted in Fig. 1.

3   The Algorithm for Automatic Annotations

In our implementation, we extend the code developed for AUGs in [7], which is publicly available [4]. Since the Groum extraction algorithm has been designed with an interest only in intra-procedural analysis, a separate Groum is extracted

```
5 ...
6 public String myMethod() {
7   String high = getData();
8   String low = encrypt(high);
9   return low;
10 }
```

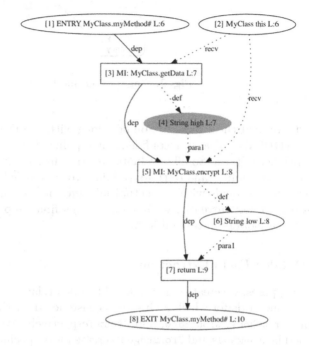

Fig. 1. Java method and its corresponding Groum.

for every method and no support for inter-procedural analyses is provided. In this section we describe in more detail our extension which allows for an inter-procedural analysis on Groums.

We employ Datalog and the tool Soufflé as the underlying reasoning engine for our approach. Datalog is a declarative, Prolog-style programming language "introduced as a query language for deductive databases in the late 70s", and Soufflé [6] is an open-source engine for Datalog that has been employed successfully for, among other things, static analysis of Java [2] and vulnerability detection [3].

Our algorithm employs three stages, as depicted in the diagram of Fig. 2. Grey boxes represent external programs, while white boxes refer to our implementation. Initially, a Groum is generated (a) for every method in the Java code base. Additional details on the extraction step can be found in previous work [7,21]. Also here, the Datalog generator (b) encodes the Groums as Datalog facts.

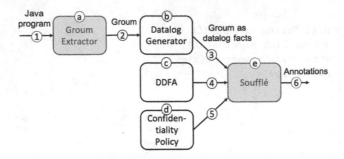

Fig. 2. Stages of our method.

Next, we send these facts to Soufflé, along with the Datalog-based data flow analysis (DDFA) (c), and a confidentiality policy (d) used for specifying the confidentiality criteria. Soufflé evaluates (e) the rules of the DDFA based on the given facts and policy, and outputs the data to be labeled (6).

The last step deals with the actual labelling of the confidential data in the Java source code. Currently, we implement this final step manually, presenting results to developers in textual form.

3.1 Datalog Facts Extraction

For our purposes, we create a hierarchy of Datalog relations for the Groum nodes, edges and methods for which a Groum is constructed: at the top level, we define relations `GroumNode`, `GroumEdge`, and `Groum` respectively. We use the information contained in `GroumNode` and `GroumEdge` to create more specific relations concerning the nodes and edges. E.g., relation `GroumDefinitionDFEdge` captures `def` edges, and `GroumMethodCallActionNode` represents an MI action node. In this way, we build a one-to-one correspondence between the AUG representation from [7] described in Sect. 2 and a set of Datalog relations.

3.2 Confidentiality Policy

The automated process for deciding which data to label needs some heuristics to base its decisions on. A reasonable indication that a piece of data is confidential is whether it is encrypted, or if it is the result of a decryption method. This represents what we refer to as the *confidentiality policy*.

As such, in our confidentiality policy we include Java APIs implementing cryptographic methods for encryption and decryption. These are methods that either have confidential *parameters* (encryption APIs) or confidential *returns* (decryption APIs). The policy can be extended by the developer with other cryptographically-related APIs or even with other methods known to return confidential data (e.g., `getDeviceId()`) or to have arguments referring to confidential data (e.g., `processUserOrder(userId)`).

Our algorithm further employs the confidentiality policy to detect the starting nodes for the DDFA (Sect. 3.3). A forward annotation propagation phase detects the data nodes influenced by these initial nodes (Sect. 3.4).

3.3   Initial Data Annotation Phase

As described in Sect. 2, a Groum contains parameter `param` and definition `def` data flow edges. These are the edges whose connecting data nodes we target, depending on whether the adjacent action nodes correspond to calls of methods contained in the confidentiality policy. As a result, in the phase of the DDFA for initial data annotation we retain all data nodes connected via a `param` edge to an MI action node denoting an encryption method invocation. The Datalog relation `ConfidentialVarsFromMethodParams` captures this.

Listing 1.

```
ConfidentialVarsFromMethodParams(method, id) ←
    MethodWithConfidentialParams(method, from),
    ParameterDFEdge(method, to, from).
```

Further, we retain all data nodes connected via a `def` edge to an MI action node representing a call to a decryption method. The Datalog relation `ConfidentialVarsFromMethodReturn` captures this.

Listing 2.

```
ConfidentialVarsFromMethodReturn(method, id) ←
    MethodWithConfidentialReturn(method, to),
    DefinitionDFEdge(method, from, to).
```

For example, in the code below, `h` is annotated by our algorithm as confidential as it is the argument of encryption function `encrypt`.

```
String h = getData();
String l = encrypt(h);
```

Observation. The cryptographic methods (or methods added by the developer in the confidentiality policy) whose implementation is part of the codebase under investigation are treated differently, as a Groum is generated for them. This is in contrast with the case when the methods are just API calls and hence no Groum is generated. In the former case, we do not use the intra-procedural `def` and `param` edges to mark the data nodes denoting confidential data, but instead the inter-procedural data flow edges `InputParamEdge` and `OutputParamEdge` which we describe in more detail in paragraph *Inter-procedural DFA* of the next subsection.

3.4   Data Annotation Propagation Phase

In order to evaluate our approach we also implement a forward propagation of the labels, as not all taint trackers support this step. The nodes retained during the initial data annotation phase are used as starting nodes for propagating the confidential labels forward in the graph, by following the data flow paths.

Put rather simply, Groums are control flow graphs extended with data nodes and contain no explicit data flow edges, i.e., there are no edges connecting data nodes with other data nodes. However, this is exactly what we need for our second stage of the DDFA—data annotation propagation through the data flow path.

Hence, we extend Groums with additional edges connecting data nodes, both intra- and inter-procedurally. Thus, two data nodes are connected (intra- or inter-procedurally) if there is a data dependence relation between the `from` node and the `to` node, i.e., the value of node `from` flows-to or influences the value of node `to`.

We discuss each case of dependence, intra- and inter-procedurally separately, starting with the former.

Intra-procedural DFA. At the moment, we support the intra-procedural cases listed below. Note we also model data flows via exceptions (not listed in the rules below).

Listing 3.

```
IntraDFEdge(method, from, to) ←
  (ReceiverDFEdge(method, from, recv),
   DefinitionDFEdge(method, recv, to))
  ;
  (ParameterDFEdge(method, from, m),
   DefinitionDFEdge(method, m, to),
   ¬IsGroum(method, m))
  ;
  (ConditionDFEdge(method, from, cond),
   ControlFlowBlock(method, cond, join),
   cond < id <= join,
   DefinitionDFEdge(method, id, to)).
```

Observe from the last case of relation `IntraDFEdge` that our analysis takes into account control dependencies, whereas typical taint analyses consider only data dependencies for tainting. This means that a control flow block (such as conditional branches or loops) guarded by confidentially-labeled data will taint everything (re-)defined inside it. More specifically, assuming `h` is marked as confidential in the program below, `l` will be marked as confidential as well, as their corresponding data nodes will be connected through an `IntraDFEdge`.

```
if (h > 0) { l = 1; } else { l = 0; }
```

In this regard, our analysis performs an over-approximation, as in the example which follows, a slight variation of the previous one, 1 is marked as confidential, although at runtime it will be influenced by h only if h > 0.

```
if (h > 0) { l = 1; }
```

Inter-procedural DFA. Unfortunately, the original implementation of Groums in [7] does not provide support for inter-procedural analyses, as a separate graph is generated for every method of the program being analysed and no relation between them is provided. Thus, there are no inter-procedural (data flow) edges, and no call-graph is given.

In order to capture inter-procedural data flows, we extend the initial Groum analysis with three new types of edges that connect previously disconnected Groums by creating three new Datalog relations:

- `CallDependenceEdge`—between an MI action node in the caller Groum and the start node of the corresponding callee Groum of the method invoked in the action node.
- `InputParameterEdge`—between a data node denoting a parameter to an MI action node in the caller Groum and its corresponding argument node in the callee Groum of the method invoked in the action node.
- `OutputParameterEdge`—between a return action node in the callee Groum and the data node defined by an MI action node in the caller Groum denoting the method depicted by callee Groum.

Further, based on these new edges, we define relation `InterDFEdge` for connecting data nodes in different Groums:

Listing 4.

```
InterDFEdge(caller, from, callee, to) ←
  (InputParameterEdge(caller, from, callee, param),
   DefinitionDFEdge(callee, param, to))
  ;
  (OutputParameterEdge(caller, to, callee, return),
   ParameterDFEdge(callee, from, return)).
```

Annotation Propagation. We obtain all data nodes originating in the nodes computed during the initial phase by following the data flow paths obtained from relations `IntraDFEdge` and `InterDFEdge` (a path is defined as the transitive closure of an edge relation). The relation `ConfidentialDFPath` is responsible for this.

Listing 5.

```
ConfidentialDFPath(caller, from, callee, to, cxt) ←
  (DFPath(caller, from, callee, to, cxt),
   NodeFromInitialPhase(caller, from)
   ;
   ConfidentialDFEdge(caller, from, callee, to, cxt)
```

```
1 public void backwardInter(String s) {
2   String h1 = "high";
3   String l = myMethod(h1);
4 }
5
6 public String myMethod(String h2) {
7   return encrypt(h2);
```

Fig. 3. Inter-procedural example.

```
;
ConfidentialDFPath(caller, from, m, id, cxt),
DFPath(m, id, callee, to, _)),
¬IsDeclassified(callee, to).
```

Note that not all data nodes belonging to a data flow path originating in the data nodes returned by the initial phase of DDFA may require annotations. Assume the following code:

```
enc = encrypt(pwd);
```

DDFA will rightfully mark `pwd` as in need of annotation, as it is the argument of an encryption method. In addition, the DDFA will create a data flow edge between the parameter node `pwd` and the defined variable `enc`. Since `pwd` is annotated, `enc` would become annotated as well, although there is no need for it, as encryption methods act as declassifiers and no information can be learned about the encrypted value.

This is the role of relation `IsDeclassified` called during the creation of a `ConfidentialDFPath`, to check whether a data node should be marked as declassifier. If a node is marked as such, then all the nodes on the data flow path are discarded and as consequence, not marked for receiving annotations.

This backward step also works inter-procedurally. For example, in function `backwardInter` in Fig. 3, `h1` is properly marked as confidential, because it is used as a parameter of `myMethod`, and the parameter of `myMethod` is marked as confidential as an argument of a sanitiser function.

Observe relation `ConfidentialDFPath` takes a 5th argument—cxt, which is used to distinguish between different calls to a certain callee method taking place in the same caller method. E.g., our analysis is able to distinguish between the two calls to the method `foo` in the snippet below:

```
int x = foo(a);
int y = foo(b);
```

4   Evaluation

We have implemented the DDFA analysis in Datalog. The actual Datalog code for the deduction rules consists of approximately 650 lines of code. The Datalog

```
protected void doGet(HttpServletRequest req, HttpServletResponse
    resp) throws IOException {
  String name = req.getParameter(FIELD_NAME);
  Object o1 = name;
  Object o2 = name.concat("abc");
  Object o3 = "anc";

  PrintWriter writer = resp.getWriter();
  writer.println(o1);                          /* BAD */
  writer.println(o2);                          /* BAD */
  writer.println(o3);                          /* OK */
}
```

Fig. 4. Test case Aliasing4 from SecuriBench-microbenchmark.

facts generator is implemented on top of the existing AUG Java implementation from [7] and consists of approximatively 350 additional lines of code. In this section we report results obtained in two scenarios: using a publicly available benchmark and on previously annotated Java code within Amazon code bases.

4.1   SecuriBench

In addition to programs extending the basic structure of the examples described in the previous sections, our analysis was tested on the SecuriBench-microbenchmark [5]. SecuriBench-microbenchmark contains minimal test cases, each of them checking a specific ability of the static analyser. For example, Aliasing4 (depicted in Fig. 4) checks for simple aliasing with casts. The test case is annotated with "BAD" or "OK", indicating what should be flagged or not. In this case, our analysis behaves correctly, it detects the two illicit outputs but not the last one which is valid.

Note that this benchmark is not designed for assessing how precise the labelling is performed, it only evaluates the label propagation. For example, in Aliasing4, we have marked req.getParameter as being a method with confidential return. Therefore the labelling part of our algorithm marks name as confidential, and the label propagation part then propagates it forward.

The results of our analysis are shown in Table 1, by reporting on 12 categories. The first column presents the category, the second the number of true positives (TPs) detected by our analysis compared to the total, while the last column depicts the false positives (FPs) given by our analysis.

Our analysis was able to flag most of the *aliasing* (10/12) and *basic* (54/60) cases, with only 2 FPs. 5 of the missed cases and the 2 FPs are due to lack of field and array sensitivity, other 3 are due to the fact that we do not mark constructors, such as new FileWriter as public sinks. These results show that our DDFA analysis is able to handle complex control flows such as the one in example Basic28, in which there are 39 branchings, nested in various combinations up to 9 times deep.

Table 1. SecuriBench-micro benchmark

Category	TP/Total	FP
Aliasing	10/12	0
Arrays	2/9	1
Basic	54/60	2
Collections	0/14	1
Data structures	0/5	0
Factory	3/3	0
Inter	8/16	0
Pred	3/3	4
Sanitizer	3/4	3
Session	0/3	0
Strong updates	0/1	0

Table 2. Reconstructed annotation

Service	Found/Total	Analysis time (s)
S1	0/1	5.53
S2	1/1	3.85
S3	1/2	3.86
S4	2/2	3.71
S5	1/1	3.72
S6	2/2	3.99
S7	2/3	4.11

4.2 Reconstructing Existing Annotations

A further data point for the evaluation of our approach is provided by considering code that has been previously annotated with labels to characterise confidential information. In particular, we have considered 7 existing software packages implementing Amazon services and we have extracted the Java implementation of classes that contained annotated variables using the Checker framework [1]. Overall, we identified seven files containing 12 annotated variables. Our analysis was able to find 9 out of the 12 annotated variables.

Table 2 reports the number of annotations found by our algorithm versus the total number of annotations present and the execution time (all the experiments have been performed on a standard 2019 Macbook laptop with 16 Gb of Ram). The size of each class ranges between 60 and 426 lines of code; the names of services have been anonymised.

5 Discussion and Limitations

One key feature of our method resides in working with a graph-based representation of the program, and its modeling in Datalog. This renders our approach (almost) language-independent. Once a Groum conversion is applied to a program expressed in a language other than Java, our Datalog analysis would require minimal interventions before it could annotate those programs as well.

5.1 Limitations

Our analysis is work in progress and, as discussed below, it cannot provide completeness guarantees and it does not deal with persistent memory storage. However, as seen in the preliminary results discussed in the previous section, it already shows some promising results. There are several limitations worth mentioning.

First, with the exception of the backward propagation of declassifiers, our framework performs a forward analysis only, so it misses to label data when backwards steps are required. For instance, in the program below, the DDFA will label as confidential the return value of `foo(pwd)`, but not `pwd`.

```
encryptedPassword = encrypt(foo(pwd));
```

Second, when performing the backward step for detecting the arguments of encryption methods, our analysis only looks at the last definition of those arguments, and it does not inspect how they were formed. For example, in the program below, our analysis only annotates `h2`.

```
String l1 = "Something_Public";
String h1 = "Something_Secret";
String h2 = l1 + h1;
String l2 = encrypt(h2);
```

The analysis could be extended to cover this case by performing a backwards analysis as well, but without additional information provided by the developer, it would lead to additional false positives. E.g., in the program above, it would falsely annotate `l1`.

Consider again function `backwardInter` from Fig. 3. Although `myMethod` is considered a declassifier, as it returns the encryption of its argument, due to our computing of the transitive closure of the edge relations, `l` ends up falsely marked as confidential.

The approach presented in this paper targets Java and therefore we support dynamic memory allocation, even if we are not fully precise in terms of context sensitivity. For instance, adding call-sensitivity context would further improve DDFA's precision. Consider the program below:

```
String userId = getUserId();
String l1 = foo("abc");
String h = foo(userId);
String l2 = foo("xyz");
```

First, the user ID (returned by method with confidential returns `getUserId`) is stored in variable `userId`, then method `foo` is invoked three times each with parameters `"abc"`, `userId`, and `"xyz"` respectively, and its results are stored in variables `l1`, `h`, and `l2` respectively. The analysis should only label as confidential `h`, but it labels as confidential `l2` as well, as the returned value of method `foo` is marked as confidential in its Groum due to the dependency to confidential `userId`.

Finally, as we previously mentioned, our analysis does not currently support field sensitivity.

5.2   Other Approaches

Improving Precision. As discussed in the previous sections, our algorithm uses a single Groum for every method invoked and encodes additional information to capture context-call sensitivity and to distinguish between different invocations of the same method.

Another approach would be to use a Groum for every method invocation. The resulting inter-procedural graph may *explode*, but the algorithm's precision would improve. An investigation on how the performance may be affected in this case would also be required. The implementation of this variant, as well as an analysis on the trade-offs between the two approaches is left for future work.

Upgrade to Information Flow Analysis Tool. A natural extension of our algorithm is to transform it into an information flow analysis tool, by expanding the confidentiality policy to include methods that should be considered as public sinks. Then, we could get an information flow analysis by extending the algorithm with a relation which simply checks that no annotated nodes in the graph are parameter nodes of the public methods.

6   Related Work

There is a substantial body of work in this area. In this section, we discuss and compare our method with some of the related work.

Automatic Labelling of Confidential Data. Merlin [18] infers information-flow specifications in .NET code using a data propagation graph to model inter-procedural data flows. In contrast to our approach, Merlin uses probabilistic constraints, potentially resulting in an exponential number of constraints that are then approximated to achieve scalability. Zhu et al. [27] present an approach to infer confidentiality annotations for library calls without the corresponding source code being available, but still assumes other sources and sinks in the program to be annotated.

Groums. Groums (Graph-based Object Usage Model) [21], which form the basis of our approach, were initially designed for automatically inferring API usage patterns from an API's usage in a code base. Groums were later also used for detecting API-misuse [7].

Information-Flow Control. Information-flow control [16,23] is an active area of research focused on detecting information leaks in programs providing stronger security guarantees than taint trackers. There exist both dynamic and static approaches to information-flow control for many languages, such as Jif [20], Joana [14], and Paragon [9] as extensions of Java, LIO [10,26] and FlowCaml [22] for languages in the ML family, as well as JSFlow [15], a dynamic information-flow tracker for EcmaScript [12]. All of the above approaches require some amount of user annotation to indicate which inputs to a program are confidential. The approach presented in this paper can be used to automate this annotation process, assuming the availability of Groums, and can potentially simplify the use of information-flow control in practice.

Taint Tracking. Taint tracking is a practical approach to information-flow control that intentionally ignores [24] some information leakage resulting from less explicit features of program semantics such as control-flow, termination, and concurrency. Taint tracking can be applied both statically [17] as well as dynamically [25]. Similar to the approach here, Li et al. [17] present a static taint tracking system based on program dependency graphs (PDGs), which have similarities with Groums. This representation would allow an approach similar to the one presented here to automate the labelling of confidential inputs and outputs. Many taint-tracking systems have been applied to real-world applications: TaintDroid [13] and FlowDroid [8] are taint-tracking systems for Android applications. The Checker Framework [1] allows building custom type checking extensions for Java programs and includes support for taint tracking. Similar to information-flow control approaches, such systems typically require manual annotation to indicate which sources and sinks are confidential. The approach here can be used to lessen the annotation burden to developers, potentially enabling an easier use of taint tracking on real world software.

7 Conclusion

We have presented a method for automatically annotating confidential data in Java programs. Our method uses a graph-based program representation based on Groums to mark the data nodes denoting the confidential information, based on a confidentiality policy. This policy is designed to mark as confidential data which either is encrypted or results from decryption operations. The confidentiality policy also allows for developer extensions to capture more cases of interest. We have implemented our approach using Datalog and we have assessed the current features and limitations against publicly available examples. We have also validated the approach using existing internal code bases, reproducing 75% of the existing annotations.

We see our work as an initial step in the construction of a fully automated tool to generate annotations for confidential data, with the long-term goal aim of enabling zero-touch information flow analysis.

Acknowledgments. This work was partially supported by the Wallenberg AI, Autonomous Systems and Software Program (WASP) funded by the Knut and Alice Wallenberg Foundation.

References

1. Checker framework. https://checkerframework.org/manual/
2. Doop framework. https://bitbucket.org/yanniss/doop/src/master/
3. Java Vulnerability Detection. https://labs.oracle.com/pls/apex/f?p=labs:49:::::P49_PROJECT_ID:122
4. MUDetect. https://github.com/stg-tud/MUDetect
5. SecuriBench-micro. https://github.com/too4words/securibench-micro
6. Soufflé. https://souffle-lang.github.io
7. Amann, S., Nguyen, H.A., Nadi, S., Nguyen, T.N., Mezini, M.: Investigating next steps in static API-misuse detection. In: MSR 2019, 26–27 May 2019, Montreal, Canada (2019)
8. Arzt, S., et al.: Flowdroid: precise context, flow, field, object-sensitive and lifecycle-aware taint analysis for android apps. In: PLDI 2014, Edinburgh, United Kingdom, 09–11 June 2014, pp. 259–269 (2014)
9. Broberg, N., van Delft, B., Sands, D.: Paragon - practical programming with information flow control. J. Comput. Secur. **25**(4–5), 323–365 (2017)
10. Buiras, P., Vytiniotis, D., Russo, A.: HLIO: mixing static and dynamic typing for information-flow control in haskell. In: Proceedings of the 20th ACM SIGPLAN International Conference on Functional Programming, ICFP 2015, Vancouver, BC, Canada, 1–3 September 2015, pp. 289–301 (2015)
11. Christakis, M., Bird, C.: What developers want and need from program analysis: an empirical study. In: Proceedings of the 31st IEEE/ACM International Conference on Automated Software Engineering, pp. 332–343 (2016)
12. ECMA International: Standard ECMA-262 - ECMAScript Language Specification. 5.1 edn, June 2011
13. Enck, W., et al.: Taintdroid: an information-flow tracking system for realtime privacy monitoring on smartphones. In: Proceedings of 9th USENIX Symposium on Operating Systems Design and Implementation, OSDI 2010, 4–6 October 2010, Vancouver, BC, Canada, pp. 393–407 (2010)
14. Hammer, C., Snelting, G.: Flow-sensitive, context-sensitive, and object-sensitive information flow control based on program dependence graphs. Int. J. Inf. Secur. **8**(6), 399–422 (2009)
15. Hedin, D., Birgisson, A., Bello, L., Sabelfeld, A.: JSFlow: tracking information flow in JavaScript and its APIs. In: SAC (2014)
16. Hedin, D., Sabelfeld, A.: A perspective on information-flow control. In: Software Safety and Security - Tools for Analysis and Verification, pp. 319–347 (2012)
17. Li, B., Ma, R., Wang, X., Wang, X., He, J.: DepTaint: a static taint analysis method based on program dependence. In: Proceedings of the 2020 4th International Conference on Management Engineering, Software Engineering and Service Sciences, pp. 34–41 (2020)
18. Livshits, V.B., Nori, A.V., Rajamani, S.K., Banerjee, A.: Merlin: specification inference for explicit information flow problems. In: PLDI 2009, Dublin, Ireland, 15–21 June 2009, pp. 75–86 (2009)

19. Mover, S., Sankaranarayanan, S., Olsen, R.B.P., Chang, B.E.: Mining framework usage graphs from app corpora. In: 25th International Conference on Software Analysis, Evolution and Reengineering, SANER 2018, Campobasso, Italy, 20–23 March 2018 (2018)
20. Myers, A.C., Zheng, L., Zdancewic, S., Chong, S., Nystrom, N.: Jif 3.0: Java information flow, July 2006. http://www.cs.cornell.edu/jif
21. Nguyen, T.T., Nguyen, H.A., Pham, N.H., Al-Kofahi, J.M., Nguyen, T.N.: Graph-based mining of multiple object usage patterns. In: ESEC/FSE, 2009, Amsterdam, The Netherlands, 24–28 August 2009 (2009)
22. Pottier, F., Simonet, V.: Information flow inference for ML. In: Conference Record of POPL 2002: The 29th SIGPLAN-SIGACT Symposium on Principles of Programming Languages, Portland, OR, USA, 16–18 January 2002, pp. 319–330 (2002)
23. Sabelfeld, A., Russo, A.: From dynamic to static and back: riding the roller coaster of information-flow control research. In: Pnueli, A., Virbitskaite, I., Voronkov, A. (eds.) PSI 2009. LNCS, vol. 5947, pp. 352–365. Springer, Heidelberg (2010). https://doi.org/10.1007/978-3-642-11486-1_30
24. Schoepe, D., Balliu, M., Pierce, B.C., Sabelfeld, A.: Explicit secrecy: a policy for taint tracking. In: IEEE European Symposium on Security and Privacy, EuroS&P 2016, Saarbrücken, Germany, 21–24 March 2016, pp. 15–30 (2016)
25. Schwartz, E.J., Avgerinos, T., Brumley, D.: All you ever wanted to know about dynamic taint analysis and forward symbolic execution (but might have been afraid to ask). In: 31st IEEE Symposium on Security and Privacy, S&P 2010, 16–19 May 2010, Berleley/Oakland, California, USA, pp. 317–331 (2010)
26. Stefan, D., Russo, A., Mitchell, J.C., Mazières, D.: Flexible dynamic information flow control in haskell. In: Proceedings of the 4th ACM SIGPLAN Symposium on Haskell, Haskell 2011, Tokyo, Japan, 22 September 2011, pp. 95–106 (2011)
27. Zhu, H., Dillig, T., Dillig, I.: Automated inference of library specifications for source-sink property verification. In: Shan, C. (ed.) APLAS 2013. LNCS, vol. 8301, pp. 290–306. Springer, Cham (2013). https://doi.org/10.1007/978-3-319-03542-0_21

A Quantile-Based Watermarking Approach for Distortion Minimization

Maikel Lázaro Pérez Gort[(✉)], Martina Olliaro, and Agostino Cortesi

Ca' Foscari University of Venice, DAIS, Via Torino 155, 30172 Mestre, Venice, Italy
{maikel.perezgort,martina.olliaro,cortesi}@unive.it

Abstract. Distortion-based watermarking techniques embed the watermark by performing tolerable changes in the digital assets being protected. For relational data, mark insertion can be performed over the different data types of the database relations' attributes. An important goal for distortion-based approaches is to minimize as much as possible the changes that the watermark embedding provokes into data, preserving their usability, watermark robustness, and capacity. This paper proposes a quantile-based watermarking technique for numerical cover type focused on preserving the distribution of attributes used as mark carriers. The experiments performed to validate our proposal show a significant distortion reduction compared to traditional approaches while maintaining watermark capacity levels. Also, positive achievements regarding robustness are visible, evidencing our technique's resilience against subset attacks.

Keywords: Distortion reduction · Numeric distribution · Quantile · Robust watermarking · Watermark capacity

1 Introduction

With the easy access and spreading of digital content through the Internet, data copyright protection faces more and more challenges every day. Digital watermarking has become a handy tool to deal with false ownership claims and illegal data copy distribution. The general idea of watermarking techniques consists of adding hidden content (i.e., the watermark) into the protected data. Under demands, watermarks can be extracted and used as evidence of rightful ownership and data tampering, among others. Considering that watermarking is not based on blocking access or copying data, their portability benefits (e.g., allowing data to reach the target communities) are never affected. For the sake of authenticity and trust, usability and intellectual property of data must be protected at all costs.

According to the distortion criterion, watermarking techniques can be classified as distortion-free or distortion-based [2,16]. Distortion-free techniques generate the watermark from a particular digital asset copy (or embed it into the

E. Aïmeur et al. (Eds.): FPS 2021, LNCS 13291, pp. 162–176, 2022.
https://doi.org/10.1007/978-3-031-08147-7_11

data without performing updates) [14,17]. In contrast, distortion-based techniques perform watermark embedding by modifying the data as long as changes are permissible and do not compromise their usability [9].

Distortion-based watermarking techniques are characterized by two main processes: (i) watermark embedding, (ii) and its extraction. The embedding process first encodes the watermark and then performs its injection into the data. If the encoding uses a meaningful source (e.g., an image file, an audio stream, or a text document) for watermark generation, the watermark is classified as meaningful. Otherwise, it is classified as meaningless [7]. Instead, the extraction process detects every mark from the data and then carries out their extraction to proceed with the watermark reconstruction. Some techniques only perform the detection phase, stating the presence or absence of the watermark in the data [4]. Performing both embedding and extraction processes requires at least one parameter defined as the Secret Key. This parameter must remain secret, and it has to keep the same value for both processes [1].

In most cases, distortion-based approaches are oriented to ownership protection and must be resilient against attacks focused on compromising watermark detection. For this reason, they are classified as robust techniques.

One of the major challenges for distortion-based techniques is guaranteeing data usability despite the changes performed on them. This is hard to achieve considering that according to the robustness requirement, a significant number of marks must be inserted into the data to allow the watermark signal persistence despite attacks. Then, the higher the number of marks inserted, the higher the distortion over the data. Thus, the number of marks embedded into the digital assets (defined as watermark capacity) is inversely proportional to the watermark imperceptibility in the data. Indeed, the imperceptibility requirement is expected to be accomplished as long as the distortion does not cause degradation of data usability.

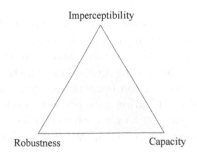

Fig. 1. Trade-off among robustness, imperceptibility, and capacity requirements [10].

There is a trade-off that watermarking techniques must deal with regarding robustness, capacity, and imperceptibility requirements (see Fig. 1). The strong link among them and the equality of their relevance for the technique's success is represented as an equilateral triangle. As long as one of them is affected, the others will be impacted for better or worst. For example, a common approach for distortion reduction is to reduce the watermark capacity, negatively affecting the technique's robustness. Indeed, it is not possible to significantly increase the imperceptibility without having a negative influence over robustness.

1.1 Paper Contribution

In this paper, we propose a strategy to benefit watermark imperceptibility in techniques embedding marks in numerical attributes (a.k.a., numerical cover type watermarks) of database relations, without affecting watermark capacity.

Our main goal is to preserve the numerical distribution of the columns used as carriers as much as possible, avoiding some values from moving from quantiles defined to control the distribution. When the new value containing the mark changes quantile after the embedding, the marking should not be rolled back since this would reduce the watermark capacity. Instead of allowing values changes between quantiles, we propose a mechanism for performing mark embedding in other carriers' distributions allowed regions.

The experiments performed show a significant enhancement of imperceptibility once numerical distribution is kept as similar as possible with respect to the original unwatermarked columns. We used scatter statistical metrics to compare the effects of watermark embedding of our approach vs. conventional embedding. Also, we applied the Kullback-Leibler divergence to measure the relative entropy between the distribution of the original data and the one resulting from the watermark embedding. Since the watermark capacity is not affected, robustness improves, making it more difficult for attackers to compromise watermark signal detection.

1.2 Paper Structure

The rest of the paper is organized as follows. Section 2 offers details of the theoretical background, presenting commonly used notations in the relational data watermarking research field. Also, in this section, the related work (mostly focused on approaches oriented to distortion-reduction) is given. Section 3 presents our proposal, depicting the benefits and downsides of each strategy of quantile-based numerical distribution preservation. Section 4 presents the experimental results, mainly oriented to show the behavior of robustness, capacity, and imperceptibility watermark requirements. Section 5 concludes.

2 Theoretical Background

Contrary to multimedia data, effects of the watermark (WM) embedding into relational data are not perceived directly by human systems (e.g., human visual system, human auditory system). Instead, a Middle Coded-based Layer (MCL) composing management information systems processes the data and delivers it to users in more suitable formats such as digital reports. This has an important consequence. Indeed, WM imperceptibility does not depend on human systems limitations but on the processes implemented by MCL, which are often based on business rules. Following that principle, it may appear that WM capacity benefits from the inability of direct human perception over relational data changes. Nevertheless, as long as digital systems generate outputs from the watermarked data (having others using them as inputs), the slightest changes will drive drastic consequences.

Among their classification criteria, relational data watermarking defines the technique type according to the data type of attribute selected in the relation R to perform the WM embedding (also known as mark carriers). Some techniques use textual attributes, being classified as textual cover type approaches (e.g., Al-Haj & Odeh [3], Pérez Gort et al. [6]). Others are focused on numerical cover types (e.g., Rani et al. [12], Hou & Xian [8], Zhao et al. [18]), etc. For numerical cover type approaches, it is very common to perform WM embedding by inserting each mark in one position selected from a given range of less significant bits (lsb) of the carrier attribute numerical value binary representation.

Even if just the first lsb is changed, the impact at column level could be higher compared to at attribute-value level. Also, depending on the MCL implemented processes, changes might not be tolerable if a general description of the behavior of the data is used for decision making. Some changes at single-value level might appear tolerated, but the effects over the whole set of data might contradict database purposes.

2.1 Related Work

In 2002, Agrawal & Kiernan [2] highlighted for the first time the need for watermarking relational data for ownership protection and formalized the so-called AHK watermarking algorithm. Precisely, based on the condition that some attribute's values can tolerate changes (as long as data usability is preserved), they proposed to mark only numeric columns. Embedding is performed at bit level, where carriers are pseudo-randomly selected according to a Secret Key (SK). However, this technique has proved to be vulnerable to simple attacks (e.g., bit flipping and updates attacks) due to the meaningless of WM information (i.e., bit pattern). Usability control is based on the number of lsb available for marking in an attribute and the number of marked tuples, while constraints deployed over the database are ignored.

Statistic metrics describing the numerical distribution featuring the attribute selected for WM embedding are a good reference to appreciate the general changes performed compared to the distribution before the embedding.

In 2004, Sion et al. [15] proposed a numerical cover type technique performing embedding of marks at bit level. For this case, usability maintenance is done by data statistics preservation. Also, the marking of selected tuples is performed according to database constraints and an error range allowed for data, using the Mean Squared Error (MSE) as reference. Nevertheless, this proposal requires tuple ordering to define subsets identifying some tuples as group bounds, being vulnerable to subset reverse order, tuple updates, and deletion attacks.

In 2010, Sardroudi & Ibrahim [13] proposed a new watermarking technique using as WM source a binary image. Given a relation, their schema embeds marks only in one numerical attribute, focusing on guaranteeing robustness and minimizing data variation by flipping the first *lsb* depending on the value of the mark embedded. This technique shows good results against subset reverse order attacks. Nevertheless, capacity is often affected by the partial embedding of the watermark, making it vulnerable to other malicious operations such as subset update attacks.

Pérez Gort et al. [11], in 2017, proposed a technique extending Sardroudi & Ibrahim's scheme, where the embedding is performed over more than one attribute per tuple according to one parameter defined as Attribute Fraction (AF). In this case, distortion reduction at bit level is also performed, but flipping all *lsb*s to the right of the one selected for mark embedding, depending on their values and the value of the mark. Nevertheless, reducing distortion at the bit level does not always benefit the numerical distribution of the carrier column. In that sense, WM embedding is performed blindly and the general quality of data could be compromised.

Techniques based on the AHK [2] algorithm select $\omega \approx \eta/\gamma$ tuples to mark out of the η stored in the relation R, being $\gamma \in [1, \eta]$ the Tuples Fraction (TF) representing the inverse of the marking density. For each tuple selected, an attribute (out of ν attributes) is chosen and the binary representation of the contained value is used for inserting the mark. Sardroudi & Ibrahim's [13] technique increases the link between the watermark source and R. To this aim, each pixel *pseudo-randomly* selected from the binary image used as WM source is *xored* with one of the most significant bits (*msb*) of a range given as parameter (denoted as β) of the value where the mark will be embedded. Finally, the *lsb* position is selected from a given number of bits available for marking (denoted as ξ), and the mark generated is embedded into it. Considering the approaches just mentioned embed only one mark per tuple, Pérez Gort et al. [11] extends the embedding to more than one attribute by defining AF (denoted as $\delta \in [1, \nu]$), where $\delta = 1$ forces all attributes of the selected tuples to be marked.

3   Proposed Approach

Note that none of the approaches discussed in the previous section analyzes the distortion caused by WM embedding from a numerical distribution point of view. This is a critical issue since, depending on the distribution variation, data can result useless after the embedding, according to the data owner's goals. In this work, besides taking care of the distortion from the binary level perspective, also different proposals are presented to preserve each attribute's distribution. Our main goal is to maintain as similar as possible the resulting distributions after WM embedding with respect to the one each attribute had before R being distorted.

Formally, let us denote by $\mathcal{D}_i$ the distribution of the attribute i before the WM embedding, and $\mathcal{D}_i'$ after the embedding. If we denote by $\equiv$ the equivalence relation between distributions, we aim to achieve the following condition:

$$\forall i \in [0, v - 1] : \mathcal{D}_i \equiv \mathcal{D}_i' \tag{1}$$

We start by fragmenting each distribution $\mathcal{D}_i$ in g quantiles (see Fig. 2a)) to prevent the distribution from suffering high variations during the WM embedding.

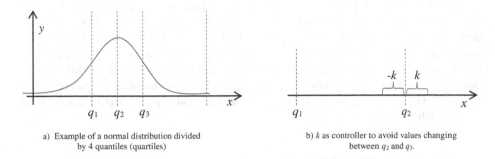

a) Example of a normal distribution divided   b) k as controller to avoid values changing
by 4 quantiles (quartiles)   between q_2 and q_3.

Fig. 2. Numerical distribution split into 4 quantiles (known as quartiles).

Besides the number of quantiles g, also a threshold to control the set of values restricted to be marked in the limits of the quantile (denoted as k) is considered in order to prevent distribution variations (see Fig. 2b)).

The main lines of action followed in this work are: (i) reversing the embedding and preventing the value from being marked, (ii) performing the embedding by assigning values to other distributions as long as quantile changes are not carried out. Each one of these alternatives is detailed below.

3.1   First Action: Mark Embedding Cancellation

Once a value v is selected to be marked, its quantile is located according to $[q_l, q_u] = \mathcal{Q}(\mathcal{D}_i, v, g)$, where $\mathcal{Q}$ is the function returning the quantile boundaries in the distribution $\mathcal{D}_i$, split in g fragments. Also, q_l and q_u corresponds to the lower and upper quantile bounds, respectively. Then, the embedding of the mark m is performed according to $\mathcal{E}(m, v) = v'$, being $\mathcal{E}$ the embedding function given in [11], and v' the resulting distorted value. Finally, if $v' \notin [q_l + k, q_u - k]$, embedding is rolled back and the algorithm proceeds checking the rest of R.

The main downside of this action is the WM capacity reduction (if WM length is too high with respect to η) due to rolling back the embedding of some marks. Nevertheless, WM recognition will be carried out as long as the number of tuples in R is higher than WM length.

3.2   Second Action: Change the Target Distribution

The second action is focused on saving those marks rolled back from the embedding in the previously described action (cf. Sect. 3.1). The attributes in the selected tuple will be presented as a cyclic structure where A_{v-1} will precede A_0 (being A_i the ith attribute of R). Then, if the value v' for A_i is out of its quantile, the embedding is rolled back, and the attribute $A_{(i+1)}$ is selected for the embedding. Moreover, attribute values in the ranges $[q_l, q_l + k]$ and $[q_u - k, q_u]$ are not considered for the embedding since it is very likely that v' will belong to the same range.

Finally, values of ξ and k are selected according to $k \geq [\xi]_{10}$ (being $[\xi]_{10}$ the decimal notation of the number of lsbs). This way, high pseudo-random embedding (which increases the difficulty for attackers to compromise WM detection) and a significant distortion reduction (with respect to methods not fragmenting $\mathcal{D}_i$ in quantiles) will be achieved. Precisely, capacity is maintained while distortion resulting from WM embedding is reduced both at the binary level of v' (by applying the strategy given in [11]) and at the statistical distribution level of each attribute used as carrier.

4   Experimental Results

In the following, we present the experimental evaluation of the quantile-based watermarking actions for distortion reduction formalized in Sect. 3. Moreover, we discuss their benefits and downsides.

4.1   Experimental Setup

The data set used to perform the embedding and extraction of the watermark was *Forest Cover Type* [5], consisting of 581,012 tuples with 54 numerical attributes. Each one of the actions discussed in Sect. 3 was implemented based on a client/server architecture. The client layer was developed with Java 1.8 programming language and Eclipse Integrated Development Environment (IDE) 4.20. For the server layer was used Oracle Database 18C engine with Oracle SQL Developer 20.4 as Database Management System (DBMS) IDE. The runtime environment was a 2.11 GHz Intel i5 PC with 16.0 GHz of RAM with Windows 10 Pro OS.

We compare our results with a technique developed by Pérez Gort et al. [11] based on the AHK algorithm [2] and Sardroudi & Ibrahim's approach [13]. As mentioned in Sect. 2, the watermarking technique discussed in [11] uses a binary image to generate the watermark being embedded into R, and extends marks embedding to multiple attributes per tuple without considering numerical distortion preservation.

Figure 3 depicts the watermark sources we used, which are the binary images of the Chinese character Dáo (20 × 21 pixels) and of the character E (10 × 10 pixels), respectively. Despite being binary images, missed pixels due to partial embedding, benign updates or attacks were highlighted using the red color for a clearer appreciation of the damage caused to the watermark.

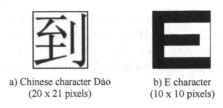

a) Chinese character Dào   b) E character
(20 x 21 pixels)   (10 x 10 pixels)

Fig. 3. Binary images used as watermark sources.

The metrics to analyze the quality of the extracted watermark with respect to the original image used for the WM generation were the correction factor (CF)[1] and the Structural Similarity Index (SSIM)[2] defined in [6].

$$M = |\mu - \mu'| \tag{2}$$

$$\Sigma = |\sigma - \sigma'| \tag{3}$$

The amount of distortion caused over each numerical attribute was measured by comparing the values of the mean μ and the standard deviation σ of the unwatermarked columns' numerical distribution with respect to the ones of the new distribution resulting from the embedding, denoted by μ' and σ', respectively. Note that WM embedding allowing absolute distribution preservation is achieved when $M = 0$ and $\Sigma = 0$.

Furthermore, for cases when two different distributions present similar values of μ and σ we used the Kullback-Leibler divergence (D_{KL}), as depicted in Eq. (4), where $P_{\mathcal{D}_i}$ and $P_{\mathcal{D}'_i}$ represent the discrete probability distributions of the columns $\mathcal{D}_i$ and $\mathcal{D}'_i$ respectively, and $\mathcal{X}$ indicates the probability space on which the distributions are defined.

$$D_{KL}(P_{\mathcal{D}_i} \| P_{\mathcal{D}'_i}) = \sum_{x \in \mathcal{X}} P_{\mathcal{D}_i}(x) \log \left(\frac{P_{\mathcal{D}_i}(x)}{P_{\mathcal{D}'_i}(x)} \right) \tag{4}$$

4.2 Watermark Capacity Variations

The first requirement analyzed, featuring WM, is the capacity. A distortion reduction can be achieved by embedding fewer marks, which is not recommended since this will also reduce robustness.

Table 1 compares the capacity values obtained when the watermarking technique described in [11] is applied to the chosen data set, and when the same technique is enhanced by our actions. In particular, **NoQuant** captures the capacity when the quantile-based approach to watermark is not used, **NoEmb**

---

[1] CF $\in [0, 100]$ where 0 means total lack of correlation, and 100 the exact match between the extracted image with the original one.

[2] SSIM $\in [0, 1]$ where 0 represents the lack of similarity between the embedded and the extracted images, and 1 the presence of perfect similarity.

refers to the capacity obtained when mark embedding is canceled if quantile changes occur (cf. Sect. 3.1), and **Redist** to the capacity gained when distorted values are adjusted to prevent them from changing quantiles (cf. Sect. 3.2). For each case, the image of the synchronized WM and the correspondent SSIM and CF values are given.

Table 1. Watermark capacity varying γ.

γ	NoQuant		Proposals			
			NoEmb		Redist	
1	0.99	0.99	0.99	0.99	0.99	0.99
	99.76	99.00	99.76	99.00	99.76	99.00
5	0.99	0.99	0.99	0.99	0.99	0.99
	99.76	99.00	99.76	99.00	99.76	99.00
10	0.99	0.99	0.99	0.99	0.99	0.99
	99.76	99.00	99.76	99.00	99.76	99.00
20	0.99	0.99	0.97	0.99	0.99	0.99
	99.76	99.00	99.04	99.00	99.76	99.00
40	0.96	0.99	0.93	0.99	0.96	0.99
	97.14	99.00	95.71	99.00	97.14	99.00

The parameters' values for watermark synchronization were set as SK = *s3cur1ty2021*, $\delta = 5$, $\beta = 3$, and $\xi = 1$. Also, for the approaches fragmenting numerical distribution in quantiles we used $q = 4$ and $k = 1$. The experiments were carried out under a subset of *Forest Cover Type* data set composed by the first 30.000 tuples and 10 attributes.[3]

---

[3] The subset selection was done to establish comparisons with other published results.

From the data reported in Table 1, can be concluded that: (i) The watermark capacity is not compromised when quantile-based embedding is performed (even for the line of action based on canceling mark insertion) , and (ii) by using high γ values, the distortion caused by embedding is reduced without compromising the watermark recognition (especially for cases of watermark with small lengths).

In general, results achieved by canceling marks embedding experience a slight WM capacity reduction but, in terms of distortion, this strategy becomes highly recommended (especially when $\xi > 1$).[4] Nevertheless, for preventing WM capacity reduction, the embedding of canceled marks in **NoEmb** is carried out in other locations on R by the strategy depicted in column **Redist**.

4.3 Imperceptibility Improvements

Regarding imperceptibility, by using $\xi = 1$ and $k = 1$ when applying the actions proposed in this work, there is evidence of a reduction of the distortion caused by the embedding in terms of M, preserving benefits and downsides in terms of Σ. Table 2 shows the values registered for M and Σ of each column of R, highlighting in blue color the results depicting lower distortion and in red color the ones causing more changes with respect to the approach not using quantiles.

Table 2. Distortion caused by WM embedding ($\gamma = 1$, $\xi = 1$, $k = 1$).

Attribute	NoQuant		Proposals			
			NoEmb		Redist	
	M	Σ	M	Σ	M	Σ
ATTR_01	8.50×10^{-3}	5.26×10^{-3}	8.20×10^{-3}	5.50×10^{-3}	8.23×10^{-3}	5.38×10^{-3}
ATTR_02	4.13×10^{-3}	5.01×10^{-4}	3.17×10^{-3}	1.08×10^{-3}	2.80×10^{-3}	6.33×10^{-4}
ATTR_03	7.00×10^{-3}	3.83×10^{-3}	1.19×10^{-2}	5.41×10^{-3}	2.90×10^{-3}	3.16×10^{-3}
ATTR_04	4.82×10^{-2}	1.25×10^{-2}	4.92×10^{-2}	1.46×10^{-2}	4.92×10^{-2}	1.46×10^{-2}
ATTR_05	4.93×10^{-3}	4.64×10^{-3}	5.50×10^{-3}	3.81×10^{-3}	4.53×10^{-3}	4.12×10^{-3}
ATTR_06	2.16×10^{-2}	9.56×10^{-3}	2.15×10^{-2}	9.57×10^{-3}	2.15×10^{-2}	9.62×10^{-3}
ATTR_07	2.56×10^{-2}	1.18×10^{-2}	1.64×10^{-2}	5.03×10^{-3}	1.84×10^{-2}	7.42×10^{-3}
ATTR_08	2.86×10^{-2}	1.42×10^{-2}	2.28×10^{-2}	8.11×10^{-3}	1.86×10^{-2}	9.31×10^{-3}
ATTR_09	8.30×10^{-3}	2.89×10^{-3}	7.60×10^{-3}	2.13×10^{-3}	6.93×10^{-3}	1.97×10^{-3}
ATTR_10	1.19×10^{-2}	2.34×10^{-3}	1.21×10^{-2}	2.50×10^{-3}	1.20×10^{-2}	2.53×10^{-3}

The presence of higher variation in some values of Table 2 is mainly due to the use of $\xi = 1$, which causes less distortion with respect to $k = 1$. Nevertheless, these values make the techniquesvadjust vulnerable against bit flipping attacks,

---

[4] The effect of the considered watermarking approaches over data distortion is discussed in Sect. 4.3.

being a perfect option for attackers to achieve WM removal without compromising data quality. Table 3 shows results by increasing the value of both ξ and k according to the recommendation given in Sect. 3. In this case, the robustness of our watermarking actions improves, whereas distortion experiments a significant reduction.

Table 3. Distortion caused by WM embedding ($\gamma = 1$, $\xi = 3$, $k = 4$).

Attribute	NoQuant		Proposals			
			NoEmb		Redist	
	M	Σ	M	Σ	M	Σ
ATTR_01	1.16×10^0	1.00×10^1	2.18×10^{-2}	9.96×10^{-3}	2.17×10^{-2}	1.00×10^{-2}
ATTR_02	6.85×10^{-1}	9.94×10^{-2}	2.77×10^{-3}	3.13×10^{-3}	4.33×10^{-3}	1.85×10^{-3}
ATTR_03	0	0	0	0	0	0
ATTR_04	6.16×10^{-2}	8.31×10^{-2}	6.23×10^{-3}	5.47×10^{-3}	6.23×10^{-3}	5.47×10^{-3}
ATTR_05	4.47×10^{-3}	9.87×10^{-3}	4.47×10^{-3}	9.87×10^{-3}	4.47×10^{-3}	9.87×10^{-3}
ATTR_06	3.08×10^0	4.32×10^0	2.30×10^{-2}	7.15×10^{-3}	2.28×10^{-2}	7.08×10^{-3}
ATTR_07	1.31×10^{-1}	1.37×10^0	1.45×10^{-2}	1.49×10^{-2}	1.30×10^{-2}	1.19×10^{-2}
ATTR_08	5.49×10^{-2}	1.21×10^0	1.17×10^{-2}	9.58×10^{-3}	1.10×10^{-2}	1.03×10^{-2}
ATTR_09	6.17×10^{-2}	2.56×10^{-1}	1.19×10^{-2}	7.52×10^{-3}	1.19×10^{-2}	7.25×10^{-3}
ATTR_10	6.57×10^{-1}	1.00×10^0	2.27×10^{-2}	7.29×10^{-3}	2.30×10^{-2}	7.57×10^{-3}

Table 4. Registered values of D_{KL} for experiments of Table 2.

Attribute	NoQuant	Proposals	
		NoEmb	Redist
ATTR_01	1.40×10^{-2}	1.39×10^{-2}	1.38×10^{-2}
ATTR_02	3.57×10^{-3}	3.54×10^{-3}	3.40×10^{-3}
ATTR_03	1.08×10^{-3}	1.78×10^{-3}	5.61×10^{-4}
ATTR_04	9.61×10^{-2}	9.09×10^{-2}	9.09×10^{-2}
ATTR_05	3.24×10^{-3}	3.29×10^{-3}	3.14×10^{-3}
ATTR_06	4.98×10^{-2}	4.98×10^{-2}	4.98×10^{-2}
ATTR_07	3.22×10^{-3}	1.99×10^{-3}	1.59×10^{-3}
ATTR_08	3.18×10^{-3}	2.80×10^{-3}	1.80×10^{-3}
ATTR_09	1.70×10^{-3}	1.88×10^{-3}	1.52×10^{-3}
ATTR_10	4.61×10^{-2}	4.60×10^{-2}	4.60×10^{-2}

Table 5. Registered values of D_{KL} for experiments of Table 3.

Attribute	NoQuant	Proposals	
		NoEmb	Redist
ATTR_01	1.26×10^{-2}	1.19×10^{-2}	1.18×10^{-2}
ATTR_02	2.59×10^{-3}	2.37×10^{-3}	2.28×10^{-3}
ATTR_03	0	0	0
ATTR_04	6.83×10^{-2}	6.20×10^{-2}	6.20×10^{-2}
ATTR_05	1.67×10^{-3}	1.67×10^{-3}	1.67×10^{-3}
ATTR_06	4.91×10^{-2}	4.86×10^{-2}	4.86×10^{-2}
ATTR_07	2.53×10^{-3}	1.45×10^{-3}	9.87×10^{-4}
ATTR_08	2.42×10^{-3}	1.18×10^{-3}	7.08×10^{-4}
ATTR_09	2.19×10^{-3}	1.73×10^{-3}	1.28×10^{-3}
ATTR_10	4.42×10^{-2}	4.39×10^{-2}	4.39×10^{-2}

Tables 4 and 5 show the values of the D_{KL} metric for the experiments of Tables 2 and 3. The obtained results lead to the conclusion that the distributions resulting from applying the proposed lines of actions are more similar to the original data distributions than when the embedding is performed without considering quantiles.

4.4 Watermark Robustness Impact

Reducing distortion while preserving WM capacity has a positive impact on robustness. By performing the watermark embedding using $\gamma = 1$ and $\delta = 5$, all approaches guaranteed the WM signal total recovery for subset attacks based on inserting (or deleting) up to 90% of tuples with respect to the number of tuples stored in R. Instead, by using $\gamma = 10$, resilience against subset attacks will remain high. Nevertheless, because of WM capacity reduction, detected WM signal starts depicting small degradation when more than 80% of tuples are deleted (see Fig. 4).

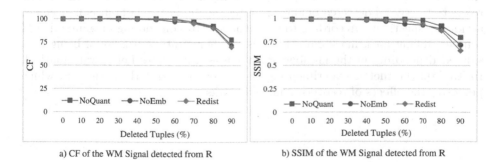

a) CF of the WM Signal detected from R

b) SSIM of the WM Signal detected from R

Fig. 4. Quality of WM detected in R after different degree of subset deletion attacks.

Another feature of our strategies contributing to resilience against bit-flipping attacks is the increasing of the pseudo-random nature of WM embedding process. By selecting different numerical distributions in R, according to values in the database, and by increasing ξ and k, attackers face additional challenges for marks detection.

Besides the small variations in terms of robustness against subset deletion attacks for higher values of γ, a general appreciation in terms of WM capacity with respect to the distortion caused during WM embedding shows the benefits of proposed lines of action compared to traditional embedding. Figure 5 depicts the rate of WM quality (in terms of CF) vs. distortion. Considering that different attributes change values during the embedding, and that Fig. 5 reflects the whole distribution for each one of them, M_A and Σ_A were obtained from the average of M and Σ of all numeric columns used as carriers for each approach.

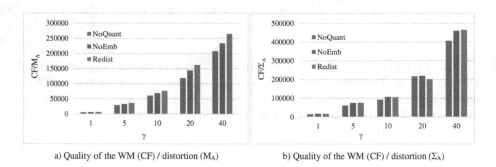

a) Quality of the WM (CF) / distortion (M_A)   b) Quality of the WM (CF) / distortion (Σ_A)

Fig. 5. Rate of detected WM quality/embedding distortion by varying γ.

4.5   Benefits of Selecting Meaningful Watermark Sources

Even for the action of rolling back mark embedding when quantile changes are spotted, WM capacity damages are not critical when WM length is not high, and meaningful WM sources are used. Table 6 shows the benefits obtained by considering symmetry criteria and neighboring pixels for the restoration of the extracted WM signal. Precisely, **PrevEnhancement** and **Enhancement** refers to the signal detected before and after the application of our enhancement actions, respectively. According to this behavior, by considering meaningful WM sources, rolling back mark embedding is another strategy worthy of being considered depending on the number of attributes and tuples being watermarked. In Table 6, the metric experimenting the increment regularly is the CF, which perceives the effects of recovering missed marks.

Table 6. WM signal enhancement (for meaningful WM sources).

γ	PrevEnhancement		Enhancement	
	SSIM	CF	SSIM	CF
20	0.97	99.04	0.98	99.28
40	0.93	95.71	0.91	97.14
60	0.81	82.85	0.83	91.66
80	0.78	79.76	0.74	90.23
100	0.59	64.04	0.59	84.52

5   Conclusions

In this paper, we proposed a quantile-based watermarking technique for relational data oriented to preserve the distribution of numerical attributes selected for mark embedding. Our approach follows two main lines of action: (i) rolling back mark embedding that violates quantile value preservation and (ii) seeking alternative embedding places for those marks causing a marked value changing quantile. Experimental results validate the relevance of *lsb* number and the threshold used for securing quantiles boundaries, for reducing the distortion while performing WM embedding. Furthermore, our technique shows an improvement in robustness while preserving WM capacity and increasing its imperceptibility.

Acknowledgement. This work has been partially supported by the project "VIR2EM - VIrtualization and Remotization for Resilient and Efficient Manufacturing" - POR FESR VENETO 2014–2020.

References

1. Agrawal, R., Haas, P.J., Kiernan, J.: Watermarking relational data: framework, algorithms and analysis. VLDB J. **12**(2), 157–169 (2003)
2. Agrawal, R., Kiernan, J.: Watermarking relational databases. In: VLDB 2002: Proceedings of the 28th International Conference on Very Large Databases, pp. 155–166. Elsevier (2002)
3. Al-Haj, A., Odeh, A.: Robust and blind watermarking of relational database systems. J. Comput. Sci. **4**(12), 1024–1029 (2008)
4. Barni, M., Bartolini, F.: Watermarking Systems Engineering: Enabling Digital Assets Security and Other Applications. CRC Press, Boca Raton (2004)
5. Colorado-State-University: Forest CoverType, The UCI KDD Archive. Information and Computer Science. University of California, Irvine, June 1999. http://kdd.ics.uci.edu/databases/covertype/covertype.html
6. Gort, M.L.P., Olliaro, M., Cortesi, A., Uribe, C.F.: Semantic-driven watermarking of relational textual databases. Expert Syst. Appl. **167**, 114013 (2021)
7. Halder, R., Pal, S., Cortesi, A.: Watermarking techniques for relational databases: survey, classification and comparison. J. Univers. Comput. Sci. **16**(21), 3164–3190 (2010)

8. Hou, R., Xian, H.: A graded reversible watermarking scheme for relational data. Mob. Netw. Appl. 1–12 (2019)

9. Naz, F., et al.: Watermarking as a service (WaaS) with anonymity. Multimedia Tools Appl. **79**(23), 16051–16075 (2020)

10. Nematollahi, M.A., Vorakulpipat, C., Rosales, H.G.: Digital Watermarking: Techniques and Trends. Springer, Heidelberg (2017)

11. Pérez Gort, M.L., Feregrino Uribe, C., Nummenmaa, J.: A minimum distortion: high capacity watermarking technique for relational data. In: Proceedings of the 5th ACM Workshop on Information Hiding and Multimedia Security, pp. 111–121 (2017)

12. Rani, S., Koshley, D.K., Halder, R.: Partitioning-insensitive watermarking approach for distributed relational databases. In: Hameurlain, A., Küng, J., Wagner, R., Dang, T.K., Thoai, N. (eds.) Transactions on Large-Scale Data- and Knowledge-Centered Systems XXXVI. LNCS, vol. 10720, pp. 172–192. Springer, Heidelberg (2017). https://doi.org/10.1007/978-3-662-56266-6_8

13. Sardroudi, H.M., Ibrahim, S.: A new approach for relational database watermarking using image. In: 5th International Conference on Computer Sciences and Convergence Information Technology, pp. 606–610. IEEE (2010)

14. Siledar, S., Tamane, S.: A distortion-free watermarking approach for verifying integrity of relational databases. In: 2020 International Conference on Smart Innovations in Design, Environment, Management, Planning and Computing (ICSIDEMPC), pp. 192–195. IEEE (2020)

15. Sion, R., Atallah, M., Prabhakar, S.: Rights protection for relational data. IEEE Trans. Knowl. Data Eng. **16**(12), 1509–1525 (2004)

16. Sun, S., Xu, Y., Wu, Z.: Research on tampering detection of material gene data based on fragile watermarking. In: Sun, X., Wang, J., Bertino, E. (eds.) ICAIS 2020. CCIS, vol. 1252, pp. 219–231. Springer, Singapore (2020). https://doi.org/10.1007/978-981-15-8083-3_20

17. Xu, Y., Shi, B.: Copyright protection method of big data based on nash equilibrium and constraint optimization. Peer-to-Peer Netw. Appl. **14**(3), 1520–1530 (2021). https://doi.org/10.1007/s12083-021-01096-4

18. Zhao, M., Jiang, C., Duan, J.: Reversible database watermarking based on differential evolution algorithm. In: 2019 International Conference on Artificial Intelligence and Advanced Manufacturing (AIAM), pp. 120–124. IEEE (2019)

EXMULF: An Explainable Multimodal Content-Based Fake News Detection System

Sabrine Amri⑩, Dorsaf Sallami$^{(\boxtimes)}$⑩, and Esma Aïmeur⑩

Department of Computer Science and Operations Research (DIRO),
University of Montreal, Montreal, Canada
{sabrine.amri,dorsaf.sallami}@umontreal.ca, aimeur@iro.umontreal.ca

Abstract. In this work, we present an explainable multimodal content-based fake news detection system. It is concerned with the veracity analysis of information based on its textual content and the associated image, together with an Explainable AI (XAI) assistant. To the best of our knowledge, this is the first study that aims to provide a fully explainable multimodal content-based fake news detection system using Latent Dirichlet Allocation (LDA) topic modeling, Vision-and-Language BERT (VilBERT) and Local Interpretable Model-agnostic Explanations (LIME) models. Our experiments on two real-world datasets demonstrate the relevance of learning the connection between two modalities, with an accuracy that exceeds 10 state-of-the-art fake news detection models.

Keywords: Fake news · Multimodal detection · Explainability

1 Introduction

In today's digital era, information is easily accessible at our fingertips. Technological advancements such as the creation of the World Wide Web have made it possible to share data across the globe in a matter of seconds. However, the veracity of the content is not always guaranteed [1], which also allows the rapid spread of fake news, misinformation and disinformation.

Fake news can easily reach and impact a large number of users in a short time. It can be presented in different types and forms of data which promotes its negative impact on OSN users and threatens their security and privacy. Forms of fake news may include false text such as hyperlinks or embedded content and multimedia such as manipulated images, videos and audios.

Studies have shown that it is still difficult for individuals to verify the veracity of a given news content based solely on automatic models, and without further explanation [14]. Additionally, humans achieved an average accuracy of 54% in the task of deception judgment [5]. Therefore, identifying fake news has shifted to explainable and interpretable automatic detection models in the last few years.

Supported by Canada's Natural Sciences and Engineering Research Council (NSERC).

© Springer Nature Switzerland AG 2022
E. Aïmeur et al. (Eds.): FPS 2021, LNCS 13291, pp. 177–187, 2022.
https://doi.org/10.1007/978-3-031-08147-7_12

To address these issues, this paper introduces a content-based fake news detection system that contains three automated processes to address: 1) multimodal topic modeling, 2) multimodal content-based detection, and 3) multimodal explainable detection. Having this in mind, the main contributions of this paper are then to:

(i) Analyze multimodal data within the news content.
(ii) Elaborate a multimodal topic modeling analysis based on the Latent Dirichlet Allocation (LDA) topic model to measure the topic similarity between the text and the image within the online news content.
(iii) Use multimodal data to detect fake news based on Vision-and-Language BERT (VilBERT).
(iv) Generate appropriate multimodal explanations based on Local Interpretable Model-agnostic Explanations (LIME).
(v) Implement and evaluate our system using two publicly available multimodal datasets (i.e. Twitter and Weibo).

Our system includes then topic representation models, text classification models, image processing models and explainable deep learning models. The remainder of the paper is organized as follows. Section 2, briefly summarizes the related work. Section 3 presents the details of our system named as EXMULF. In Sect. 4, the experimental configurations and results are detailed and discussed. Finally, Sect. 5 concludes our paper with some discussion on the future directions.

2   Related Work

The present study is built on two existing research axes. First, on methods seeking to detect fake news based on analyzing the multimodal content (e.g. text and image) automatically, without any human assistance. Second, on expanding fake news classification models by means of explainable AI (XAI) and visual analytics in order to help OSN users to understand how a certain classification result was obtained. In this section, we briefly review the related work on multimodal content-based fake news detection and explainable fake news detection. In our system we consider both aspects (i.e., multimodality and explainability).

2.1   Multimodal Content-Based Fake News Detection

Up to now, numerous studies in fake news detection started using visual information, as auxiliary information in their detection methods to infer the veracity of online news. They are named multimodal approaches since they analyze textual data and visual data extracted from the news content. Some of them focus on the correlation between the attached images and the credibility of the news text [8,12,15,22,26,29,30], while others only use one or the other data type [24,28]. For that various techniques ranging from neural networks [8,12,15,22,26,28,30], semantic analysis [15,22,29], sentiment analysis [18] and web scraping [24] were used.

2.2 Explainable Fake News Detection

Explainable ML is a well-established state-of-the-art approach employed in fake news detection [9,13,14,16]. Multiple researchers [3,6,11,14,16,19,20,27] are trying to incorporate explainability in their prediction models for fake news detection tasks to clarify the outcome of their models. A comparison between these approaches with emphasis on the techniques and datasets used is provided in Table 1. On the other hand, multiple studies on explainable machine learning are dedicated to investigating and evaluating existing fake news prediction models [2,9,13], including looking into which important features contribute to the models' prediction from the explainable machine learning perspective.

Table 1. A comparison between the explainable fake news detection approaches.

Reference	Approach	Techniques used	Datasets used
Shu et al. [19]	DEFEND	Attention neural network	PolitiFact, GossipCop
Reis et al. [16]	–	SHAP	BuzzFace
Yang et al. [27]	XFake	MIMIC, ATTN, PERT	An annotated benchmark dataset in the German language
Lu et al. [11]	GCAN	Co-Attention Network	Twitter datasets: Twitter15, Twitter16
Przybyła et al. [14]	–	Machine learning: linear method trained on stylometric features, a recurrent neural network method	Fake News Corpus dataset
Bhattarai et al. [3]	TM framework	Tsetlin Machine (TM)	PolitiFact, GossipCop
Denaux et al. [6]	–	NLP: semantic similarity and stance detection	Clef18, FakeNewsNet, coinform250
Silva et al. [20]	Propagation2Vec	Network embedding learning	PolitiFact, GossipCop

3 EXMULF: Explainable Multimodal Content-Based Fake News Detection System

In this section, we present the details of the proposed system for an explainable multimodal content-based fake news detection, named as EXMULF: (EXplainable MULtimodal Fake news detection). It consists of three major components: 1) a topic modeling component, 2) a multimodal content-based fake news detection component (multimodal detector), and 3) a multimodal explainable detection component (multimodal explainer).

Figure 1 illustrates an overview of the adopted methodology. Specifically, the news content is first provided as input to our system. The text available in the associated image (when applicable) is extracted. Both texts available in the news content and in the associated image are processed for text analysis. The associated image is also processed for image analysis. Then the obtained multimodal data (i.e. text and image) are passed to the topic modeling component for topic similarity detection to measure the similarity between both text and image topics. If the captured topics were different, then the news is classified as fake and an explanation based on this will be provided by the multimodal explainer component. Otherwise, the multimodal data obtained will be passed to the multimodal detector component to predict the news veracity based on analyzing the latent task-agnostic joint representations of the text and the associated image. These results are then processed by the multimodal detector component to predict the veracity of the news content. Finally, the decision, the prediction model as well as the extracted text and image are processed by the multimodal explainer component to generate relevant interpretable explanations to provide to the OSN users.

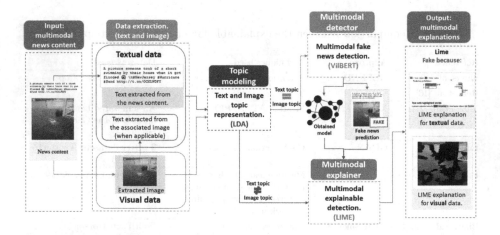

Fig. 1. EXMULF methodology overview.

4   Experimental Results and Discussion

In this section we provide, the experimental details, the interpretation of the results, as well as a comparison with the state of art methods.

4.1   Datasets

We used two publicly available real-world benchmark datasets for our experiments: Twitter[1] and Weibo[2]. Table 2 shows the distribution for both datasets after the preprocessing phase.

Twitter Dataset. The preprocessing of this dataset included the removal of single modality instances, the preprocessing of textual data (i.e. the removal of punctuation, symbols and emoji from the text, as well as translating non-English text into English), and the preprocessing of images (i.e. resizing all images to the same equal size and extracting the text within the image (when applicable)).

---

[1] https://github.com/MKLab-ITI/image-verification-corpus.
[2] https://drive.google.com/file/d/14VQ7EWPiFeGzxp3XC2DeEHi-BEisDINn/view.

Table 2. Statistics of the datasets used.

Dataset	Train		Test	
	Fake	Real	Fake	Real
Twitter	6841	5009	2564	1217
Weibo	3748	3783	1000	996

Weibo Dataset. For this dataset, the preprocessing phase was inspired by the same preprocessing presented by Wang et al. [25]. In fact, for image data duplicate images and odd-sized images have been removed to ensure the integrity of the dataset. For the textual data, we proceeded in the same way as for the Twitter dataset considering the Chinese language.

4.2 The LDA Topic Modeling

The LDA topic modeling component, is based on using the Latent Dirichlet Allocation (LDA) [4] which is a probabilistic modeling approach. It consists of topic modeling of both text and image within the online news. Using such approach is motivated by the fact that the inconsistency (incoherence) between text and image topics in an online news can be a major sign that the news is fake. In this section we overview each task separately.

Topic Modeling for Textual Data. It consists of preprocessing the text (Tokenization, stop words removal, lemmatization, and stemming), computing the TF-IDF (term frequency-inverse document frequency), and specifying the number of topics to train the base LDA model. Then, The topic coherence [17] was used as an intrinsic evaluation metric for the resulting model.

Topic Modeling for Image Data. Topic modeling for images presented a unique difficulty since it must interpret both visual and linguistic data, which are two entirely distinct types of data. To do this, the LDA method was employed to extract topics from the vocabulary of text data, as well as a fine-tuned pretrained VGGNet16 model [21] which was used to identify patterns from images, and then the model was trained to predict themes for the supplied images. To evaluate the model, we load the true topics and the predicted topics and calculate the accuracy. Thus, an accuracy of 54% was achieved.

4.3 Multimodal Detector

Baselines. To evaluate the performance of VilBERT on the fake news detection task, we compared it against other models, single-modality and multimodal models.

1. **single-modality models**:
   (a) **Text only**: To evaluate the text-based detection model, a fine-tuned $BERT_{BASE}$, a pretrained $BERT_{BASE}$ and a $BERT_{T+IT}$ models were used with inputs, the text with the news, the text within the image and a combination of both texts, respectively. For Weibo dataset, we used bert-base-chinese because it is trained on cased Chinese simplified and traditional text.
   (b) **Image only**: In this case, only the images have been processed. For that reason, VGG-19 and ResNet-34 [7] were used.
2. **multimodal models**: To evaluate the multimodal model, a fusion model that concatenates $BERT_T$ and ResNet-34 features was defined, then a Multilayer Perceptron (MLP) was trained on top of it. Then, to evaluate the results obtained, other existing multimodal models that were trained on the same datasets that we used was selected (i.e. SpotFake, AMFB, FND-SCTI, HMCAN, and BDANN) and this to compare our results with.

A fair comparison was then made based on four commonly used evaluation metrics for fake news detection as presented in Table 3. Namely the classification accuracy, precision, recall and F1-score metrics stated by the corresponding authors.

Table 3. Results.

Dataset	Model		Accuracy	Fake news			Real news		
				Precision	Recall	F1	Precision	Recall	F1
Twitter	Text only	$BERT_T$	0.572	0.602	0.586	0.597	0.543	0.553	0.544
		$BERT_{T+IT}$	0.577	0.612	0.574	0.598	0.551	0.564	0.556
	Image only	ResNet-34	0.624	0.712	0.567	0.6	0.558	0.72	0.62
		VGG-19	0.596	0.698	0.522	0.593	0.531	0.698	0.597
	Multi-modal	Fusion	0.7695	0.820	0.726	0.779	0.719	0.798	0.748
		SpotFake [22]	0.7777	0.751	0.900	0.82	0.832	0.606	0.701
		AMFB [8]	0.883	0.89	**0.95**	0.92	**0.87**	0.76	0.741
		HMCAN [15]	0.897	**0.971**	0.801	0.878	0.853	**0.979**	**0.912**
		BDANN [30]	0.830	0.810	0.630	0.710	0.830	0.930	0.880
		VilBERT	**0.898**	0.934	0.92	**0.926**	0.859	0.88	0.869
Weibo	Text only	$BERT_T$	0.680	0.731	0.715	0.709	0.667	0.676	0.669
		$BERT_{T+IT}$	0.682	0.739	0.72	0.71	0.672	0.684	0.673
	Image only	ResNet-34	0.694	0.701	0.634	0.698	0.698	0.711	0.699
		VGG-19	0.633	0.640	0.635	0.637	0.637	0.641	0.639
	Multi-modal	Fusion	0.8152	0.865	0.734	0.88	0.764	0.889	0.74
		SpotFake [22]	0.8923	0.902	**0.964**	0.932	0.847	0.656	0.739
		AMFB [8]	0.832	0.82	0.86	0.84	0.85	0.81	0.83
		FND-SCTI [29]	0.834	0.863	0.780	0.824	0.815	0.892	0.835
		HMCAN [15]	0.885	0.920	0.845	0.881	0.856	0.926	**0.890**
		BDANN [30]	0.842	0.830	0.870	0.850	0.850	0.820	0.830
		VilBERT	**0.9204**	**0.946**	0.948	**0.946**	**0.879**	**0.893**	0.885

Although VilBERT was originally designed for various vision-and-language challenges, recent research has indicated that learning visiolinguistic feature representations may be transferred across tasks [10]. As a result, we fine-tune ViL-BERT across datasets by passing the element-wise product of the final image and text representations into a learned classification layer. The results as shown in Table 3 demonstrate that our suggested method outperforms the baseline models described above in terms of accuracy.

4.4 Multimodal Explainer

For the explanation part, LIME was used for both image and text. For image data, see Fig. 2, the explanations are built by designing a new dataset of perturbations around the instance to be explained using the quickshift segmentation algorithm [23]. The quickshift segmentation is a mode-seeking algorithm that treats pixels as samples in a 5-dimensional space (3 color dimensions and 2 space dimensions).

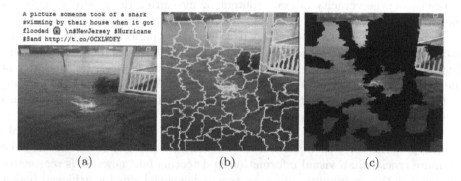

Fig. 2. LIME explanations for image data. (a) presents the original fake tweet (b) shows the superpixels that are generated using the quickshift segmentation algorithm (c) shows the area of the image that produced the prediction of the class (fake, in our case)

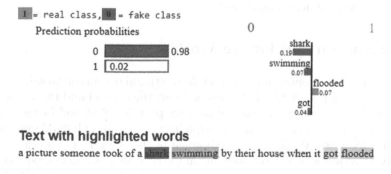

Fig. 3. LIME explanations for textual data.

Then, the class of the newly generated images was predicted using the model obtained. After that, the cosine similarity and the weighted linear regression were used to measure the importance (i.e. the weights) of each perturbation in the prediction of the corresponding class. LIME then returns as an explanation the area of the image (superpixels) which has a stronger relationship with the correct prediction class (i.e. fake, real).

On the other hand, we use LIME Text Explainer for textual data. For this, we can add a separate text instance to the interpreter. The return value summarizes the contribution of each word to the assignment of the text instance to a specific class (i.e. fake, real), see Fig. 3.

4.5 Discussion of the Results Obtained

Our study shows the promising aspect of leveraging topic representation to distinguish fake and real news by measuring topics similarity of both text and image. Indeed, topic modeling for both textual and visual content in fake news detection present a unique difficulty. However, it has yielded interesting results in predicting the veracity of news content by measuring the coherence between the captured topics.

It is also noteworthy that the detection models perform differently for the two datasets. In fact, they achieve better results with the Weibo dataset. These findings can be related to the fact that, in the Weibo dataset, the majority of the images seem to be more involved. Furthermore, Weibo is a Chinese dataset, so following segmentation, the length of certain sentences exceeds the sentence length of the Twitter dataset.

Although results of the single-modality models show that the image-only models perform worse than the text-only models, revealing that text seems to be far more crucial than visual information in detecting fake news. It is reasonable to conclude that combining image to text is beneficial since it achieved higher performance. Specifically, the pretrained ViLBERT outperforms other baselines because it uses early, deep fusion and has undergone multimodal pretraining rather than just separate unimodal visual and textual pretraining. This implies that the ability to understand the semantic link between visual and linguistic data is transferable across activities.

5 Conclusion and Future Work

In this paper, we propose an explainable multimodal content-based fake news detection system EXMULF that takes as input the textual and the visual information within the content of the online news post (i.e. text and image), detects whether this post is fake or real, and explains the reasoning behind system decisions to OSN users. We focus on the content of the news as it is a crucial factor for early detection as it is fully available in the early stages unlike auxiliary information (i.e. social engagement, user response, propagation patterns, etc.) which can only be obtained after the news has spread. The experimental results show that combining textual, visual and text-image topic modeling analysis, together with multimodal explainability is very efficient for the fake news detection task. Future work may include audio and video as multimodal input data. In addition, we plan to expand the visual representations to further increase the effectiveness of explainability provided to OSN users. To do so, more evaluations will be made to improve the performance of the multimodal explainer.

References

1. Aïmeur, E., Hage, H., Amri, S.: The scourge of online deception in social networks. In: 2018 International Conference on Computational Science and Computational Intelligence (CSCI), pp. 1266–1271. IEEE (2018). https://doi.org/10.1109/CSCI46756.2018.00244
2. Alharbi, R., Vu, M.N., Thai, M.T.: Evaluating fake news detection models from explainable machine learning perspectives. In: ICC 2021-IEEE International Conference on Communications, pp. 1–6. IEEE (2021)
3. Bhattarai, B., Granmo, O.C., Jiao, L.: Explainable TSETLIN machine framework for fake news detection with credibility score assessment. arXiv preprint arXiv:2105.09114 (2021)
4. Blei, D.M., Ng, A.Y., Jordan, M.I.: Latent DIRICHLET allocation. J;. Mach. Learn. Res. **3**, 993–1022 (2003)
5. Bond, C.F., Jr., DePaulo, B.M.: Accuracy of deception judgments. Pers. Soc. Psychol. Rev. **10**(3), 214–234 (2006). https://doi.org/10.1207/s15327957pspr1003_2
6. Denaux, R., Gomez-Perez, J.M.: Linked credibility reviews for explainable misinformation detection. In: Pan, J.Z., et al. (eds.) ISWC 2020. LNCS, vol. 12506, pp. 147–163. Springer, Cham (2020). https://doi.org/10.1007/978-3-030-62419-4_9
7. He, K., Zhang, X., Ren, S., Sun, J.: Deep residual learning for image recognition. In: Proceedings of the IEEE Conference on Computer Vision and Pattern Recognition, pp. 770–778 (2016)
8. Kumari, R., Ekbal, A.: AMFB: Attention based multimodal factorized bilinear pooling for multimodal fake news detection. Expert Syst. Appl. **184**, 115412 (2021). https://doi.org/10.1016/j.eswa.2021.115412
9. Kurasinski, L., Mihailescu, R.C.: Towards machine learning explainability in text classification for fake news detection. In: 2020 19th IEEE International Conference on Machine Learning and Applications (ICMLA), pp. 775–781. IEEE (2020). https://doi.org/10.1109/ICMLA51294.2020.00127
10. Lu, J., Goswami, V., Rohrbach, M., Parikh, D., Lee, S.: 12-in-1: multi-task vision and language representation learning. In: Proceedings of the IEEE/CVF Conference on Computer Vision and Pattern Recognition, pp. 10437–10446 (2020)
11. Lu, Y.J., Li, C.T.: GCAN: graph-aware co-attention networks for explainable fake news detection on social media. arXiv preprint arXiv:2004.11648 (2020)
12. Meel, P., Vishwakarma, D.K.: Han, image captioning, and forensics ensemble multimodal fake news detection. Inf. Sci. **567**, 23–41 (2021). https://doi.org/10.1016/j.ins.2021.03.037
13. Mohseni, S., et al.: Machine learning explanations to prevent overtrust in fake news detection. arXiv preprint arXiv:2007.12358 (2020)

14. Przybyła, P., Soto, A.J.: When classification accuracy is not enough: explaining news credibility assessment. Inf. Process. Manage. **58**(5), 102653 (2021). https://doi.org/10.1016/j.ipm.2021.102653
15. Qian, S., Wang, J., Hu, J., Fang, Q., Xu, C.: Hierarchical multi-modal contextual attention network for fake news detection. In: Proceedings of the 44th International ACM SIGIR Conference on Research and Development in Information Retrieval, pp. 153–162 (2021). https://doi.org/10.1145/3404835.3462871
16. Reis, J.C., Correia, A., Murai, F., Veloso, A., Benevenuto, F.: Explainable machine learning for fake news detection. In: Proceedings of the 10th ACM Conference on Web Science, pp. 17–26 (2019). https://doi.org/10.1145/3292522.3326027
17. Röder, M., Both, A., Hinneburg, A.: Exploring the space of topic coherence measures. In: Proceedings of the Eighth ACM International Conference on Web Search and Data Mining, pp. 399–408 (2015). https://doi.org/10.1145/2684822.2685324
18. Shah, P., Kobti, Z.: Multimodal fake news detection using a cultural algorithm with situational and normative knowledge. In: 2020 IEEE Congress on Evolutionary Computation (CEC), pp. 1–7. IEEE (2020). https://doi.org/10.1109/CEC48606.2020.9185643
19. Shu, K., Cui, L., Wang, S., Lee, D., Liu, H.: defend: Explainable fake news detection. In: Proceedings of the 25th ACM SIGKDD International Conference on Knowledge Discovery and Data Mining, pp. 395–405 (2019). https://doi.org/10.1145/3292500.3330935
20. Silva, A., Han, Y., Luo, L., Karunasekera, S., Leckie, C.: Propagation2vec: embedding partial propagation networks for explainable fake news early detection. Inf. Process. Manage. **58**(5), 102618 (2021). https://doi.org/10.1016/j.ipm.2021.102618
21. Simonyan, K., Zisserman, A.: Very deep convolutional networks for large-scale image recognition. arXiv preprint arXiv:1409.1556 (2014)
22. Singhal, S., Shah, R.R., Chakraborty, T., Kumaraguru, P., Satoh, S.: Spotfake: a multi-modal framework for fake news detection. In: 2019 IEEE Fifth International Conference on Multimedia Big Data (BigMM), pp. 39–47. IEEE (2019). https://doi.org/10.1109/BigMM.2019.00-44
23. Vedaldi, A., Soatto, S.: Quick shift and kernel methods for mode seeking. In: Forsyth, D., Torr, P., Zisserman, A. (eds.) ECCV 2008. LNCS, vol. 5305, pp. 705–718. Springer, Heidelberg (2008). https://doi.org/10.1007/978-3-540-88693-8_52
24. Vishwakarma, D.K., Varshney, D., Yadav, A.: Detection and veracity analysis of fake news via scrapping and authenticating the web search. Cogn. Syst. Res. **58**, 217–229 (2019). https://doi.org/10.1016/j.cogsys.2019.07.004
25. Wang, Y., et al.: EANN: Event adversarial neural networks for multi-modal fake news detection. In: Proceedings of the 24th ACM SIGKDD International Conference on Knowledge Discovery & Data Mining, pp. 849–857 (2018). https://doi.org/10.1145/3219819.3219903
26. Xue, J., Wang, Y., Tian, Y., Li, Y., Shi, L., Wei, L.: Detecting fake news by exploring the consistency of multimodal data. Inf. Process. Manage. **58**(5), 102610 (2021). https://doi.org/10.1016/j.ipm.2021.102610
27. Yang, F., et al.: Xfake: explainable fake news detector with visualizations. In: The World Wide Web Conference, pp. 3600–3604 (2019). https://doi.org/10.1145/3308558.3314119
28. Yuan, H., Zheng, J., Ye, Q., Qian, Y., Zhang, Y.: Improving fake news detection with domain-adversarial and graph-attention neural network. Decision Support Systems, p. 113633 (2021). https://doi.org/10.1016/j.dss.2021.113633

29. Zeng, J., Zhang, Y., Ma, X.: Fake news detection for epidemic emergencies via deep correlations between text and images. Sustain. Urban Areas **66**, 102652 (2021). https://doi.org/10.1016/j.scs.2020.102652
30. Zhang, T., et al.: BDANN: Bert-based domain adaptation neural network for multimodal fake news detection. In: 2020 International Joint Conference on Neural Networks (IJCNN), pp. 1–8. IEEE (2020). https://doi.org/10.1109/IJCNN48605.2020.9206973

IoT Security

A Comparative Analysis of Machine Learning Techniques for IoT Intrusion Detection

João Vitorino$^{(\boxtimes)}$ (ID), Rui Andrade (ID), Isabel Praça$^{(\boxtimes)}$ (ID), Orlando Sousa (ID), and Eva Maia (ID)

Research Group on Intelligent Engineering and Computing for Advanced Innovation and Development (GECAD), School of Engineering, Polytechnic of Porto (ISEP/IPP), 4249-015 Porto, Portugal
{jpmvo,rfaar,icp,oms,egm}@isep.ipp.pt

Abstract. The digital transformation faces tremendous security challenges. In particular, the growing number of cyber-attacks targeting Internet of Things (IoT) systems restates the need for a reliable detection of malicious network activity. This paper presents a comparative analysis of supervised, unsupervised and reinforcement learning techniques on nine malware captures of the IoT-23 dataset, considering both binary and multi-class classification scenarios. The developed models consisted of Support Vector Machine (SVM), Extreme Gradient Boosting (XGBoost), Light Gradient Boosting Machine (LightGBM), Isolation Forest (iForest), Local Outlier Factor (LOF) and a Deep Reinforcement Learning (DRL) model based on a Double Deep Q-Network (DDQIN), adapted to the intrusion detection context. The most reliable performance was achieved by LightGBM. Nonetheless, iForest displayed good anomaly detection results and the DRL model demonstrated the possible benefits of employing this methodology to continuously improve the detection. Overall, the obtained results indicate that the analyzed techniques are well suited for IoT intrusion detection.

Keywords: Internet of Things · Intrusion detection · Supervised learning · Unsupervised learning · Reinforcement learning

1 Introduction

The digital transformation is associated with the Internet of Things (IoT) concept, which describes decentralized and heterogeneous systems of interconnected devices. This field converges wireless sensor networks, real-time computing, embedded systems and actuation technologies [1]. Industrial IoT (IIoT) is a subfield of IoT focused on industrial assets and the automation of manufacturing processes. Due to the integration of physical and business processes, as well as control and information systems, IIoT is bridging the gap between Operational Technology and Information Technology [2].

However, the convergence of previously isolated systems and technologies faces tremendous security challenges. IoT devices commonly have software and communication protocol vulnerabilities, in addition to weak physical security and resource

E. Aïmeur et al. (Eds.): FPS 2021, LNCS 13291, pp. 191–207, 2022.
https://doi.org/10.1007/978-3-031-08147-7_13

constraints [3, 4]. Consequently, malware attacks pose a major threat to IoT systems. A self-propagating malware, such as Mirai, can compromise a large number of suscepti- ble devices and establish a botnet to launch several cyber-attacks [5]. The cyber-attacks targeting IoT systems can be divided into two categories: passive and active. Passive attacks do not impact the operation of the system, mainly consisting of eavesdrop- ping and traffic analysis. On the other hand, active attacks can range from probing and man-in-the-middle to brute-force and Denial-of-Service (DoS) [6, 7].

Due to the exposure of IoT to malicious activity, a reliable intrusion detection is indispensable. An Intrusion Detection System (IDS) dynamically monitors an environ- ment with the purpose of identifying suspicious activity, so that possible threats can be mitigated [8]. The application of machine learning techniques to an IDS is a promising strategy to tackle the growing number and increasing complexity of cyber-attacks.

The developed work addressed nine malware captures of the IoT-23 dataset in both binary and multi-class classification scenarios. Three distinct types of techniques were analyzed and compared: supervised, unsupervised and reinforcement learning. The developed models consisted of three supervised models, Support Vector Machine (SVM), Extreme Gradient Boosting (XGBoost) and Light Gradient Boosting Machine (LightGBM), two unsupervised models, Isolation Forest (iForest) and Local Outlier Fac- tor (LOF), and a Deep Reinforcement Learning (DRL) model based on a Double Deep Q-Network (DDQN), adapted to the intrusion detection context.

This paper is organized into multiple sections. Section 2 provides a survey of pre- vious work on machine learning techniques for intrusion detection. Section 3 describes the utilized dataset and models, including the data preprocessing steps and evaluation metrics. Section 4 presents an analysis of the results obtained in each scenario. Finally, Sect. 5 addresses the main conclusions and future research topics.

2   Related Work

In recent years, IoT intrusion detection has drawn attention from a research perspective. As both cyber-attacks and the techniques used to detect them evolve, an increasing number of research topics come to light. Therefore, it is essential to understand the results and conclusions of previous work.

Chaabouni et al. [8] provided a comprehensive survey of research published up to the year of 2018. The authors reviewed previous studies aimed at IoT, highlighting the advantages and limitations of the developed machine learning models.

More recently, Zolanvari et al. [9] utilized a testbed mimicking an industrial plant to train several models for anomaly detection. The best overall performance was achieved by Random Forest, which obtained a True Positive Rate (TPR) of 97.44%. However, only SVM reached a False Positive Rate (FPR) of 0.00, representing no false alarms.

Jan et al. [10] proposed the use of SVM to detect attacks that influence IoT network traffic intensity, which is common in DoS. The performance of different SVM kernels was analyzed on simulated datasets with only three features: the minimum, maximum and median values of the packet arrival rate. Even though the Linear kernel reached 98.03% accuracy with a small training time, this approach lacks the ability to detect attacks that do not increase neither decrease traffic intensity.

Bakhtiar et al. [11] employed the lightweight C4.5 algorithm to search for DoS attacks by directly analyzing the packets captured in a device and creating a decision tree. Despite achieving an accuracy of 100%, the average time required to process each one was 0.0351 s on their testbed. Consequently, only 18.15% of the transmitted packets were analyzed, which revealed the drawback of a packet-based approach.

Verma and Ranga [12] addressed classifier ensembles, comparing several models on the CIDDS-001, UNSW-NB15 and NSL-KDD datasets. 10-fold cross-validation was performed and the highest average accuracy, 96.74%, was obtained by the Classification And Regression Trees algorithm, which creates a decision tree. However, XGBoost reached the very close value of 96.73% and obtained the best average TPR, 97.31%.

Yao et al. [13] proposed the use of LightGBM to perform a lightweight analysis in IoT devices, followed by more resource-intensive models in other devices. The authors noted that since LightGBM is embedded with feature selection, the bandwidth required to transmit the data is reduced. On their dataset, LightGBM achieved an accuracy of 93.2% and an F1-score of 95.6% for a flow-based approach.

Eskandari et al. [14] used unsupervised models to perform anomaly detection by building a baseline of benign flows. LOF and iForest were compared in their testbed with probing, brute-force and DoS attacks. Their macro-averaged F1-scores were 78.4% and 92.5%, respectively, which indicates the suitability of the latter for the detection of unknown attacks when trained with normal network traffic only.

The key drawback of both supervised and unsupervised techniques is that if the cyber-attacks are modified or the network topology is updated, which includes the addition of a new device, the models must be retrained to take into consideration the new traffic patterns. To tackle this challenge, reinforcement learning can be adapted to the intrusion detection context.

Gu et al. [15] proposed an entropy-based approach to continuously optimize a threshold for anomaly detection. An agent interacted with the network environment, receiving TPR and FPR as the rewards for each selected threshold. It employed Q-Learning, which is an off-policy learner because it is improved regardless of the agent's actions.

Despite not being aimed at IoT, Lopez-Martin et al. [16] analyzed the performance of several techniques that combine reinforcement learning with deep learning to create DRL models with improved stability. The utilized agents directly predicted the class of the network flows received from the environment. Regarding the reward function, the authors noted that a simple 1/0 reward for correct/incorrect predictions led to a better performance. The best results were achieved by a DDQN, with F1-scores of 91.20% and 93.94% on the NSL-KDD and AWID datasets, respectively.

To the best of our knowledge, no previous work has comparatively analyzed supervised, unsupervised and reinforcement learning techniques on the IoT-23 dataset.

3 Methods

This section describes the utilized dataset and models, as well as the employed data preprocessing steps and the considered evaluation metrics. The work was carried out on a machine with 16 GB of RAM, an 8-core CPU and a 6 GB GPU. The implementation relied on the Python programming language and the following libraries: *Numpy* and *Pandas* for general data manipulation, *Scikit-learn* for the implementation of SVM, iForest and LOF, *Xgboost* for the implementation of XGBoost, *Lightgbm* for the implementation of LightGBM and *Tensorflow* for the implementation of the DRL model.

3.1   Dataset

The IoT-23 dataset [17] was created by the Stratosphere Research Laboratory and is publicly available. It consists of twenty-three labeled captures of malicious and benign network flows, caused by malware attacks targeting IoT devices between 2018 and 2019. This is an extremely valuable dataset because it manifests real IoT network traffic patterns and provides a large quantity of labeled malicious flows.

From the twenty-three captures, six were selected due to their distinct characteristics. Since Capture-1-1 displayed a large number of recorded flows and the best balance between malicious and benign labels, it was renamed as 1-1-full and three smaller balanced subsets were established: 1-1-large, 1-1-medium and 1-1-small.

Table 1 provides an overview of the malware type and class proportions of the utilized datasets. The labels PartOfAHorizontalPortScan and C&C-FileDownload were shortened to POAHPS and C&C-FD, respectively.

Table 1. Main characteristics of the utilized datasets.

Dataset	Malware type	Total samples	Malicious class samples	Malicious class label
1-1-full	Hide and Seek	1,008,749	539,465	POAHPS
			8	C&C
1-1-large	Hide and Seek	400,000	199,996	POAHPS
			4	C&C
1-1-medium	Hide and Seek	200,000	99,999	POAHPS
			1	C&C
1-1-small	Hide and Seek	20,000	10,000	POAHPS
20-1	Torii	3,210	16	C&C-Torii
21-1	Torii	3,287	14	C&C-Torii
34-1	Mirai	23,146	14,394	DDoS
			6,706	C&C
			122	POAHPS
42-1	Trojan	4,427	3	FileDownload
			3	C&C-FD
44-1	Mirai	238	14	C&C
			11	C&C-FD
			1	DDoS

3.2 Data Preprocessing

Besides the creation of the three additional subsets, a preprocessing stage was required before the data was usable (see Fig. 1). This stage was applied to all nine datasets, taking into consideration their distinct characteristics.

A pertinent aspect is that if a class only contains a single sample, it cannot be simultaneously used to train and evaluate a model. Therefore, that individual sample must be discarded. This is the case of the 1-1-medium and 44-1 datasets, when used for multi-class classification. Regarding 1-1-medium, it becomes only suitable for binary classification because only the POAHPS malicious class remains. Consequently, only 1-1-full, 1-1-large, 34-1, 42-1 and 44-1 were utilized in the multi-class scenario.

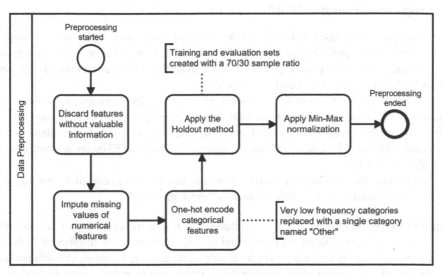

Fig. 1. Overview of data preprocessing stage (Business Process Model and Notation).

3.3 Evaluation Metrics

The performance of a model can be evaluated using the values reported by the confusion matrix. It reports the number of True Positives (TP), True Negatives (TN), False Positives (FP) and False Negatives (FN) regarding the predicted classes. Using binary classification as an example, the considered metrics and their interpretation are described below [18, 19].

Accuracy measures the proportion of correctly classified network traffic. However, a high value can be achieved even when a minority class is disregarded. For instance, a high accuracy can be reached in datasets unbalanced towards benign traffic without any malicious activity being detected.

Precision measures the proportion of predicted attacks that were actual attacks, which indicates the relevance of a model's predictions. On the other hand, Recall, which corresponds to TPR, measures the proportion of actual attacks that were correctly predicted, reflecting a model's ability to identify malicious activity.

FPR is a valuable metric because it accounts for false alarms, which must be avoided. It measures the proportion of benign traffic that was incorrectly predicted to be an attack, leading to unnecessary mitigation efforts.

Overall, the most trustworthy metric is the F1-score, also referred to as F-measure. It calculates the harmonic mean of Precision and Recall, considering both FP and FN. Therefore, a high F1-score indicates that malicious activity is being correctly identified and there are low false alarms.

These metrics, except for Accuracy, can be macro-averaged to treat all classes equally. Since the minority classes are given the same relevance as the overrepresented, macro-averaging is well suited for unbalanced datasets.

3.4 Supervised Learning Models

Due to the promising results obtained in the surveyed work, three supervised techniques were selected to be evaluated on the IoT-23 dataset. The configurations of the developed models resulted from a grid search of possible hyperparameter combinations for both binary and multi-class classification scenarios.

To obtain the optimal configuration for each dataset and scenario, a 5-fold cross-validation was performed. Therefore, a model was trained with 4/5 of a training set and validated with the remaining 1/5 in each iteration. Due to its adequacy for unbalanced data and consolidation of Precision and Recall, the macro-averaged F1-score was selected as the validation metric.

After their optimization, the models were retrained with the complete training sets and a final evaluation was performed with the evaluation sets.

Support Vector Machine. SVM [20] attempts to find a hyperplane that successfully segregates two classes in an n-dimensional space, where n is the number of features. Even though it only inherently performs binary classification, a One-vs-All scheme was employed to handle multi-class classification. Table 2 summarizes the configuration.

Table 2. Summary of SVM configuration.

Parameter	Value
Kernel	Linear
Loss function	Squared Hinge
Dual	False
C	0.001 to 0.1

The parameter search led to the use of the Linear kernel with the Squared Hinge loss function, evidencing the linear separability of the data. Since the number of samples is significantly higher than the number of features across all datasets, Dual was set to *False* to solve the primal optimization problem.

This model relies on the C parameter, a value inversely proportional to the strength of the regularization. It was set to lower values on the larger datasets and higher values on the smaller datasets, in the range of 0.001 to 0.1.

Extreme Gradient Boosting. XGBoost performs gradient boosting using an ensemble of decision trees. A level-wise growth strategy is employed to split nodes level by level, seeking to minimize a loss function. Table 3 summarizes the configuration.

Table 3. Summary of XGBoost configuration.

Parameter	Value
Method	Histogram or exact
Loss function (Objective)	Cross-entropy
Max depth	5
Feature subsample	0.7
Min loss reduction (Gamma)	0.01
Min child weight	1.2 to 100.0
N° of estimators	60 to 80
Learning rate	0.001 to 0.01

The acknowledged Cross-Entropy loss function was used for both binary and multiclass classification. To build the decision trees on the smaller datasets, the Exact method was utilized to account for all possible node splits. On the larger datasets, the Histogram method was selected because it computes fast histogram-based approximations.

The key parameters are the number of estimators and the learning rate. The first represents the number of decision trees, whereas the latter controls how quickly the model adapts its weights to the training data. Overall, the number of estimators was set to a relatively large value and the learning rate to a small value, avoiding a fast convergence to a suboptimal solution.

Light Gradient Boosting Machine. LightGBM [22] also utilizes an ensemble of decision trees to perform gradient boosting. A leaf-wise strategy is employed for a best-first approach, directly splitting the leaf with the maximum loss reduction. Consequently, despite having similar parameters to XGBoost, these have different effects on its performance. Table 4 summarizes the configuration.

The key advantage of this model is the ability to use Gradient-based One-Side Sampling (GOSS) to build the decision trees, which is computationally lighter than the remaining methods and therefore provides a faster and reliable convergence.

The Cross-Entropy loss function was also used and the learning rate was set to a small value on most datasets. However, the smaller and more unbalanced sets required it to be increased to counteract the shortage of training data.

Table 4. Summary of LightGBM configuration.

Parameter	Value
Method	GOSS
Loss function (Objective)	Cross-entropy
Max depth	5
Max leaves	25
Feature subsample	0.7
Min loss reduction (Split gain)	0.01
L2 regularization (Lambda)	1.0
Min child samples	2 to 2000
N° of estimators	60 to 100
Learning rate	0.001 to 0.04

3.5 Unsupervised Learning Models

Two unsupervised techniques were also selected because of their promising results in the surveyed work. Even though the developed models only perform one-class classification with unlabeled data, they can be compared to the remaining models in the binary scenario. Therefore, their optimization process was similar to the supervised approach, employing cross-validation to assess their configurations on unlabeled subsets.

Isolation Forest. An iForest isolates anomalies through an ensemble of decision trees. The samples are repeatedly split by random values of random features until outliers are segregated from normal observations. Table 5 summarizes the configuration.

Table 5. Summary of iForest configuration.

Parameter	Value
N° of estimators	100
Max features	1.0
Max samples	100 to 250
Contamination	0.001 to 0.05

This model relies on the contamination ratio of the training set, which must not exceed 50%. Consequently, the number of samples intended to be anomalies must be lower than the number of remaining samples, otherwise outliers cannot be detected.

For 20-1, 21-1, 42-1 and 44-1, the ratio was set to the approximate percentage of malicious flows of the training sets. Even though 1–1-full and 34-1 do not fit the 50% requirement, 1-1-large, 1-1-medium and 1-1-small have exactly 50/50 proportions.

Despite being theoretically suitable, the model underperformed with such high contamination. To overcome this obstacle, the samples with a malicious label were randomly subsampled to reduce the contamination of their training sets. The optimized ratio was 0.05, with approximately 5% malicious and 95% benign samples.

Local Outlier Factor. LOF [24] detects anomalies by measuring the local density deviation. This strategy identifies samples with a significantly lower density than their neighbors, which correspond to local outliers that would otherwise remain undetected.

Even though LOF only identifies anomalies on the initial data it receives by default, Novelty was set to *True* to enable it to detect outliers on new data, based on the neighborhoods computed in its training. Table 6 summarizes the configuration.

Table 6. Summary of LOF configuration.

Parameter	Value
Novelty	True
Algorithm	K-dimensional tree
Metric	Euclidean
Leaf size	30
N° of neighbors	35 to 520
Contamination	0.001 to 0.05

The parameter search led to the values of the remaining parameters, as well as the use of the K-Dimensional Tree algorithm and the Euclidean metric. Regarding the contamination ratio of the training data, the approach employed for iForest was replicated.

The key parameter of this model is the number of neighbors, which regulates the size of the neighborhoods and therefore affects the measurement of the local density deviation. It was set to a higher value as the size of the dataset increased.

3.6 Deep Reinforcement Learning Model

To adapt the reinforcement learning methodology to the intrusion detection context, it was necessary to create a suitable training environment and develop a learning process for an agent. Due to the characteristics of this methodology, a manual optimization of several aspects was performed instead of cross-validation.

Regarding the training environment, when the agent observes a state and performs an action, predicting a class, it advances into the next state and provides a reward for the performed action. Due to the conclusions reached in [16], a simple 1/0 reward is calculated for correct/incorrect predictions.

Regarding the agent, an incremental episode-based learning process was developed, where each episode contains multiple steps (see Fig. 2). It was based on a DDQN [25] because this technique introduced several improvements to the training of an Artificial Neural Network (ANN). Therefore, the following concepts were applied:

- **Exploration** – During the initial training, the agent implements the Epsilon-Greedy method to choose predictions of the utilized ANN or random actions according to an exploration ratio. This method avoids a fast convergence to a suboptimal solution.
- **Experience Replay** – Instead of immediately updating the ANN's weights after an interaction with the environment, the agent stores those experiences in a finite memory. Then, a minibatch of past experiences is randomly sampled from the memory to train the ANN. Consequently, the interaction phase is logically separated from the learning phase, which mitigates the risk of catastrophic interference.
- **Target network** – Instead of using the same ANN for predicting the actions and the target values during experience replay, the agent employs two separate networks. An active network is continuously trained while a target network is used to calculate soft targets, being a copy of the first with delayed synchronization. This approach improves the generalization of the model by minimizing the instabilities inherent to the incremental training of an ANN.

In addition to the reward for the current action, a DDQN also calculates the expected future rewards during experience replay. However, since the correctness of future predictions is not relevant to the classification of a network flow, these were not calculated.

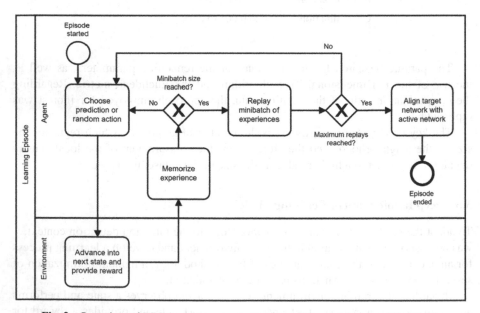

Fig. 2. Overview of DRL learning episode (Business Process Model and Notation).

Several parameters were manually optimized to regulate the developed learning process and the training of the agent. Table 7 summarizes the configuration.

The exploration rate was set to 0.2, which corresponds to 80% predictions and 20% random actions. The rate is decayed by 0.01 after each experience replay until a minimum of 0.05 is reached, effectively decreasing the random actions as the weights are adapted to the training data. The best balance between underfitting and overfitting was achieved with 2 replays per episode, each cycling through a minibatch for 20 epochs.

The size of a minibatch is the number of randomly sampled past experiences in an experience replay. Considering the small size of most utilized datasets, it was set to 2.5% of the size of a training set. Due to the greater size of the 1-1-full, 1-1-large and 1-1-medium datasets, this percentage was decreased. To strengthen the training of the agent, memory size was set to $1.5\times$ the minibatch size, which corresponds to 3.75% of the size of a training set. Therefore, the agent can retrain with up to half of the already replayed experiences.

To perform the final evaluation, the most up-to-date network is retrieved from the agent. For that purpose, the learning process is stopped when the model's loss is stabilized. Stabilization is achieved when the average loss of the experience replays of the most recent episode is within the same range as the previous episodes. The number of previous episodes to compare and the stability range were set to 3 and 0.05, respectively, which gives margin for a slight variance.

Table 7. Summary of DRL learning process configuration.

Parameter	Value
Exploration rate	0.2
Exploration rate decay	0.01
Min exploration rate	0.05
Replays per episode	2
Replay epochs	20
Min stable episodes	3
Stability range	0.05
Minibatch size	2.5% of set
Memory size	3.75% of set

Regarding the active and target networks, both consist of a four-layered ANN. The Adam optimization algorithm is used to minimize the Cross-Entropy loss, with a learning rate of 0.001 to avoid a fast convergence to suboptimal weights.

The input layer node size is the number of utilized features, expressed as NF. Next, there are two hidden layers with 20 neurons each and the computationally efficient Rectified Linear Unit (ReLU) activation function. Finally, the binary output layer uses the Sigmoid activation function and a single node. For multi-class output, the layer is created with the Softmax function and a node size matching the total number of classes to be predicted, expressed as NC. Table 8 describes the employed structure.

Table 8. Employed ANN structure.

Layer	Size	Activation
Dense	NF	-
Dense	20	ReLU
Dense	20	ReLU
Dense	1 or NC	Sigmoid or Softmax

4   Results and Discussion

This section presents and analyses the results obtained in the binary and multi-class classification scenarios, comparing the performance of the developed models.

4.1   Binary Classification

For the binary scenario, a comparison was performed between the F1-scores obtained in the cross-validation and the final evaluation. The obtained results are summarized in Tables 9 and 10, respectively.

In the 5-fold cross-validation, the supervised models, namely SVM, XGBoost and LightGBM, achieved scores near 100% when training with a large quantity of balanced data. The main distinction between the three models is visible on 21-1, where XGBoost only reached approximately 89.98%, despite SVM and LightGBM both obtaining 97.99%. On 34-1, a dataset unbalanced towards malicious flows, LightGBM obtained the highest score, a value of 99.73%.

In contrast with the supervised models, the scores of iForest and LOF were significantly lower on most of the larger datasets. Nonetheless, these unsupervised models achieved a good performance on the smaller and more unbalanced sets. LOF obtained better results than iForest on 1-1-small, 21-1 and 34-1. On 21-1, it surpassed XGBoost with a score of 91.66%. However, iForest outperformed LOF on all the remaining sets and even reached approximately 100% on 42-1.

Table 9. F1-scores of the binary cross-validation (5-fold average).

Model	1-1-full	1-1-large	1-1-medium	1-1-small	20-1	21-1	34-1	42-1	44-1
SVM	**100**	**100**	**100**	**100**	**100**	**97.99**	99.30	**100**	**97.84**
XGBoost	99.99	99.99	99.99	99.99	**100**	89.98	98.14	**100**	**97.84**
LightGBM	**100**	99.99	99.99	99.99	**100**	**97.99**	**99.73**	**100**	**97.84**
iForest	76.62	71.88	71.82	73.36	93.75	68.15	88.20	**100**	88.79
LOF	62.18	61.88	61.03	80.64	93.54	91.66	97.43	79.97	87.89

In the final evaluation, the supervised models achieved a good generalization. However, the lower scores on 20-1 and 21-1 indicate a slight overfitting on those smaller sets. On 44-1, the smallest of the analyzed datasets, only SVM increased its score.

A significant improvement is visible on the results of iForest on the larger sets, as well as on 20-1, where it reached 100%. This indicates it is well suited for the detection of anomalies on unseen data. On the other hand, LOF obtained lower scores on all datasets except 44-1. On this last set, its score was also increased to approximately 100%, possibly due to the small number of new samples to be classified.

The DRL model almost reached the results of the supervised models on the larger sets. However, it is pertinent to note that the smaller the training set, the lower the obtained score. This suggests that a large quantity of data is required for the developed learning process to be effective in an initial training.

Table 10. F1-scores of the binary evaluation.

Model	1-1-full	1-1-large	1-1-medium	1-1-small	20-1	21-1	34-1	42-1	44-1
SVM	**100**	**100**	**100**	**100**	95.43	**94.42**	99.43	**100**	**100**
XGBoost	99.99	99.99	99.99	99.99	95.43	**94.42**	98.84	**100**	96.28
LightGBM	**100**	99.99	**100**	**100**	95.43	**94.42**	**99.76**	**100**	96.28
iForest	96.46	94.80	94.68	95.37	**100**	89.95	75.08	**100**	90.91
LOF	53.46	53.40	54.66	80.18	89.95	87.45	96.80	49.96	**100**
DRL	99.91	99.91	99.97	99.98	78.49	83.28	98.65	83.31	75.39

Overall, the analyzed supervised and DRL models were reliable on most datasets, despite their slight performance decrease on some of the smaller sets. On the other hand, the unsupervised models were more advantageous for the smaller training sets, especially the ones highly unbalanced towards benign flows (see Fig. 3).

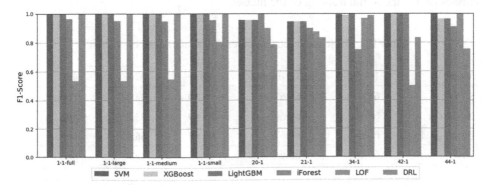

Fig. 3. Comparison of the F1-scores of the binary evaluation.

4.2 Multi-class Classification

For the multi-class scenario, an equivalent comparison was performed using the macro-averaged F1-scores, which are summarized in Tables 11 and 12. Due to the inability of unsupervised models to perform multi-class classification, these were not analyzed.

In the 5-fold cross-validation, the supervised models achieved very high scores on 34-1 and 44-1. LightGBM reached the highest score on 34-1, as in the previous scenario. On the other hand, very poor results were obtained on the particularly unbalanced sets. Since 1-1-full, 1-1-large and 42-1 contain minority classes with a very low number of samples, the models were not able to learn how to correctly classify them while training with 4/5 of the training sets.

Table 11. Macro-averaged F1-scores of the multi-class cross-validation (5-fold average).

Model	1-1-full	1-1-large	34-1	42-1	44-1
SVM	**66.67**	**80.00**	95.67	59.97	**97.66**
XGBoost	66.66	**80.00**	97.30	46.67	96.44
LightGBM	66.66	**80.00**	**98.77**	**59.99**	**97.66**

In the final evaluation, the supervised models reached scores of approximately 100% on 44-1 and similar results to the cross-validation on 34-1, which indicates a good generalization. However, their scores were decreased to near 66% on 1-1-large, due to the neglect of the underrepresented class. Furthermore, only LightGBM correctly classified one of the two minority classes of 42-1, whereas the remaining models failed to detect both. Since poor results were obtained on both validation and evaluation sets, the lack of training samples of those classes may be leading to underfitting.

The results obtained by the DRL model were very similar to the remaining models on most datasets, but significantly lower on 34-1 and 44-1. This indicates that the employed learning process cannot successfully account for multiple underrepresented classes during the initial training of the model.

Table 12. Macro-averaged F1-scores of the multi-class evaluation.

Model	1-1-full	1-1-large	34-1	42-1	44-1
SVM	**66.67**	**66.67**	95.89	33.31	**100**
XGBoost	66.66	66.66	95.59	33.33	**100**
LightGBM	66.66	**66.67**	**99.64**	**66.65**	**100**
DRL	66.64	66.64	63.75	33.38	88.38

Overall, the analyzed models achieved a good multi-class classification performance on the datasets with relatively balanced class proportions (see Fig. 4). The key obstacles remain the lack of training data and the underrepresented classes. Therefore, for these models to be able to distinguish between the different types of cyber-attacks, it is crucial to train them with a greater number of flows of each type.

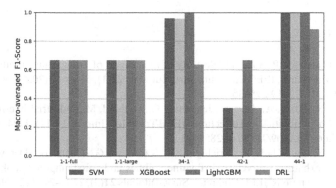

Fig. 4. Comparison of the macro-averaged F1-scores of the multi-class evaluation.

5 Conclusions

The developed work addressed IoT intrusion detection from a machine learning perspective. Nine malware captures of the IoT-23 dataset were utilized in a binary classification scenario and five of those in a multi-class scenario as well.

After a data preprocessing stage, three supervised models, SVM, XGBoost and LightGBM, two unsupervised models, iForest and LOF, and one DRL model based on a DDQN were analyzed and compared to assess their applicability to an IDS in an IoT system. Both a 5-fold cross-validation and a final evaluation were performed with the macro-averaged F1-score as the metric.

The supervised models achieved the most reliable performance in both scenarios, reaching higher scores when trained with a greater number of malware attack examples. LightGBM stood out for displaying the best generalization to several evaluation sets, especially in the multi-class scenario.

Despite the significantly lower results of the unsupervised models, these seem advantageous for the detection of very low-frequency malware attacks. Furthermore, iForest achieved a good overall performance, which highlights its suitability for anomaly detection when trained with smaller and more unbalanced datasets.

The DRL model adapted to the intrusion detection context demonstrated that the reinforcement learning methodology can reach the performance of supervised techniques while also providing a learning process capable of continuously improving the detection. Therefore, the model can be adapted to changes in the traffic patterns, caused by updates to the network topology or by modifications to the cyber-attacks.

As a future research topic, these three distinct types of machine learning techniques can be combined in an IDS to strengthen their benefits and overcome their individual drawbacks. Additionally, the development of DRL learning processes with rewards obtained from user feedback or other systems is a promising strategy to provide a more reliable and robust IoT intrusion detection.

Acknowledgments. The present work was done and funded in the scope of the European Union's Horizon 2020 research and innovation program, under project SeCoIIA (grant agreement no. 871967). This work has also received funding from UIDP/00760/2020.

References

1. Butun, I., Osterberg, P., Song, H.: Security of the Internet of Things: vulnerabilities, attacks, and countermeasures. IEEE Commun. Surv. Tutorials **22**(1), 616–644 (2020). https://doi.org/10.1109/COMST.2019.2953364
2. Sisinni, E., Saifullah, A., Han, S., Jennehag, U., Gidlund, M.: Industrial internet of things: challenges, opportunities, and directions. IEEE Trans. Ind. Inform. **14**(11), 4724–4734 (2018). https://doi.org/10.1109/TII.2018.2852491
3. Neshenko, N., Bou-Harb, E., Crichigno, J., Kaddoum, G., Ghani, N.: Demystifying IoT security: an exhaustive survey on IoT vulnerabilities and a first empirical look on Internet-scale IoT exploitations. IEEE Commun. Surv. Tutorials **21**(3), 2702–2733 (2019). https://doi.org/10.1109/COMST.2019.2910750
4. Al-Masri, E., et al.: Investigating Messaging Protocols for the Internet of Things (IoT). IEEE Access **8**, 94880–94911 (2020). https://doi.org/10.1109/ACCESS.2020.2993363
5. Srivastava, A., Gupta, S., Quamara, M., Chaudhary, P., Aski, V.J.: Future IoT-enabled threats and vulnerabilities: state of the art, challenges, and future prospects. Int. J. Commun. Syst. **33**(12) (2020). https://doi.org/10.1002/dac.4443
6. Panchal, A.C., Khadse, V.M., Mahalle, P.N.: Security issues in IIoT: a comprehensive survey of attacks on IIoT and its countermeasures. In: Proceedings of the 2018 IEEE Global Conference on Wireless Computing Networking, GCWCN 2018, pp. 124–130 (2019). https://doi.org/10.1109/GCWCN.2018.8668630
7. Tahsien, S.M., Karimipour, H., Spachos, P.: Machine learning based solutions for security of Internet of Things (IoT): a survey. J. Netw. Comput. Appl. **161** (2020). https://doi.org/10.1016/j.jnca.2020.102630
8. Chaabouni, N., Mosbah, M., Zemmari, A., Sauvignac, C., Faruki, P.: Network intrusion detection for IoT security based on learning techniques. IEEE Commun. Surv. Tutorials **21**(3), 2671–2701 (2019). https://doi.org/10.1109/COMST.2019.2896380
9. Zolanvari, M., Teixeira, M.A., Gupta, L., Khan, K.M., Jain, R.: Machine learning-based network vulnerability analysis of industrial Internet of Things. IEEE Internet Things J. **6**(4), 6822–6834 (2019). https://doi.org/10.1109/JIOT.2019.2912022
10. Jan, S.U., Ahmed, S., Shakhov, V., Koo, I.: Toward a lightweight intrusion detection system for the Internet of Things. IEEE Access **7**, 42450–42471 (2019). https://doi.org/10.1109/ACCESS.2019.2907965
11. Bakhtiar, F.A., Pramukantoro, E.S., Nihri, H.: A lightweight IDS based on j48 algorithm for detecting DoS attacks on IoT middleware. In: 2019 IEEE 1st Global Conference on Life Science Technology LifeTech 2019, pp. 41–42 (2019). https://doi.org/10.1109/LifeTech.2019.8884057
12. Verma, A., Ranga, V.: Machine learning based intrusion detection systems for IoT applications. Wirel. Pers. Commun. **111**(4), 2287–2310 (2019). https://doi.org/10.1007/s11277-019-06986-8
13. Yao, H., Gao, P., Zhang, P., Wang, J., Jiang, C., Lu, L.: Hybrid intrusion detection system for edge-based IIoT relying on machine-learning-aided detection. IEEE Netw. **33**(5), 75–81 (2019). https://doi.org/10.1109/MNET.001.1800479

14. Eskandari, M., Janjua, Z.H., Vecchio, M., Antonelli, F.: Passban IDS: an intelligent anomaly-based intrusion detection system for IoT edge devices. IEEE Internet Things J. **7**(8), 6882–6897 (2020). https://doi.org/10.1109/JIOT.2020.2970501
15. Gu, T., Abhishek, A., Fu, H., Zhang, H., Basu, D., Mohapatra, P.: Towards learning-automation IoT attack detection through reinforcement learning. In: 21st IEEE International Symposium on a World of Wireless, Mobile and Multimedia Networks, WoWMoM 2020, pp. 88–97 (2020). https://doi.org/10.1109/WoWMoM49955.2020.00029
16. Lopez-Martin, M., Carro, B., Sanchez-Esguevillas, A.: Application of deep reinforcement learning to intrusion detection for supervised problems. Expert Syst. Appl. **141**, 112963 (2020). https://doi.org/10.1016/j.eswa.2019.112963
17. Garcia, S., Parmisano, A., Erquiaga, M.J.: IoT-23: a labeled dataset with malicious and benign IoT network traffic (2020). https://doi.org/10.5281/ZENODO.4743746
18. Khraisat, A., Gondal, I., Vamplew, P., Kamruzzaman, J.: Survey of intrusion detection systems: techniques, datasets and challenges. Cybersecurity **2**(1), 1–22 (2019). https://doi.org/10.1186/s42400-019-0038-7
19. Liu, H., Lang, B.: Machine learning and deep learning methods for intrusion detection systems: a survey. Appl. Sci. **9**(20) (2019). https://doi.org/10.3390/app9204396
20. Hearst, M.A., Dumais, S.T., Osuna, E., Platt, J., Scholkopf, B.: Support vector machines. IEEE Intell. Syst. their Appl. **13**(4), 18–28 (1998). https://doi.org/10.1109/5254.708428
21. Chen, T., Guestrin, C.: XGBoost: a scalable tree boosting system. In: Proceedings of the 25th ACM SIGKDD International Conference on Knowledge Discovery & Data Mining, vol. 13–17-August, pp. 785–794 (2016). https://doi.org/10.1145/2939672.2939785
22. Ke, G., et al.: LightGBM: a highly efficient gradient boosting decision tree. Adv. Neural Inf. Process. Syst. **2017**, 3147–3155 (2017)
23. Liu, F.T., Ting, K.M., Zhou, Z.H.: Isolation forest. In: IEEE International Conference on Data Mining, pp. 413–422 (2008). https://doi.org/10.1109/ICDM.2008.17
24. Breunig, M., Kriegel, H.-P., Ng, R., Sander, J.: LOF: identifying density-based local outliers. ACM SIGMOD Rec. **29**, 93–104 (2000). https://doi.org/10.1145/342009.335388
25. Van Hasselt, H., Guez, A., Silver, D.: Deep reinforcement learning with double Q-learning. In: Thirtieth AAAI Conference on Artificial Intelligence, pp. 2094–2100 (2016)

An Automatized Identity and Access Management System for IoT Combining Self-Sovereign Identity and Smart Contracts

Montassar Naghmouchi[1,2], Hella Kaffel Ben Ayed[1], and Maryline Laurent[2(✉)] ⓘ

[1] Faculty of Science of Tunis, University of Tunis El Manar, Tunis, Tunisia
montasser.naghmouchi@etudiant-fst.utm.tn,
hella.kaffel@fst.utm.tn
[2] Samovar, Télécom SudParis, Institut Polytechnique de Paris, Palaiseau, France
Maryline.Laurent@telecom-sudparis.eu

Abstract. Nowadays, open standards for self-sovereign identity and access management enable portable solutions that are following the requirements of IoT systems. This paper proposes a blockchain-based identity and access management system for IoT – specifically smart vehicles- as an exemplar use-case, showing two interoperable blockchains, Ethereum and Hyperledger Indy, and a self-sovereign identity model.

Keywords: Self-Sovereign Identity · Identity and Access Management · Automatized authorization

1 Introduction

For IoT ecosystems that require a scalable, resilient, lightweight, and secure Identity and Access Management (IAM) technologies to ensure the privacy of user-data, it is essential to implement systems that are owned directly by the device owners themselves. In the case of smart vehicles, it is logical that vehicle owners have full control over their identities, those of their vehicles and to be able to manage authorization methods since cars are private properties. Such systems are enabled with a combination of consortium or public blockchains and a Self-Sovereign Identity model (SSI).

This paper proposes a Blockchain-based IAM system that makes use of the SSI model to provide ledger-rooted identities for users and IoT devices, specifically smart vehicles. Moreover, it explores a crucial property for blockchain technology, which is interoperability. In a matter of fact, two different blockchains are used in our system - Ethereum and Hyperledger Indy - due to different capabilities provided by the two platforms.

The remaining of the paper is structured as follows. Section 2 introduces the background on SSI and related open standards. Section 3 presents our system architecture and design. Section 4 provides an insight on blockchain interoperability and how we handle it in our proposal. Finally, we conclude our work in Sect. 5. Acronyms used are listed in Table 1.

© Springer Nature Switzerland AG 2022
E. Aïmeur et al. (Eds.): FPS 2021, LNCS 13291, pp. 208–217, 2022.
https://doi.org/10.1007/978-3-031-08147-7_14

Table 1. Acronyms.

Acronym	Meaning
DID	Decentralized Identifier
DPKI	Decentralized Public Key Infrastructure
IAM	Identity and Access Management
JSON-LD	JavaScript Object Notation for Linked Data
RWoT	Rebooting the Web of Trust
SSI	Self-Sovereign Identity
VC	Verifiable Credential

2 Background on Self-Sovereign Identity and Open Standards

Self-Sovereign Identity (SSI) refers to the digital movement that recognizes that an individual should own and control their digital identity without relying on a third party. Online users are more aware of the value of their data and adequate privacy measures around them.

The SSI model defines the following roles:

- An *issuer*, which is an entity that creates credentials for users.
- A *holder*, which is a user in possession of a credential, either by ownership or by delegation from the owner.
- A *verifier*, which is the entity that verifies a credential presented by a holder willing to obtain a service from a service provider.

The SSI model relies on four (4) key standards: Decentralized Identifiers (DID), Verifiable Credentials (VC), Decentralized Public Key Infrastructures (DPKI) and a DID Authentication protocol (DID Auth).

2.1 Decentralized Identifiers (DID)

DID is a W3C standard [1] that serves as an identifier for a subject. A DID is resolved into a DID Document that describes the identified subject. The DID Document is a JSON-LD data, that includes the public keys owned by the subject, service endpoints and verification methods.

A DID satisfies the following core properties: 1) permanent, i.e. which does not change or can not be re-assigned, 2) resolvable, i.e. which can be looked up to discover metadata, 3) cryptographically-verifiable, i.e. which authorship and ownership can be proved, and 4) decentralized, i.e. which do not need any central registration authority.

The DID is generated from the public key of the subject, so that the ownership of the DID can be accomplished using the private key that is cryptographically bound to a public key published in the DID Document.

2.2 Decentralized Public Key Infrastructure (DPKI)

Since DIDs rely on public keys, it is essential to have a Public Key Infrastructure to manage keys related to identifiers. Moreover, this infrastructure must be decentralized. DPKI or Decentralized Key Management System defines protocols to generate, store and manage public and private keys that help generate decentralized identifiers and prove ownership over them. Blockchain, as a key-value storage system can already play the role of a DPKI [2].

2.3 Verifiable Credentials (VC)

Verifiable credential (VC) [3] is another standard by W3C. A VC is a JSON-LD composed of assertions, about some user' identity attributes. It is issued by an issuer and held by a holder. A VC includes the issuer's public key and signature and is used to obtain services from service providers based on some claims included in that credential. It supports selective disclosure, zero-knowledge proofs and it is revocable.

2.4 DID Authentication Protocol

DID Auth is an authentication protocol proposed by RWoT to prove the ownership or the authorship over a DID record using the authentication material specified in the DID Document (i.e. knowledge of the private key associated to the public key published in the DID document). A DID Auth process may contain verifiable credentials, as part of the exchange. DID Auth allows to establish an authenticated channel between the two parties which are usually the verifier and the holder [4].

3 Our System Architecture and Design

This section focuses on the chosen example, the blockchain-based IAM system for smart vehicles. We present the IAM model and discuss functional and security requirements. We also present the design choices and a detailed system workflow.

3.1 System Model and Vehicle Sharing Use Case

The smart vehicle sharing use-case is considered for illustrating the need for an automatized access control based on the SSI model. In this use-case, a smart vehicle owner, be it a physical person or a corporate, is able to create credentials allowing other users to gain access and usage privileges to the vehicle for various possible purposes: rental, exchange, car-sharing, vehicles for work-mission etc.

Following the SSI model, our system refers to the actors, as depicted in Fig. 1:

- Vehicle owner: The owner of a vehicle is an **issuer** capable of issuing a credential for a holder authorizing access and usage of the vehicle.
- User: An entity wishing to gain access to a vehicle, once the request is made to the vehicle owner and the credential is created for the user, they are considered as a **holder** as long as the credential is valid.

- Smart contract: The **verifier** in our use-case is an Ethereum smart contract (cf. Sect. 3.6). The smart contract is linked to a given vehicle (one or many) and is charged of verifying the credentials presented by holders. Access is granted according to the access policies defined in the smart contract that are compared against the content of the presented verifiable credentials.
- Service Provider: The service being the vehicle usage, confers smart vehicles to service providers. These vehicles must have identifiers in the system (DIDs controlled by their owners) and have connectivity to invoke and read access decision made by verifiers, that are smart contracts.
- SSI infrastructure: Hyperledger Indy blockchain platform is used as an identity layer for our system (cf. Sect. 3.5). This supposes that a running Hyperledger Indy blockchain is maintained by different entities (to ensure decentralization). It can either be a consortium blockchain or a public one, depending on the implementation and real world requirements specified in a business model to ensure that vehicle owners and users are incentivized to join and use the network.
- Access Management component: Ethereum Blockchain, running smart contracts as verifiers, is the access management component and acts as an authorization layer for our system. These smart contracts can be published on the public Ethereum network and utilized by the decentralized authorization application as a blockchain back-end.

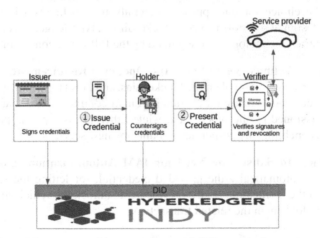

Fig. 1. Overview of the system architecture, along with SSI actors, other system components and standards

3.2 Functional and Security Requirements

The main requirements to be fulfilled by our system are:

- Scalability: due to the number of actors – issuers, holders, and cars – distributed over a territory and the high volume of transactions, the scalability requirement is a high priority in our system.

- Openness: the objective is to let the solution be available to as many users as possible with low entry levels, as soon as the physical persons are registered into the SSI Hyperledger Indy system.
- Availability: the IAM should remain available for serving new requests and should not be vulnerable to Single Point of Failure (SPOF) attacks.
- Automatization of the IAM: due to the number of actors, and possible transactions, this is of high interest to have the transactions processed automatically and autonomously by smart contracts.
- Accountability: Any transactions processed by our system must be logged and traced with high integrity proof guarantee for later dispute resolution.
- Flexible access policy management: access policies for vehicles should be easily updated by the owner and also fine grained for each vehicle to have a potentially customized access policy.
- Security: access to the vehicle must be conditioned by obtaining a valid credential and must not be bypassed through some fake credentials for instance.
- Privacy: identities of actors and transaction contents should remain confidential to avoid the system to leak personal data.

3.3 Design Choices

Due to scalability, availability, traceability and automatization requirements, as identified in Sect. 3.2, the choice for our approach naturally fell on blockchain technologies. Moreover, the design of solution over two blockchains – Hyperledger Indy and Ethereum - and smart contract technologies were guided by the following considerations:

Two Blockchain Technologies to Serve the Openness Requirement. The need for openness leads to the selection of public blockchains, and thus Hyperledger Indy for supporting SSI function and Ethereum for running smart contracts. Note that Hyperledger Indy is a permissioned public blockchain, while Ethereum is a public permissionless blockchain thus enabling any corporates to build any new services.

Smart Contracts to Satisfy the Need for IAM Automatization. Smart contracts enable to verify automatically the provided credential, for letting the smart car service know about the verification result and whether to unlock the vehicle and for writing onto Ethereum blockchain the related transaction.

3.4 The Workflow Description

All involved entities (issuers, holders, and smart vehicles) are registered in Hyperledger Indy and are provided with a DID. All the interactions between entities are setup with a DID Auth to mutually authenticate and exchange credential or credential requests as shown in Fig. 2.

The issuer is responsible for publishing his smart contract(s), either one smart contract for each vehicle or one smart contract for a group of cars. The cars are configured for contacting one smart contract (at least). It might also happen that car owners cooperate to jointly publish a smart contract. Note that we can have services (in the form of smart contracts) provided by other entities should the vehicle owner chooses to use an existing smart contract developed by another party. This creates an open market for smart contract development as they can generate fees to reward developers.

The vehicles are configured for contacting at least one smart contract for authorization decisions. When a holder needs to access to the service (step 1 in Fig. 2), an interaction occurs with the issuer through Hyperledger Indy, and an authenticated channel is established. The issuer can then issue a verifiable credential for the requesting holder (step 2), including specific conditions for the smart contract and the vehicle to refine the access policy for that specific holder, i.e. authorized time slots, a specific vehicle. In step 3 of Fig. 2, the holder goes near to the vehicle and presents the credential contained in a mobile wallet (via NFC, Bluetooth ...) which is forwarded to the Ethereum smart contract (verifier). The smart contract refers to Hyperledger Indy to verify the ownership, the authorship, and the non-revocation of the credential (step 5). The verifier also checks the credential against a list of access policies – as the credential contains claims – specified by the issuer. Note that the smart contract has exclusive invocation properties, restricted to the issuer and to the vehicles(s) controlled by that smart contract. In step 6, the smart vehicle is informed by the smart contract about the resulting decision which is written into the Ethereum blockchain. The vehicle then can unlock the doors or maintain the doors locked.

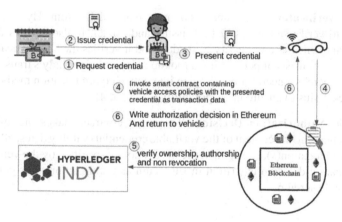

Fig. 2. System workflow. Describing basic steps and interactions between entities in the system.

3.5 Identity Management with Hyperledger Indy

Hyperledger Indy is an open source project maintained by The Linux Foundation, and designed as an identity blockchain to work as an infrastructure for decentralized identities. It implements the standards introduced in Sect. 2 and enables a decentralized identification and authentication thanks to DIDs and public key cryptography. In the proposed system, Hyperledger Indy supports the identification function. After an identity registration transaction is received from the vehicle owner (issuer) or the vehicle renter (holder) and is validated by a trust anchor, their DID identifiers are created and registered into the blockchain. Both Issuer and Holder manage their DIDs through a wallet application which enables them to interact with the Hyperledger Indy blockchain. The wallet stores all the DIDs under the control of the wallet owner, the related private keys, the verifiable credentials, as well as the messages exchanged between entities (credential offers, credential requests, private messages).

Revocation tails for the issued credentials are also published on the ledger. These transactions represent the current state of a verifiable credential and are used to manage the revocation of credentials

3.6 Access Management with Ethereum

The smart vehicle, considered as a service provider, delegates the credential verification and the authorization decisions to the verifier, which is an Ethereum smart contract. When a holder is physically near to the vehicle, DID Auth interaction can occur via an NFC, WiFi or Bluetooth connectivity to establish a secure communication channel between the holder and the vehicle and to enable the holder to present a verifiable presentation using claims from different credentials from their wallet. The smart car invokes the verifier smart contract on Ethereum with the verifiable presented claims as transaction data.

At this point, the smart contract verifier executes two major phases, described below in a chronological order.

Credential Verification. The smart contract reads data from Hyperledger Indy Blockchain to verify signatures of both issuer and holder. It also verifies the hash of the credential to ensure the integrity of its data and it verifies the non-revocation status. This processing consists of performing a lookup in Hyperledger Indy's transactions. For this purpose, there is a need for building an interactive communication method between the two blockchains to ensure interoperability (cf. Sect. 4).

Accountable Authorization Decision. The smart contract makes the authorization decision by checking the content of the verifiable credential (validity dates, allowed vehicle(s), allowed location(s), ...) against the access policy specified by the vehicle owner. The authorization decision is written in Ethereum as a transaction, thus generating an access-log on Ethereum.

4   Blockchain Interoperability Between Hyperledger Indy and Ethereum

The proposed architecture relies on two separate blockchains with separate ledgers. Interoperability in blockchain is a new trending topic in academic research since 2014 [5]. The lack of standards for blockchain systems results in Blockchain interoperability issue, which is required to ensure the openness of blockchain systems and their integration in existent systems and environments. It also permits to eliminate digital islands and contributes to enhance blockchains scalability. Interoperability resolves heterogeneity, mainly in terms of governance (public/private/consortium), openness (permissioned/permissionless), consensus algorithm and cryptographic assets like cryptocurrency and token.

4.1 Interoperability Solutions for Blockchains

With new blockchains created, each having different consensus protocols, different purposes, different capabilities and different use cases, interoperability solutions between blockchains are gaining more attention. So far, the existing methods to inter-operate blockchains are:

– Sidechains: Multiple blockchains are used to improve the system scalability. Each Multiple blockchains are used to improve the system scalability. Each Blockchain is responsible for managing a portion of the load. Generally, sidechains are secondary blockchains that are connected to a mainchain (consortium blockchain). For example, in an IoT context, Sidechains permit a finer granularity to a blockchain system where each sidechain handles a set of devices [6]. The consortium blockchain is responsible for maintaining a log of successful or failed data access requests from a consortium member to another. This can also be seen in blockchain-sharding that allows parallel transaction execution by having subsets of nodes working in parallel.
– Cross chain communication: Different blockchains are integrated in the same system or communicate with other systems, regardless of the technologies. This scenario refers to multiple needs: connect multiple blockchains to a consortium blockchain, connect blockchain engines to each other, asset swap/exchange/trading between two different blockchains, create cross-chain assets and to notify a blockchain about events happening in another blockchain. There are two cases of cross-chain asset exchange and communication: (1) Isomorphic cross-chains where the two blockchains use the same consensus algorithm, (2) Heterogeneous cross-chains where the two blockchains use different consensus algorithms [5].

Interoperability is achieved by the following components:

– Relayers: transmit messages between two chains or two blockchains. Relayers need a communication protocol to define how to transmit notifications and transactions between two blockchains. Cross-chain Communication Protocol (CCCP), is used in case of isomorphic cross-chains and Cross-Blockchain Communication Protocol (CBCP) in the case of Heterogeneous cross-chains [5].
– Notary nodes: nodes that are common between two blockchains. A notary node runs two blockchain clients at the same time. It can read from both ledgers and perform cross-chain transactions between the two blockchains. It has transaction forwarding capability. Notary nodes signs transactions with a majority of 2/3 to forward them from one blockchain A to a blockchain B. The main use case is exchanging assets.
– Other methods: Such as smart contracts reading from another blockchain (BTC Relay) and APIs exposing transactions between two blockchains. APIs have the ability to fetch transaction data from a blockchain and expose it to be consumed by any other party, for example a web client. In our solution, we are not performing any cross-chain transactions or asset exchange between the two blockchains, so we are relying on a HTTP API to expose the Hyperledger Indy transactions to the outside world.

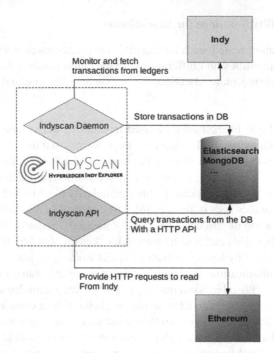

Fig. 3. Inter-operating Ethereum and Hyperledger Indy with APIs

4.2 The Proposed Interoperability Solution

Our solution relies on a HTTP API to expose the Hyperledger Indy transactions to the outside world. Inspired by the indyscan.io [7, 8], we propose the re-use of components in the repository to create a method for smart contracts on Ethereum to query transactions recorded on Hyperledger Indy. The architecture, depicted in Fig. 3, relies on two important components found in the indyscan project: the indyscan daemon and the indyscan API. The indyscan daemon monitors the Hyperledger Indy blockchain and fetches transactions from the ledger. Later on, these transactions are stored in a database like MongoDB or Elasticsearch. Indyscan API then queries the database and provides a HTTP API enabling a consumer to perform HTTP requests to read from that database. Smart contracts on Ethereum consume this API, either directly or via an oracle.

5   Conclusion

This paper proposes an SSI compliant Identity and Access management system for a vehicle-sharing use-case. The system is based on two blockchains that are complementary, where each blockchain plays a suitable role based on its capabilities. The proposed architecture is fully decentralized and presents a system with tamper-proof identity data and permanent transparent access history for better audit and accountability. Thanks to open standards, the system is inter-operable and in compliance with modern digital identity and privacy requirements.

The choice of a self-sovereign identity model allows users to truly own and control their identities and vehicles' identities. This makes our architecture more suitable for systems with high privacy requirements. The security by design and availability features of blockchains also make this proposal a more resilient solution. The two separate blockchains with two separate ledgers provide better accountability and easier audit as blockchains have transparent data. At the same time, user's privacy is kept due to the usage of off-chain encrypted data storage, and different cryptographical methods like selective disclosure and zero-knowledge proofs. In terms of scalability, Hyperledger Indy is scalable by design with two types of nodes: validators and observers.

Managing authorization and verification with smart contracts allows for a more dynamic autonomous access control for vehicles. Access policies can be remotely updated by updating a smart contract. Some smart contracts templates can also remain publicly at the disposal of vehicle owners. The smart contracts are automated and require no intervention from humans which adds more trust between an issuer and a holder in terms of enforcing an agreement between the two parties. As for the Indy-Ethereum communication, an intermediate database is used to store the transactions from Hyperledger Indy and an HTTP API is provided for smart contracts on Ethereum to automatically verify the credentials.

Ongoing work focuses on optimizing the interoperability between the two blockchains. Furthermore, the proposal can be extended to manage identity and access for other types of devices more constrained and limited than smart cars.

References

1. Reed, D., et al.: Decentralized Identifiers DID 1.0
2. Law, J., et al.: Decentralized Key Management System Design and Architecture v4 (2019)
3. Sporny, M., et al.: Verifiable Credential Data Model 1.0 (2019)
4. Sadabello, M. et al: Introduction to DID Auth (2018)
5. Belchior, R., et al.: A Survey on Blockchain Interoperability: Past, Present, and Future Trends (2020)
6. Jiang, Y., et al.: A cross-chain solution to integrating multiple blockchains for IoT Data Management (2019). Sensors **19**(9), 2042 (2019). https://doi.org/10.3390/s19092042
7. Indyscan website. https://indyscan.io/home/SOVRIN_MAINNET. Accessed 01 Apr 2021
8. Indyscan Github repository. https://github.com/Patrik
9. Oktian, Y.E., et al.: Hierarchical multi-blockchain architecture for scalable internet of things. Electronics **9**(6), 1050 (2020). https://doi.org/10.3390/electronics9061050

PERMANENT: Publicly Verifiable Remote Attestation for Internet of Things Through Blockchain

Sigurd Frej Joel Jørgensen Ankergård, Edlira Dushku$^{(\boxtimes)}$ (iD),
and Nicola Dragoni (iD)

DTU Compute, Technical University of Denmark (DTU),
2800 Kgs. Lyngby, Denmark
s164443@student.dtu.dk, {edldu,ndra}@dtu.dk

Abstract. Remote Attestation (RA) is a security mechanism that allows a centralized trusted entity (Verifier) to check the trustworthiness of a potentially compromised IoT device (Prover). With the tsunami of interconnected IoT devices, the advancement of *swarm* RA schemes that efficiently attest large IoT networks has become crucial. Recent swarm RA approaches work towards distributing the attestation verification from a centralized Verifier to many Verifiers. However, the assumption of trusted Verifiers in the swarm is not practical in large networks. In addition, the state-of-the-art RA schemes do not establish network-wide decentralized trust among the interacting devices in the swarm. This paper proposes PERMANENT, a Publicly Verifiable Remote Attestation protocol for Internet of Things through Blockchain, which stores the historical attestation results of all devices in a blockchain and allows each interacting device to obtain the attestation result. PERMANENT enables devices to make a trust decision based on the historical attestation results. This feature allows the interaction among trustworthy devices (or with a trust score over a certain threshold) without the computational overhead of attesting every participating device before each interaction. We validate PERMANENT with a proof-of-concept implementation, using Hyperledger Sawtooth as the underlying blockchain. The conducted experiments confirm the feasibility of the PERMANENT protocol.

Keywords: Remote Attestation · Internet of Things · Blockchain · Public verifiability

1 Introduction

With the rapid evolution of the Internet-of-Things (IoT), many smart devices are increasingly becoming interconnected, working together in remote locations and performing many collaborative tasks without human intervention. Often IoT devices perform safety-critical operations and process sensitive information, thus, these devices are continuously targeted from many cyber attacks [17,19,25,30].

© Springer Nature Switzerland AG 2022
E. Aïmeur et al. (Eds.): FPS 2021, LNCS 13291, pp. 218–234, 2022.
https://doi.org/10.1007/978-3-031-08147-7_15

While it is challenging to protect resource-constrained devices with conventional security mechanisms, Remote Attestation (RA) has emerged as a lightweight security method that verifies whether devices have been compromised or not. Traditional RA is a challenge-response protocol between a trusted party called Verifier (*Vrf*) and an untrusted remote device called Prover (*Prv*). Specifically, at the attestation time, the *Vrf* sends a challenge to the *Prv*, the *Prv* responds by sending reliable evidence about its software state to the *Vrf*. This evidence consists of performing a software measurement (i.e., computing a checksum or hash) usually over the static memory content of a device which allows the *Vrf* to detect the malware presence on *Prv*'s device. However, traditional challenge-response RA protocols pose scalability challenges for large IoT systems [3].

In order to overcome the scalability challenges of RA, many swarm RA schemes ([4,5,8], to mention only a few) have been proposed in the literature to allow a trusted *Vrf* to attest large-scale IoT networks. The state-of-the-art RA approaches typically rely on the presence of multiple Verifiers in the swarm for verification. Nevertheless, the assumption of trusted Verifiers is often not practical in large networks. Moreover, the existing RA schemes do not establish network-wide decentralized trust among the interacting devices in the swarm.

Contribution of the Paper. We argue that, to establish trust in multi-party large IoT networks, blockchain is a promising technology [14]. In particular, the immutability of blockchain guarantees the reliability of IoT data stored in blockchain transactions. Moreover, all the historical transactions stored in the blockchain are traceable. While these properties are important in improving IoT data security in general, they can potentially play a key role in securing attestation evidence of IoT devices.

To the best of our knowledge, this paper proposes the first RA protocol that uses blockchain technology to make RA publicly verifiable. Specifically, instead of relying on any single trusted third party, we rely on permissioned blockchains [18] to establish trust in a decentralized manner. In our approach, devices perform self-attestation [11,22,27] which gets triggered by a timer stored in the device's trusted component. Then, we leverage the timer of Proof-of-Elapsed-Time (PoET) consensus mechanism to combine it with the device's timer used for self-attestation in order to reach consensus without additional interactions. The proposed protocol utilizes the blockchain-based history of the devices attestation to evaluate the trustworthiness of IoT devices. The paper brings the following two main contributions:

1. The paper designs PERMANENT, a novel RA protocol which leverages blockchain technology to make the attestation result publicly verifiable and decentralized. PERMANENT decides devices' trustworthiness based on their entire historical attestations evidence. This feature serves as a building block to enable secure interactions among IoT devices.
2. The paper presents the proof-of-concept implementation of PERMANENT. PERMANENT has been implemented and tested with HyperLedger Sawtooth using Proof-of-Elapsed-Time (PoET) as a consensus mechanism. Experiments confirm the feasibility of the proposed solution.

Outline. The remainder of this paper is organized as follows. Section 2 presents different RA approaches and compares PERMANENT with relevant ones. System model and adversary model are described in Sect. 3 and Sect. 4, respectively. Next, PERMANENT protocol is detailed in Sect. 5 and its proof-of-concept implementation presented in Sect. 6. Protocol limitations are discussed in Sect. 7. Finally, Sect. 8 concludes the paper.

2 Related Works

In general RA is classified into three categories: software-based, hardware-based and hybrid RA. Software RA [6,29] does not require specialized hardware components but instead uses timing requirements to ensure the attestation code has not been tampered with. However, software-based RA schemes rely on strong adversarial assumptions and do not provide secure storage for protecting device's keys and the attestation code. To tackle this drawback, hardware-based RA relies on specialized hardware components like Trusted Platform Module (TPM) [7] to provide a root-of-trust. TPM consists of a coprocessor that performs software measurements during system boot and securely stores RA cryptographic keys. However, such a specialized hardware component for RA is expensive and not practical for IoT devices. Hybrid RA [10,16] relies only on minimal additional hardware components, such as Read-Only Memory (ROM) and memory protection unit (MPU). The hardware components of hybrid approaches are cheaper, making them more suitable for an IoT setting. Thus, the current state-of-the-art RA protocols are based on hybrid architecture.

Self-triggering RA. Instead of following a classical on-demand challenge-response protocol, self-attestation schemes self-trigger the attestation based on a timer resided in a trusted component. **SEED** [22] is a non-interactive RA protocol where the RA time is determined from a pseudo-random number generator (PRNG), for which both the *Prv* and the *Vrf* have the seed. Once the timer is triggered, the *Prv* performs RA. Then, the *Prv* uses the shared symmetric key to sign the RA result along with the RA time so that the *Vrf* can check the *Prv*'s trustworthiness and RA freshness. **ERASMUS** [11] is a RA protocol that aims to solve the problem of on-demand RA requiring a device to stop normal operations to perform RA. In ERASMUS, the *Prv* uses a reliable read-only clock to perform RA at pre-defined times. The *Prv* then stores the RA results locally in its memory, and the *Vrf* can collect a set of consecutive RA results. In this way, the *Vrf* can identify a mobile adversary that tries to hide itself during RA.

Swarm RA. Swarm RA schemes (e.g., [3–5,8]) focus on attesting a group of devices efficiently. **SEDA** [8] constructs the network as a spanning tree to allow efficient propagation of RA request and aggregation of the RA responses. The aggregated RA result is then sent to a centralized trusted *Vrf*. **SANA** [5] extends SEDA by employing a multi-signature scheme that aggregates the RA results among a large group of devices. The usage of multi-signature makes the RA publicly verifiable in SANA because anyone who knows that public key can verify the aggregated RA result. In general, swarm RA schemes are on-demand protocols initiated by a trusted *Vrf*.

Table 1. Remote attestation schemes using blockchain

RA scheme	Public/Private	Consensus	Blockchain	RA	Decentralized
BARRET	Public	PoW	Ethereum	Any	No
TM-COIN	Public	PoW	Own	Hardware	No
DAN	Private	PBFT	HyperLedger Fabric	Hardware	No
PERMANENT	**Private**	**PoET**	**HyperLedger Sawtooth**	**Hybrid**	**Yes**

Distributed RA. Distributed services RA schemes (e.g., [12,13,15]) aim to attest a group of interacting devices that compose a *distributed IoT service*. **RADIS** [13] performs control-flow RA of synchronous distributed services by representing the entire control-flow execution of a distributed service as a single hash value. **SARA** [15] attests asynchronous distributed IoT services in a publish/subscribe IoT network. Both RADIS and SARA attest distributed services while relying on the presence of a centralized trusted *Vrf*. Instead, the distributed RA schemes (e.g., [2,21,24]) overcome the need for a centralized trusted *Vrf*, e.g., a base station, to handle RA. In particular, devices in the network play the role of the *Prv* and the *Vrf*. As such, devices in the network attest each other. **DIAT** [2] performs control-flow RA for each pair of devices. In **US-AID** [21], devices perform mutual attestations and store the result of their neighbour to assess the health status of the entire network. In **ESDRA** [24], each *Prv* gets attested by three different neighbours that assign a score to the *Prv*. In the end, the *Prv*'s score is reported to cluster-heads and then to the *Vrf*. In distributed RA schemes, the verification process is distributed across many Verifiers, but the RA results are not publicly verifiable.

2.1 Remote Attestation Using Blockchain

BARRET [9] aims to mitigate computational Denial of Service attacks by utilizing an Ethereum blockchain. It works by forcing the *Vrf* to pay a computational fee to send a RA request, which is the fee for mining a blockchain block. Since Verifiers have to pay this fee, they cannot send thousands of (valid) RA requests to a *Prv*. In BARRET, a *Vrf* sends a RA request to the blockchain, and the blockchain smart contract forwards this RA request to the *Prv*. Once the *Prv* receives the request, it performs RA, submits the result to the blockchain, and sends it to the *Vrf*. Then, the *Vrf* checks and submits the verification result to the blockchain. **TM-COIN** [26] is a hardware-based RA scheme utilizing blockchain to store the RA results. Here, a *Vrf* challenges a *Prv*, and the *Prv* stores the evidence in the blockchain. At any time, the *Vrf* can check the blockchain to see if a *Prv* is trustworthy. TM-COIN uses its own blockchain architecture, a public blockchain with Proof-of-Work (PoW) consensus algorithm. However, it is not a completely decentralized system since the miners are still responsible for performing the PoW and verifying the RA response.

Table 2. Overview of consensus algorithms efficiency

Algorithm	Family	Throughput	Scalability	Overhead
Proof-of-Work (PoW)	Proof-of-X	Low	Low	Computational
Proof-of-Authority (PoA)	Proof-of-X	Low	High	None
Proof-of-Stake (PoS)	Proof-of-X	Low	Low	None
Proof-of-Elapsed-Time (PoET)	**Proof-of-X**	**Low**	**High**	**None**
Proof-of-Capacity (PoC)	Proof-of-X	Low	Low	None
Proof-of-Burn (PoB)	Proof-of-X	Low	Low	None
Proof-of-Importance (PoI)	Proof-of-X	Low	Low	None
Byzantine Fault Tolerance (BFT)	Voting	High	Low	Communications
Crash Fault Tolerance (CFT)	Voting	High	High	Communications

DAN [23] is a hardware-based RA scheme that uses a Trusted Platform Module (TPM) as a root-of-trust. It clusters devices into organizations where each organization has a number of peer nodes responsible for interactions with the blockchain. Here, a *Vrf* sends a challenge to the device and waits for the RA result. The peer node is responsible for adding the result to the blockchain. In DAN, the proof-of-concept implementation relies on HyperLedger Fabric and the peer nodes are containers running on consumer desktops.

Discussion. Table 1 shows an overview of the three RA schemes utilizing blockchain technology. It shows that two of them, BARRET and TM-COIN, use public blockchains with PoW consensus algorithm. In contrast, DAN uses a private blockchain with a Practical Byzantine Fault Tolerance (PBFT) consensus. Furthermore, TM-COIN and DAN rely on specialized hardware components, while BARRET abstracts away from the RA and hardware requirements. All three schemes rely on trusted Verifiers to verify RA response and/or super nodes to handle blockchain interactions. Thus, they are not completely decentralized. Different from the existing blockchain-based RA schemes, PERMANENT aims to provide a decentralized RA using a Hyperledger Sawtooth as a permissioned blockchain with Proof-of-Elapsed-Time (PoET) as a consensus mechanism.

2.2 Blockchain Consensus Protocols

In designing a blockchain network, the choice of the consensus protocol is crucial mainly due to its significant impact on performance. Table 2 presents an overview of the consensus algorithms efficiency. While voting-based consensus protocols provide a better performance, they introduce a communications overhead, which is costly in an IoT environment. The PoX category has two protocols, PoET and PoA, which both have high scalability, but they have a low throughput (Transactions per second), which makes them poor choices if there are many transactions to be added to the blockchain. However, in the RA context, the throughput is a low priority metric because RA does not occur very often. To this end, PoET is a suitable consensus protocol with good performance, offering both low computational and low communications overhead. In PoET consensus, each network participant is given a random timer and the participant that has the shortest time (the timer that expires first) becomes the block leader and produces the new block. Thus, PoET brings an advantage in our proposed RA protocol: We leverage PoET's timer to combine it with the *Prv*'s timer (protected by the trusted component) used for self-attestation. In this way, when the timer triggers RA, it also allows the device to add a new block in the blockchain with the corresponding RA result. Additionally, in comparing different blockchains architectures, the study in [28] shows that HyperLedger Sawtooth clearly outperforms other HyperLedger blockchains in an IoT setting. Thus, in this paper, we choose HyperLedger Sawtooth with PoET consensus algorithm.

3   System Model

We consider a peer-to-peer (P2P) IoT network where untrusted IoT devices interact among themselves. In such a system, each device must be authenticated in order to join the permissioned blockchain network that uses Proof-of-Elapsed-Time (PoET) consensus mechanism. Devices that are part of the network have permission to add blocks in the blockchain. Unauthenticated entities have only read permissions to the blockchain data. Each participating IoT device acts both as a Prover (*Prv*) and Verifier (*Vrf*). Note that we assume that devices are trusted in the beginning when they authenticate to join the blockchain network (e.g., they can be enforced to perform attestation), but they can be compromised later, so in general we consider a network of untrusted devices.

We assume the presence of a Network Operator (*OP*) that guarantees the secure bootstrap of RA protocol and blockchain code deployed on each device. *OP* computes the checksum (i.e., collision-resistant hash) of the device's legitimate software and stores the corresponding valid measurement inside each device. In addition, the *OP* ensures secure key distribution among devices.

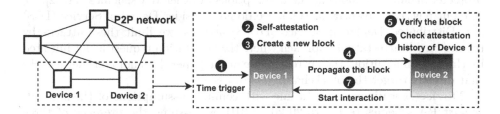

Fig. 1. Overview of interactions between two devices in the blockchain network

We consider the interactions among untrusted devices in a P2P blockchain network, and for simplicity, Fig. 1 depicts the interactions among two devices in the network. The RA procedure starts when the timer of Device 1 gets triggered (Step ❶). Then, Device 1 performs self-attestation by computing the software measurement and comparing the computed result against the pre-stored legitimate attestation value (1 if it matches and 0 otherwise) (Step ❷), and adds the boolean attestation result in a new blockchain block (Step ❸). When the new block is published to the blockchain, it is broadcasted and propagated throughout the network (Step ❹). When the peers (e.g., Device 2 in Fig. 1) receive the new block, they verify it by checking the device's signature and the signed timer (Step ❺). Later, when Device 2 wants to communicate to another device in the network (e.g., Device 1), it first checks the blockchain for the historical results of the device's attestation and then decides its trustworthiness (Step ❻). If the device is trustworthy above a pre-defined threshold, then these two devices proceed with their interaction (Step ❼).

4   Adversary Model and Security Requirements

4.1   Adversary Model

In line with the adversary model described in [1,3], and in particular, with other swarm and self-attestation schemes (e.g., [5,8,11,22]), we consider an adversary with the following capabilities.

- **Software adversary** (Adv_{sw}): A Adv_{sw} exploits a vulnerability on Prv's software and compromises the Prv by executing malicious code.
- **Communication adversary** (Adv_{comm}): The Adv_{comm} can forge, drop, delay, and eavesdrop the exchanged messages among devices.
- **Mobile adversary** (Adv_{mob}): A Adv_{mob} tries to avoid detection by deleting itself just before the execution of the attestation protocol starts.
- **Replay attack:** Any of the adversaries above can precompute a valid attestation response and responds with the old valid attestation response to hide malware presence.

Assumptions. We assume that a Adv_{sw} does not compromise the hardware-protected memory. Following the assumptions of other RA schemes [11,22], we rule out physical adversaries. While we do not consider Denial of Service (DoS) and Distributed Denial of Service (DDoS) attacks, we limit these attacks by relying on self-attestation approach where the attestation request is not initiated by the Vrf. In addition, the current scope of the paper does not consider attacks that directly target the blockchain.

Device Requirements. In line with common assumptions of the state-of-the-art RA schemes (e.g., [15,20,20,22,31]), we assume the presence of three trusted components inside a Prv.

- **Read-Only Memory (ROM).** The code of PERMANENT protocol and blockchain reside in a ROM memory region, preventing software adversaries Adv_{sw} from tampering with the code.

- **Secure key storage.** This memory region stores securely the attestation keys and the timer. It guarantees that device key is accessed only by the PERMANENT protocol resided in ROM. The timer is the component responsible for scheduling RA, thus, it must be tamper-proof and unpredictable by an adversary. To enforce unpredictability, a pseudo-random number generator (PRNG) is used for the time scheduler. Only PERMANENT protocol and blockchain code have read permissions in this memory region.
- **Real Time Clock (RTC).** RTC is a real-time write-protected clock that a software adversary cannot modify. RTC ensures that an attestation response is generated at the current time and the adversary is not reusing old software measurements.

4.2   Security Requirements

Considering the adversarial model described in Sect. 4, we define the required security properties in a blockchain-based RA protocol as follows.

- **Integrity.** The protocol should provide reliable evidence guaranteeing that the attestation response of the Prv corresponds to software measurements of the Prv at the attestation time (0 when the Prv is malicious, 1 otherwise).
- **Integrity of communication data.** The protocol should ensure the Prv's exchanged data cannot be altered without it being detectable by other devices participating in the network.
- **Freshness.** The protocol should ensure that the attestation time is random and confidential. Any given attestation result should be reliably linked to a new attestation time.

5   PERMANENT: Protocol Proposal

This section describes in detail the four distinct phases that compose the proposed PERMANENT protocol: (1) Bootstrap, (2) Attestation, (3) Verification, and (4) History-based Trust Decision. Table 3 summarizes the terms used in PERMANENT protocol.

5.1   Bootstrap

The Bootstrap Phase of PERMANENT is an offline procedure executed only once at the beginning of the system deployment. During this phase, the operator OP is responsible for securely deploying the devices, distributing and managing the keys, and installing certificates on the devices. In particular, each device Prv is initialized with an asymmetric signing key pair (SK_{Prv}, PK_{Prv}) and an identity certificate $cert(PK_{Prv})$ signed by OP, guaranteeing that PK_{Prv} belongs to Prv. This certificate is stored in the genesis block, so it cannot be altered and is always available for devices to retrieve. Furthermore, each device is initialized with the Op's public key PK_{OP} to be able to verify $cert(PK_{Prv})$

Table 3. Notation summary of PERMANENT protocol

Term	Description
Vrf	Verifier
Prv	Prover
OP	System operator
SK_{Prv}	Secret key of prover
PK_{Prv}	Public key of prover
$Block$	The blockchain block containing the attestation data
$PRNG$	Pseudo-random number generator
$Timer$	Scheduled time
$Seed$	The seed of PRNG
$CreatedOn$	Timestamp of the blockchain block
Ψ	Calculated trust score
α_i	The result of the i'th attestation
n	The number of attestation results stored in the blockchain
$cert(PK_{Prv})$	Identity certificate of prover
$SeedGenerator()$	A random generator function

of other devices without storing the public key of every participating device. Furthermore, the OP stores a threshold value inside the device to indicate that the device can interact only with other network devices with a trust score above this pre-defined threshold value.

5.2 Attestation

In the following, we describe the attestation of a P2P network with interconnected IoT devices. In such a system, only authenticated device join the permissioned blockchain network and add blocks to the blockchain. However, the blockchain data are publicly readable even from unauthenticated entities. Alternatively, we can consider an IoT system with an edge layer consisting of higher-end edge devices with a larger computational power and storage capacity than the IoT devices. In that case, only a subset of devices deploys the blockchain. To preserve the generality of the approach, in this paper we consider a distributed P2P network where each authenticated device participates in the blockchain.

In PERMANENT, the attestation gets initialized by a timer inside the device. The timer has two functions, scheduling function and triggering function for the attestation. The scheduling function uses a pseudo-random number generator (PRNG) for scheduling the attestation at unpredictable time within a pre-defined time interval. The seed of the PRNG is generated by a random generator function $SeedGenerator()$. We combine the self-attestation procedure and the blockchain to use the same timer.

In PERMANENT, the device performs self-attestation, which means the attestation result is verified by the device itself (secured by a trusted component) and the output of attestation is 0 or 1 (failed or successful attestation). Once the device completes the attestation, it creates a new blockchain block containing the necessary information required to verify the result and device identity. Then, a Merkle Hash Tree is constructed in order to create the header for the block. After the block has been created, it is propagated throughout the network using a gossip protocol. When the block is published, the scheduled time and the seed for the timer is signed and sent along with the block. Based on the PRNG properties, other devices participating in the blockchain use the seed to reproduce the scheduled time and verify that the device was actually allowed to add a new block to the blockchain.

Block Design for Attestation. The attestation block contains all the data produced during attestation transactions along with the hash of the previous block added during block creation as shown in Fig. 2. In particular, the attestation block contains an identifier (i.e., id or public key) for the device that submitted the attestation result, the attestation result, the scheduled time, and the created time. The scheduled time is used during the verification phase to verify the validity of the attestation and detect replay attacks. The created time is used later for the history-based trust decision.

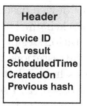

Fig. 2. Data structure for attestation block

5.3   Verification

The verification of published blocks is a three-step procedure: certificate verification, signature verification, and scheduled time verification. In the PoET consensus protocol, a new block is added only when there is the respective devices turn. Thus, the wait time (i.e., the scheduled time) should be verified before adding the block to the blockchain in order to prevent participants from adding a block at arbitrary times. In order to verify the scheduled time, the time and the seed is signed with the private key of the publishing device, using their private key. Since the other devices receive the seed when the block is published, they are able to reproduce and verify the scheduled time. Figure 3 shows the flow of the block verification. The verification procedure starts with a device receiving the scheduled time $Timer$, the seed $Seed$, both signed with Prv's secret key SK_{Prv}, along with the block $Block$. Upon receiving these data, the device first

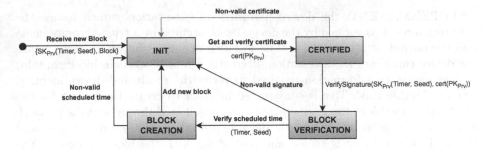

Fig. 3. State machine - block verification

verifies the certificate. If the certificate is valid, then it verifies the signature of the scheduled time and seed. Once the signature is verified, the device proceeds with the verification of the scheduled time against the creation time $CreatedOn$ of the block to ensure the device was allowed to publish a block at this time. If any of the checks fail, then the block is rejected and the device returns the $Init$ state, waiting for the next block to be published.

5.4 History-Based Trust Decision

The objective of history-based trust decision is to allow devices to decide whether or not to collaborate with another device based on the historical records of the devices attestation stored in the blockchain. The historical records allow the trust decision beyond the recent attestation result. Furthermore, the timestamped blocks in the blockchain allow the attestations to be weighed based on their age, for instance, that older attestations have a lower impact on the trust score.

In PERMANENT, the history-based trust score is a weighted average, where the weight is calculated based on the age of the attestation. In particular, PERMANENT calculates the trust score by taking how long after the genesis block the attestation result was made and divide it by how much time has actually passed since the genesis block was created. Moreover, in PERMANENT, successful attestations have a value of one, while failed attestations have a value of minus one. This means that if a device failed an attestation a long time ago, and after that it has passed successful attestations after that, then the failed attestation should not have the same impact as if the device failed more recently. Note that we assume that after a device has failed the attestation the Network Operator will bootstrap/update the device. In general, the update process is considered out of scope of the RA objective. Thus, we do not provide further process details, but we assume that a recent failed result is a stronger indicator than an old one.

Equation 1 shows the calculation of the trust score.

$$\Phi = \frac{\sum_{i=1}^{n} \left(\frac{CreatedOn_i - CreatedOn_{genesis}}{now - CreatedOn_{genesis}} \right) \times \alpha_i}{n} \mid \alpha_i = \begin{cases} 1 \text{ iff Attestation passed} \\ -1 \text{ iff Attestation failed} \end{cases}$$

$$(1)$$

where Φ is the resulting trust score, $CreatedOn_i$ is the created on timestamp of the block for attestation i'th, $CreatedOn_{genesis}$ is the created on timestamp of the genesis block, now is the timestamp of the current time, α_i is the result of the i'th attestation and n is the number of attestation results stored in the blockchain. In this equation, α is one if the attestation passed and minus one if it failed.

Figure 4 shows the evolution of the range of trust scores based on the number of attestations evenly distributed over its lifetime. The maximum trust score is shown with green and is the score if all attestations are passed. While all failed attestations are shown in red. Any mix of passed and failed attestation will be within the range between the green and the red graphs.

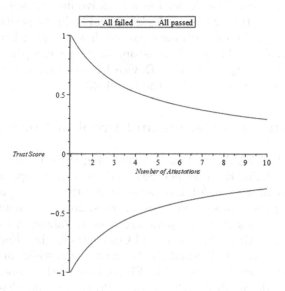

Fig. 4. Trust score range

Due to the weight, the range of the trust score decreases over time. From Fig. 4 it is clear that when time passes the devices cannot obtain the same score as when they are newly deployed. This causes some challenges when trying to compare two devices with different ages, even if both devices have passed all attestations.

To mitigate this and make the comparison more clear, the final trust score is divided by the maximum trust score the device in question can obtain, as in Eq. 2. In this context, the final trust score shows how close the device is to its maximum trustworthiness. Thus, when two devices passed all their attestations, they will have the same final trust score and will be considered equally trustworthy.

$$\Psi = \frac{\Phi}{\Phi_{max}} \qquad (2)$$

where Ψ is the final trust score, Φ is the trust score calculated in Eq. 1, and Φ_{max} is the maximum trust score the device can achieve.

The maximum trust score Φ_{max} is calculated as in Eq. 1, but with α always equal to one. This means the maximum trust score is determined by the number of attestations and how long ago they where made. The calculation of the maximum trust score is done as in Eq. 3.

$$\Phi_{max} = \frac{\sum_{i=1}^{n} \left(\frac{CreatedOn_i - CreatedOn_{genesis}}{now - CreatedOn_{genesis}} \right)}{n} \tag{3}$$

The final trust score can be in the range $[-1, 1]$. It will be negative if the total weighed failed attestations have a higher value then the total weighed passed attestations. This means if a device has a negative final trust score, it is highly untrustworthy. To be trustworthy, a device should be in the positive range, where a threshold for needed trustworthiness can be chosen, e.g., a final trust score of $\Psi \geq 0.5$. Furthermore, the final trust score allows for comparing devices, such that $\Psi_1 = 0.3 > 0.1 = \Psi_2$ means that Device 1 is more trustworthy than Device 2, even though they are both below the threshold.

6   Implementation Details and Proof of Concept

We implemented PERMANENT in Python, using Hyperledger Sawtooth as the underlying blockchain. Hyperledger Sawtooth is a well supported blockchain platform, which can use the PoET consensus algorithm. Docker has been used to deploy each component in separate containers, simulating a network of devices.

The system consists of six components, namely, Validator, Rest-API, Transaction Processor, Settings Processor, and Consensus Engine. Each of these components are deployed in individual Docker containers, while an IoT device can include each component as depicted in Fig. 5. Four of the aforementioned components (i.e., Validator, Rest API, Settings Processor, and Consensus Engine) come with the HyperLedger Sawtooth platform and require no changes, while two components (i.e., Client and Transaction Processor) are custom and contain the logic of the application.

6.1   Client

The Client contains the code for interacting with the blockchain. In particular, it is the entity that creates the attestation result and submits it to the blockchain. When the Client starts, it first sets up event subscriptions to listen and receive events from the Validator. After the subscriptions, the Client runs an initial attestation. Then, the Client continuously check if there is a scheduled attestation.

Attestation. The attestation of the Client has three steps: scheduling/triggering, computing attestation result, and publishing the result in the

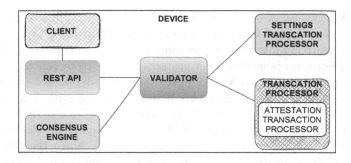

Fig. 5. Hyperledger Sawtooth components for a single device

blockchain. In this implementation, the scheduling is done by using a crypto-graphically secure pseudo-random generator. Specifically, once an attestation is performed, the schedule is updated by adding a random time to the previously scheduled time. The seed is generated as a random number using the /dev/urandom Linux random number generator. Then, the seed is sent along with the attestation result to allow other devices that know the last scheduled time and the seed to compute and verify the current scheduled time. To compute the attestation, we perform the static software measurement of the device. After the result has been computed, the Client wraps the result, device id, created on date, seed and scheduled time in a transaction with a message identifier, showing it is a *publish attestation* transaction. The Client then wraps the transaction in a batch and sends it to the Rest API.

6.2   Transaction Processor

The transaction processor has two parts: one part handles the business logic for the Attestation transaction family and the other one handles the Diffie-Hellman transaction family. Each of these two parts consists of three components: the *Handler*, *Payload* and *State*. The *Handler* contains the business logic for the transaction family and is the smart contract for the family. The *Payload* defines what the transactions for the family must look like. The *State* contains the getting and setting of the blockchain state data, as well as serializing and deserializing the data.

Attestation. The only business rule for attestations to be accepted to the blockchain is that they have to follow the specified format. This means attestations should specify the attestation message, construct a defined attestation payload and the transaction, and the batch has to be signed by a key accepted in the blockchain network.

7   Limitations

While PERMANENT protocol allows devices to store historical results in the blockchain, the proposed solution also has some limitations.

PERMANENT relies on the PoET consensus algorithm due to the low computational and communications overhead that this algorithm provides. However, PoET has a relatively low throughput compared to other consensus algorithms. This could present an issue if the RA protocol is required to run very frequently in a large-scale network. However, RA protocols typically do not run very often to require high throughput. Thus, this limitation is not critical in the setting where attestations are not performed very often.

Another well-known open research challenge in applying blockchain technology in IoT is the increased memory requirements. Since the blockchain is a distributed ledger, every device needs to store the entire blockchain database with the results of all the devices. If devices have a long lifetime and/or run many attestations, this database could expand rapidly, possibly beyond the available memory of the devices.

Furthermore, the blockchain solution introduces extra cryptographic operations. Cryptographic operations are known to be resource expensive for IoT devices. So the extra security of the blockchain comes at the computational cost of the extra cryptographic operations. However, it may require fewer attestations that also use cryptographic operations, so the total amount of operations might be the same or less over a longer period.

8   Conclusions and Future Work

This paper proposes PERMANENT, a decentralized and publicly verifiable remote attestation protocol that relies on blockchain technology. Instead of deciding the trustworthy state of a device based on the latest attestation result, the proposed protocol uses the history of attestations to validate the trustworthiness of each IoT device and calculate the corresponding trust score. We presented the proof-of-concept implementation of the proposed protocol with HyperLedger Sawtooth using Proof-of-Elapsed-Time (PoET) as a consensus mechanism, demonstrating the feasibility of the solution.

While in this paper, we assumed that devices that are trustworthy above a threshold can proceed their interactions, in our future work we will extend the protocol by providing technical details of group session key establishment among trusted devices. Moreover, as future work, we plan to perform some performance optimizations in the proof-of-concept implementation and conduct an empirical analysis of the protocol's performance. Another main area of our future work will be investigating and designing even more efficient blockchain architectures for IoT devices. Furthermore, we will explore and investigate the possibility of attesting devices with lightweight cryptographic operations while providing strong security guarantees.

Acknowledgment. This work is supported by Danish Industry Foundation through project "CIDI - Cybersecure IoT in Danish Industry" (project number 2018-0197) and the European Union's Horizon 2020 Research and Innovation program under Grant Agreement No. 952697 (ASSURED).

References

1. Abera, T., et al.: Invited - things, trouble, trust: on building trust in IoT systems. In: Proceedings of the 53rd Annual Design Automation Conference, pp. 1–6 (2016)
2. Abera, T., Bahmani, R., Brasser, F., Ibrahim, A., Sadeghi, A., Schunter, M.: DIAT: data integrity attestation for resilient collaboration of autonomous system. In: Proceedings of the Network and Distributed System Security Symposium (2019)
3. Ambrosin, M., Conti, M., Lazzeretti, R., Rabbani, M., Ranise, S.: Collective remote attestation at the internet of things scale: state-of-the-art and future challenges. IEEE Commun. Surv. Tutor. **22**(4), 2447–2461 (2020)
4. Ambrosin, M., Conti, M., Lazzeretti, R., Rabbani, M.M., Ranise, S.: PADS: practical attestation for highly dynamic swarm topologies. In: Proceedings - 2016 International Workshop on Secure Internet of Things (SIoT). pp. 18–27 (2018)
5. Ambrosin, M., Conti, M., Ibrahim, A., Neven, G., Sadeghi, A.R., Schunter, M.: SANA: secure and scalable aggregate network attestation. In: Proceedings of the 2019 ACM SIGSAC Conference on Computer and Communications Security, pp. 731–742 (2016)
6. Ankergård, S.F.J.J., Dushku, E., Dragoni, N.: State-of-the-art software-based remote attestation: opportunities and open issues for Internet of Things. Sensors **21**(5) (2021)
7. Arthur, W., Challener, D.: A Practical Guide to TPM 2.0: Using the Trusted Platform Module in the New Age of Security. Apress, Berkeley (2015). https://doi.org/10.1007/978-1-4302-6584-9
8. Asokan, N., et al.: SEDA: scalable embedded device attestation. In: Proceedings of the 22nd ACM SIGSAC Conference on Computer and Communications Security, pp. 964–975 (2015)
9. Bampatsikos, M., Ntantogian, C., Xenakis, C., Tomopoulos, S.C.: BARRETT blockchain regulated remote attestation. In: Proceedings - 2019 IEEE/WIC/ACM International Conference on Web Intelligence, pp. 256–262 (2019)
10. Brasser, F., El Mahjoub, B., Sadeghi, A.R., Wachsmann, C., Koeberl, P.: TyTAN: tiny trust anchor for tiny devices. In: Proceedings of the 52nd Annual Design Automation Conference, pp. 1–6 (2015)
11. Carpent, X., Rattanavipanon, N., Tsudik, G.: Remote attestation via self-measurement. ACM Trans. Des. Autom. Electron. Syst. **24**(1) (2018)
12. Conti, M., Dushku, E., Mancini, L.V.: Distributed services attestation in IoT. In: Samarati, P., Ray, I., Ray, I. (eds.) From Database to Cyber Security. LNCS, vol. 11170, pp. 261–273. Springer, Cham (2018). https://doi.org/10.1007/978-3-030-04834-1_14
13. Conti, M., Dushku, E., Mancini, L.V.: RADIS: remote attestation of distributed IoT services. In: Proceedings 6th International Conference on Software Defined System (SDS), pp. 25–32 (2019)
14. Dai, H.N., Zheng, Z., Zhang, Y.: Blockchain for Internet of Things: a survey. IEEE Internet of Things J. **6**(5), 8076–8094 (2019)
15. Dushku, E., Rabbani, M.M., Conti, M., Mancini, L.V., Ranise, S.: SARA: secure asynchronous remote attestation for IoT systems. IEEE Trans. Inf. Forensics Secur. **15**, 3123–3136 (2020)
16. Eldefrawy, K., Tsudik, G., Francillon, A., Perito, D.: SMART: secure and minimal architecture for (establishing dynamic) root of trust. In: Proceedings of the 19th Annual Network & Distributed System Security Symposium. Network Security (NDSS), pp. 1–15 (2012)

17. Favaretto, M., Tran Anh, T., Kavaja, J., De Donno, M., Dragoni, N.: When the price is your privacy: a security analysis of two cheap IoT devices. Adv. Intell. Syst. Comput. **925**, 55–75 (2020)
18. Garcia Lopez, P., Montresor, A., Datta, A.: Please, do not decentralize the internet with (permissionless) blockchains! In: 2019 IEEE ICDCS, pp. 1901–1911 (2019)
19. Giaretta, A., De Donno, M., Dragoni, N.: Adding salt to pepper: a structured security assessment over a humanoid robot. In: Proceedings of ARES 2018 (2018)
20. Halldórsson, R.M., Dushku, E., Dragoni, N.: ARCADIS: asynchronous remote control-flow attestation of distributed IoT services. IEEE Access **9**, 144880–144894 (2021)
21. Ibrahim, A., Sadeghi, A.R., Tsudik, G.: US-AID: unattended scalable attestation of IoT devices. In: Proceedings of the IEEE 37th Symposium on Reliable Distributed Systems, pp. 21–30 (2018)
22. Ibrahim, A., Sadeghi, A.R., Zeitouni, S.: SeED: secure non-interactive attestation for embedded devices. In: Proceedings of the 10th ACM Conference on Security and Privacy in Wireless and Mobile Networks WiSec 2017, pp. 64–74 (2017)
23. Jenkins, I.R., Smith, S.W.: Distributed IoT attestation via blockchain. In: Proceedings - 20th IEEE/ACM International Symposium on Cluster, Cloud and Internet Computing, CCGRID 2020, pp. 798–801 (2020)
24. Kuang, B., Fu, A., Yu, S., Yang, G., Su, M., Zhang, Y.: ESDRA: an efficient and secure distributed remote attestation scheme for IoT swarms. IEEE Internet of Things J. **6**(5), 8372–8383 (2019)
25. Neshenko, N., Bou-Harb, E., Crichigno, J., Kaddoum, G., Ghani, N.: Demystifying IoT security: an exhaustive survey on IoT vulnerabilities and a first empirical look on internet-scale IoT exploitations. IEEE Commun. Surv. Tutor. **21**(3), 2702–2733 (2019)
26. Park, J., Kim, K.: TM-Coin : Trustworthy management of TCB measurements in IoT. In: 2017 IEEE PerCom Workshops, pp. 654–659. IEEE (2017)
27. Rabbani, M.M., Dushku, E., Vliegen, J., Braeken, A., Dragoni, N., Mentens, N.: RESERVE: Remote Attestation of Intermittent IoT Devices. In: Proceedings of the 19th ACM Conference on Embedded Networked Sensor Systems (SenSys), pp. 578–580 (2021)
28. Rasolroveicy, M., Fokaefs, M.: Performance evaluation of distributed ledger technologies for IoT data registry: A comparative study. In: 2020 Fourth World Conference on Smart Trends in Systems, Security and Sustainability 2020, pp. 137–144 (2020)
29. Seshadri, A., Perrig, A., Doorn, L.v., Khosla, P.: SWATT: softWare-based attestation for embedded devices. In: IEEE S & P 2004, pp. 272–282 (2004)
30. Sokolov, S., Gaskarov, V., Knysh, T., Sagitova, A.: IoT security: threats, risks, attacks. In: Mottaeva, A. (ed.) Proceedings of the XIII International Scientific Conference on Architecture and Construction 2020. LNCE, vol. 130. Springer, Singapore (2021). https://doi.org/10.1007/978-981-33-6208-6_6
31. Østergaard, J.H., Dushku, E., Dragoni, N.: ERAMO: effective remote attestation through memory offloading. In: IEEE International Conference on Cyber Security and Resilience (IEEE-CSR), pp. 73–80 (2021)

Cut It: Deauthentication Attacks on Protected Management Frames in WPA2 and WPA3

Karim Lounis[1]([✉]), Steven H. H. Ding[2], and Mohammad Zulkernine[1]

[1] Queen's Reliable Software Technology Lab, Queen's University,
Kingston, ON, Canada
{karim.lounis,mz}@queensu.ca
[2] L1NNA Research Laboratory, School of Computing, Queen's University,
Kingston, ON, Canada
steven.ding@queensu.ca

Abstract. Deauthentication attacks on Wi-Fi protocol (IEEE 802.11) were pointed out in early 2003. In these attacks, an attacker usually impersonates a Wi-Fi access point (a.k.a., authenticator) and sends spoofed deauthentication frames to the connected Wi-Fi supplicants. The connected supplicants receive the frames and process them as if they were sent by the legitimate access point. These frames instruct - connected Wi-Fi supplicants to invalidate their current association and authentication to the access point and get disconnected from the Wi-Fi network. This is possible due to the absence of authentication in management frames (which includes deauthentication frames) in the currently used Wi-Fi security mechanisms (i.e., WPA and WPA2). To thwart these attacks, as well as, many other Denial-of-Service attacks, in 2009, an amendment, standardized IEEE 802.11w, was published as a set of new security mechanisms and procedures to enforce authentication, data freshness, and confidentiality on certain management frames. This amendment uses PMF (Protected Management Frames) to provide authentication of management frames and prevent the occurrence of many management frame spoofing-related attacks, including deauthentication attacks. Although only a few Wi-Fi-certified devices have incorporated IEEE 802.11w as an optional mechanism, the new Wi-Fi security mechanism, WPA3, has made IEEE 802.11w mandatory to provide a better security against those Denial-of-Service attacks. In this paper, we demonstrate through various attack scenarios the feasibility of deauthentication attacks on PMF-enabled WPA2-PSK and WPA3-PSK networks. We provide interpretations to explain the reason behind the feasibility of the attacks and describe possible countermeasures to prevent the attacks.

Keywords: Wi-Fi security · WPA3 security · Wi-Fi attacks · PMF · Wi-Fi Denial-of-Service attacks · Deauthentication attack

© Springer Nature Switzerland AG 2022
E. Aïmeur et al. (Eds.): FPS 2021, LNCS 13291, pp. 235–252, 2022.
https://doi.org/10.1007/978-3-031-08147-7_16

1   Introduction

Wi-Fi networks have been susceptible to Denial-of-Service (DoS) attacks at both the physical layer (e.g., jamming attacks) and the MAC-layer (e.g., deauthentication and disassociation attacks [12]). Also, tools to launch these attacks are freely available on the Internet. Technically, there are two main reasons why Wi-Fi networks have been vulnerable to DoS attacks: (1) The wireless medium is not confined by physical boundaries like it is in wired Ethernet networks. Therefore, attacks can be generated from an outside range of an access point (e.g., from a nearby building or from inside a parked vehicle). (2) Wi-Fi management and control frames are neither encrypted nor authenticated as per the IEEE 802.11 specifications. In fact, the original reasoning was that there are management frames that are expected before a Wi-Fi supplicant is associated with an access point, and hence protecting frames with encryption and authentication and sending them to Wi-Fi supplicants that knew nothing about the access point credentials did not sound logical for IEEE 802.11 designers. As a consequence, the lack of authentication in these frames allowed attackers to spoof the frames and generate various types of Wi-Fi Denial-of-Service (DoS) attacks [12].

To mitigate these Denial-of-Service attacks, in particular, deauthentication attacks, in 2009, an amendment, standardized IEEE 802.11w [1], was published to provide a set of new security mechanisms to augment certain management frames with authentication, data freshness, and confidentiality. This amendment uses PMF (Protected Management Frames) to provide authentication of certain management frames, called RMF (Robust Management Frames), and prevent the Denial-of-Service attacks that rely on spoofing management frames. Even though the standard has been around since 2009, it is really unfortunate to find that many Wi-Fi devices in 2021 still not have incorporated the IEEE 802.11w amendment. Only a few number of Wi-Fi certified devices have implemented IEEE 802.11w as an optional mechanism to be used in WPA2 networks. Fortunately, the IEEE 802.11w standard has been made mandatory in WPA3 certified devices to provide a higher security against many Denial-of-Service attacks.

In this paper, we demonstrate different attack scenarios to cause deauthentication of PMF-enforced WPA2 and WPA3 supplicants. We analyze the causes of the attacks and provide possible countermeasures to prevent the attacks.

The remainder of this paper is organized as follows. In Sect. 2, we discuss the related work. In Sect. 3, the IEEE 802.11w amendment is briefly presented. We demonstrate various deauthentication attack scenarios in Sect. 4. We conclude the paper in Sect. 5.

2   Related Work

There has been some research work that demonstrated that IEEE 802.11w was not completely effective. Ahmad et al. [2] demonstrated three Denial-of-Service attacks on IEEE 802.11w, namely, BIP (Broadcast Integrity Protocol) vulnerability, Security Association (SA)-query manipulation, and association starvation. The first one is an insider attack where a malicious supplicant uses the shared broadcast key (which is supposed to be used only by the access point) to generate protected broadcast deauthentication and disassociation frames. The second attack consists of maliciously initiating an SA-query procedure and jamming the legitimate supplicant to prevent it from responding to the SA-query requests causing a deadlock. The third attack consists of preventing a supplicant from associating to an access point by sending a fake association frame with Reason Code 30 and a large association come-back time, e.g., 300 s. Eian et al. [3] outlined the feasibility of an authentication attack, where a spoofed open system authentication request would cause the access point to disassociate the supplicant and drop its received data. This would force the supplicant to re-associate and restart the 4-way-handshake. Nevertheless, most Wi-Fi device manufacturers have fixed this issue. A new authentication request would not change the status of an associated supplicant. Wang et al. [4] briefly discussed some known Denial-of-Service attacks that are still possible on IEEE 802.11w during the 4-way-handshake. For example, by injecting a fake EAPoL message (a.k.a., EAPoL M_1[1]) during the 4-way-handshake and before the supplicant replies to the first legitimate EAPoL message that it receives from the access point, an attacker could force the supplicant to derive the pairwise transient key (PTK) each time it receives a newly forged EAPoL message. Additionally, injecting spoofed deauthentication frames during the 4-way-handshake, e.g., after exchanging the EAPoL M_1, would abort the authentication process. Valli et al. [5] performed a formal security analysis of the IEEE 802.11w during the 4-way-handshake phase using CasperFDR. They pointed out the feasibility of man-in-the-middle attacks to compromise certain security properties of the 4-way-handshake and disclose keys used for group communication and protected broadcast messages. Schepers et al. [6] developed a framework to test and fuzz Wi-Fi devices for vulnerabilities. They used the developed tool to demonstrate that certain 802.11w capable access points are vulnerable to deauthentication by exploiting the vulnerability CVE-2019-16275. This vulnerability makes certain access points reply with a protected broadcast deauthentication frame when a spoofed association request frame is injected with a destination address set to broadcast. They used the tool to detect whether certain devices were vulnerable to KRACKs [14]. Ram et al. [7] discussed through a patent how an attacker can disconnect a PMF-enforced supplicant from an access point by forcing the supplicant to switch the radio channel through a spoofed probe response (with a channel switching element) during the execution of an SA-query procedure. This is to prevent the supplicant from responding to the SA-query requests that are being sent on the original channel. The SA-query procedure would time out, causing the disconnection of the supplicant. Lounis et al. [8–11] demonstrated various Denial-of-Service attacks on WPA2-PSK and WPA3-PSK when PMF is enforced. These attacks target the authentication phase by injecting spoofed authentication messages in a race condition to prevent and deprive the supplicant of successfully getting authenticated and associated with the access point.

---

[1] There are 4 EAPoL messages that are exchanged between the supplicant and the authenticator during the 4-way-handshake. Based on their order, these messages are often referred to as EAPoL M_1, M_2, M_3, and M_4.

As IEEE 802.11w is a set of MAC-layer procedures, physical-layer threats, e.g., jamming, are not concerned and hence are still feasible. Last but not least, it is important to note that most of the attacks presented in [2–7,9–11] are attacks that need to be launched before or during the execution of the 4-way-handshake, where the session keys are derived at the end. This means that most of them would not work if the supplicant is already associated with an access point and is exchanging encrypted data. In this paper, the attacks that we present target PMF-protected supplicants that are associated and are exchanging encrypted data to cause their disconnection.

3   IEEE 802.11w Amendment

Before IEEE 802.11w[2] (a.k.a., Protected Management Frames, or PMF[3]), only data frames could be protected in Wi-Fi. Management and control frames were used without any protection. The IEEE 802.11w amendment came to provide certain protection to some specific management frames, known as Robust Management Frames (RMF). These frames include, deauthenticaiton frames, disassociation frames, and certain action frames, e.g., QoS action frames and Block ACK frames. Also, the mechanism provides protection, through Security Association teardown protection (a.k.a., Security Association Query Procedure, cf., next subsection), to association and authentication frames exchanged during an existing connection to prevent disconnection of connected Wi-Fi supplicants.

The IEEE 802.11w provides data integrity and freshness for broadcast and multicast robust management frames through the use of the Broadcast Integrity Protocol (BIP). This protocol uses the Message Integrity Code (MIC) to protect the integrity of the frames and provide freshness to prevent the replay of old frames. Tampered or replayed frames are passively discarded when they are detected. This for example mitigates broadcast deauthentication attack, where all connected supplicants get instantly disconnected after processing (without any verification) a spoofed deauthentication frame. On the other hand, unicast robust management frames benefit from data confidentiality in addition to data integrity and data freshness protection.

Because IEEE 802.11w provides protection to only some management frames, DoS attacks based on other management frames (i.e., Class 1 frames) are unfortunately still possible (e.g., race condition-based attacks [8–11]). Additionally, attacks based on control frames (e.g., RTS/CTS[4]-based attacks [12]) are still

---

[2] IEEE 802.11w only applies to Wi-Fi networks running Robust Security Networks (RSN), i.e., using WPA-TKIP or WPA-CCMP (WPA2 and WPA3).

[3] Note that PMF should not be confused with Cisco MFP (Management Frame Protection), which was developed in 2005. In MFP, there are two modes: (1) Infrastructure mode, where the access point sings beacon frames and other broadcast management frames (to detect Rogues). (2) Client mode, where the AP signs management frames that are sent to the client in addition to beacon and broadcast management frames.

[4] The request to send (RTS) and clear to send (CTS) is a mechanism used to reserve the radio channel to send time-sensitive packets and prevent collisions.

possible since IEEE 802.11w deals only with management frames. Furthermore, if an attacker manages to crack the network password (and hence the keys), it will be able to forge authenticated management frames and may succeed in generating DoS attacks. This also means that an insider malicious supplicant may abuse the mechanism and run successful DoS attacks since it knows the network password (although may need to capture some 4-way-handshakes).

3.1 Security Association Query Procedure

IEEE 802.11w amendment introduced an association spoofing protection mechanism to prevent replay attacks from tearing down an existing Wi-Fi supplicant's association to an access point. It consists of two mechanisms: (1) Association come-back time, and (2) SA-query procedure.

When an authenticator (i.e., access point) receives an association request from a supplicant that is already associated with the authenticator (i.e., in IEEE 802.11 State 3[5]), the latter responds with a rejective association response stating the reason "Association rejected temporarily; try again later (Code 30)". This association response incorporates an association come-back time, a.k.a., timeout interval value (TIV), that informs the supplicant to comeback and re-associate after the expiration of that association come-back time and in the case where the SA-query procedure is unsuccessful. In fact, just after the rejection, the authenticator initiates the SA-query procedure by sending SA-query requests (which are 12-byte protected action frames) until it receives a valid SA-query response (also a 12-byte protected action frame) from the supplicant or the association come-back time expires. If no valid SA-query response is received and the association come-back time expires, the access points consider that the supplicant is no longer associated and requires a re-association. Otherwise, if a valid SA-query response was received, the authenticator drops the received association request and considers it as a spoofed request that was generated by an attacker. This maintains the association of the supplicant. This SA-query procedure against a spoofed association request is illustrated by the MSC[6] of Fig. 1.

The SA-query procedure is basically used for the following: (i) Prevent an attacker from tearing down an existing supplicant's association using spoofed association frames. (ii) Allow a previously associated supplicant to securely re-associate to an authenticator after loosing the keys or encountering a local failure. (iii) Prevent an attacker from disassociating/deauthenticating associated supplicants from an access point using disassociation/deauthentication frames.

---

[5] There are three IEEE 802.11 states in which a supplicant can be: (1) State 1, where the supplicant is not authenticated and not associated with any access point. (2) State 2, where the supplicant is authenticated but not associated. (3) State 3, where the supplicant is both authenticated and associated.

[6] MSC (Message Sequence Chart) is a graphical language for the description of the interaction between different components of a system. This language is standardized by the ITU (International Telecommunication Union).

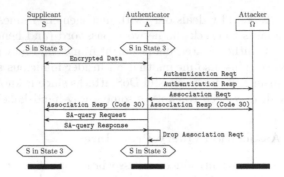

Fig. 1. Security association-query procedure initiated against a spoofed association request sent by an attacker Ω on an associated supplicant S, where State 3 indicates the IEEE 802.11 state of "Authenticated & Associated". State 1 and State 2 indicate the state of "Unauthenticated & Unassociated" and "Authenticated & Unassociated".

Overall, if an unprotected frame is received, the SA-query procedure is used to authenticate the communicating parties and take the correct decision. Receiving unprotected frames could happen due to the presence of an attacker spoofing management frames, or legitimate supplicants having lost their keys for some reasons.

4 Deauthentication Attacks on IEEE 802.11w

In this section, we present different deauthentication attacks on IEEE 802.11w, in general, and Protected Management Frames (PMF), in particular. These attacks are of type Denial-of-Service (DoS) as they all aim to disconnect a Wi-Fi supplicant from an access point when PMF is used in WPA2-PSK and WPA3-PSK. We first present the experimental environment that we have used to generate the attacks, and then individually present each attack, how it was generated (for reproducibility), and provide our interpretations w.r.t. the feasibility of the attack. We also discuss how each attack can be mitigated. In Subsect. 4.1, we present deauthentication attack scenarios that are based on the use of unicast deauthentication frames. In Subsect. 4.2, we present deauthentication attack scenarios that are based on fake authentication sessions and association frames.

Table 1 illustrates the Wi-Fi devices (with their characteristics) that we have used during the experiments. Additionally, Table 2 shows the estimated time in seconds to succeed in different deauthentication attack scenarios. The average time (avg) is computed over 20 consecutive and independent attack attempts for each attack scenario. In the next paragraph, we present the experimental environment that we have used to generate the attacks and analyze the causes of their feasibility.

Experimental Environment. To realize our attacks, we have used two types of Wi-Fi networks, one operating WPA2-PSK with PMF enabled on a Cisco

Table 1. Wi-Fi devices (with their characteristics) used during the experiments.

Wi-Fi device	Operating system or Firmware version	Device type	Wi-Fi security	PFM capable
Apple MacBook Pro M1	Apple macOS Big Sur (versions 11.4, 11.5.1, & 11.5.2)	Laptop (Supplicant)	WPA2-PSK & WPA3-PSK	Yes
Apple MacBook Pro i5	Apple macOS Big Sur (version 11.5.2)	Laptop (Supplicant)	WPA2-PSK & WPA3-PSK	Yes
Apple iPhone 11 Pro Max	Apple iOS (version 14.7.1-18G82)	Smartphone (Supplicant)	WPA2-PSK & WPA3-PSK	Yes
Huawei Nova 5T	Google Android (version 10.0)	Smartphone (Supplicant)	WPA2-PSK	Yes
Cisco WAP150	WAP150-A-K9-NA V02 (version 1.1.3.2)	Access point (Authenticator)	WPA2-PSK	Yes
TP-Link AX6000	TP-Link 1.2.3 Build 20210511 rel.76452(5553)	Access point (Authenticator)	WPA2-PSK & WPA3-PSK	Yes
HP ProBook 6560b	Linux Ubuntu (version 20.04 LTS)	Laptop (Attacker)	WPA2-PSK	No

WAP150 access point[7], and the second network running WPA3-PSK (PMF enforced by default) on a TP-LINK AX6000 wireless router. Moreover, we have used different types of supplicants as illustrated in the first group of rows of Table 1. These supplicants are PMF-capable. Further, for the attacker, we have used an HP PROBOOK 6560B laptop that runs LINUX UBUNTU 20.04LTS. We have used *airodump-ng, aireplay-ng, macchanger*, and some *Scapy-based python scripts* to launch the attacks and capture the wireless traffic. We have analyzed the traffic using the *Wireshark* packet analyzer.

4.1 Deauthentication Using Unicast Deauthentication Frames

Observation. In IEEE 802.11w, when an associated supplicant/access point receives an unprotected deauthentication frame, it starts the SA-query procedure to check whether the access point/supplicant has truly sent that deauthentication frame (e.g., in the case where the access point/supplicant has lost the session keys) or the frame was sent by an unauthorized party that is impersonating the access point or supplicant. If the access point or supplicant responds correctly to the SA-query request, the supplicant/access point concludes that the received frame was a spoofed one and discards it. Otherwise, if no response was received within an SA-timeout, the supplicant/access point resend the SA-query request again. If no response is received for a second time, the supplicant/access point assumes that the access point/supplicant has lost the session keys (for some reason) and considers the unprotected deauthentication frame as a legitimate frame. The supplicant/access point usually sends a protected disassociation frame to conclude the session. The number of SA-query requests that are sent during the

---

[7] The CISCO WAP150 is a Wi-Fi access point that uses MFP (Management Frame Protection), which is the Cisco implementation of PMF.

Table 2. Estimated time in seconds to succeed in different deauthentication attack scenarios. The average time (avg) is computed over 20 consecutive and independent attack attempts for each attack scenario.

Deauthentication attack scenario on IEEE 802.11w Supplicants		WPA2-PSK (Cisco WAP150)	WPA3-PSK (TP Link AX6000)
Send bidirectional spoofed unicast and unprotected deauthentication frames (Command 1 in Table 3)	Apple MacBook Pro M1	[03–32] (avg: 15.70)	[05–28] (avg: 14.45)
	Huawei Nova 5T	[03–27] (avg: 11.70)	Unsupported
	Apple iPhone 11 Pro Max	[03–56] (avg: 14.40)	[03–44] (avg: 24.15)
	Apple MacBook Pro i5	[05–41] (avg: 17.80)	[06–50] (avg: 23.10)
Send bidirectional spoofed unicast and unprotected disassociation frames (Code 1 in Table 3)	Apple MacBook Pro M1	[03–29] (avg: 08.30)	[03–60] (avg: 26.10)
	Huawei Nova 5T	[03–18] (avg: 08.85)	Unsupported
	Apple iPhone 11 Pro Max	[04–33] (avg: 14.50)	[04–60] (avg: 25.80)
	Apple MacBook Pro i5	[04–27] (avg: 10.80)	[06–46] (avg: 25.50)
Send spoofed unicast deauthentication/disassociation frames to the access point (Code 2 & 3 in Table 3)	Apple MacBook Pro M1	[10– 30] (avg: 16.05)	[05–9] (avg: 11.25)
	Huawei Nova 5T	[03–56] (avg: 14.70)	Unsupported
	Apple iPhone 11 Pro Max	[08–53] (avg: 22.70)	[03–58] (avg: 21.20)
	Apple MacBook Pro i5	[05–25] (avg: 14.80)	[08–43] (avg: 20.50)
Send spoofed unicast deauthentication/disassociation frames to the supplicant (Code 2 & 3 in Table 3)	Apple MacBook Pro M1	No disconnection	No disconnection
	Huawei Nova 5T	No disconnection	Unsupported
	Apple iPhone 11 Pro Max	No disconnection	No disconnection
	Apple MacBook Pro i5	No disconnection	No disconnection
Use complete fake open system authentication and association (Command 3 in Table 3)	Apple MacBook Pro M1	[04–10] (avg: 06.50)	[03–20] (avg: 10.70)
	Huawei Nova 5T	[07–123] (avg: 47.35)	Unsupported
	Apple iPhone 11 Pro Max	[04–10] (avg: 07.35)	[05–60] (avg: 19.10)
	Apple MacBook Pro i5	[04–18] (avg: 06.40)	[07–32] (avg: 16.70)
Use injected association request frames with capability 0 × 0431 (Code 2 in Table 3)	Apple MacBook Pro M1	[02–09] (avg: 03.90)	[03–04] (avg: 03.40)
	Huawei Nova 5T	[03–24] (avg: 14.50)	Unsupported
	Apple iPhone 11 Pro Max	[03–10] (avg: 05.20)	[03–06] (avg: 04.40)
	Apple MacBook Pro i5	[02–08] (avg: 03.60)	[03–05] (avg: 03.95)
Use injected association response frames with reason code 0 × 001e (Code 3 in Table 3)	Apple MacBook Pro M1	[02–06] (avg: 03.60)	[02–07] (avg: 04.05)
	Huawei Nova 5T	No disconnection	Unsupported
	Apple iPhone 11 Pro Max	[03–13] (avg: 05.02)	[03–06] (avg: 04.60)
	Apple MacBook Pro i5	[02–08] (avg: 04.15)	[04–10] (avg: 05.75)
Use injected association response frames with reason code 0 × 001f (Code 6 in Table 3)	Apple MacBook Pro M1	[02–09] (avg: 03.50)	[02–05] (avg: 04.05)
	Huawei Nova 5T	No disconnection	Unsupported
	Apple iPhone 11 Pro Max	[03–08] (avg: 04.95)	[04–08] (avg: 04.75)
	Apple MacBook Pro i5	[02–08] (avg: 03.75)	[04–08] (avg: 04.65)

SA-query procedure may depend on the implementation of IEEE 802.11w on Wi-Fi certified devices by different manufacturers.

As part of our experiments, we have discovered that it was possible to cause a deauthentication and force the PMF-enforced supplicants to get disconnected using spoofed deauthentication and disassociation frames. We have observed that by generating a large number of spoofed unprotected unicast deauthentication frames or disassociation frames, sent to both the access point and the supplicant (i.e., bidirectional injection), the access point usually ends up sending a protected disassociation frame to the supplicants. It then ignores the supplicant's protected action frames (which are encrypted SA-query requests/responses). The supplicants continue sending their frames (encrypted SA-query requests/responses) to the access point, and since the latter is not responsive, the SA-procedure times out and the supplicants disconnect from the access point by sending a protected disassociation frame. It is important to note that sending spoofed frames to both the access point and the supplicants would initiate the SA-query procedure on both sides. Interestingly, we have also discovered that using spoofed unicast and unprotected deauthentication/disassociation frames, sent only to the access

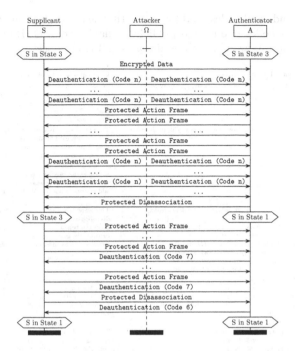

Fig. 2. Deauthentication attack using unprotected unicast deauthentication frames on PMF (WPA2 and WPA3), where State 1 and State 3 indicate the IEEE 802.11 state of "Unauthenticated & Unassociated" and "Authenticated & Associated", respectively. State 2 is "Authenticated & Unassociated".

point on behalf of the supplicants, would cause a disconnection of the supplicants. However, when we have sent these frames to the supplicants on behalf of the access point, the attack did not succeed and no disconnection was observed.

Attack Generation. To generate the attack, we have used the attacker laptop (HP PROBOOK 6560B) and configured it to impersonate both the access point and the supplicants by setting its MAC address to the ones of the spoofed parties. Then, by connecting the supplicants to the access points, we have generated a large number of spoofed unprotected unicast deauthentication frames[8] (using Command 1 in Table 3) and captured the subsequent wireless traffic (using Command 2 in Table 3). After few seconds, we have managed to disconnect the supplicants from the access points. Next, with the help of *Wireshark*, we have analyzed the exchanged wireless packets and tried to understand the reason that caused the disconnection. Additionally, we have used different *scapy scripts* (viz., Code 1, 2, and 3 in Table 3) to achieve the same goal of disconnecting the supplicants. For example, we have used Code 1 to send a flood of unicast and bidirectional disassociation frames. We have found that after

---

[8] We have used different Reason Codes [0–254] and the impact was the same. For the experiments of Table 2, we have used Reason Code 10.

Table 3. Commands and codes used for generating deauthentication attacks. We have made the complete codes (Code 1–6) publicly available over a GitHub repository [13]. Commands 1, 2, and 3, are part of the *aircrack-ng* Linux toolset.

Command & Code	Command/Code Syntax	Command/Code Semantics
Command 1	aireplay-ng -0 5 $-a$ mac_{ap} $-c$ mac_{sp} $--deauth$-rc n wlan0	In this command, the option -0 5 indicates deauthentication to be run 5 times, $-a$ the access point MAC address, $-c$ the supplicant's MAC address, $--deauth$-re n the reason code (e.g., n=7 is "Class 3 frame received from non-associated STA"), and wlan0 the Wi-Fi interface
Command 2	airodump-ng $-c$ 6 $--bssid$ mac_{ap} $-w$ ./file.pcap wlan0	The option $-c$ 6 indicates the radio channel 6 to listen on (i.e., the one used by the access point), $--bssid$ the access point MAC address, $-w$ the pcap file location where to store the captured wireless traffic, and wlan0 the Wi-Fi interface
Command 3	aireplay-ng -1 5 $-a$ mac_{ap} wlan0	In this command, the option -1 5 indicates the generation of fake authentications using the IEEE open system (i.e., no security) each 5 s (reassociation), $-a$ the access point MAC address, and wlan0 the Wi-Fi interface
Code 1	dot11=Dot11x(type=0, subtype=10, addr1=bssid, addr2=supp, addr3=bssid) dot11=Dot11y(type=0, subtype=10, addr1=supp, addr2=bssid, addr3=bssid) framex=RadioTap()/dot11x/Dot11Disas() framey=RadioTap()/dot11y/Dot11Disas() sendp(framex, iface=wlan0, count=500, inter=0.1) sendp(framey, iface=wlan0, count=500, inter=0.1)	This scapy-based python code snippet creates and sends 500 disassociation frames on both directions, i.e., to the access point (on behalf of the supplicant) and to the supplicant (on behalf of the access point). This code has the same impact and consequences as those of Command 1
Code 2	dot11=Dot11(type=0, subtype=12, addr1=bssid, addr2=supp, addr3=bssid) frame=RadioTap()/dot11/Dot11Deauth(reason=254) sendp(frame, iface=wlan0, count=500, inter=0.1)	This scapy-based python code snippet creates and sends 500 deauthentication frames with reason code 254 (unknown) to the access point on behalf of the supplicant. To send the frame to the supplicant on behalf of the access point, we switch the values of addr1 and addr2
Code 3	dot11=Dot11(type=0, subtype=10, addr1=bssid, addr2=supp, addr3=bssid) framex=RadioTap()/dot11/Dot11Disas() sendp(frame, iface=wlan0, count=500, inter=0.1)	This scapy-based python code snippet creates and sends 500 spoofed unicast disassociation frames to the supplicant on behalf of the access point. To send the frame to the supplicant on behalf of the access point, we switch the values of addr1 and addr2
Code 4	dot11=Dot11(type=0, subtype=0, addr1=bssid, addr2=supp, addr3=bssid) frame=RadioTap()/dot11/Dot11AssoReq(cap=0x0431, listen_interval=0x000a)/Dot11Elt(ID=0, info="SSID") sendp(frame, iface=wlan0, count=500, inter=0.1)	This scapy-based python code snippet creates and sends 500 association request frames to the access point on behalf of a PMF-capable supplicant. This code proved to be more efficient than Command 3 in succeeding the attack within a shorter time. For example, when launched against the APPLE MAC-BOOK PRO M1, it took between 3 and 4 s to disconnect it (3.40 s on average)
Code 5	dot11=Dot11(type=0, subtype=1, addr1=supp, addr2=bssid, addr3=bssid) frame=RadioTap()/dot11/Dot11AssoResp(cap=0x0431, status=0x001e)/Dot11Elt(ID=0, info="SSID") sendp(frame, iface=wlan0, count=500, inter=0.1)	This scapy-based python code snippet creates and sends 500 association response frames with Reason Code 30 to the supplicant on behalf of the access point. This code proved to affect more the re-association of the supplicant once disconnected. This is probably due to the association come-back time
Code 6	dot11=Dot11(type=0, subtype=3, addr1=supp, addr2=bssid, addr3=bssid) frame=RadioTap()/dot11/Dot11AssoResp(cap=0x0431, status=0x001f)/Dot11Elt(ID=0, info="SSID") sendp(frame, iface=wlan0, count=500, inter=0.1)	This scapy-based python code snippet creates and sends 500 association response frames with Reason Code 31 to the supplicant on behalf of the access point. This code had the same impact as Code 5

sending a certain amount of spoofed frames (around 130 frames), the supplicants got disconnected. Furthermore, using Code 2 and 3, we were able to cause the disconnection by sending unidirectional spoofed deauthentication/disassociation frames. The attack flow using bidirectional deauthentication frames is illustrated in the MSC of Fig. 2 (where $n \in \{0, \ldots, 254\}$ is arbitrary chosen reason code).

Attack Interpretation. When analyzing the wireless traffic that we have captured using *Wireshark*, we have observed that there was a large number of protected action frames (SA-query requests and responses) exchanged between the access points and the supplicants during the injection of the spoofed deauthentication/disassociation frames. Most of the time, the supplicants were not responding to any of the requests. After few seconds, the access points sent a protected disassociation frame to the supplicants, which set the supplicants' status at the access points' association table to "non-associated and unauthenticated" (i.e., IEEE 802.11 State 1). Right after that, the supplicants started sending protected action frames (SA-query requests/responses) which got rejected by the access points using deauthentication frames with a reason "Received Class 3 frame from non-associated STA (Code 7)" (since action frames are Class 3 frames). After multiple rejections, the supplicants concluded with a protected disassociation frame (to disassociate themselves from the access point) since no response was received and the SA-query procedure timed out. The access points replied with a deauthentication frame with a reason "Received Class 2 frame from unauthenticated STA (Code 6)".

As per the IEEE 802.11w, a party that is involved in an SA-query procedure would send a protected disassociation frame if the latter does not receive any response to its SA-query requests and the SA-query procedure timeout elapses. In our experiments, we believe that the access points (and sometimes the supplicants) concluded the session due to the fact of not receiving SA-query responses to their SA-query requests. There are many hypotheses as to why this has occurred:

1. One party could not respond to new SA-query requests as long as their locally generated SA-query requests have not yet been sent or responded to. In fact, the specification that not explicitly dictate what a party that has initiated the SA-query procedure does if it receives an SA-query request from the other party. Nevertheless, the success of the attack using unidirectional deauthentication/disassociation frames (i.e., using Code 2 and 3), makes this hypotheses weaker since the SA-query procedure is only initiated on one side.
2. One party is not able to access the channel on time and to send their SA-query responses due to the flood of spoofed frames generated by the attacker. This would make the SA-query timeout expire and cause disassociation.
3. Some of the SA-query responses or requests got into a collision with the attacker's frames making the party that is expecting SA-query responses believe that the requested party cannot respond to their SA-query requests, which would timeout the SA-query procedure and cause the disassociation.
4. It is possible that the implementation of IEEE 802.11w on certain devices (including access points) is not robust enough to perfectly handle a large number of SA-query requests and responses mixed along with the spoofed management frames, which would cause the disassociation.
5. If the quality of the radio signal is weak (e.g., due to long distance or noise), it is possible that many of the SA-query requests and responses get lost and do not reach their destination. This would lead to the expiry of the SA-query procedure timeout and cause a disassociation.

Table 2 (Row 1, 2, 3, and 4), shows the time it took to successfully accomplish deauthentication attack using different attack patterns. For example, in Row 1 (bidirectional unicast spoofed and unprotected deauthentication frames) and in the case of the APPLE MACBOOK PRO M1, it took between 3 and 32 s for the attack to succeed on the CISCO WAP150 running WPA2-PSK with PMF enabled. In 20 successful attempts, the average time was 15.70 s. It took between 5 and 28 s for the same attack to succeed on the TP-LINK AX6000 running WPA3-PSK. Where in the case of the HUAWEI NOVA 5T, it took between 3 and 26 s for the attack to succeed (12.35 s on average) on the CISCO WAP150. Since the HUAWEI NOVA 5T does not support WPA3-PSK, the attack on this particular supplicant could not be evaluated on the TP-LINK AX6000 access point.

Furthermore, as per the impact of the attacks, we note that after a successful deauthentication, we have observed that the supplicants had serious difficulties to rejoin the network again when the attacks continue. In fact, each time the supplicants try to re-authenticate and re-associate to the access points, the supplicants as well as the access points, get distracted by the flood of deauthentication frames and fail to accomplish the authentication and remain disconnected.

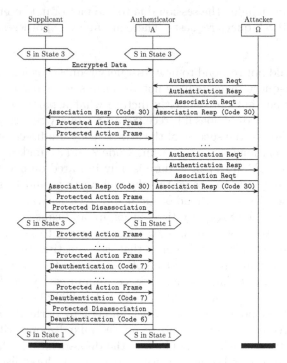

Fig. 3. Deauthentication attack using fake open system authentication on PMF (WPA2 and WPA3), where State 1 and State 3 indicate the 802.11 state of "Unauthenticated & Unassociated" and "Authenticated & Associated", respectively. State 2 (not used here) is "Authenticated & Unassociated".

4.2   Deauthentication Using Fake Authentication Session

Observation. In IEEE 802.11w, when an access point receives an unprotected associated frame from a supplicant that is already associated with it, it starts the SA-query procedure with an association come-back time to check whether the supplicant has truly sent that association frame (in the case where the supplicant has lost the session keys) or the frame was sent by an unauthorized party that is impersonating the supplicant. If the supplicant responds correctly to access point's SA-query requests before the association come-back time is up, the access point concludes that the received frame was a spoofed one and discards it. Otherwise, if no response was received for any of the generated SA-query requests and before the association come-back time runs out, the access point assumes that the supplicant has lost the session keys and allows a re-association from the supplicant after the association come-back time.

During our experiments, in particular, when we have used the APPLE devices as supplicants (viz., Row 1, 2, and 3 in Table 1), we have discovered that it was possible to quickly disconnect the supplicants from the access points due to what it seems to be an implementation flaw. By initiating a fake authentication session using the IEEE 802.11 open system mode, the access points rejected the association with a reason "Association Request Rejected Temporarily; Try Again Later (Code 30)". This has made the access points and the supplicant exchange protected action frames (encrypted SA-query requests/response) to check the legitimacy of the new association, which totally conforms to the standard (i.e., SA-query procedure of 802.11w). However, we have noticed that the supplicants (specifically, APPLE devices) did not always react to the rejected association frame as per the standard (i.e., wait for an SA-query request and respond to it), but rather sent a protected disassociated frame to the access points and then started sending their protected action frames (possibly, SA-query responses) as if they remained associated. The access points processed the disassociation frame and changed the status of the supplicants in the access points' association table to Unauthenticated (State 1). For each action frame sent by the supplicants after their disassociation, the access point replied by sending unprotected deauthentication frames with a reason "Received Class 3 frame from non-associated STA (Code 7)". Subsequently, the supplicants continued sending protected action frames (which indicates that they are still considering themselves associated with the access point, i.e., in State 3) and then concluded with another protected disassociation frame (to disassociate themselves from the access points). The access points replied with a deauthentication frame with a reason "Received Class 2 frame from unauthenticated STA (Code 6)".

With respect to the Huawei Nova 5T, the attack was successful although it took longer for the disconnection to take place compared to the case of APPLE devices. Nevertheless, the disconnection in this case occurred in the same way as it had occurred in the deauthentication attacks presented in the previous section. Due to the absence of SA-query responses, a timeout occured, causing the disconnection of the supplicant.

Attack Generation. By connecting the supplicants to the access points, we have started generating fake open system authentication sessions with the access point (using Command 3 in Table 3) and captured the subsequent wireless traffic (using Command 2 in Table 3). After few seconds, we have managed to disconnect the supplicants from the access points. Furthermore, to optimize the attack, we have used some *scapy-based scripts* (viz., Code 4, 5, and 6 in Table 3). Code 4 performs what Command 3 does but without going through the authentication phase. It only sends a spoofed association request to the access points on behalf of the supplicants to receive a legitimate association response from the access point. Code 5 and 6 save the transmission of 3 frames by only sending the association response frame with Reason Code 30 (i.e., "Association request rejected temporarily; try again later") or 31 (i.e., "Robust management frame policy violation"), respectively. Nevertheless, these two last attack patterns (i.e., Code 5 and 6) succeeded only on APPLE devices and did not cause a disconnection on the HUAWEI NOVA 5T. The attack flow using complete fake authentication and association on APPLE devices is illustrated in the MSC of Fig. 3. We provide our interpretations in the next paragraph.

Attack Interpretation. After analyzing the wireless traffic that we have captured, we have observed that all APPLE devices supplicant do not always react, as per the standard, to a an association response with Reason Code 30 sent by the access point. Indeed, we have discovered that after a couple of fake authentications and associations (sometimes at the first attempt), these devices sent a protected disassociation frame to the access point after receiving a protected action frame (an encrypted SA-query request), changing their status in the access point's association table. This has made all future supplicants' frames (mostly Class 3 frames, e.g., action frames) being ignored by the access point, which made the supplicants disconnect after several attempts. This seems to be an implementation flaw as it is completely incorrect to send a protected disassociation frame (declaring disassociation) and then start replying to SA-query requests. This does not conform to the standard and it is making the attack accomplishment quicker compared to other devices from a different vendor. Furthermore, we believe that this incorrect behavior of sending a protected disassociation frame is related to the SA-query procedure implementation. In fact, we managed to reproduce the same behavior by just injecting spoofed association responses with status code 30 and 31. These two reason codes are only used in IEEE 802.11w (viz., Code 5 and 6 in Table 3). We have reached out to Apple Product Security and they asked us to run the attacks on their latest macOS version (macOS Monterey v12.0 Beta) [15]. We have tried the attacks on this latest version after we installed it on MacBook Pro i5. The incorrect behavior of sending a protected disassociation frame and remaining associated seemed to be fixed in this new version of macOS. These attacks did not succeed. Notwithstanding, deauthentication attacks that we have discussed in the previous section were still successful as they engender a different behavior.

Table 2 (Row 5, 6, 7, and 8), shows the time it took to successfully accomplish deauthentication attacks using fake open system authentication and some of its variant and optimized attack patterns. For example, in Row 5 (use complete fake open system authentication and association) and in the case of the APPLE MACBOOK PRO M1, it took between 4 and 10 s for the attack to succeed on the CISCO WAP150 running WPA2-PSK with PMF enabled. In 20 successful attempts, the average time was 6.50 s. Additionally, it took between 3 and 20 s for the same attack to succeed on the TP-LINK AX6000 running WPA3-PSK. The average time was even lower, between 3 to 4 s, when we have used Code 4, 5, and 6. This codes are optimized versions of the attack pattern of Command 3. The execution time of Command 3 on HUAWEI NOVA 5T was longer. It took between 7 and 123 s (47.35 s on average) to disconnect the supplicant from the CISCO WAP150. A much better average execution time of 14.50 s was obtained using Code 4 for this supplicant. Code 5 and 6 did not cause any disconnection.

4.3 Further Result Analysis

Based on the obtained experimental results, we do not deny that IEEE 802.11w is indeed a security amendment for the IEEE 802.11i standard to prevent many Denial-of-Service attacks, including, deauthentication attacks, to be successfully executed within one second. However, we do claim that the current implementations of IEEE 802.11w do not stand against certain attack patterns. We have demonstrated how it was possible to disconnect associated supplicants within one minute using a flood of spoofed unprotected management frames.

With respect to the vulnerability that we have discovered on certain APPLE devices, the vulnerability seemed to be fixed in the upcoming version of APPLE operating systems, such as, macOS Monterey v12.0 Beta and iOS 15 Beta. This has been confirmed by Apple Product Security department [15]. Thus, until these Beta versions become available to the public as an update, it is still possible to cause deauthentication of certain PMF-enforced APPLE devices within 3 to 4 s. As a countermeasure to this vulnerability, we strongly urge APPLE device users to update their systems as soon as the update becomes available to be immune from these attacks.

As per the attacks that rely on creating a flood of deauthentication or disassociation frames to cause the disconnection, we have placed five hypotheses in Sect. 4.1 (although we have weakened Hypothesis 1) as for why the disconnection had occurred. Since in most cases, if not all, the SA-query procedure is aborted by the access point by sending a protected disassociation frame (possibly after the SA-query procedure timeout expires), we thought that the issue may reside on the access point. Thus, it may be a good idea to use the APPLE MACBOOK PRO I5 that runs the Beta version of macOS (which is claimed to be secure), as an access point (i.e., Wi-Fi hotspot) and try the attacks. To that end, we have used the APPLE MACBOOK PRO M1 as a supplicant and run the first three attacks of Table 2. The results were as follows:

- When bidirectional spoofed deauthentication frames were used (Command 1), there were 20 disconnections out of 21. It took between 5 and 141 s to cause the disconnection. The average time was around 46.90 s, which is considerably longer than the case of the TP-LINK AX6000 access point for the same supplicant.

- When bidirectional spoofed disassociation frames were used (Code 1), all attack attempts caused a disconnection. It took between 5 and 129 s to cause the disconnection. The average time was around 51.60 s, which is also longer than the case where the TP-LINK AX6000 access point was used.
- When unidirectional spoofed deauthentication and disassociation frames were used (Code 2 & 3), we have found that 40% of the attack attempts did not cause a disconnection. Based on the cases where a disconnection occurred, the average time was around 103.80 s, which is much longer than 11.25 s that we have obtained on the TP-LINK AX6000 access point.

Although all 5 hypotheses presented in Sect. 4.1 are logical, these latter results propel us to claim that Hypothesis 4 is more likely to be true. As APPLE's latest version of macOS (Monterey v12 Beta) proved to have a more robust resilience against these attacks when used as a Wi-Fi hotspot, it is clear that the implementation of the SA-query procedure by different vendors has indeed an impact on hardening or easing the feasibility of those attacks. Furthermore, the fact that the access point generally disassociates the supplicants after the expiry of the SA-query timeout, implies that it is not receiving the expected SA-query responses on time. This could indicate a lack of robustness by the supplicants' current implementation of IEEE 802.11w in handling a large number of SA-query requests that are interfered with other frames.

Therefore, we recommend to device manufacturers to consider evaluating the robustness of their implementation of the IEEE 802.11w amendment and perform intensive testings as of whether their implementations could handle non-standardized behaviors, such as floods of SA-query requests/responses.

5   Conclusion

Deauthentication attacks on Wi-Fi networks constituted a tiresome security threat for many years. Attackers were able to remotely disconnect legitimate devices from a secured Wi-Fi network by merely sending spoofed management frames of type deauthentication and disassociation. In 2009, the IEEE 802.11w amendment came to put an end to many Wi-Fi Denial-of-Service attacks, including deauthentication attacks, through the use of PMF (Protected Management Frames). Later on, some researchers demonstrated the feasibility of certain Denial-of-Service (DoS) attacks on IEEE 802.11w Wi-Fi network. Most of these attacks target the authentication and association phase to deprive devices from getting successfully connected to the network. Only a few of these attacks aimed to cause the disconnection of already connected PMF-enforced devices.

In this paper, we have demonstrated, through various attack patterns, the feasibility of deauthentication attacks on IEEE 802.11w Wi-Fi networks that adopt either WPA2 or WPA3. We have started by briefly presenting the most important concepts of IEEE 802.11w amendment. Then, through numerous experiments, we have demonstrated different deauthentication attack scenarios on PMF-enforced Wi-Fi networks. As part of our experiments, we have identified a vulnerability on certain APPLE devices that could make deauthentication happen within 4 s. After coordinating with Apple products security department, the vulnerability has been fixed in the upcoming version of their systems. Furthermore, we have discussed some hypotheses to why some of the presented attacks were successful. We have recommended to device manufacturers to carefully evaluate the robustness of their implementation of IEEE 802.11w on their devices w.r.t. handling a large number of SA-query requests and responses. In fact, on certain IEEE 802.11w implementations, we have observed a better resilience against the attacks compared to other implementations.

References

1. IEEE. Wireless LAN Medium Access Control (MAC) and Physical Layer (PHY). Amendment 4: Protected Management Frames. IEEE Std. 802.11w-2009 (2009)
2. Ahmad, M.S., Tadakamadla, S.: Short paper: security evaluation of IEEE 802.11w specification. In: Proceedings of the 4th ACM Conference on Wireless Network Security, pp. 53–58 (2011)
3. Eian, M.: Fragility of the robust security network: 802.11 denial of service. In: Proceedings of the 7th International Conference on Applied Cryptography and Network Security, pp. 400–416, Springer, Berlin (2009). https://doi.org/10.1007/978-3-642-01957-9
4. Wang, W., Wang, H. Weakness in 802.11w and an improved mechanism on protection of management frame. In: Proceedings of the 2011 International Conference on Wireless Communications and Signal Processing, pp. 1–4 (2011)
5. Valli, K.V., Krishnam, R.K.V.: Formal verification of IEEE 802.11w authentication protocol. In: The 2nd International Conference on Communication, Computing & Security (ICCCS-2012), vol. 6, pp. 716–722, Elsevier (2012)
6. Schepers, D., Vanhoef, M., Ranganathan, A.: DEMO: a framework to test and fuzz Wi-Fi devices. In: Proceedings of the 14th ACM Conference on Security and Privacy in Wireless and Mobile Networks, WiSec 2021, pp. 368–370, ACM (2021)
7. Ram, M., Kaushik, A.: Deauthenticating and disassociating unauthorized access points with spoofed management frames. United States Patent: US9681299B2, pp. 1–17 (2017)
8. Lounis,K.: Security of short-range wireless technologies and an authentication protocol for IoT. Ph.D. thesis, Queen's University (2021)
9. Lounis, K., Zulkernine, M.: Exploiting race-condition for Wi-Fi denial of service attacks. In: 13th International Conference on Security of Information and Networks, SIN 2020, Istanbul, Turkey, 4–7 November 2020, pp. 1–8 (2020)
10. Lounis, K., Zulkernine, M.: Bad-Token: denial of service attacks on WPA3. In: Proceedings of the 12th International Conference on Security of Information and Networks, Article no. 15, pp. 1–8, ACM (2019)
11. Lounis, Karim, Zulkernine, Mohammad: WPA3 connection deprivation attacks. In: Kallel, Slim, Cuppens, Frédéric., Cuppens-Boulahia, Nora, Hadj Kacem, Ahmed (eds.) CRiSIS 2019. LNCS, vol. 12026, pp. 164–176. Springer, Cham (2020). https://doi.org/10.1007/978-3-030-41568-6_11
12. Lounis, K., Zulkernine, M.: Attacks and defenses in short-range wireless technologies for IoT. IEEE Access J. **8**, 88892–88932 (2020)

13. Lounis, K.: Python-based Scapy scripts for deauthentication attacks on PMF (2021). https://github.com/KarimLounis/Scapy-Scripts
14. Vanhoef, M., Piessens, F.: Key reinstallation attacks: forcing nonce reuse in WPA2. In: Proceedings of the ACM Conference on Computer and Communications Security, pp. 1313–1328, ACM (2017)
15. Lounis, K., Nick: A possible security vulnerability in Wi-Fi PMF on MacOS. Private Email Communications, July 24th to September 1th (2021)

Lightweight Authentication and Encryption for Online Monitoring in IIoT Environments

Armando Miguel Garcia$^{(\boxtimes)}$ and Matthias Hiller

Fraunhofer AISEC, Garching, Germany
{armando.miguel.garcia,matthias.hiller}@aisec.fraunhofer.de

Abstract. Emerging industrial technologies building upon lightweight, mobile and connected embedded devices increase the need for trust and enforcing access control in industrial environments. We propose an approach which combines Physical Unclonable Functions (PUFs), firmware fingerprinting and Attribute-Based Encryption (ABE) for enabling authentication and fine-grained access control of the data generated on the IoT end nodes. This approach is evaluated using an experimental setup and its feasibility for online monitoring in industrial environments is demonstrated. The proposed architecture adds a processing overhead of under 1% on a low-cost microcontroller and a communication latency of 144 ms over a long-range wireless link, while having a low power consumption and protecting against multiple cyber-threats.

Keywords: Industrial Internet of Things (IIoT) · Attribute-based encryption · Physical unclonable function · Industry 4.0 · Access control · Cloud manufacturing

1 Introduction

Sensor nodes are integral parts of the Industry 4.0, as they interact with manufacturing equipment and forward the measured data to other devices in the network. They are part of the Industrial Internet of Things (IIoT), which represents the interconnected network of industrial devices communicating with each other without human intervention, i.e., Machine-to-Machine Communication, thus enabling processes to run autonomously [1].

While processing sensitive data and lacking computational resources for complex security schemes, sensor nodes are attractive targets for cyber-attacks from inside and near the shop-floor, which is especially critical in open or very wide settings. Such cyber-attacks often result in theft of proprietary information, extortion, and tampering of devices across the production chain [2,3]. Therefore it is critical to not only focus on the safety and reliability of industrial environments but also on the security of the processed data.

In this work, we propose and demonstrate an end-to-end approach for securing data-chains involving sensor nodes in industrial environments. The main contributions of this work are as follows:

© Springer Nature Switzerland AG 2022
E. Aïmeur et al. (Eds.): FPS 2021, LNCS 13291, pp. 253–262, 2022.
https://doi.org/10.1007/978-3-031-08147-7_17

- A security architecture for end-to-end secure communication within industrial environments, which enables monitoring and forensics-friendly encryption of measurement data.
- An experimental evaluation for demonstrating the feasibility of our architecture in terms of performance, latency and power consumption.

2 Related Work

The growing usage of IIoT devices for cloud manufacturing has increased the importance of communication security and access control.

The use of public-key cryptography and digital certificates is a widespread practice for authenticating the identity of devices within a network. However, the latter is often not suitable for IIoT due to high levels of processing power, latency and storage required. In [4], a signature approach without certificates is presented, this approach is nonetheless vulnerable to known-message attacks.

Attribute-Based Encryption (ABE) was first introduced by Sahai and Waters for enhancing access-control capabilities by making use of attributes and access policies [5].

In [6], Yao et al. proposed a lightweight KP-ABE scheme for constraint devices based on elliptic curves instead of bilinear pairings. A fault in this scheme was explained in [7], and a solution was also proposed.

A lightweight authentication mechanism based on pre-shared keys and performing hash and XOR operations only, is presented in [8]. This work assumes an infrastructure in which the nodes are equipped with a secure element and are authenticated by gateways equipped with a Trusted Platform Module (TPM).

Authentication methods also attests the device hardware e.g., by means of a Physical Unclonable Function (PUF) [9]. Those functions exploit very small variations during the manufacturing process of the devices for granting them unique identities. For example, a hardware-based solution for implementing a trusted gateway using PUFs is presented in [10].

In [11], a method for verification of firmware integrity is presented, which also addresses roving malware. This method splits the program memory in blocks, which are verified independently in a shuffled manner, this allows for the verification process to be interrupted without the risk of compromising the result. However, the verification of each block must be performed atomically.

3 System Architecture

3.1 Use Case

The IIoT infrastructure serves as the interface between the manufacturing process and the IT-infrastructure. The functional architecture is shown in Fig. 1, which integrates of manufacturing tools and microcontrollers for enabling authentication and end-to-end encryption from the sensor nodes, and the back-end within the corporate network.

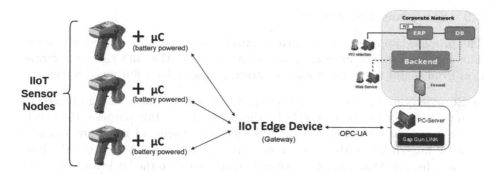

Fig. 1. Handheld tool use case showing the proposed architecture.

Our exemplary use case comprises handheld mobile devices for measuring physical properties during the quality control process, e.g., in the scope of automotive or aerospace manufacturing. The current process for taking measurements relies on such equipment being connected to its docking station after all measurements of a session have been taken. The proposed architecture is composed by three main components:

- **Sensor Node:** the coupling point between the physical and information domains. It is a mobile or stationary device to securely acquire the measurement data.
- **Gateway:** the collusion point between the IIoT and conventional IT infrastructure. The principal task for the devices in this layer is the secure forwarding of data.
- **Backend:** the main destination and place of rest for the generated data. This data can be stored encryptedly and retrieved on demand for verification, analysis, audits, etc.

3.2   Threat Model

According to IEC 62443-3-3, the attacker level is divided into four levels and defined by four main characteristics: means, resources, capabilities and motivation [12]. Our attacker is classified as a level 3 attacker, which drives intentional attacks with sophisticated means and moderate resources, has specific skills regarding industrial environments and communication protocols, and possesses a moderate motivation.

This attacker level corresponds to outsiders (rival organizations, terrorist groups and hacktivists) and insiders (trusted persons, contractors, suppliers, and current or former employees) attempting to disrupt the production environment, and to eavesdrop on the communication for stealing intellectual property, e.g., through the introduction of one or multiple rogue devices into the network.

3.3 Setup and Enrollment

The proposed approach starts with an enrollment process for devices and users. The enrollment distributes credentials for authentication and gathers information from sensor nodes to validate received messages later during operation.

- **Sensor Node**: as a data producer entity, the measurement data gathered and reported needs to be verifiable by the backend. For this purpose, the enrollment process for the sensor node includes the sharing of hardware and software fingerprints with the backend. Those fingerprints are generated within the sensor node and must be securely transmitted to the backend, e.g., using a wired connection in a secure environment. The sensor node then receives a list of attributes from the backend, which enables the subsequent encryption of data.
- **Gateway**: as a data forwarding entity, the gateway needs credentials for communicating securely with the IIoT platform. For this purpose, a PKI certificate is generated by the backend and forwarded to the gateway through a secure connection.
- **User**: to enable a combined user-asset authentication, every user within the system is provided with a PKI SmartCard with a certificate generated by the backend, to combine the identities of the device and the user using it.

3.4 Authentication

The mobility of the sensor node and its interaction with sensitive data makes it attractive for cyber-attacks and tampering attempts. Our approach involves the following authentication mechanisms to reduce the attack surface:

- **Hardware-Authenticity:** authenticates that the underlying hardware was previously registered into the system. This is implemented through a Physical Unclonale Function (PUF). The PUF-Response is extracted at start-up and used for computing an evidence, which is sent to the backend. The backend then verifies the authenticity of the hardware with the information obtained during the enrollment process.
- **Firmware-Integrity:** indicates if the firmware was not manipulated and is measured by performing an initial fingerprinting during the enrollment process and a continuous self-attestation during run-time. The integrity of the firmware can be verified by comparing the fingerprint with the initial one.
- **Worker's Identity:** indicates if a user possesses the credentials for working with the corresponding sensor node and is obtained through a digital signature involving the SmartCard and PIN of the user. As the backend issues the permissions, it is able to verify the correctness of the signature and the user credentials.

3.5   Encrypted Communication

The proposed architecture is based on a uni-directional communication link between the sensor node and the backend during operation. This communication is encrypted using ABE, which facilitates the management of private keys and enables access control over the generated data for each measurement session. As ABE often results in higher computational costs than conventional symmetric encryption mechanisms, a Key Encapsulation Mechanism (KEM) is implemented, i.e., a symmetric key is encrypted with ABE and the remaining communication traffic is then protected with symmetric encryption. As the ABE-encryption not involves private keys, impersonation attacks must be considered, i.e., an adversary pretends to be the sensor node in order to produce false data. To prevent such attacks, our implementation introduces an additional message containing the authentication evidences of the sensor node. Table 1 summarizes the different types of messages.

Table 1. Types of messages sent from the sensor node to the backend.

Message	Plaintex content	Encrypted content	Attributes
Security Header	Message ID List of attributes	Message ID Hash of ABE-Encr. Payload Hardware Fingerprint Firmware Fingerprint Signature over Time & Date	High-Level Access Device ID Time & Date
ABE-Encrypted Payload	Message ID List of attributes	Message ID AES Key	Device ID Time & Date
AES-Encrypted Payload	Message ID	Message ID Measured Value Time & Date Device Serial Number	–

Figure 2 presents an overview of the communication flow between the sensor node and backend. This communication flow takes place once for every work order and contains the following two phases:

- **Initialization Phase:** two messages are sent to the backend for initialization: The first is the ABE-Encrypted Payload, which carries the AES-key for encrypting the measurement data during the operation phase, and the second is the Security Header, which carries authentication information for validating the device and the user. For enabling different levels of access, messages are ABE-encrypted with a different set of attributes.
- **Operation Phase:** After every measurement, the gathered data is encrypted using AES and sent to the backend.

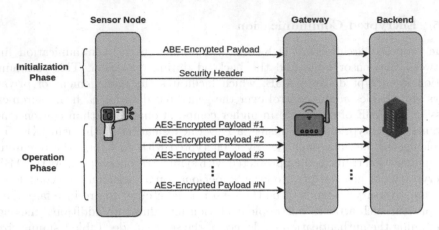

Fig. 2. Overview of unidirectional communication flow.

4   Implementation and Evaluation

We demonstrate the feasibility of the proposed approach in an experimental setup. Figure 3 shows the main components of the setup, which are briefly described below.

4.1   Experimental Setup

Components

Microcontroller: The core of the sensor node is a SiFive's E310 RISC-V microcontroller. It carries out the different authentication mechanisms, obtains the measured data, performs encryption by means of ABE and communicates with the gateway via LoRa.

Physical Sensor: An Infrared-Thermometer PCE-895 was taken as the coupling point between the physical and digital world. It measures temperatures in with a resolution of $+/-0.1\,°C$ and communicates the result of the measurement over a Serial Peripheral Interface (SPI) to the microcontroller.

LoRa Transceivers: The transmission of messages on the sensor node is performed via SX1261 LoRa Transceivers, which are specifically designed for low-power applications requiring long range communication, which is suitable for measurements on different locations within a shop-floor.

SmartCard Reader: The interface to the SmartCard is a SEC1210 Smart-Card Reader. This chip communicates with the SmartCard using the standard ISO/IEC 7816, and acts as a bridge for requesting the signature of data.

Gateway: The gateway is comprised by a Microchip's PolarFire SoC, a Linux-capable processor, and forwards encrypted messages from the sensor nodes to the backend over an OPC-UA channel.

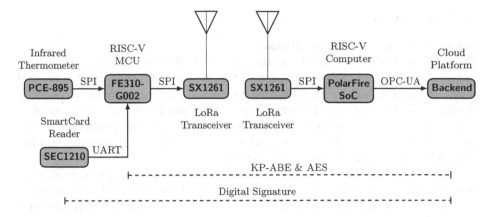

Fig. 3. Implementation overview.

Security Measures

Hardware Fingerprint: The on-chip SRAM within a device, and also our microcontrollers, exhibits a unique pattern after initialization, i.e., after power-up, which is used as SRAM PUF [13] and cannot be simply observed by outsiders. The PUF produces a 128-bit fingerprint, which is stored in volatile memory and protected by the Memory Protection Unit (MPU).

Firmware Fingerprint: Most of the existing firmware fingerprinting methods verify entire blocks of memory sequentially. This forces the system to verify an entire memory block before continuing the program execution and opens a vulnerability towards roving malware due to the deterministic order of the memory blocks being verified. The implemented scheme has a single-memory-address level of granularity and is based on a Pseudo-Random Function (PRF) for determining the order in which memory addresses are verified. The addresses are merged with their contents and an incremental counter for determining the next address to be verified, thus chaining the entire program memory while also considering the order in which they are visited via the counter. The memory addresses are verified at regular intervals by means of an interruption, during which multiple addresses are verified.

Encryption: The ABE-encryption in our implementation is based on the pairing-free KP-ABE Scheme described in [6]. This scheme avoids the computation of bilinear pairing and only applies point-scalar multiplication operations on elliptic curves. It derives a key from a point of the elliptic curve, which is then utilized for symmetric encryption of the plaintext. The data can be decrypted when the access structure of a key is satisfied by a certain ciphertext, as it facilitates to reconstruct the curve point and the symmetric key.

4.2   Evaluation

Evaluation - Initialization Phase

The implementation of a KEM and the separation of activities into initialization and operation phases allows for concentrating the most processing intensive and power consuming tasks, i.e., ABE encryption and the transmission of Security Header and ABE-Encrypted Payload over LoRa, into the initialization phase.

During their initialization, mobile sensor nodes have the possibility of still being attached to a docking station, which leads to the power consumption not being a critical indicator during this phase.

The CPU time for encrypting the messages sent during the initialization phase increments linearly with the amount of attributes involved in the encryption process. The encryption time with respect to the amount of attributes at a system clock of 320 MHz is shown below:

Attributes	1	2	4	8	16	32	64	128	256	512
Time (s)	0.073	0.11	0.18	0.32	0.60	1.1	2.3	4.5	8.9	18

Evaluation - Operation Phase

We apply the following performance indicators to our experimental setup to assess the practical feasibility of our approach for monitoring of measurement data during the operation phase:

Processing Overhead: The value is measured as the difference between the amount of MIPS (Million Instructions Per Second) for performing the tasks of authentication and encryption during the operation phase, and the total amount of MIPS available on the reference system.

The resulting processing overhead is related to the amount of instructions per second required for (a) continuous firmware fingerprinting and (b) AES encryption in CCM mode. The tests were conducted using a clock speed of 320 MHz for the microcontroller, a message size of 32 bytes and a verification of 1000 memory addresses per second. The obtained processing overhead corresponds to 0.044 MIPS, which is equivalent to 0.11% for a reference system having 40 MIPS of processing power available.

Power Consumption: This is the total power consumption needed during the operation phase for the continuous firmware fingerprinting, the encryption of measurement data and its transmission over LoRa.

Table 2 shows the resulting power consumption for different clock and transmission power configurations. Configuration A results in an average power consumption of 2.28 µWh per measurement, almost twice as much as the configurations having a less powerful transmission. Those results indicate that the driving factor for the power consumption during the operation phase is the transmission power.

Table 2. Power consumption during the operation phase.

Parameter	Config. A	Config. B	Config. C	Magnitude
MCU clock speed	320	320	16	MHz
MCU current	150	150	8	mA
LoRa TX power	15	10	10	dBm
LoRa power	107.3	49.5	49.5	mW
Max. power required	646.4	588.6	120	mW
Average consumption	2.28	1.13	1.13	μWh/Measurement

Communication Latency: This is the added delay to the communication link from the sensor node to the backend when applying the proposed authentication and encryption methods. This delay is measured from the beginning of a transmission at the sensor node to the end of the reception of the data by the gateway. The main parameters for this communication are: a preamble of 8 symbols, a code rate of 4/5, an explicit header, the presence of a CRC, and DR5 as data rate, i.e., SF7/125 kHz.

Under the given operating conditions, the obtained latency for the secure communication over LoRa corresponds to 144 ms. When compared to a wireless, unprotected communication link between sensor node and backend, the latency overhead amounts to 30.6 ms, i.e., only 30.6 additional milliseconds when implementing the proposed security features.

4.3   Discussion on Security and Portability

The proposed approach protects against the insertion of rogue devices through to the PUF; against impersonation attacks thanks to the authentication information in the security header; against replay attacks due to the signature over date & time; against man-in-the-middle attacks, e.g., malicious gateways, through the hash included in the security header.

Due to the attribute-based access control, this architecture can be expanded for allowing usage at intermediate stages of the data chain, e.g., for data verification and visualization at the shop-floor. This can be enabled by giving intermediate parties access rights for decryption the ABE-Encrypted Payload. This also requires the inclusion of an additional key in the Security Header for signing a hash of the AES-Encrypted Payload on every transmission, thus avoiding the introduction of a fake AES-key by a compromised intermediate party.

This approach also has the potential of being ported to other industries and applications requiring mobility and lightweight security via uni-directional communication channels, e.g., healthcare for remote diagnoses, transportation and logistics for monitoring of objects across the supply chain, and energy and utilities for assessment and management of actual demand.

5   Conclusion

In this paper, we proposed a lightweight authentication and encryption architecture for end-to-end protection of measurement data within industrial environments. The proposed approach is characterized by low processing overhead, low power-consumption and low latency overhead, while enabling fine-grained access control on encrypted data and being resistant against insertion of rogue devices, collusion attacks, impersonation attacks, replay attacks, man-in-the-middle attacks. This architecture was also evaluated with an experimental setup, thus demonstrating its feasibility for implementation in industrial environments.

Acknowledgement. This paper is supported by European Union's Horizon 2020 research and innovation programme under grant agreement No. 871967, project SeCoIIA (Secure Collaborative Intelligent Industrial Assets).

The authors would like to thank the Chair of Security in Information Technology at the Technical University of Munich for the collaboration on the PUF authentication which was developed in the Project SecForCars 16KIS0795.

References

1. Tao, F., et al.: Cloud computing and internet of things-based cloud manufacturing service system. IEEE Trans. Industr. Inf. **10**, 1435–1442 (2014)
2. Yu, X., Guo, H.: A Survey on IIoT Security. APWCS, Singapore (2019)
3. Dallon Adams, R.: Ransomware Attacks by Industry, Continent and More. Tech Republic (2020)
4. Karati, A., Islam, S.H., Karuppiah, M.: Provably secure and lightweight certificateless signature scheme for IIoT environments. IEEE Trans. Industr. Inf. **14**(8), 3701–3711 (2018)
5. Sahai, A., Waters, B.: Fuzzy identity-based encryption. In: Cramer, R. (ed.) EUROCRYPT 2005. LNCS, vol. 3494, pp. 457–473. Springer, Heidelberg (2005). https://doi.org/10.1007/11426639_27
6. Yao, X., Chen, Z., Tian, Y.: A lightweight attribute-based encryption scheme for the internet of things. Future Gener. Comput. Syst. **49**, 104–112 (2014)
7. Tan, S.Y., Yeow, K.W.: Enhancement of a lightweight attribute-based encryption scheme for the internet of things. IEEE IoT J. **6**, 6384–6395 (2019)
8. Esfahani, A., et al.: A lightweight authentication mechanism for M2M communications in industrial IoT environment. IEEE IoT J. **6**(1), 288–296 (2019)
9. Yilmaz, Y., Gunn, S.R., Halak, B.: Lightweight PUF-based authentication protocol for IoT devices. In: IVSW (2018)
10. Frisch, C., Tempelmeier, M., Pehl, M.: PAG-IoT: a PUF and AEAD enabled trusted hardware gateway for IoT devices. In: ISVLSI (2020)
11. Carpent, X., Rattanavipanon, N., Tsudik, G.: Remote attestation of IoT devices via SMARM: Shuffled measurements against roving malware. In: HOST (2018)
12. International Electrotechnical Commission. Industrial communication networks - Network and system security - IEC 62443-3-3 (2013)
13. Böhm, C., Hofer, M., Pribyl, W.: A microcontroller SRAM-PUF. In: 2011 5th International Conference on Network and System Security (2011)

Attacks and Code Security

Detecting Attacks in Network Traffic Using Normality Models: The Cellwise Estimator

Felix Heine[✉], Carsten Kleiner, Philip Klostermeyer, Volker Ahlers,
Tim Laue, and Nils Wellermann

Hannover University of Applied Sciences and Arts, Hannover, Germany
{felix.heine,carsten.kleiner,philip.klostermeyer,volker.ahlers,tim.laue,
nils.wellermann}@hs-hannover.de

Abstract. Although machine learning (ML) for intrusion detection is attracting research, its deployment in practice has proven difficult. Major hindrances are that training a classifier requires training data with attack samples, and that trained models are bound to a specific network.

To overcome these problems, we propose two new methods for anomaly-based intrusion detection. Both are trained on normal-only data, making deployment much easier. The first approach is based on One-class SVMs, while the second leverages our novel Cellwise Estimator algorithm, which is based on multidimensional OLAP cubes. The latter has the additional benefit of explainable output, in contrast to many ML methods like neural networks. The created models capture the normal behavior of a network and are used to find anomalies that point to attacks. We present a thorough evaluation using benchmark data and a comparison to related approaches showing that our approach is competitive.

Keywords: Network intrusion detection · Machine Learning · Anomaly Detection · Multidimensional data · OLAP cubes · Iceberg condition

1 Introduction

In this paper, we introduce a novel approach to anomaly-based intrusion detection systems (IDS). Most commercial IDS are based on static rules that need to be maintained and are thus being called rule-based. In the research community, many approaches try to exploit machine learning (ML) to build what is often called an anomaly-based IDS. A common claim is that anomaly-based approaches are capable of detecting new types of attacks, in contrast to rule-based IDS, that can only detect known attacks. While the latter is true for sure, the correctness of the former claim depends on the exact method.

The GLACIER project has been funded by the German Federal Ministry of Education and Research under grant no. 16KIS0950.

E. Aïmeur et al. (Eds.): FPS 2021, LNCS 13291, pp. 265–282, 2022.
https://doi.org/10.1007/978-3-031-08147-7_18

Many publications use some form of classification, either binary or multi-class classification, to build a model that is used to detect attacks [6], with neural networks and decision trees being among the most popular algorithms. However, a classifier needs training data containing samples for each attack type that it should later detect. This means such a model is also not capable to detect novel types of attacks whose patterns do not resemble attacks from the training data.

Furthermore, it is unclear how to deploy such approaches in practice. Experiments from Al-Riyami et al. [3] show that it is in general not possible to use models trained on one network in another network. This implies that deployment must include a training process using data from the target network. However, to train a classifier, this data must include attack samples, which need to be labeled as such. This makes deployment extremely complex, rendering these approaches impractical.

To mitigate this problem, we propose to apply one-class classification to network intrusion detection. One-class classification uses normal-only training data and builds a model of the normal data to later detect deviations from the learned normal behavior. This approach implies that there is no need to include attacks in the training data, making the deployment process much easier.

We compare two different one-class classification methods. On one hand, we use the well-known **one-class support vector machine (OSVM)** algorithm [18], and on the other hand an approach developed at our group called **cellwise estimator (CE)**. The latter is based on modeling traffic patterns of the network on various aggregation levels, e.g. traffic between two hosts, traffic using a certain protocol, traffic between two sub-nets, traffic from a single host using a certain protocol, and so forth. The original idea stems from our paper [9], however in this publication, we introduce an important extension called **default cells** that model how likely new traffic patterns are. This means we focus on attacks that show up as unusual traffic patterns, e.g. DoS attacks, port scans, data exfiltration, lateral movement, C2 communication, see [22]. As we only use traffic meta data and no content, encrypted traffic is no issue.

A main benefit of CE compared to most ML methods including OSVM is **explainability**, which is crucial for practical application, since it helps security operations center (SOC) staff to understand alerts and react better [2]. With typical ML methods, the user has no clue *why* an alert has been issued. We, in contrast, can generate explanations for anomalies, thus moving towards explainable security [24].

Furthermore, we evaluate both methods using benchmark data and compare the results to related results from the literature. The evaluation shows that CE performs better than OSVM on the UNSW benchmark, with the additional benefit of explainability. Overall, we present the following **contributions**:

- Two methods for intrusion detection that use normal-only data for training: the CE and OSVMs
- A comparative evaluation of these methods and discussion of the results
- A comparison to the detection quality of a rule-based IDS (Suricata)

The paper is organized as follows. In Sect. 2, we give an overview of related work in terms of intrusion detection systems using machine learning with a specific eye on anomaly-based approaches. We move on explaining the concept of the CE and the application of OSVMs in Sect. 3. In Sect. 4, we present and discuss our evaluation results. Finally, we conclude and present an outlook to future work.

2   Related Work

There is a plethora of evaluations of different classification algorithms used for machine learning-based intrusion detection [4,14,20]. For this section, we primarily chose publications that used network data for their evaluation, since this is also the main type of data we focused on using during our own evaluation and which benchmarked their approach using the UNSW-NB15 dataset [15] to improve comparability with our research.

Nixon et al. [17] evaluated the potential of unsupervised autoencoder neural networks with different layer depths as a low-cost alternative for anomaly detection. They used two different approaches to determine the anomaly threshold from data streams and evaluated their approach on the KDD'99 and UNSW-NB15 datasets. For UNSW-NB15 they reported an accuracy of 0.791 and a F1 score of 0.703. As a benchmark, they compared their results to Naïve Bayes and Hoeffding Adaptive Tree approaches, which achieved an accuracy of 0.929 (NB) and a F1 score of 0.832 (HAT) at a much higher computational cost.

Tama et al. [1] proposed a two-stage meta classifier with a hybrid feature selection beforehand and two meta classifiers, i.e., Rotation Forest and Bagging. They evaluated their contribution using the suggested UNSW-NB15$_{test}$ split from the main dataset and achieved the best results using 19 features, including *service* and *state*. They reported an accuracy value of 0.85797, false positive rate (FPR) of 0.117 and precision/recall of 0.88/0.868 at best.

Tufan et al. [23] created an anomaly-based flow-level IDS pipeline by using an ensemble learning model approach, consisting of two machine learning algorithms, namely a base classifier using Naïve Bayes, a k-nearest neighbors algorithm, logistic regression, and a SVM into a convolutional neural network (CNN), as a case study specifically on probing attack types (e.g., ping sweeping, port scans) and used the reconnaissance attack category from the UNSW-NB15 dataset as a benchmark. They introduced a feature selection workflow and with a smaller set of 10 features, including *dsport*, *state* and *service*, they reported an impressive F1 score of 0.9902 and an area under curve (AUC) value of 0.9990 in their results section for this attack type.

Gharaee et al. [7] used an SVM approach for anomaly detection in combination with a genetic algorithm for feature selection. They evaluated their algorithm on the KDD'99 and UNSW-NB15 datasets for different attack types. In a similar manner Chowdhury et al. [5] combined SVM-based anomaly detection with simulated annealing to select three random features. They evaluated their algorithm on the UNSW-NB15 dataset, achieving an accuracy of 0.9876, a FPR of 0.0009, and a false negative rate of 0.0115. Zhang et al. [26] used a one-class SVM (OSVM) approach, which trains an anomaly detection model with normal data only. They use the KDD'99 dataset for evaluation, making their results not directly comparable to ours.

Khan et al. [11] conducted a study in which five different supervised ML classifiers have been benchmarked using the UNSW-NB15 dataset, namely Decision Tree, a Random Forest classifier, a Gaussian Naïve Bayes classifier, an AdaBoost classifier and a Gradient Boost classifier. They achieved their best results using the Random Forest approach and reported an accuracy of 0.986 and a F1 score of 0.983. Prior to this, a feature extraction was carried out, but it was not elucidated which features were ultimately selected in the process.

3 Concept

In this chapter, we describe both how we use **One-class SVMs** to find attacks, and how the **Cellwise Estimator** works.

We start with a general overview. The basic setting in both approaches is that we use training data that contains only normal (i.e. attack-free) flows from the target network. From this training data, we derive a model that describes the normal operation of the network. Using this model, we score new traffic during the inference phase. The score expresses how well the new traffic matches the normality model. In the evaluation, we figure out how well the scores (i.e. normality of traffic) reflect whether the traffic contains attacks or not.

This is a fundamentally different approach compared to the typical machine learning approach of training a classifier. In this approach, the classifier sees examples for each type of attack during training and tries to identify similar patterns later.

An important assumption underlying this approach is that deviations from the learned normal behavior of the network will, at least to some part, be related to attacks. This implies that the attack-free part of the network data is in some form regular, i.e. that the traffic follows a common pattern, at least to some amount. As such, the method might work even better in industrial networks where machines communicate in a regular fashion compared to office networks where humans communicate.

To train both the OSVM and the CE, *hyperparameters* need to be configured. These parameters influence exact behavior and thus the detection capabilities. To validate hyperparameter settings, labeled validation data is required. In consequence, this means that our requirements are not completely fulfilled. However, this is an intrinsic problem of all anomaly-based approaches. An interesting approach is to adapt the hyperparameters during operation as suggested by [17] for the threshold. The CE has a slight benefit as we obtained already good results with standard settings, while a grid search was necessary for the OSVM to work properly.

3.1   One-Class SVM

OSVMs are a special kind of SVMs that are trained on normal-only records. They model an area in the data space where normal records reside. The inference data is scored based on its distance to the normal area in the data space [26].

As SVMs can only handle numeric data, we need to convert all categorical columns of the data to numeric columns. We use one-hot encoding to accomplish this, however, some columns like port numbers have high cardinality leading to high-dimensional data. As a remedy, in the case of ports, we only use the well-known ports and convert the other ports (>1024) to frequency groups depending on how often the port occurs in the training data.

We also tested Isolation Forests [13] as an alternative, however OSVMs yielded superior results thus we only include OSVMs in the paper due to lack of space.

3.2   Cellwise Estimator

In this section, we describe the cellwise estimator. For more details please refer to its original proposal in [9]. However, the original proposal does not include the concept of default cells, that proved to be very important in the evaluation.

The base idea is to use various aggregation levels in an automated fashion to model network traffic. Data cubes [8] and Online Analytical Processing (OLAP) [12] offer an appropriate model. In this terminology, **dimensions** are categorical attributes that define aggregation levels, like IP address, port, protocol etc., and **metrics** are continuous attributes that are aggregated, e.g. summed up, like a connection count or the sum of the transferred data amount in bytes.

Assume we have four dimensions *srcip, destip, destport*, and *protocol*. Then, a **cell** is described by a four-tuple containing one entry for each dimension: either a specific value for this dimension, or a star $*$ meaning *any*. Thus the cell (1.2.3.4, $*$, 443, tcp) contains all tcp traffic on port 443 originating from IP 1.2.3.4 to any destination host. The set of all cells is called a **cube**.

The time dimension is handled by chopping the data into time slices of a configurable size, e.g. 20 min or one hour. During training, for each cell a time series is collected with one value per time slice. During inference, each time slice is converted to a data cube and evaluated as soon as it is complete, i.e. during operation, new alerts are generated for each time slice independently.

For each cell, we store one or more models that describe the normal traffic pattern in this cell. Here, various classes of models (Gaussian, time series, etc.) are possible in general. A Gaussian model for the cell (1.2.3.4, $*$, 443, tcp) could for example describe the normal amount of traffic in the cell during a defined time period.

Three problems have to be solved. Firstly, even with a moderate number of dimensions, the number of possible cells is quite large; in general, we have $\prod_{i=1}^{N}(|A_i| + 1)$ possible cells where N is the number of dimensions and $|A_i|$ is the cardinality of dimension i (e.g., the number of different IP addresses). Secondly, many of the more specific cells will have no or only very sporadic data making it difficult to find a robust model. Thirdly, we do not know how to score traffic that does not match an existing model.

To solve these problems, we first define an **iceberg condition** that the training data for a cell must meet for the cell to be included in the final model. In our experiments, we only use cells where traffic occurs regularly, excluding all sporadic patterns. Assume that host 1.2.3.4 communicates with 5.6.7.8 regularly using tcp port 443 (https). Thus a cell (1.2.3.4, 5.6.7.8, 443, tcp) is built. There is no other host that 1.2.3.4 contacts via 443/tcp regulary, i.e. no other cell (1.2.3.4, *target*, 443, tcp) is build for other target IP addresses. Note that there are efficient algorithms to find all cells fulfilling an iceberg condition [25]. The set of all iceberg cells is called an **iceberg cube**.

Continuing the example, assume that during the inference phase, there is traffic from 1.2.3.4 to 3.4.5.6 via 443/tcp. This traffic would only show up in aggregated cells like (1.2.3.4, *, 443, tcp), where it might not be detected. Thus the question is: is it normal for host 1.2.3.4 to contact other hosts apart of 5.6.7.8 via 443/tcp? To answer this, we introduce **default cells**. In this case the default cell is (1.2.3.4, ?, 443, tcp). During training, all traffic from 1.2.3.4 via 443/tcp that does not match an iceberg cell is collected. Finally, a model for this traffic is build. This means that we can score how unusual the contact to 3.4.5.6 is, depending on whether host 1.2.3.4 has contacted other hosts apart of 5.6.7.8 in the past. Note that no iceberg condition is applied to default cells. Instead, the set of default cells is derived from the iceberg. Thus a default cell can also be an empty cell during training, making new traffic occurring in this cell during inference very suspicious. To summarize, the default cell (1.2.3.4, ?, 443, tcp) contains all data from the cell (1.2.3.4, *, 443, tcp) that is not in a specific cell (1.2.3.4, *ip*, 443, tcp) of the iceberg.

Default cells enable the model to differentiate better between entities that have regular communication patters with only a few targets (typically servers, production systems), and entities that have many spontaneous connections like human-operated office PCs. Furthermore, the combinatorial approach of the cells makes it possible to perform this differentiation on various levels, i.e. to model that the communication patterns of some host on port 443 are very noisy, while the patterns on port 22 (ssh) are quite regular, as the user browses various different web-pages while contacting only a single ssh server. In the consequence, browsing a new web page would not trigger an alert, while contacting a new ssh server would do so.

Overall, the training process runs through the steps of the `train_ce()` function shown in Listing 1.1. First, all cells in the iceberg cube are computed using a configurable condition. From the iceberg cube cells, the default cells are derived. The union of the iceberg cells and the default cells is the set of all cells that we are going to compute models for. Then, all training records are assigned to each matching cell. Having collected the data for each cell, we are ready to build a statistical model for each cell. The model cube returned only contains the model parameters and no training records any more.

Listing 1.1. Training and Inference Procedures of the CE.

```
1  FUNCTION train_ce(train_data, iceberg_cond):
2      iceberg_cube := build_iceberg(train_data, iceberg_cond)
3      default_cube := create_default_cells(iceberg_cells)
4      model_cube := iceberg_cube UNION default_cube
5      assign_records_to_cells(model_cube, train_data)
6      FOR EACH cell IN model_cube:
7          build_models(cell)
8      RETURN model_cube
9
10 FUNCTION inference_ce(model_cube, inference_data, threshold):
11     assign_records_to_cells(model_cube, inference_data)
12     anomalies := list()
13     FOR EACH cell IN model_cube:
14         evaluate_model(cell)
15         IF score(cell) > threshold:
16             anomalies.append(cell)
17     anomaly_groups := group_anomalies(anomalies)
18     RETURN anomaly_groups
```

The inference phase is described in the `inference_ce()` function. It starts by assigning the inference data to the cells. Using the statistical models, an anomaly score is calculated for each cell separately that tells us how unusual the data in this cell is. A configurable threshold then determines whether the score is large enough to qualify as an anomaly. All anomaly cells are collected.

In a final phase, the anomaly cells are grouped into anomaly groups. This is necessary as an anomaly might be visible in multiple cells due to the hierarchical nature of the cube data. As an example, large amounts of connections towards host 1.2.3.4 on port 443 *might* also show up as anomalies in cells (*, 1.2.3.4, 443, tcp), (*, 1.2.3.4, *, tcp), and (*, 1.2.3.4, *, *). On one hand, this is a kind of redundancy; on the other hand, different cells might give different hints to the analyst. As a solution, we do not remove redundant cells but rather bundle them as **anomaly groups** using the most generic cell as root. In the example, (*, 1.2.3.4, *, *) is the root for the group. For each anomaly in the group, text is generated that describes the cell, the cell model and explains why the cell data is considered unusual. Such texts look like this:

```
Anomaly from a rare source ip to destination port 143.
A rare value for 'source ip' in this context is any value except:
    '59.166.0.0', '59.166.0.1', [...]
The following anomalies were found:
- Connection count (value 39) is not within 0.00 +- 0.01 * 4.
```

This indicates that data has been found in a default cell that has been empty during training. The threshold (configurable) is four times the standard deviation of the Gaussian distribution. For constant values, we set the standard deviation to 0.01 to avoid division by zero errors. A GUI could provide a drill through feature to show the data underlying each cell and each cell model, i.e. as a time series.

Finally, we note that the CE approach is generic: it could also be applied to anomaly detection in other domains as long as there are suitable dimensions in the data to define aggregation levels. However, in this paper, we focus on the IDS domain.

3.3   Comparison and Output

The One-class SVM approach and the CE are quite different approaches. The base granularity of network data is a flow record (a single connection). An OSVM builds a model that looks at each record individually and assigns it a score. In contrast, we group the records to different aggregation levels and compare the aggregated values to models built during training for the same aggregation levels. This means that the output is on a different scale: individual connections vs. groups of connections. This does not exclude that we cannot issue alerts about individual connections, in cases that there is only a single connection in a cell, e.g. in a default cell that is supposed to be empty (no traffic expected). However, connections that belong together are grouped in a natural way and thus reduce the overall number of alerts. We will show the result of this reduction in the evaluation.

4   Evaluation

In this section we present evaluation results of the CE as well as other detection approaches. We have tested the CE with the following publicly available datasets: UNSW-NB15 [15], CICIDS2017 [19], TON IoT [16]. Even though each of these datasets has its own issues, those are the best datasets publicly available to our knowledge. Due to space constraints, we cannot present all evaluation results here, hence we will focus on the most representative examples.

4.1   Effectiveness of CE

In this subsection we will discuss the quality of the attack detection of our CE approach on the mentioned datasets.

Note that the CE has a large set of hyper-parameters, such as time slice size, iceberg conditions, used cell types, cell aggregation function as well as cell model specific parameters, only the most influential of which we can discuss here due to space limitations. Our experiments showed that different iceberg conditions do not have a big impact on the results and will thus not be analyzed further. In addition, when changing the size of the time slices used during training and inference, we did observe changes in detection quality, but no general pattern. Due to this non-uniform behaviour we will use time slices of 20 min for the remainder of this work to make the results comparable. Note that this behavior of the hyper-parameters is considered specific for the data sets used in this paper.

When applying the CE to other data and/or domains, these parameters are likely relevant. This requires further investigation (cf. Sect. 5.2).

We use the well-known receiver operating characteristic (ROC) curves displaying the behavior of the true positive rate (TPR) of the algorithm as a function of the FPR along with the AUC as quality measure. A random classifier achieves a straight line from (0,0) to (1,1) and thus an AUC of 0.5 whereas a perfect classifier has an AUC of 1.0.

For the UNSW-NB15 dataset, we used the fields *srcip*, *dstip*, *dsport*, *proto*, *state* in our tests. The CICIDS17 dataset has a lot more numerical features overall, but is missing the *state* field, so we tested the CE on *srcip*, *sport*, *dstip*, *dsport* and *proto*. The network part of the TON IoT dataset was also missing the *state* field while having a *service* field, so we tested the CE on the fields *srcip*, *sport*, *dstip*, *dsport*, *proto* and *service*. We only use a single count metric that indicated the number of flows in the current aggregation. Using this metric, a Gaussian model is build for each cell.

We have focused our feature selection on those features which facilitate User and Entity Behavior Analysis (UEBA) [10, Req. 2] and which are processable by our prototype. This set of features differs from the sets other approaches tend to use, since some of them use automated feature selection for their evaluation and most of their choices do not contain standard flow identifying characteristics like *srcip, sport, dstip* or *dsport*, thereby forfeiting the advantages of UEBA.

For the UNSW-NB15 dataset, we used a cross-validation approach, with data from all but one hour used for training and data from the remaining hour for testing. For this, we chose a subset of the dataset from 2:00 until 12:00 on day 2, as this range contains continuous data without gaps. That means that e.g. results for 3 to 4 have been obtained by using training day 2 from hour 2 to 3 and 4 to 12 and testing on data from hour 3 to 4. According to our approach, attacks are removed from the training part of the data. Figure 1 shows the corresponding ROC curves as mean of the cross-validation iterations. Note that here the AUC is computed based on flows by adding up scores from all cells containing the flow. This is done in order to be able to compare results to other approaches later, even though the computation works on cells as explained in Sect. 3.

The approach without default cells (left side) results in bad detection quality, as we obtain an AUC of only 0.62. However, the AUC is much higher if we include default cells to detect attacks, making them a key detection feature of the CE. With a mean AUC of 0.98, we can conclude that the CE can detect attacks well using default cells.

The CICIDS17 dataset includes five days of network traffic between a Monday and a Friday, with a different set of simulated attacks on each day, except Monday. Instead, this day serves as a reference with benign traffic only, so we chose to train the model on this day and to test on the other ones without cross-validation. Training and testing happened between 1 am and 1 pm.

Taking a look at overall ROC curves with 292906 attack flows and 2511658 benign flows, we achieved a maximum AUC value of 0.995. However, if we take

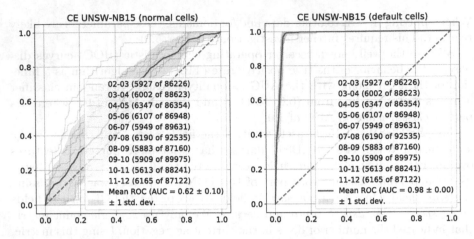

Fig. 1. UNSW overall result for normal and default cells.

a closer look onto isolated AUC values for different types of simulated attacks, we can observe rather different values for individual attacks.

The left part of Fig. 2 shows exemplary curves for the attack type of fuzzers in the UNSW dataset. This attack type produces a large number of flows towards a target host or socket (the respective flow counts are also shown in Fig. 2). This graph shows good detection capabilities of the CE with a mean AUC of 0.97. For other attack types in this dataset the AUC values are similar, irrespective of the number of flows belonging to the attack. This behavior can not be observed in the results on the CICIDS dataset, shown in the right part of Fig. 2. There we can see that the detection capabilities differ for different types of attacks. In particular the Heartbleed attack consisting of only very few flows has a very low AUC. In general, the CE struggles to detect attacks with small flow numbers as those likely go unnoticed even with default cells. For the UNSW dataset this has not been the case, probably because those few flows have been between previously unseen endpoints, so that they have been detected as abnormal.

Reporting too many anomaly cells could cause resource problems when applying the CE in a SOC. Thus, it would be desirable to report as few anomaly cells as possible while still covering the largest possible number of attacks. To assess how well anomaly cells and attack flows overlap we will use two measures, namely:

– Recall as percentage of attack flows that occur in at least one cell with an anomaly score
– Precision as percentage of the anomaly cells containing an attack

In the left part of Fig. 3, the precision and recall values are displayed for different thresholds. The threshold value determines the anomaly score above which a cell is considered an anomaly. These scores are now computed on cell- not on flow-level in line with the concept of the CE. Naturally, if we raise this threshold we miss some of the attack flows as they are only contained in cells with

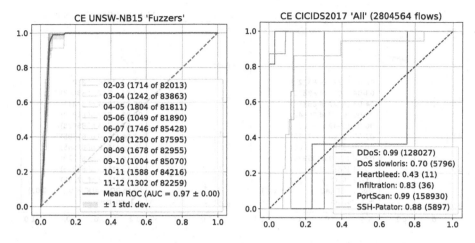

Fig. 2. UNSW results for attack type Fuzzers and CICIDS results for all attack types

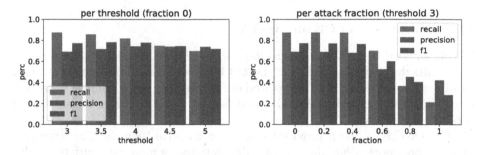

Fig. 3. Detailed analysis of anomaly cell quality and importance

small anomaly score, reducing the recall. On the other hand, the graph shows that the precision increases with a higher threshold as cells are more likely to contain an attack, if the anomaly score is larger.

Another important measure is *how interesting* a cell containing an attack is, meaning how many of the flows in an anomaly cell are actually attack flows. Cells with few number of attack flows may lead to huge workload in an SOC while only addressing very few relevant flows. So, ideally the fraction of attack flows in the anomaly cells should be high. As conclusion from above (F1-measure is almost constant for different thresholds), it makes sense to continue with the smallest threshold tested (i.e. 3) focusing on higher recall and analyze the precision and recall values as a function of the fraction of attack flows. The result is shown in the right part of Fig. 3. We can see that up to a fraction of 0.4 the precision, recall and F1 scores are somewhat high, then drop and are rather low (below 0.5) from 0.8 onward. This means that about half of the anomaly cells reported consist of at least 50% attack flows. This is a very good result, as those cells capture attacks very well, so treatment of these cells will be an efficient way to treat these attacks.

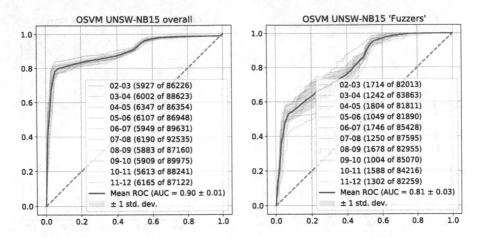

Fig. 4. OSVM results for UNSW using connection meta-data.

4.2   Comparison of CE and OSVM

In this subsection we will compare the results of the CE presented above with the results the OSVM approach (cf. Sect. 3.1). In addition to the actual detection quality assessment, it has to be pointed out again, that the advantage of the CE in general is the explainable model used for the detection, whereas the OSVM acts like a black box.

The OSVM has been provided with more features than the CE, since providing more information about each individual flow is more appropriate for this algorithm. Namely, *sbytes, dbytes, spkts, dpkts, srcip* and *dstip* have been provided as numeric attributes and *dsport_cat, dsport_fcat, sport_cat, sport_fcat* as categorical or frequency categorical attributes from the UNSW dataset. The OSVM has been trained on a sample of 100000 flows due to its very high training time, but results have been similar to using the full training set.

The results are displayed in Fig. 4. The left graph showing detection capabilities over all types of attacks should be compared with Fig. 1 (right side) for the CE. We can see that the AUC is higher for the CE than for the OSVM, but both perform well. Due to the different approach (CE grouping flows into cells, whereas OSVM classifies individual flows) the graph of the CE shows a more step-wise behavior for some test sets, whereas the OSVM graph is more continuous. However, the CE reaches the TPR of 1.0 much earlier which is important for attack detection as detecting all attacks is desirable. This should come at the smallest possible false positive rate to avoid costly unnecessary work in the SOC. A positive aspect of the OSVM is the small variance of the detection quality with regard to the actual time slot under investigation, which has only been achieved in the CE by using default cells.

As for the CE we have also examined the behavior of the OSVM over different types of attacks. The right graph in Fig. 4 shows the curve for the fuzzers attack type which had slightly lower detection quality than average for the CE (cf. left

Table 1. Number of alerts generated from detection for methods (per hour)

Method	Overall	Alerts	False	Alerts
	μ	σ	μ	σ
CE	336	50	107	53
OSVM	12084	3745	7282	3735

part of Fig. 2). The graph shows that the sub-par behavior is the same for the OSVM and actually the difference in the detection quality is much larger here than it is overall between CE and OSVM (fuzzers: AUC 0.81 vs. 0.97, overall: 0.90 vs. 0.98). We can conclude that the detection of fuzzers seems to be difficult in general and this is not a specific behavior of the CE. Similarly to the overall evaluation, we see again that the OSVM's curve is more delicate, yet reaches the TPR much later than that of the CE. For this attack type there is also a much larger variation over the different testing intervals than for the OSVM overall. This is comparable to the variation of the CE. In general, the standard deviation is larger for the OSVM, e. g. on the attack type Analysis with very small number of flows per attack the AUC result has been 0.90 with a standard deviation of 0.17. This again emphasizes the higher difficulty of detecting attacks with small numbers of flows.

Another big advantage of the CE can be inferred from Table 1, namely the number of generated alerts is significantly lower for the CE than for the OSVM. The total number of alerts is about 3% and the number of false alerts about 1.5% of those in the OSVM. This is very important from a practical perspective as each alert requires the attention of people in the SOC and the less alerts need attention the less personnel in the SOC is required. The difference is also due to the approach: whereas the OSVM generates an alert for each suspicious flow, the CE only generates an alert for a significant number of flows together that are reflected in a single cube cell.

In summary, we can conclude that the CE has a detection quality that is even better than the OSVM, while providing the additional advantage of an explainable detection model as opposed to a black box and in addition reducing the number of alerts requiring attention from the SOC.

4.3 Comparison to Other IDS

We have also experimented with the well-known IDS Suricata[1] which is rule-based, i.e. requires detection rules for the attacks and will thus only detect previously known attacks. The detection quality depends significantly on the ruleset fed into Suricata. In order to compare the results to our CE, which does not require rules for known attacks, we have used Suricata on the UNSW-NB15 dataset with the publicly available Proofpoint Emerging Threats open rule set[2].

---

[1] https://suricata.io/.

[2] https://rules.emergingthreats.net/.

Table 2. Results for Suricata and UNSW-NB15 (day 2)

Severity	Alerts	Recall	Prec	FPR
≤ 1	779	0.01	0.95	0.00
≤ 2	2,211	0.03	0.94	0.00
≤ 3	2,729	0.04	0.94	0.00
Anomalies	38,844	0.03	0.04	0.04

Suricata rules refer to a variable HOME_NET, which has to be set. For the UNSW-NB15, we used the following subnets: 192.168.0.0/16, 10.40.0.0/16, 59.166.0.0/16, 149.171.126.0/24; cf. the network diagram in [15].

Representative results are shown in Table 2. Suricata classifies alerts by severity with 1 being most important, the number of alerts shown is summated. The results show a very high precision of the generated alerts and almost no false positives. Thus, the alerts generated by Suricata are always relevant.

The issue with the generated alerts in Suricata as opposed to detections by CE and OSVM is the extremely low recall. Only an extremely small fraction of potential attacks are detected and the problem is worse the higher the severity is selected. This leads to f1-measures around 0.02 (severity 1) to 0.07 (severity 3) which are significantly lower than the values of the CE shown in Fig. 3.

Suricata additionally detects anomalies which represent unexpected content in packet structure or protocol and might be considered as potential attacks to increase the recall. However, as shown in Table 2, there is a very high number of anomalies, but those do not really help in detecting attacks as can be seen from both low precision and recall. Even though the FPR is still low the ratio of undetected attacks is still very high. In summary, Suricata with the given ruleset issues valuable high-precision alerts but misses most of the attacks. Thus it needs to be complemented with an anomaly-based system like the CE.

5   Conclusion

In this section, our results are summarized and and an outlook on future work is given.

5.1   Summary

This paper introduces two novel approaches to detecting attacks in network traffic that operate on a normal behavior model of the network. The advantage of such approaches is that any kind of attack, even if not seen previously, can be detected as long as it has an impact on the traffic in a network which is likely true for almost any relevant attack. The approach to use a one-class support vector machine has shown to provide good detection capabilities, however at the expense of generating a high number of alerts, since it reports every suspicious network flow. Also, it does not provide reasoning as to why this flow is suspicious.

The main contribution of this paper is the second approach using a Cell-wise Estimator described in Sect. 3. As has been shown in Sect. 4 the detection capabilities of the CE are even better than the OSVM, achieving an AUC value of 0.98 over all attack types in the UNSW-NB15 dataset. In addition, the CE aggregates suspicious flows into cells, resulting in a significantly lower number of alerts (roughly 1/50 of the OSVM). Moreover, the cells contain information about the reason for flagging them as suspicious, significantly simplifying the work of the security analyst. Finally, the training as well as the analysis time has been significantly lower for the CE when compared to the OSVM (training about 1/30 of the time, analysis 1/3).

The detection quality of both approaches varies over different kinds of attacks, however for all kinds it is much better than that of widely used IDSs such as Suricata. Even though not all hyper-parameters of the CE have yet been completely optimized, the system at the current state is already very powerful.

5.2 Future Work

Even given the promising results presented above, there is a lot of work remaining. As has been explained, the optimization of all hyper-parameters of the CE approach is not yet complete. In particular, we had experiments where the detection quality varied over different sizes of time slices used to create the model. There may be a relation to the actual length of an attack, as an attack spanning over a full time slice might be considered normal behavior. On the other hand large time slices might lead to short attacks staying unnoticed because a cell's anomaly score might remain below the threshold. This relationship has to be analyzed further to be able to optimize this hyper-parameter. Also, using other aggregation functions to compute the scores of a cell beyond the currently used count, as well as cell models of higher complexity than the Gaussian models, is a promising route for future research.

For the used sample datasets as well as in practical usage scenarios feature engineering could be improved in the future. Other research shows that selecting a different set of features for a specific dataset (e.g. [21] for the CICIDS) might also improve the correctness of the prediction scores for other types of attacks. This could be applied here as well. Also, for a practical deployment, general rules on how to determine the relevant features to train the model need to be developed. The need to train the model for a specific network is still there and seems impossible to overcome.

A general issue with the sample datasets available is that the number of attacks is potentially higher than in real-world situations. Thus, a more realistic evaluation scenario would be to add individual attacks to a clean normal behavior dataset and then determine the detection capabilities. However, information about which flow belongs to which attack would be required, which is currently not available for the sample datasets.

Building a model might also benefit from larger training time ranges than have been available in the sample datasets used. The longer the training, the more precise the model will become, potentially resulting in even better detection. On the other hand, it is important that the data used to learn the normal behavior consists of benign data only. This is more difficult to achieve, the longer the training period is in real circumstances.

Although in this paper we have used default cells only in the classification of network anomalies, we believe that both the method and the approach of using default cells are transferable to other areas of classification as well.

References

1. Adhi Tama, B., Comuzzi, M., Rhee, K.H.: TSE-IDS: a two-stage classifier ensemble for intelligent anomaly-based intrusion detection system. IEEE Access 7, 1–10 (2019). https://doi.org/10.1109/ACCESS.2019.2928048
2. Akinrolabu, O., Agrafiotis, I., Erola, A.: The challenge of detecting sophisticated attacks: Insights from SOC analysts. In: Proceedings of the 13th International Conference on Availability, Reliability and Security. ARES 2018, ACM, New York, NY, USA (2018). https://doi.org/10.1145/3230833.3233280
3. Al-Riyami, S., Coenen, F., Lisitsa, A.: A re-evaluation of intrusion detection accuracy: Alternative evaluation strategy. In: Proceedings of the 2018 ACM SIGSAC Conference on Computer and Communications Security, CCS 2018, pp. 2195–2197. ACM, New York, NY, USA (2018). https://doi.org/10.1145/3243734.3278490
4. Buczak, A.L., Guven, E.: A survey of data mining and machine learning methods for cyber security intrusion detection. IEEE Commun. Surv. Tut. 18(2), 1153–1176 (2016). https://doi.org/10.1109/COMST.2015.2494502
5. Chowdhury, M.N., Ferens, K., Ferens, M.: Network intrusion detection using machine learning. In: Proceedings of International Conference on Security Management (SAM), pp. 1–7 (2016)
6. Faraj, O., Megías, D., Ahmad, A.M., Garcia-Alfaro, J.: Taxonomy and challenges in machine learning-based approaches to detect attacks in the internet of things. In: Proceedings of the 15th International Conference on Availability, Reliability and Security. ARES 2020, ACM, New York, NY, USA (2020). https://doi.org/10.1145/3407023.3407048
7. Gharaee, H., Hosseinvand, H.: A new feature selection IDS based on genetic algorithm and SVM. In: 2016 8th International Symposium on Telecommunications (IST), pp. 139–144 (2016). https://doi.org/10.1109/ISTEL.2016.7881798
8. Gray, J., et al.: Data cube: a relational aggregation operator generalizing group-by, cross-tab, and sub-totals. Data Mining Knowl. Disc. 1(1), 29–53 (1997). https://link.springer.com/article/10.1023/A:1009726021843
9. Heine, F.: Outlier detection in data streams using OLAP cubes. In: Kirikova, M., et al. (eds.) ADBIS 2017. CCIS, vol. 767, pp. 29–36. Springer, Cham (2017). https://doi.org/10.1007/978-3-319-67162-8_4
10. Heine, F., Laue, T., Kleiner, C.: On the evaluation and deployment of machine learning approaches for intrusion detection. In: 2020 IEEE International Conference on Big Data (Big Data), pp. 4594–4603, December 2020. https://doi.org/10.1109/BigData50022.2020.9378479

11. Khan, S., Sivaraman, E., Honnavalli, P.B.: Performance evaluation of advanced machine learning algorithms for network intrusion detection system. In: Dutta, M., Krishna, C.R., Kumar, R., Kalra, M. (eds.) Proceedings of International Conference on IoT Inclusive Life (ICIIL 2019), NITTTR Chandigarh, India. LNNS, vol. 116, pp. 51–59. Springer, Singapore (2020). https://doi.org/10.1007/978-981-15-3020-3_6

12. Kimball, R., Ross, M.: The Data Warehouse Toolkit: The Complete Guide To Dimensional Modeling. John Wiley & Sons, Hoboken (2011)

13. Liu, F.T., Ting, K.M., Zhou, Z.H.: Isolation-based anomaly detection. ACM Trans. Knowl. Disc. Data **6**(1), 1–39 (2012). https://doi.org/10.1145/2133360.2133363

14. Mishra, P., Varadharajan, V., Tupakula, U., Pilli, E.S.: A detailed investigation and analysis of using machine learning techniques for intrusion detection. IEEE Commun. Surv. Tut. **21**(1), 686–728 (2019). https://doi.org/10.1109/COMST.2018.2847722

15. Moustafa, N., Slay, J.: UNSW-NB15: a comprehensive data set for network intrusion detection systems. In: 2015 Military Communications and Information Systems Conference, pp. 1–6, November 2015. https://doi.org/10.1109/MilCIS.2015.7348942

16. Moustafa, N.: A new distributed architecture for evaluating AI-based security systems at the edge: network TON_IoT datasets. Sustain. Cities Soc. **72**, 102994 (2021). https://doi.org/10.1016/j.scs.2021.102994

17. Nixon, C., Sedky, M., Hassan, M.: Autoencoders: a low cost anomaly detection method for computer network data streams. In: Proceedings of the 2020 4th International Conference on Cloud and Big Data Computing, pp. 58–62, August 2020. https://doi.org/10.1145/3416921.3416937

18. Schölkopf, B., Platt, J.C., Shawe-Taylor, J.C., Smola, A.J., Williamson, R.C.: Estimating the support of a high-dimensional distribution. Neural Comput. **13**(7), 1443–1471 (2001). https://doi.org/10.1162/089976601750264965

19. Sharafaldin, I., Lashkari, A.H., Ghorbani, A.A.: Toward generating a new intrusion detection dataset and intrusion traffic characterization. In: ICISSP, pp. 108–116 (2018). https://doi.org/10.5220/0006639801080116

20. Singh, G., Khare, N.: A survey of intrusion detection from the perspective of intrusion datasets and machine learning techniques. Int. J. Comput. App. 1–11 (2021). https://doi.org/10.1080/1206212X.2021.1885150

21. Singh Panwar, S., Raiwani, Y.P., Singh Panwar, L.: Evaluation of network intrusion detection with features selection and machine learning algorithms on CICIDS-2017 dataset. In: International Conference on Advances in Engineering Science Management and Technology (ICAESMT) (2019). https://doi.org/10.2139/ssrn.3394103

22. Strom, B.E., Applebaum, A., Miller, D.P., Nickels, K.C., Pennington, A.G., Thomas, C.B.: Mitre attack®: Design and philosophy (2020). https://attack.mitre.org/docs/ATTACK_Design_and_Philosophy_March_2020.pdf

23. Tufan, E., Tezcan, C., Acarturk, C.: Anomaly-based intrusion detection by machine learning: a case study on probing attacks to an institutional network. IEEE Access. **9**, 50078–50092 (2021). https://doi.org/10.1109/ACCESS.2021.3068961

24. Viganò, L., Magazzeni, D.: Explainable security. In: 2020 IEEE European Symposium on Security and Privacy Workshops (EuroS PW), pp. 293–300 (2020). https://doi.org/10.1109/EuroSPW51379.2020.00045

25. Xin, D., Han, J., Li, X., Wah, B.W.: Star-cubing: computing iceberg cubes by top-down and bottom-up integration. In: Freytag, J.C., Lockemann, P., Abiteboul, S., Carey, M., Selinger, P., Heuer, A. (eds.) Proceedings 2003 VLDB Conference, pp. 476–487. Morgan Kaufmann, San Francisco, January 2003
26. Zhang, M., Xu, B., Gong, J.: An anomaly detection model based on one-class SVM to detect network intrusions. In: 2015 11th International Conference on Mobile Ad-hoc and Sensor Networks (MSN), pp. 102–107 (2015). https://doi.org/10.1109/MSN.2015.40

A Modular Runtime Enforcement Model Using Multi-traces

Rania Taleb, Sylvain Hallé[(✉)], and Raphaël Khoury

Laboratoire d'informatique formelle,
University of Quebec at Chicoutimi, Saguenay, Canada
shalle@acm.org

Abstract. Runtime enforcement seeks to provide a valid replacement to any misbehaving sequence of events of a running system so that the correct sequence complies with a user-defined security policy. However, depending on the capabilities of the enforcement mechanism, multiple possible replacement sequences may be available, and the current literature is silent on the question of how to choose the optimal one. In this paper, we propose a new model of enforcement monitors, that allows the comparison between multiple alternative corrective enforcement actions and the selection of the optimal one, with respect to an objective user-defined gradation, separate from the security policy. These concepts are implemented using the event stream processor BeepBeep and a use case is presented. Experimental evaluation shows that our proposed framework can dynamically select enforcement actions at runtime, without the need to manually define an enforcement monitor.

1 Introduction

Runtime enforcement is the process of monitoring a program during its execution, and intervening as needed to ensure compliance with a user-specified security policy [13]. The process differs from runtime *verification* in that the monitor is expected to provide a valid replacement for any misbehaving trace, rather than simply signal a violation. In recent years, the growing presence of smart contracts has sparked a renewed interest in runtime enforcement [8]; indeed, since smart contracts cannot be modified after deployment, runtime enforcement is the only remedial mechanism available to handle a deviation from the expected behavior.

The notion of enforcement is commonly defined in terms of two properties: *soundness* and *transparency* [19,25]. Soundness imposes that the output of the monitor must respect the underlying security policy; on its side, transparency states that if the original security policy was already valid, then the replacement sequence must be equivalent, with respect to some equivalence relation. In addition, Khoury *et al.* suggested that the transformations performed on invalid traces also be bounded by an equivalence relation or a preorder [22]. Indeed, one would rarely accept a security enforcement mechanism that corrects an invalid trace by replacing it with a completely unrelated valid trace. This line of research

© Springer Nature Switzerland AG 2022
E. Aïmeur et al. (Eds.): FPS 2021, LNCS 13291, pp. 283–302, 2022.
https://doi.org/10.1007/978-3-031-08147-7_19

has also stressed the need for a process that selects the optimal corrective action, from a set of possible alternatives that are available to the monitor.

Many formal models of enforcement have been proposed in the past to capture the behavior of monitors [2,19,20,23,25]. In most of them, a single mathematical structure (usually an automaton or some other type of finite state machine) is tasked with the entirety of the enforcement process: reading the input, transforming it through a process of substitutions, insertions, deletions and/or truncations, and ensuring compliance of the resulting output trace with respect to both soundness and transparency. As a consequence, elaborate proofs are often required to ensure that the output of the monitor is indeed sound and transparent (see e.g. [22]).

The present paper offers a different take on the problem, and introduces a model of runtime enforcement composed of three separate stages. The first stage transforms events of an (invalid) input trace into a set of traces, obtained by applying each possible modification one is allowed to apply. The second stage filters this set to keep only the traces that do not violate a specified security policy, while the third stage ranks the remaining traces based on an objective gradation we term the *enforcement preorder*, and picks the highest-scoring trace as its output.

This design provides a high level of modularity. First, the expression of the allowed modifications to the trace, the security policy itself and the enforcement preorder can all be expressed independently, using a different formal notation if need be. Second, the model does not require a specific enforcement monitor to be manually synthesized for each policy to enforce: corrective actions are computed, selected and applied dynamically. Finally, the model does not impose a single valid output, and rather allows multiple corrective actions to be compared against the enforcement preorder provided by the user.

The remainder of this paper is organized as follows: Sect. 2 provides a more detailed statement of the problem this paper seeks to address, while simultaneously reviewing previous work on the topic. Then, in Sect. 3, we present a new model of monitors for runtime enforcement. Section 4 illustrates the flexibility of the approach with a use case adapted from the literature, and presents a concrete implementation of the principle as an extension of the BeepBeep event stream processing library [18]. Concluding remarks are given in Sect. 5.

2   State of the Art in Runtime Enforcement

Let Σ be a finite or countably infinite set of elements called *events*. The set of all finite sequences from Σ, also called *traces*, is given as Σ^*. Given a trace $\sigma \in \Sigma^*$, we use the notation $\sigma[i]$ to range over the elements of σ, where i represents the event at the i-th position (the first event is at $i = 0$). The notation $\sigma[i..]$ denotes the remainder of the sequence starting from action $\sigma[i]$ while $\sigma[..i]$ denotes the prefix of σ, up to its i-th position. The concatenation of two sequences σ and σ' is given as $\sigma \cdot \sigma'$. The empty sequence is denoted ϵ, and $\sigma \cdot \epsilon = \epsilon \cdot \sigma = \sigma$. As usual, the notation $\sigma' \preceq \sigma$ denotes that σ' is a prefix of σ.

Given two sets of events Σ_1, and Σ_2, a trace transducer is a function $\tau :$ $\Sigma_1^* \to \Sigma_2^*$, with the added condition that for every $\sigma, \sigma' \in \Sigma^*$, $\sigma' \preceq \tau(\sigma)$ implies $\sigma' \preceq \tau(\sigma \cdot x)$ for every $x \in \Sigma_1$. In other words, a transducer takes as input a sequence of events, and progressively outputs another sequence of events. Given an arbitrary transducer $\tau : \Sigma_1^* \to \Sigma_2^*$ and a sequence $\sigma \in \Sigma_1^*$, we define $\tau_\sigma : \Sigma_1^* \to$ Σ_2^* as $\tau_\sigma(\sigma'') = \tau(\sigma \cdot \sigma'')$. Intuitively, τ_σ is a device abstracting the "internal state" of the transducer τ after ingesting the events from the prefix σ.

Of particular importance in this paper is an enforcement monitor, which is defined as a transducer $\tau : \Sigma^* \to \Sigma^*$. A security policy is a subset $S \subseteq \Sigma^*$ of sequences called the *valid* sequences. An enforcement monitor is said to satisfy the *soundness* condition if $\tau(\sigma) \in S^*$ for every $\sigma \in \Sigma^*$. Additionally, depending on the type of monitor used, it may be subject to other constraints that limit the freedom of the monitor to substitute one sequence for another (a property we call *transparency*).

A long line of research focuses on delineating the set of properties that are (or are not) enforceable by monitors operating under a variety of constraints [2, 22, 25]. A key finding of these works is that the enforcement power of monitors is affected both by the capabilities of the monitor as an enforcement mechanism, and by the license given to the monitor to alter the input sequence (the transparency requirement). A thorough survey of runtime enforcement, stressing its connection to runtime verification, is given by Falcone *et al.* [13].

2.1 Monitor Capabilities

In his initial formulation, Schneider [25] considered a monitor that observes the sequence of events produced by the target program, and reacts by aborting the execution (truncating the execution sequence) upon encountering an event which, if appending that event to the ongoing execution, would violate the security policy. Ligatti *et al.* [2] consider more varied models of monitors, capable of inserting events in the execution stream, of suppressing the occurrence of some events while allowing the remainder of the execution to proceed, or both. Another characterization, in which some events lie beyond the control of the monitor, was proposed by Khoury *et al.* [20].

Extending the available capabilities given to a monitor to alter the input trace greatly extend its enforcement power, but may in counterpart introduce several possible corrective courses of action to restore compliance with a policy. For instance, a trace where a *send* action occurs immediately after a file is being *read* violates a policy stipulating that no information can be sent on the network after reading from a secret file, unless the sending is recorded in a log beforehand. Multiple corrective actions are hence possible: aborting the execution before the *send* action (truncation); inserting an entry in the log (insertion); or suppressing either the *read* or the *send* action (suppression).

In this line of research, the monitor is usually modeled as a finite state machine, which dictates its behavior according to the input action and its current state. Care must be taken to ensure that this FSM correctly enforces the policy and is concordant with the limitations imposed on the monitor's capabilities. Falcone *et al.* [14] showed that a finer automaton model, with explicit store and dump operations, can enforce policies in the *response* class from the safety-progress classification [6]. Their model also lends itself to implementation in a more straightforward manner than previous models.

Another line of research examines how memory constraints affect the enforcement power of monitors. Thali *et al.* [28] study the enforcement power of monitors with bounded memory; Fong *et al.* [15] study a monitor that only records the shallow history (i.e. the unordered set of events) of the execution, while Beauquier *et al.* [3] study the enforcement power of a monitor with finite, but unbounded memory. On their side, the monitors proposed by Ligatti *et al.* and Bielova *et al.* have the capacity to store an unbounded quantity of program events, simulating the execution until it can ascertain that the ongoing execution is valid; however, this course of action may not always be possible in practice. In contrast, Dolzhenko *et al.* propose a model of monitoring in which the monitor is required to react to each action performed by the target program as it occurs [10].

2.2   Transparency Constraints

In the original definition of runtime enforcement reported above, the notion of transparency only imposes that the monitor must maintain the semantics of *valid* sequences [2], which can lead to undesirable behavior. As an example, consider the policy "an opened file is eventually closed", and a sequence in which multiple files are consecutively opened and closed, except the final file which is opened, but not closed. The monitor may correct the situation either by appending a close action at the end of the sequence, or by deleting the opening of the ultimate file and any subsequent file actions (reads and writes). However, the monitor could also enforce the property by removing every well-formed pair of files being opened and closed, or even by adding to the sequence new events not present in the original. This is because the definition of enforcement entails that the monitor can replace an invalid sequence with *any* valid sequence, even one completely unrelated to the original execution.

Transparency constraints refer to mechanisms by which the available enforcement actions of a monitor are restricted according to some requirement. For example, Bielova *et al.* create sub-classes that further constrain the monitor's handling of invalid executions [5]. First is the class of monitors that are limited to delaying the execution of some program events, but may not insert new events into the execution; second, monitors that may only insert the delayed part of the execution on an all-or-nothing basis; third, monitors limited to output some prefix of invalid sequences. They compare the set of properties that are enforceable in each case.

Khoury *et al.* also consider constraints on invalid sequences, and introduce the notion of "gradation" of solutions [22]. Sequences are arranged on a partial order, independent of the security policy being enforced, which makes it possible to state that some corrective actions are preferable to others. For example, a policy stating that every acquired resource must eventually be relinquished could be enforced by forcibly removing the resource from the control of a principal and reallocating it to another user; a monitor could then seeking to allocate the resource equitably between all users, or to minimize the amount of time the resource is idle. In a similar vein, Drábik *et al.* [12] propose to associate each action taken by the monitor with a cost, and to seek optimal cost. Their notion of transparency binds the monitor in its handling of both valid and invalid sequences; it is defined as a function $f : \Sigma^* \to \mathbb{R}$, which the monitor must either maximize or minimize, depending on its formulation. This is the work that is most closely related to the current study.

A few elements stand out in this line of research. First, most approaches impose on the designer to create a finite state machine that enforces the desired policy, and respect any limitations on the capabilities of the monitor (with the exception of [14], which provides a monitor synthesis algorithm). This is a non-trivial task, made even harder when some guarantee of optimal enforcement cost is sought. Furthermore, elaborate proofs are often required to ensure that the enforcement of the property is correct, transparent and optimal. The use of a fixed cost for each program action is limiting. One may prefer a more flexible gradation of solutions, in which the value associated with a solution is more context-specific.

3   A Modular Runtime Enforcement Pipeline

In this paper, we present an alternate model of runtime enforcement with the aim to transform the input sequence in order to ensure both the respect of the security policy as well as provide assurance that the corrected sequence is optimal with respect to a separate transparency requirement. The key idea of this model is to separate the various operations of enforcement into independent computation steps. The high-level schematics of the model are illustrated in Fig. 1. Various transducers are represented as boxes illustrated with different pictograms, depending on their definition. These transducers are organized along a "pipeline" where events flow from left to right. A link between two transducers indicates that the output of the first is given as the input to the second.

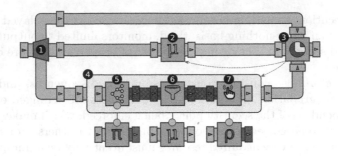

Fig. 1. The stages of the runtime enforcement framework.

An input event sequence is first forked into three separate copies, as represented by box #1 in the figure. One copy is fed to an instance of a transducer μ called the *monitor* (box #2), which determines whether the input trace violates the security policy. Another copy is fed to an enforcement pipeline (box #4), itself decomposed into three phases. First, a single event sequence is turned into multiple event sequences by applying the possible corrective actions produced by a proxy transducer π (#5); this set of sequences is then filtered out so that only sequences satisfying the security policy evaluated by μ are kept (#6). The last phase sends the remaining sequences into a ranking transducer ρ, and picks the one with the highest rank as specified by the enforcement preorder (#7).

The last step of the pipeline is represented by box #3, which is called a *gate*. Based on the output from the monitor (box #2), the gate either outputs elements of the original trace directly (if it is valid), or switches to the output from the enforcement pipeline emitting a corrected sequence. Depending on the actual sequence of events produced by the gate, the internal state of the upstream transducers may need to be forcibly updated; this process, called *checkpointing*, is represented by the backwards red arrows. In the remainder of this section, we describe the stages of this pipeline in more detail.

3.1 Production of Corrected Traces

As discussed earlier, an enforcement monitor can apply a combination of several modifications to an input trace. These possible alteration actions are encapsulated into a conceptual entity that we call a proxy π, corresponding to the first stage of the enforcement pipeline represented by box #4.

Formally, the proxy is a transducer $\pi : \Sigma^* \to (2^{\Sigma^*})^*$. It takes as input the original execution trace and emits for each input event a set of all possible event sequences that can override that event. For example, a proxy that is allowed (but not obligated) to insert an event b before an occurrence of event a could be defined in such a way that for every $\sigma \in \Sigma^*$, $\pi(\sigma \cdot a) = \pi(\sigma) \cdot \{ba, a\}$. Note how the trace obtained from σ is appended by a set of two possible event sequences: one where b is inserted, and one where it is not. Since each "event" of the output is made of a set of sequences, we shall call them *sequence sets*. In this respect, it can be seen as a generalization of an earlier model, which was introduced to handle uncertainty and missing events as sets of possible worlds called "multi-events" [27].

It is important to stress that the proxy only models the enforcement capabilities of a monitor, irrespective of the actual property that is meant to be enforced. That is, if an enforcement monitor is allowed to remove any event from the trace, then the proxy will generate output traces where each event may or may not be present. Stated differently, the goal of the proxy is to generate all the possible modifications of the input trace that are potentially available to enforce a given property. An interesting feature of this model is to enable "non-standard" enforcement capabilities. For instance, classical delete automata can delete any event at any moment. Our abstract definition of a proxy could express a finer-grained capability, such as the fact that only successive b events following an initial b may be deleted (formalized as $\pi(\sigma \cdot bb) = \pi(\sigma) \cdot \{\epsilon, b\}$, and $\pi(\sigma) = \sigma$ otherwise). Since the proxy is not tied to a specific notation and has the leeway to output any sequence set it wishes, it offers a high capacity to precisely circumscribe available enforcement actions.

One can see in Fig. 1 is that the output of transducer π is not fed directly to the second phase of the enforcement pipeline. Rather, its output is post-processed so that traces of sequence sets are converted into a more compact representation called a *prefix tree*; each path in such a tree represents one possible sequence in the set. For the purpose of the enforcement pipeline, a special representation of these trees has been adopted, such that their contents can be transmitted in the form of a sequence of events. Let $\mathcal{V}\langle T \rangle$ denote the set of vectors of elements in T. For a given vector $v \in \mathcal{V}\langle T \rangle$, let $v[i]$ denote the element at position i in that vector. Define $\mathcal{T} = \mathcal{V}\langle \mathcal{V}\langle \Sigma \rangle \rangle$ as the set of prefix tree elements, which are vectors of vectors of events. A prefix tree sequence is a trace $v_0, v_1, \ldots, v_n \in \mathcal{T}^*$, such that $v_0 = [[]]$, and for each $i \in [1, n]$:

$$|v_i| = \sum_{j=0}^{|v_{i-1}|} |v_{i-1}[j]|$$

The intuition behind this condition is that the j-th vector within a prefix tree element corresponds to the list of children attached to the j-th symbol in the prefix tree element that precedes it. As an example, the prefix tree in Fig. 2 corresponds to the sequence of prefix tree elements $[[]], [[a, b, c]], [[a, b], [a, b, c], [a]]$. Note that a symbol may be ϵ, so that a tree of given depth does not necessarily represent sequences of equal lengths. This representation makes it possible for a transducer to output a sequence of elements that represents the progressive construction of a prefix tree representing multiple event sequences. The task of box #5 in Fig. 1 is precisely to receive each sequence set produced from π, and turn it into the appropriate prefix tree element.

3.2   Filtering of Valid Traces

The purpose of this setup becomes apparent
in the next phase of the enforcement pipeline.
The set of event traces generated by the proxy
captures all the possible replacements of the
original input trace. However, some of them
are valid according to a given security policy,
and others are not; one must therefore remove
from the possible sequences produced by the
proxy all those that violate the policy. To this
end, this phase involves a monitor $\mu : \Sigma^* \to$
$\mathbb{B}_4$, where $\mathbb{B}_4 \triangleq \{\top, \top^?, \bot^?, \bot\}$ is the set of 4-
valued verdicts that follows the interpretation

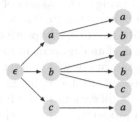

Fig. 2. Graphical representation of
a prefix tree, for the multitrace
$\{aa, ab, ba, bb, bc, ca\}$.

of RV-LTL [1]. In a nutshell, $\bot$ (resp. $\top$) is
emitted for a prefix if the property is irremediably violated (resp. satisfied),
while $\top^?$ indicates that the property is currently satisfied but could be violated
in the future (and dually for $\bot^?$).

The task of filtering invalid traces is represented by box #6 in the pipeline. It
receives as its input a sequence of prefix tree elements, and produces as its output
a modified sequence of prefix tree elements, where any branches corresponding
to prefixes violating the security policy are pruned out. If the monitor produces
$\bot$ anywhere along a path, the node producing this verdict and all its descendants
in the prefix tree are replaced by a placeholder $\Diamond$, indicating that these nodes
should not be considered. If a path ends with the monitor producing $\bot^?$, the last
node of that path is replaced by $\Diamond$. For example, suppose that the security policy
imposes that a trace never start with b. In the tree of Fig. 2, the leftmost b node
must therefore be deleted. In this particular case, the output of the filtering step
would be the sequence of prefix tree elements $[[], [[a, \Diamond, c]], [[a, b], [\Diamond, \Diamond, \Diamond], [a]]$. In
contrast, a property stating that a must eventually be followed by b would result
in the sequence $[[], [[a, b, c]], [[\Diamond, b], [\Diamond, b, c], [a]]$. As a result, all remaining paths
in the prefix tree correspond to prefixes of the trace that result in the monitor
producing either $\top$ or $\top^?$.

Conceptually, it suffices to run a fresh instance of μ on each path of the
induced prefix tree, and to remove a node (as well as all its descendants) as
soon as μ appends $\bot$ to its output. However, the process needs to be done
incrementally, since the contents of the prefix tree are produced one element at
a time. Algorithm 1 shows how this can be done. The algorithm receives a vector
of monitor instances and a prefix tree element of same size. The μ_{σ_i} represent
the state of monitor μ after processing the paths ending in each leaf of the prefix
tree, and the v_i are the children events to be appended to each of these leaves.
For each μ_{σ_i} and v_i, the algorithm iterates over each event x in v_i and adds to
an output vector m the monitor instance $\mu_{\sigma_i \cdot x}$, which is the result of feeding x
to μ_{σ_i}. If the resulting output trace contains $\bot$, this path violates the security
policy and the event x is replaced by $\Diamond$. Otherwise, the event is added to the
output vector, and the process repeats. The end result is a new pair of vectors

m and v, where v is the filtered prefix tree element obtained from $[v_0, \ldots, v_n]$, and m is the vector of monitor states for each leaf of this element.

Algorithm 1. Incremental filtering	**Algorithm 2.** Output trace selection
procedure FILTER($[\mu_{\sigma_1}, \ldots, \mu_{\sigma_n}]$, $[v_0, \ldots, v_n]$)	1: **procedure** UPDATE($[(\rho_{\sigma_1}, s_1), \ldots, (\rho_{\sigma_n}, s_n)]$, $[v_0, \ldots, v_n]$)
$\quad v \leftarrow [\ ], m \leftarrow [\ ]$	2: $\quad m \leftarrow [\ ]$
$\quad$ **for** $i \leftarrow 1, n$ **do**	3: $\quad$ **for** $i \leftarrow 1, n$ **do**
$\quad\quad v' \leftarrow [\ ]$	4: $\quad\quad$ **for** $x \in v_i$ **do**
$\quad\quad$ **for** $x \in v_i$ **do**	5: $\quad\quad\quad s = -\infty$
$\quad\quad\quad$ ADD($m, \mu_{\sigma_i \cdot x}$)	6: $\quad\quad\quad$ **if** $x \neq \Diamond$ **then**
$\quad\quad\quad$ **if** $\mu_{\sigma_i}(x)$ contains $\bot$ **then**	7: $\quad\quad\quad\quad s \leftarrow$ LAST($\rho_{\sigma_1}(x)$)
$\quad\quad\quad\quad$ ADD($v', \Diamond$)	8: $\quad\quad\quad$ ADD($m, \rho_{\sigma_i \cdot x}$)
$\quad\quad\quad$ **else if** $i = n$ **and** $\mu_{\sigma_i}(x)$ ends with $\bot^?$	9: $\quad$ **return** m
$\quad\quad\quad\quad$ ADD($v', \Diamond$) **else** ADD(v, v')	10: **end procedure**
$\quad$ **return** (m, v)	
end procedure	

As with the previous step, note that this operation is independent of the formal notation used to represent the security policy. It is applicable as long as the monitor is a computational entity outputting a sequence of elements in $\mathbb{B}_4$, and that stateful copies of itself can be cheaply produced.

3.3 Selection of the Optimal Output Trace

This final phase of the enforcement pipeline relies upon a special transducer, called the selector, which receives as input a sequence of prefix tree elements, and attempts to select the "optimal" one, based on a transparency condition. This phase involves a ranking transducer $\rho : \Sigma^* \to \mathbb{R}$, which assigns a numerical score to a trace. The principle of the selector is simple: each path in the filtered prefix tree is evaluated by ρ, and the path that maximizes the score is selected and returned as the output.

The operation of the selector, depicted in Fig. 1 as box #7, is described by procedure UPDATE in Algorithm 2. This time, the procedure receives a prefix tree element $[v_0, \ldots, v_n]$ and a vector of pairs, each containing a ranking transducer instance ρ_{σ_i} and the score s_i this transducer has produced after processing σ_i. The algorithm then proceeds in a similar way as for FILTER: each transducer instance is fed with each child in sequence, and the updated instance and its associated score are added to the new vector m. Applying this procedure successively on each prefix tree element, and feeding the output vector m back into the next call to UPDATE produces a vector, from which the output trace σ_i can be chosen based on the highest score s_i in all pairs.

3.4   Merging Valid vs. Corrected Trace

The last step of the pipeline, called the *gate* and represented by box #3, takes care of letting the input trace through as long as it does not violate the security policy, and to switch to the output of the enforcement pipeline only in case of a violation. This is why the gate receives as its inputs the original event trace, the output from the enforcement pipeline, as well as the verdict of the monitor μ for events of the input trace (box #2) that allows it to switch between the two. More precisely, the gate returns an input event directly if and only if μ does not produce the verdict $\bot$ or $\bot^?$ upon receiving this event. Otherwise, this event is kept into an internal buffer, and the gate awaits for an event or a sequence of events to be returned by the enforcement pipeline of box #4, which is output instead. As long as μ returns a false or possibly-false verdict, input events are added to the buffer and also fed to the enforcement pipeline. In such a way, the enforcement pipeline is allowed to ingest multiple input events and replace them by another sequence.

This mode of operation ends at the earliest occurrence of two possible situations. The first is if the monitor resumes returning either $\top$ or $\top^?$. In such a case, the input events in the buffer are deemed to be a safe extension of the ongoing trace, and are sent to the output. The second situation is if the enforcement pipeline produces a corrective sequence as its output. This indicates that the sequence of buffered input events must be discarded, and replaced by the output of the enforcement pipeline. After either of these two situations occur, the input buffer is cleared, and control is returned to the input trace.

However, doing so requires a form of feedback from the downstream gate to the upstream transducers, so that their internal state be consistent with the trace that has actually been output, and not the input trace that has been observed. To illustrate this notion, consider a simple security property stating that every a event must be followed by a b. If the input trace is ac, the first a event is output directly, as this prefix does not violate the policy. The next event, c, makes the prefix violate the policy; the gate therefore switches to the output of the enforcement pipeline. Suppose that this pipeline produces as its output the corrective sequence bc, which inserts a b before the c. This sequence restores compliance with the policy, and events from the input trace can again be let through. However, the monitor μ of box #2, in charge of evaluating compliance of the trace, is still in an error state (having read ac); its verdict will therefore be incorrect for the subsequent incoming events.

This entails that one must be able to "rewind" μ and put it in the state it should after reading the real output trace (abc), so that it produces the correct verdict for the next events. It is the purpose of the feedback mechanism illustrated by the red arrows in Fig. 1, and which we call *checkpointing*. Along with the transducer μ of box #2, a copy μ_σ is kept of that transducer, in the state it was after reading σ (the "checkpoint"). Intuitively, σ represents the sequence of events that have actually been output by the pipeline. As events are received, μ updates its internal state accordingly, but μ_σ is preserved. This copy is updated only when the downstream gate instructs it to, by providing a segment of newly output events σ'. When this occurs, both the checkpoint μ_σ and the internal state of μ are replaced by $\mu_{\sigma \cdot \sigma'}$. A similar feedback process occurs for the enforcement pipeline of box #4.

On its side, the gate notifies these transducers of a new checkpoint every time it outputs an event from the original input trace, or when a corrected segment from the enforcement pipeline is chosen instead. This makes sure that the whole system is always in sync with the contents of the actual output sequence.

3.5 Event Buffering

A final aspect of the architecture that needs to be discussed is the notion of buffering. The default behavior of the selector (box #7) is to keep accumulating prefix tree elements without producing an output, until a signal to pick a trace is given to it. This makes it possible to consider corrective actions generated by the proxy that may involve replacing a sequence of input events by another sequence of output events. However, the question remains as to how and when this signal should be emitted. The proposed architecture deliberately leaves this parameter open, enabling a user to select among various possibilities. We enumerate a few of them in the following.

The first is a greedy choice: every time the selector receives a prefix tree element, it picks the event that maximizes the evaluation of the ranking trans-ducer (evaluated from the beginning of the trace) and immediately outputs it. The second strategy is to pick an output trace once a given threshold length is observed. Prefix tree elements are buffered until k are received, after which the best path in the tree is selected (note that this path itself may be shorter than k due to the presence of ϵ symbols). Yet another possibility is to buffer events until one of the traces reaches a threshold score. Finally, one last possibility is to base the decision to pick a trace on a condition evaluated on the prefix tree itself –for example by evaluating an auxiliary monitor $\delta : \Sigma^* \to \mathbb{B}_4$ on each path. As an example, one could decide to pick a trace whenever a specific event is observed in one of the paths.

4   Discussion

In this section, we discuss the advantages of the proposed enforcement model, illustrate its use with a simple use case, and describe a software implementation of these concepts.

4.1   Use Case

As an example, we consider a variant of the running example from Colombo et al. [8], which stems from a study of the remedial actions that can be taken to recover from violations of the terms of smart contracts. The example dictates the interaction between 3 types of principals: the casino, players and dealers. The casino provides a venue where dealers can set up games in which players can participate. Players then join by depositing a participation fee in the bank's account and guessing the result of a coin toss. After a prespecified time has elapsed, the dealer reveals the result and pays out the winners. A player who correctly guessed the parity of the number gets back twice his participation fee, paid by the dealer. If a player looses, he forfeits his participation fee, which is divided equally between the dealer and the casino.

The following set of events can occur in a trace of the casino: $NewGame(A)$ indicates the onset of a game by dealer A, $Bet(A)$ indicates that player A has placed a bet. The occurrence of the $EndGame()$ event indicates the end of game, and enjoins the selector to cease buffering events, and take corrective action if needed. A payment from A to B will be noted by the event $Pay(A, B)$. All bets are worth are two dollars, and the $Pay()$ event transfers a single dollar. We write $Bet(\cdot)$ as a shorthand for $\bigvee_x Bet(x)$, for all players x in the game. We likewise write $Pay(A, \cdot)$ (resp. $Pay(\cdot, A)$) for any payment in which principal A is the recipient (resp. donor).

Monitor. The policy that underpins this scenario is as follows: while a game is in progress, the balance of the dealer's account can never fall below the sum of the expected payouts. There are multiple ways this policy can be stated, but a particularly appropriate notation is through a system of stream equations over typed stream variables as defined in LOLA [9]. A stream expression may involve the value of a previously defined stream. The language provides the expression ite($b; s_1; s_2$), which represents an if-then-else construct: the value returned depends on whether the predicate of the first operand evaluates to true. It also allows a stream to be defined by referring to the value of an event in another stream k positions behind, using the construct $s[-k, x]$. If $-k$ corresponds to an offset beyond the start of the trace, value x is used instead.

Defining the security policy using LOLA becomes straightforward. The original event stream of casino events is first pre-processed to produce the Boolean streams e, b, p^+ and p^-, indicating whether an event is respectively an $EndGame$, a bet placed by a player, a payment from the player to the casino, or the reverse situation.

$$t_1 := \text{ite}(e; 0; \text{ite}(b; t_1[-1, 0] + 2; t_1[-1, 0]))$$
$$t_2 := \text{ite}(p^+; t_2[-1, k] + 1; \text{ite}(p^-; t_2[-1, k] - 1; t_2[-1, k]))$$
$$\varphi := \text{ite}(\varphi[-1, \top], (t_2 - t_1) \geq 0, \bot)$$

The first equation defines a stream that keeps the count of the potential payouts to players. This counter is reset to 0 whenever a game ends; otherwise, it is incremented by 2 whenever a player places a bet, and keeps its value otherwise. The second equation keeps track of the dealer's balance, assuming the trace starts with an initial balance k. Stating that the potential payouts should never exceed the current balance then becomes the Boolean stream defined as φ, whose output can be used as the monitor verdict for the security policy.

Proxy. The policy can be enforced by refusing (suppressing) bets when the dealer's assets are insufficient to cover them, or by lending (inserting) funds to the dealer's account. If a dealer is running multiple games simultaneously, the casino may also enforce the policy by prematurely ending some games, in the hopes that the winnings incurred by the dealer may allow him to accept further bets on other games. Refusing the bets submitted by a player incurs its own trade-off, since a player whose bets are consistently rejected may eventually take his business to a competing casino. For example, π can be defined as a Mealy machine such as the one shown in Fig. 3; depending on the current state and current input event, the machine may delete or insert other events.

Selector. This policy exposes itself to several interrelated courses of actions, with the choices made by the monitor restricting its future course of action: canceling a game may turn off future patrons, refusing a bet incurs the loss of future revenue, reducing the monitor's freedom to reimburse players when the dealer defaults might further irritate some players. The enforcement pipeline will be forced to choose between these

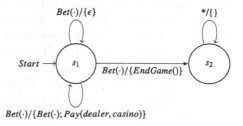

Fig. 3. Representation of a possible proxy enforcing the casino use case.

courses of action in order to attain one of several goals. This time, we opt for an extension of LTL called TK-LTL. We briefly recall the semantics of its important operators; the reader is referred to [21] for complete details.

TK-LTL extends the semantics of LTL with several syntactic structures aimed providing a quantitative evaluation of different aspect of the trace. The feature upon which we rely the most is the counter $\widehat{C}^v_\varphi$, where φ is an LTL formula and v ranges over the truth values of LTL, returns the number of suffixes of the input trace for which the evaluation of φ evaluates to v. Arithmetic operators or functions can be freely applied to the outputs of multiple counters over the same sequence to compute information about the trace. In addition to counters, the semantics of TK-LTL includes quantifiers. One of them is the propositional quantifier, and is written as $\mathcal{P}$. The formula $\mathcal{P}_{\sim k}\widehat{C}$ thus evaluates to $\top$ if the comparison $n \sim k$ holds where n is the value returned by $\widehat{C}$. For example, let $\sigma = aaaba$ be a trace; the formula $\mathcal{P}_{=3}\widehat{C}^\top_a$ evaluates to $\top$ at positions $i = 3$ and $i = 4$, and to $\bot$ elsewhere.

The process of expressing the enforcement preorder is straightforward, and most of the possible requirements can be formulated as relatively simple formulas. For instance, the TK-LTL subformula $\widehat{C}^\top_{Bet(\cdot)}$ counts the total number of bets that are placed, and can be used as a transparency constraint if the casino's main concern is to maximize the total number of bets that are placed. A monitor that seeks to achieve this goal will thus avoid suppressing bet events from the input stream. Conversely, the formula $\widehat{\mathcal{C}}^{\top}_{Pay(casino,\cdot)} - \widehat{\mathcal{C}}^{\top}_{Pay(\cdot,casino)}$ expresses an alternative transparency requirement, namely maximizing gains for the casino.

4.2   Design Considerations

The modular design of the enforcement pipeline offers several advantages. Notably, it simplifies the creation of the monitor, since the process of manipulating the sequence is now separate from the process of the selecting a valid replacement. A main benefit of the method we propose is that the behavior of the enforcement monitor need not be coded explicitly. Instead, the behavior of the enforcement monitor is simply the result of the selector seeking to optimize the evaluation of the enforcement preorder.

The model also makes it possible to select the optimal replacement sequence, according to a criterion separate from the security policy, and which can be stated in a distinct formalism. The model also allows users to compare multiple alternative corrective enforcement actions, and select the optimal one with respect to an objective gradation. Finally, since the alteration of the input trace is done independently of its downstream verification for compliance with the policy, the model also does away with the need for a proof of correctness of the synthesized enforcement monitor, as is usually done in related works on the subject.

As we also stressed in Sect. 3, the proposed architecture is independent of the formal representation of each component. As a matter of fact, we deliberately chose three different notations for the proxy, monitor and ranking transducer of the casino use case to illustrate this feature. This flexibility makes it possible to support other types of enforcement requirements. For instance, consider a monitor whose objective is to produce a valid output that is as close to the input as possible. This is a fairly intuitive requirement, but difficult to implement using existing solutions. In the proposed framework, this requirement can be enforced by assigning a cost to each transformation performed by the monitor (adding an event or suppressing an event) and having the monitor minimize the overall enforcement cost for the entire sequence. Even more flexibility can be achieved by assigning different cost to each action as needed, or by assigning a different cost to suppression and insertion.

4.3   Implementation and Experimental Results

In the previous sections, we endeavored to describe the runtime enforcement model in an abstract way that is not tied to any specific system or formalism, and to give users the freedom of choosing the formal notation of their choice for each component of the pipeline. Nevertheless, a software implementation of this model has been developed as a Java library that extends the BeepBeep event stream processing engine [18].

This extension, which amounts to a little more than 2,600 lines of Java code, provides a new `Processor` class (the generic entity performing stream processing in the BeepBeep) called `Gate`. This class must be instantiated by defining four parameters. The first three are the transducers μ, π and ρ representing the monitor, proxy and ranking transducer described earlier. In line with the formal presentation of Sect. 3, the pipeline makes no assumption about the representation of these three transducers. Any chain of BeepBeep processors is accepted, provided they have the correct input/output types for their purpose. For instance, an existing BeepBeep extension called Polyglot [16] makes it possible to specify the monitor using finite-state machines, LTL, LOLA, or Quantified Event Automata [24], while another one can be used to define the ranking transducer by means of a TK-LTL expression. However, the user is free to pick from all of the available BeepBeep processors to form a custom chain for any of these components. Since every Processor instance in BeepBeep can create a stateful copy of itself at any moment, the checkpointing feature required by our proposed model is straightforward to implement.

The last parameter that must be defined is the strategy that decides how the filter and selector buffer and release events, as discussed in Sect. 3.5. Concretely, this is done by specifying a method named `decide`, which is called every time a new prefix tree element is received by the selector. By default, the enforcement monitor accepts an integer k and picks an output trace after k calls (with $k = 1$ corresponding to the immediate greedy choice); overriding this method produces a different behavior implementing another strategy. In the experiments, it was arbitrarily set to $k = 8$.

The rest of the operations are automated. Once a `Gate` is instantiated, it works as a self-contained processor which, internally, operates the pipeline described in Fig. 1. To the end user, this processor can be used as a box receiving a sequence of events in Σ and producing another sequence of events in Σ, which automatically issues corrected sequences when a policy violation occurs. It can be freely connected to other processor instances to form potentially complex computation chains.

To test the implemented approach, we performed several experiments made of a number of scenarios, where each scenario corresponds to a source of events, a property to monitor, a proxy applying specific corrective actions, a filter, and a ranking selector applying specific enforcement preorder. The set of experiments has been encapsulated into a LabPal testing bundle [17], which is a self-contained executable package containing all the code required to rerun them [26]. In addition to the *Casino* use case described earlier, our experiments include the following.

Simple: An abstract scenario where the source of events is a randomly generated sequence of atomic propositions from the alphabet $\Sigma = \{a, b, c\}$. Different proxies are considered for the purpose of the experiments: adding any event at any time, deleting any event at any time, adding/deleting only event a, or adding two events at a time. These proxies are meant to illustrate the flexibility of our framework to define possible corrective actions. Similarly, various policies are also considered: one corresponding to the LTL formula $\mathbf{G}\,(a \rightarrow (\neg b\,\mathbf{U}\,c))$, another that stipulates that events a must come in pairs, and a last corresponding to the regular expression $(abc)^*$. Finally, the enforcement preorder in this scenario assigns a penalty (negative score) by counting the number of inserted and deleted events in a candidate trace. This leads the pipeline to favor solutions that make the fewest possible modifications to the input trace.

File Lifecycle: The second scenario is related to the operations that can be made on a resource such as a file, and is a staple of runtime verification literature [7]. A trace of events is made of interleaved operations open, close, read and write on multiple files. The policy is notable in that it is *parametric*: it splits the trace into multiple sub-traces (one for each file), and stipulates that each file follows a presrcibed lifecycle (read and write are allowed only between open and close, and no write can occur after a read). The scenario reuses a proxy and ranking transducer from *Simple*.

Museum: This example is taken from Drabik *et al.* [11], and illustrates quantified security policy enforcement. Events of the trace represent adults, children and guards going in and out of a museum. The policy specifies that access is forbidden for any children if no guard is currently present in the museum. The interest of this scenario lies in the possible variations for the proxy and enforcement preorder. A proxy can either insert a guard, prevent a guard from going out, or prevent a child from getting in. The possible enforcement preorders can be to minimize the number of modifications to the trace (as before), to maximize the number of children that enter the museum, or to minimize the number of time steps where guards are "idle" (present while no children are there).

For each variation of a scenario, we ran the enforcement pipeline on a randomly generated trace of length 1,000 of the corresponding type. The experiments are meant to assess the overhead, both in terms of running time and memory consumption, incurred by the presence of the proxy and the selector. A downloadable instance containing all the experiments described in this paper can be obtained online[1]. All the experiments were run on a Intel CORE i5-7200U 2.5 GHz running Ubuntu 18.04, inside a Java 8 virtual machine with the default 1964 MB of memory.

The results are summarized in Table 1. As one can see, the number of input events processed per second ranges in the hundreds to the thousands. Overall, one can conclude that the overhead incurred by the use of the pipeline is reasonable. For instance, in a real-world setting such as a blockchain, the limiting factor is more likely to be the number of transactions per second supported by the infrastructure itself; as a single example, the Ethereum network handles at most a few dozen transactions per second on the main net [4]. On its side, memory overhead remains relatively low with a few kilobytes, with a maximum demand of about 120 kB for a single scenario. Upon examination of the data, we observed that this corresponds to a single peak during the whole execution, with memory consumption otherwise remaining mostly below 10 kB.

Global overhead varies based on the actual combination of policy, proxy and ranking transducer. For instance, the $(abc)^*$ policy, when used on a proxy that only has the power to insert events into the trace, results in the slowest throughput. This scenario represents an extreme case since at any moment in

---

[1] https://github.com/liflab/multitrace-enforcement-lab.

the trace, a single next event is valid. Since the input trace is randomly generated, the probability that an input event not be the expected one is about 2/3, meaning that the pipeline must perform a corrective action on almost every event.

Table 1. Summary of throughput (in events/sec.) and maximum memory consumption (in bytes) for each scenario.

Event source	Policy	Proxy	Scoring formula	Throughput	Max memory
Casino	Casino policy	Casino proxy	Maximize bets	2380	9824
			Maximize gains	490	7976
			Minimize changes	2325	8814
Files	All files lifecycle	Delete any	Minimize changes	78	9580
Museum	Museum policy	Museum proxy	Maximize children	4347	9580
			Minimize changes	480	7984
			Minimize idle guards	1694	9580
a-b-c	(abc)*	Delete any	Minimize changes	628	9580
		Insert any	Minimize changes	18	8692
	After a, no c until b	Delete any	Minimize changes	869	8236
		Insert any	Minimize changes	67	119076
		Insert any b	Minimize changes	485	10344
	Stuttering a's	Delete any	Minimize changes	952	9580
		Insert any	Minimize changes	602	9396

The action of a proxy can also be examined in further detail. Figure 4a shows the cumulative number of deleted, inserted and output events produced as the input trace is being read, for a variant of the museum scenario. Although difficult to see due to the scale of the plot, the output event line increases in an irregular staircase pattern. This is caused by the fact that the gate withholds events at moments where the policy is temporarily violated. One can also observe that, for this scenario, the enforcement pipeline inserts and deletes events in a relatively equal (and small) proportion.

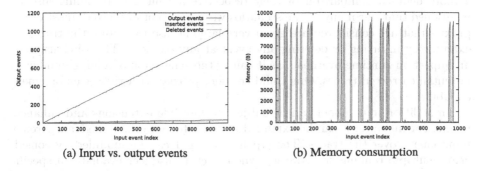

(a) Input vs. output events   (b) Memory consumption

Fig. 4. Runtime statistics for the execution of an enforcement pipeline on a variation of the museum scenario.

On its side, Fig. 4b shows the memory used by the pipeline at each point in the execution. Memory remains near zero as long as the input trace does not violate the property; as a matter of fact, these flat regions exactly match the locations in Fig. 4a where no change occurs on both inserted and deleted events. The memory plot also shows spikes, which correspond to the moments in the trace where the enforcement pipeline kicks in and starts generating possible corrected sequences. Once one such sequence is chosen and emitted, all data structures are cleared and memory usage drops back to zero. These observations are consistent with the expected operation of the pipeline described in Sect. 3.

5   Conclusions

In this paper, we presented a flexible runtime enforcement framework to provide a valid replacement to any misbehaving system and guarantee that the new sequence is the optimal one with respect to an objective criterion we call transparency constraints. A proxy interposed between the input sequence and the monitor is used to generate all the possible replacements. A monitor then eliminates invalid options, while a selector identifies the optimal replacement sequence with respect to a transparency constraint, separate from the security policy. We described a novel formalism to state this constraint; the implementation of these concepts as an extension leveraging the BeepBeep event stream processing engine, and run through a range of different scenarios, has shown that the enforcement of a property can be done dynamically at runtime without the need to manually define an enforcement monitor specific to the use case considered.

Therefore, the precise behavior of the pipeline can be seen as being emergent from the interplay of its components. Moreover, we stressed how this modular design makes it possible to easily replace any element of the framework (policy, proxy, preorder) by another. As a matter of fact, each individual transducer used in the scenarios benchmarked in Sect. 4.3 requires at most a few dozen lines of code. This genericity opens the way to the future study of a broad range of enforcement mechanisms under a uniform formal framework, and to a more detailed comparison of their respective advantages. It should also be mentioned that, for many of the scenarios we experimentally tested, most of the proxies that are considered are given very large license to modify the trace, for example by inserting or deleting any event at any moment. This obviously has an impact on runtime overhead, as it causes the generation of a large number of potential corrected traces. One could consider proxies with tighter enforcement capabilities.

In addition, our model can be subject to multiple extensions and enhancements. For instance, it can be extended to evaluate more than one transparency requirement over the traces. The pipeline of Fig. 1 can be modified by considering multiple ranking transducers, where each transducer evaluates a specific transparency requirement and assigns a numerical score to each output trace of the proxy based on the enforcement preorder. One could also consider relaxing the classical definition of transparency, and allow modifications to a trace that are not triggered only by hard violations of a policy.

Finally, the treatment of partial and ambiguous events known as gaps that may be present in an input trace could be an area of future research. A proxy could be used to model different types of data degradation in order to fill in the gaps in the trace with all potential events as we did in [27]. The same or another proxy could be used to enforce the desired policy, then the filter filters the traces and the selector quantifies the traces and chooses the optimal one. As a result, our framework will be useful in a variety of situations including enforcing policies over corrupted logs or any other data source with insufficient information.

References

1. Bauer, A., Leucker, M., Schallhart, C.: Comparing LTL semantics for runtime verification. J. Log. Comput. **20**(3), 651–674 (2010)
2. Bauer, L., Ligatti, J., Walker, D.: More enforceable security policies. In: In Foundations of Computer Security (2002)
3. Beauquier, D., Cohen, J., Lanotte, R.: Security policies enforcement using finite and pushdown edit automata. Int. J. Inf. Sec. **12**(4), 319–336 (2013)
4. Betti, Q., Montreuil, B., Khoury, R., Hallé, S.: Smart Contracts-Enabled Simulation for Hyperconnected Logistics, pp. 109–149. Springer International Publishing, Cham (2020). https://doi.org/10.1007/978-3-030-38677-1_6
5. Bielova, N., Massacci, F.: Do you really mean what you actually enforced? - edited automata revisited. Int. J. Inf. Sec. **10**(4), 239–254 (2011)
6. Chang, E., Manna, Z., Pnueli, A.: The safety-progress classification. In: Bauer, F.L., Brauer, W., Schwichtenberg, H. (eds.) Logic and Algebra of Specification, pp. 143–202. Springer, Berlin Heidelberg, Berlin, Heidelberg (1993). https://doi.org/10.1007/978-3-642-58041-3_5
7. Chen, F., Meredith, P.O., Jin, D., Rosu, G.: Efficient formalism-independent monitoring of parametric properties. In: ASE, pp. 383–394. IEEE Computer Society (2009)
8. Colombo, C., Ellul, J., Pace, G.J.: Contracts over smart contracts: recovering from violations dynamically. In: Margaria, T., Steffen, B. (eds.) ISoLA 2018. LNCS, vol. 11247, pp. 300–315. Springer, Cham (2018). https://doi.org/10.1007/978-3-030-03427-6_23
9. D'Angelo, B., et al.: LOLA: runtime monitoring of synchronous systems. In: TIME, pp. 166–174. IEEE Computer Society (2005)
10. Dolzhenko, E., Ligatti, J., Reddy, S.: Modeling runtime enforcement with mandatory results automata. Int. J. Inf. Secur. **14**(1), 47–60 (2014). https://doi.org/10.1007/s10207-014-0239-8
11. Drábik, P., Martinelli, F., Morisset, C.: Cost-aware runtime enforcement of security policies. In: Jøsang, A., Samarati, P., Petrocchi, M. (eds.) STM 2012. LNCS, vol. 7783, pp. 1–16. Springer, Heidelberg (2013). https://doi.org/10.1007/978-3-642-38004-4_1
12. Drábik, P., Martinelli, F., Morisset, C.: A quantitative approach for inexact enforcement of security policies. In: Gollmann, D., Freiling, F.C. (eds.) ISC 2012. LNCS, vol. 7483, pp. 306–321. Springer, Heidelberg (2012). https://doi.org/10.1007/978-3-642-33383-5_19

13. Falcone, Y., Mariani, L., Rollet, A., Saha, S.: Runtime failure prevention and reaction. In: Bartocci, E., Falcone, Y. (eds.) Lectures on Runtime Verification. LNCS, vol. 10457, pp. 103–134. Springer, Cham (2018). https://doi.org/10.1007/978-3-319-75632-5_4

14. Falcone, Y., Mounier, L., Fernandez, J.C., Richier, J.L.: Runtime enforcement monitors: Composition, synthesis, and enforcement abilities. Form. Methods Syst. Des. **38**(3), 223–262 (2011)

15. Fong, P.W.L.: Access control by tracking shallow execution history. In: S&P 2004, pp. 43–55. IEEE Computer Society (2004)

16. Hallé, S., Khoury, R.: Writing domain-specific languages for BeepBeep. In: Colombo, C., Leucker, M. (eds.) RV 2018. LNCS, vol. 11237, pp. 447–457. Springer, Cham (2018). https://doi.org/10.1007/978-3-030-03769-7_27

17. Hallé, S., Khoury, R., Awesso, M.: Streamlining the inclusion of computer experiments in a research paper. Computer **51**(11), 78–89 (2018)

18. Hallé, S.: Event Stream Processing With BeepBeep 3: Log Crunching and Analysis Made Easy. Presses de l'Université du Québec (2018)

19. Hamlen, K.W., Morrisett, J.G., Schneider, F.B.: Computability classes for enforcement mechanisms. ACM Trans. Program. Lang. Syst. **28**(1), 175–205 (2006)

20. Khoury, R., Hallé, S.: Runtime enforcement with partial control. In: Garcia-Alfaro, J., Kranakis, E., Bonfante, G. (eds.) FPS 2015. LNCS, vol. 9482, pp. 102–116. Springer, Cham (2016). https://doi.org/10.1007/978-3-319-30303-1_7

21. Khoury, R., Hallé, S.: Tally keeping-LTL: an LTL semantics for quantitative evaluation of LTL specifications. In: IRI 2018, pp. 495–502. IEEE (2018)

22. Khoury, R., Tawbi, N.: Corrective enforcement: a new paradigm of security policy enforcement by monitors. ACM Trans. Inf. Syst. Secur. **15**(2), 10 (2012)

23. Mallios, Y., Bauer, L., Kaynar, D., Ligatti, J.: Enforcing more with less: formalizing target-aware run-time monitors. In: Proceedings of the International Workshop on Security and Trust Management, pp. 17–32, September 2012

24. Reger, G., Cruz, H.C., Rydeheard, D.: MarQ: Monitoring at Runtime with QEA. In: Baier, C., Tinelli, C. (eds.) TACAS 2015. LNCS, vol. 9035, pp. 596–610. Springer, Heidelberg (2015). https://doi.org/10.1007/978-3-662-46681-0_55

25. Schneider, F.B.: Enforceable security policies. ACM Trans. Inf. Syst. Secur. **3**(1), 30–50 (2000)

26. Taleb, R., Hallé, S., Khoury, R.: Benchmark measuring the overhead of runtime enforcement using multi-traces (LabPal package) (2022)

27. Taleb, R., Khoury, R., Hallé, S.: Runtime verification under access restrictions. In: Bliudze, S., Gnesi, S., Plat, N., Semini, L. (eds.) FormaliSE@ICSE 2021, pp. 31–41. IEEE (2021)

28. Talhi, C., Tawbi, N., Debbabi, M.: Execution monitoring enforcement for limited-memory systems. In: PST, PST 2006, Association for Computing Machinery, New York, NY, USA (2006)

A Tight Integration of Symbolic Execution and Fuzzing (Short Paper)

Yaëlle Vinçont[1,2], Sébastien Bardin[2(✉)], and Michaël Marcozzi[2]

[1] Université Paris-Saclay, CNRS, ENS Paris-Saclay, Inria, Laboratoire Méthodes Formelles, Gif-sur-Yvette, France
yaelle.vincont@universite-paris-saclay.fr
[2] Université Paris-Saclay, CEA, List, Saclay, France
{yaelle.vincont,sebastien.bardin,michael.marcozzi}@cea.fr

Abstract. Most bug finding tools rely on either fuzzing or symbolic execution. While they both work well in some situations, fuzzing struggles with complex conditions and symbolic execution suffers from path explosion and high constraint solving costs. In order to enjoy the advantages from both techniques, we propose a new approach called *Lightweight Symbolic Execution* (LSE) that integrates well with fuzzing. Especially, LSE does not require any call to a constraint solver and allows for quickly enumerating inputs. In this short paper, we present the basic concepts of LSE together with promising preliminary experiments.

Keywords: Software testing · Symbolic execution · Fuzzing

1 Introduction

Context. *Automatic test generation* is a major topic in software engineering and security. Currently, most test generation techniques and tools studied by researchers and applied in industry rely on some form of either *symbolic execution* [2,9,11] or *fuzzing* [12,13]. Symbolic execution generates so-called *seeds* (test inputs) covering as many execution paths as possible, by analyzing each of them symbolically, in order to infer a corresponding path constraints that is then solved by an off-the-shelf solver. Fuzzing relies on massive and cheap seeds generation. While the first fuzzers were akin to blackbox random testing, *greybox (mutation-based) fuzzing* [14,16,18] takes the technique one step further by adding a feedback loop, where new seeds are produced by randomly mutating previous seeds deemed as interesting (e.g. covering new parts of code).

Problem. Symbolic execution can explore arbitrarily deep parts of the program, thanks to its powerful constraint derivation and solving machinery. Yet, it scales badly as soon as the number of paths in the program is large and the constraints are difficult to solve. On the contrary, the randomness of fuzzing enables quick and easy seed generation, independent of program size or complexity. Yet, fuzzing will usually fail to explore (in acceptable time) parts of the code protected by

© Springer Nature Switzerland AG 2022
E. Aïmeur et al. (Eds.): FPS 2021, LNCS 13291, pp. 303–310, 2022.
https://doi.org/10.1007/978-3-031-08147-7_20

complex conditions (e.g. deeply nested conditions or hard-coded "magic bytes" checks). Symbolic execution and fuzzing exhibit rather complementary strengths and weaknesses, calling for a proper integration between the two techniques.

Goal and Challenges. *Our objective is precisely to develop a mixed test generation technique reaching a sweet spot between the power of symbolic execution and the lightness of greybox fuzzing.* More precisely, we want to build an *efficient* approach able to reason about complex code, while generating seeds much more quickly and easily than symbolic execution would.

Related Work. Several recent works [3,4,10,15,17] follow roughly the same goal. Many of these approaches [15,17] combine an off-the-shelf fuzzer together with an off-the-shelf symbolic executor, i.e. they do not integrate the two techniques at the *conceptual* level. We aim at introducing a correct seed generation technique which genuinely *integrates* the concepts from symbolic execution with those of fuzzing.

Proposal. We introduce two novel ideas to tackle this problem: *Lightweight Symbolic Execution* and *Constrained Fuzzing.* Lightweight Symbolic Execution (LSE) is a variant of Symbolic Execution where the target constraint language is restricted to an *easily-enumerable* fragment. As a consequence, deriving (correct) path constraints in this language is more complicated but seeds exercising a given path are then easy to enumerate, and do not require any SMT solver. Second, a Constrained Fuzzer operates over a seed and an easy-to-enumerate constraint in order to massively generate seeds exercising the intended path. Overall, LSE will lead the exploration past specific conditions and towards interesting parts of the code, while the constrained fuzzer will efficiently create seeds, including solutions to the constraints. This allows us to explore the program without systematically relying on symbolic analysis, and removes the need for an SMT solver to create seeds satisfying the constraints.

Contribution. As a summary, our contribution is three-fold:

– We introduce *Lightweight Symbolic Execution* (LSE), a flavor of symbolic execution tailored for tight integration with fuzzing. LSE relies on the novel notion of *easily-enumerable* path predicates, and avoids the need for any external constraint solver;
– We show how Lightweight Symbolic Execution can be smoothly integrated with fuzzing, through the novel idea of Constrained Fuzzing, communicating through easily-enumerable path predicates, yielding fast (solver-less) seed enumeration together with targeted symbolic reasoning;
– Finally, we have implemented these ideas in an early prototype named CON-FUZZ, built on top of BINSEC [5,6] and AFL [18], and provide promising preliminary experiments against standard tools.

We believe that these preliminary results show the potential of LSE and Constrained Fuzzing. Still, the experimental evaluation needs to be consolidated on larger benchmarks and compared to the latest advances in fuzzing. This is left as future work.

2   Symbolic Execution

Symbolic execution [2,9,11] runs the program over symbolic input instead of concrete values. Along the execution, symbolic execution maintains two pieces of information about the state of the program: a *symbolic state* Σ – a map binding variables to their symbolic value – and a *path constraint* φ – a predicate over the input symbols, describing the condition for a seed to reach the current instruction. On branching instructions, symbolic execution forks in order to explore all possible paths (up to a given bound). When one of the forked analyses reaches the program end, the resulting path constraint is a predicate over the input, so that executing any of its solutions follows the path of all the branching choices made in this analysis. That constraint can be tackled by an off-the-shelf solver. If the constraint has a solution, the solver will return a seed which covers the path. If there is no solution, it means that the path is unfeasible.

The execution tree on the right of Fig. 1 shows the symbolic state and path predicate for each of the (numbered) instructions in the program on the left. In this tree, x_0 is the symbol corresponding to the program input returned by the read_int function, and forking happens due to the condition **if** (x >= 5).

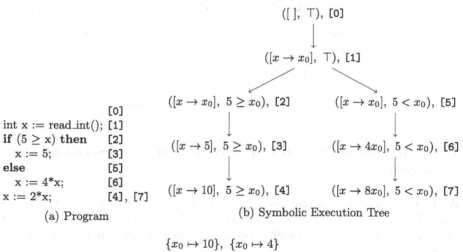

```
                       [0]
int x := read_int();   [1]
if (5 >= x) then       [2]
    x := 5;            [3]
else                   [5]
    x := 4*x;          [6]
x := 2*x;              [4], [7]
```

(a) Program

(b) Symbolic Execution Tree

$$\{x_0 \mapsto 10\}, \{x_0 \mapsto 4\}$$

(c) Possible seeds returned by a constraint solver

Fig. 1. Symbolic execution of a sample program

3   Coverage-Based Fuzzing

Fuzzing [12,13] is a brute-force software testing technique aimed at triggering faults and vulnerabilities by running the program on a very large number of quickly-generated random seeds. In coverage-based greybox fuzzing [16,18], the seed generation process (detailed in Fig. 2) is lightly directed in order to max-imize the code coverage of the produced seeds. The fuzzing tool—or fuzzer—maintains a seed database, which can be initialized by the user. The fuzzing procedure is then basically a loop, executed for as long as possible, where every new iteration selects a seed within the test database, applies a slight syntactical modification to it (a.k.a. *mutation*) and runs the program on the mutated seed. If the program run fails, the fuzzer successfully found a bug-triggering seed. If not, code coverage data is collected and analyzed. If the mutated seed covered parts of the code that had not been explored by previous iterations, it is considered to be *"interesting"* and added to the seed database. Otherwise, it is discarded. The coverage data is also used during the seed selection phase, in order to bias the picking towards seeds that recently increased coverage. The rationale behind this heuristic is that by mutating such seeds, there is a higher chance of exploring the newly uncovered parts of the program.

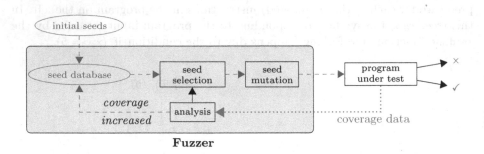

Fig. 2. Coverage-based fuzzing process

4   Lightweight Symbolic Execution and Constrained Fuzzing

We first present an example showing the potential issues faced by fuzzing and symbolic execution (Sect. 4.1). Then we provide an overview of our approach (Sect. 4.2) and finally we describe promising preliminary experimental results (Sect. 4.3).

4.1   Motivating Example

We describe the issues behind fuzzing and symbolic execution and the bene-fits of our approach by discussing how the KLEE symbolic execution engine [1] and the AFL fuzzer [18], two popular and representative tools, struggle at generating seeds for the sample program in Fig. 3, while our implementation of lightweight symbolic execution and constrained fuzzing (CONFUZZ) performs well. In a nutshell, the sample program contains (lines 9–12) a loop which dramatically increases the number of paths considered by KLEE, as well as (lines 16–18) a set of nested equality conditions over the inputs, which might take AFL a long time to cover.

AFL. The two main issues that will prevent AFL from quickly finding seeds penetrating the three nested conditionals are the following. First, the fuzzer does not know how to mutate the seeds in order to enter the conditionals, meaning that it will typically have to try a large number of mutations before succeeding. Second, since it does not understand why a given seed increases coverage, the fuzzer may apply mutations that will destroy this ability. For example, it may mutate "a42" into "042", which does not satisfy the first condition anymore. Meanwhile, the loop does not cause any problem to AFL, as it focuses on branch rather than path coverage.

```
1   int main(int argc, char** argv) {
2
3     char buf[64];
4     int x, y;
5
6     read(0, buf, 64);
7
8     int cpt;
9     for (cpt = 10; cpt < 30; cpt++) {
10      if (buf[cpt] == cpt % 20)
11        y += 1;
12    }
13
14    printf("%i\n", y);
15
16    if (buf[0] == 'a')
17      if (buf[4] == 'F')
18        if (buf[7] == '6')
19          x = 1;
20        else
21          x = 2;
22      else
23        x = 3;
24    else
25      x = 4;
26
27    printf("%i\n", x);
28
29    return 0;
30  }
```

Fig. 3. Sample program

KLEE. For KLEE, solving the specific conditions from lines 16 to 18 is not an issue, as it will simply infer the corresponding path predicates – such as $i[0] = $ 'a', and then create a seed using a constraint solver. On the other hand, KLEE will actively try to explore every possible path of the loop, yielding path explosion.

4.2   Our Approach: ConFuzz

CONFUZZ relies on two key components: *Lightweight Symbolic Execution* (LSE) and *Constrained Fuzzing* (CF). These two components communicate through the key notion of *easily-enumerable path predicate*. CF identifies interesting runs (like a classical fuzzer) and derives targets to be sent to LSE from these runs. LSE is in charge of deriving easily-enumerable constraints for these targets in the code. CF is then back in charge, to quickly enumerate solutions of such constraints.

Easily-Enumerable Path Predicates. We want LSE to create *path predicates* in order to produce seeds reaching targets in the code. For CF to solve such predicates, we need them to be *easily-enumerable*, i.e. creating n solutions is linear w.r.t. the number of inputs and n. For that, we restrict our constraint language for path predicates to conjunctions of interval constraints ($k \leq x \leq k'$)

and equality constraints between variables ($x = y$). Then, we rely on backward domain propagation to translate actual path constraints to our language, together with concretization (forcing a symbolic variable to take an observed concrete runtime value) for some hard-to-handle constraints, such as disequality. Figure 4 shows an example of the path predicate created by LSE (φ_2), i.e. translated from the actual predicate φ_1 to our constraint language. While not complete, φ_2 is correct: all its satisfying seeds follow the path from φ_1.

```
t = {x : 0 ; y : 1 ; z : 2 ;
     t : 4 ; v : 5}
a := x + 3;
if (a ≤ 4) then
    b := y;
    c := t;
else
    b := 2;
if (b != z) then
    d := 4;
else if (c != v)
    d := 3
```

```
declare x, y, z, t, v;
define a = x + 3;
assert (a ≤ 4);
define b = y;
define c = t;
assert (b == z);
assert (c ≠ v);
define d = 3;
```

$$x \leq 1$$
$$\wedge\ y = z$$
$$\wedge\ t \neq v$$

$$x \leq 1$$
$$\wedge\ y = z$$
$$\wedge\ t = 4$$
$$\wedge\ v = 5$$

(a) program P | (b) trace (σ) | (c) path predicate (φ_1) | (d) easily-enumerable path predicate (φ_2)

Fig. 4. Example of an easily-enumerable path predicate

Integrating Lightweight Symbolic Execution and Constrained Fuzzing. Figure 5 illustrates how the two techniques communicate. In practice, communication is asynchronous, as both techniques run in parallel. When the fuzzer finds an interesting seed, it sends the trace as well as the target (a branch condition to be inverted) to LSE. LSE will analyze such information and infer constraints, which will be sent back to the fuzzer, to be associated to the seed in the database.

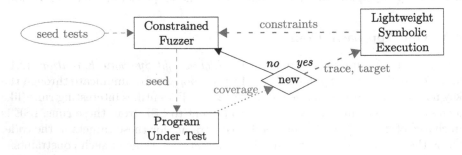

Fig. 5. Overview of CONFUZZ

4.3   Preliminary Experiments

Sample Program from Fig. 3. We consider two settings, depending on whether the loop can be unrolled at most 20 iterations, or at most 0 iterations. We run KLEE, AFL and AFL++ [8] (a popular fork of AFL) 10 times each over the sample program with a timeout of 20 min, and compare the time necessary for each tool to reach 100% branch coverage (if a tool reaches less, we count 20 min). We also carry the experiment with our CONFUZZ prototype.

Results are presented in Table 1 and fulfill our expectations: fuzzers are not impacted by the loop but struggle on nested constraints (showing here poor performance and significant variability), while KLEE has a hard time going from 0 iteration to 20. On the other hand, we can observe that CONFUZZ performs very well here (quick time for full coverage, low variability) and is not impacted by the loop. Interestingly, CONFUZZ generates here roughly 6× more seed than KLEE, but only 4 of them come from a symbolic reasoning, highlighting the capacity of CONFUZZ to trigger symbolic reasoning only when needed.

Table 1. Comparison of KLEE, AFL and CONFUZZ on our sample program

			AFL	AFL++	KLEE	CONFUZZ
0 iterations - 20 min	Nb success/Nb tries		9/10	10/10	10/10	10/10
	Time (s) to cover all branches	Avg	247	14	0.3	1.0
		Min	15	0.5	0.2	0.7
		Max	TO	92	0.5	1.4
		Dev (σ)	348	26	0.1	0.2
20 iterations - 20 min	Nb success/Nb tries		9/10	10/10	10/10	10/10
	Time (s) to cover all branches	Avg	246	96	133	1.4
		Min	2.2	14	121	1.2
		Max	TO	627	155	1.9
		Dev (σ)	355	177	9.5	0.2

AFL - average number of executions	10,433,816
AFL++ - average number of executions	14,239,200
KLEE - average number of generated seeds	1,101,764
CONFUZZ - average number of executions	6,131,172
CONFUZZ - average number of traces sent to LSE	4

LAVA-M. We report the performance of CONFUZZ on 3/4 programs from the standard LAVA-M fuzzing benchmark [7] (5 runs of 1h) – our prototype crashes on the last example. On base64 (3kloc, 44 injected faults), CONFUZZ reports on average 38.8 fault per run (min: 38, max: 39), while KLEE finds 10 (min: 8, max: 11), AFL++ finds 0.2 (min: 0, max: 1) and AFL reports 0 fault. On md5sum (3kloc, 57 injected faults), CONFUZZ reports on average 9 bugs (min: 8, max: 11), where KLEE, AFL++ and AFL do not find any bug. On uniq (3kloc, 28 inbjected faults), CONFUZZ reports 26.9 faults on average (min: 15, max: 29), better than KLEE (avg: 5, min: 5, max: 5), AFL++ (avg: 0.4, min: 0 min, max: 1) and AFL (avg: 0, min: 0, max: 0).

5 Conclusion

We have introduced and discussed Lightweight Symbolic Execution (LSE), a variant of Symbolic Execution tailored to tight integration with fuzzing thanks to its focus on fast solution enumeration – yielding Constrained Fuzzing. We report promising early experiments against standard tools, demonstrating the potential of these novel ideas. Future work includes consolidating the experimental evaluation with larger benchmarks and the latest advanced fuzzers as competitors, as well as providing a full formalization of the approach.

References

1. Cadar, C., et al.: KLEE: unassisted and automatic generation of high-coverage tests for complex systems programs. In: OSDI (2008)
2. Cadar, C., Sen, K.: Symbolic execution for software testing: three decades later. Commun. ACM **56**(2), 82–90 (2013)
3. Chen, P., Chen, H.: Angora: efficient fuzzing by principled search. In: 2018 IEEE Symposium on Security and Privacy (SP), pp. 711–725. IEEE (2018)
4. Chen, P., Liu, J., Chen, H.: Matryoshka: fuzzing deeply nested branches. In: Conference on Computer and Communications Security (2019)
5. David, R., et al.: A dynamic symbolic execution toolkit for binary-level analysis. In: Proceedings of the 23rd IEEE International Conference on Software Analysis, Evolution, and Reengineering, SANER 2016. IEEE (2016)
6. Djoudi, A., Bardin, S.: BINSEC: binary code analysis with low-level regions. In: Baier, C., Tinelli, C. (eds.) TACAS 2015. LNCS, vol. 9035, pp. 212–217. Springer, Heidelberg (2015). https://doi.org/10.1007/978-3-662-46681-0_17
7. Dolan-Gavitt, B., et al.: Lava: large-scale automated vulnerability addition. In: IEEE Symposium on Security and Privacy (SP) (2016)
8. Fioraldi, A., Maier, D., Eißfeldt, H., Heuse, M.: AFL++: Combining incremental steps of fuzzing research. In: WOOT (2020)
9. Godefroid, P., Levin, M.Y., Molnar, D.A.: SAGE: whitebox fuzzing for security testing. Commun. ACM **55**(3), 40–44 (2012)
10. Huang, H., Yao, P., Wu, R., Shi, Q., Zhang, C.: Pangolin: incremental hybrid fuzzing with polyhedral path abstraction. In: Security and Privacy (2020)
11. King, J.C.: Symbolic execution and program testing. Commun. ACM **19**(7), 385–394 (1976)
12. Manès, V.J.M., et al.: The art, science, and engineering of fuzzing: a survey. IEEE Trans. Softw. Eng. **47**, 2312–2330 (2019)
13. Miller, B.P., Fredriksen, L., So, B.: An empirical study of the reliability of UNIX utilities. Commun. ACM **33**(12), 32–44 (1990)
14. Rawat, S., Jain, V., Kumar, A., Cojocar, L., Giuffrida, C., Bos, H.: VUzzer: application-aware evolutionary fuzzing. In: 24th Annual Network and Distributed System Security Symposium, NDSS (2017)
15. Stephens, N., et al.: Driller: augmenting fuzzing through selective symbolic execution. In: NDSS (2016)
16. Website. Libfuzzer (2021). https://llvm.org/docs/LibFuzzer.html
17. Yun, I., Lee, S., Xu, M., Jang, Y., Kim, T.: QSYM : a practical concolic execution engine tailored for hybrid fuzzing. In: 27th USENIX Security Symposium (USENIX Security 2018). USENIX Association (2018)
18. Zalewski, M.: American fuzzy lop (2021). http://lcamtuf.coredump.cx/afl/

At the Bottom of Binary Analysis: Instructions

Guillaume Bonfante[1] and Alexandre Talon[2(✉)]

[1] Université de Lorraine - LORIA, Nancy, France
`guillaume.bonfante@loria.fr`
[2] Univ. Grenoble Alpes, CNRS, Grenoble INP, G-SCOP, 38000 Grenoble, France
`alexandre.talon@grenoble-inp.fr`

Abstract. We present here a careful exploration of the set of instructions for the x86 processor architecture. This is a preliminary step towards a systematic comparison of SMT-based retro-engineering tools. The latter arose in the context of binary code retro-engineering. All these tools rely themselves on more elementary disassembly tool. In this contribution, we attack the problem at its most atomic level: the instructions. We prepare, trading off between the size of the list and the correctness of the future comparison, a good list of instructions.

Keywords: Retro-engineering · Disassembly tools · x86

1 Introduction

Deep analysis of binaries, and especially malware, lead to many difficult questions that are quite often undecidable. For instance, what is the value of `eax` when the program's control reaches instruction `jmp eax`? The reconstruction of a control flow graph (CFG), dead code identification, searching for buffer overflow are other examples of the phenomenon. All these issues are not computable due to Rice's Theorem.

Nevertheless, these questions remaining open, researchers explored some partial solutions. There are many possibilities, exemplified by their respective underlying tools.

First, we must mention disassembly tools such as IDA[1], Ghidra[2], but also their more atomic versions: `capstone`[3], `zydis`[4] or even `xed`[5]. All these tools are capable of extracting assembly code out of a binary executable or a piece of

---

[1] https://hex-rays.com/IDA-pro/.
[2] https://ghidra-sre.org.
[3] http://www.capstone-engine.org.
[4] https://zydis.re.
[5] https://intelxed.github.io.

G. Bonfante—Experiments have been conducted at LHS - LORIA.
A. Talon—Supported by DGA - Direction Générale de l'Armement.

© Springer Nature Switzerland AG 2022
E. Aïmeur et al. (Eds.): FPS 2021, LNCS 13291, pp. 311–320, 2022.
https://doi.org/10.1007/978-3-031-08147-7_21

memory. Actually, for the first two tools of the list, they will perform some further analysis of the binary: they will rebuild – at least partially – the control flow graph, function structures, virtual table, imports, export table, and so on. All these tools start with the same step: they must extract and recognize instructions from a sequence of bytes.

In another branch of retro-engineering tools, the idea is to provide a logical model of the behavior of the processor so that the above-mentioned questions can be reformulated in terms of logical formulae and solved using SMT solvers. These are the original targets of the current study: the tools involving a logical model of (the behavior of) the processor that is compatible with SMT solvers. Let us call them SMT/symbolic tools.

It would be hard to mention all the contributions on solving retro-engineering issues via SMT solvers, but let us mention a few of them and their associated tools. Take for instance "Capture The Flag" style of issues, in [8], Springer and Feng show how to use `angr` to find the user's input that will lead to the "wrong path". To compute user data that will reach some particular point, `angr` (see [6]) performs some symbolic computation and solves the obtained constraints with the help of an SMT solver engine. `Triton` (see [5]) is another example of such an SMT/symbolic tool. In [4], Salwan, Bardin and Potet propose another typical application. They show how to deobfuscate some virtualized code.

Again, on the problem of deobfuscation of virtualized code, we mention the work of Souchet and Girault [7] based on `miasm`, another example of SMT/symbolic tools. In their blog post, they describe how to cope with nanomites, an anti-analysis trick that is used by the famous packer "Armadillo". Finally, the last but not the least of the tools under our scope is `binsec`. In [2], Girol, Farinier and Bardin consider another application of symbolic computations: bug tracking. The tool `binsec` is at the core of their "robust reachability" exploration.

To sum up, all these tools need to describe symbolically the behavior of the processor. To do that, they describe the semantics of each processor instruction. However, the documentation by Intel [1] is quite huge and complex, thus prone to errors which can be propagated to disassembly tools. In the long term, we propose to build a platform to evaluate properly retro-engineering tools involving instruction semantics or syntax.

In principle, one has to run the tool on each instruction and then to verify the correction of the tool on this instruction. However, that would mean we already have access to the ground truth, that is to the actual semantics or syntax of the instruction. But we do not. Thus, the idea of the platform is to perform a relative verification rather than an absolute one. Given two tools with same purpose, we propose a comparison between them. Our idea is that if they disagree on some instruction, for sure *one* of them is wrong. If they agree, we may hope that both are right. Such a hope should be stronger when the tools are developed independently.

However, such an approach is unfeasible in practice if done naively. Indeed, we are immediately overwhelmed by the number of processor instructions. The first issue is that instructions may involve immediates, that is integers stored within up to 32 bits. But, the number of registers (say around 20 for 64 bits x86 architectures) cannot be neglected since instructions may involve combinations with three of them. To give an idea, extracting the SMT formulae for 10 000 instructions for two of the above mentioned SMT/symbolic tools, and then comparing the formulae with an SMT solver takes on average 30 min.

Thus, we have first turned our attention to an intermediate goal: grouping instructions into broader classes. This is the topic of the present contribution. Suppose that tools X and Y agree on `add eax, 0x1234`, they probably agree on `add eax, 0x2345` too. That corresponds to the abstraction `add eax, imm` where `imm` denotes some integer stored in two bytes. That forms a first class of instructions. But we could go one step further in the abstraction by grouping all instructions of the shape `add reg, imm` where `reg` represent a register and that leads to a second (wider) class of instructions.

The more abstractions we perform, the more chances that the class is too wide for our goal: two tools could agree on some instructions of the class and disagree on others from the same class. In other words, there is a balance between the level of abstraction and correction of the verification. We must choose a compromise according to the situation: how long do the tests last. For instance, disassembling 10 000 instructions with `capstone` takes 10ms. To conclude, the level of abstraction is a parameter we can choose for our platform. The trade-off we can obtain at apparently no cost on the precision is what we discuss here.

In practice, how to enumerate the instructions? We could follow Intel's documentation. But even a simple enumeration of instructions is not easy. This has been already observed by Mahoney and McDonald, see [3] for a good presentation of the problem (with a completely other purpose: steganography, that is creating a valid executable used for hiding some information inside its instruction bytes). Furthermore, this work has actually already been done several times before by disassembly tool such as `capstone` or `zydis`. They both extract instructions out of some buffer of bytes. Moreover, they both give information about the structure of instructions. So, we may think of using such tools to enumerate instructions. As a by-product of instruction enumeration, we could observe differences between two disassembly tools: `capstone` and `zydis`. Ensuring that they recognize generally the same instructions is a ground to, in the future, compare the semantics of the instructions.

2   Listing the Instructions

In this section we first describe the structure of an instruction, then the different types or arguments and the number of possibilities for each type. Since some arguments can take a huge number of values, we present a way to abstract them and give the reduced number of combinations, once we apply our optimizations.

An instruction is two-fold: it can be seen as a machine code (a sequence of bytes), and in a more abstract way as an assembly instruction, which we define below. Let us first note that different assembly instructions can correspond to the same sequence of bytes: even if they are morally identical, mov eax, [2*eax] and mov eax, [2*eax+0] correspond to the unique sequence "8B 04 45 00 00 00 00". The reverse is also true: "F2 90" and "90" both correspond to the nop instruction. We will use indifferently machine code and assembly instructions.

At first sight, one may say that there are around five hundred different operations or so. This is the number of different opcodes. But we have to go further in details: an instruction contains more than its opcode alone.

2.1　Structure of Assembly Instructions

An *instruction* can be decomposed in the following format[2]:

$$
\begin{aligned}
instruction &::= prefix_1 \ldots prefix_k \; opcode \; arg_1 \ldots arg_l \\
arg &::= imm | reg | mem \\
mem &::= (seg[reg_1 + scale * reg_2 + disp], size) \\
prefix &::= \mathtt{rep}, \mathtt{lock}, \ldots \\
opcode &::= \mathtt{add}, \mathtt{jmp}, \mathtt{call}, \ldots \\
seg &::= \mathtt{cs}, \mathtt{ds}, \mathtt{es}, \ldots \\
reg &::= \mathtt{eax}, \mathtt{ebx}, \ldots
\end{aligned}
$$

where *imm* denotes some immediate (an integer on up to 32 bits), the same goes for the displacement *disp*, and *scale* $\in \{1, 2, 4, 8\}$. In the clause defining the memory argument above, the segment register *seg* and *scale* * *reg_2*, are optional. At least one among the base register and the displacement must be present.

The number of different instructions is pretty huge: the set of 2^{32} immediates is already so large that calling an SMT solver for each instruction is infeasible.

2.2　Instructions Enumeration

Prefixes Enumeration. Let us consider the leftmost part of instructions: the prefix combinations. Prefixes usually change the semantics of the instruction: for instance making it a loop (like the rep prefix, 0xF2 and 0xF3).

There are in total 13 prefixes, sorted into 5 categories. A priori, there is no bound on the number of prefixes of an instruction, a prefix can be even duplicated. The only limitation is actually the size of an instruction, that is 15. Naively, leaving one byte for the opcode, that makes around $13^{14} \approx 4 \cdot 10^{15} \approx 2^{52}$ possibilities. It is obvious that this number needs to be reduced.

However, according to the documentation, for each category, only the rightmost one (or the leftmost one, depending on the processor) will be effective. To reduce the number of prefix combinations, we take advantage of the fact that in

---

[2] More technical details can be found in http://ref.x86asm.net/coder32.html.

practice, 1) only the last read prefix from each group is used and 2) the order of prefixes between two groups is not important. So, we only allow instructions for which there is at most one prefix per group and when the groups of the prefixes respect some arbitrary fixed order. This parameter of our abstraction reduces the number of prefixes combinations from 10^{15} to 112.

Actually, there are on average fewer than 112 prefixes combinations per instruction because some prefixes are illegal with some opcodes. For instance, the lock prefix 0xF0 is illegal on many instructions like F0 8B C0 = mov eax, eax.

To reduce more the number of instructions, we could ignore useless combinations of prefixes. For instance, the segment prefixes (0x2E, 0x3E, 0x26, 0x36, 0x64 and 0x65) have no effect when the function has no memory argument. 26 40 and 40 both mean inc eax. The same goes for the prefixes changing the address or operand size (0x66 and 0x67) when non applicable. The REP prefixes (0xF2 and 0xF3) have no effect on most instructions. We could skip "useless" combination of prefixes: reject any sequence of bytes if its assembly version is already in our list.

Argument Enumeration. Some opcodes have no argument, like nop and ret. Others generally have a source and a destination arguments. Some take two registers, like mov eax, ebx or a register and a memory address like mov eax, [4*ebx+ecx+1]. Others may also take a constant like add eax, 0x1742.

Let us begin with the registers. An x86 processor has 8 general-purpose registers plus others used in floating point arithmetic, and other specific registers like cr1, dr1, tr3...

Many instructions expect their arguments in the so-called ModR/M format. For better comprehension, we describe it here. The ModR/M encoding is stored on one byte: three bits for the "reg" part which encodes which register is concerned (as source or destination, depending on the opcode), two bits for the "mod" and the remaining three bits for the "R/M" part. The "reg" part can also designate 8-bit parts of the general registers according to the opcode: 83 C3 03 encodes add ebx, 0x3 while 80 C3 03 means add bl, 0x3. In both cases the ModR/M byte is 0xC3. Also, the prefix 0x66 changes the given 32-bit register to its lower 16 bits: 89 D8 is mov eax, ebx and 66 89 D8 is mov ax, bx.

The "mod" + "R/M" parts combined designate either a register or a memory address such that the corresponding memory cell is read or written to. While some ModR/M gives addresses like [edx], others allow for other parameters: a displacement (disp) and/or a SIB (scale base index). The disp is simply a constant on 1, 2 or 4 bytes the value of which shifts the address, like [edx + 0x1742] for a disp on two bytes. We can also have a disp alone like in [0x17421742], with no register. Let us now describe the SIB. It encodes addresses of the shape $[base + scale * index]$ where $base$ and $index$, encoded on three bits, can be any of the eight general-purpose registers (except for esp as index). The scale is encoded on two bits and can be equal to 1, 2, 4 or 8.

To sum up, the source and destination operands of an instruction are generally expressed using the ModR/M system, including sometimes a disp value, and/or a SIB value. The ModR/M takes one byte, the SIB one byte, and the disp can have a size of 1, 2 or 4 bytes. Assuming all ModR/M values expect a SIB byte and a 32-bit displacement, we obtain $256^{1+1+4} = 2^{48} \approx 2.8 \cdot 10^{14}$ possibilities. With a careful analysis, taking into account forbidden patterns, we obtain that there are around $9 \cdot 10^{12}$ valid possibilities for the ModR/M+SIB+disp combinations.

We could take the whole ModR/M+SIB/disp combination as parameter for our abstraction, hence taking one representative out of $9 \cdot 10^{12}$ for almost all instructions using the ModR/M encoding. The ModR/M+SIB is an encoding, hence not that straightforward. Moreover, some ModR/M values are illegal with some opcodes but not others (see Sect. 4). Therefore, to keep a more simple code, and to avoid accepting illegal values of ModR/M, we decided not to abstract the ModR/M byte, nor the SIB one. However, we take the displacement as a parameter in our abstraction: add eax, [ebx+0x28] and add eax, [ebx+0x37] are simply add eax, [ebx+$imm8$] to us. The same applies respectively to the class of 16-bit and 32-bit displacements. Using this abstraction we obtain 6376 different classes (instead of $9 \cdot 10^{12}$) of ModR/M+SIB+disp combinations of an instruction.

There remains a set of arguments to consider: the immediates. They appear for instance in mov ecx, 0x1234 and add edx, 0xabcd1234. We treat them as for the case of displacements: we consider add edx, 0xabcd1234 as add edx, $imm32$. For a given instruction, each immediate on k bits can have 2^k values, so if a prefix+opcode combination expects a 32-bit immediate, thanks to this abstraction we divide by $2^{32} \approx 4 \cdot 10^9$ the number of instructions using this prefix+opcode combination.

Illustration of the List. We give a small extract of our list of instructions in Fig. 1. We can see on lines (2) to (5) that the instruction includes some immediates on 32 bits, and in (4) also a disp on 8 bits. Thanks to our abstractions, we do not list the values for these constants. This allows us to save 256^4 lines for (2) and (3), 256^5 for (4) and 256^8 for (5).

(1)	53	(push ebx)
(2)	8b 84 83	(mov eax,[ebx+eax*4+imm32])
(3)	8b 8c 85	(mov ecx,[ebp+eax*4+imm32])
(4)	69 40	(imul eax,[eax+disp8],imm32)
(5)	69 80	(imul eax,[eax + imm32_1], imm32_2)

Fig. 1. A few instructions as they appear on our list. ".." denotes any byte value.

Final Number of Instructions. What we described above consists in finding a compromise between enumerating all possible instructions to be tested on disassembly tools, and reducing their number by keeping only one instruction by equivalence class according to some parameter of abstraction. This is a trade-off between precision and the final number of instructions we enumerate. We believe, as we explained, that we kept the precision and obtained a reasonable number of instructions with that in mind.

In the end, enumerating the opcodes along with ModR/M and SIB bytes, and with valid prefixes in order, one per group, we obtain a total of 72 million instructions (one representative per class), 72 174 844 to be precise. In this list, we kept useless prefixes as long as they are in order and at most one per group. We must specify that this list includes the deprecated AMD 3DNow! extension but not the (too many) VEX, EVEX, MVEX and XOP instructions.

As we said at the beginning, our number of instructions depends on which parameters we used for the abstraction. For instance, without a limit of one prefix per group, we would have had a really huge number of instructions. Then if we only limit at one prefix per group, we obtain $6.8 \cdot 10^{24}$ instructions. If we also forbid the prefix combinations which are the same up to a permutation, this number goes down to $3.0 \cdot 10^{24}$. By keeping only one representative for all disp values, we list $2.6 \cdot 10^{16}$ instructions: a big improvement, but not enough. The size of the list decreases to 72 million if we also abstract the immediates (our final choice). We could then abstract the SIB values to obtain a smaller list of 262 000 instructions, or 23 700 if we also abstract the ModR/M, that is keeping only the opcode and the one per group ordered prefixes combination. To sum up, according to the needs and constraints, any parameter of the abstraction can be switched on and off, resulting in a different number of instructions.

3   Representing the Abstractions: The Automata

Each time we want to compare two tools (e.g. `capstone` versus `zydis` or `binsec` versus `triton`), we need to perform some specific instruction abstraction, that is an abstraction for which the tools will answer in a coherent way for all the elements of each class of instructions.

We may consider several abstractions. If we want to verify that `capstone` and `zydis` agree on the size of the instructions, we may take one abstraction while we may use another one if we want to verify that they agree on the registers read or written. For the first case, we have no need to process the SIB of the instruction whereas for the second case we need this information, resulting in smaller equivalence classes.

3.1   General Automaton Representation

We could represent our list of instructions as a list, but there is a much more compact way of representing our abstractions: an automaton. Such an automaton consists of a directed acyclic graph whose edges are labeled by bytes: it reads a flow of bytes which corresponds to a path in the graph starting from the root, until reaching a leaf with a value corresponding to the information for the instruction. The automaton is more compact than the list. At least (but not exclusively) for a same opcode we store once all the common prefixes when building the automaton, hence saving some space. We can see this in Fig. 2(a) illustrates this: the 8b first byte is shared between two instructions.

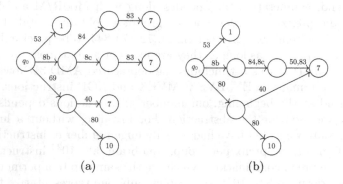

Fig. 2. The automaton built from Fig. 1 (a) and its optimized version (b). The leaves indicate the sizes of the instructions.

3.2   Examples of Specific Automata

We can also build more specific automata to obtain some disassembly information like the size, the mnemonic, or the target information of a jump for instance. Here we describe another way to perform the abstraction: set the goal and automatize the creation of the classes.

Let us assume we want to know the size of any instruction. We propose to first build, from any level of abstraction (so that the list of instruction is reasonable), an automaton where each leave stores a integer between 0 (illegal instruction) and 15: the size of the instruction read. We can imagine that from 72M instructions to only 16 different leaves, many subpaths will be shared by a lot of instructions. For instance, add and sub, among many others, will have the same size if given the same arguments.

Once the first version of the automaton is built, we optimize it by merging equivalent subarborescences, using classical techniques (see Fig. 2(b)).

We mention here another level of abstraction we can consider, which may or may not be used depending if we want a full correctness or if we allow to answer something when reading an invalid instruction. We could consider that two nodes of the automaton are equivalent not only if the have the same outgoing arcs, but also if they simply have the same set of out-neighbors. For instance, if node u has three outgoing arcs towards nodes u_1, u_2 and u_3 and if node v has two outgoing arcs towards u_1 and u_3, we consider u and v to be equivalent. Doing this, we created some new paths from v to u_2, but any existing path is preserved, so that we answer correctly to the instructions of our list. This allows us to obtain a smaller automaton, in terms of number of nodes, with the drawback of not detecting invalid instructions.

We built (and optimized) the automata to provide the following sorts of information: the size of the full instruction (and whether it is a valid instruction), its mnemonic, its "type", the number of "operands", the type of each such i-th "operand", and the information about jumps (including calls). For a jump target, we give the position of its first byte in the instruction, its size, whether the immediate is a signed or unsigned integer, and whether the jump is relative or absolute. Here by operand we mean the operands with status explicit or implicit in zydis (never or almost never the eflags for instance). For the i-th operand automaton, we give the register, the size and position of first byte if it is an immediate, or the memory address as some scale, index and bas, plus some displacement (size and position of first byte) if any. These automaton enable us, given a flow of bytes corresponding to instructions, to retrieve the useful data for each instruction: we have the type, position and size of the operands so that we can read the values of the immediates inside the instruction. So they can be used together as a fast alternative to the disassembly tools.

The choice to have several automata and not a big one was made on purpose: storing all the information in one automaton would be much bigger. Indeed, for instance many instructions have eax as "first" operand, many have ebx as "second" operand, but not so many have both eax and ebx in this order. As we explained earlier: the more different information we put in one automaton, the smaller the equivalence class we obtain, hence a bigger automaton.

We obtain, using Zydis to build the list with the relevant data, the following information (number of different leaves values): 698 mnemonics, from 0 to 4 operands, a size from 0 (invalid instruction) to 14 for the instructions, 27 different encodings for the target of a jump. We find also respectively 32 523, 22 543, 35 and 5 different values for the first to the fourth operands.

Apart from the number of leaves, $i.e.$ the number of different values, the number of internal nodes is also interesting. Compressing the automata as we described earlier, we obtain 167 internal states for the mnemonic, 463 for the instruction size, 99 for the number of operands, 39 for the jump information, and respectively 701, 625, 95 and 22 for the information about the first to the fourth operands. The level of compression of the automaton we can achieve also gives us information about the complexity of the list of instructions according to the parameter studied. It gives information about how some instructions share a common subsequence as a suffix, with the same parameter value.

4   Concluding Remarks

We introduced in this paper the notion of a list of instructions abstracted by some parameters. We explain how to reach a sufficient level of abstraction to obtain a list of 72 million (equivalence classes of) instructions. This list will be used in a future paper to compare the semantics of instructions given by four tools: `angr`, `binsec`, `miasm` and `triton`. In that paper, we will even go further, considering indirectly two instructions with the same assembly string to be equivalent. We will also, in some way, consider `add eax, 0x17` and `add ebx, 0x17` to be equivalent, by deducing the result of the second from the first one by replacing all references to `eax` by references to `ebx`.

Using the automata we describe in Sect. 3.2 in a malware detection tool, we could observe a few differences between `capstone` (v4.0.2) and `zydis` (v3.1.0) even if they most generally agree. We found some instructions accepted by `capstone` and not by `zydis`. One example is `8e 0f 10 2c`: `capstone` says it is a `mov cs, word ptr [edi]` while `zydis` returns the error "bad register", meaning that the opcode does not accept this value of ModR/M. We tested this instruction on our computers to verify whether or not they raise some "Illegal instruction". On the example above, the instruction is not valid, agreeing with `zydis`. However, one of the issues we must face is the evolution of processors. Indeed, the set of instructions varies across time. It is not easy to delineate the "right" set of (x86) instructions. Some instructions appear, like the AMD 3DNow! in 1998 and then become deprecated in 2010. Some specific instructions can disappear, for instance there is no `push ds` in 64-bit architectures.

Acknowledgments. We thank Fabrice Sabatier who gave us some examples of "nasty" instructions.

References

1. Intel 64 and IA-32 Architectures Software Developer Manuals. https://software.intel.com/content/www/us/en/develop/articles/intel-sdm.html
2. Girol, G., Farinier, B., Bardin, S.: Not all bugs are created equal, but robust reachability can tell the difference. In: Silva, A., Leino, K.R.M. (eds.) CAV 2021, Part I. LNCS, vol. 12759, pp. 669–693. Springer, Cham (2021). https://doi.org/10.1007/978-3-030-81685-8_32
3. Mahoney, W., McDonald, J.T.: Enumerating x86-64 - it's not as easy as counting. https://www.unomaha.edu/college-of-information-science-and-technology/research-labs/_files/enumerating-x86-64-instructions.pdf
4. Salwan, J., Bardin, S., Potet, M.-L.: Symbolic deobfuscation: from virtualized code back to the original. In: Giuffrida, C., Bardin, S., Blanc, G. (eds.) DIMVA 2018. LNCS, vol. 10885, pp. 372–392. Springer, Cham (2018). https://doi.org/10.1007/978-3-319-93411-2_17
5. Saudel, F., Salwan, J.: Triton: a dynamic symbolic execution framework. In: Symposium sur la sécurité des technologies de l'information et des Communications, pp. 31–54 (2015)
6. Shoshitaishvili, Y., et al.: SoK: (State of) the art of war: offensive techniques in binary analysis. In: IEEE Symposium on Security and Privacy (2016)
7. Souchet, A., Girault, É.: Taming a wild nanomite-protected MIPS binary with symbolic execution: No such crackme. https://doar-e.github.io/blog/2014/10/11/taiming-a-wild-nanomite-protected-mips-binary-with-symbolic-execution-no-such-crackme
8. Springer, J., Chang Feng, W.: Teaching with angr: a symbolic execution curriculum and CTF. In: USENIX Workshop ASE 2018 (2018)

K-Smali: An Executable Semantics for Program Verification of Reversed Android Applications

Marwa Ziadia, Mohamed Mejri, and Jaouhar Fattahi(✉)

Department of Computer Science and Software Engineering, Laval University,
2325, rue de l'Université, Québec City, QL G1V 0A6, Canada
jaouhar.fattahi.1@ulaval.ca

Abstract. One of the main weaknesses threatening smartphone security is the abysmal lack of tools and environments that allow formal verification of application actions, thus early detection of any malicious behavior, before irreversible damage is done. In this regard, formal methods appear to be the most natural and secure way for rigorous and unambiguous specification as well as for the verification of such applications. In previous work, we proposed a formal approach to build the operational semantics of a given Android application by reverse engineering its assembly code, which we called *Smali+*. In this paper, we rely on the same idea and we enhance it by using a language definitional framework. We choose K framework to define Smali semantics. We briefly introduce the K framework. Then, we present a formal K semantics of Smali code, called K-Smali. Semantics includes multi-threading, threads scheduling and synchronization. The proposed semantics supports linear temporal logic model-checking that provides a suitable and comprehensive formal environment for checking a wide range of Android security-related properties.

Keywords: Android applications · K Framework · Formal semantics · Formal verification · Smali

1 Introduction

Android platform users are increasingly exposed to attacks on the Android environment via untrusted applications. The McAfee 2020 report confirms that fake applications are the most active mobile threat category, generating almost half of all malicious telemetry, with a 30% increase from 2018 [1]. SMS trojan such as *AsiaHitGroup* and *GGTracker* are prime examples of attacks that manifest at the application level (e.g. *Fake Player* application). This may cause financial losses to the user by sending text messages to premium-rate numbers without their knowledge. Spying by taking photos, recording videos or audios, retrieving the history of the application, recording phone conversations, and tracking user location are among a large range of threats that jeopardize Android users through rogue applications. Several research initiatives have been recently put forward to handle these concerns. Their goal is mainly to detect misbehaving applications and to enforce the security within them. Nevertheless, it is virtually impossible to assess efficiency or deficiency or prove the validity of a given system in the absence of a formal specification. According to Stefanescu et al. [2], which we

© Springer Nature Switzerland AG 2022
E. Aïmeur et al. (Eds.): FPS 2021, LNCS 13291, pp. 321–337, 2022.
https://doi.org/10.1007/978-3-031-08147-7_22

endorse, analysis tools for a programming language should be based on the formal semantics of that language. The informal semantics are subject to interpretation by different tool developers, and there is generally no guarantee that these interpretations are consistent with the specification. However, even in the presence of a formal specification, language definitional frameworks are highly needed. They are generally provided with a guideline to formalize a given language, which allows avoiding human errors and omissions that can slip in. They also permit to produce reliable results and to test the resulting formal semantics against a set of sample programs. Nevertheless, this type of framework should meet a set of criteria. Firstly, it must be easy to use and should provide human-readable semantics. Secondly, it must be sufficiently adapted to perform formal reasoning and provide automated proofs. Moreover, it should be able to define language-related features, such as concurrency. The framework should also be generic so that it is not tied to a specific language, and modular so that it does not need to be modified if new features are added. Ideally, the framework should also include its own analyzer for the language being analyzed so that the use of an external software program is not mandatory. The $\mathbb{K}$ framework [3] is a prime example of tools satisfying most of these requirements. It provides a user-friendly rewrite-based language for defining formal operational semantics of programming languages. Figure 1 shows different modules that can be applied on any language having $\mathbb{K}$ semantics, such as LTL model checking, symbolic execution, and program verification. The first thing we can notice is the large choice of tools (e.g. compilers, interpreters, state-space explorers, and test-case generators) that can be automatically derived from *one* reference formal definition of the language. It is a wise way to eliminate the need to squander resources on designing and implementing expensive custom tools. Different approaches define multiple semantics for one language, each designed for a purpose (e.g. program verification, symbolic execution, etc.), which is an uneconomical and labor-intensive way. In previous work [4], we put forward an operational semantics for Smali that we called $Smali^+$. Smali is an assembly-like code generated from reverse-engineering Android applications. $Smali^+$ includes the most important Dalvik features such as multithreading, method invocation, and object creation. However, this formal approach used to generate formal semantics is not executable, error-prone, and lacks a semantics engineering framework with the characteristics mentioned above. Furthermore, verifying and proving the correctness of such formal semantics requires manual development of custom tools (such as interpreters and compilers), usually with no guarantee. The resulting program may end up manifesting unexpected behaviors and, in some cases, leading to irreversible consequences [3]. In this paper, we choose the $\mathbb{K}$ framework for Smali code formalization. The main goal is to provide an executable and expressive formal semantics with which program analysis, security policy enforcement, and property verification can be performed. We name the resulting semantics $\mathbb{K}$-Smali. Additionally, using $\mathbb{K}$, the obtained semantics can be used to check security properties specified as Linear temporal logic (LTL) [5,6] formulas. These properties reflect the healthy behaviors of an application that attacks, originating from SMS Trojans or Android spyware for example, try to transgress. For complete details on Smali, reverse engineering and compilation steps of an Android application, we kindly refer the reader to [4]. Our contribution consists of full-fledged semantics for Android applications, entirely compatible with the $\mathbb{K}$ framework so that it inherits all its powerful compilation, testing, and verification tools. We have been a lot motivated by different 𝕂 semantics for several real languages such as Java [7], PHP [8], and C [9]. We see that they have been used as trusted reference models for the defined language.

This paper is organized as follows. In Sect. 2, we briefly introduce the 𝕂 framework. In Sect. 3, we present 𝕂-Smali. That is, we present the general and detailed configuration, syntax, and semantics rules. In Sect. 4, we indicate how we verify some important security-related properties using 𝕂 on the derived semantics. Section 5 reviews and discusses related research work. Finally, in Sect. 6, we draw some conclusions and trace some directions for future work.

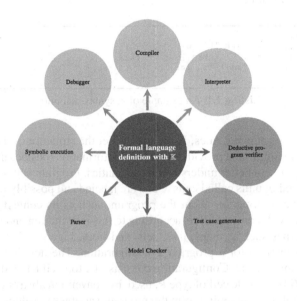

Fig. 1. 𝕂 Framework features [10]

2 Overview on 𝕂 Framework

𝕂 is a rewriting-based definitional semantic framework for programming languages. It provides a complete methodology for their design and specification. The 𝕂 specification consists of three main steps: a syntax definition, a configuration definition, and a semantic definition. Once these steps are completed and saved in files with *k* extension, the command *kompile* is used to compile each definition. The command *krun* invokes an interpreter with which program models can be simulated and tested. Several options can be added to this command to generate models on which formal verification tools for parsing, interpretation, deductive formal verification, symbolic execution, and model checking can be applied. Figure 1 illustrates all these features. Syntax in 𝕂 is written with the conventional Backus-Naur Form (BNF) notation. Listing 1.1 represents an example of a 𝕂 source file containing a program *P* syntax definition. As shown, non-terminals are starting with uppercase letters and preceded by the keyword *syntax*, whereas terminals are represented inside two quotes. For example, in line 2, a program *Pgm* is defined as a list of semicolon-separated instructions. Syntax declaration can be tagged with attributes. These attributes are specified in square brackets at the end of a given definition and are meant to provide additional information to the parser. The strictness constraint, for example, specifies how the arguments of the language construct should be evaluated. In line 3, the "strict(2)" attribute indicates to the parser that only the second argument (i.e. Exp) should be evaluated. When no number is provided with this attribute, such as in line 4, all argument positions are considered strict (i.e. they are evaluated in any fully interleaved order). $\mathbb{K}$ framework offers some basic types such as *Bool*, *Int*, *String*, *Float*, etc. as well as the *Id* type (Identifier), which facilitates the language specification.

```
1  module P-Syntax
2      syntax Pgm   ::= List "{" Inst "," ; " "}"
3      syntax Inst  ::= Id " " Exp [strict(2)]
4      syntax Exp   ::= "mul" "(" Int Int")" [strict]
5  end module
```

Listing 1.1. An example of $\mathbb{K}$ syntax definition

Before defining semantic rules, $\mathbb{K}$ requires to set the structure of the program state by setting its configuration. It provides additional information (besides the syntax) about the definite language to better understand its semantics. Program states in $\mathbb{K}$ configurations are organized in units called cells. Cells are labeled and possibly nested. Each cell contains semantic information about the program, such as its context, memory, environment, etc. The cell content differs according to this information and can hold several algebraic data types such as maps, lists, sets, and trees. Figure 2 shows the generated graphical representation for a program P configuration. The notation inside the cells represents their initial state. Configuration consists of a top cell labeled ⊤, holding two sub-cells: a *$ PGM* variable cell of type *k*, used, by convention always for computation, a *Memory* cell holding a mapping form the program variables to values, initially empty. The asterisk symbol "*" used with the *Inst* sub-cell specifies its multiplicity.

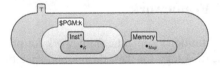

Fig. 2. $\mathbb{K}$ configuration example

Once syntax and configuration are defined, semantics rules should be set. Defining semantics for the language consists of a set of $\mathbb{K}$ rewrite rules that drive the execution of programs. One can describe a $\mathbb{K}$ rewrite rule as a transition over configurations, that starts with a configuration holding the original program and ends with a new one maintaining the result. Each rule in $\mathbb{K}$ is preceded by the keyword *rule* and has the following form:

$$\text{rule } lhs \Rightarrow rhs$$

where *lhs* represents the left-hand side of the rule and *rhs* is the right-hand side. Listing 1.2 provides an example of semantics definition. The module *P-semanitcs* represents the semantics definition of the *P* program presented in Listing 1.1. Line 3 represents a rewrite rule definition for multiplication. Notice the ellipses "..." in the rewrite rule definition. It is actually used for a volatile part of the term, which corresponds to the part that the current rule does not take into account.

```
1  module P-Semantics
2  imports P-Syntax
3    rule <T> <PGM><Inst> I1:Int * I2:Int ⇒ I1 *Int I2 </Inst></PGM>... </T>
4  end module
```

Listing 1.2. An example of K semantics definition

The K rewrite rule defined in Listing 1.2 affects one cell in the program *P* configuration (i.e. *Inst* cell) as follows:

$$\text{rule} \left\langle \frac{\text{I1}:Int * \text{I2}:Int}{\text{I1} *_{Int} \text{I2}} \right\rangle_{Inst}$$

The line expresses a rewrite. Terms above and below the line represent the left-hand side (*lhs*) and the right-hand side (*rhs*) of the rule, respectively. The rest of the configuration context is inferred automatically.

3   K-Smali

3.1   Syntax

As previously mentioned, formal modeling Smali code was the subject of earlier work [4]. To make this paper self-contained, this subsection details just the definitions, instructions, and terms that are newly considered in K-Smali. Listing 1.3 corresponds to a K source file used to define K-Smali. It provides basic syntactic categories and the syntax of selected instructions. Following the disassembly process, all internal source Java classes are separated from their including class, each class in a *.smali* file. The Manifest file allows the identification of the application's entry point. We suppose that its syntax consists only of the keyword *.manifest* followed by a method reference *MethodRef* referring to the method's full name as well as the fully qualified name of its including class. This method represents the entry point from which the program starts execution (line 78). Each class in the *.smali* file is defined by a class header *ClassHeader* indicating all information about the class: possible comments; its fully qualified name (starting always by "L" and ending by ";" line 33), its direct super-class fully qualified name (if exists), access flags indicating its visibility; its corresponding Java source class (identified by the *.source* keyword) and finally a set of implemented interfaces.

[!t]

```
  1  module SMALI-SYNTAX
  2    syntax Program      ::= SmaliFiles ManifestFile
  3    syntax SmaliFiles   ::= List{SmaliFile," "}
  4    syntax SmaliFile    ::= Class
  5    syntax Class        ::= ClassHeader Fields Methods
  6    syntax ClassHeader ::= Comments ".class" AccessFlags ClassName SuperClass
                             SourceClass Interfaces
  7    syntax SuperClass  ::= Comments ".super" SuperClassName | Empty
  8    syntax SourceClass::= Comments ".source" String | Empty
  9    syntax Comments ::= List{Comment," "}
 10    syntax Comment    ::= r"\\#.*"                      [token]
 11    syntax Fields     ::= List{Field," "}
 12    syntax Field      ::= Comments ".field" AccessFlags FieldName ":" Type ValueOp
 13    syntax ValueOp ::= Value | Empty
 14    syntax Methods ::= List{Method," "}
 15    syntax Method  ::= Comments ".method" AccessFlags  MethodNameSign MethodBody ".
                          end method"
 16    syntax MethodNameSign ::= MethodName MethodSignature
 17    syntax MethodSignature ::= MethodInTypes MethodRetType
 18    syntax MethodInTypes ::= "(" Types ")" | "(" ")"
 19    syntax MethodRetType ::= Type  | VoidType
 20    syntax Type::= PrimitiveType|ObjectType|ArrayType
 21    syntax PrimitiveType::="Z"|"B"|"C"|"D"|"F"|"I"|"J"|"S"
 22    syntax VoidType     ::= "V" /* void type*/
 23    syntax ObjectType ::= LName  /* Object reference*/
 24    syntax ArrayType ::="["PrimitiveType|"["ObjectType|"["ArrayType"
 25    syntax Value ::= Bool | Int | Float | String
 26    syntax AccessFlags ::= List{AccessFlag," "}
 27    syntax AccessFlag::= "public"|"private"|"protected" |"final"|"abstract"|"static"
 28    syntax ClassName ::= LName
 29    syntax SuperClassName ::= LName
 30    syntax MethodName ::= Name | "constructor" "<init>"
 31    syntax FieldName::=Name
 32    syntax Name ::= Id
 33    syntax LName ::= r"L[_a-zA-Z0-9]*[_a-zA-Z0-9]*;"[token]
 34    syntax MethodRef ::= ClassName"->" MethodNameSignature
 35    syntax FieldRef   ::= ClassName"->" FieldName
 36    syntax Parameters::= List{Parameter,","}
 37    syntax Parameter ::= RegName
 38    syntax MethodBody ::=  List{Statement," "}
 39    syntax Statement   ::= Instruction | Directive
 40    syntax Instruction ::= "goto" ":" Label
 41                        |":" Label
 42                        |"nop"
 43                        |"sparse-switch" RegName "," ":" Switchtab
 44                        |"const" RegName "," Val
 45                        |"const-string" RegName "," String
 46                        |"move" RegName "," RegName
 47                        |"new-instance" RegName "," ClassName
 48                        |"new-array" RegName "," RegName "," ArrayType
 49                        | Sget RegName "," FieldRef
 50                        | Sput RegName "," FieldReference
 51                        |"iget" RegName "," RegName "," FieldRef
 52                        |"iput" RegName "," RegName "," FieldRef
 53                        |"aget" RegName "," RegName "," RegName
 54                        |"aput" RegName "," RegName "," RegName
 55                        |"if-eq" RegName "," RegName "," ":" Label
 56                        |"if-lt" RegName "," RegName "," ":" Label
 57                        | BinOp RegName "," RegName "," RegName        [left]
 58                        | UnOp RegName "," RegName
 59                        |"invoke-static" "{"Parameters"}" "," MethodRef
 60                        |"invoke-virtual" "{"Parameters"}""," MethodRef
 61                        |"move-result" RegName
 62                        |"retrun-void"
 63                        |"return" RegName
 64                        |"monitor-enter" RegName
 65                        |"monitor-exit" RegName
 66    syntax Sput  ::= "sput" |"sput-object"
 67    syntax Sget  ::= "sget" | "sget-object"
 68    syntax Binop ::= "add" | "sub" | "mul" | "div" |...
 69    syntax Unop  ::= "neg" | "not" | "int-to-long" |...
 70    syntax Val   ::= Int
 71    syntax Switchtab ::= ".sparse-switch" Tablecases ".end sparse-switch"
 72    syntax Tablecases ::= List {Tablecase," "}
 73    syntax Tablecase ::= Value "->" ":" Label
 74    syntax StringId , Label ::= Id
 75    syntax Empty ::= " "
 76    syntax ManifestFile::=".manifest" MethodRef
 77  end module
```

Listing 1.3. K source file for K-Smali syntax

A *Comment* is a regular expression r"<regExp>" that starts with # and followed by any character (.) zero or many times (*). Notice that the attribute [token] used when defining a comment and the fully qualified name of a class (lines 10 and 33) signals that the associated sort will be occupied by domain values, which is a set of literal values (string and integer). A class definition includes its fields and methods as well.

A method is defined by a set of access flags that determines its scope, a full name, a signature, and a body. A method name signature consists of the method input *MethodIntypes* and output *MethodRetTypes* types. Fields are a list of *field* identified by the keyword *.field*, access flags, a name, a type, and a value (if exists). The method body is a list of blank-separated statements. Statements are either directives or instructions. A directive could be *.locals* followed by an integer, indicating the number of the local register in the method. The directive *.registers* specifies the total number of registers in the method (including local and parameter registers). Considered instructions include unconditional and conditional jumps with, respectively, *goto*, *if-eq*, *if-lt* and *sparse-switch* instructions. All jumping to a given label (*:Label*) identifying the concerned instruction. We also consider instructions of moving a constant string and constant integer to a destination register with, respectively *const-string* and *const* instructions. Exchange between registers is modeled with *move* instruction from source to a destination register. Objects and arrays creation, arithmetic and subroutine instructions as method invocation and return (void and non-void) instructions are also part of the K-Smali language. Notice that the attribute [left] can be used for binary operations like addition which is left-associative (line 57). K-Smali includes as well read/write static fields (*sget, sput*), instance fields (*iget, iput*), and array elements (*aget, aput*) instructions. Finally, threads synchronization for shared objects instructions are modeled by *monitor-enter* and *monitor-exit* followed by the register name *RegName*, which actually holds the object to be reserved reference. For more details, such as interface definition, primitive types notations in Smali, we invite the reader to see [4].

3.2 Configuration

Figure 3 illustrates the configuration of a disassembled DEX file in a high-level overview. A Smali program configuration consists of a top level cell ⊤ holding four main cells: **Threads**, **Classes**, **RegisterMethods**, and **Heap**. The **Threads** cell represents the concurrent behavior of the program. It consists of the executing thread represented by the *Thread* sub-cell and a list of runnable threads in the *Scheduler* sub-cell. All information required for multithreading (synchronization, scheduling and communication), including the currently executing details, are in this sub-cell. Each thread is identified by an identifier *id*, a *RunTime* field computing each executed instruction, and a *status* representing its state. A thread state can be "run" for a running thread, a "runnable" for a thread waiting to be selected by the scheduler, or an object reference "*Ref*" for a blocked thread waiting for the release of this object. **Classes** cell is harboring one or multiple class(es). **RegisterMethods** cell is an independent cell (since registers are reserved and released each time a method returns). The **Heap** cell corresponds to a shared memory used to store the dynamically created objects and arrays.

Figure 4 provides the detailed configuration for sub-cells. A running thread is identified by an identifier *Id*, a *k* cell for the execution context (i.e. the computation to be executed), and a *ReturnResult* cell for its return value. Each class in *Class* cell is defined by its fully qualified class name, its direct super-class fully qualified name, an access flag indicating its visibility, and a map cell *Fieldsclass* mapping the class fields names to values. The *Class* cell includes either a *Methods* cell for all methods (zero or more) in the class. A *method* cell includes its full name, access flags, and a body, which is

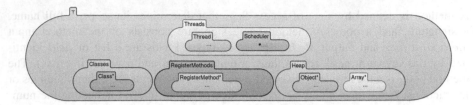

Fig. 3. $\mathbb{K}$-Smali global configuration

denoted by *code* cell and consists of a mapping from *Ids* (identifiers) to corresponding statements. *RegisterMethod* cell holds two sub-cells, the register reference and a mapping register names to values. An *Object* cell records the object reference in the heap, its class full name, a mapping (class) fields to values, and a *Reservedobject* indicator (an integer) cell used for threads synchronization. An "undefined" value indicates a free object (i.e. its associated monitor is not acquired by any thread), whereas a thread identifier *id* value designates a reserved one by the specified thread reference. The *Array* cell records the array name and size, and a mapping form indexes names to values.

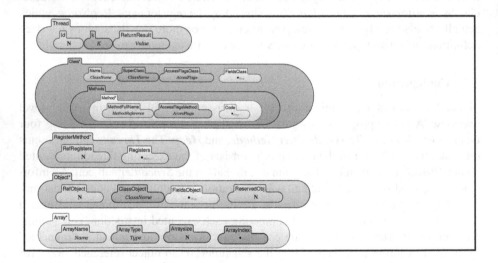

Fig. 4. $\mathbb{K}$-Smali sub-cells configuration

3.3 Semantics

Hereafter, we present the operational semantics of Smali in $\mathbb{K}$. It is represented as a set of independent rewrite rules. As our semantics is quite vast (it encompasses more than 50 rules), we will present only rules expressing the most important features. In each rule, we can capture three main repetitive execution phases : (1) the execution of the selected statement in the *code* sub-cell, (2) the selection of next statement to execute in the sub-cell K, (3) the thread executing the current instruction T must be selected by the scheduler. Which means that it must have the state "*run*" and the identifier *id*. This condition is checked by the side condition of each rule. In addition to rewrite rules, $\mathbb{K}$ definitions include functions. Most of these functions are used to manage the side-conditions of rewrite rules, in particular, for logical predicates.

The rule $R_{invoke-virtual}$ invokes an instance method.

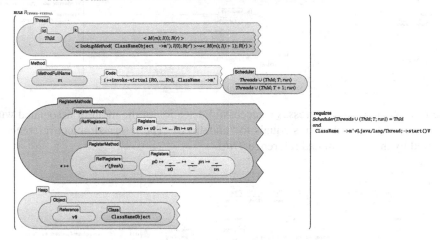

The caller method passes arguments to the callee by setting its parameter registers. The class of the object whose method is being called (or the receiving object's class) is first retrieved from the heap through its reference. The rule $R_{lookupMethod}$ is called to search the method *m'* in the class *ClassName* and upwards to its super-class chain.

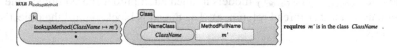

If the method is not in the class, then lookup in the super-class *scn*.

This rule checks also if the invoked method is different from *start()* method of the class *Thread*, which is used to start a thread and treated separately with the rule $R_{Create-thread}$. The rule $R_{create-thread}$ creates a new thread object and adds it to the scheduler list.

330   M. Ziadia et al.

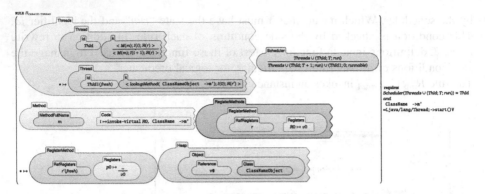

The rule $R_{\text{monitor-enter}}$ expresses a successful detention of the monitor associated with the object *Ref* since its status equals to "undefined". The reserved object reference is updated by the owner thread reference *ThId*.

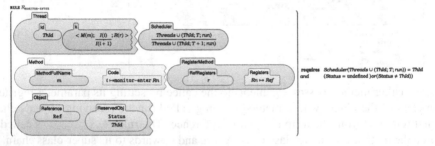

The rule $R_{\text{monitor-enter(block)}}$ models a failed attempt to a shared object (the object status equals to another thread reference). The thread is blocked until the object's monitor is released.

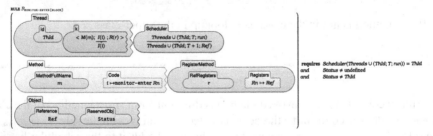

The rule $R_{\text{monitor-exit}}$ represents a thread that releases the owned monitor for the object in *Rn* (the status is rewritten by the "undefined" value).

where:

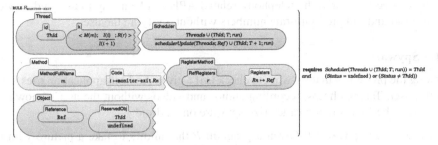

$schedulerUpdate(\{\}; Ref) = \{\}$
$schedulerUpdate(\{(ThId; T; Ref)\} \cup Threads; Ref) = \{(ThId; T; run)\} \cup schedulerUpdate(Threads; Ref)$
$schedulerUpdate(\{(ThId; T; Status)\} \cup Threads; Ref) = \{(ThId; T; Status)\} \cup schedulerUpdate(Threads; Ref)$ If $Status \neq Ref$

The Function *schedularUpdate( )* releases all blocked threads waiting for this object since it is now free.

4   Program Verification

In addition to defining an executable formal semantics of Smali, our second objective is to formally verify Smali programs using $\mathbb{K}$ and the built-in tools for parsing and program verification. To verify properties on a given Android application, we need a $\mathbb{K}$-Smali *program P*, a *property S* to be proved, and finally testing if *P* satisfies or not the property *S* using the command *krun* and the appropriate option. For property specification, $\mathbb{K}$ offers a wide range of options. In sum, the logical foundation of the $\mathbb{K}$ framework's verification infrastructure is matching logic for static properties [11] and reachability logic for the dynamic ones (from version 4 and up). Therefore, properties can be specified as reachability logic assertions using $\mathbb{K}$ rewrite rules. They can also be written as preconditions and post-conditions in Hoare triples [2], temporal logic formulas LTL, Modal logic, formulas in first-order logic, or any other logical formalism. $\mathbb{K}$ offers Linear Temporal Logic (LTL) model checking via compilation into Maude programs through its Maude [12, 13] backend available in version 3.5 and down. Security-related properties such as confidentiality, access control, information flow, etc. can be checked in general. For Android, we may need more fine-grained properties specific to its typical features and security-sensitive services. Most existing approaches rely on the analysis of API calls to detect malicious behaviors of a given Android application (e.g. in [14–18]). Executing sensitive operations, such as sending SMS messages, recording audios and videos, tracking the geographical position of the user are all performed through calls to API methods. Verifying properties for each time these APIs are used will certainly increase the false positive rate. Instead, it would be more judicious to express the temporal order in which these APIs are invoked. In this sense, model-checking is the most suitable technique for verifying temporal properties [14]. Many spyware exploit the system services to collect or disclose private data. As a result, they become able to track the geographic location of the device, eavesdrop on conversations, take photos, and record videos without the user's knowledge. The SMS sending APIs are also among the most sensitive APIs in Android. Such a feature can be mislead by attackers to send SMSs to premium-rate numbers without the user's consent. DogWars

[19], for instance, is an application containing a Trojan that sends SMSs to all contacts on the device. Similarly, the telephony-related APIs can be a way to use paid services in Android and call premium-rate numbers without notifying the user.

4.1 Spyware

Among the properties that we want to check is if a given Android application tries to spy on the user. Taking photos, recording audios and videos without the user's knowledge are among behaviors that characterize spyware on Android.

- *Program to be verified:* Given a program *P* that allows to take a picture with the instruction *invoke-virtual* of the method *TakePicture* from the fully-qualified class name *Landroid/hardware/Camera*. The invocation of this API can only be exploited to take a picture without the user's knowledge. Except that, invoking the method *setPreviewDisplay* or *setPreviewTexture* from the same class before allows to display the camera preview. In this way, the user will be aware that the camera is open and tries to take a photo. APIs representing these two features are mainly invoked by as illustrated in the following example.

```
1  invoke-virtual{v1,v2},Landroid/hardware/Camera;↦setPreviewDisplay(Landroid
   /view/SurfaceHolder;)V
2  invoke-virtual{v0,v2,v2,v1},Landroid/hardware/Camera;↦takePicture(Landroid
   /hardware/Camera$ShutterCallback;Landroid/hardware/Camera$
   PictureCallback;Landroid/hardware/Camera$PictureCallback;)V
```

Listing 1.4. Taking a picture and displaying camera preview APIs

- *Property specification:* An LTL formula can express the desired behavior and requires the order of having the API *SetPreviewDisplay* or *SetPreviewTexture* **before** the API *TakePicture*. This way we can check if the program can spy on the user or not. To define this property, we need to express the past logic using both past LTL (ptLTL) and future LTL logic (LTL) modalities. Temporal logic (LT) gathers LTL and ptLTL modalities [20]. An LTL formula representing this behavior could be defined as follows:

$$\Box(takePicture \rightarrow \odot(setPreviewDisplay \lor setPreviewTexture))$$

The LTL formula starts with the LTL operator $\Box$ which means *"always"*. The operator $\odot$ represents the past logic (ptLTL) and means *"previously"*. The operator $\lor$ expresses disjunction. Intuitively, the formula states that *"If takepicture happens now, setPreviewDisplay or setPreviewTexture must (always) have happened (previously)"*. Similarly, by not using the method *setPreviewDisplay* from *Landroid/media/MediaRecorder;*, the user will not be warned when the application attempts to record video or audio surreptitiously. The following LTL formula expresses this behavior:

$$\Box(setVideoSource \lor setAudioSource \rightarrow \odot setPreviewDisplay)$$

4.2 SMS Trojan

SMS trojans cause financial losses to users by sending SMS messages to premium-rate numbers without the user's consent. Hiding of received SMS messages is possible by aborting broadcast intents. In fact, after invoking the API *sendTextMessage* with a premium number, the attacker intercepts and calls the *abortBroadcast* function to remove billing-related notification messages from respective service providers. This way, the attacker can make sure that the user will not be able to detect that an SMS has been sent.

– *Property specification:* This property can be expressed by the formula below:

$$\Box(\neg abortBraodcast \rightarrow \Diamond sendTextMessage)$$

The ptLTL operator $\Diamond$ means *"eventually"* in the past. In order to detect the possibility of an SMS Trojan, the formula ensures that *"each time the abortBroadcast function is preceded with a sendTextmessage* method, this action will not be permitted". Intuitively, it ensures that the user will be notified each time he receives an SMS.
– *Krun command: Krun* command is used to execute a program having the $\mathbb{K}$ semantics of the language. LTL formulas can also be verified through LTL model checking with this command plus the option "−−ltlmc" as follows:

$$krun\ P.smali\ --ltlmc\ LTLformula$$

The option "−−ltlmc" is used with the command *Krun* to indicate that the specified program (*P.smali*) is model-checked with the following LTL formula (*LTLformula*). The outcome is *True* if the property holds. Otherwise, a counter-example representing an execution violating the property is exhibited.

5 Comparison with Related Work

Android application analysis tools can be grouped into two categories of approaches: test-based and formal semantics-based approaches, hereafter discussed.

Test-Based Approaches. Several efforts have focused on the Android security issue without a formal foundation at both the specification and verification levels. For example, Porter Felt et al. [21] proposed a tool, called Stowaway, to capture overprivilege in compiled Android applications to ascertain whether Android developers follow the least privilege rule. This tool collects the API calls that an application uses and associates them with permissions. They used dedicated testing tools to build the permissions map in order to spot privilege escalation. In [22], Chin et al. proposed a tool, called ComDroid, to analyze the interaction between applications in order to detect vulnerabilities and security risks in their components. In [23], Arzt et al. proposed Flowdroid, a static taint-analysis tool for Android applications. This tool models important aspects specific to Android such as application lifecycle and callbacks, which results in reducing missed leaks and false positives. What these tools all have in common is that they do not all produce formal proof that an application is secure or not, which undermines their reliability and raises questions about their validity. Another line of test-based Android malware detection is using machine learning and deep learning. The overall idea consists of building a dataset holding both malicious and benign Android application samples, from which features are extracted. Based on these inputs, classification algorithms are used for malware detection. Feng et al. [24] propose a pre-installed solution called MobiTive. They divide their system functionality into a server-side and mobile side. The first part provides a trained deep learning model and a feature dictionary built from the extracted API calls and manifest properties. In the second part, as soon as an application is downloaded, MobiTive extracts features of the API calls and manifest properties from the *classes.dex* and *manifest* files. Although the authors insist on the benefits of extracting features directly from the APK, without wasting time on converting it into a human-readable format, they use a third-party decoder library and an API parser for that, which is also time-consuming. In our approach, we use the reverse-engineering tool Apktool to retrieve the Smali code. The tool generates immediately a human-readable code (Smali), from which several features can be more easily extracted and parsed. In the same stream of thought, Kumar et al. [25] use a deep learning model to analyze and detect malware in Android Internet of Things (IoT) devices. Although their claimed high accuracy scores, none of the cited pieces of work are based on a formal specification to detect malware. Therefore, none of them can be proven correct. Moreover, the shown results are tritely bound to the given scenarios.

Formal Approaches. In addition to test-based approaches, there have been several efforts to use formal methods to analyze the code of Android applications. In [26], Khan et al. put forward a formal model to analyze data flows between Android applications using the theorem prover Coq. For that, a programming language-based security was formalized in mechanical Coq. Applications were modeled as simple terms and the system correctness comes down then to data-flow safety. Coq offers mechanical support for building and checking proof of correctness. In [27,28], Betarte et al. suggested a formal specification of Android's permission model allowing to state and prove security proprieties and enforce permission-based access control policies. Properties were proved using the Coq proof assistant. Compared to Coq, $\mathbb{K}$ supports an interpreter enabling to test and to run testing programs (executable semantics), a symbolic execution engine for the language, and parsers generated automatically from the specification. Moreover, the program definition with $\mathbb{K}$ is clearer and more concise with BNF notations, against inductive purely syntactic definitions with Coq. In sum, the $\mathbb{K}$ framework is better suited for specifying languages and verifying programs. This task is far more expensive when using Coq. This being said, Coq remains more suited to model math-oriented problems and to prove theorems. Other important studies [29–31] have been proposed. They were based on the formal semantics of Dalvik bytecode for the analysis, detection of potential vulnerabilities, or malicious behavior. Despite promising results and the power of formal methods to identify problems at an earlier stage and produce more robust languages, none of these pieces of work have been based on a language definitional framework for defining formal semantics. On the other hand, none of the aforementioned formal languages for Android application is considering the concurrent nature of the language. 𝕂-Smali fully supports multithreading. Pegasus[14] model checks temporal logic formulas, expressing an application behavior as expected by the user, against an abstraction called permission event graph (PEG). The PEG is then verified using a verification tool for compliance with the specification. Other model checkers are also proposed in [32–34] is the closest work to ours. Instead of parsing a single application, the approach is applied to a set of applications (APK) since the checked property is related to collusion between different applications. The Maude model checker checks the property for the input set of Android applications. The resulting semantics was only used to verify the collusion property. In our work, the semantics of one Android application enables us to verify many properties related to its API calls. This feature is a key static metric that enables to identify malicious behaviors, such as SMS Trojans, spyware, and many other malware. In [35], we used the 𝕂-*Smali* semantics presented in this paper as a formal basis to enforce security policies. LTL formulas expressing several properties are defined and then transformed to 𝕂-*Smali* programs, then injected into untrusted programs, compelling them to abide by the policy. The security policy enforcement process has been automated in [36] using the 𝕂 framework once again. In this work, all the enforcement steps were made by 𝕂 through a syntax, a configuration and rewrite rules. It generates, from a formula defined in 𝕂 and a 𝕂-*Smali* program, a new version of the program that behaves according to the introduced formula. We used the interpreter offered by 𝕂 to confirm this result.

6 Conclusion

In this work, we have presented 𝕂-Smali, which we believe is the most complete formal semantics of the Smali language. Using the 𝕂 framework, we have been able to improve several uncovered points in *Smali*⁺, such as the program entry point, the initialization step, and other missing details discovered when compiling the language definition. Execution, semantics debugging are all taken care of by the framework. The interpreter allows executing sample programs and debugging the semantics, which increases the reliability of the generated formal model. 𝕂-Smali includes an important feature that has been largely neglected in the state of the art, which is multithreading. This allows testing the behavior of any multi-threaded Android program. Moreover, owing to its built-in tools, 𝕂 makes it easy to verify properties on Smali programs.

References

1. Mcafee mobile threat report (2020). https://www.mcafee.com/content/dam/consumer/en-us/docs/2020-Mobile-Threat-Report.pdf
2. Stefanescu, A., Park, D., Yuwen, S., Li, Y., Rosu, G.: Semantics-based program verifiers for all languages. In: Visser, E., Smaragdakis, Y., (eds.), Proceedings of the 2016 ACM SIGPLAN International Conference on Object-Oriented Programming, Systems, Languages, and Applications, OOPSLA 2016, part of SPLASH 2016, Amsterdam, The Netherlands, 30 October–4 November 2016, pp. 74–91. ACM (2016)

3. Rosu, G., Serbanuta, T.-F.: An overview of the K semantic framework. J. Log. Algebraic Methods Program. **79**(6), 397–434 (2010)
4. Ziadia, M., Fattahi, J., Mejri, M., Pricop, E.: Smali+: an operational semantics for low-level code generated from reverse engineering android applications. Information **11**(3), 130 (2020)
5. Bae, K., Meseguer, J.: Model checking linear temporal logic of rewriting formulas under localized fairness. Sci. Comput. Program. **99**, 193–234 (2015)
6. Goranko, V., Rumberg, A.: Temporal logic. In: Zalta, E.N. (ed.), The Stanford Encyclopedia of Philosophy. Metaphysics Research Lab, Stanford University, Summer 2020 edn. (2020)
7. Bogdanas, D., Rosu, G.: K-Java: a complete semantics of Java. In: Rajamani, S.K., Walker, D., (eds.), Proceedings of the 42nd Annual ACM SIGPLAN-SIGACT Symposium on Principles of Programming Languages, POPL 2015, Mumbai, India, 15–17 January 2015, pp. 445–456. ACM (2015)
8. Filaretti, D., Maffeis, S.: An executable formal semantics of PHP. In: Jones, R. (ed.) ECOOP 2014. LNCS, vol. 8586, pp. 567–592. Springer, Heidelberg (2014). https://doi.org/10.1007/978-3-662-44202-9_23
9. Hathhorn, C., Ellison, C., Rosu, G.: Defining the undefinedness of C. In: Grove, D., Blackburn, S., (eds.) Proceedings of the 36th ACM SIGPLAN Conference on Programming Language Design and Implementation, Portland, OR, USA, 15–17 June 2015, pp. 336–345. ACM (2015)
10. Rosu, G.: $\mathbb{K}$: a semantic framework for programming languages and formal analysis tools. In: Pretschner, A., Peled, D., Hutzelmann, T., (eds.), Dependable Software Systems Engineering, vol. 50, NATO Science for Peace and Security Series-D: Information and Communication Security, pp. 186–206. IOS Press (2017)
11. Rosu, G., Chen, X.: Matching logic: the foundation of the K framework (invited talk). In: Blanchette, J., Hritcu, C., (eds.) Proceedings of the 9th ACM SIGPLAN International Conference on Certified Programs and Proofs, CPP 2020, New Orleans, LA, USA, 20–21 January 2020, p. 1. ACM (2020)
12. Clavel, M., et al.: All About Maude - A High-Performance Logical Framework. LNCS, vol. 4350. Springer, Heidelberg (2007). https://doi.org/10.1007/978-3-540-71999-1
13. Şerbănuţă, T.F., Roşu, G.: K-Maude: a rewriting based tool for semantics of programming languages. In: Ölveczky, P.C. (ed.) WRLA 2010. LNCS, vol. 6381, pp. 104–122. Springer, Heidelberg (2010). https://doi.org/10.1007/978-3-642-16310-4_8
14. Chen, K.Z., et al.: Contextual policy enforcement in android applications with permission event graphs. In: 20th Annual Network and Distributed System Security Symposium, NDSS 2013, San Diego, California, USA, 24–27 February 2013 (2013)
15. Alhanahnah, M., et al.: Detecting vulnerable android inter-app communication in dynamically loaded code. In: IEEE INFOCOM 2019 - IEEE Conference on Computer Communications, pp. 550–558, April 2019
16. Jerbi, M., Dagdia, Z.C., Bechikh, S., Said, L.B.: On the use of artificial malicious patterns for android malware detection. Comput. Secur. **92**, 101743 (2020)
17. Gao, H., Cheng, S., Zhang, W.: Gdroid: android malware detection and classification with graph convolutional network. Comput. Secur. **106**, 102264 (2021)
18. Bai, G., et al.: Towards model checking android applications. IEEE Trans. Softw. Eng. **44**(6), 595–612 (2018)
19. Mills, E.: Dog wars app for android is trojanized. https://www.cnet.com/news/dog-wars-app-for-android-is-trojanized/
20. Manna, Z., Pnueli, A.: The Temporal Logic of Reactive and Concurrent Systems - Specification. Springer, Cham (1992). https://doi.org/10.1007/978-1-4612-0931-7
21. Felt, A.P., Chin, E., Hanna, S., Song, D., Wagner, D.A.: Android permissions demystified, pp. 627–638 (2011)

22. Chin, E., Felt, A.P., Greenwood, K., Wagner, D.: Analyzing inter-application communication in android. In: Proceedings of the 9th International Conference on Mobile Systems, Applications, and Services, MobiSys 2011, pp. 239–252, New York (2011)
23. Arzt, S., et al.: Flowdroid: precise context, flow, field, object-sensitive and lifecycle-aware taint analysis for android apps. SIGPLAN Not. **49**(6), 259–269 (2014)
24. Feng, R., Chen, S., Xie, X., Meng, G., Lin, S.-W., Liu, Y.: A performance-sensitive malware detection system using deep learning on mobile devices. IEEE Trans. Inf. Forensics Secur. **16**, 1563–1578 (2021)
25. Kumar, R., et al.: IoTmalware: android IoT malware detection based on deep neural network and blockchain technology. CoRR, abs/2102.13376 (2021)
26. Khan, W., Kamran, M., Ahmad, A., Khan, F.A., Derhab, A.: Formal analysis of language-based android security using theorem proving approach. IEEE Access **7**, 16550–16560 (2019)
27. Betarte, G., Campo, J.D., Luna, C., Romano, A.: Formal analysis of android's permission-based security model. Sci. Ann. Comput. Sci. **26**(1), 27–68 (2016)
28. Betarte, G., Campo, J., Cristiá, M., Gorostiaga, F., Luna, C., Sanz, C.: Towards formal model-based analysis and testing of android's security mechanisms. In: 2017 XLIII Latin American Computer Conference (CLEI), pp. 1–10 (2017)
29. Payet, E., Spoto, F.: An operational semantics for android activities, pp. 121–132 (2014)
30. Wognsen, E., Karlsen, H., Olesen, M.C., Hansen, R.: Formalisation and analysis of Dalvik bytecode. Sci. Comput. Program. **92**, 25–55 (2014)
31. Jeon, J., Micinski, K.K.: Symdroid: Symbolic Execution for Dalvik (2012)
32. Casolare, R., Martinelli, F., Mercaldo, F., Santone, A.: Android collusion: detecting malicious applications inter-communication through sharedpreferences. Information **11**(6), 304 (2020)
33. Casolare, R., Martinelli, F., Mercaldo, F., Nardone, V., Santone, A.: Colluding android apps detection via model checking. In: Barolli, L., Amato, F., Moscato, F., Enokido, T., Takizawa, M. (eds.) WAINA 2020. AISC, vol. 1150, pp. 776–786. Springer, Cham (2020). https://doi.org/10.1007/978-3-030-44038-1_71
34. Asăvoae, I.M., Blasco, J., Chen, T.M., Kalutarage, H.K., Muttik, I., Nguyen, H.N., Roggenbach, M., Shaikh, S.A.: Detecting malicious collusion between mobile software applications: the android^{TM} case. In: Palomares Carrascosa, I., Kalutarage, H.K., Huang, Y. (eds.) Data Analytics and Decision Support for Cybersecurity. DA, pp. 55–97. Springer, Cham (2017). https://doi.org/10.1007/978-3-319-59439-2_3
35. Ziadia, M., Mejri, M., Fattahi, J.: Formal and automatic security policy enforcement on android applications by rewriting. In: Fujita, H., Pérez-Meana, H., (eds.), New Trends in Intelligent Software Methodologies, Tools and Techniques - Proceedings of the 20th International Conference on New Trends in Intelligent Software Methodologies, Tools and Techniques, SoMeT 202, Cancun, Mexico, 21–23 September 2021, vol. 337, Frontiers in Artificial Intelligence and Applications, pp. 85–98. IOS Press (2021)
36. Ziadia, M., Mejri, M., Fattahi, J.: K semantics for security policy enforcement on android applications with practical cases. In: EAI CICom 2021, editor, 2nd EAI International Conference on Computational Intelligence and Communications, 18–19 November 2021 Versailles, France, EAI CICom 2021 (2021)

Defense and Analysis

Why Anomaly-Based Intrusion Detection Systems Have Not Yet Conquered the Industrial Market?

S. Seng[1,2], J. Garcia-Alfaro[2(✉)], and Y. Laarouchi[1]

[1] EDF R&D, Palaiseau, France
`so.seng@free.fr, youssef.laarouchi@edf.fr`
[2] Télécom SudParis, Institut Polytechnique de Paris, Palaiseau, France
`joaquin.garcia_alfaro@telecom-sudparis.eu`

Abstract. In this position paper, we tackle the following question: why anomaly-based intrusion detection systems (IDS), despite providing excellent results and holding higher (potential) capabilities to detect unknown (zero-day) attacks, are still marginal in the industry, when compared to, e.g., signature-based IDS? We will try to answer this question by looking at the methods and criteria for comparing IDS as well as a specific problem with anomaly-based IDS. We will propose 3 new criteria for comparing IDS. Finally, we focus our discussion under the specific domain of IDS for critical Industrial control systems (ICS).

Keywords: Intrusion detection system · Anomaly detection · Explainable artificial intelligence · Industrial control system · Critical infrastructures

1 Introduction

Faced with cybersecurity issues, the implementation of information systems monitoring tools is increasingly needed or a compulsory requirement. Many companies are investing in setting up a SOC (Security Operation Center), equipped with a SIEM (Security Information Management System) for the recognition and management of alerts. The origin of these alerts comes from various sensors, intrusion detection probes or external contextual informations.

There are two main categories of intrusion detection probes. The first category concerns Host-based IDS (HIDS). They use system data such as files or application event logs as input data. The second category concerns Network-based IDS (NIDS) which uses network exchanges as input data. In this paper, we do not distinguish between these two categories. In fact, whether we refer to either HIDS or NIDS, we focus our study on the underlying technology used by the detection engine. Two main representative technologies are often used in the literature: either signature-based or anomaly-based detection.

Signature-based detection, also referred to as *misuse* or *knowledge*-based detection, uses pattern matching classifiers to identify the attacks, i.e., they

© Springer Nature Switzerland AG 2022
E. Aïmeur et al. (Eds.): FPS 2021, LNCS 13291, pp. 341–354, 2022.
https://doi.org/10.1007/978-3-031-08147-7_23

use signature databases or heuristics describing the attacks. Early IDS products used this type of detection engines, since it is indeed simple, fast and does not consume much material resources. This type of detection is extremely effective at detecting attacks for which there is a signature, detection heuristic, or possibly an indicator of compromise (IoC). However, due to their operation, this type of detection is incapable of detecting unknown (zero-day) attacks. In addition, it requires a frequent updating of the signature database.

Anomaly-based detection aims at detecting attacks (also unknown ones) by modeling *normal* behaviors and, then, reporting any variations or anomalies deviating from a such model. This type of detection is not very recent. Indeed, the first one was proposed by Denning in 1987 [1]. However, in real life, information systems are often complex and difficult to model. Over the years, several methodologies have been proposed to model malicious behavior. The simplest methodologies are based on statistical methods such as threshold crossings. Today, most existing solutions seem to improve traditional detection rates by using artificial intelligence (AI) algorithms and, in particular, Machine Learning (ML) algorithms.

For nearly 20 years, the scientific literature on IDS has focused on anomaly-based detection engines, in particular on the use of AI algorithms. The majority of these studies on AI-based anomaly detection algorithms present detection rates (i.e., accuracy rates) greater than 95%, with very low false-negative rates, of the order of a few percent [2]. These very good results seem to show that AI algorithms are particularly efficient and suitable for IDS. However, currently on the market, commercial offers are mainly based on signature-based detection engines and ultimately only integrate little AI [3]. This low representativeness of commercial AI-based IDS solutions constitutes a paradox.

In this position paper, we tackle this paradox: why anomaly-based IDS have not yet conquered the industrial market? We will try to answer this question by looking at the methods and criteria for comparing IDS as well as a specific problem with anomaly-based IDS. We focus our discussion under the specific domain of critical Industrial control systems (ICS) and show that this question is particularly important in this context.

The paper is structured as follows. Section 2 provides the background and elaborates further on our problem domain. Section 3 provides our answer to the question. Section 4 discusses the link of our question to the specific domain of critical industrial control systems. Section 5 concludes the work.

2   Low Adoption of ML-Based Detection in the Industry

As mentioned in the introduction, there is a vast literature and scientific studies on AI-based anomaly detection engines. Reports like [4] show that between 2000 and 2012, only a 3% of the scientific literature was concerned with signature-based solutions, while almost a 97% of the studies correspond to anomaly-based solutions, from which a high majority relied on AI methods, in particular, ML methods. We have not found more recent statistics but we are confident that with the craze and the latest advances in AI, the ratio of scientific study has remained very high for AI-based anomaly detection engines. This section will give a quick overview of existing products, both for open source and commercial solutions. Then it will try to identify causes for the low adoption of AI in existing products. Finally, we will look at the evaluation criteria for IDS.

2.1 Omnipresence of Signature-Based Detection Engines

OpenSource Products—Successful IDS products in the OpenSource community include NIDS products such as Snort [5], Zeek [6] (formerly called Bro) and Suricata [7]; and HIDS products such as ClamAV/ClamWin [8]. They all use signature-based detection engines. OpenSource IDS using anomaly-based detection engines are mainly at the level of prototypes, derived from research studies [9–14]. Only a few, like Zeek [6] are listed as anomaly-based IDS by some authors. Indeed, Zeek can be used as a development framework which can be easily extended to create new functionalities like anomaly detection. Hence, several research projects use this ability to extend Zeek for proof-of-concept development of anomaly-based algorithms[1]. However, we must note that Zeek shall be considered as a signature-based IDS, since this is its main default mode

Commercial Products—The number of commercial IDS products is considerably larger than OpenSource products [15]. A first observation that can be made on commercial IDS is that almost all of them integrate a signature-based detection engine. Indeed, such engines are generally very effective at detecting known attacks, consuming little material resources and very attractive from a corporate security standpoint.

On the contrary, very few commercial products come with an anomaly-based detection engine. At most, we can find in the market some hybrid designs, promising the two main types of detection. This may also suggest that anomaly-based detection engines are not yet self-sufficient, i.e., they are merely seen as a kind of complement to the more efficient signature-based designs. The inclusion of anomaly-based AI solutions in commercial products can also be seen as a commercial claim [16]. Most commercially available anomaly-based detection solutions are still insufficiently described to be able to assess their capabilities. It is then difficult to estimate whether this is an effective implementation or a cosmetic and marketing argument.

Commercial IDS do not generally use a single intrusion detection probe but a complete solution integrating several additional functionalities [15]. A detection engine can even be provided as a SaaS (Software as a Service), offering hybrid solutions combining multiple detection techniques. We regularly find hybrid solutions containing an intrusion detection probe incorporating a signature engine, coupled with an outsourced service performing an anomaly-based detection. This

---

[1] For instance, https://www.stratosphereips.org/zeek-anomaly-detector.

is notably the case of most antivirus-type HIDS where signature-based detection is performed by the intrusion detection probe itself and the anomaly-based detection is an outsourced service called *CloudAV* [17].

2.2   Anomaly-Based Challenges for IDS

Some authors in the related literature justify the lack of anomaly-based IDS in the industry, compared to the number of existing studies in the scientific community, by the lack of rigor in such studies [2]. It can be summarized by the following issues: (1) lack of datasets, (2) weak evaluation methods, (3) reproducibility (e.g., lack of data initialization data, replicability of the datasets and hardware configuration), (4) comparability (e.g., different types of attacks needing to be compared separately).

The lack of rigor [18] and the importance of having datasets of quality [19] is in fact a classical issue for the evaluation of AI algorithms, and ML in particular. In the cybersecurity realm, moreover, confidentiality issues can also lead to difficulties to share high quality datasets [4,20,21]. This observation particularly affects the evaluation of NIDS products. According to [22], two very old datasets such as KDD99 and NSL-KDD represented in 2020 almost a 71% of the datasets used in scientific literature. Seen by most authors as outdated evaluation datasets, they correspond moreover to a single experiment carried out by DARPA between 1998 and 1999 [23], being the latter a cleaning and improvement of the former, in particular, in terms of data labeling [20]. More recent datasets exist [3], notably CIC-IDS 2017 and CIC-IDS2018 [24] and SWaT [25]. Still, their number remains generally modest and these are still too rarely used. For architectures not covered by KDD99 or by other public datasets, e.g., for industrial architectures, the absence of existing datasets encourages simulation or data generation, even if it means moving away from real constraints.

The aforementioned issues and, more specifically, the difficulties in finding appropriate evaluation datasets, are intrinsic issues in many other AI and ML research domains, such as medicine, where access to data must respect patient privacy. However, they may constitute a major obstacle to consolidate a commercial solution, especially in industrial domains related to critical ICS, in which the incorporation of novel cybersecurity approaches have a certain lack of acceptance.

2.3   Benchmarks and Evaluation Criteria

The expected rate of false positives and false negatives, as well as the processing performance, constitute important criteria to evaluate the quality of an IDS. The processing performance is often related to the number of events per second processed by the detection engine of an IDS. In particular, it is notably used to identify whether the IDS is capable of processing events in real time. The expected rate of false positives and false negatives is often defined as follows:

- False Positive Rate (FPR): $FPR = \frac{FP}{FP+TN}$, where FP is the observed number of false positive events, and TN the true number of negative events.

- False Negative Rate (FNR): $FNR = \frac{FN}{FN+TP}$, where FN is the observed number of false negative events, and TP the true number of positive events.

The two aforementioned indicators are generally used for the evaluation of any classifier used for detection. Receiver Operating Characteristic (ROC) curves are often used to represent binary classifiers based on their FPR and FNR rates [26]. Similarly, a confusion matrix, cf. Table 1, can also be used to represent the efficiency of a classifier.

Table 1. Confusion matrix

	Actual positives	Actual negatives
Positive predictions	True positives (TP)	False positives (FP)
Negative predictions	False negatives (FN)	True negatives (TN)

In a cybersecurity and IDS context, the primary goal of a classifier is to minimize the number of false negatives (since undetected attacks lead to high risks [27]). This only goal can be a challenge because minimizing the number of false negatives usually involves to increase the number of false positives, which in turn increases the workload of human analysts.

Other criteria to quantify the efficiency of an IDS include [28,29]: (1) accuracy (directly derived from the FPR), (2) performance (i.e., processing capabilities), (3) completeness (i.e., ability to identify all existing attacks and therefore directly derived from the FNR), (4) fault tolerance (i.e., ability of the IDS to resist the attacks itself), and (5) timeliness (i.e., ability to propagate the information, e.g., when a mitigation action must be conducted right after a detection alert has been processed).

2.4 New Evaluation Criteria

We think, the aforementioned explanations and evaluation criteria are insufficient to justify the low number of anomaly-based IDS deployed in the market. We propose to define two new concepts or criteria that will be interesting to explore (1) *completeness of knowledge* and (2) *ease of implementation and maintenance*.

Completeness of knowledge differs depending on the detection technique. On one hand, the use of knowledge completeness as a criterion related to a signature-based detection engine would refer to the quality and richness (in the absence of being able to be exhaustive) of the signature database. Since signature-based techniques base their detection on the existence of attack signatures (i.e., attack identification patterns), the higher the number of unique signatures associated to the IDS, the higher as well the completeness of knowledge associated to such an IDS. This criterion may also focus on related properties of the signature database of the IDS, such as the database update mechanism or the language flexibility to define new attacks. On the other hand, the use of knowledge completeness as a criterion related to anomaly-based detection engines rather refers to the quality of the the training dataset, which is often very domain specific and hard to quantify. This criterion, Completeness of knowledge, is potentially difficult to quantify. A good approach is probably to build a index reference based on the benchmark of several existing solutions.

Ease of implementation and maintenance also depends on the specific detection technique. In fact, signature-based detection is generally agnostic to the use cases or systems they monitor. The general tendency consists in integrating as many attack signatures as possible in the signature database. Its setup and maintenance process is, hence, straightforward. On the contrary, anomaly-based detection is rather specific to use cases. The setup process requires a preliminary step needed to model the normal behavior of the events that will be monitored. The level of expertise required for maintenance and operational conditions (e.g., updates, business knowledge, definition of ML features and samples during the creation of both training and testing datasets, etc.) is definitely much higher than for signature-based detection approaches. This criterion is composed of several subjective elements and therefore difficult to quantify. It would be necessary to look in detail at each of the elements that compose it and identify applicable metrics.

All thoses aforementioned explanation and evaluation criteria lead to a possible explanation for the low adoption of AI and ML techniques in current IDS products. Next, we continue our discussion on the necessity of anomaly-based designs to provide a higher degree of explanability in their predictions, in order to conquer the market.

3   Explainability of IDS Predictions

Regardless of IDS, some machine learning algorithms operate as *black boxes* and offer little explanation of their classification decisions. This lack of explanation or justification of the decision can be a hindrance to confidence in the prediction, in the model and to transparency. This prevents the use of these technologies for certain use cases such as medicine or critical infrastructure. This difficulty in interpreting the predictions of a classifier using machine learning methods can also be a part of the answer to the lack of anomaly-based IDS.

Figure 1, extract from [30], represents an intuitive graph (i.e., not based on accurate values) of the different machine learning algorithms. In the opinion of the author, this figure makes consensus. It illustrates that Neural Network (NN) algorithms offering the best FPR and FNR rates are also those offering the least explanations, and vice versa. This difficulty is well known and has been the topic of a major research focus since 2016. Indeed, in 2016 DARPA launched the eXplainable Artificial Intelligence (XAI) program and funded $2 billion [31]. [32] identified at least 14 workshops or symposia dedicated to this thematic between 2014 and mid-2019. According to Gartner, in 2020, XAI research was among the top 25 trends for artificial intelligence in the *Hype* curve.

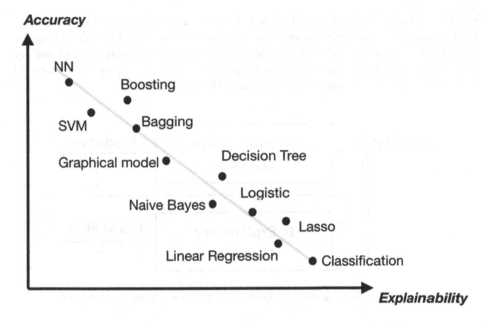

Fig. 1. Accuracy vs. Explainability of the main machine learning algorithms, extracted from [30]

The XAI topic is complex and several questions arise:

– What to explain?
– To whom should explanations be provided?
– How to provide these explanations?
– What explanations can be generated?

The answer to this last question is the one that raises the most scientific challenges. An obvious solution is to use classifiers that can provide explanations, such as decision trees, for use cases that require it. However, this limits the performances to a smaller number of classifiers and potentially the least accurate ones, as illustrated in Fig. 1. To try to provide solutions, three main research approaches are studied:

1. Couple an accuracy algorithm with an explanation algorithm
2. Local Interpretation
3. Deep Explanation: Modify the model structure to extract intermediate metrics

Couple an Accuracy Algorithm with an Explanation Algorithm. The first approach, 1) consists of keeping an existing classifier α, typically a DeepLearning (NN) classifier, and coupling it with a more explanatory classifier β. The latter then takes as input the same data as the classifier α, as well as its output prediction as shown in Fig. 2. The β classifier then, having both the input data of the model and the prediction to be obtained, would allow to improve its prediction model and potentially to obtain some explanations. This solution has the advantage of allowing the use of any α classifier and taking advantage of α's accuracy and β's explanatory capabilities. However, it is not trivial to guarantee that the explanation provided by the β classifier matches the prediction of the α classifier.

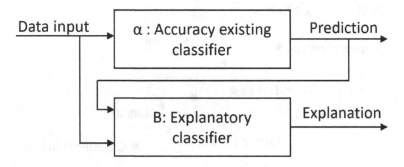

Fig. 2. Couple an accuracy algorithm with an explanation algorithm

Local Interpretation. The research approach 2) also uses an already existing classifier and consists, for a given prediction, in slightly varying the input data in order to identify local threshold values from which the classifier modifies its prediction. This method allows to identify the input data that are important for the prediction and to group them into *clusters*. The interpretation that can be made of these clusters can then constitute a possible explanation for the prediction. This interpretation is however difficult to realize and even more difficult to generalize for all possible use cases.

This technique, named LIME (Local Interpretable Model-Agnostic Explanations) was first proposed by Ribeiro et al. in [33]. It seems to be the most studied approach and is particularly efficient for image classification and explanation. The interpretation of the clusters is then assigned to a human who can then evaluate the quality of the prediction.

Deep Explanation. Finally, research approach 3) consists in improving existing algorithms or more globally classification models to allow the generation of explanations. An example of this approach is the DeepExplanation cited by Gunning in [31] and described in [34] which aims at extracting intermediate predictions whose semantic association allows the final prediction.

XAI and IDS. Research on XAI is a recent topic, the most advanced work seems to be applied to photographic image processing and is most often based on the use of an explanation human-interface which then allows a human to validate or not the prediction. About twenty articles propose to apply the principles of XAI research to IDS. The majority of them uses the LIME method. The results of these studies seem promising but still insufficient. For example, the need to interpret the clusters concept of the LIME method seems indeed appropriate to detect enumeration attacks such as DDOS or network scans, but seems hardly feasible for other types of attacks.

This explanation issue of AI-based classifiers in anomaly-based IDS does not really appear in signature-based IDS. Indeed, a signature intrinsically contains the detection criteria (the rules) and is often accompanied by descriptive elements such as the name of the associated attack or its references.

4   Discussion About ICS

4.1   Higher Cybersecurity Risks and Impacts

Until recently, Industrial control system (ICS) was a separate and disjointed domain from traditional IT, with little or no communication between these two worlds. However, for cost reasons and complexity, ICS is increasingly adopting IT technologies, especially network communication that are now based on IP technologies. In addition, latest innovations and trends in ICS management and governance, such as Enterprise 4.0, strongly encourage the interconnection between IT and ICS. These two facts offer new opportunities for cybersecurity attacks on ICS.

We believe that ICS, which were until now globally spared, are less well prepared to face cybersecurity attacks. Indeed, some specificities of ICS offer a greater exposure to cyber-attacks. First, industrial equipment designers, industrial solution integrators and operators are still not very aware of cybersecurity, which is why there are rarely effective protection measures against cybersecurity risks. Secondly, ICS are often designed for a much longer lifespan than in IT. It is common to still find ICS in operation 20 to 30 years after their initial setup. However, cybersecurity evolves quickly and requires regular software and hardware updates. But the availability of ICS is often a more important criterion than for IT, the updates of ICS are often grouped during the planned maintenance operations. Thus, a critical vulnerability on a system can sometimes be fixed several months, or even years, after the publication of a patch. This is even more true for critical ICS where a hardware or software update can jeopardize safety qualifications. In these cases, operational safety has priority over cyber security, and operators are reluctant to perform updates. Finally, ICS and especially critical ICS, due to their interaction with the physical world, can have financial, environmental and even human impacts that are much more significant than in IT. All these elements imply that the need for monitoring ICS is probably more important than for IT.

4.2   Potentially Effective Network Monitoring

On another level, some specificities about ICS seem favorable to monitoring solutions. Indeed, compared to IT systems, ICS do not evolve much. They have equipment, especially programmable logic controllers (PLC), that are deterministic in their operation. This provides industrial communication protocols with interesting properties for network monitoring [35]:

- *relatively* simple protocols;
- deterministic communication, based on iterative and continuous polling between, for example, a PLC and its sensors/actuators or between a supervisory console and its PLCs;
- strict timing requirement.

These properties make industrial communications easier and more efficient to monitor than IT communications which are often more complex, evolve rapidly and have a high variability due to human activities [36]. This facilitates the creation of anomaly detection models. However, the heterogeneity of industrial solutions, their low hardware resources and their closed (proprietary) aspects limit the possibilities for Host-based IDS.

4.3   Strong Need of Anomaly-Based IDS for ICS

The two aforementioned points about ICS, comparing to IT, 1) risks and impacts of cybersecurity are potentially much higher and 2) anomaly-based monitoring solutions can be particularly effective, are complementary and make the use of anomaly-based IDS even more important. However, here again, there are several scientific works [3, 10, 35–51] but few anomaly-based IDS are deployed. The need to explore this paradox becomes even stronger in this context. The XAI issue of anomaly-based IDS may be a part of the problematic.

5   Conclusion

This position paper has addressed why, despite their excellent results and in particular their potential capacity to detect unknown attacks, the use of artificial intelligence (AI) anomaly-based detection in IDS products, e.g., machine learning (ML) approaches, still remain marginal in the cybersecurity industry—compared to other detection approaches, such as the use of signature-based detection.

We have started our discussions by reviewing some existing background and related literature, highlighting specific problems in other AI and ML domains, such as the difficulty of building up and maintaining quality datasets (both for training and operational processing), as well as issues with traditional criteria proposed for the evaluation of IDS. The use of extended criteria, such as *completeness of knowledge* and *ease of implementation and maintenance* led our discussion to claim the necessity of exploring a new criterion, the *explainability of IDS predictions* and positioned some of the necessary rationale to be included by next-generation anomaly-based detection engines, to tackle the problem.

To sum up, we have considered that usual IDS evaluation approaches such as false negative and false positive rates, complemented by additional performance criteria, are not enough for an IDS to adopt new anomaly-based products built upon AI and ML techniques. We think that novel criteria addressing the level of quality and explainability of the predictions derived from anomaly-based detection engines is a must. We have also discussed the importance of handling this question under the specific domain of critical ICS. Indeed, those systems have increased monitoring needs and have properties that make them more favorable to anomaly detection.

For future work, it would be interesting to identify metrics to quantify the new criteria we have discussed in this paper: *completeness of knowledge*, *ease of implementation and maintenance* and especially *explainability*. Then to measure these metrics on various existing products and thus make a comparison of the existing solutions. Finally, it would be relevant to apply this approach in priority to critical ICS which are particularly adapted to anomaly-based IDS. For the latter case, it will also be necessary to overcome the issue of lack of data sets, which is more pronounced for industrial than for IT.

References

1. Denning, D.: An intrusion detection model. In: Proceedings of the Seventh IEEE Symposium on Security and Privacy, pp. 119–131 (1986)
2. Tavallaee, M., Stakhanova, N., Ghorbani, A.A.: Toward credible evaluation of anomaly-based intrusion-detection methods. Toward Credible Evaluation of Anomaly-Based Intrusion-Detection Methods, vol. 40, issue 5, pp. 516–524. Institute of Electrical and Electronics Engineers, NY Publisher, New-York (2010)
3. Conti, M., Donadel, D., Turrin, F.: A Survey on Industrial Control System Testbeds and Datasets for Security Research (2021). arXiv: 2102.05631
4. Bhuyan, M.H., Bhattacharyya, D.K., Kalita, J.K.: Network anomaly detection: methods, systems and tools. IEEE Commun. Surv. Tutor. **16**(1), 303–336 (2014). (Conference Name: IEEE Communications Surveys Tutorials)
5. Snort official web site. Snort - Network Intrusion Detection & Prevention System (2021). https://www.snort.org/
6. Zeek official web site. The Zeek Network Security Monitor (2021). https://zeek.org/
7. Suricata official web site. Suricata (2021). https://suricata-ids.org/
8. ClamavNet official web site. ClamavNet (2021). https://www.clamav.net/
9. Hurley, J., Munoz, A., Sezer, S.: ITACA: flexible, scalable network analysis. In: 2012 IEEE International Conference on Communications (ICC), pp. 1069–1073 (2012). ISSN: 1938–1883
10. Pan, S., Morris, T., Adhikari, U.: A specification-based intrusion detection framework for cyber-physical environment in electric power system. Int. J. Network Secur. **17**, 174–188, 105124 (2015)
11. Bostani, H., Sheikhan, M.: Hybrid of anomaly-based and specification-based IDS for Internet of Things using unsupervised OPF based on MapReduce approach. Comput. Commun. **98**, 52–71, 105124 (2017)
12. Korba, A.A., Nafaa, M., Ghanemi, S.: Hybrid intrusion detection framework for Ad hoc networks. Int. J. Inf. Secur. Privacy **10**(4), 1–32 (2016)
13. Lavin, A., Ahmad, S.: Evaluating real-time anomaly detection algorithms - the numenta anomaly benchmark. In: 2015 IEEE 14th International Conference on Machine Learning and Applications (ICMLA), pp. 38–44 (2015)
14. Hu, J.: Host-based anomaly intrusion detection. In: Stavroulakis, P., Stamp, M., (eds.) Handbook of Information and Communication Security, pp. 235–255. Springer, Heidelberg (2010). https://doi.org/10.1007/978-3-642-04117-4_13

15. Orans, L., D'Hoinne, J., Chessman, J.: Gartner - Market Guide for Network Detection and Response (2020). https://www.gartner.com/doc/reprints?id=1-1Z8C9OAX&ct=200612&st=sb
16. Garner-Hype. 2 Megatrends Dominate the Gartner Hype Cycle for Artificial Intelligence (2020)
17. wikipedia. Comparison of antivirus software (2021). https://en.wikipedia.org/w/index.php?title=Comparison_of_antivirus_software&oldid=1003484641. (Page Version ID: 1003484641)
18. Wainer, J., Barsottini, C.G.N., Lacerda, D., de Marco, L.R.M.: Empirical evaluation in computer science research published by ACM. Inf. Software Technol. **51**(6), 1081–1085 (2009)
19. Osorio, A., Dias, M., Cavalheiro, G.G.H.: Tangible assets to improve research quality: a meta analysis case study. In: Bianchini, C., Osthoff, C., Souza, P., Ferreira, R. (eds.) WSCAD 2018. CCIS, vol. 1171, pp. 117–132. Springer, Cham (2020). https://doi.org/10.1007/978-3-030-41050-6_8
20. Tavallaee, M., Bagheri, E., Lu, W., Ghorbani, A.A.: A detailed analysis of the KDD CUP 99 data set. In: 2009 IEEE Symposium on Computational Intelligence for Security and Defense Applications, pp. 1–6 (2009). ISSN: 2329–6275
21. Shiravi, A., Shiravi, H., Tavallaee, M., Ghorbani, A.A.: Toward developing a systematic approach to generate benchmark datasets for intrusion detection. Comput. Secur. **31**(3), 357–374 (2012)
22. Aldweesh, A., Derhab, A., Emam, A.Z.: Deep learning approaches for anomaly-based intrusion detection systems: a survey, taxonomy, and open issues. Knowl.-Based Syst. **189**, 105124 (2020)
23. Darpa. KDD Cup 1999 Data (1999)
24. Sharafaldin, I., Lashkari, A.H., Ghorbani, A.A.: Toward generating a new intrusion detection dataset and intrusion traffic characterization. In: Proceedings of the 4th International Conference on Information Systems Security and Privacy, pp. 108–116. SCITEPRESS - Science and Technology Publications, Funchal, Madeira, Portugal (2018)
25. Singapore University of Technology and Design. Secure Water Treatment (2015). https://itrust.sutd.edu.sg/testbeds/secure-water-treatment-swat/
26. Brown, C.D., Davis, H.T.: Receiver operating characteristics curves and related decision measures: a tutorial. Chemomet. Intell. Lab. Syst. **80**(1), 24–38, 105124 (2006)
27. Szczepański, M., Choraś, M., Pawlicki, M., Kozik, R.: Achieving explainability of intrusion detection system by hybrid oracle-explainer approach. In: 2020 International Joint Conference on Neural Networks (IJCNN), pp. 1–8 (2020). ISSN: 2161–4407
28. Debar, H., Dacier, M., Wespi, A.: A revised taxonomy for intrusion-detection systems. Ann. Des Télécommun. **55**(7), 361–378, 105124 (2000)
29. Ghorbani, A.A., Lu, W., Tavallaee, M.: Evaluation criteria. In: Ghorbani, A.A., Wei, L., Tavallaee, M. (eds.) Network Intrusion Detection and Prevention. ADIS, vol. 47, pp. 161–183. Springer, US, Boston, MA (2010). https://doi.org/10.1007/978-0-387-88771-5_7
30. Duval, A.: Explainable Artificial Intelligence (XAI). MA4K9 Scholarly Report, Mathematics Institute, The University of Warwick (2019)
31. Gunning, D.: Explainable Artificial Intelligence (XAI). Machine learning, p. 18 (2016)

32. Carvalho, D.V., Pereira, E.M., Cardoso, J.S.: Machine learning interpretability: a survey on methods and metrics. Electronics **8**(8), 832 (2019). Number: 8 Publisher: Multidisciplinary Digital Publishing Institute
33. Ribeiro, M.T., Singh, S., Guestrin, C.: Why should i trust you?: explaining the predictions of any classifier. In: Proceedings of the 22nd ACM SIGKDD International Conference on Knowledge Discovery and Data Mining, KDD 2016, pp. 1135–1144. Association for Computing Machinery, New York, NY, USA (2016)
34. Cheng, H., et al.: Multimedia Event Detection and Recounting, p. 12 (2014)
35. Mitchell, R., Chen, I.-R.: A survey of intrusion detection techniques for cyber-physical systems. ACM Comput. Surv. **46**(4), 55:1–55:29 (2014)
36. Cheung, S., Dutertre, B., Fong, M., Lindqvist, U., Skinner, K., Valdes, A.: Using Model-based Intrusion Detection for SCADA Networks (2006)
37. Yu, C., et al.: The implementation of IEC60870-5-104 based on UML statechart and QT state machine framework. In: 2015 IEEE 5th International Conference on Electronics Information and Emergency Communication, pp. 392–397 (2015)
38. Wickramasinghe, C.S., Marino, D.L., Amarasinghe, K., Manic, M.: Generalization of deep learning for cyber-physical system security: a survey. In: IECON 2018–44th Annual Conference of the IEEE Industrial Electronics Society, pp. 745–751 (2018). ISSN: 2577-1647
39. Beyerer, J., Maier, A., Niggemann, O.: Machine Learning for Cyber Physical Systems: Selected papers from the International Conference ML4CPS 2020. Springer (2021). Google-Books-ID: r8kQEAAAQBAJ
40. Fovino, I.N., Carcano, A., Masera, M., Trombetta, A.: Design and implementation of a secure modbus protocol. In: Palmer, C., Shenoi, S. (eds.) ICCIP 2009. IAICT, vol. 311, pp. 83–96. Springer, Heidelberg (2009). https://doi.org/10.1007/978-3-642-04798-5_6
41. Aarts, F., Kuppens, H., Tretmans, J., Vaandrager, F., Verwer, S.: Improving active Mealy machine learning for protocol conformance testing. Mach. Learn. 189–224 (2013). https://doi.org/10.1007/s10994-013-5405-0
42. Lin, H., Slagell, A., Kalbarczyk, Z., Sauer, P.W., Iyer, R.K.: Semantic security analysis of SCADA networks to detect malicious control commands in power grids. In: Proceedings of the first ACM workshop on Smart Energy Grid Security, SEGS 2013, pp. 29–34. Association for Computing Machinery, Berlin, Germany (2013)
43. Hadžiosmanović, D., Sommer, R., Zambon, E., Hartel, P.H.: Through the eye of the PLC: semantic security monitoring for industrial processes. In: Proceedings of the 30th Annual Computer Security Applications Conference, ACSAC 2014, pp. 126–135. Association for Computing Machinery, New Orleans, Louisiana, USA (2014)
44. Barbosa, R.R.R.: Anomaly detection in SCADA systems: a network based approach (2014)
45. Caselli, M., Zambon, E., Kargl, F.: Sequence-aware Intrusion Detection in Industrial Control Systems. In: Proceedings of the 1st ACM Workshop on Cyber-Physical System Security, CPSS 2015, pp. 13–24. Association for Computing Machinery, Singapore, Republic of Singapore (2015.)
46. Kerkers, M.: Assessing the Security of IEC 60870-5-104 Implementations using Automata Learning. Library Catalog: essay.utwente.nl Publisher: University of Twente (2017)
47. Udd, R., Asplund, M., Nadjm-Tehrani, S., Kazemtabrizi, M., Ekstedt, M.: Exploiting bro for intrusion detection in a SCADA System. In Proceedings of the 2nd ACM International Workshop on Cyber-Physical System Security, CPSS 2016, pp. 44–51. Association for Computing Machinery, Xi'an, China (2016)

48. Kaouk, M., Flaus, J.-M., Potet, M.-L., Groz, R.: A review of intrusion detection systems for industrial control systems. In 2019 6th International Conference on Control, Decision and Information Technologies (CoDIT), pp. 1699–1704 (2019). ISSN: 2576-3555

49. Khan, I.A., et al.: Efficient behaviour specification and bidirectional gated recurrent units-based intrusion detection method for industrial control systems. Electron. Lett. **56**(1), 27–30 (2019). Publisher: IET Digital Library

50. Olufowobi, H., Young, C., Zambreno, J., Bloom, G.: SAIDuCANT: specification-based automotive intrusion detection using controller area network (CAN) timing. IEEE Trans. Veh. Technol. **69**(2), 1484–1494 (2020). (Conference Name: IEEE Transactions on Vehicular Technology)

51. Mitchell, R., Chen, I-R.: Behavior-rule based intrusion detection systems for safety critical smart grid applications. IEEE Trans. Smart Grid **4**(3), 1254–1263 (2013). (Conference Name: IEEE Transactions on Smart Grid)

Creation and Detection of German Voice Deepfakes

Vanessa Barnekow[✉], Dominik Binder, Niclas Kromrey, Pascal Munaretto,
Andreas Schaad, and Felix Schmieder

Offenburg University of Applied Sciences, Offenburg, Germany
{vbarneko,dbinder,nkromrey,pmunaret,fschmied}@stud.hs-offenburg.de
andreas.schaad@hs-offenburg.de

Abstract. Synthesizing voice with the help of machine learning techniques has made rapid progress over the last years [1]. Given the current increase in using conferencing tools for online teaching, we question just how easy (i.e. needed data, hardware, skill set) it would be to create a convincing voice fake. We analyse how much training data a participant (e.g. a student) would actually need to fake another participants voice (e.g. a professor). We provide an analysis of the existing state of the art in creating voice deep fakes and align the identified as well as our own optimization techniques in the context of two different voice data sets. A user study with more than 100 participants shows how difficult it is to identify real and fake voice (on avg. only 37% can recognize a professor's fake voice). From a longer-term societal perspective such voice deep fakes may lead to a *disbelief by default*.

1 Introduction

Recent progress in text-to-speech synthesis resulted in the possibility to create new products such as speech assistants. However, the existing technology can also be used to synthesize fake voice of any individual as long as an attacker has enough voice material from the target to train a neural network. This can lead to criminals using synthesized voice to perform, for example, phishing attacks or fraud [2]. In this paper we will determine the effort required by an attacker to create a realistic audio deepfake in a German online teaching scenario using "off-the-shelf" methods and hardware. Therefore, we analyse the necessary technical steps for the realization of this attack, with a special focus on realistic data acquisition, which we investigate by means of a practical case study (Sect. 3). A survey was conducted asking participants to distinguish between real and fake voice samples of a professor (Sect. 4). Subsequently, we will address the question of whether and how fake voices can be detected (Sect. 5).

2 Text-to-Speech Synthesis with Tacotron 2

We base our work on the neural network architecture Tacotron 2 [3] which consists of a sequence-to-sequence feature prediction network and a modified version

© Springer Nature Switzerland AG 2022
E. Aïmeur et al. (Eds.): FPS 2021, LNCS 13291, pp. 355–364, 2022.
https://doi.org/10.1007/978-3-031-08147-7_24

of WaveNet as a vocoder. To combine both networks, mel spectrograms are used as an intermediate representation for sound. The result is a framework that synthesizes speech and nearly achieves the quality of real human speech. This means that we do not have an end-to-end learning process but rather have to train two independent neural networks on the same data instead. The vocoders are usually interchangeable and vocoder networks can be combined differently to optimize results. The only prerequisite is that the first neural network produces an output that is a suitable input for the second neural network. We did focus on the Tacotron 2 model architecture because it is the most widely implemented and still keeps up with the latest model architectures when it comes to performance and audio quality. In fact, latest models like FastPitch [4] or FastSpeech 2 [5] only achieve a Mean Opinion Score (MOS) that is slightly higher than the one that was achieved with Tacotron (Fig. 1).

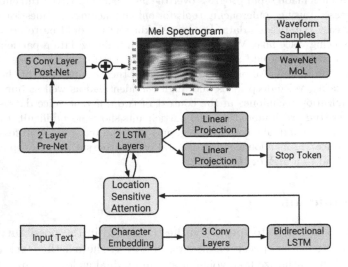

Fig. 1. Tacotron 2 architecture [3, p. 2]

The Spectrogram Prediction Network consists of an encoder that converts input character sequences into a feature representation and a decoder that uses the feature representation to predict a mel spectrogram. The encoder starts by representing the input in a 512-dimensional character embedding, which is passed through three convolutional layers. These convolutional layers model long-term context in the input character sequence. The next step is to use the output of the convolutional layers and pass it through a single bi-directional long short-term memory neural network (LSTM). This step generates the encoded features the decoder needs. The encoded features are put into a location sensitive attention network. This network later summarizes each decoder output as a fixed-length context vector. The usage of an attention network encourages the model to move forward and therefore mitigates possible problems where some subsequences are repeated or ignored. The last part of the network is the decoder that predicts the mel spectrogram. The decoder starts with a small pre-net to bottleneck the incoming information. After that, the pre-net output is passed through two uni-directional LSTM layers followed by a linear transformation of the output to predict the spectrogram. As the last step in the decoder, the predicted mel spectrogram is passed through a five layer convolutional post-net. The post-net predicts a residual that is later used to optimize the predictions by minimizing the summed Mean Squared Error (MSE) [3].

The modified version of WaveNet [6] is used to invert the predicted mel spectrogram into speech. The main difference between the old and the new version is the input that is required by the network. Whilst the old version needed linguistic features, predicted log fundamental frequency and phoneme durations, the new version only needs a mel spectrogram [3].

3 Cloning the Voice of a University Professor

Preliminary research on speech synthesis, which can be found in detail in the extended version of this paper [7], showed how considerably good samples could be generated from existing datasets with a length of two to three hours of high quality audio material. In this section, we examine whether the creation of a fake voice can be realized with audio material from online lectures, using the example of a professor.

3.1 Data Ingestion

Training neural networks usually requires a lot of training data to achieve state-of-the-art performance. It is not uncommon that network architectures like DenseNet or Inception are trained on millions of samples and approximately the same applies to the speech synthesis domain. Therefore, the first task is to collect as much audio material of the person from whom we want to clone the voice as possible. Note that a synthesized voice can only be as good as the quality of the audio files it was trained on.

For this purpose, we had three hours of audio recorded by a university professor. Half of the data originated from synchronous Zoom online lectures (with a JABRA Speak 510 as input device) and the other half was professionaly recorded in an asynchronous online lecture (with a Rhode NT1-A microphone and Arturia Audiofuse DAC). We then used aeneas[1] to automatically synchronize the transcript with the original audio file. The timestamps are then used to extract all sentences from the recording. The results are roughly 1800 audio files with lengths between 2 to 20 s as well as a new metadata file with all transcriptions. Next, we divide the metadata file in a train and validation set and we should also make sure not to surpass a lower boundary of 100 validation samples.

---

[1] https://github.com/readbeyond/aeneas.

3.2 Choosing an Implementation

The Tacotron 2 architecture was implemented by different people and institutions over the past few years. We choose the implementation from NVIDIA[2] in this work, considering the fact that they modified the architecture in such a way that it produces better results without affecting the overall performance. Furthermore, it is one of the few repositories that supports Automatic Mixed Precision (AMP) which accelerates our learning process with a factor of up to three by using dedicated tensor cores on the GPU for mixed-precision computing while preserving FP32 levels of accuracy [8]. This makes it easier to train the model multiple times and test out different datasets and hyperparameters throughout the process. If we look at the changes NVIDIA made to the original model blueprint, the first thing to notice is that only a single uni-directional LSTM layer is used in the decoder while the paper suggests two. This is a trade-off after all because on the one hand it slows down the attention learning process, but on the other hand it allows us to achieve better voice quality by further reducing the training and validation losses. Another change is the fact that dropout layers are used to regularize the LSTM layers instead of zoneout layers. In practice, it turned out that dropout layers are just as effective as their counterpart and they are considerably faster during training. However, the biggest change is the fact that the originally proposed WaveNet vocoder was replaced with WaveGlow. According to NVIDIA, this choice was made because of an improved audio quality and faster than real-time inference [9].

Note that we train our own Tacotron 2 model but for WaveGlow, we fall back to pretrained models that are provided via the NVIDIA NGC platform. The reasoning behind this is the fact that it takes multiple weeks of training to converge a WaveGlow model and there is no real advantage by doing so because pretrained models generalize well to unseen speakers and languages. Nevertheless, it has to be kept in mind that WaveGlow was initially released in 2018 and other vocoders like MelGAN [10] and Parallel WaveGAN [11] exist nowadays that may outperform WaveGlow by a fair margin.

3.3 Training

Before starting the training process, the following heuristics should be taken into account because they can greatly influence the training speed as well as the quality of our synthesized samples:

- **Warmstart:** The implementation from NVIDIA allows us to drop the embedding weights of a pretrained model by passing an additional `--warm-start` parameter to the training script. This erases the learned voice but keeps the linguistic characteristics intact that can be transferred to other speakers and languages, effectively reducing the time until convergence. We will be using a pretrained Tacotron 2 model from NVIDIA as our starting point that was trained for 1,500 epochs on the English LJSpeech corpus. Normally we expect

---

[2] https://github.com/NVIDIA/tacotron2.

to see alignment after 400 to 500 epochs, but with the help of a warmstart, we already start to see first signs after 5 to 10 epochs.

- **Learning Rate Reduction:** The initial learning rate of 1e-3 should be reduced throughout the learning process if the training loss stagnates or loss spikes can be observed. In the latter case, we should recover the last checkpoint before the spike and continue to train with a reduced learning rate. Learning rate reduction has a noticeable effect on the audio quality, especially if we train on a reduced dataset. A more modern approach would be to modify the code and use an adaptive learning rate with exponential decay as other implementations do.
- **Batch Size:** Another hyperparameter that has great impact on the results is the batch size. Larger batch sizes allow us to process more data at once and fully utilize the GPU resources, but we do not benefit from the regularization effect of smaller batch sizes. It turned out that training with a batch size between 32 and 64 is the sweet spot if we train on the full dataset but we have to reduce it to a smaller number if we reduce the length of our dataset, otherwise the model does not learn any attention.

Note that even though the validation loss may increase over time, the model can still improve in terms of voice quality. This means besides the validation loss, we should also check the alignment and quality of synthesized samples throughout the training process (Fig. 2).

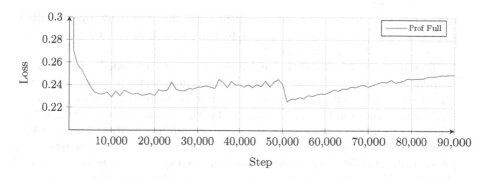

Fig. 2. Validation loss curve of the custom dataset

3.4 Inference

After finishing the training process, the checkpoints can be used for inference to generate mel spectrograms based on text. The next step is to transform the mel spectrogram to speech and as already mentioned earlier, we will use a pretrained WaveGlow model from NVIDIA for this. Similar to the pretrained Tacotron 2 model we used for a warmstart, the WaveGlow model was trained on the English LJSpeech corpus for 3,000 epochs. One thing to note is that we can add an optional denoising step during the inference by using the respective code from the WaveGlow repository. This allows us to remove some of the model bias from the final sample, effectively eliminating background noises and high whistle like sounds. We can also set the strength of the denoiser and as it turned out, a value of 0.1 is the best compromise between reducing unwanted artifacts and not affecting the speech quality itself. An alternative is to manually edit the samples ourselves by using sound editing software. In rare cases it can occur that the last frames of the generated samples sound robotic. A simple solution is to add a padding word at the end that will be cut out afterwards.

4   Survey

In order to test how convincing our deepfakes are, we conducted an online survey with 102 participants. The initially expected goal of our study was to obtain a result showing that the fake voices cannot be correctly detected in more than 50% of the cases. The survey included ten real audio files, recorded as such by the professor with a Rhode NT1-A microphone and an Arturia Audiofuse DAC using Audacity, and eleven deepfakes, with sentences he had never said, such as "Please enter A+ as a grade" or "The government fails in controlling the pandemic situation". We define six criteria to obtain the most representative survey possible in the context of this work:

1. **Unseen Words**: The deepfake sentences contained words that did not appear in the training set.
2. **Different Contents**: The real and fake audio files are made up of realistic and unrealistic statements, so as not to be able to make a statement about authenticity based on the content.
3. **Different Quality**: Since the real audio files were recorded with a professional microphone, the quality had to be degraded. So we processed the audio samples with Audacity and combined random side-effects like noise, compressor, reverb, bass and treble. The reason for this is that, on the one hand, no decision should be made based on equal sounding qualities. On the other hand, many attack scenarios are based on unprofessional equipment (e.g. phone calls, mobile phone videos, voice messages, etc.) where the quality of the audio files is poor due to room acoustics, wind and other background noises or due to the limited transmission rate.
4. **Odd Number of Audio Files**: We took 21 audio files to prevent participants from assuming an equal distribution of real and fake files when reading, for instance, 20 audio files, thus reducing an influenced decision.
5. **Listening Once**: To represent a realistic scenario, we asked (but did not force) the subjects to listen to the audio files only once and evaluate them directly. This is to avoid comparing the audio files with each other, which would make it easier to decide on the authenticity.
6. **Different Subjects**: In order to obtain a realistic picture of the survey, different groups of people between the age of 18 and 64 were questioned, some of whom were familiar with the professor's voice and some of whom were not.

The first group consisted of 19 students who knew the professor only through the online lectures. The second group was made up of 14 students who knew the professor in person. Both groups included individuals between the ages of 18 and 31. The third group consisted of 17 faculty members and colleagues of the professor, ranging in age from 29 to 64. The last and largest group, with 52 participants, included 40% under the age of 30 and about 66% overall who did not know the professor's voice.

Within the scope of this work, the following analysis is based on basic statistical techniques and does not include other in-depth analysis techniques. During the survey, participants rated the audio files using a scale with the options "real", "rather real", "rather fake", "fake" and "no idea". Table 1 shows an overview of all results. The answers with "no idea" (14% of all answers) have not been included in the evaluation and "rather fake" and "rather real" have only been weighted half as much. For each group and for all groups in total, the number of participants, the percentage of correctly identified real and fake audio files, and the detected deepfakes are given. Additionally, a confusion matrix visualizes the number of correctly or incorrectly guessed audios based on the majority vote. The results of the survey are surprisingly good, considering that the model was only re-trained with 3 h of audio. On average, a deepfake was only correctly detected 37% of the time, exceeding our initial hypothesis of 50% (fair coin toss). It is noticeable that the first two groups have a higher identification rate than the others. This could be because they are all students who know the professor's voice very well and were more motivated to achieve a good result. Based on their age, it can be expected that they have average better hearing than group 3 and 4. In addition, they are active in the IT field, so they have a better feeling about this topic. Furthermore, it can be assumed that the question instructions on single listening were partly ignored.

Table 1. Survey results of all groups (F = fake and R = real)

		G1		G2		G3		G4		Total	
Participants		19		14		17		52		102	
Correctly identified		57%		67%		38%		33%		43%	
Deepfake detected		55%		63%		27%		27%		37%	
Confusion matrix		Actual label									
		F	R	F	R	F	R	F	R	F	R
Guessed label	F	6	5	7	4	3	8	3	8	4	7
	R	4	6	3	7	5	5	6	4	6	4

Some participants gave us feedback that they decided on the basis of quality (noise, reverb, tinny sound, etc.), as they could not detect any differences in prosody. It is also important to keep in mind that participants are aware of the presence of deepfakes. In real life, people do not think about the possibility of fake material, also time pressure or other social engineering techniques are often applied to the victim, which makes it more difficult for humans to detect.

5   Detection

Since our previous results have shown that realistic voices can be cloned with existing methods and already comparatively small data sets of a few hours, the motivation to find adequate detection measures is accordingly high. In this section, we examine the audio data we have created to determine if and how technical measures can be applied to automatically detect synthetically generated voice. We demonstrate how correlation-based properties of audio tracks are used to create speech profiles, and how these profiles can be used to identify the differences between the real speaker and the synthesized voice. Subsequently, we will perform cluster-based anomaly detection on the basis of these profiles to detect synthesized voices.

5.1   Bispectral Analysis

The bispectrum is a higher order time series analysis technique that can be applied to a single time series. For a triplet of frequencies, it measures the reversibility in time and the symmetry about the mean of its flux distribution. The bispectrum is calculated as a complex number and consists of a magnitude and a phase (the biphase) [12]. In our case, the single time series of interest is the audio signal of individual samples, which we inspect using bispectral analysis. The application of this method to distinguish real and synthetic voices was demonstrated in [13]. The authors compared the voices of common voice assistants with those of real people and custom WaveNet models and concluded that this method is highly effective. We adopt relevant parts of their methodology to check whether this represents a suitable measure to detect the synthetic voices created in our work. To implement the bispectrum analysis, the Python *stingray* library was used. For the purpose of the demonstrations contained in this section, we use a subsample of the data we generated as well as a subsample of the original data. These subsamples contain respectively 100 randomly selected real and synthetic samples of the chancellor dataset and all samples of the professor dataset that were used for the survey (Sect. 4).

5.2   Anomaly Detection

To generate appropriate features for the detection of the deepfakes, we adopt the methodology shown in [13], which includes the mean, variance, skewness and kurtosis for both the magnitude and the phase of the bispectral analysis. Instead of a supervised algorithm, we deliberately use a clustering procedure to detect synthesized voices as anomalies, based on the standardized features. We base this decision on the previous observation that strong deviations of real and fake voices are recognizable for different voice profiles. Our procedure is therefore based on the assumption of having audio samples of a target's real voice and matching them with a potential fake. Using the DBSCAN clustering algorithm and match the obtained clusters with the known real voice data resulted in a model that was able detect synthesized voice samples with a precision of 80%.

6 Conclusion

We investigated the feasibility of generating German fake voices using established machine learning methods. Modern text-to-speech models are openly accessible and require only a basic understanding of the technology. The hardware required for creating synthesized voice can be acquired with a budget starting at 3000 Euros. With regard to training data acquisition, it became apparent that audio data from public figures was easy to obtain. For example, we did report in earlier work [7], that transcribed data sets of 18.7 h of the German Chancellor Merkel are freely available.

For a more realistic attack scenario, a custom dataset of a university professor was created in the context of this paper. This consisted of less than three hours of audio material partially taken from online teaching activities. Despite the reduced amount of training data, our training framework was able to generate realistic samples. In a survey we conducted with 102 participants, only 37% on average were able to detect the artificially generated voices of the professor.

In comparison, technical detection based on the features of bispectral analysis provided significantly better results, as fakes could be detected with a precision of up to 80%. We consider this approach to be particularly practical because it requires only a few samples (21 for the professor's example), unlike supervised methods that require large amounts of data. Since each sample is only a few seconds long, this detection method can thus be applied individually to any attack scenario, even if only a few minutes of the audio material to be examined are available.

The misuse of this technology can cause severe damage to individuals, organizations or even society as a whole and reduce trust in systems. To prevent this, in the worst case enabling a general *disbelief by default*, we will need more reliable detection methods in the future.

References

1. Wang, Y., et al.: Towards end-to-end speech synthesis (2017)
2. Stupp, C.: Fraudsters Used AI to Mimic CEO's Voice in Unusual Cybercrime Case (2019). https://www.wsj.com/articles/fraudsters-use-ai-to-mimic-ceos-voice-in-unusual-cybercrime-case-11567157402. Accessed 14 July 2021
3. Shen, J., et al.: Natural TTS synthesis by conditioning Wavenet on MEL spectrogram predictions (2018)
4. Łańcucki, A.: Fastpitch: Parallel text-to-speech with pitch prediction (2021)
5. Ren, Y., et al.: Fastspeech 2: Fast and high-quality end-to-end text to speech (2021)
6. van den Oord, A., et al.: A generative model for raw audio, Wavenet (2016)

7. Barnekow, V., Binder, D., Kromrey, N., Munaretto, P., Schaad, A., Schmieder, F.: Creation and detection of german voice deepfakes (2021)
8. NVIDIA. Deep Learning Performance Documentation (2021). https://docs.nvidia.com/deeplearning/performance/mixed-precision-training. Accessed 31 Mar 2021
9. Prenger, R., Valle, R., Catanzaro, B.: A flow-based generative network for speech synthesis, Waveglow (2018)
10. Kumar, K., et al.: Generative adversarial networks for conditional waveform synthesis, Melgan (2019)
11. Yamamoto, R., Song, E., Kim, J.-M.: Parallel wavegan: a fast waveform generation model based on generative adversarial networks with multi-resolution spectrogram (2020)
12. Maccarone, T.J.: The biphase explained: understanding the asymmetries in coupled fourier components of astronomical time series. Monthly Notices Roy. Astron. Soc. **435**(4), 3547–3558 (2013). ISSN: 0035-8711. https://doi.org/10.1093/mnras/stt1546
13. AlBadawy, E.A., Lyu, S., Farid, H.: Detecting AI-synthesized speech using bispectral analysis. In: CVPR Workshops, pp. 104–109 (2019)

Asset Sensitivity for Aligning Risk Assessment Across Multiple Units in Complex Organizations

Carla Mascia[1]($\boxtimes$) ⓘ and Silvio Ranise[1,2] ⓘ

[1] University of Trento, Trento, Italy
{carla.mascia,silvio.ranise}@unitn.it
[2] Bruno Kessler Foundation, Trento, Italy

Abstract. A cyber-risk assessment conducted in a large organization may lead to heterogeneous results due to the subjectivity of certain aspects of the evaluation, especially those concerning the negative consequences (impact) of a cyber-incident. To address this problem, we propose an approach based on the identification of a set of sensitivity features, i.e. certain attributes of the assets or processing activities that are strongly related to the levels of impact of cyber-incidents. We apply our approach to revise the results of a Data Protection Impact Assessment, a mandatory activity for complying with GDPR, conducted in a medium-to-large organization of the Italian Public Administration, and we obtain encouraging results.

Keywords: Risk assessment · Impact evaluation · Sensitivity and data protection

1 Introduction

Risk based approaches are increasingly adopted in a variety of security privacy management processes including authentication (see, e.g., [11]), access control (see, e.g., [4]), and data protection (see, e.g., the General Data Protection Regulation, GDPR). In all such situations, it is crucial to assess the risk level. Usually, risk levels are obtained by combining the likelihood and impact of an adverse event (see, e.g., [10]), such as the theft of authentication credentials, users with compromised devices accessing sensitive data thus exposing them to leakage, or data breaches containing personal information. While techniques and resources for establishing the likelihood of cyber-incidents are available – consider, for instance, the methodology for prioritizing weaknesses[1] based on the Common Weakness Enumeration (CWE) database – the same cannot be said for impact. This is because the evaluation of the impact level for a cyber-incident requires to consider both technical and non-technical aspects depending on the stakeholder with respect to whom we evaluate the impact. Indeed, several different

---

[1] https://cwe.mitre.org/community/swa/priority.html.

© Springer Nature Switzerland AG 2022
E. Aïmeur et al. (Eds.): FPS 2021, LNCS 13291, pp. 365–375, 2022.
https://doi.org/10.1007/978-3-031-08147-7_25

stakeholders are involved in today IT systems, services, and applications and cyber-incidents may be perceived in very different ways (see, e.g., [7]). Additionally, the impact evaluation may be subjective when, in the case of the GDPR, it involves the fundamental rights and freedom of people. To make the situation even more complex, large organizations may involve several different departments and people with different sensibilities in the risk assessment process. This implies that impact evaluation results – and, as a consequence, also risk levels – may be heterogeneous despite the attempts of organizations to provide indications and guidelines. This may lead to the under- or over-estimation of risk; the former may expose assets and processes to attacks, while the latter may impose the adoption of unnecessary (and costly) security and privacy measures and, at the same time, hinder the flow of information and ultimately business continuity.

To address this situation, we propose an approach to derive the impact level by identifying a set of *sensitivity features* that are related to assets and processes involved in the risk assessment. Examples of sensitivity features are the type and the size (in terms of the number of users) of the system the user wants to access for both risk based authentication and access control, data subject categories (e.g., citizens, patients, minors) and types of personal data (e.g., genetic data, racial or ethnic origin). The notion of sensitivity feature is a generalization of sensitivity level in Multi-Level Security policies such as the Bell and LaPadula model [3]. In these policies, sensitivity levels are associated to the negative consequences that a security violation may have on one of the stakeholders of a system. Our generalization consists of first identifying a set of features to which we associate weights – intuitively, the higher the weight, the larger the impact – and then measuring the sensitivity $S(x)$ of an asset or data processing activity x. Actually, S gives an estimate of the impact of a cyber-incident on x and it is computed by considering only the features and the related weights that are relevant to x. We also explain how to integrate our approach in methodologies for both quantitative and qualitative risk assessment (see, e.g., [10]).

To illustrate the practicability of our methodology, we discuss how it can be used to conduct a change analysis of the Data Protection Impact Assessment (DPIA) in a medium-to-large organization of the Italian Public Administration sector. The organization is subdivided into little more than one hundred departments, that deal with around 1500 data processing activities. Each department has appointed a person in charge to contribute to the DPIA for those data processing activities managed by that unit. It is thus unlikely that the results of the risk assessment are consistent and homogeneous given the high number of different employees involved in the process and the subjectivity in evaluating negative consequences on the fundamental rights and freedom of natural persons. We show how the impact of several data processing activities was under-estimated, potentially exposing the organization to fines from the Italian Data Protection Authority. We shared our results with the the Data Protection Unit (DPU), that is in charge of orchestrating the DPIA activities of the various departments in the organization. Based on these, the DPU produced a revised version of the

DPIA with more homogeneous risk levels, resulting from the systematic evaluations of the impact based on a set of security features derived from the relevant articles and related Recitals of the GDPR.

This work is organized as follows: in Sect. 2 we briefly describe ISRAM, an information security risk assessment. In Sect. 3, we present our new methodology to quantify the sensitivity and the impact with respect to it of an asset or data processing activity. In Sect. 4, we show a real application of our methodology.

2 Preliminaries

An Information Security Risk Assessment (ISRA) determines the level of security risk that exists within an organization (see, e.g., [1,2,9]). The underlying risk model of many of them is based on the following fundamental risk formula [6,8]:

$$\text{Risk} = \text{Likelihood of OSB} \times \text{Impact of OSB}, \tag{1}$$

where OSB stands for occurrence of security breach.

The Information Security Risk Analysis Method (ISRAM) (see [5]) is an ISRA that is performed by conducting a survey composed of questions and answer choices related to the information security problem. Manager, directors, and technical personal may be candidates for answering the survey questions. The risk formula (1) for ISRAM is given by

$$\text{Risk} = \left(\frac{\sum_m \left[T_1 \left(\sum_i w_i a_i \right) \right]}{m} \right) \cdot \left(\frac{\sum_n \left[T_2 \left(\sum_j w_j a_j \right) \right]}{n} \right), \tag{2}$$

where i (resp. j) is the number of questions for the survey of likelihood (resp. impact) of occurrence, m (resp. n) is the number of participants who participated in the survey of likelihood (resp. impact) of occurrence, w_i (resp. w_j) is the weight of the question i (resp. j), a_i (resp. a_j) the numerical value of the selected answer choice for question i (resp. j), T_1 (resp. T_2) is the risk table for the survey of likelihood (resp. impact) of occurrence, that scales the points obtained carrying out the survey into an integer between 1 and 5.

3 Our Methodology

As observed in the introduction, often, risk analysis comes upon different issues connected to the objectivity and homogeneity of the results within an organization. One aspect strictly related to all the others is the sensitivity of the data involved in an asset. Since estimating the likelihood that a risk event occurred is less prone to subjectivity, we will focus on the impact. Our methodology consists of three main steps: determination of the sensitivity features, preparation and conduction of a survey, and determination of the sensitivity impact.

3.1   Determination of the Sensitivity Features

It takes as input the set $\mathcal{P}$ of all the assets and data processing activities of a company. Following the GDPR together with national laws and criteria decided by the company itself, it returns an exhaustive list $\mathcal{L}$ of all attributes, involved in any asset or activity of $\mathcal{P}$, that are related to the impact of a cyber-incident. Clearly, collecting all such features requires a full control and knowledge of the data. We call the attributes in $\mathcal{L}$ as *sensitivity features*, or briefly *features*.

3.2   Preparation and Conduction of a Survey

After determining all the relevant features that can affect the impact assessment, a survey preparation and conduction process is required. The survey is aimed at identifying all the sensitive features involved in an asset. The possible answers are just two, either *yes* or *no*. The participants of the survey should be either the risk controllers, which can be managers and staff that directly deal with the data, or the data subjects. Summarizing, this step takes as input $\mathcal{L}$ and prepares a survey $\mathcal{Q}$ with questions Q_j such that for each $j \in \mathcal{L}$ and $P \in \mathcal{P}$, if j is a feature involved in P, the answer is $a_{j,P} = Q_j(P) = 1$ (yes), otherwise $a_{j,P} = 0$ (no). It returns the set $\{a_{j,P}\}_{j\in\mathcal{L},P\in\mathcal{P}}$.

3.3   Determination of the Sensitivity Impact

The purpose of this last phase is to establish the influence of the features for the impact assessment. In case of a data breach, the exposure of some type of data is more dangerous than the exposure of others. For this reason, features must be divided into different categories. A weight value w_j is assigned to the feature $j \in \mathcal{L}$. Weight values are associated to the sensitivity levels: the more the feature is sensitive, the higher the weight value is. Moreover, if two features belong to the same category, then they are supposed to receive the same weight. Putting together the knowledge of the occurrence of features and the overall weight calculated from them, one derives an impact evaluation depending on the sensitivity.

In mathematical terms, this step takes as input $\mathcal{P}, \mathcal{L}$, and $\{a_{j,P}\}_{j\in\mathcal{L},P\in\mathcal{P}}$. First, we define the set $\{w_j\}_{j\in\mathcal{L}}$ of the weights by using expert knowledge or indications and guidelines derived from various sources including organizational policies and legal documents (e.g., in the application presented in Sect. 4, we use selected articles of the GDPR and associated Recitals). Then, for a data processing activity $P \in \mathcal{P}$, we compute the impact value by means of a function $\mathcal{I} = T \circ \mathcal{S} : \mathcal{P} \rightarrow \mathbb{R}$, with $\mathcal{S} : \mathcal{P} \longrightarrow \mathbb{R}$ and $T : \mathbb{R} \longrightarrow \{1, 2, 3, 4, 5\}$. Let $P \in \mathcal{P}$, we define

$$\mathcal{S}(P) = \sum_{j\in\mathcal{L}} w_j a_{j,P} \tag{3}$$

as the sensitivity of P. Additionally, T encodes an impact table that maps the sensitivity $\mathcal{S}(P)$ to an integer between 1 and 5 that represents the impact value that a cyber-incident may have on P in increasing order of negative consequences, namely negligible (1), minor (2), important (3), serious (4), and catastrophic (5). Indeed, both determining the feature weights and the impact table T are key operations for the successful application of our methodology. Thus, in the following, we discuss which factors should be considered in the process of defining the weights and propose a method to derive T by interpolating a (logarithmic) function f and then identify a set of intervals, that forms a partition of the co-domain of f, to be associated with the integers ranging from 1 to 5.

Weights Determination and Relationship Analysis. The features in $\mathcal{L}$ should be divided into different categories, according to their degree of sensitivity. For this, we can split them into three different groups: *high*, *medium*, and *low*.

Denote by ω_L, ω_M, and ω_H the weights assigned to low, medium, and high-sensitivity features, respectively. To emphasize the distinction of the three groups of features, we suggest to set their weights as follows:

$$\omega_H = k \cdot \omega_M = k^2 \cdot \omega_L, \tag{4}$$

for $k > 1$. The greater k is, the higher the impact with respect to the sensitivity; this means that the latter will strongly depend on the high-sensitivity features.

In some cases, features need an additional investigation and adjustment of their weights. Indeed, it can happen an overlap in the set of features: both a data subject and the sensitive data that the data subject itself reveals have been included in the set of the features (e.g., inmates and judicial data, patients and health-related data); two strictly related sensitive data have been included in the set of the features (e.g., current health status data and medical history, person's sex life and sexual orientation).

The risk analysts have first to recognize all such pairs of features and consider the event that the two elements of such a pair appear simultaneously in an asset. One should examine the statistical significance of the event. If the likelihood of occurrence of the event among all the assets is irrelevant, namely under a previously determined threshold, it could be reasonable to disregard it and keep both features. Otherwise, the risk analysts could proceed in three different ways:

i. Consider only one of them when the overlap occurs. This is the recommended choice when the overlap is statistically significant to mitigate the risk of overestimating the sensitivity of the assets.

ii. Consider both of them, with the pre-set weights. Even if the two features are strictly related, both of them contribute to increase the sensitivity of the asset. For instance, consider a register with the data of all employees of an organization. The sensitivity should be higher if there are both the criminal record's subject and the possible criminal offences than if there is only clean/criminal record's subject.

iii. Consider both of them, changing the weights only when the overlap occurs. This is a compromise between the two strategies above. When the two features appear simultaneously, one can reduce their weights to avoid counting them twice but still consider their simultaneous occurrence.

Of course, being the solution iii a trade-off between the other two, it represents the most likely candidate for adoption in several contexts. But it requires a preliminary and accurate analysis by experts, to avoid the risk of too subjective evaluations.

Impact with Respect to Sensitivity Evaluation. As in many risk models, the impact score is an integer from 1 to 5, where 1 denotes the minimum impact, 5 the maximum impact, and the other values denote increasing scores. Estimating the impact with respect to the sensitivity of a data processing activity $P \in \mathcal{P}$ requires first to determine its sensitivity. By Eq. (3), the sensitivity $\mathcal{S}(P)$ of P is calculated as the sum of the weight values of the features involved in it. The real number $S = \mathcal{S}(P)$ must be scaled into one of the five values for the impact, by using a function $T : \mathbb{R} \to \{1, \ldots, 5\}$. To this aim, T converts sensitivity to meaningful, quantitative and scaled values for the impact. We do this as follows. Let A_0 and A_5 denote the minimum and the maximum possible value for the sensitivity, respectively, where A_0 can be set to 0 and A_5 depends on $|\mathcal{L}|$, that is $A_5 = \sum_{j \in \mathcal{L}} w_j$. We determine five intervals $(A_i, A_{i+1}]$, for $i = 0, \ldots, 5$, such that if $S \in (A_i, A_{i+1}]$ then the impact is equal to $i + 1$, namely $T(S) = i + 1$.

Impact Table Determination. Determining the A_i's is the crucial part of our methodology. We would like to define a function f such that the impact with respect to S is given by $\lceil f(S) \rceil$, namely by the approximation of $f(S)$ with the lowest integer that is not less than $f(S)$. Choosing a linear function f corresponds to the naive way of splitting the interval $[A_0, A_5]$ in five intervals of equal length. This could lead to incorrect values for the impact. Suppose that the total number of the high-sensitivity features is far greater than the number of the others. This implies that A_5 is very large, and P gets a high value for the impact only if it involves a huge amount of high-sensitivity features. Determining objectively the right thresholds of the intervals, or equivalently f, is a task requiring a certain care. But for the first and last interval it turns up to be easier than the others. Moreover, knowing A_1 and A_4, one may compute a more fitting and precise function f. Therefore, A_1 and A_4 have to be fixed by the risk analysts, where A_1 is the maximum value for the sensitivity in order to get the minimum impact, and A_4 is the maximum value for the sensitivity to get an impact equal to 4. In addition, due to the choices of the feature weights, the lengths of the intervals should be increasing, and small changes in the sensitivity should not entail a change of the corresponding impact value. The logarithm function fits all these conditions. Therefore, to find out A_i for $i = 2, 3$, we compute, by interpolation, the function

$$f(x) = B \ln(x) + C, \qquad \text{satisfying} \qquad \begin{cases} f(A_1) = 1, \\ f(A_4) = 4. \end{cases}$$

After solving the linear system for B and C, the values A_2 and A_3 are the minimum values of S such that $\lceil f(S) \rceil = 3$ and $\lceil f(S) \rceil = 4$, respectively.

4 Validating Our Methodology with a Real-World Data Set

An organization which deals with potential high-sensitivity data processing activities is required to perform a Data Process Impact Assessment (DPIA). An established approach in information security is to evaluate the risk using formula (1) with respect to the three fundamental security properties: confidentiality (C), integrity (I), and availability (A), that is

$$\text{Risk}_Z = (\text{Likelihood of OSB})_Z \times (\text{Impact of OSB})_Z, \quad \text{for } Z \in \{C, I, A\}.$$

The final risk is the maximum of the values above. Our strategy provides for including the computation of the risk with respect to the sensitivity (S):

$$\text{Risk}_S = (\text{Likelihood of OSB}) \times (\text{Impact of OSB})_S,$$

where Likelihood of OSB is the maximum of the likelihoods of OSB with respect to the three fundamental security properties, and $(\text{Impact of OSB})_S$ denotes the impact with respect to sensitivity, namely $(\text{Impact of OSB})_S = \mathcal{I}(P)$. The final risk is hence given by $\text{Risk} = \max\{\text{Risk}_C, \text{Risk}_I, \text{Risk}_A, \text{Risk}_S\}$.

To validate our methodology, we applied it to the results of a DPIA conducted in a real organization, as showed in the rest of the section.

4.1 Data

We conducted our experiment in a medium-to-large sized organization within the Italian Public Administration. It is subdivided in a little more than one hundred departments, that deal with almost 1,500 data processing activities. Whenever it is clear from the context, we refer to data processing activities as simply *activities*. All the managers were requested to list all the activities under their control and information regarding each of them. In particular, a complete description of any activity was provided, making explicit, among other factors, the data subject categories, sensitive personal data, and type of data processing activity. This process provided us with 36 different sensitivity features that were divided in three groups containing low, medium, and high-sensitivity features, respectively. Our classification is showed in Table 1 and was made by complying with Article 4(13), (14) and (15) and Article 9 and Recitals (51) to (56) of the GDPR that identify the following personal data as subject to specific processing conditions: personal data revealing racial or ethnic origin, political opinions, religious or philosophical beliefs; trade-union membership; genetic data, biometric data processed solely to identify a human being; health-related data; data concerning a person's sex life or sexual orientation.

4.2 Analysis of the Previous Results

The original DPIA was made by following ISRAM (recall Sect. 2): a survey was submitted to all managers in order to evaluate the impact of activities with

Table 1. Classification of the sensitivity features.

Features		
High sensitivity	Medium sensitivity	Low sensitivity
Biometric Data	Co-interconnection	Associations
Current-health status data	Data on a person's sex life	Candidates
Disabled people	Data on a person's sexual orientation	Citizens
Genetic data	Data sharing with third parties	Consulting suppliers and collaborators
History-health status data	Data transfer in non-eu countries	Local public administration employees
Patients	Diffusion	Military police
Previous-health status data	Inmates	Parents
	Judicial records	Physical persons
	Minors	Private employees
	Other beliefs	Public employees
	Philosophical beliefs	Public entities
	Political opinions	Students
	Profiling	Teachers
	Racial or ethnic origin	
	Religious beliefs	
	Trade-union membership	

respect to confidentiality, integrity, and availability of data. At the same time, an external IT company estimated the likelihood of security breaches with respect to the three key security aspects. At the end, all the activities received a risk score. At first glance, the risk scores were very optimistic: 98.9% of the activities was classified as low risk, that is they scored the minimum value, and the remainder 1.1% as low-medium risk.

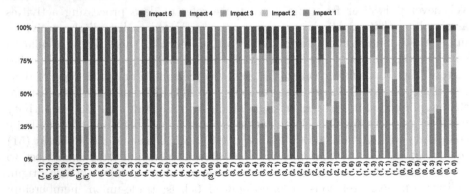

Fig. 1. The percentage bar diagram for the impact without considering sensitivity.

After a deeper analysis, it become clear that the impact assigned to the majority of them was incoherent with respect to their sensitivity, as showed in the percentage bar diagram in Fig. 1. Each bar (m, n) represents all the activities that involve exactly m high-sensitivity and n medium-sensitivity features. The bars are individually scaled so that they stack up to 100%. Moreover, each bar is subdivided depending on the percentage of activities marked with impact equal to i, for $i = 1, \ldots, 5$. One expects the dominance of the red and dark red colors, that corresponds respectively to impact value 4 and 5, on the left of the diagram, where all the activities with the highest number of high-sensitivity features are located. But, looking at Fig. 1, this is not the case and several activities with more than 4 high-sensitivity attributes have been evaluated to be low-impact. This suggests that the impact level of several activities had been underestimated by using subjective evaluations.

Henceforth, we call briefly impact of an activity the maximum of its impact values with respect to confidentiality, integrity, and availability.

4.3   Application of Our Methodology

After identifying and classifying all the features as displayed in Table 1, the next step was to assign a weight to each one of them. In Eq. (4), we fixed $k = 5$ and we associate 0.2, 1, and 5 with low, medium, and high-sensitivity features, respectively. Moreover, we conduct the relationship analysis described in Subsect. 3.3 and, in our case, we adopted the solution ii. In accordance with the notation introduced in Subsect. 3.3, we got $A_5 = 53.6$, and we set $A_1 = 2$ and $A_4 = 19.8$. This means that the impact is minimum when the activity involves at most either 10 low-sensitive features or 2 medium-sensitivity features, and the impact is maximum when the processing involves at least either 13 medium-sensitivity features and one high-sensitivity feature or 4 high-sensitivity features. With these values, we got, by interpolation, $f(x) = 1.35 \ln(x) + 0.07$. Given the sensitivity of an activity, the corresponding impact with respect to sensitivity is showed in Table 2.

Table 2. The impact table T for the impact with respect to the sensitivity.

Sensitivity	Qualitative scale	Quantitative scale
$0 - 2$	Negligible consequences	1
$2.2 - 4.4$	Minor consequences	2
$4.6 - 9.4$	Important consequences	3
$9.6 - 19.8$	Serious consequences	4
$20 - 53.6$	Catastrophic consequences	5

4.4   Analysis of the Results Obtained with Our Methodology

We compared our results with the ones previously computed. Table 3 (Left) shows the percentage of activities that attained a given impact value, before and after having integrated the sensitivity impact. But, it could be more meaningful to observe how the values changed because of the integration of the sensitivity impact.

Table 3. Left: Distribution of the impact. Right: Counting activities for any value.

Impact	Before	After
1	53%	32.9%
2	16.1%	12.7%
3	21.3%	28.7%
4	5.2%	15.9%
5	4.5%	9.8%

Before \ After	1	2	3	4	5
1	518	50	152	81	32
2		149	50	41	13
3			249	64	21
4				63	18
5					70

Table 3 (Right) captures this information: in position (i, j), namely in the i-th row and j-th column of the table, one finds the number of activities that before integrating sensitivity have obtained impact equal to i and after integrating sensitivity have obtained impact equal to j. It emerges that 833 activities were evaluated low-impact, but considering the sensitivity, 265 of these activities were assigned at least an impact value equal to 3. This means that adopting our methodology we were able to identify and correct all those cases in which sensitivity was underestimated. Sharing these results with the organization started an internal revision process of the impact values that largely confirmed our findings and produced a new version of the DPIA.

References

1. Agrawal, V.: A comparative study on information security risk analysis methods. JCP **12**(1), 57–67 (2017)
2. Behnia, A., Rashid, R.A., Chaudhry, J.A.: A survey of information risk analysis methods. Smart Comput. Rev. **2**, 79–94 (2012)
3. Bell, D.E., LaPadula, L.J.: Secure computer systems: mathematical foundations, No. MTR-2547-VOL-1. MITRE CORP BEDFORD MA (1973)
4. Bijon, K.Z., Krishnan, R., Sandhu, R.: A framework for risk-aware role based access control. In: Proceedings of the IEEE Conference on Communications and Network Security, pp. 462–469. National Harbor, MD, USA, 14–16 October 2013
5. Karabacak, B., Sogukpinar, I.: ISRAM: information security risk analysis method. Comput. Secur. **24.2**, 147–159 (2005)
6. McEvoy, N., Whitcombe, A.: Structured risk analysis. In: Davida, G., Frankel, Y., Rees, O. (eds.) InfraSec 2002. LNCS, vol. 2437, pp. 88–103. Springer, Heidelberg (2002). https://doi.org/10.1007/3-540-45831-X_7
7. Mollaeefar, M., Siena, A., Ranise, S.: Multi-stakeholder cybersecurity risk assessment for data protection. In: Proceedings of the 17th International Joint Conference on e-Business and Telecommunications - SECRYPT, pp. 349–356 (2020)
8. National Institute of Standards and Technology (NIST). Risk management guide for information technology systems (2001). Special Publication 800-30
9. Shukla, N., Sachin, K.: A comparative study on information security risk analysis practices. IJCA Special Issue on Issues and Challenges in Networking, Intelligence and Computing Technologies ICNICT **3**, 28–33 (2012)

10. Vose, D.: Risk Analysis: A Quantitative Guide. Wiley (2008)
11. Wiefling, S., Dürmuth, M., Lo Iacono, L.: What's in score for website users: a data-driven long-term study on risk-based authentication characteristics. In: Borisov, N., Diaz, C. (eds.) FC 2021. LNCS, vol. 12675, pp. 361–381. Springer, Heidelberg (2021). https://doi.org/10.1007/978-3-662-64331-0_19

An Extensive Comparison of Systems for Entity Extraction from Log Files

Anubhav Chhabra$^{(\boxtimes)}$ (iD), Paula Branco (iD), Guy-Vincent Jourdan (iD),
and Herna L. Viktor (iD)

School of Electrical Engineering and Computer Science, University of Ottawa,
Ottawa, ON, Canada
{achha096,pbranco,gjourdan,hviktor}@uottawa.ca

Abstract. Log parsing is the process of extracting logical units from
system, device or application generated logs. It holds utmost importance
in the field of log analytics and forensics. Many security analytic tools rely
on logs to detect, prevent and mitigate attacks. It is critical for these tools
to extract information from large volumes of logs from multiple evolving sources. Log parsers typically require human intervention as regular
expressions or grammar need to be provided to extract knowledge. Teams
of experts are required to keep these rules up-to-date in a time-consuming
and costly process that is prone to errors and fails when new logs are
added. On the other hand, strategies based on machine learning can automate the parsing of logs, thereby reducing time consumption and human
labour. In this paper, we perform an extensive and systematic comparison of different log parsing techniques and systems based on machine
learning approaches. These include baseline learning solutions such as
Perceptron, Stochastic Gradient Descent, Multinomial Naive Bayes, a
graphical model: Conditional Random Fields, a pre-trained sequence-
to-sequence model: NERLogParser, and a pre-trained language model:
BERT. Moreover, we experiment with the Transformer Neural Network,
modelling the Named Entity Recognition task as a sequence-to-sequence
generation task, an approach not previously tested in this domain. An
extensive set of experiments is carried out in in-scope and out-of-scope
datasets aiming at estimating the performance in log files from known
and unknown log sources. We use multiple evaluation schemes in order
to: (i) compare the different systems; and (ii) understand the quality
of the information extracted, providing deeper insights on the advantages and disadvantages of the different systems. Overall, we found that
sequence-to-sequence models tend to perform better both in in-scope and
out-of-scope data.

Keywords: Log parsing · Log analytics · Log forensics · Named
Entity Recognition · Deep learning · Transformer Neural Network

1 Introduction

Logging is the process of outputting information related to events that take
place in a system, device or application. Extracting logical units from these logs

© Springer Nature Switzerland AG 2022
E. Aïmeur et al. (Eds.): FPS 2021, LNCS 13291, pp. 376–392, 2022.
https://doi.org/10.1007/978-3-031-08147-7_26

is termed log parsing. Security Information and Event Management (SIEM) and other security analytic tools at the heart of modern Security Operation Centers (SOCs) do rely on logs and log parsing to detect, prevent and mitigate attacks. These systems must be able to integrate logs from many sources, keep up with the constant addition of new devices, and update existing ones [7]. Log Parsing also plays a crucial role in the field of log forensics and analytics. The unstructured nature of logs makes it hard to perform analytics and find insights. On the other hand, parsed logs have a fixed key-value format which makes performing these operations easier.

The most trivial solution to parse the logs is to apply regular expressions or grammar (e.g. [2,12]) to extract fields from the logs and then proceed to forensics. However, these solutions require regular human intervention as regular expressions or grammar must be constantly added and/or updated to extract knowledge. This raises important problems associated to costs and ineffectiveness. In effect, these approaches become expensive in terms of time and human effort requiring large teams of experts. Moreover, the developed regular expressions may still fail when logs from new sources are added.

Leveraging Machine Learning to prepare an automated solution can help reduce the manual effort and time required to write and maintain different rules used in parsing the log files. The log parsing problem can be framed as a Named-Entity-Recognition (NER) problem where each token in the log is tagged as part of an entity. However, no systematic comparison of the performance of these solutions has been put forward. Moreover, the capability of extracting knowledge from log files from sources unseen in training has not been extensively evaluated.

In this paper we carry out an experimental comparison of different machine learning approaches to solve the problem of Entity Extraction from log files. These include baseline approaches such as Perceptron, Stochastic Gradient Descent, Multinomial Naive Bayes, a graphical model: Conditional Random Fields [17], a pre-trained sequence-to-sequence model: NERLogParser [14], a transformer-based sequence-to-sequence model [16] and a pre-trained language model: BERT [5]. We also tested the generalization capacity of the different systems when prompted with new log instances whose format was not previously seen in the training stage. To achieve this we use two non-overlapping datasets, the in-scope and out-of-scope datasets. We use the in-scope dataset for training, validation and testing purposes, whereas the out-of-scope dataset originates from different sources and is solely used to evaluate the robustness of the systems when new log files are provided.

We employ multiple evaluation schemes that allow to compare the various systems and to better understand the quality of the information extracted. Our main goal is twofold: (i) test and evaluate an extensive and diverse set of learning approaches to tackle the NER problem in the context of logs files, and (ii) evaluate the robustness and quality of the information extracted from the different methods when considering both previously seen and unseen log formats.

This paper is structured as follows. Section 2 reviews different log parsing techniques used in our experiments. In Sect. 3 we discuss the datasets used in our work. The experimental settings and results are discussed in Sect. 4. Finally, the conclusions and future work are presented in Sect. 5.

2   Log Parsing Techniques for Named Entity Recognition

This section starts by describing the IOB tagging for NER. Then, we review and discuss four groups of methods to tackle our task including: word-based, graphical, sequence to sequence and language-based models. All the methods included in our experiments are presented here, as well as other related works.

2.1   IOB Tagging for Named Entity Recognition

NER can be formulated as a multiclass classification problem, where the input consists of a token present in the log instance, and the output is a tag in the IOB format. IOB tagging [10] consists of 3 types of tags: I-ENT, B-ENT, and O (where ENT represents an entity). If just a single token represents an entity, then it is tagged as I-ENT. Whereas, if an entity spans over multiple tokens, the first token is tagged as B-ENT, and the remaining token are annotated with I-ENT. Tag O is used to depict a token that does not belong to any of the entities. Figure 1 depicts the IOB tagging for a sample log instance. In this example we observe that we have two tokens representing the entity time (TIM), thus, the first token is tagged as B-TIM and the second a I-TIM. In the case of the entity Host (HOS) which is represented by a single token we observe the tag I-HOS associated with this token.

Fig. 1. Example of IOB tagging of a log instance.

2.2   Word-Based Methods

Baseline machine learning approaches can be trained on a token level using a token-to-tag mapping to address our task. We consider the following approaches: Multinomial Naïve Bayes, Stochastic Gradient Descent and Perceptron. We use the Scikit-learn package's default classifiers, and parameters, as seen in [14]. The token-tag pairs are extracted from the log instances present in the training dataset. The token-to-tag mapping may have a one-to-many relationship, meaning that a single token may map to multiple possible IOB tags. Once the token-to-tag mapping is prepared, the tokens are converted to one-hot-encoded vectors resulting in a sparse matrix which is then fed to all the baseline methods for training.

2.3   Graphical Model: Conditional Random Fields

Conditional Random Fields (CRF) [17] is an undirected graphical model, which is a well-known approach in sequence-related natural language processing (NLP) tasks. Traditional word-based NER methods are unable to capture the dependencies between a word and its neighbours. In contrast, CRF capture the context of the neighbouring words, resulting in better sequence prediction. To achieve this CRF models use feature functions as their key point. A feature function takes as arguments: the input sequence, current index position, and multiple features of a word and its neighbours; some examples of these features are the IOB tag of the previous and current word. CRF defines a conditional probability of an output sequence given an input sequence as shown in Eq. 1.

$$p(Z_{1:n}|X_{1:n}) = \frac{1}{K} exp(\sum_{n=1}^{N} \sum_{i=1}^{F} \lambda_i f_i(Z_{n-1}, Z_n, X_{1:n}, n)) \tag{1}$$

where $K = \sum_{Z_{1:n}} exp(\sum_{n=1}^{N} \sum_{i=1}^{F} \lambda_i f_i(Z_{n-1}, Z_n, X_{1:n}, n))$, f_i are feature functions and λ represents the importance of a particular feature function. In the above equation, N represents the total number of words present in the sequence and F depicts the number of different feature functions taken into consideration.

From Eq. 1 we observe that a weighted summation of all the feature functions for a particular word position in the sequence is performed, then, we repeat it for all the possible words in the sequence. At last, the value is divided by a normalization factor K. Parameter λ can be learned using gradient descent, maximizing the conditional likelihood. The sklearn-crfsuite package and its default parameters were used to implement this model.

2.4   Sequence to Sequence Learning

The sequence to sequence learning problem involves mapping a variable-length input sequence to a variable-length output sequence. The input and output sequence length may match or not depending upon the use-case being solved.

Depending upon the length of the input and the output, the architecture of the sequence-to-sequence model may vary. Figure 2 depicts two different model architectures that may be used to tackle the problem. Architecture 1 shows the encoder-decoder model where the length of the input and output sequence can vary. On the other hand, Architecture 2 depicts a model that can be employed to use cases where both sequences' lengths match. The encoder-decoder model showed remarkable results in sequence to sequence learning for machine translation. In [4] RNN is used as the founding block of the encoder and decoder sub-modules whereas in [15] LSTM is proposed. The encoder is responsible for encoding the entire input sequence into a fixed-length context vector that is passed to the decoder block, which outputs the tokens of the output sequence one step at a time.

The key limitation of such encoder-decoder approaches is related to decoding large sequences: the fixed-length context vector may not carry enough adequate information for decoding long sequences [1]. To solve this problem, the notion of attention was used. [1] proposed that rather than passing a single fixed-length context vector, a set of attention weights should be passed to the RNN/LSTM unit in the decoder at each time step. This set of attention weights allows the model to search for input sequence segments relevant to the current target word being predicted. All the architectures discussed above are recurrent and work sequentially at a word level, and this makes it hard for the model to learn sequences in parallel [16].

NERLogParser [14] is a different solution for NER using sequence-to-sequence models based on the Bi-directional LSTM. NERLogParser is an automatic tool capable of parsing logs while handling various log files. This tool is available as a Python package and can directly be used to parse logs. The package offers a pre-trained model on a more extensive dataset, which supersets the dataset we have access to and that we used in our experiments to train different solutions. We include NERLogParser in our experiments using the provided pre-trained model. The underlying architecture of NERLogParser is based on the Bidirectional LSTM (BLSTM) [6]. BLSTM uses two LSTMs taking both directions into account and hidden representations from both the LSTMs are concatenated together and are used at the time of training and inference. Figure 3 depicts the underlying architecture of NERLogParser. This architecture is similar to Architecture 2 mentioned in Fig. 2 in terms of mapping the input to output.

Words cannot be directly fed to the BLSTM architecture, thus, a feature representation is required. The authors used GloVe embeddings [9], precisely the glove.6B, an embedding trained on 6 billion tokens with a size of 300. An embedding is a lookup table that contains an n-dimensional feature representation of different words; similar words have similar representations and tend to be closer in their feature space. NERLogParser also makes the use of character-level input representation [8] of a word. The character-level representation helps create embedding for unknown words and helps to learn different subwords contained within in words. The authors employ a BLSTM network for preparing the character-level word representation, which is concatenated to the GloVe embedding and then fed to the network for training.

Another solution in this group is the Transformer Neural Network (transformer) [16] which relies on an attention mechanism, eliminating the need for recurrent units such as RNN or LSTM. Since the transformer does not require any recurrent units it is easy to achieve parallelism. The transformer reads all the tokens in an input sequence at once, thus reducing the training times. Figure 4 shows the architecture of the transformer neural network, which contains two key blocks: an encoder and a decoder that we describe next.

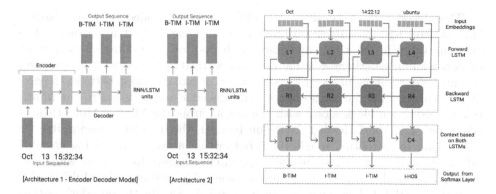

Fig. 2. Sequence to sequence models   **Fig. 3.** NERLogParser architecture

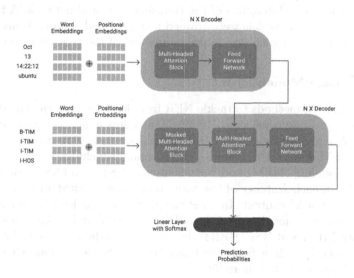

Fig. 4. Transformer architecture

The encoder block receives the aggregation of the input embeddings of all the words in the input sequence with the positional embeddings. The positional embeddings carry information about the absolute position of a word in a sequence. This is required in the transformer as opposed to what happens for the RNN/LSTM. The Encoder block firstly passes the embedding vectors through a Multi-Headed attention block. This block is responsible for computing the attention weights and outputs a vector that has encoded information about how a word of an input sequence is contextually related to other words within the input sequence; this is termed self-attention. The output vector is then passed through a feed-forward network whose output is then fed to the decoder.

The decoder block consists of 2 different multi-headed attention blocks: Masked Multi-Headed attention block and Multi-Headed attention block. The first one takes in the word embedding with position embedding of the output sequence and masks the words that are to be learned by the model. Self-attention is computed, resulting in a vector containing contextual relation between the predicted words in the output sequence. The Encoder output is fed to the Multi-Headed attention block along with the output from the Masked-Multi-Headed attention. The Multi Headed Attention block in the decoder is responsible for calculating the attention weights and outputting a vector containing encoded information about which segments of the input sequence to consider while predicting a particular word in the output sequence. The output of the Multi-headed attention block is fed to the feed-forward network. Finally, the decoder's output is fed through a linear layer with a softmax activation function to get the next predicted output token. We use the PyTorch framework to explore and experiment with various architectures of the transformer neural network. A total of 24 different transformer models were trained using manual combinations of hyperparameters. Table 1 depicts the hyperparameters of the best performing model.

2.5 Language Model: BERT

The final group of methods to tackle NER from log files concerns language models. In this setting we considered BERT [5], a language model pre-trained on the complete Wikipedia English and BookCorpus data, having a total vocabulary of over 3,000M words. Pre-training BERT mainly includes two tasks: Masked Language Modeling (MLM) and Next Sentence Prediction (NSP). In MLM 15% of the words in each sentence of the entire corpus are masked and then predicted using nearby words' context. In NSP the goal is to predict whether a sentence follows the other or not. Pre-Training BERT includes minimizing the aggregated loss of both MLM and NSP. BERT showed state-of-the-art results for 11 different NLP tasks including Sentence Classification, Sentence Pair Classification, Question Answering, and more [5].

BERT can be used for a sentence tagging task and can be adapted to a log parsing use case by fine-tuning the model parameters using a dataset of interest. In our experiments, we used the BERT-base-uncased model from the huggingface library. The training data is firstly pre-processed to its subword-tokenized form using the WordPiece Tokenizer, resulting in a sequence of subword tokens. The first subword of a token is mapped to the token's IOB tag, and the rest of the subwords are mapped to the tag "X". Once the wordpiece tokens are prepared, they are converted to a sequence of integers(indices) and are padded to a fixed length. The exact process is repeated for the IOB tags. The wordpiece token sequence and IOB tag sequence are then fed to BERT, and a full-fine tuning of all the model layers is performed. Table 1 shows the hyperparameters used to perform the full fine-tuning.

Table 1. Hyperparameters used on transformer and BERT models.

Model	Hyperparameters
Transformer	learning_rate: 7e–5, batch_size: 64, embedding_size: 512, num_heads: 8, num_encoder_layers: 6, num_decoder_layers: 6, dropout: 0.1, dim_feedforward: 4, num_epochs: 60
BERT	batch_size: 32, learning_rate: 3e–5, num_epochs: 2

3   In-Scope and Out-of-Scope Datasets

For the different learning solutions, we aim at evaluating their robustness and quality of information extracted when considering log files with formats previously seen and unseen by the models. To achieve this, we consider two different datasets: the in-scope and the out-of-scope datasets. The in-scope dataset is used for training, validation, and testing purposes. In contrast, the out-of-scope dataset is built from an entirely different distribution of log files and is solely used to evaluate the robustness of systems for new unseen logs. The use of these two datasets will allow us to assess the generalization ability of each model under new log formats.

The in-scope dataset is a subset derived from the dataset used in NERLog-Parser [14] and consists of approximately 120K log instances obtained from 10 different sources (Auth, Bluegene, Daemon ,Debug, Dmesg, Kernel , Message, Proxifier, Web and Zookeeper logs). The distribution of the number of logs and number of entities for the in-scope dataset is shown in Table 2. The in-scope dataset is split into training, validation, and test sets using a 60-20-20 split scheme, resulting in a training set with a total of 73,195 instances.

The out-of-scope dataset consists of log instances that belong to 8 different sources (Cisco ASA, Cisco IOS, Linux Secure, Linux Apache, Nginx, Windows Application, Windows System and Windows Security Logs). Table 3 shows the sources and the distribution of logs and entities for the out-of-scope dataset.

The log instances belonging to the in-scope dataset have 23 entities, whereas there are 37 entities present in the out-of-scope dataset. Since the out-of-scope dataset contains entities not present in the training dataset, evaluation is based on the following 11 common entities present in both the datasets: timestamp, hostname, service, ip_address, dash, auth, command, status_code, num_bytes, referrer and client_agent.

The initial log data is consists of the log instances from various sources. PyParsing library is used to develop grammar and expressions to annotate the log instances in the IOB format. The dataset is then transformed into a CSV file, each row representing a pair of input and output sequences. Input and outputs sequences represent the tokens of log and its IOB tags respectively.

Table 2. Distribution of the number of logs and entities for the in-scope dataset.

Log file	No. instances	No. entities	Entities present in the logs
Auth	16669	5	timestamp, hostname, service, subservice, message
Daemon	9809	5	timestamp, hostname, service, subservice, message
Debug	1722	6	timestamp, hostname, service, unix_time, subservice, message
Dmesg	7218	3	unix_time, subservice, message
Kernel	34246	6	timestamp, hostname, service, unix_time, subservice, message
Message	11338	6	timestamp, hostname, service, unix_time, subservice, message
Proxifier	10107	6	timestamp, service, arch, domain_or_ip, status, message
Web	10883	9	ip_address, dash, auth, timestamp, command, status_code, num_bytes, referrer, client_agent
Zookeeper	10000	5	timestamp, dash, status, job, message
Bluegene	10001	8	socket, number, timestamp, core, source, service, level, message
Total	**121993**		

4   Experimental Evaluation

4.1   Performance Assessment Metrics

Evaluation of NER systems may be performed at an entity-level or a token-level. We use an entity-level evaluation as the end goal of an NER system is to correctly classify an entity over a span of tokens. [11] uses the same to calculate the precision, recall, F1-score and evaluate the various NER systems. Chinchor et al. [3] proposed the following different scoring categories to calculate precision, recall and F1-score in this evaluation scenario:

- COR (Correct): prediction and ground truth entity match;
- INC (Incorrect): prediction and ground truth entity do not match;
- PAR (Partial): prediction and ground truth entity are somewhat similar;
- MIS (Missing): ground truth is not captured by the system;
- SPU (Spurious): system's prediction not present in the ground truth;
- POS (Possible) = COR + INC + PAR + MIS;
- ACT (Actual) = COR + INC + PAR + SPU.

The evaluation methodology that we use [13] introduces four evaluation schemes which use the scoring categories previously mentioned to calculate the precision, recall and F1-score for any NER system. These evaluation schemes are:

Table 3. Distribution of number of logs and entities for the out-of-scope dataset.

Log file	No. instances	No. entities	Entities present in the logs
Cisco ASA	1691	5	timestamp, hostname, colon, facility_severity_mnemonic, message
Cisco IOS	2999	6	timestamp, hostname, colon, service, facility_severity_mnemonic, message
Linux Secure	3000	13	timestamp, hostname, service, ip_address, dash, auth, http_request_timestamp, http_command, status_code, num_bytes, referrer, client_agent, message
Linux Apache	3000	9	ip_address, dash, auth, timestamp, http_command, status_code, num_bytes, referrer, client_agent
Nginx	3000	17	ip_address, dash, auth, timestamp, http_command, status_code, num_bytes, referrer, client_agent, http_x_forwarded_for, request_time, upstream_response_time, scheme, scheme_protocol, url, http_range, sent_http_x_varnish_cache
Win App Events	1392	12	timestamp, logname, source_name, event_code, event, event_name, computer_name, task_category, op_code, keywords, record_number, message
Win Sys Events	3000	15	timestamp, logname, source_name, event_code, event, event_name, computer_name, user, security_identifier, security_identifier_type, task_category, op_code, record_number, keywords, message
Win Sec Events	3000	12	timestamp, logname, source_name, event_code, event, event_name, computer_name, task_category, op_code, record_number, keywords, message
Total	**21082**		

- Strict Evaluation: exact boundary string and entity-type match.
- Exact Evaluation: exact boundary string match, irrespective of entity type match.
- Partial Evaluation: partial boundary string match irrespective of entity type.
- Entity Type Evaluation: entity type matching.

We must highlight that the strict evaluation scheme we use is not related to the well-known strict notion used in deep learning. In this case "strict" refers to an evaluation method that takes into account the complete matching of tokens and tags. A more detailed example is provided in Table 4.

The strict evaluation is the more demanding scheme and our main basis for performance assessment, but all schemes provide a different perspective of the NER performance task. For example, a NER system getting a F1-score of 1 in the entity type evaluation and 0.98 in the strict evaluation suggests that there can be a few cases where there is discrepancy in the boundary matches of the surface string. A NER system getting a high F1-score in the exact evaluation and a low F1-score in strict evaluation can suggest that most of the boundary string matches are correct whereas the entity-type matching is not correct.

For each of the evaluation schemes the precision, recall and F1-score are calculated in different ways. Equations 2 and 3 depict the precision and recall for strict and exact evaluation schemes, whereas, Equations 4 and 5 formulate the precision and recall for partial and entity-type evaluation schemes. We differentiate the two definitions by appending a suffix (A or B).

$$Prec_A = \frac{|COR|}{|ACT|} \quad (2) \qquad\qquad Rec_A = \frac{|COR|}{|POS|} \quad (3)$$

$$Prec_B = \frac{|COR| + (0.5 * |PAR|)}{|ACT|} \quad (4) \qquad Rec_B = \frac{|COR| + (0.5 * |PAR|)}{|POS|} \quad (5)$$

Table 4 shows a complete example of how the scoring is performed for the different evaluation schemes. Entity and Surface String pairs for ground truth and system's prediction are compared with each other and the scoring is performed using the categories already discussed. Each row in the table represents scoring for a single entity and surface string pair. This scoring is applied to all the pairs of entity and surface strings for all the log instances present in a log file. After the scoring is completed, the frequency of each scoring category ($|COR|$, $|INC|$, $|PAR|$, $|MIS|$, $|SPU|$, $|ACT|$, $|POS|$) is computed across all the four evaluation schemes. To calculate precision for the strict evaluation we use Eq. 2, calculate the frequency of each scoring category across the strict column and this provides a result of $Prec_A = \frac{1}{4}$ because $|COR| = 1$ and $|ACT| = |COR| + |INC| + |PAR| + |SPU| = 4$ in the example shown. The precision for entity-type evaluation scheme can be calculated using Eq. 4 which provides us with $Prec_B = \frac{3}{4}$ because for entity-type evaluation $|COR| = 3$ and $|ACT| = 4$. Similarly, the values of precision, recall and F1-score can be calculated for all the evaluation schemes.

Table 4. An example of the scoring categories for the different evaluation schemes.

Ground truth		System's prediction		Evaluation schemes			
Entity	Surface string	Entity	Surface string	Strict	Exact	Partial	Entity type
Time	01-12-2028 13:11:46	Time	01-12-2028	INC	INC	PAR	COR
Host	ubuntu	Host	13:11:46 ubuntu	INC	INC	PAR	COR
Service	CRON[8354]:	Time	CRON[8354]:	INC	COR	COR	INC
Sub-Service	pam_unix(cron:session):	Sub-Service	pam_unix(cron:session):	COR	COR	COR	COR
Message-Type	<info>			MIS	MIS	MIS	MIS

4.2 Experimental Settings

We evaluated 7 different models (3 word-based models, 1 graph-based model, 2 sequence-to-sequence models and 1 pre-trained language model) on the in-scope and out-of-scope datasets presented in Sect. 3. We used the evaluation framework described in Sect. 4.1 to calculate the precision, recall and F1-score for 4 different evaluation schemes (strict, exact, partial and entity-type). The hyperparameters used are described in Sect. 2 for each one of the techniques.

4.3 Results and Discussion

In this section we start by presenting and discussing the in-scope dataset results, followed by an analysis of the results on the out-of-scope dataset.

In Scope Dataset Results: Table 5 depicts the performance evaluation for the in-scope dataset. The transformer neural network outperforms all the other approaches, getting a strict F1-score of 0.999893. It is followed by the NER-LogParser and CRF having 0.999889 and 0.9998269 strict F1-scores. We must highlight that NERLogParser has an advantage when compared against the other competitor approaches because this pre-trained model used a superset of our in-scope dataset for the training stage. BERT achieves a strict F1-score of 0.999731, which is also close to the approaches mentioned above. Overall, the graphical, sequence-to-sequence and language models performed equally well, with a strict F1-score above 0.999. This high performance is verified across all the evaluation schemes considered. Although these models are similar in performance, their sizes exhibit a large variation with CRF using the smallest disk space of 230 KB, whereas BERT occupies the highest space of 427.82 MB.

Naive Bayes, Perceptron and Stochastic Gradient Descent achieve a strict F1-score of 0.77942, 0.75068 and 0.66086, respectively, in the in-scope dataset. This high performance achieved by our baseline word-based approaches, suggests that there could be a strong overlap between the vocabulary of training and testing datasets which could be biasing the results. To confirm our hypothesis, we investigated the vocabulary sizes of both sets and calculated the intersection between the two. Out of 26,014 tokens present in the test vocabulary, 16,453 tokens are also a part of the training dataset; there is an overlap of approximately 63%, which justifies the performance of the word-based methods. The baseline word-based approaches do not show an uniform performance across the different evaluation schemes. For example, looking at the exact F1-score achieved by Perceptron, we notice that it performed well in finding the boundary matches (i.e. where an entity should start and end). However, the entity-type F1-score suggests that some of the entities that the model predicts are wrong. The SGD and Naive Bayes models show an improvement tendency as the evaluation scheme shifts from strict to entity-type. This behaviour could mean that both the models perform well in predicting the entities, whereas they could have missed their corresponding boundaries.

Out of Scope Dataset Results: Tables 6 and 7 depict the strict and exact evaluation for eight different log file sources present in the out-of-scope dataset. Due to space constraints, similar tables for the partial and entity type evaluation schemes are provided in https://github.com/anubhav562/An-Extensive-Comparison-of-Systems-for-Entity-Extraction-from-Log-Files. Overall, the transformer model performed better than all the other approaches. It outperforms all the other approaches in parsing three out of the eight log files by achieving 0.6856, 0.995, and 0.0102 strict F1-scores for Cisco IOS, Linux Apache, and Nginx log files, respectively. NERLogParser secured the highest strict F1-score of 0.691 for the Linux Secure log file, whereas BERT peformend better on the Cisco ASA files with a strict F1-score of 0.997. The traditional word-based approaches performed poorly for all of the out-of-scope log files. CRF shows poor performance for most log files except Linux Secure and Apache, where it achieves a strict F1-score of 0.6894 and 0.7988. All classifiers performed poorly for the three Windows log files where all the strict F1-scores were 0.

Table 5. Performance results for in-scope data.

Model	Metric	Strict	Exact	Partial	Entity-type	Model size
Naive Bayes	Precision	0.79343	0.81549	0.82714	0.81672	
	Recall	0.7659	0.78719	0.79843	0.78838	25.1 MB
	F1-score	0.77942	0.80109	0.81253	0.8023	
Perceptron	Precision	0.71256	0.81973	0.82983	0.73276	
	Recall	0.79311	0.91239	0.92363	0.81559	12.5 MB
	F1-score	0.75068	0.86358	0.87422	0.77196	
SGD	Precision	0.67884	0.70128	0.73164	0.73956	
	Recall	0.6438	0.66508	0.69387	0.70138	12.5 MB
	F1-score	0.66086	0.6827	0.71226	0.71997	
CRF	Precision	0.9997781	0.9997781	0.9997781	0.9997781	
	Recall	0.9998757	0.9998757	0.9998757	0.9998757	230 KB
	F1-score	0.9998269	0.9998269	0.9998269	0.9998269	
NERLogParser	Precision	0.9998846	0.9998846	0.9998846	0.9998846	
	Recall	0.9998935	0.9998935	0.9998935	0.9998935	29.5 MB
	F1-score	0.999889	0.999889	0.999889	0.999889	
Transformer	Precision	0.999893	0.999893	0.999893	0.999893	
	Recall	0.999893	0.999893	0.999893	0.999893	259 MB
	F1-score	**0.999893**	**0.999893**	**0.999893**	**0.999893**	
BERT	Precision	0.999641	0.999531	0.999531	0.999641	
	Recall	0.999823	0.999832	0.999832	0.999823	427.82 MB
	F1-score	0.999731	0.999681	0.999681	0.999731	

The in-scope dataset does not contain any logs related to the Windows operating system. On the other hand, we have considered the windows-based logs as a part of the out-of-scope dataset to evaluate the performance of classifiers on unseen data. The timestamp is the only common entity between the windows logs and the in-scope data, so we evaluate the parsing of windows-based log files by considering the timestamp alone. All the classifiers were unable to parse the timestamp in the windows log files. This poor performance may be explained by the presence of: (1) some months, dates, and years not present in the training data; (2) timestamps in a format that the models have never seen.

None of the classifiers showed a good performance in parsing the Nginx log file; all the classifiers achieved a strict F1-score below 0.015. The Nginx log instances contain seventeen different entities, out of which nine are present in the training data. The performance of the classifiers was evaluated on these common entities. We investigated the Nginx file and found out that most of the logs in the file are pipe ("|") delimited. The presence of a pipe ("|") delimiter causes the tokens to get concatenated. Hence, many individual tokens do not get parsed, resulting in a drop of exact F1-score across all the systems.

Table 6. Strict evaluation for out-of-scope data (NB: Naive Bayes; Perc: Perceptron; NERLogP: NERLogParser; Transf: Transformer).

Log files	Metric	NB	Perc	SGD	CRF	NERLogP	Transf	BERT
Cisco ASA	Precision	0	0	0	0	0.667	0.6666	0.997
	Recall	0	0	0	0	1	0.9923	0.997
	F1-score	0	0	0	0	0.8	0.7975	**0.997**
Cisco IOS	Precision	0	0	0	0	0.589	0.5688	0.00053
	Recall	0	0	0	0	0.689	0.8629	0.00066
	F1-score	0	0	0	0	0.635	**0.6856**	0.00059
Linux Secure	Precision	0.142	0.032	0.145	0.9696	1	0.9698	0.7028
	Recall	0.0756	0.0786	0.0694	0.5348	0.528	0.4407	0.6193
	F1-score	0.0987	0.0457	0.0939	0.6894	**0.691**	0.6060	0.6584
Linux Apache	Precision	0.1662	0.0587	0.1875	0.9598	0.975	0.9993	0.9821
	Recall	0.1050	0.1062	0.1039	0.6841	0.96	0.9907	0.9711
	F1-score	0.1287	0.0756	0.1337	0.7988	0.968	**0.9950**	0.9766
Nginx	Precision	0.0053	0.0011	0.0053	0	0.0138	0.0351	0.0121
	Recall	0.0017	0.0018	0.0017	0	0.0060	0.0060	0.0067
	F1-score	0.0026	0.0013	0.0026	0	0.0083	**0.0102**	0.0086
Win App Events	Precision	0	0	0	0	0	0	0
Win Sys Events	Recall	0	0	0	0	0	0	0
Win Sec Events	F1-score	0	0	0	0	0	0	0

The Linux Apache log instances consist of nine entities that are all present in the training dataset. The structure of these logs is the same as Weblogs, which is part of the training dataset. These log files are generated from different sources, resulting in them having different vocabularies yet maintaining a similar sequential structure. All the word-based methods perform poorly, with a strict F1-score below 0.14. Since the Linux Apache logs belong to a different source, there is not a considerable amount of overlap in the vocabulary, which accounts for the poor performance of these methods. The other approaches perform well in parsing the entire log file, with CRF having a strict F1-score of 0.7988 and all the deep learning methods with a strict F1-score above 0.96. A similar trend can be observed for the Linux Secure logs where all the word-based methods achieve a strict F1-score below 0.1, whereas all the other approaches obtain a score above 0.6. The deep learning approaches worked well for parsing the Cisco ASA, and the Cisco IOS log files, whereas all the other approaches performed poorly with a strict F1-score of 0. The exact, partial, and entity-type F1-scores of the word-based approaches for Cisco ASA and Cisco IOS log files suggest that these models neither performed well on boundary nor entity matching. Overall, the results suggest that the attention mechanism employed by the transformer neural network helps it outperform the other approaches in both datasets. We also notice that tackling the NER problem using sequence-to-sequence models is

Table 7. Exact evaluation for out-of-scope data (NB: Naive Bayes; Perc: Perceptron; NERLogP: NERLogParser; Transf: Transformer).

Log files	Metric	NB	Perc	SGD	CRF	NERLogP	Transf	BERT
Cisco ASA	Precision	0	0.0886	0	0.3333	0.667	0.6666	1
	Recall	0	0.5	0	0.0845	1	0.9923	1
	F1-score	0	0.1506	0	0.1349	0.8	0.7975	**1**
Cisco IOS	Precision	0	0.1188	0	0	0.589	0.5688	0.00053
	Recall	0	0.5	0	0	0.689	0.8629	0.00066
	F1-score	0	0.1920	0	0	0.635	**0.6856**	0.00059
Linux Secure	Precision	0.1471	0.2531	0.1507	0.9734	1	0.9698	0.8148
	Recall	0.0783	0.61582	0.0721	0.5369	0.528	0.4407	0.7180
	F1-score	0.1022	0.3587	0.0976	0.6921	0.691	0.6060	**0.7633**
Linux Apache	Precision	0.2080	0.3364	0.2353	0.9713	0.981	0.9994	0.9839
	Recall	0.1315	0.6088	0.1303	0.6922	0.965	0.9908	0.9729
	F1-score	0.1611	0.4334	0.1677	0.8084	0.973	**0.9951**	0.9783
Nginx	Precision	0.0510	0.2459	0.0459	0	0.3477	0.1623	0.2798
	Recall	0.017	0.4108	0.0152	0	0.1509	0.0278	0.1561
	F1-score	0.0255	**0.3077**	0.02286	0	0.2105	0.0475	0.2004
Win App Events	Precision	0	0	0	0	0	0	0
Win Sys Events	Recall	0	0	0	0	0	0	0
Win Sec Events	F1-score	0	0	0	0	0	0	0

the most rewarding in terms of performance and generability to unseen sources of log files. The Transformer and NERLogParser perform competitively well, outperforming all the other approaches on in-scope and out-of-scope datasets.

5   Conclusion and Future Work

In this paper, we carry out an extensive and systematic comparison of different techniques for parsing log files modeling the problem as a NER task. Multiple approaches are explored, including three word-based classifiers; a graphical model: CRF; a pre-trained sequence-to-sequence model: NERLogParser; a sequence-to-sequence transformer model; and a pre-trained language model: BERT.

In our experiments we use in-scope and out-of-scope datasets. The in-scope dataset is used for training, validation, and testing purposes whereas, the out-of-scope dataset is used for evaluating the robustness of the systems when dealing with log files from new unseen sources. Multiple evaluation schemes are used for performance assessment. All approaches except the word-based methods perform exceptionally well on the in-scope dataset. On the out-of-scope dataset, only the sequence-to-sequence models generalize well. The transformer model outperforms all the other approaches on in-scope and out-of-scope datasets.

For our future work, we plan to investigate techniques that lead to improvements in the parsing of unseen logs. We will also address the issue of log files with different delimiters by building a delimiter classifier.

References

1. Bahdanau, D., Cho, K., Bengio, Y.: Neural machine translation by jointly learning to align and translate. arXiv preprint arXiv:1409.0473 (2014)
2. Chen, K., Clark, A., De Vel, O., Mohay, G.: ECF-event correlation for forensics. In: First Australian Computer, Network and Information Forensics Conference, pp. 1–10. We-B Centre. com (2003)
3. Chinchor, N., Sundheim, B.M.: MUC-5 evaluation metrics. In: Fifth Message Understanding Conference (MUC-5): Proceedings of a Conference Held in Baltimore, 25–27 Aug 1993, Maryland (1993)
4. Cho, K., et al.: Learning phrase representations using RNN encoder-decoder for statistical machine translation. arXiv preprint arXiv:1406.1078 (2014)
5. Devlin, J., Chang, M.W., Lee, K., Toutanova, K.: BERT: pre-training of deep bidirectional transformers for language understanding. arXiv preprint arXiv:1810.04805 (2018)
6. Graves, A., Schmidhuber, J.: Framewise phoneme classification with bidirectional LSTM networks. In: Proceedings of the 2005 IEEE International Joint Conference on Neural Networks, vol. 4, pp. 2047–2052. IEEE (2005)
7. Hossain, S.M.M., Couturier, R., Rusk, J., Kent, K.: Automatic event categorizer for SIEM. In: CASCON 2021 (2021)
8. Lample, G., Ballesteros, M., Subramanian, S., Kawakami, K., Dyer, C.: Neural architectures for named entity recognition. arXiv preprint arXiv:1603.01360 (2016)
9. Pennington, J., Socher, R., Manning, C.D.: GloVe: global vectors for word representation. In: Proceedings of the 2014 Conference on Empirical Methods in Natural Language Processing (EMNLP), pp. 1532–1543 (2014)
10. Ramshaw, L.A., Marcus, M.P.: Text chunking using transformation-based learning. In: Armstrong, S., Church, K., Isabelle, P., Manzi, S., Tzoukermann, E., Yarowsky, D. (eds.) Natural Language Processing Using Very Large Corpora, TLTB, vol. 11, pp. 157–176. Springer, Dordrecht (1999). https://doi.org/10.1007/978-94-017-2390-9_10
11. Sang, E.F., De Meulder, F.: Introduction to the CONLL-2003 shared task: language-independent named entity recognition. arXiv preprint cs/0306050 (2003)
12. Schatz, B., Mohay, G., Clark, A.: Rich event representation for computer forensics. In: Proceedings of the Fifth Asia-Pacific Industrial Engineering and Management Systems Conference (APIEMS 2004). vol. 2, pp. 1–16. Queensland University of Technology Publications (2004)
13. Segura Bedmar, I., Martínez, P., Herrero Zazo, M.: SemEval-2013 task 9: extraction of drug-drug interactions from biomedical texts (DDIExtraction 2013). Association for Computational Linguistics (2013)
14. Studiawan, H., Sohel, F., Payne, C.: Automatic log parser to support forensic analysis (2018)

15. Sutskever, I., Vinyals, O., Le, Q.V.: Sequence to sequence learning with neural networks. In: Advances in Neural Information Processing Systems, pp. 3104–3112 (2014)
16. Vaswani, A., et al.: Attention is all you need. In: Advances in Neural Information Processing Systems, pp. 5998–6008 (2017)
17. Wallach, H.M.: Conditional random fields: an introduction. Technical Reports (CIS), p. 22 (2004)

Choosing Wordlists for Password Guessing: An Adaptive Multi-armed Bandit Approach

Hazel Murray[1]([envelope])[iD] and David Malone[2][iD]

[1] Munster Technological University, Cork, Ireland
Hazel.Murray@cit.ie
[2] Maynooth University, Maynooth, Ireland
David.Malone@mu.ie

Abstract. A password guesser often uses wordlists (e.g. lists of previously leaked passwords, dictionaries of words in different languages, and lists of the most common passwords) to guess unknown passwords. The attacker needs to make a decision about what guesses to make and in what order. In an online guessing environment this is particularly important as they may be locked out after a certain number of wrong guesses. In this paper, we employ a multi-armed bandit model to show that an adaptive strategy can actively learn characteristics of the passwords it is guessing, and can leverage this information to dynamically weight the most appropriate wordlist. We also show that this can be used to identify the nationality of the users in a password set, and that guessing can be improved by guessing using passwords chosen by other users of the same nationality.

Keywords: Passwords · Password guessing · Multi-armed bandit · Learning · Cybersecurity

1 Introduction

Passwords are a widely used form of authentication online. However, one major weakness is that human chosen passwords can often be guessed by attackers. In fact, with the regular occurrence of leaks of password datasets [9], attackers are provided with an increasing amount of data to inform password guesses. It is important for security advocates and researchers to understand the capabilities of attackers given they have access to this data. This way, we can create countermeasures to protect the security of users.

Guessing passwords either involves formulating new words to try as guesses or using existing *wordlists* that include common password choices, words based on language dictionaries and datasets of previous password leaks. A human attacker

This work was supported in part by Science Foundation Ireland under Grant 13/RC/2077_P2.

E. Aïmeur et al. (Eds.): FPS 2021, LNCS 13291, pp. 393–413, 2022.
https://doi.org/10.1007/978-3-031-08147-7_27

who is guessing password will look for clues such as language, nationality and composition policies that might indicate a good wordlist to use in order to guess a *password set*, i.e. a set of unknown passwords. In this paper we are interested in investigating whether we can automate this learning and use it to inform wordlist choice. To our knowledge, this learning problem has not been studied before.

The order in which guesses are made can be important for a password guesser. Often they may only be able to make a small number of guesses before they will become locked out. Therefore, a quick learning strategy to maximise rewards is valuable. In this paper, we will show the speed of our learning strategy and compare it to the optimal rate of password compromise, a term we will discuss in more detail later.

Users choosing a password are known to be influenced by common factors. For example, users from similar demographics will often choose similar passwords [1, 6,13]. In addition, users have been observed choosing passwords that reflect the nature of the website they are choosing the password for [17,27]. In this paper, we investigate whether an automated learning algorithm can identify these idiosyncrasies within a password set and if it can leverage this knowledge in order to improve the success of password guessing rates.

In this paper, our contributions are as follows:

- Our algorithm suggests guesses to be made against a population of users in an online or offline attack. After each guess, it uses the relative success of all previous guesses to identify how well each wordlist matches the passwords (see Sect. 3.1). Importantly, it requires no a-priori training.
- In many previous wordlist approaches, a single ordered wordlist is created. In our method, wordlists are separated based on their source or characteristics. This allows for effective guessing from the promising wordlists, which is tailored to the characteristics of the password set.
- Its adaptive nature allows it to react to new information and tailor the guessing strategy accordingly. We show that within 1–10 guesses the model can determine useful information about the password set. We also see that the guesses are relatively close to an optimal strategy.
- Given a password set formed by users predominantly of a single nationality, our model can accurately recognise this characteristic and tailor the guessing to use an appropriate wordlist. We also show that this improves guessing, revealing that choosing a wordlist made up of other users from that same nationality can improve guessing over using a general wordlist (even when language differences are not a factor).

In this paper, we describe our full multi-armed bandit model and demonstrate its effectiveness through simulations and real-world guessing. We begin in Sect. 2 with an overview of related work. Then, in Sect. 3, the multi-armed bandit (MAB) problem is placed in the context of password guessing. In this section, we also describe the set-up of the Maximum Likelihood Estimation design and validation. In Sect. 4, we investigate the general guessing performance of the multi-armed bandit model. Section 5 shows that the MAB can identify demographic information and leverage this for guessing. We discuss our overall results in Sect. 6 and conclude in Sect. 7. The authors also include all their code for implementing the multi-armed bandit in the following repository [16].

2 Related Work and Background

For a long time researchers have been interested in modelling and improving password guessing. The first strategic methods involved dictionary attacks (that is, using a set wordlist to make guesses). These were proposed by Morris and Thompson in 1979 [15] and are still widely used today in the form of John the Ripper [19] and HashCat [25].

Developing on the simple dictionary method, in 2005, Narayanan and Shmatikov employed Markov models to enable faster guessing [18]. A Markov model can predict the next character in a sequence based on the current character. In 2009, Weir et al. used probabilistic context-free grammars (PCFG) to guess passwords [28]. PCFGs characterise a password according to its "structures". Structures can be password guesses or word mangling templates that can take dictionary words as input. In 2013, Dürmuth et al. proposed an updated password guessing model based on Markov models, called OMEN [4]. As part of their initial paper they demonstrated an OMEN specific method for merging personal information with a wordlist of guesses [2].

In 2016, Wang et al. developed a targeted password guessing model which seeds guesses using users' personally identifiable information [26]. Wang et al. leverage existing probabilistic techniques including Markov models and PCFG as well as Bayesian theory. They create tags for specific personally identifying information (PII) associated with a user. In their most successful version, TarGuess-I, they use training with these type-based PII tags to create a semantic aware PCFG. Independently, Li et al. also created a method for seeding password guesses with personal information. Their guessing also extended the probabilistic context free grammar method [11].

Also in 2016, the use of artificial neural networks for password guessing was proposed by Melicher et al. [14]. Artificial Neural networks are computation models inspired by biological neural networks. Artificial neural networks are a machine learning technique particularly useful for fuzzy classification problems and generating novel sequences (such as a password not in the training data). Melicher et al. show that their neural network method can be more effective than both Markov and PCFG methods. In addition, because neural networks can be highly compressed, they show that they can be used to efficiently carry out client-side password strength checking. In 2017, Houshmand and Aggarwal created a method for merging multiple grammars for wordlist-based PCFG models [8].

In 2019, Hitaj et al. proposed using deep generative adversarial networks (GAN) to create password guesses [7]. A generative adversarial network pits one neural network against another in a zero-sum game. PassGAN is able to autonomously learn the distribution of real passwords from leaked passwords and can leverage these to generate guesses. In contrast to Markov and PCFG models, PassGAN does not require a-priori knowledge of password structures.

In 2018, Xia et al. suggested a deep learning model which combines PCFG with the neural network LSTM [29]. This method, called GENPass, was designed to overcome the limitation of neural networks that means they can not, in their raw form, be used for cross-site attacks. This was an important contribution as leveraging passwords leaked from one website to use to guess the same users' passwords on another site is a common attack. Pal et al. in 2019, developed a password manipulation tool called PASS2PATH [20]. Leveraging the knowledge that users alter and reuse their passwords, this model can transform a base user password into targeted password guesses.

Probably the most similar to our work is work by Pasquini et al. [21,22]. They introduced the idea of "password strong locality" to describe the grouping together of passwords that share fine-grained characteristics. This password locality can be leveraged to train their learning model to generate passwords that are similar to those seen and to help with password guessing. Our model differs from previous work in that previous work has tried to create effective words to be guessed against passwords and has used learning techniques to inform how to create these words. In our work, we assume lists of guesses exist in the form of multiple wordlists, our learning technique informs which wordlist will be most effective for guessing the particular password set, and how to combine guesses from multiple wordlists in order to utilise them effectively.

Users' passwords are inherently guessable as they often take predictable forms which are impacted by the users' language and the website they were created for. In 2012, Malone and Maher investigated passwords created for different websites and found that nationality plays a role in user's choice of passwords [13]. They also found that passwords often follow a theme related to the service they were chosen from. For example, a common LinkedIn password is "LinkedIn". This result was further investigated by [27].

Researchers have also studied password sets which are in particular languages. Sishi et al. studied the strength and content of passwords derived from seven South African languages [24]. Li et al. completed a large scale study of Chinese web passwords [12]. Weir et al. used Finnish passwords as a basis for studying the use of PCFG in the creation of password guesses and mangling rules [28]. Dell et al. [3] included both Italian and Finnish password sets and guessed them using English, Italian and Finnish wordlists. They draw conclusions on the general strength of the passwords and the diminishing returns nature of guessing. In this work, we have chosen password sets from three nationalities: Irish, English and German. Despite Irish and English users both being predominantly English speaking, we were able to show that leveraging the nationality to choose a relevant wordlist, still had an impact on improving the guessing.

3   The Multi-armed Bandit Problem

The multi-armed bandit problem describes the trade-off a gambler faces when faced with a number of different gambling machines. Each machine provides a random reward from a probability distribution specific to that machine. The crucial problem the gambler faces is how much time to spend *exploring* different machines and how much time to spend *exploiting* the machine that seems to offer the best rewards. The objective of the gambler is to maximize the sum of rewards earned through a sequence of lever pulls.

In our scenario, we regard each wordlist as a bandit which will give a certain distribution of successes. We want to explore the returns from each wordlist and also exploit the most promising wordlist, in order to make effective guesses. With each guess we learn more about the distribution of the password set we are trying to guess. Leveraging this knowledge, we can guess using the wordlist that best matches the password set distribution, thus maximising rewards.

3.1   Password Guessing: Problem Set-up

Suppose we have n wordlists. Each wordlist $i = 1 \ldots n$, has a probability distribution p_i, and $\sigma_i(k)$ denotes the position of password k in wordlist i. So, the probability assigned to password k in wordlist i is $p_{i,\sigma_i(k)}$.

Suppose we make m guesses where the words guessed are k_j for $j = 1 \ldots m$. Each of these words is guessed against the N users in the password set and we find N_j, the number of users' passwords compromised with guess number j.

To model the password set that we are trying to guess, we suppose it has been generated by choosing passwords from our n wordlists. Let q_i be the proportion of passwords from wordlist i that generated the password set. Our aim will be to estimate $q_1, \ldots, q_n$ noting that

$$\sum_i^n q_i = 1 \quad \text{and} \quad q_i \geq 0. \tag{1}$$

This means that the q_i are coordinates of a point in a probability simplex. If the password set was really composed from the wordlists with proportions q_i, the probability of seeing password k in the password set would be

$$Q_k := \sum_{i=1}^n q_i p_{i,\sigma_i(k)}. \tag{2}$$

Given the N_j, we will use Q_k to build a maximum likelihood estimator.

3.2   Maximum Likelihood Estimation

Given this problem set-up, we will construct a likelihood function which will describe the likelihood that a given set of parameters $q_1, \ldots, q_n$ describe the password set. In this section, we introduce the likelihood estimator, prove that a unique maximum value exists and demonstrate convergence to this maximum.

Likelihood Function. We construct the following likelihood for our model with m guesses:

$$\mathcal{L} = \binom{N}{N_1 \cdots N_m (N - N_1 \cdots - N_m)} Q_{k_1}^{N_1} Q_{k_2}^{N_2} \cdots Q_{k_m}^{N_m}$$
$$\times (1 - Q_{k_1} \cdots - Q_{k_m})^{N - N_1 \cdots - N_m}, \tag{3}$$

where the first term is the multinomial coefficient representing each way the remaining guesses could be structured. The second term denotes how many times password k_j is expected to be seen in the password set, Q_k, to the power of how many times it was actually seen. The final term represents the remaining guesses and states that they account for the remaining users' passwords in the password set that have not yet been compromised.

Our goal is to maximise this likelihood function by choosing good estimates for $q_1, \ldots q_n$ based on our observed rewards from each previous guess. Note, with each guess we learn more about q_i for all the wordlists. In fact, one of the features of this model compared to a traditional multi-armed bandit model is that when we make a guess we learn something about all the wordlists.

We can take the log of the likelihood function to create a simplified expression. In addition, we can remove the multinomial which is simply a constant for any values of $\vec{Q}$. This leaves us with:

$$\log \mathcal{L} = \text{const} + N_1 \log Q_{k_1} + N_2 \log Q_{k_2} \cdots + N_m \log Q_{k_m}$$
$$+ (N - N_1 - \cdots - N_m) \log (1 - Q_{k_1} - \cdots - Q_{k_m}). \tag{4}$$

We will show that the log-likelihood function, $\log \mathcal{L}$, is concave. This means that the likelihood function has a unique maximum value [23], making it a good candidate for numerical optimisation.

Theorem 1 (Concavity of log likelihood function). *The log likelihood function $\log \mathcal{L}$ for $\mathcal{L}$ defined in Eq. 3 is concave.*

Proof. Required to prove that $\log \mathcal{L}(\alpha \vec{q} + (1-\alpha)\vec{r}) \geq \alpha \log \mathcal{L}(\vec{q}) + (1-\alpha) \log \mathcal{L}(\vec{r})$. We begin by simplifying the notation used in the Likelihood function by converting to vector notation.

Let $g(\vec{Q}) = \sum_{j=1}^{m+1} N_j \log Q_j$ where $N_{m+1} = N - \sum_{j=1}^{m} N_j$ and $Q_{m+1} = 1 - \sum_{j=1}^{m} Q_j$.

As before (Eq. 3), $Q_j = \sum_{i=1}^{n} q_i p_{i,\sigma_i(k_j)}$ and therefore $Q_{m+1} = 1 - \sum_{j=1}^{m} \sum_{i=1}^{n}$

$q_i p_{i,\sigma_i(k_j)} = \sum_{i=1}^{n} q_i (1 - \sum_{j=1}^{m} p_{i,\sigma_i(k_j)})$.

Observe, we can define a matrix P so $\vec{Q} = P\vec{q}$ and $\log \mathcal{L}(\vec{q}) = \sum_{j=1}^{m+1} N_j \log Q_j = g(\vec{Q})$.

Therefore, we can now rewrite

$$\log \mathcal{L}(\alpha \vec{q} + (1 - \alpha)\vec{r}) = g\left(P(\alpha \vec{q} + (1 - \alpha)\vec{r})\right) = g\left(\alpha P\vec{q} + (1 - \alpha)P\vec{r}\right)$$

$$= \sum_{j=1}^{m+1} N_j \log(\alpha (P\vec{q})_j + (1 - \alpha)(P\vec{r})_j) \geq \sum_{j=1}^{m+1} N_j (\alpha \log(P\vec{q})_j + (1 - \alpha)\log(P\vec{r})_j)$$

$$= \alpha \sum_{j=1}^{m+1} N_j \log(P\vec{q})_j + (1 - \alpha) \sum_{j=1}^{m+1} N_j \log(P\vec{r})_j = \alpha g(\vec{Q}) + (1 - \alpha)g(\vec{R})$$

$$= \alpha \log \mathcal{L}(\vec{q}) + (1 - \alpha)\log \mathcal{L}(\vec{r}).$$

As the log-likelihood function is concave, there will be a unique maximum likelihood value. We will use gradient descent to find the q_i that maximises $\mathcal{L}$ after m guesses subject to the constraints (1). We iteratively change the estimated q_i values, $\hat{q}_i$.

Gradient Descent. As we apply iterations of gradient descent to estimate the parameters $q_1, \ldots, q_n$ which maximise the likelihood function, we must maintain the constraints of the system. In particular,

$$\sum_{i=1}^{n} q_i = 1 \quad \text{and} \quad q_i \geq 0.$$

To meet these constraints, we project the gradient vector onto the probability simplex and then adjust our step size so that we stay within that space.

With each iteration of our gradient descent we move a step in the direction which maximises our likelihood function. The gradient is scaled by a factor α (described in Sect. 3.3) to give a base step size. This is further scaled by an amount β to ensure the move from $\vec{p}$ to $\vec{p} + \alpha \beta \vec{g}$ satisfies $\beta \leq 1$, $\beta \|\vec{g}\| \leq 1$ and $\vec{p} + \beta \vec{g}$ lies with in the simplex.

Gradient Descent Validation. The goal of the gradient descent is to converge towards the maximum of the likelihood function and thus find the proportions q_i that provide the best explanation of the distribution of the password set seen after m guesses. For initial validation of the gradient descent performance we take four different leaked password datasets as wordlists.

The datasets we used are leaked passwords from users of hotmail.com, flirtlife.de, computerbits.ie and 000webhost.com. They contain 7300, 98912, 1795 and 15,252,206 users' passwords respectively. The datasets were compromised by various methods so the lists may only contain a random, and possibly biased, sample of users [17]. As far as we can tell only the 000webhost dataset imposed composition policies on users' passwords [5].

We took a random sample of 1000 users' passwords from the 98912 users in the Flirtlife dataset. In [17], it was shown that when guessing a sample of leaked passwords from a website, the most effective guesses come from the passwords of other users of that same site. Therefore, if gradient descent is effective we expect it to show that the sample most closely compares to the Flirtlife wordlist.

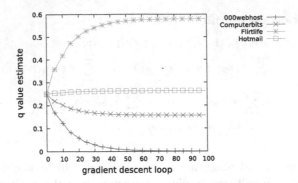

Fig. 1. Estimating the distribution of a password set using information from 1 guess and $\alpha = 0.1$.

In Fig. 1, we show the q value estimates during the convergence of the gradient descent for the likelihood function seeded with just one guess. This single guess was the password *123456* because it is widely considered to be the most commonly used password. We began by setting the $\hat{q}$-values to $1/n = 0.25$, and then used 100 steps of gradient descent with a scaling of $\alpha = 0.1$ on the step size to estimate the proportions. We recorded the q_i values that during the gradient descent gave the maximum Likelihood value. This way we remember the best value if we overstep the maximum.

The password *123456* occurred in all four password sets but using the distribution of those datasets the likelihood function was able to determine that the proportion in the sample best matched the proportion in Flirtlife. If we were guessing the full Flirtlife dataset with several guesses, rather than just a sample from it with one guess, then this proportion will be closer to 100%.

In the above example, all 1000 passwords came from a random sample of Flirtlife. We will investigate in later examples whether the maximum likelihood estimation can determine the breakdown of where passwords come from when composed of different wordlists.

3.3   Multi-armed Bandit Design and Validation

Let us now suggest some choices faced when designing a password guessing multi-armed bandit. We need to choose how to repeatedly apply our gradient based maximum likelihood estimation and also we must say how we will choose guesses. We are interested in which of these variations produces the best results.

Gradient Descent Initialization Variables. We expect the gradient descent to improve with each guess made since every guess provides it with more information. There are a number of ways of initialising the gradient descent after each guess provides new information. The following are three different methods for choosing the initialisation value:

Random. Randomly pick starting values for $\hat{q}_i$, subject to Eq. (1),

Average. Choose the average starting value, i.e. assume the passwords are uniformly distributed between the n wordlists, so $\hat{q}_i = 1/n$,

Best. Use our previous best estimate for the $\hat{q}$-values, based on the gradient descent results for the previous guess.

Gradient Descent Base Step Size. We looked at a number of techniques for choosing our base step size α for gradient descent, including a constant value of α, an α that resulted in a constant l_2 step size and an adaptive method. In supplementary material for this paper [16], we demonstrate that a **constant** $\alpha = 0.1$ was a reasonable choice for our model.

Informing Our Guess Choices. Once we have generated our estimate of the $\hat{q}$-values, we want to use them to inform our next guess. We suggest three options for how to choose our next guess:

Random. Randomly choose a wordlist and guess the next most popular password in that wordlist.

Best wordlist. Guess the next most popular password from the wordlist with the highest corresponding $\hat{q}$-value.

Q-method. Use information from the $\hat{q}$-values combined with the frequencies of the passwords in the wordlists to inform our next guess.

These options have different advantages. In the first option, we randomly choose a wordlist to guess from, but we are still taking the most probable guess from the wordlist we choose. This option emphasises the continued exploration of all the wordlists. In the second option, we are choosing the wordlist we believe accounts for the largest proportion of the password set.

The last option is specifically basing password guess choices using Eq. (2). It uses our predicted $\hat{q}$-values to estimate the probability of seeing each word k. If, for example, we have a word k which has frequency $f_1(k)$ in wordlist 1 but also occurs in wordlist 2 and 3 with frequencies $f_2(k)$ and $f_3(k)$ respectively. Using (2), where $p_{i,\sigma_i(k)} = f_i(k)/size\ of\ wordlist\ i$, we can compute the total probability of this word occurring in the password set. This method should determine which word k has the highest probability of being in the password set and use this word as our next guess.

We will now look at some examples of the performance of our multi-armed bandit model against simulated password sets. Guessing against simulated password sets allows us to identify whether the multi-armed bandit model is capable of identifying the characteristics of a password set (i.e. the q_i) with synthetic data. It also allows us to compare and contrast the effectiveness of the model variables.

In these simulations we guess one word at a time and then compute the estimated weight of each wordlist. We also report separately the number of users compromised after each guess is made. If the scheme is effective it should be able to approximate the true distribution of the password set. We also expect to find that the "Q-method" of guessing is more effective than a random wordlist choice. We may also find that it is better or as good as simply guessing using the estimated "best" wordlist.

In each of the below plots we have used the constant alpha method for computing the gradient step size and set this value to 0.1. We also show the q value estimates plot for the best combination of initialisation and guess choice methods. We discuss the alternative methods in supplementary material [16].

Validation Password Set 1: 60% Flirtlife, 30% Hotmail, 10% Computerbits. We begin by creating a password set made up of 10,000 users' passwords; 60% were selected randomly from the flirtlife.de dataset, 30% from the hotmail.com dataset and 10% from the computerbits.ie dataset.

In Fig. 2(l), we plot the estimated q-values after the gradient descent was completed for each guess. For this graph, the gradient descent was initialised using average $\hat{q}$-values, $\hat{q}_i = 1/3$, and the Q-method was used for guessing. The actual proportions are shown as solid horizontal lines. Even after a small number of guesses we have good predictions for how the password set is distributed between the three wordlists.

In Fig. 2(r), we show the number of users successfully compromised as the number of guesses increases. The successes are the average over fifty runs to reduce the variance in the random guessing method. Results are shown for each combination of initialisation and guessing method. As one might expect, picking guesses from a random wordlist resulted in the lowest success rates. Both the Q-method and guessing from the best wordlist resulted in successes close to the optimal line. After 100 guesses these methods had compromised 795 users, in comparison to the 870 users compromised by guessing the correct password in the correct order for every guess.

Validation Password Set 2: 60% 000webhost, 30% Hotmail, 10% Computerbits. In Fig. 3(l), we show the estimated q-values for a 10,000 user password set made from 000webhost, Hotmail and Computerbits with a 6:3:1 split. Again, we get good estimates for the q-values. In Fig. 3(l), 000webhost is accurately weighted as accounting for the largest proportion of password set. However, in Fig. 3(r) when we guess solely from the best ranked wordlist (dashed lines) we get lower guessing returns than when we randomly choose a wordlist to guess from (dotted lines). While we believe this is a consequence of the 000webhost, unlike the other password sets, being constrained by composition restrictions [17], it does highlight an important distinction between optimising our model for effective guessing and optimising to best represent the characteristics within the password set.

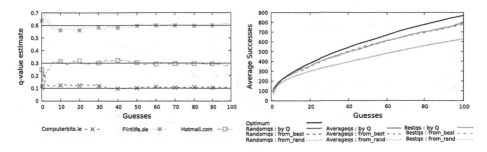

Fig. 2. Validation password Set 1. Left: q-value estimates (initialization: average $\hat{q}$-values, Guessing: Q-method). Right: Guessing returns for validation.

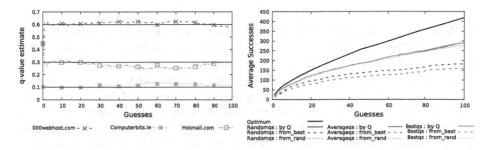

Fig. 3. Validation password Set 2. Left: q-value estimates (initialization: average $\hat{q}$-values, Guessing: Q-method). Right: Guessing returns for validation.

It is worth noting that the Q-method of guessing would also be influenced by the high ranking of 000webhost passwords and their low guessing success. However, it still performs slightly better than the random method, and significantly better than guessing from the best wordlist (avg. results over 100 trials).

Validation Password Set 3: 60% Hotmail, 30% Flirtlife, 10% Computerbits. In Fig. 4(l), we show the estimated q-values for a 10,000 user password set made from Hotmail, Flirtlife and Computerbits with a 6:3:1 split. The approximation for the Computerbits wordlist falls slightly below the correct level and the Flirtlife estimate is slightly above. The approximation for the strongest wordlist, Hotmail, is accurate. The estimates have mostly converged by guess 10 and there is little divergence after that point.

Figure 4(r) shows the guessing success rate for this password set. We see that the Q-method fares better than the random and best wordlist methods. In fact, it is close to the optimal guessing method. By the end of the guessing the Q-method has compromised an average of 1106 users. An optimal strategy at this point would have compromised 1223 users. The best wordlist method compromised an average of 980 users and random compromised an average of 962 over 5 runs. We see little difference in success rates for the different initialisation methods within each guess choice.

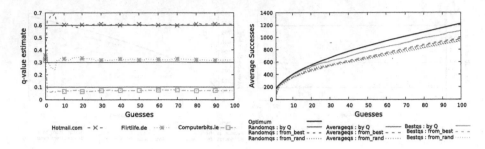

Fig. 4. Validation password Set 3. Left: q-value estimates (initialization: average $\hat{q}$-values, Guessing: Q-method). Right: Guessing returns for validation.

Validation Password Set 4: 55% Hotmail, 30% Flirtlife, 10% 000webhost, 5% Computerbits. The final password set we look at is composed of 10,000 users' passwords from 4 different wordlists. In Fig. 5(l), we display the estimated q-values. The model gives an accurate approximation of the q-values. Figure 5(r), shows the successes when guessing this password set. Again, we see that the Q-method is effective at guessing, this time performing significantly better than the other guessing methods. We notice that the successes are close to the optimal. Particularly for the first 20 guesses, the Q-method compromised 303 users in comparison to 317 compromised by optimal guessing.

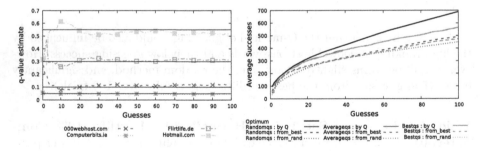

Fig. 5. Validation password Set 4. Left: q-value estimates (initialization: average $\hat{q}$-values, Guessing: best wordlist). Right: Guessing returns for validation.

Summary of Results for Validation Password Sets. The multi-armed bandit scheme is able to match characteristics in a password set to characteristics in the wordlists used for guessing. We have seen that for a variety of synthetic examples, guessing using the multi-armed bandit technique can be effective both for compromising users and estimating how the passwords have been chosen.

In all examples we saw that guessing using the Q-method is consistently effective in comparison to other wordlist selection methods. In general, we found that the initialization method had little bearing on the success results. This stems from our concave log-likelihood function, meaning that, for most set-ups, we converge to a single maximum when estimating the distributions.

These initial results demonstrate that the relationship between password choice and user cohorts is tangible and identifiable by automation. We are now motivated to investigate whether the multi-armed bandit can offer efficient guessing returns when guessing a real password set.

4   Password Guessing for Real Password Sets

Given a set of leaked passwords, that we have no a-priori knowledge about, it is unlikely that the password data set is exactly a weighted combination of datasets that we have already seen. However, we can still assess whether the multi-armed bandit can learn which wordlists to choose guesses from in order to guess efficiently. In this section, we investigate which of our methods for choosing guesses from the wordlists are most effective. In particular, we expect that the Q-method of choosing passwords between wordlists could offer a guessing improvement over both a random choice of wordlist and choosing from the predicted "best" wordlist.

Recall that the Q-method uses the weighting of wordlists and the proportion of each password in those wordlists to decide on the next guess.

For this investigation we used two leaked password sets. The 2009 rockyou.com password leak which included 32 million plaintext user credential and the 2012 yahoo.com Yahoo Voices password leak which included 453,492 plaintext users' passwords. These are old password sets that have been well studied in the literature and therefore offer effective comparison between guessing strategies and allow easy replication of our results. In this paper, we show the results for the Rockyou data, though similar results were seen for Yahoo.

4.1   Rockyou.com Password Set

In this section we describe the guessing of the Rockyou password set. Four wordlists were used: Computerbits, Hotmail, Flirtlife and 000webhost.

Figure 6(l) shows the estimated breakdown of Rockyou between the four wordlists. Hotmail is assigned the highest rating with 000webhost, flirtlife and computerbits falling below it respectively. In terms of the breadth of the audience demographic in each of the wordlists, this assessment of the breakdown seems logical. The nationality specific websites such as computerbits.ie and flirtlife.de fall lowest and 000webhost.com, which enforces composition restrictions, fares slightly worse than hotmail.com.

Figure 6(r) shows the guessing successes for the Rockyou password set guessed using the four wordlists. There is little differentiation between the initialisation methods. However, the guess choice method significantly impacts the number of successes. The optimum number of successes for 100 guesses against the Rockyou password set is 1,483,668 (100% of optimum, 4.55% of total users) compromised.

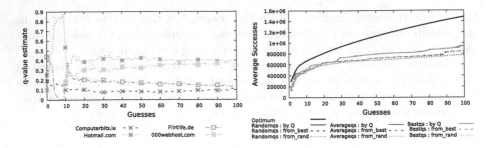

Fig. 6. Rockyou. Left: q-value estimates (initialization: average $\hat{q}$-values, Guessing: Q-method). Right: guessing returns for rockyou.com

The Q-method compromised an average of 945,371 (64% optimum, 2.9% total) users. Choosing from the estimated best wordlist compromised 846,772 (57% optimum, 2.6% total) users on average, and choosing a random wordlist resulted in the lowest number of average successes at 781,164 (53% optimum, 2.4% total). We can see the Q-method performs better than the next best method by compromising just under 100,000 more users.

Comparison to Single Wordlist Guessing. Here we investigate the value of using a multi-armed bandit, over simply guessing using each wordlist individually. In Fig. 7, we compare using the Q-method (solid purple line) to guessing using each wordlist separately. The Q-method performs well, compromising 945,371 (64% optimum, 2.9% total) users in comparison to 804,731 (54% optimum, 2.5% total), 703,041 (47% optimum, 2.2% total), 603,783 (41% optimum, 1.9% total) and 64,024 (4.3% optimum, 0.2% total) from Flirtlife, Hotmail, Computerbits and 000webhost respectively.

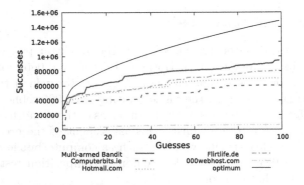

Fig. 7. Single wordlist guessing returns for rockyou.com versus multi-armed bandit

Compare the ordering in Fig. 6(l) to that in Fig. 7. Notice that, the weightings assigned to the wordlists do not necessarily correspond to a better guessing result when the wordlists are used individually. This is because our multi-armed bandit has been designed with the goal of matching characteristics not optimising guessing. It will give rewards to wordlists if the password set does not contain a password and a wordlist also does not contain the password. But this is not necessarily indicating that this wordlist will be better at guessing, only that it is a good match. If optimising guessing-returns is the goal, then we suggest experimenting with our model in order to weight successes more than failures.

5   Identifying Demographics

Though real password data may not be simple combinations of previously seen wordlists, it is possible that the weights estimated by our scheme reveal information about the demographics of the users in the dataset. It is well known that users' demographics, such as nationality and language, play an important role in their password choices [1,6,13]. Indeed, this is information that human password guessers might look for when determining their guessing strategies. Specifically, we will consider whether, given a password set formed by users predominantly from a single nationality, the multi-armed bandit can recognise which wordlist best matches this locality? Does using passwords generated by other users from that same nationality improve guessing?

5.1   Matching Nationality Characteristics

We test the ability of our scheme to identify national characteristics using two password sets and two nation-specific wordlists. We have chosen the password sets to be Irish and German users. Irish users are mainly English-speaking and both English and German are Indo-European languages using the Latin alphabet. Our challenge will be to see if we can identify the nationality of a password set by linking it to a nation-specific wordlist (in preference to international wordlists). Clearly, a simple method could tell the difference between, say, Chinese and English passwords. We are interested in the more challenging setting of distinguishing between Irish users' passwords and English users' passwords when the spoken language is the same, or between English and German passwords where both use the Latin alphabet. In this section, we will show that our learning methods are able to identify these subtle distinctions.

The two password sets we will try guessing are the computerbits.ie password set and the flirtlife.de password set. Computerbits.ie is made up of 1785 Irish users. Flirtlife.de is made up of 98,912 predominantly German and Turkish users. The two wordlists were drawn from the large set of 31 password leak datasets known as Collection #1 [10]. One of these password sets was selected and from this we extracted all the passwords whose corresponding email address contained the country code top-level domain ".ie" and separately ".de". These formed our nationality specific user wordlists from Ireland and Germany with 90,583 and 6,541,691 users respectively.

Irish Passwords. We are interested in whether the multi-armed bandit will match the distribution of the Irish password set computerbits.ie to the extrapolated Irish wordlist taken from the subset of Collection #1 (denoted *"Irish users"* from now on). To test this we ran the multi-armed bandit set-up as per the optimal parameters found in Sect. 3.3.

In Fig. 8(l), we included three wordlists, the hotmail.com leaked passwords, the flirtlife.de password set and the *Irish users*. Hotmail.com is an international website. However, it is suspected that the Hotmail users in the dataset we have were compromised by means of phishing scams aimed at the Latino community. Flirtlife is a dating site with predominantly German and Turkish users. Figure 8(l) plots the breakdown estimated by the multi-armed bandit. From the first guess it estimates that the passwords in the computerbits.ie set match closely to the passwords chosen by the *Irish users*. Notice that some weighting is assigned to the Hotmail wordlist but essentially none to the flirtlife.de password set.

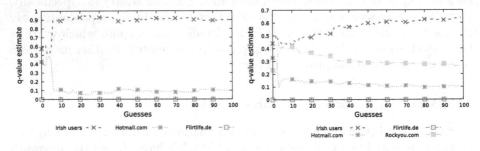

Fig. 8. q-value estimates for the Irish password set from Computerbits.i.e. Left: estimated using three wordlists. Right: estimated using four wordlists.

In Fig. 8(r), we included four wordlists. The additional wordlist is the Rockyou.com password set leaked in 2009. It includes 32 million users' passwords and had an international audience. The language used on Rockyou applications was English. Given the common spoken tongue in Ireland is English and that the Rockyou password set is often used as an effective base to seed guessing, we expect the Rockyou users to be somewhat representative of the Irish Computerbits users.

Figure 8r shows the estimated breakdown for the computerbits.ie passwords. In the beginning Rockyou is assigned a weighting nearly as high as the *Irish users*. However, the value of Rockyou declines as the number of guesses increases. In all combinations of initialisation and guess methods, the multi-armed bandit was able to identify that the Computerbits passwords most closely matched the Irish subset of users.

German Passwords. We now try to guess the flirtlife.de password set using the wordlist of *German users*. While flirtlife.de is a German dating site, its main users were both German and Turkish. Therefore, we expect there to be a less strong link between the German wordlist and the flirtlife.de passwordset than there was for computerbits.ie and the Irish wordlist.

Figure 9 plots the flirtlife.de weightings for three wordlists: *German users*, Rockyou.com and hotmail.com. Up to 50 guesses, most weighting is assigned to the Rockyou wordlist. However, after 50 guesses, the German users' passwords overtake Rockyou and remain slightly ahead up to at least guess 200.

The multi-armed bandit was still able to identify that the Flirtlife passwords best matched the German users wordlist. However, the effect does not take place until the high frequency passwords, up to 50, have been guessed. Rockyou is a large password set and will generally give a good indication of passwords chosen by a general population [17]. Because Flirtlife is made up of users from two nationalities and languages: German and Turkish, it is possible that the value that a solely German dictionary offers is not enough to counteract the general guessing strength of the Rockyou wordlist.

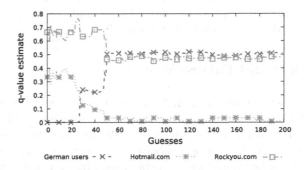

Fig. 9. *q*-value estimates for the German password set from flirtlife.de estimated using three wordlists.

5.2 Password Nationality to Inform Guessing

We saw that the multi-armed bandit can link a password set to a wordlist based on characteristics within the passwords and reveal the nationality of the users. Does using passwords generated by other users of the same nationality improve guessing?

Irish Users. In Fig. 10(l), we guess the passwords in the Irish computerbits.ie password set. The black line shows the returns for an optimum first 100 guesses. We also guess them using the order and passwords from the full Collection #1 password set that the *Irish users* and *German users* were chosen from. We label this full dataset *"all users"*. We made 100 guesses against the 1795 users in the Computerbits password set. The top 100 most popular words were chosen in order from each wordlist. The wordlist composed of only Irish users performed better at guessing than the wordlist with all users' passwords in it. We also include the guessing success for our multi-armed bandit model. It performs as well as guessing using the *Irish users* set.

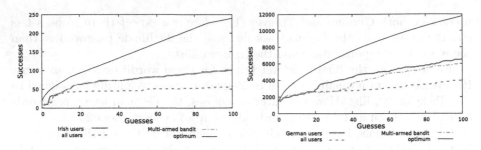

Fig. 10. Compares successes between guessing using a full wordlist of passwords and just those passwords belonging to users of the same nationality. Left: Guessing the Irish password set Computerbits. i.e. Right: Guessing the German password set Flirtlife.de.

German Users. In Fig. 10(r), we guess the Flirtlife password set using two wordlists similar to above. We can see that using just the German users' passwords ranked in order, is more effective than using *all users* passwords. The multi-armed bandit model performs better than simply using the distribution of *all users'* passwords to rank and order guesses.

6   Discussion and Future Work

For synthetic password sets, our multi-armed bandit was able to identify the wordlist that best linked to the passwordset it was guessing. This identification was achieved often within the first 10 guesses. We also saw that the scheme could automatically identify the sort of demographic information, such as nationality, that a password cracker would use to identify suitable wordlists, suggesting that the multi-armed bandit has the potential to be as good as a human at wordlist selection.

We see at least three potential offensive use-cases for such a guessing model. 1. The first approach is the most direct and utilises the real-time convergence of the MAB. An online guesser guessing a selection of users passwords from a website, will learn from each success and use it to inform the next guess made against all users. 2. An attacker could gather information by applying the multi-armed bandit to an offline leaked dataset of users from a given organisation. They could use MAB to determine the optimum choice of wordlist and then could carry out a tailored attack on other users from the same organisation. This has the potential to be effective as passwords created by users of the same organisation can significantly improve guessing returns [17]. 3. This same approach could be used in an online attack where a selection of users are used to learn characteristics, guessing until the accounts are locked. Once the MAB has highlighted the appropriate wordlist, then the wordlist can be used against other users, avoiding triggering lockout on potentially more valuable users.

This guessing model provides evidence for the importance of guiding users away from passwords which reflect nationality or website. It also demonstrates that passwords differ measurably depending on their source use. This indicates that websites should consider blocklisting passwords in a way that is tailored to their particular subject matter and users. In particular, websites who have experienced previous password leaks could work at restricting future users from using passwords which occurred with a high frequency in that leak.

We believe there is potential to further apply and expand this work. For example, the multi-armed bandit might be used to identify password policies enforced by matching them to datasets created under different composition policies. The multi-armed bandit could also be extended so that it does not depend on the exact probabilities for the words in a wordlists, and so then would work with guesses seeded from other sources, say based on users' personal information. Finally, it would be interesting to evaluate the system when used with a larger number of wordlists to assess how it scales.

7 Conclusion

Our multi-armed bandit model has proven effective in learning which wordlists best represent the composition of a set of passwords. It was therefore able to identify which wordlist would provide the most effective password guesses. This also allows it to learn features of a password set, allowing insight into the composition rules enforced, the website a leak originated from, the nationality of the users, or other characteristic information. The scheme demonstrates that this information gathering can now be done in an automated way and no longer requires a "human-in-the-loop".

References

1. AlSabah, M., Oligeri, G., Riley, R.: Your culture is in your password: an analysis of a demographically-diverse password dataset. Comput. Secur. **77**, 427–441 (2018)
2. Castelluccia, C., Chaabane, A., Dürmuth, M., Perito, D.: When privacy meets security: leveraging personal information for password cracking. arXiv preprint arXiv:1304.6584 (2013)
3. Dell'Amico, M., Michiardi, P., Roudier, Y.: Password strength: an empirical analysis. In: INFOCOM, 2010 Proceedings IEEE, pp. 1–9. IEEE (2010)
4. Dürmuth, M., Angelstorf, F., Castelluccia, C., Perito, D., Chaabane, A.: OMEN: faster password guessing using an ordered Markov enumerator. In: Piessens, F., Caballero, J., Bielova, N. (eds.) ESSoS 2015. LNCS, vol. 8978, pp. 119–132. Springer, Cham (2015). https://doi.org/10.1007/978-3-319-15618-7_10
5. Golla, M., Dürmuth, M.: On the accuracy of password strength meters. In: CCS 2018, pp. 1567–1582 (2018)
6. Han, W., Li, Z., Yuan, L., Xu, W.: Regional patterns and vulnerability analysis of Chinese web passwords. IEEE Trans. Inf. Forensics Secur. **11**(2), 258–272 (2015)

7. Hitaj, B., Gasti, P., Ateniese, G., Perez-Cruz, F.: PassGAN: a deep learning approach for password guessing. In: Deng, R.H., Gauthier-Umaña, V., Ochoa, M., Yung, M. (eds.) ACNS 2019. LNCS, vol. 11464, pp. 217–237. Springer, Cham (2019). https://doi.org/10.1007/978-3-030-21568-2_11

8. Houshmand, S., Aggarwal, S.: using personal information in targeted grammar-based probabilistic password attacks. In: DigitalForensics 2017. IAICT, vol. 511, pp. 285–303. Springer, Cham (2017). https://doi.org/10.1007/978-3-319-67208-3_16

9. Hunt, T.: Pwned websites. https://haveibeenpwned.com/PwnedWebsites

10. Hunt, T.: Collection #1 (2019). https://www.troyhunt.com/the-773-million-record-collection-1-data-reach. Accessed 09 Sept 2020

11. Li, Y., Wang, H., Sun, K.: A study of personal information in human-chosen passwords and its security implications. In: IEEE INFOCOM 2016-The 35th Annual IEEE International Conference on Computer Communications, pp. 1–9. IEEE (2016)

12. Li, Z., Han, W., Xu, W.: A large-scale empirical analysis of Chinese web passwords. In: 23rd USENIX Security Symposium (USENIX Security 14), pp. 559–574 (2014)

13. Malone, D., Maher, K.: Investigating the distribution of password choices. In: Proceedings of the 21st International Conference on World Wide Web, pp. 301–310. ACM (2012)

14. Melicher, W., et al.: Fast, lean, and accurate: modeling password guessability using neural networks. In: 25th USENIX Security Symposium (USENIX Security 16), pp. 175–191 (2016)

15. Morris, R., Thompson, K.: Password security: a case history. Commun. ACM 22(11), 594–597 (1979)

16. Murray, H.: MAB repository (2019). https://github.com/HazelMurray/multi-armed-bandit-guessing

17. Murray, H., Malone, D.: Convergence of password guessing to optimal success rates. Entropy 22(4), 378 (2020)

18. Narayanan, A., Shmatikov, V.: Fast dictionary attacks on passwords using time-space tradeoff. In: Proceedings of the 12th ACM Conference on Computer and Communications Security, pp. 364–372. ACM (2005)

19. Openwall: JtR. https://www.openwall.com/john

20. Pal, B., Daniel, T., Chatterjee, R., Ristenpart, T.: Beyond credential stuffing: password similarity models using neural networks. In: 2019 IEEE Symposium on Security and Privacy (SP), pp. 417–434. IEEE (2019)

21. Pasquini, D., Cianfriglia, M., Ateniese, G., Bernaschi, M.: Reducing bias in modeling real-world password strength via deep learning and dynamic dictionaries. arXiv preprint arXiv:2010.12269 (2020)

22. Pasquini, D., Gangwal, A., Ateniese, G., Bernaschi, M., Conti, M.: Improving password guessing via representation learning. arXiv preprint arXiv:1910.04232 (2019)

23. Rockafellar, R.T.: Convex Analysis. Princeton University Press (1970)

24. Sishi, S.: An investigation of the security of passwords derived from African languages. Masters Thesis (2019)

25. Steube, J., Gristina, G.: Hashcat. https://hashcat.net

26. Wang, D., Zhang, Z., Wang, P., Yan, J., Huang, X.: Targeted online password guessing: an underestimated threat. In: Proceedings of the 2016 ACM SIGSAC Conference on Computer and Communications Security, pp. 1242–1254 (2016)

27. Wei, M., Golla, M., Ur, B.: The password doesn't fall far: how service influences password choice. Who Are You?! Adventures in Authentication Workshop (2018)

28. Weir, M., Aggarwal, S., De Medeiros, B., Glodek, B.: Password cracking using probabilistic context-free grammars. In: 2009 30th IEEE Symposium on Security and Privacy, pp. 391–405. IEEE (2009)
29. Xia, Z., Yi, P., Liu, Y., Jiang, B., Wang, W., Zhu, T.: GENPass: a multi-source deep learning model for password guessing. IEEE Trans. Multimedia **22**(5), 1323–1332 (2019)

Author Index

Printed in the United States
by Baker & Taylor Publisher Services